Victoria Crosses on the Western Front
Cambrai to the Battle of St Quentin

Victoria Crosses on the Western Front
Cambrai to the Battle of St Quentin

20 November 1917–23 March 1918

Paul Oldfield

Pen & Sword
MILITARY

First published in Great Britain in 2018 by
Pen & Sword Military
an imprint of
Pen & Sword Books Ltd
47 Church Street
Barnsley
South Yorkshire
S70 2AS

Copyright © Paul Oldfield 2018

ISBN 978 1 47382 711 0

A CIP catalogue record for this book is available from the British Library

Typeset in Ehrhardt by
Mac Style
Printed and bound in the UK by TJ International Ltd, Padstow, Cornwall

Pen & Sword Books Ltd incorporates the imprints of Pen & Sword
Archaeology, Atlas, Aviation, Battleground, Discovery, Family History,
History, Maritime, Military, Naval, Politics, Railways, Select,
Social History, Transport, True Crime, and Claymore Press,
Frontline Books, Leo Cooper, Praetorian Press, Remember When, Seaforth
Publishing and Wharncliffe.

For a complete list of Pen & Sword titles please contact
PEN & SWORD BOOKS LIMITED
47 Church Street, Barnsley, South Yorkshire, S70 2AS, England
E-mail: enquiries@pen-and-sword.co.uk
Website: www.pen-and-sword.co.uk

Contents

Chapter 3: Local Operations Winter 1917–18 (Master Maps 1 & 2)

Chapter 4: First Battles of the Somme 1918 – Battle of St Quentin
(Master Maps 3, 5, 6 & 7)

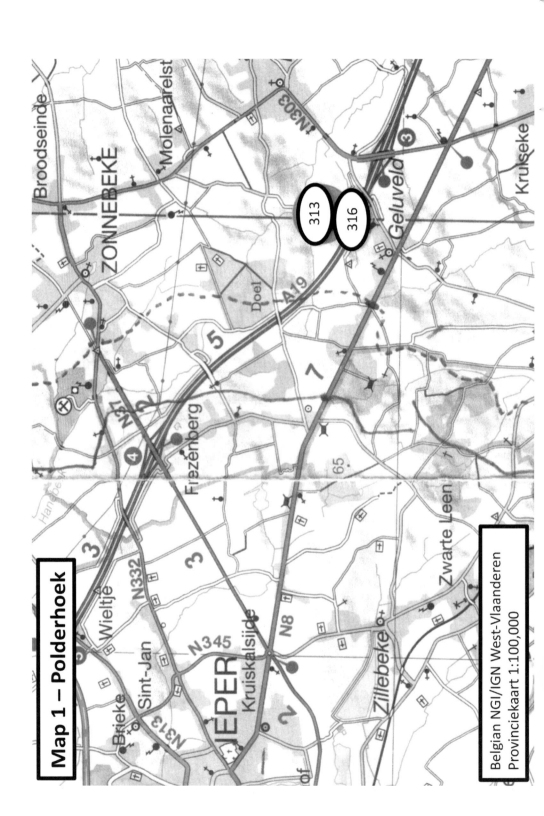

Map 1 – Polderhoek

Belgian NGI/IGN West-Vlaanderen
Provinciekaart 1:100,000

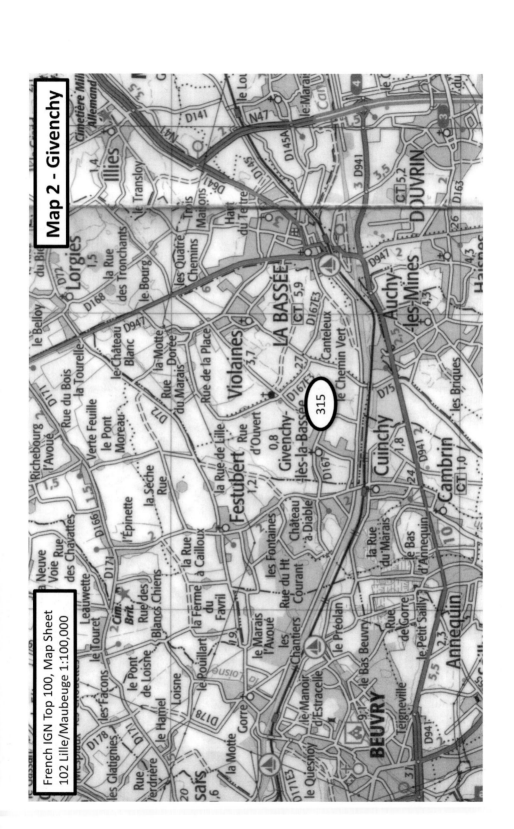

Map 2 - Givenchy

French IGN Top 100, Map Sheet
102 Lille/Maubeuge 1:100,000

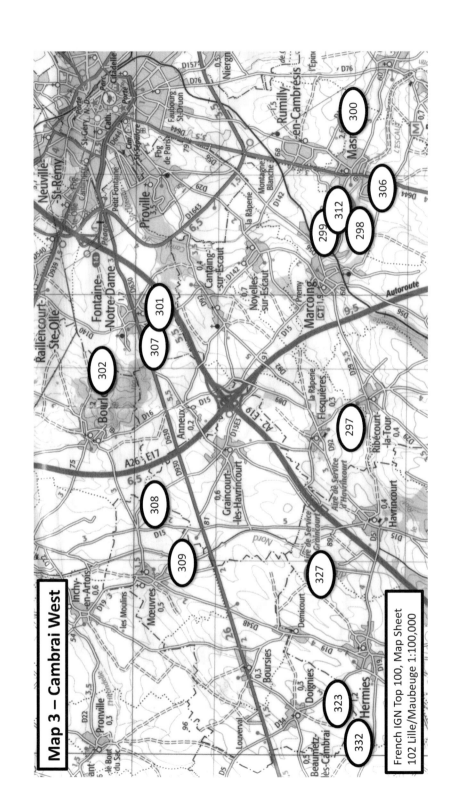

Map 3 – Cambrai West

French IGN Top 100, Map Sheet
102 Lille/Maubeuge 1:100,000

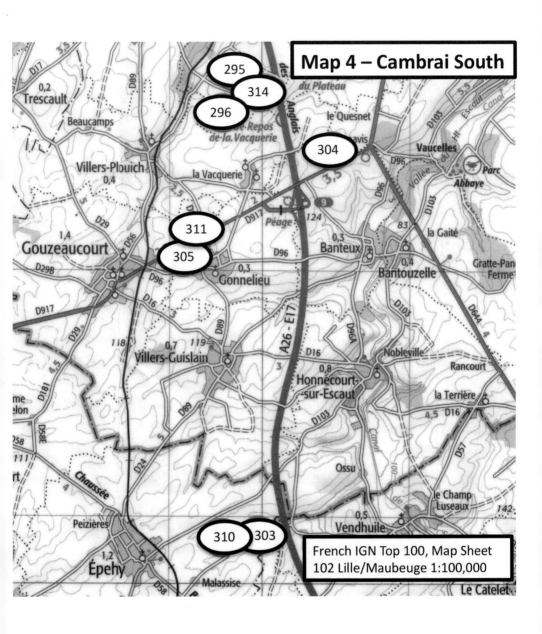

Map 4 – Cambrai South

French IGN Top 100, Map Sheet
102 Lille/Maubeuge 1:100,000

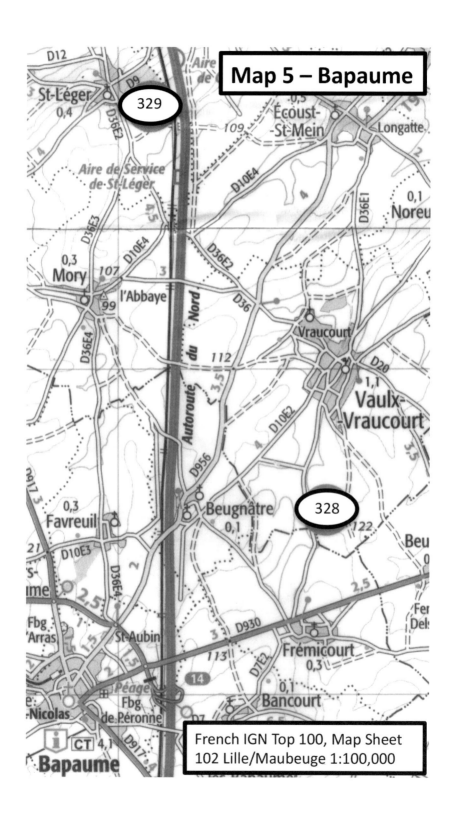

Map 5 – Bapaume

French IGN Top 100, Map Sheet
102 Lille/Maubeuge 1:100,000

Map 6 – St Quentin West

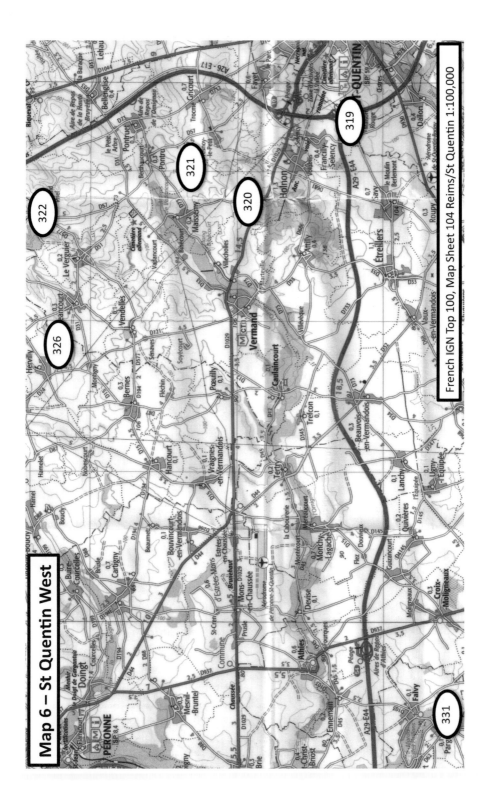

French IGN Top 100, Map Sheet 104 Reims/St Quentin 1:100,000

Map 7 – St Quentin South

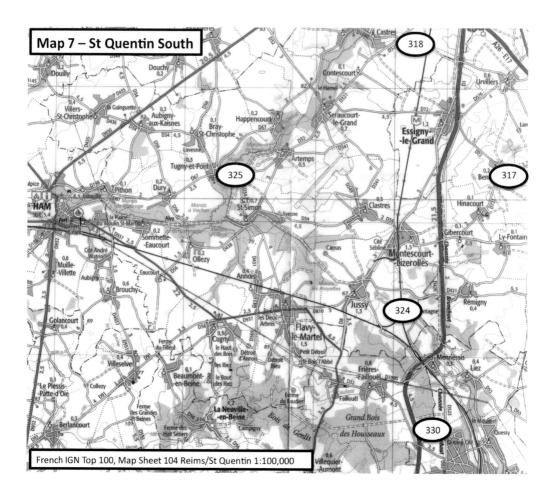

French IGN Top 100, Map Sheet 104 Reims/St Quentin 1:100,000

Abbreviations

AA	Anti-Aircraft
ADC	Aide-de-Camp
ADS	Advanced Dressing Station
AFC	Australian Flying Corps
AIF	Australian Imperial Force
AMF(L)	ACE (Allied Command Europe) Mobile Force (Land)
AMICE	Associate Member of the Institution of Civil Engineers
ASC	Army Service Corps
ATS	Auxiliary Territorial Service
AWOL	Absent without leave
Att'd	Attached
BA	Bachelor of Arts
BCh or ChB	Bachelor of Surgery
BEF	British Expeditionary Force
BMA	British Medical Association
Brig-Gen	Brigadier-General
BSc	Bachelor of Science
Bty	Battery (artillery unit of 4–8 guns)
Capt	Captain
CB	Companion of the Order of the Bath
CB	Confined to Barracks
CBE	Commander of the Order of the British Empire
CCF	Combined Cadet Force
CCS	Casualty Clearing Station
CEF	Canadian Expeditionary Force
CIE	Companion of the Order of the Indian Empire
C-in-C	Commander-in-Chief
CMG	Companion of the Order of St Michael & St George
CO	Commanding Officer
Col	Colonel
Cpl	Corporal
CQMS	Company Quartermaster Sergeant
CRA	Commander Royal Artillery
CRE	Commander Royal Engineers

CSgt	Colour Sergeant
CSEF	Canadian Siberian Expeditionary Force
CSI	Companion of the Order of the Star of India
CSM	Company Sergeant Major
CStJ	Commander of the Most Venerable Order of the Hospital of Saint John of Jerusalem
Cty	Cemetery
CVO	Commander of the Royal Victorian Order
CWGC	Commonwealth War Graves Commission
DAAG	Deputy Assistant Adjutant General
DBE	Dame Commander of the Order of the British Empire
DCL	Doctor of Civil Law
DCLI	Duke of Cornwall's Light Infantry
DCM	Distinguished Conduct Medal
DCO	Draft Conducting Officer
DFC	Distinguished Flying Cross
DL	Deputy Lieutenant
DLI	Durham Light Infantry
DSC	Distinguished Service Cross
DSO	Distinguished Service Order
Dvr	Driver
ENT	Ear, Nose and Throat
FInstCE	Fellow of the Institution of Civil Engineers
FM	Field Marshal
FRAS	Fellow of the Royal Astronomical Society
FRCP	Fellow of the Royal College of Physicians
FRCS	Fellow of the Royal College of Surgeons
FRCSE	Fellow of the Royal College of Surgeons of England
FRS	Fellow of the Royal Society
FRSM	Fellow of the Royal Society of Medicine (also FRSocMed)
FSA	Fellow of the Society of Actuaries
GC	George Cross
GCB	Knight Grand Cross of the Order of the Bath
GCMG	Knight Grand Cross of the Order of St Michael & St George
Gen	General
GOC	General Officer Commanding
GOC-in-C	General Officer Commanding in Chief
GSO1, 2 or 3	General Staff Officer Grade 1 (Lt Col), 2 (Maj) or 3 (Capt)
HAC	Honourable Artillery Company
HE	High Explosive
HLI	Highland Light Infantry
HMHS	Her/His Majesty's Hospital Ship

HMS	Her/His Majesty's Ship
HMT	Her/His Majesty's Transport/Troopship/Hired Military Transport
HMNZT	Her/His Majesty's New Zealand Transport/Troopship
HRH	His/Her Royal Highness
HS	Hospital Ship
JP	Justice of the Peace
KBE	Knight Commander of the Most Excellent Order of the British Empire
KCB	Knight Commander of the Order of the Bath
KCIE	Knight Commander of the Order of the Indian Empire
KCMG	Knight Commander of St Michael and St George
KCVO	Knight Commander of the Royal Victorian Order
KGStJ	Knight of Grace of the Most Venerable Order of the Hospital of Saint John of Jerusalem
Kia	Killed in action
KJStJ	Knight of Justice of the Most Venerable Order of the Hospital of Saint John of Jerusalem
Kms	Kilometres
KOSB	King's Own Scottish Borderers
KOYLI	King's Own Yorkshire Light Infantry
KRRC	King's Royal Rifle Corps
KSLI	King's Shropshire Light Infantry
LCpl	Lance Corporal
LG	London Gazette
LLB	Legum Baccalaureus (Bachelor of Laws)
LLD	Legum Doctor (Doctor of Law)
Lt	Lieutenant
Lt Col	Lieutenant Colonel
Lt Gen	Lieutenant General
LTh	Licentiate in Theology
Maj	Major
Maj Gen	Major General
MA	Master of Arts
MB	Bachelor of Medicine
MB BCh	Bachelor of Medicine, Bachelor of Surgery (also MBChB MBBS MBBChir)
MBE	Member of the Order of the British Empire
MC	Military Cross
MCh	Master of Surgery
MD	Medical Doctor
MGC	Machine Gun Corps
MID	Mentioned in Despatches

M.Inst.CE	Member of the Institute of Civil Engineers (MIE)
MM	Military Medal
MO	Medical Officer
MOD	Ministry of Defence
MP	Member of Parliament
MRCP	Member of the Royal College of Physicians
MRCS	Member of the Royal College of Surgeons
MSM	Meritorious Service Medal
MT	Motor Transport
MVO	Member of the Royal Victorian Order
NSW	New South Wales
NZEF	New Zealand Expeditionary Force
OBE	Officer of the Order of the British Empire
OC	Officer Commanding
OP	Observation Post
OStJ	Officer of the Most Venerable Order of the Hospital of Saint John of Jerusalem
OTC	Officers' Training Corps
PC	Police Constable
PoW	Prisoner of War
PPCLI	Princess Patricia's Canadian Light Infantry
PPS	Parliamentary Private Secretary
Pte	Private
QAINSR	Queen Alexandra's Imperial Nursing Service Reserve
QC	Queen's Counsel
RA	Royal Artillery
RAAF	Royal Auxiliary Air Force/ Royal Australian Air Force
RAC	Royal Agricultural College
RAC	Royal Armoured Corps
RAF	Royal Air Force
RAFVR	Royal Air Force Volunteer Reserve
RAMC	Royal Army Medical Corps
RASC	Royal Army Service Corps
RCT	Royal Corps of Transport
RE	Royal Engineers
REME	Royal Electrical and Mechanical Engineers
RETC	Royal Engineers Training Centre
RFA	Royal Field Artillery
RFC	Royal Flying Corps
RGA	Royal Garrison Artillery
RHA	Royal Horse Artillery
RLC	Royal Logistic Corps

RMO	Regimental Medical Officer
RMS	Royal Mail Ship/Steamer
RN	Royal Navy
RNR	Royal Naval Reserve
RSL	Returned and Services League
RSM	Regimental Sergeant Major
RSPCA	Royal Society for the Prevention of Cruelty to Animals
RTO	Railway Transport Officer
SAI	South African Infantry
Sgt	Sergeant
SMLE	Short Magazine Lee Enfield
SNCO	Senior non-commissioned officers
SOE	Special Operations Executive
Spr	Sapper
SS	Steam Ship
TA	Territorial Army
TD	Territorial Decoration
TF	Territorial Force
TMB	Trench Mortar Battery
Tr	Trench
VAD	Voluntary Aid Detachment
VD	Volunteer Decoration
VC	Victoria Cross
VIP	Very Important Person
WAAF	Women's Auxiliary Air Force
WAAC	Women's Auxiliary Army Corps
WG	Welsh Guards
WO1 or 2	Warrant Officer Class 1 or 2
YMCA	Young Men's Christian Association

Introduction

The sixth book in this series covers the Battle of Cambrai, the first three days of the German spring offensive in March 1918 and a few minor actions elsewhere on the Western Front between 20th November 1917 and 23rd March 1918. Thirty-eight VC recipients are included. As with previous books, it is written for the battlefield visitor as well as the armchair reader. Each account provides background information to explain the broad strategic and tactical situation, before focusing on the VC action in detail. Each is supported by a map to allow a visitor to stand on, or close to, the spot and at least one photograph of the site. Detailed biographies help to understand the man behind the Cross.

As far as possible chapters and sections within them follow the titles of battles, actions and affairs as decided by the post-war Battle Nomenclature Committee. VCs are numbered chronologically 295, 296, 297 etc from 20th November 1917. As far as possible they are described in the same order, but when a number of actions were fought simultaneously, the VCs are covered out of sequence on a geographical basis in accordance with the official battle nomenclature.

Refer to the master maps to find the general area for each VC. If visiting the battlefields it is advisable to purchase maps from the respective French and Belgian 'Institut Géographique National'. The French IGN Top 100 and Belgian IGN Provinciekaart at 1:100,000 scale are ideal for motoring, but 1:50,000, 1:25,000 or 1:20,000 scale maps are necessary for more detailed work, e.g. French IGN Série Bleue and Belgian IGN Topografische Kaart. They are obtainable from the respective IGN or through reputable map suppliers on-line.

Ranks are as used on the day. Grave references have been shortened, e.g. 'Plot II, Row A, Grave 10' will appear as 'II A 10'. There are some abbreviations, many in common usage, but if unsure refer to the list provided.

I endeavour to include memorials to each VC in their biographies. However, two groups have been omitted. First, every VC is commemorated in the VC Diary and on memorial panels at the Union Jack Club, Sandell Street, Waterloo, London. To include this in every biography would be unnecessarily repetitive. Second, commemorative paving stones are being laid in every VC's birthplace in the British Isles on, or close to, the 100th anniversary of their VC action. Most of the dedication ceremonies will take place after the book goes to print and so it is not possible to include them.

Thanks are due to too many people and organisations to mention here. They are acknowledged in 'Sources' and any omissions are my fault and not intentional. However, I would like to pay a particular tribute to fellow members of the 'Victoria Cross Database Users Group', Doug and Richard Arman, without whom I could not complete these books.

Paul Oldfield
Wiltshire
December 2017

Chapter One

The British Attack at Cambrai

The Tank Attack – 20th November 1917

295 Rfn Albert Shepherd, 12th King's Royal Rifle Corps (60th Brigade, 20th Division), Villers-Plouich, France

296 Capt Richard Wain, A Battalion, Tank Corps (2nd attached 3rd Tank Brigade), Marcoing, France

297 LCpl Robert McBeath, 1/5th Seaforth Highlanders (152nd Brigade, 51st Division), Cambrai, France

298 Lt Col John Sherwood-Kelly, Norfolk Regiment att'd 1st Royal Inniskilling Fusiliers (87th Brigade, 29th Division), Marcoing, France

299 Sgt Charles Spackman, 1st Border (87th Brigade, 29th Division), Marcoing, France

300 Lt Harcus Strachan, Fort Garry Horse (Canadian Cavalry Brigade), Masnières, France

Following the German withdrawal to the Hindenburg Line in the spring of 1917, the Cambrai front had remained static. Cambrai was a key supply point for the German Siegfried Stellung (Hindenburg Line) and capturing the nearby Bourlon Ridge would threaten the rear of the German line to the north. Third Army commenced planning for an offensive in the area when it took over the front at the end of May.

The only obstacle of any significance was the St Quentin Canal running north to south. However, the formidable Hindenburg defences, running northwest to southeast, also had to be taken into account. The Hindenburg Line consisted of three separate areas. The outpost zone of strongpoints included a number of fortified villages and farms. Behind it was the battle zone, the forward edge of which was a trench three metres wide and over two metres deep to stop tanks. In front was a belt of wire up to ninety metres wide and the support trench was similarly protected. At the rear of the battle zone was another complete defensive system with front and support trenches. The third area, beyond the Hindenburg system, known as the Masnières–Beaurevoir Line, comprised another complete system. The whole added up to an immensely strong defensive position; but if a breakthrough could be achieved, it would threaten the whole German line as far north as the Sensée river.

The decision to launch the attack was taken in mid October and tanks were withdrawn from Flanders, where they had not been a success due to the ground conditions. There was a shortage of manpower in the BEF due to heavy casualties

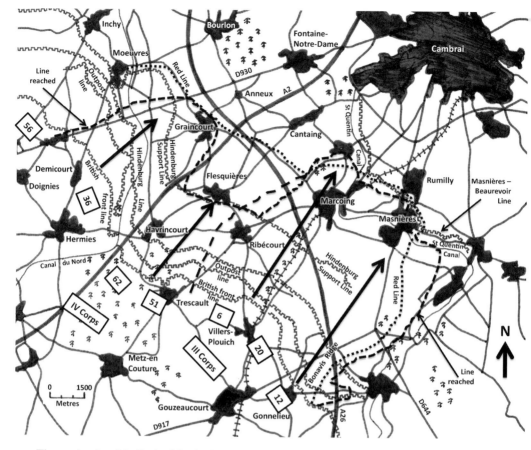

The opening day of the Battle of Cambrai on 20th November 1917. Although the objectives were not reached everywhere, the advance still represented an outstanding achievement when compared with previous offensives. Only the Red Line, the third and final objective, is shown.

in Flanders, two divisions being sent to Italy and extending the front to relieve more French divisions. As a result there were insufficient troops to continue the Flanders campaign (Third Ypres) and carry out the Cambrai offensive simultaneously. The former was shut down.

Enormous effort went into maintaining secrecy and staffs were taken into confidence at the last possible moment. Camouflage was paramount and the RFC overflew the British areas frequently to spot give away signs. From dusk on 17th November the roads were crammed with equipment and material moving forward to the concentration areas, but to German eyes in daylight, traffic appeared normal.

The Tanks Corps was eager to show what it could do when the ground was not a mass of waterlogged shell craters. Tanks were to be employed in large numbers with a strong reserve held back to exploit success. In the early stages they were to cut lanes through the wire for the infantry. Some tanks were equipped to pull wire obstacles aside in order to allow free passage of the cavalry units. Three tank brigades were allocated for the offensive, totalling 476 machines. Two-thirds of the tanks were allocated to the first objective and one third for the second.

Infantry and tanks trained together in a new method of attack, with the tanks leading in sections of three. The first tank approached the enemy line, turned left and fired along the trench to keep the defenders occupied, while the second tank dumped its fascine into the trench, crossed it and turned left to assist the first tank. The third tank crossed the fascine in the front line trench to the support trench, where it deposited its fascine and engaged the defenders there. The infantry advanced fifty metres behind the tanks to mop up residual resistance. Aircraft patrols carried parachute smoke bombs to drop over enemy counterattack formations, which were then to be engaged by artillery and machine gun barrages.

In order to achieve surprise and maintain the ground for the tanks to pass over, there was no preliminary bombardment or even registering of guns. Only normal daily rates of fire were permitted. The artillery would rely instead upon accurate survey, improved target location (aerial photography, sound ranging and flash spotting) and predicted shooting, supported by technical measurements such as barometric pressure, temperature, wind speed and direction and barrel wear. The forward movement of the artillery was strictly controlled until the day of the offensive. The last of the 1,003 guns moved into location at 2 a.m. on the morning of the attack.

Third Army had nineteen infantry divisions in six corps, three tank brigades and the Cavalry Corps. All but six of the infantry divisions had already been involved in the Flanders battles. From south to north the Corps took over their frontages in the order VII, III, IV, VI and XVII, with V Corps in reserve. The initial attack was to be launched from the Bonavis Ridge on the right to the Canal du Nord on the left by III and IV Corps. The other Corps were to demonstrate to keep the enemy in doubt where the main blow would fall. The majority of the fighting tanks were allocated to III Corps (216) and IV Corps (108). There were three objectives. The first (Blue Line) included the outpost zone and the front Hindenburg system, the second (Brown Line) included the Hindenburg support system and the third (Red Line), in III Corps' area, included the Masnières–Beaurevoir Line.

The breach was to be widened by both Corps extending their outer flanks and V Corps in reserve was to come up on the right of IV Corps to occupy the high ground beyond the Sensée river. The Cavalry Corps' task was to isolate Cambrai and then to push on to take crossings over the Sensée. VI Corps, was to launch a subsidiary attack against the original Hindenburg support line between Bullecourt and the Sensée. Together with the main assault by III and IV Corps, this would present the enemy with a continuous attack frontage of 27,400m. In addition it was planned for the French to pass through the breach and swing south.

The infantry concentration began on 15th November. New divisions taking over the line were forbidden to send patrols beyond their own wire, in order not to alert the enemy. The final move forward began at 7 p.m. on the 19th. To avoid noise and attention, the tanks moved forward at one mile per hour to reach their lying-up places about 900m from the forward enemy positions. By 5.30 a.m. on 20th

November all were in position. Five divisions and over 300 tanks were poised ready to strike and the Germans had no inkling of what was coming.

At 5.30 a.m. the Germans opened a heavy barrage on the attack frontage near Havrincourt Wood, but it died down at 6 a.m. At 6.10 a.m. the peace was again shattered when hundreds of British aircraft and tanks went into action, followed by the leading infantry battalions. Ten minutes later, in the murky light of dawn, the barrage fell on a stunned enemy. Description of the fighting will be from south to north.

III Corps was led by three divisions, with 12th Division on the right, 20th Division in the centre and 6th Division on the left. When both flanks were secure, 29th Division was to pass through and occupy the Masnières–Beaurevoir Line (Red Line) from the eastern edge of Masnières to Nine Wood. The two divisions on the right were supported by four battalions of 3rd Tank Brigade, with A Battalion attached from 2nd Tank Brigade for the operation. The left division was supported by the rest of 2nd Tank Brigade.

12th Division was allocated seventy-two tanks of C and F Tank Battalions to crush the wire and deal with machine guns. The only serious opposition was from Bleak House, which was taken in a combined attack by tanks and infantry. By 8 a.m. the first objective had been secured and, after a planned pause of forty-eight minutes, the advance continued. Some fierce resistance was met in areas missed by the barrage, but all objectives were taken.

In the centre, 20th Division attacked along Welsh Ridge into the valley beyond, led by 60th and 61st Brigades and supported by sixty tanks of I and A Tank Battalions. One company of A Battalion was detached to support 29th Division later in the day. 61st Brigade on the right met little resistance and the first objective was secured by 10 a.m. The Hindenburg support system was manned by reserves and those who had been rallied from the forward zones, but despite this the intermediate objective on the La Vacquerie Line and the second objective were taken by 11.30 a.m.

60th Brigade on the left was led by 6th Oxfordshire & Buckinghamshire Light Infantry and 12th King's Royal Rifle Corps, right and left respectively. Each battalion was supported by a section of 60th Machine Gun Company, a mortar team of 60th Trench Mortar Battery and nine tanks of A Battalion. The tanks were to operate in groups of three in a triangular formation. The infantry were to follow behind, exploiting the gaps crushed by the tanks through the enemy wire obstacles. Platoons were to advance in section files led by the bomber section, followed by the rifle grenadier section, rifle section and the Lewis gun section in the rear.

D Company, 12th King's Royal Rifle Corps was to take the German outpost line (Farm Trench) while A and C Companies, left and right respectively, were to take the Hindenburg Line. B Company, in reserve, was to deal with the junction of the Hindenburg and Marcoing Lines, where heavy resistance was expected. Seventy-five minutes after zero the support battalions, 6th King's Shropshire Light Infantry on the right and 12th Rifle Brigade on the left, were to continue the advance from the

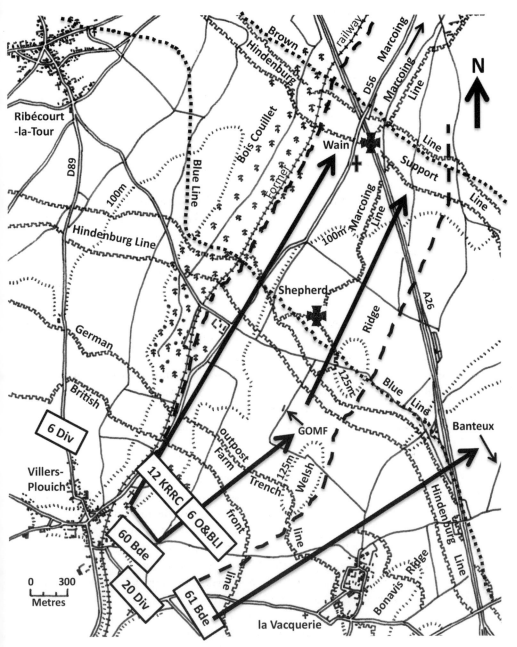

20th Division on 20th November 1917. Good Old Man Farm has been abbreviated to 'GOMF'. The cross alongside the D56, close to the scene of Richard Wain's VC action, is where he was buried. To reach the site of Wain's VC action, leave Marcoing southwest on the D56 towards Villers-Plouich. Go over the A26 autoroute and after 150m park on the right where there is some hard standing. Turn round and look back towards the bridge over the autoroute. The front trench of the Hindenburg Support Line ran across the road here. As close as can be established, Wain's VC action was in the field to the right of the D56, almost on the autoroute. To reach the site of Shepherd's VC action continue southwest towards Villers-Plouich for 1,800m and turn left onto a track just before the buildings on the right. Follow this track up the hill to the very top, where there is hard standing on the right to park. Look back the way you came. Shepherd's VC action was in the fields to the right of the track, about 500m away. The terrain here is utterly featureless and there is now no sign of the mound captured by Shepherd.

Blue Line to a point about 1,400m short of Marcoing (Brown Line). Each battalion would have three tanks leading, plus any tanks still serviceable from the first wave. On reaching the Brown Line, the tanks that were earlier responsible for the Blue Line were to pass through and advance rapidly to Marcoing in order to seize the vital crossings over the canal east of the railway bridge and west of Masnières.

12th King's Royal Rifle Corps married up with its tanks and was in position by 2.15 a.m. The enemy front line (Farm Trench) was taken without difficulty and D Company remained there while the advance continued. C Company came under fire from Good Old Man Farm, but managed to continue; and A Company on the left also met some resistance. Despite this opposition, the Battalion took its first objective on the Banteux to Ribécourt track.

B Company, under Captain Archibald Hoare, set off for the Battalion's final objective. The first enemy trench was taken, but resistance stiffened in the support line. Leaving one platoon to deal with it, Hoare continued with two platoons towards the third and final trench line. Between the support line and the final objective was a mound containing a strongpoint at the junction of the Hindenburg Line and the Marcoing Line. 6th Oxfordshire & Buckinghamshire Light Infantry had not advanced as far and all the enemy's attention was on B Company. Hoare attacked the mound, but all his officers and NCOs became casualties and he was mortally wounded (died 27th November 1917 and buried in Tincourt New British Cemetery – III A 13). **Rifleman Albert Shepherd**, Hoare's orderly and company runner, took command. Earlier in the day, although ordered not to, he had rushed a machine gun single-handed, killing two of the crew with a grenade and capturing the gun. Having dispersed the men into fire positions Shepherd went back seventy metres to bring up a tank to deal with the enemy and then led the company forward. Once the mound had been subdued an officer managed to get forward and led B Company to the objective, supported by the tank. By then the Company was only thirty-four

Looking northwest from the highest point on the Banteux to Ribécourt track. The ability to see Orival and Bourlon Woods, six and nine kilometres away respectively, speaks volumes about the skilful use the Germans made of the ground to site the Hindenburg Line. Albert Shepherd's VC action was at the junction of the Marcoing Line with the rear of the Hindenburg Line. There is no longer any trace of the mound.

strong out of the ninety-nine men who went into action. D Company also reached its objective on the left.

At 7.20 a.m., 6th King's Shropshire Light Infantry on the right and 12th Rifle Brigade on the left, supported by six tanks, followed behind the leading battalions to attack the Brigade's second objective, the Brown Line. On 12th Rifle Brigade's right, A Company was pinned down by a strongpoint containing five machine guns and a trench mortar. Until passing the Blue Line the tanks of A Battalion encountered little opposition. Thereafter they came under heavy fire from field guns and trench mortars, resulting in eleven tanks receiving direct hits. **Captain Richard Wain**, commanding 1 Section, 1 Company directed his tank, A2 *Abou Ben Adam II* (named after a poem by Leigh Hunt (1784–1859)), to advance directly at the strongpoint while a party of 12th Rifle Brigade tried to work around it.

Wain's tank was commanded by Lieutenant Christopher Duncan MC, 4th North Staffordshire attached Tank Corps. The other two tanks in 1 Section were hit at point blank range by the mortar. *Abou Ben Adam II* was hit five times, the last shot disabling it and killing Duncan and 40060 Private/First Driver John Browning (both commemorated on the Cambrai Memorial) and wounding the remainder of the crew. When the smoke cleared, Wain discovered that only he and one other crewman, both of whom were wounded, could move. They staggered from the tank and saw that the infantry were held up 180m behind. Wain salvaged a Lewis gun from the knocked-out tank and rushed the strongpoint single-handed. Half the garrison surrendered and he captured two machine guns and four trench mortars. He fired upon the remainder of the retreating garrison with a captured rifle until he was hit in the head by a bullet. The infantry arrived but he refused assistance from the stretcher-bearers while he organised the clearing of the strongpoint. Only then did he allow them to take him away, but he died soon afterwards. No difficulties were encountered elsewhere and all objectives were secured soon after 11 a.m.

The precise location of Wain's VC action has been in some doubt. Some accounts specify Good Old Man Farm, but others indicate it took place in the Hindenburg Line support trench or the Hindenburg Support Line. The former is about 600m beyond Good Old Man Farm, the latter about 2,200m beyond. One account gives

Taken from the D56 roadside 1,200m southwest of the bridge over the Autoroute. Wain's VC action was on the Hindenburg Support Line front line to the right of the D56 almost on the autoroute.

a grid reference (L24a36), but this is east of Marcoing on the far side of the St Quentin Canal and makes no sense. However, if there was a small mistake and the grid reference was actually L34a36, this is less than 200m from where Wain's body was buried at L34a03. The weight of evidence indicates the action was in the Hindenburg Support Line system and not at Good Old Man Farm (L9a72). Confusion may have arisen originally as the directions given to Wain's tanks were to proceed in the direction of Good Old Man Farm towards Marcoing. In this context, Good Old Man Farm is a point through which the advance was to pass, rather than an objective.

Looking along the axis of 1/5th Seaforth Highlanders' advance on 20th November 1917 from the D29 roadside about 300m north of the Hindenburg Line. McBeath's VC action was beyond the trees in the centre, behind 'Grand Ravin'.

59th Brigade in reserve moved forward to extend the defensive flank on Bonavis Ridge and support the tanks racing to secure the Masnières crossings. Tanks from A Battalion reached Marcoing at 10.50 a.m. and an officer cut the demolition charge wires under the railway bridge. During the night the bridge near Mon Plaisir Farm was seized, although its presence had not been known about earlier, when it was most needed.

The story was similar in 6th Division on the left of III Corps. Here Brigadier General Hugh Elles personally led the tanks forward, flying a huge Tank Corps flag. By 11 a.m. 6th Division was on its second objective and forty minutes later the reserve brigade was heading for Premy Chapel, assisted by tanks from H Battalion. This objective was taken with few casualties by noon. Marcoing was also cleared with tank support.

3rd Tank Brigade lost eight men killed, seventy-seven wounded and four missing on 20th November. Of the 146 tanks available that morning, twenty-two received

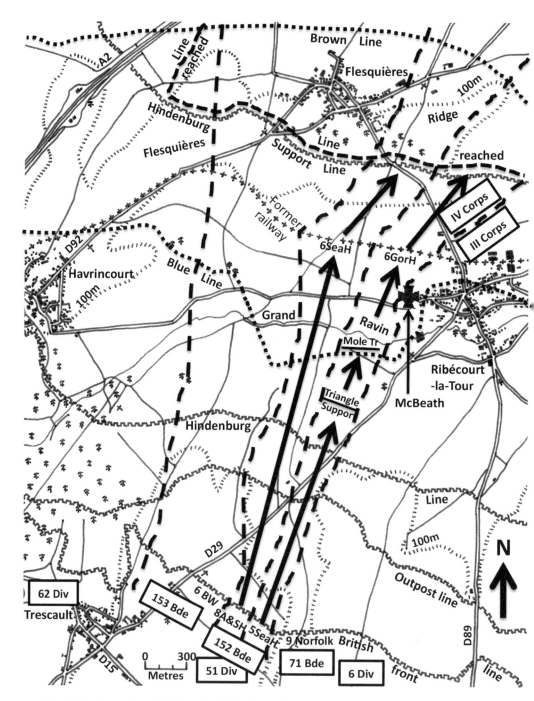

51st Division's attack on 20th November 1917. Enter Ribécourt from the south on the D89. Pass the church on the right and 75m beyond turn left into Rue Michel Sauvage, signed 'Salle des Fêtes'. Continue for 450m until the buildings end. This is the area where McBeath's VC action took place.

direct hits, fifteen ditched, one sank in the canal at Masnières and sixteen had mechanical breakdowns, but ninety-two were ready to continue operations.

IV Corps was led by 51st Division on the right and 62nd Division on the left, while on the left of the Canal du Nord 36th Division was to keep pace and roll up the Hindenburg Line. Four hours after zero 51st Division was to advance from the second objective on Cantaing and Fontaine and 62nd Division on Graincourt, Anneux and the western end of Bourlon Ridge.

In 51st Division, 152nd Brigade led on the right, 153rd Brigade on the left and 154th Brigade was in reserve. 152nd Brigade on the right was preceded through the German outpost line and wire by thirty-four tanks of E Battalion. It was led on the right by 1/5th Seaforth Highlanders and on the left by 1/8th Argyll & Sutherland Highlanders. On the right flank was 9th Norfolk (71st Brigade) and on the left was 1/6th Black Watch (153rd Brigade).

1/5th Seaforth Highlanders, led by C and D Companies, secured the German front line, Triangle Support and Mole Trench by 7.50 a.m. with almost no opposition. A Company, following from Stafford Support, paused in Grand Ravin while the first objective was secured and then led the advance to the final objective. A Company and 9th Norfolk on the right were held up by machine guns in the western outskirts of Ribécourt and the company commander called for a Lewis gun team to deal with it. **Lance Corporal Robert McBeath** volunteered and set off with his Lewis gun and a revolver. He located the first machine gun after covering about 140m and shot the gunner with the revolver from twenty metres. He then discovered several more machine guns in action and, with the assistance of a tank, attacked them and drove the defenders into a deep battalion HQ dugout. Regardless of the danger he rushed in after the enemy, shot one German who tried to resist at the bottom of the stairs and took the other thirty-five occupants prisoner, together with five machine guns. Sending the prisoners to the rear, he went back into the dugout and accounted for two more Germans hiding there.

The way forward was cleared for the advance of both units and the objective on the railway embankment was secured just two hours after zero. When a German aircraft flew over the newly won position, the forward platoons were withdrawn 200m before the line was shelled. 1/5th Seaforth Highlanders ended the day with a bag of four field guns, nine machine guns and 254 prisoners for twenty-five casualties.

On the left, 1/8th Argyll & Sutherland Highlanders had more fighting, but still reached its objective on the railway at 9.10 a.m. At 9.17 a.m. the advance was continued by the leading companies of 1/6th Gordon Highlanders on the right and 1/6th Seaforth Highlanders on the left, supported by twenty-six tanks. By 10 a.m. the Hindenburg Support system front line had fallen and the support companies passed through. However, most of the tanks were knocked out by field guns firing from close range as they reached the crest of the Flesquières Ridge. The infantry came under heavy fire from Flesquières. With no tanks to support the advance and

The western edge of Ribécourt. McBeath's VC action was probably where these buildings now stand.

cut gaps through the wire, the infantry advance ground to a halt. 1/6th Gordon Highlanders withdrew behind Flesquières Ridge and dug in. 1/6th Seaforth Highlanders was checked by fire from the support line of the Hindenburg Support system (Flesquières Trench) and three attempts were made to continue the attack. The Battalion almost succeeded in gaining the eastern end of Flesquières village and, covered by fire from some immobilised tanks, a small foothold was made in Flesquières Trench, near the southeast end of the village.

On the left, 153rd Brigade's first objective fell about 9.45 a.m., although fighting continued to clear Grand Ravin. Ten tanks led the advance to the second objective. On the right, the front trench of the Hindenburg Line was taken and contact was established with 152nd Brigade about 10.10 a.m. On the left there was hard fighting in Cemetery Alley before the front trench of the Hindenburg Support Line was secured about 10.35 a.m. The Brigade was checked by fire from Flesquières and the leading tanks were knocked out before breaching the wire. The village was broken into but the hold could not be maintained and Flesquières Trench was organised for defence using machine guns salvaged from derelict tanks.

51st Division continued attacks against Flesquières throughout the afternoon. Late in the day six tanks got into the village, but came out as the infantry went in and mutual support was lost. The enemy rushed out of their dugouts and threw the attackers back. HQ IV Corps issued orders to attack Flesquières from the south, but by nightfall little had happened. Flesquières was taken next day against little opposition and the advance continued almost two miles to the sunken road from Premy Chapel to Graincourt. 154th Brigade passed through and continued to Cantaing. By the time 152nd Brigade was relieved on 23rd November, it had taken about 1,200 prisoners, twelve guns/howitzers, thirty-seven machine guns and thirty-six trench mortars. Casualties amounted to ninety-two killed, 495 wounded and fifteen missing.

Grand Ravin

1/5ᵗʰ Seaforth Highlanders axis

Opposite the Havrincourt Salient, 62nd Division's right got off to a bad start due to tank delays. Despite this, the outpost zone was cleared and Havrincourt and the Hindenburg front trenches were secured by 10.15 a.m. The left ran into heavy fire from Havrincourt Château, but had taken part of Havrincourt and the first objective by 9 a.m. By 10.30 a.m. the whole of the Division's second objective had fallen to the point where the Hindenburg front system crossed the Canal du Nord. The reserve brigade took Graincourt and the factory on the Cambrai–Bapaume road. At the end of the day the Division was short of its final objectives in Anneux and close to Bourlon Wood, but had enjoyed reasonable success otherwise.

West of the Canal du Nord, 36th Division advanced at 8.35 a.m. when 62nd Division drew level with the Spoil Heap on the right. This feature was taken with little loss and by 11.20 a.m. the Demicourt–Graincourt road had been reached, 2,300m beyond the start line. Resistance stiffened in the Hindenburg front system, but by 3.30 p.m. the leading troops were in line with the advanced elements of 62nd Division beyond the Cambrai–Bapaume road. 56th Division kept up on the left, but proper contact was not established until 2 a.m. on the 21st.

By midday on 20th November almost all of III and IV Corps were on their objectives some 3,650m into enemy territory. Only at Flesquières was there failure. This great success was achieved with comparatively few casualties. Most of the enemy artillery had been knocked out and British guns were moving into position to support the next advance.

29th Division (III Corps reserve) moved from assembly trenches between Gonnelieu and Beaucamp to occupy the vacated front line at zero hour. At 8.30 a.m. it began to move forward and about 10.30 a.m. the Division commenced its advance to seize objectives at Masnières, Marcoing and Nine Wood. It was then to cross the St Quentin Canal and occupy the Masnières–Beaurevoir Line trenches.

On the right, 88th Brigade advanced on Masnières. All the tanks were knocked out or broke down, but the infantry captured the offending guns after a short delay.

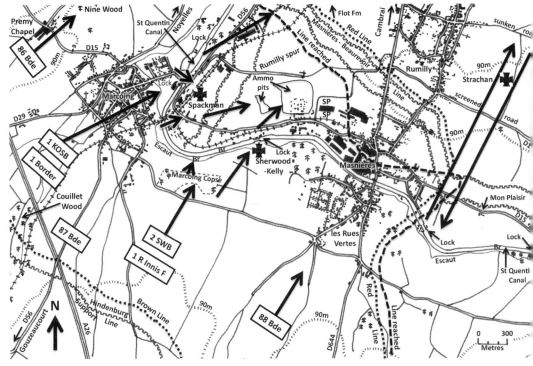

The area of 29th Division's attack on 20th November 1917. Br = location of a bridge in 1917 and SP = strongpoint. There is a café in Marcoing between the centre and the canal lock bridge on the Masnières road.

Two companies crossed the canal east of Masnières, but on the far bank they ran into stiff resistance and were halted. A tank of F Battalion (*Flying Fox*) attempted to rush the bridge between les Rues Vertes and Masnières, but it collapsed and the infantry were unable to establish a bridgehead. The reserve battalions made their way into the village and at 2.15 p.m. elements of 5th Cavalry Division also rode into les Rues Vertes.

An intact lock was discovered southeast of the bridge and men were passed over it in single file. Meanwhile the left of 88th Brigade crossed the canal west of Masnières, but was in insufficient strength to take the two trench lines of the Masnières–Beaurevoir Line. The troops dug in where they were. At 10 p.m. orders were issued for the troops north of the Canal to attack Masnières from the east and clear it before morning.

87th Brigade, in the centre, headed for Marcoing via the eastern slopes of the Couillet Wood valley. The leading battalions, 2nd South Wales Borderers on the right and 1st King's Own Scottish Borderers on the left, were to secure the canal crossings and form bridgeheads. Having achieved that, the support battalions, 1st Royal Inniskilling Fusiliers and 1st Border, right and left respectively, were to pass through and take the trenches between the Masnières–Cambrai road and the canal bend southeast of Noyelles. Each battalion had a section of the Brigade Machine Gun Company attached.

On the right, 2nd South Wales Borderers dealt with snipers in Marcoing Copse with the assistance of a tank, prior to closing up to the Escaut River and crossing the

The canal lock east of Marcoing from the enemy bank. John Sherwood-Kelly led his men across here and onto the higher ground behind the camera. Note the obvious bullet strikes on the building at the extreme right. Leave Masnières on the D15 Rue de Marcoing and pass some large silos on the left. 250m beyond, turn left into a slip road signed 'Ecluse de Bracheux'. It crosses the former railway line, now a cycle path, and leads down to the canal lock.

light railway bridge. However, on moving towards the canal lock east of Marcoing, the Battalion was delayed considerably by heavy machine gun fire from houses at the eastern end of Marcoing on the far bank, which also held up 1st Newfoundland (88th Brigade) on the right.

1st Royal Inniskilling Fusiliers was ordered forward at 10.30 a.m. and it too, together with B Company, 1st Border, was unable to cross the canal. **Lieutenant Colonel John Sherwood-Kelly** ran under fire to a tank and brought it up to the canal along the eastern edge of Marcoing Copse, where he directed its fire against machine gun posts in the buildings on the far bank. Having set this in motion he

Contemporary photograph of the lock from the southern bank. The bullet-struck building in the previous picture is left of centre.

personally led the first company across the lock. The opposition was overcome and three companies of 2nd South Wales Borderers were then able to cross the canal by a light bridge to the west of the lock and took up positions about 230m to the north of the waterways. The fourth company of 2nd South Wales Borderers lined the northern edge of Marcoing Copse. Later in the afternoon contact was established with 1st Newfoundland.

Meanwhile Sherwood-Kelly made a reconnaissance under heavy fire of the high ground held by the enemy, while the rest of the Battalion crossed the Canal and formed up. This was completed by 2 p.m. Sherwood-Kelly decided to attack immediately and the Battalion set off with A and B Companies leading. On leaving the cover of the canal bank, the Battalion came under heavy fire from ammunition pits and houses along the Masnières–Cambrai road. The enemy fell back, fighting from pit to pit. The advance was pushed on for 450m by short rushes. Sherwood-Kelly crossed to the left flank with a Lewis gun team, forced his way through the obstacles and set up the Lewis gun to cover the Battalion as it cut its way through the wire. He then led the attack on the ammunition pits, which were defended stubbornly. The enemy fell back to a second line of pits but many were killed or captured. The two companies in the centre kept up covering fire while a company on each flank worked around the enemy. The Battalion then charged from three sides simultaneously and the Germans retired to the Marcoing–Cambrai road. Two strongpoints held out, one with two machine guns and the other with three, but they were eventually taken with the assistance of 1st Border, which had come up on the left of 1st Royal Inniskilling Fusiliers. The position was cleared and five machine guns and forty-six prisoners were taken, in addition to a large number of enemy dead. However, as the advance approached a belt of wire thirty metres wide

From the road between Marcoing and les Rues Vertes looking north. The St Quentin Canal runs across the centre of the picture. Only fragments of Marcoing Copse still exist. There were fewer trees in 1917 and crossing this ground would have been completely exposed to fire from the higher ground on the far side of the canal.

Eastern edge of the
former Marcoing Copse

Sherwood-Kelly

in front of the Masnières–Beaurevoir Line, the Battalion came under heavy rifle and machine gun fire from houses on the Masnières–Cambrai road. This position was too strong and the Battalion withdrew a hundred metres. A tank came up to assist but, with darkness falling, further action was cancelled for the night. Touch was made with 1st Border on the left, but no troops could be found on the right, so the company on that flank withdrew to face the Masnières–Cambrai road. The right centre company withdrew into support and the Battalion dug in. Total casualties for the day were 147.

1st Border arrived at its concentration area on Borderer Ridge near Gouzeaucourt at 3 a.m. At 7 a.m. the Battalion moved off behind 1st King's Own Scottish Borderers, proceeding to the west of the Gouzeaucourt–Marcoing railway to the start line in a sunken road running north from Villers Plouich. A number of casualties were sustained after the Battalion arrived there at 8 a.m. At 10.05 a.m. news arrived that the Hindenburg Support Line had fallen. At 10.20 a.m. the advance by 1st King's Own Scottish Borderers continued, supported by a number of tanks. 1st Border followed in diamond formation, with A Company leading, B Company on the right flank, C Company on the left flank and D Company in reserve. The Battalion kept 350m behind 1st King's Own Scottish Borderers and the advance progressed with almost no enemy resistance being encountered until nearing Marcoing. There was a halt just short of Marcoing to allow 1st King's Own Scottish Borderers time to clear opposition and establish two crossings over the canal. Opposition west of the canal was forced back over it. The main railway bridge was saved from destruction by sappers cutting the charge leads. Two companies of 1st King's Own Scottish Borderers crossed over to the east bank, leaving the other two companies to mop up on the west side.

At noon 1st Border entered Marcoing with A and D Companies pushing across the railway bridge. C Company crossed at the lock to the northeast at 12.12 p.m., having silenced a machine gun covering the lock bridge. Soon after crossing, a

Lock buildings
St Quentin Canal
Masnières

In Marcoing follow the road to Masnières over the canal bridge, noting the lock on the right side. Immediately after the bridge turn right, signed for Masnières D15, and immediately turn left up a slip road (Rue de la Gare) leading to the former railway station. There is plenty of room to park there. The canal lock and bridge are in the left distance, with the station approach road in the centre. The station building is hidden behind the bushes on the right next to the parked car.

machine gun was encountered on the railway station platform. **Sergeant Charles Spackman** attacked the gun, starting from 180m away and despite there being no cover at all. With his first shot he hit the gunner and then raced forward some distance before halting and shooting the second gunner. He finally rushed the position and bayoneted the third crewman and captured the gun.

The advance continued, with A and D Companies east of the railway and C Company to the west, while B Company was involved in taking Marcoing Copse with 1st Royal Inniskilling Fusiliers. C Company cleared two machine guns covering the lock from the northeast. A Company met the first serious opposition on the right when it reached the sunken road leading to the ammunition pits on the

The old station building in Marcoing, where Charles Spackman captured the machine gun, is fenced off and its future appears to be in doubt. Most of the tracks have been lifted. British telephone boxes get everywhere!

Looking southeast over the St Quentin Canal lock bridge at Marcoing. The station building is behind the trees at the highest point in the centre.

lower slopes of the Rumilly Spur. As 1st Royal Inniskilling Fusiliers had not yet arrived, a defensive flank was formed by D Company to prevent A Company being outflanked. B Company crossed the canal by the bridge and was in reserve on the western embankment of the railway station. Soon after 1.30 p.m. a combined attack by 1st Royal Inniskilling Fusiliers and A Company cleared the ammunition pits and a line was established from the canal. Plans were made for a combined attack by both battalions, but it was not possible for 1st Royal Inniskilling Fusiliers to get forward due to enfilade fire and it was getting dark. The attack was cancelled, but this message did not reach C Company, 1st Border, which attacked with a tank. The enemy line southwest of Flot Farm was penetrated but, due to heavy machine gun fire from the right flank the Company had to withdraw. A line of strongpoints was then established held by C, A and D Companies.

At 11.40 a.m. the Canadian Cavalry Brigade leading 5th Cavalry Division southwest of Gouzeaucourt was ordered to advance to Masnières and maintain contact with the infantry to its front. It was acknowledged that the situation between Masnières and Marcoing was unclear. At 12.07 p.m. the Fort Garry Horse led the advance. At 2 p.m. the Canadian Cavalry Brigade commander, Brigadier General John Seely, arrived at les Rues Vertes and conferred with Brigadier General Herbert Nelson, commanding 88th Brigade. Initial reports indicated that tanks were crossing the canal and the infantry had reached their objectives. Seely ordered the Fort Garry Horse forward, but by the time the Regiment arrived in the southwest of les Rues Vertes about 2.15 p.m. it was clear that the main bridge over the canal was broken. The enemy defending Masnières was also resisting strongly.

Assisted by local inhabitants and the Brigade Machine Gun Squadron, the Fort Garry Horse improvised a crossing suitable for horses at the lock to the southeast of Masnières. At 3.30 p.m. B Squadron, Fort Garry Horse began crossing, having suffered seven casualties during the construction and in crossing some marshy ground before the lock. Half an hour later B Squadron set off for the ridge east of Rumilly. At that time the bridge southeast of Mon Plaisir Farm had not been discovered, even though it appeared on maps carried by HQ 88th Brigade and its coordinates were indicated in 29th Division's operation order. The bridge was not taken until that night.

GOC 2nd Cavalry Division came forward and it was concluded that the lock was unsuitable for passing over large numbers of horses. In any case daylight was fading and the infantry had yet to secure their objectives, so there was no point in the cavalry racing ahead. The advance of the Fort Garry Horse was cancelled and the Canadian Cavalry Brigade was instead ordered to assist the infantry in holding a bridgehead at Masnières. Two riders were sent to recall B Squadron. One was the Fort Garry Horse CO, Lieutenant Colonel Robert Paterson DSO, and the other was Corporal Ryan of the Machine Gun Squadron, who had already been wounded in the arm. They followed the direction indicated by the infantry, but were unable to catch up. Paterson's horse was injured in a fall into a sunken road and he returned with some wounded and six prisoners. Ryan returned with a wounded cavalryman.

Meanwhile B Squadron had galloped north-eastwards through a gap in the German wire cut by the infantry. The Squadron then came under heavy fire and the commander, Captain Duncan Campbell MC, was killed (Flesquières Hill British Cemetery – VI B 16), and two others were also hit. **Lieutenant Harcus Strachan** took command and continued the advance. Southeast of Rumilly the Squadron cut its way through a screened road under heavy fire from Rumilly on the left and from pillboxes on the nearby spur. Strachan ordered the Squadron to charge a gun battery. The gunners managed to destroy one of the three guns, while another fired one round at point blank range but missed. The gun crews were killed or captured, but not before the Squadron suffered more casualties from flanking machine

Drive north from Masnières on the D644 towards Cambrai. At a roundabout with large flowerpots turn right and continue on this road for about one kilometre. When the road runs out keep going eastwards for another 400m to the sunken part of the lane held by Strachan and B Squadron. At the small copse at the top of the hill there is space to turn round. The photograph was taken from the sunken lane held by Strachan, on the right, looking southwest. Rumilly church is right of centre. The water tower on the horizon on the left is on the screened road. Masnières is in the dead ground beyond.

The sunken lane looking west.

gun fire. The gallop continued, with disorganised German infantry parties being overtaken and attacked. Any survivors were left in the belief that more cavalry units would soon be following. The Squadron took cover in a sunken road about 900m east of Rumilly until darkness fell, when it was realised that no support was coming.

Parties of Germans tried to outflank the position and were engaged successfully, but Strachan realised that they had to get away and sent two messengers back with reports on the situation. After dark the horses were stampeded (only five were unwounded) to confuse the Germans and Strachan led back the surviving cavalrymen on foot. Four German parties were dispersed at bayonet point on the way and more casualties were inflicted. Lieutenant William Cowen, who was wounded in the neck, became detached and returned first with nineteen men and nine prisoners. Strachan brought in another thirteen men. In addition to the prisoners brought back by the cavalry, a considerable number of Germans gave themselves up to the infantry after B Squadron had charged through them earlier. An order in the

evening from HQ 5th Cavalry Division to take Rumilly was cancelled later and the Canadian Cavalry Brigade pulled back into bivouacs. Eventually sixty-eight of the 127 men in B Squadron who set out returned. Of the remainder, sixteen were killed or died of wounds. In addition to Strachan's VC, B Squadron was awarded eleven other gallantry awards – three MCs, two DCMs, two MM Bars and four MMs.

On 29th Division's left, 86th Brigade secured the trenches on the near side of the canal, from the bend southeast of Noyelles to Nine Wood, and gained touch with 6th Division at Premy Chapel. On the right, assistance was given to 87th Brigade in clearing part of Marcoing. By 3.15 p.m. the Brigade's objective was secured. Patrols pressed on, but the Germans blew up the bridges at Noyelles, although the village was occupied around 4 p.m.

At the end of the day Third Army had advanced three to four miles along a frontage of six miles. Two complete trench systems in the Hindenburg Line had been overcome in less than four hours. This achievement was unprecedented on the Western Front and news of the victory caused church bells to be rung throughout the British Isles. The enemy had suffered heavy losses and over 4,200 prisoners had been taken, together with over a hundred guns, for less than 4,000 British casualties.

The new tactics had worked, but there were worrying signs. Not all the objectives had been taken. The Masnières–Beaurevoir Line had not been breached. Bourlon Ridge was still in enemy hands and 51st Division was held up in front of Flesquières, resulting in a troublesome salient in the British lines. In addition, tank losses had been severe, with 179 already out of action. Haig's next priority was to secure Bourlon Ridge, after taking Flesquières, then breach the Masnières–Beaurevoir Line to allow the cavalry through and for the French formations concentrated at Péronne to widen the attack front.

Capture of Bourlon Wood – 23rd–28th November 1917

301 Sgt John McAulay, 1st Scots Guards (2nd Guards Brigade, Guards Division), Fontaine-Notre-Dame, France
302 Pte George Clare, 5th Lancers (3rd Cavalry Brigade, 2nd Cavalry Division), Bourlon Wood, France

The first day of the Cambrai offensive on 20th November had been a resounding success. Flesquières was occupied at 6 a.m. on the 21st, completing the seizure of the second objective. Later in the day Cantaing and Anneux were taken, as was a section of the Hindenburg Support system east of the Canal du Nord.

That evening Haig closed down III Corps' operations across the St Quentin Canal in order to press forward against Bourlon Ridge. Unless this feature was taken the British would be forced to withdraw, as the forward troops were in poor defensive positions. Whatever the outcome, the British could not afford to become

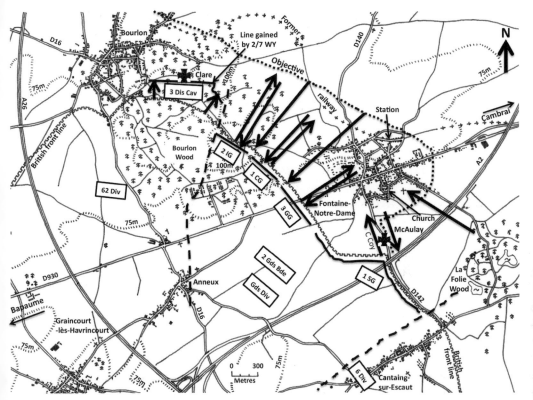

In Fontaine-Notre-Dame turn off the D930 Bapaume–Cambrai road southwards towards Cantaing on the D142. Just before going under the A2 autoroute, park carefully on the grass verge. Turn round to look back along the sunken road, the scene of John McAuley's VC action. Drive through Bourlon on the D16E1 northeastwards. Where the road swings to the left turn right, signed for 'Stade Municipale'. Continue past the Stade for 200m and park at the track junction. Walk along the track leading to the southwest for 250m to a track junction and small clearing, which appears to be used for fly tipping building waste. This is approximately where George Clare's VC action took place.

involved in a long wasting fight. The ridge had to be taken quickly, but it would not fall without a properly coordinated attack and the time needed to set this up would allow the Germans to recover. The next major attack was set for 23rd November, but early on the afternoon of the 22nd the Germans retook Fontaine-Notre-Dame from 51st Division. Meanwhile, 36th and 56th Divisions made further gains in the Hindenburg Line front system west of the Canal du Nord.

On 23rd November, IV Corps attacked along its entire frontage, but 51st Division on the right was thrown back from Fontaine-Notre-Dame. 40th Division, right centre, reached the northern edge of Bourlon Wood and entered the village, but the Germans regained it and by mid afternoon the troops were digging in. 36th Division, left centre, gained most of Moeuvres before being forced back to the southern edge and 56th Division on the left made some limited progress northwest of Tadpole Copse.

HQ Third Army was unaware of the extent of the gains, but any opportunity to exploit success was to be seized. 1st Cavalry Division was placed at the Army's disposal and a composite battalion took over a portion of 40th Division's line. 2nd Cavalry Division stood by in case mounted action was required. In the hope that Fontaine-Notre-Dame and Bourlon could be taken, the Guards Division was brought up to replace the tired 51st Division. The relief took place in snow and rain, but by 1 a.m. on 24th November, 1st Guards Brigade was holding the Division's front.

Orders were issued for 40th Division to capture Bourlon village on 24th November. The left was to be covered by 36th and 56th Divisions, while the Guards Division on the right remained on the defensive. Early in the day the British about Bourlon were subjected to a series of strong attacks, but they drove the Germans back. At 3 p.m. elements of 40th Division attacked Bourlon village not knowing that the attack had been cancelled. Three companies of 14th Highland Light Infantry passed through the village and consolidated the railway line to the north, where they were cut off.

The priority on 25th November was to link up with 14th Highland Light Infantry and secure Bourlon village. The attack ran into problems immediately and by 9.30 a.m. the isolated Battalion had been overwhelmed. Fighting in the Wood made little progress against enemy counterattacks. During the night 62nd Division relieved 40th Division in Bourlon Wood and in front of the village. Haig confirmed that Third Army was to secure Bourlon Ridge but, once observation over the British rear areas had been denied to the enemy, this would be the last effort for the year.

The Guards Division was to take Fontaine-Notre-Dame and the northeast corner of Bourlon Wood. For the operation 2nd Guards Brigade relieved 1st Guards Brigade and had fourteen tanks attached to it. The Division's frontage was shortened on the right by 6th Division (III Corps) taking over some of the line. Further assistance was to be provided by 62nd Division on the left, which was to secure the northern part of Bourlon Wood and the village. 62nd Division's front was shortened by 2nd Division, which had relieved 36th Division on the right.

It snowed during the day and night before the attack (26th November) and trudging forward to the attack positions was exhausting. There was no opportunity for reconnaissance by junior commanders and it was very late before they arrived in their attack positions. By zero hour (6.20 a.m.) on 27th November the snow had turned to drizzly rain.

2nd Guards Brigade attacked with three battalions in line. On the right, astride the Bapaume–Cambrai road, 3rd Grenadier Guards was to take Fontaine-Notre-Dame. In the centre, 1st Coldstream Guards was to seize the ground up to the railway between Bourlon Wood and Fontaine-Notre-Dame station. 2nd Irish Guards on the left was to attack Bourlon Wood. During the relief prior to the attack this Battalion came under very heavy fire and suffered about forty casualties. While these three battalions made the main attack, 1st Scots Guards was to secure the right flank in contact with 3rd Grenadier Guards. As soon as the first objective was taken, it was to send one company and a machine gun to the western part of Fontaine-Notre-Dame to hold the sunken road leading from the northeast of Cantaing.

As soon as the artillery and machine gun barrage came down, the troops moved off without waiting for the tanks. It was still dark. They were hit immediately by machine gun and artillery fire and casualties were heavy. The leading companies on the right of 3rd Grenadier Guards, south of the Cambrai road were almost annihilated by fire from La Folie Wood. Despite these setbacks, the centre of Fontaine-Notre-Dame was gained at 7.15 a.m., although the village was not completely cleared of the enemy and fire was still coming from the sunken road leading to Cantaing.

On the right, 1st Scots Guards continued the front south-eastwards. Left Flank Company was on the left, C Company in the centre and B Company on the right, with Right Flank Company in support. Shortly before 7 a.m. it seemed that the other battalions had reached the first objective, where they were to pause for half an hour. C Company was sent up the sunken road towards the southern edge of Fontaine-Notre-Dame to link up with 3rd Grenadier Guards. However, the reconnaissance, conducted in a snowstorm the previous night, did not notice that the road was not sunken after the first fifty metres. There was no cover beyond and the road was exposed to the machine guns in La Folie Wood. It was thought that by crawling, the worst of the fire would be avoided. This was true for fire from La Folie, but not from the southern part of Fontaine, which had yet to be cleared by 3rd Grenadier Guards. C Company advanced into intense fire, in particular from a machine gun in Fontaine-Notre-Dame church.

All the officers were killed or wounded and command devolved to **Sergeant John McAulay**. He carried his mortally wounded company commander (Lieutenant Arthur Middleton Kinnaird MC, son of 11th Baron Kinnaird, is buried in Ruyaulcourt Military Cemetery) 350m to the safety of a dugout. He was twice knocked over by bursting shells on the way. Kinnaird knew he was dying and whispered a farewell message to McAulay to relay to his mother. McAulay took other wounded men back to positions of safety and also killed two of the enemy who tried to stop him. Patrols failed to get in touch with 3rd Grenadier Guards on the left and the attack stalled less than 150m from the village. Having failed to get into the village, McAulay reorganised the men and beat off a counterattack from the left, which left fifty enemy dead. Reinforcements were requested and two platoons of B Company arrived. OC B Company took command of both companies and at dusk the troops were withdrawn in good order to their start positions. 1st Scots Guards suffered seventy-seven casualties, mainly in C Company.

The rest of the Brigade had also suffered badly. 1st Coldstream Guards ran into obstinate resistance, but the final objective was reached. Heavy fighting continued in the rear and there were considerable gaps between companies. On the left, 2nd Irish Guards went straight through to its final objective in the northeast of Bourlon Wood. It was in touch with 1st Coldstream Guards on the right but the left flank was in the air and no contact was made with 62nd Division. 4th Grenadier Guards (3rd Guards Brigade) was sent forward to reinforce the success, with its companies

From the D142 roadside bank looking north towards Fontaine-Notre-Dame. The short length of sunken lane is in the foreground.

being distributed between all three assault battalions. Despite the heavy losses incurred, 2nd Guards Brigade took over 600 prisoners.

The Brigade was unable to resist two heavy counterattacks. One was against the left of 1st Coldstream Guards and right of 2nd Irish Guards. The second was against the left of 3rd Grenadier Guards and the right of 1st Coldstream Guards. Small parties of Germans also worked around the rear of the Guards' line, as it had not yet been consolidated. 4th Grenadier Guards had yet to deploy its companies. A counterattack from La Folie swept through the outposts and entered Fontaine-Notre-Dame from the southeast, where it was joined by Germans emerging from the cellars. As a result of the counterattacks the whole Brigade was forced to withdraw, fighting all the way back. Only 460 men from the three assault battalions returned to the start line, which was held by 4th Grenadier Guards. By 1 p.m. the fighting in the Guards Division area was over, with nothing to show for the enormous losses incurred. That night 2nd Guards Brigade was relieved by 1st and 3rd Guards Brigades, except for 1st Scots Guards, which remained in the line until the night of the 28th/29th. 2nd Guards Brigade's casualties for the period 26th–28th November were ninety-six killed, 495 wounded and 489 missing.

On the left, 62nd Division's objective was the northern part of Bourlon Wood and the village as far as the railway. The advance was hampered by thick undergrowth and flanking fire. The main street was reached but no further progress could be made against heavy fire from the railway line. A counterattack at 4.30 p.m. was driven back, but the attack was called off and the positions held were consolidated. The highest part of the Bourlon Ridge had been taken, but the enemy still overlooked the British battery positions. The total British gain at Cambrai was a strip nine miles wide and four miles deep. However, it formed a salient into the German lines that was not easy to defend.

While the main British attention was on the fighting in the IV Corps area, the Germans had been preparing a counteroffensive. These preparations were apparent, but warnings were largely ignored by HQ III Corps and HQ Third Army. On the night of 28th/29th November the Guards and 62nd Divisions were relieved by 59th and 47th Divisions respectively. At the same time, 4th and 5th Dismounted Cavalry Battalions from 2nd Cavalry Division were withdrawn, but 3rd Dismounted Cavalry Battalion (3rd Cavalry Brigade), remained in position until the following night.

3rd Dismounted Cavalry Battalion had formed on 24th November when 3rd Cavalry Brigade had been warned to have a dismounted battalion on standby with a strength of 650. The CO and Battalion HQ came from 4th Hussars and each of the regiments in the Brigade provided a company of five officers and 200 other ranks. There were also eight machine guns from the Brigade Machine Gun Squadron. The company from 5th Lancers was commanded by Captain John Batten-Pooll, brother of Captain Arthur Batten-Pooll VC, Royal Munster Fusiliers.

By 25th November it was clear that the Brigade was not needed in the mounted role and it pulled back to camp at Fins. 3rd Dismounted Cavalry Battalion remained in support of 40th Division, with a strength of 590 all ranks, plus the eight machine gun teams. The target of 650 could not be achieved due to the requirement to have one man leading two horses as the rest of the Brigade pulled back. Early on the evening of the 26th the Battalion moved to dugouts by the Canal du Nord, about 2,700m north of Havrincourt. Next evening it moved into the support line about 135m from the northern edge of Bourlon Wood. By 7 p.m. on 28th November it had relieved 4th Dismounted Cavalry Battalion in the front line and spent the night digging in. The line held was that taken by 2/7th West Yorkshire in the attack by 62nd Division on 27th November.

The position was shelled heavily throughout the night, particularly half an hour before daylight. Throughout this time **Private George Clare** fearlessly exposed himself to all manner of fire as he tended the wounded and carried them back to

This track junction and clearing are approximately where George Clare's VC action took place.

a dressing station 450m behind the line. At one time all members of one of two listening posts, 135m in front of the front line and to the flank of Clare's position, were wounded. Clare left his trench and dashed over the open ground to reach the post unscathed. He bandaged the wounded and then manned the post singlehandedly until relieved. He carried the most badly wounded man, Lance Corporal Glascoe, to the shelter of a tree while he went in search of a stretcher and assistance. Returning with help he carried Glascoe to the dressing station, where he learned that the enemy was firing gas shells over the wood into the valley behind. The wind was blowing the gas towards the front line up the hill. Clare was exhausted, but set out from the right of the line and worked his way along the front to warn every post of the danger. Although exposed to enemy fire throughout, he reached the end of the line in safety. This prompt action saved many casualties. However, a few hours later he was killed when a shell landed close to him. The Battalion was relieved at 9 p.m. on 29th November by 17th London (47th Division) and marched back to Flesquières. The Battalion suffered sixty-six casualties on 28th–29th November, out of a Brigade total of 125.

Chapter Two

The German Counterattack at Cambrai

30th November

303 Sgt Cyril Gourley, D/276th Brigade RFA (55th Division), East of Épehy, France
304 Lt Col Neville Elliott-Cooper, 8th Royal Fusiliers (36th Brigade, 12th Division), East of la Vacquerie, France
305 Lt Samuel Wallace, C/63rd Brigade RFA (12th Division), Gonnelieu, France
306 Capt Robert Gee, 2nd Royal Fusiliers (86th Brigade, 29th Division), Masnières, France
307 LCpl John Thomas, 2/5th North Staffordshire (176th Brigade, 59th Division), Fontaine-Notre-Dame, France
308 Capt Walter Stone, 17th Royal Fusiliers (5th Brigade, 2nd Division), Moeuvres, France
309 Capt Allastair McReady-Diarmid, 17th Middlesex (6th Brigade, 2nd Division), Moeuvres, France
310 L/Dafadar Gobind Singh, 28th Light Cavalry att'd 2nd Lancers (Gardner's Horse) (5th (Mhow) Cavalry Brigade, 4th Cavalry Division), East of Épehy, France
311 Capt George Paton, 4th Grenadier Guards (3rd Guards Brigade, Guards Division), Gonnelieu, France
312 Capt Arthur Lascelles, 14th Durham Light Infantry (18th Brigade, 6th Division), Masnières, France
314 2Lt James Emerson, 9th Royal Inniskilling Fusiliers (109th Brigade, 36th Division), North of la Vacquerie, France

Despite the initial spectacular success of the British offensive at Cambrai on 20th November, little further was gained thereafter. The offensive was closed down on 27th November and an infantry division, two artillery brigades, a RFC wing and three tank brigades were withdrawn from Third Army. On 28th and 29th November reports indicated that a German counteroffensive was imminent. GHQ believed that Third Army was capable of containing the attack because of the battering the Germans had received over the previous months in Flanders and at Cambrai. The German aim at Cambrai was to retake the salient lost on 20th November by attacking the northern and southern flanks simultaneously.

An air of complacency pervaded the British high command. On the right of Third Army's front, HQ VII Corps alerted HQ Third Army to the coming attack, but with little reaction. The Corps' frontage of over twelve kilometres was held

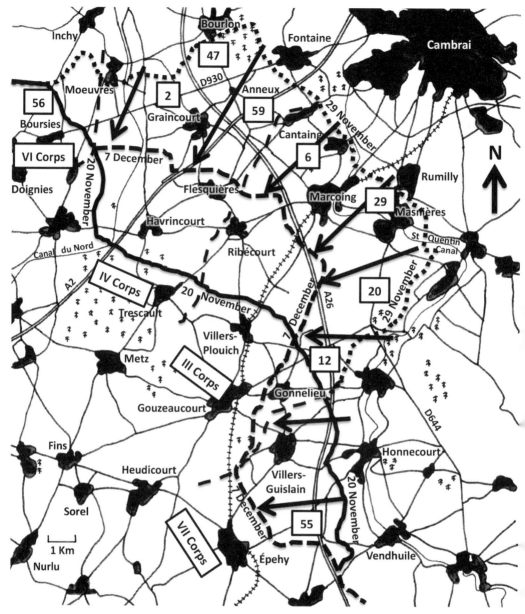

The German counteroffensive at Cambrai. The line at the start of the British attack on 20th November is shown, in addition to the line on the 29th, i.e. the furthest extent of the British gains and also on 7th December, where the front stabilised at the end of the German counteroffensive.

weakly by just two brigades of 55th Division. The only reserves available were tired divisions that had been through the recent offensive.

VII Corps stood by for an attack from 5.30 a.m. on 30th November. The artillery bombarded the enemy trenches, but all was quiet and patrols found nothing unusual. At 6 a.m. the enemy guns opened fire and the barrage grew heavier as gas was mixed

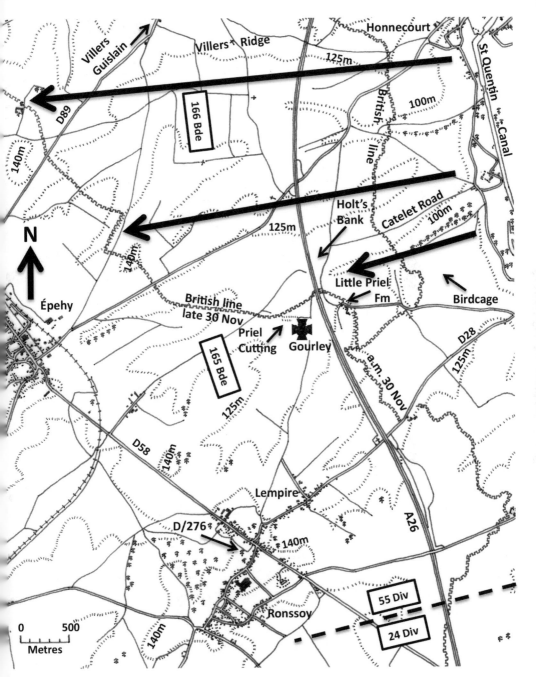

Drive through Vendhuile southwest on the D28. Cross the St Quentin Canal, continue up the hill for 800m and turn right onto a rough track that leads to Little Priel Farm. The track is passable by car with care. Pass the farm and the track swings right, parallel with the A26. Follow it down the hill and turn left under the autoroute. Turn immediately left and continue southwards for 300m. On the right is a rather indistinct track. Follow it on foot as it curves to the right to reach a low embankment. Straight ahead is a shallow re-entrant. This is where Priel Cutting was in 1918 but it has since been filled in and ploughed over. The British front line was just to the north of the Cutting, in the vicinity of which was the section of guns of D/276th Battery.

From Gourley's gun position near Little Priel Farm. There is nothing left of Priel Cutting except for a shallow re-entrant.

with the HE. The morning was dark and misty and no enemy concentrations were detected by the RFC. At 7 a.m. German infantry began moving forward and a few minutes later SOS signals from the British front line brought down the protective barrage.

On the right of 55th Division was 165th Brigade. The German blow fell on the left of the Brigade, which was forced back 900m. At Little Priel Farm, which was lost and retaken later in the day, the enemy came under point blank fire from a 4.5″ Howitzer section of D/276th Battery RFA. It began engaging the advancing Germans on SOS Guillemont at 7.10 a.m. in response to SOS signals from the front line. From 7.30 a.m. it came under counter-battery fire and 681795 Sergeant Edward James Thornley went to find the gun position officer, Lieutenant Harry Reginald Ridealgh MC, for instructions. However, Ridealgh was seriously wounded and Thornley arranged for his removal and cleared the detachments out to a flank. Thornley then consulted a trench mortar officer who told him that the enemy was practically on top of them. Ridealgh instructed Thornley to do what he could and to hang on for as long as possible.

The Germans were seen advancing along Holt's Bank and 114983 Gunner Clough Hartley suggested they go back to the guns and engage them. Thornley then gained the agreement of CO 1/6th King's to engage the enemy advancing along Holt's Bank rather than continue with the SOS task on Birdcage. By the time Thornley returned to the gun position the ten-man section was scattered. Some had taken cover in dugouts in Priel Cutting while others attempted to get the wounded away. Thornley collected four men (Corporal Howard, 681791 Gunner Fred Backhouse (signaller), 167717 Gunner Thomas Arthur Jevons (signaller) and Hartley) and got one howitzer back into action. They fired about twenty rounds into the enemy over

open sights until a machine gun, firing from close range from a flank, forced them into cover. They then had to return to Battery HQ, having removed the breech mechanism and dial sight.

When communication with this section was lost the Battery Commander, Major John Hudson MC, received information through a runner, 681787 Bombardier Joseph Austin Pinnington. He learned that the officer was wounded, the howitzers had been temporarily abandoned and the enemy was closing in. He sent a reliable SNCO, **Sergeant Cyril Gourley**, with instructions to re-establish the line and keep the howitzers in action for as long as possible. On his way Gourley detailed a signaler, 656259 Gunner Alfred George Oram, to work forward along the telephone line and on arrival at the section position, about 10.30 a.m., he set two other signalers (Jevons and Backhouse) to work back down the line. Gourley then collected all the men he could find and held them in cover in readiness for a lull in the firing.

At about 11 a.m. the barrage moved south towards the three signallers attempting to repair the wire. Gourley reported to CO 1/6th King's to seek information and they agreed that the gunners would provide a slow rate of fire on the Birdcage. This they did, using one howitzer at a time and moving the detachments around. The gunners then put one howitzer out of action by removing and burying the breech mechanism lever. At 12 p.m. a 1/6th King's officer, Captain Geoffrey Glynn Blackledge MC, asked Gourley if he could do anything about the enemy coming down Holt's Bank and Cottesmore Road (not identified, but may be Catelet Road running northeast from Holt's Bank). Gourley collected Sergeant Thornley and four other men (Gunner Hartley, 681770 Bombardier Thomas Edge, 72339 Gunner Charles Oliver and 199319 Gunner Reginald Charles Evans), and pulled the remaining howitzer out of its pit and moved it twenty metres. They opened fire on the enemy only 370m to the front and flank. There were also snipers to the rear. After firing twenty rounds, three enemy aircraft appeared and engaged the gunners with machine-guns. They also appear to have reported the position and about one hundred 4.2″ shells fell around them. The crew took cover and Gourley again reported to CO 1/6th King's, who asked him to stay in readiness.

Fifteen minutes later Gourley and Gunner Hartley fired another eight rounds before being driven off again. Lieutenant Mitchell Biggart arrived at about 2 p.m., having been sent by the Battery Commander to take over the section, and reported to CO 1/6th King's. The Germans were again seen on Holt's Bank and in front of it. Biggart led Gourley, Thornley, Edge, Hartley and Oliver out to the howitzer at 2.30 p.m. with each man carrying two shells. Gourley was No.1, Edge laid and fired, Biggart loaded, Thornley prepared the charges and the other two carried up more ammunition. Despite close range rifle and machine gun fire, they fired off another twenty rounds. Two machine guns opened fire from the left flank, forcing them into the cover of the gun pit twenty metres away, leaving Bombardier Edge to fire three rounds, between each dashing for cover and returning to fire the next round. The gun sights were recovered and the men made their way to Battalion HQ. At 4 p.m. the enemy was seen running over Villers Ridge, south of Villers-Guislain. Battalion HQ feared an attack through Priel Cutting and the gunners assisted the infantry to build a barricade and carry ammunition and bombs. After dark the Battery Commander sent a party to assist in recovering the guns along Lempire Road to Battalion HQ, where the limbers married up and brought them back. They went into action almost immediately in the main Battery position. In addition to Gourley's VC, Lieutenant Biggart received the MC, Sergeant Thornley and Bombardier Edge the DCM and the MM was awarded to Corporal Howard, Bombardiers Edge and Pinnington, and Gunners Backhouse, Evans, Hartley, Jevons, Oliver and Oram.

On 55th Division's left, 166th Brigade took the full brunt of the German onslaught. Some posts held out for an hour, but most were swept away and it seemed as if the enemy might break through. By 9 a.m., 164th Brigade in reserve was moving to a blocking position, but it was very weak. Stout resistance slowed the enemy, but did not halt them. Reinforcements from 24th Division in the south and 4th and 5th Cavalry Divisions moved forward in preparation to counterattack, but despite 55th Division being so weak it managed to establish a new line by the end of the day. Even so the enemy was able to advance about four kilometres at its deepest point.

Third Army allocated 1st Cavalry Division to VII Corps, but reinforcements from First Army would not arrive until the next day. Two French divisions were positioned behind the right of VII Corps in case an attack developed against 24th Division. 61st Division was brought forward to the area between Metz and Heudicourt, from where it could support IV, III or VII Corps.

III Corps was exhausted from the previous ten days' fighting. It had four divisions (12th, 20th, 29th and 6th) in the line when the attack fell upon it an hour later than in VII Corps to the south. The loss of the Banteux Ravine in the north of 55th Division's area (VII Corps) allowed the Germans to drive deep into III Corps' right flank held by 12th Division. Its front extended 4,500m from north of Turner Quarry to Lateau Wood. 12th Division's position was not ideal, having

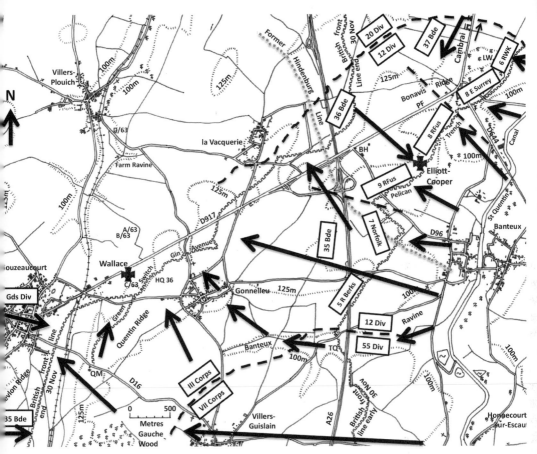

Overview of the action in 12th Division's area on 30th November 1917. The following abbreviations are used on this and the following map – TQ = Turner Quarry, BH = Bleak House, QM = Quentin Mill, LW = Lateau Wood and PF = Pavé Farm.

resulted from the salient formed by the successful advance on the 20th. Because of this the lines of communication lay almost parallel to the front line. All three brigades were holding the front, with 35th Brigade on the right, 36th Brigade in the centre and 37th Brigade on the left. 11th Middlesex (36th Brigade) and 6th Queen's (37th Brigade) were held in reserve near Heudicourt. The Division had three field artillery groups, one to support each brigade. As the enemy advanced, the loss of Villers-Guislain and Gouzeaucourt destroyed all links to the brigade HQs.

On the right, 35th Brigade's front was held by 7th Norfolk on the left and 5th Royal Berkshire on the right. 7th Suffolk and 9th Essex were in support. The Brigade came under fire from 6.45 a.m. onwards and at 6.50 a.m. the enemy bombardment fell on Villers-Guislain. At 7.10 a.m. news arrived that the attack had spread to 12th Division's front and attacks on the Brigade began at 7.30 a.m. 169th Army Brigade RFA reported infantry falling back through its positions near Villers-Guislain cemetery. German infantry swarmed over the hill, while more advanced up Banteux Ravine towards the southeast of Gonnelieu. This thrust hit 7th Suffolk in support on the right of the Division. Only an officer and about fifty other ranks managed to fight their way out. A portion of this attack continued up the valley and

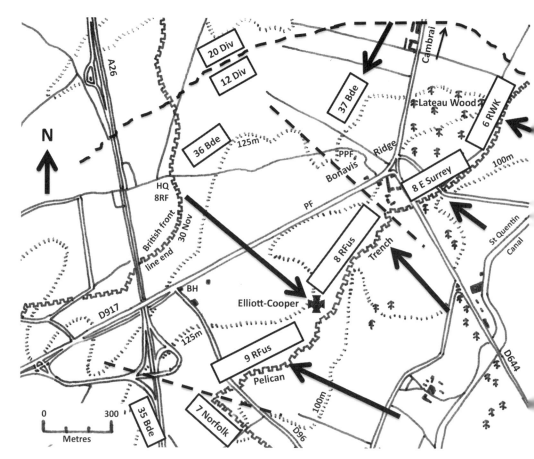

Drive northeast along the D917 towards Cambrai. Just after the turning onto the A26 autoroute on the right take the left signed for la Vacquerie. After 150m turn right and follow this track around to the left up the hill and down the other side to a t-junction. Turn right, cross over the autoroute and 150m further on is an open area where you can park. This is approximately where Battalion HQ of 8th Royal Fusiliers was located and from where Neville Elliott-Cooper launched the counterattack onto the high ground to the southeast. In addition to the abbreviating in the previous map, there is one other – PPF = Pam Pam Farm.

was joined by some of the enemy who had been deflected from Villers-Guislain. They advanced unopposed into Gouzeaucourt, overrunning HQ 29th Division.

To the northeast of Villers-Guislain, in a valley below the cemetery, was Brigadier General B Vincent's HQ 35th Brigade. It had to pull back at 10 a.m. to a small ridge about 200m from the HQ dugouts. It continued the rearward move through Gauche Wood, holding off the enemy until ammunition gave out. It then fell back to Revelon Ridge, where it was reinforced by 11th Middlesex and shortly afterwards by 6th Queen's coming up from Heudicourt. The 12th Division's artillery Right Group HQ, under Lieutenant Colonel RC Coates DSO, was in a dugout close to HQ 35th Brigade. He and his adjutant narrowly avoided being taken prisoner, but the orderly officer, who was telephoning the batteries, was captured.

Revelon Ridge was held and a 400 strong party of Divisional details under Major Johnson, 9th Essex, went forward to Vaucelette Farm, where they found an officer and sixty men of the Loyal North Lancashire (55th Division) holding out. The enemy was held there and prevented from moving southwest from Chapel Crossing. In the afternoon Brigadier General Vincent organised a counterattack without artillery support. It advanced 900m and on the left was in contact with the Guards Division, which had retaken Gouzeaucourt. 35th Brigade also remained in contact with 36th Brigade on its left and prevented a breakthrough. It held this line until relieved on 4th December.

In the centre, 36th Brigade's front south of the Gouzeaucourt–Cambrai road (D917) was held by 9th Royal Fusiliers on the right and 8th Royal Fusiliers on the left. 7th Royal Sussex was in support. The bombardment began at 6.45 a.m. and infantry assaults followed at 7.40 a.m. The Germans attacked 9th Royal Fusiliers by advancing up the spur from Banteux and bombing along Pelican Trench from the south. The attacks were held but the retirement of the left of 35th Brigade forced the right of 36th Brigade to withdraw in compliance. The enemy followed rapidly and pushed on to near the Cambrai road. A counterattack by 9th Royal Fusiliers pushed them back 200m and established a line across the Hindenburg Line. D Company, 9th Royal Fusiliers was cut off holding strongpoints covering Bleak House. Except for an officer and thirteen men, all were lost.

B and A Companies, 8th Royal Fusiliers held the Battalion's line and the northern end of Pelican Trench. At 7.00 a.m. a heavy bombardment fell on Bonavis Ridge, followed by smoke. At 7.45 a.m. large numbers of enemy were seen advancing from the St Quentin Canal. At 8.00 a.m., B and A Companies were attacked by Germans appearing suddenly from their right rear, as a result of the advances made against 35th Brigade. They were overrun and only twelve men fought their way back to the reserve line. D Company, which was moving up in support, was forced back. Bonavis Ridge was seized and the enemy was within fifty metres of the reserve line held by C Company, close to Battalion HQ. Despite being unarmed, **Lieutenant Colonel Neville Elliott-Cooper** mounted the parapet and called on the HQ staff, C Company and remnants of D Company, a total of only 140 men, to follow him. They charged into the enemy and, although hopelessly outnumbered, pushed them back 550m over the Cambrai road before the Germans rallied. Elliott-Cooper saw

From the bridge over the A26 autoroute near 8th Royal Fusiliers' Battalion HQ looking southeast over the open and featureless terrain of the counterattack.

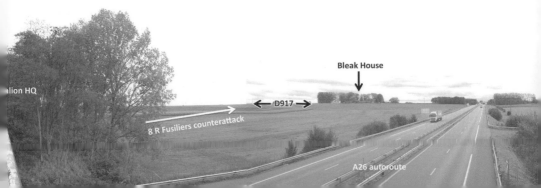

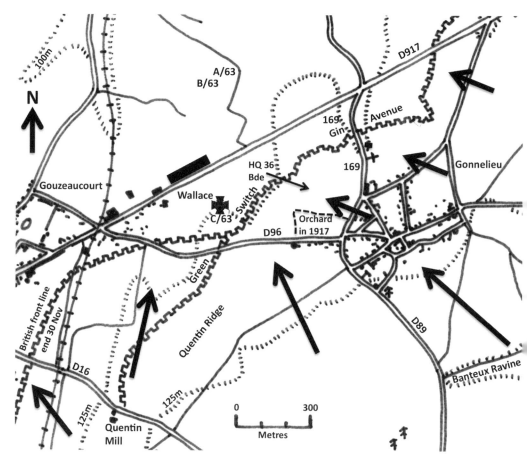

Leave Gonnelieu westwards on the D96. Pass the water tower on the left and continue for another 400m to where there are a number of places to pull off the road safely. C/63rd Battery RFA was in the field to the north of this spot about 170m from the road.

the impossibility of consolidating where they were and ordered his small force back as their casualties began to mount. Elliott-Cooper was badly wounded forty metres in front of his troops and was taken prisoner.

The counterattack released a number of D Company men taken prisoner earlier and brought to a halt the enemy's advance on this part of the battlefield. The remnants of the Battalion took up positions in the reserve line southeast of la Vacquerie in contact with 9th Royal Fusiliers on the right. It drove off several enemy advances. At 10 a.m., 7th Royal Sussex moved into the centre of the reserve

From C/63rd Battery's position looking east towards Gonnelieu. Green Switch ran across the picture about 180m in front of the camera position.

line, with remnants of both Royal Fusilier battalions on either side, and was also in contact with 37th Brigade on the left. A secure front was established and the enemy was held with ease thereafter. Firing died down after dusk. By the end of the day 8th Royal Fusiliers had suffered 257 casualties.

Due to the shape of 12th Division's front, HQ 36th Brigade was in 35th Brigade's area west of Gonnelieu, which also held a dressing station and some rear details. The Right Group of 12th Division's artillery consisted of the four batteries of 63rd Brigade RFA and two batteries of 169th Army Brigade RFA. The latter batteries were situated south and north of Gin Avenue near Gonnelieu cemetery. Just to the south of them was a 6″ Howitzer battery. A, B and D Batteries, 63rd Brigade RFA were further north of Gonnelieu and C/63rd Brigade was 550m to the west. Between 5 a.m. and 7 a.m. each battery fired 200 rounds of harassing fire against Honnecourt to assist 55th Division. At 6.45 a.m. the batteries were ordered to fire the SOS mission in front of 55th Division as the Germans closed in.

The Germans appeared without warning at Gonnelieu and soon occupied it, taking many prisoners. At 8.30 a.m. the Germans appeared at the northern edge of Gonnelieu. The two 169th Army Brigade RFA batteries at first withdrew their men under heavy shellfire, but SOS fire was ordered and the guns were manned again and engaged the enemy at a range of about 360m. The 6″ Howitzer battery had to be abandoned and two 18 Pounders disabled them with direct hits. The Brigade HQ details and part of 69th Field Company RE moved up the road to the cemetery in a pre-arranged manoeuvre, but several men were lost on the way. A machine gun team of 235th Machine Gun Company falling back came into action at the cemetery. It caused massive casualties to the advancing Germans until every man was killed. At the same time the two 169th Army Brigade RFA batteries put up a valiant defence. When one battery ran out of ammunition, efforts were made to manhandle the guns to the Cambrai road to the north under heavy machine gun fire. This was unsuccessful and when the other battery ran out of ammunition all the guns had to be abandoned. Casualties were heavy but they had held back the enemy for over an hour. At the last possible moment the breechblocks and dial sights were removed and taken with the gunners as they fell back with the infantry.

HQ 36th Brigade was west of the orchard north of the village. At 10 a.m. it was forced to pull back over the Cambrai road and later to Farm Ravine and Villers-Plouich, where communications were re-established with HQ 12th Division. Before leaving, the commander of 36th Brigade, Brigadier General CS Owen, arranged for Green Switch to be held by 70th Field Company RE, Brigade HQ details and two companies of 5th Northamptonshire (Pioneers), all under the command of

Quentin Ridge

Gouzeaucourt →

Major James Dunlop Gemmill RE (MC for this action). C/63rd Brigade RFA was about 180m west of Green Switch. About 10.30 a.m. the Germans advanced from Gonnelieu and from Quentin Mill towards the Cambrai road. A and B/63rd Brigade RFA ran their guns onto the crest of the ridge north of the Cambrai road to engage this threat.

C/63rd Brigade RFA was threatened from both flanks and the crest in front by the German advance. It would be in action throughout the rest of the day under shell, aircraft and small arms fire. Earlier it had provided harassing fire against Honnecourt and at about 8.45 a.m. reports were received that the enemy was just south of Gonnelieu. Casualties in the Battery were light until about 10.30 a.m. when enemy riflemen and machine guns came into range. At 10.35 a.m. the enemy appeared 550m behind the Battery, crossing Quentin Ridge. **Lieutenant Samuel Wallace** turned one of the guns round and drove the enemy back over the ridge. The Battery came under heavy shellfire and many casualties were sustained, including the battery commander (Major Raymond Douglas Belcher DSO, died of wounds 7th December – Mont Huon Military Cemetery, Le Treport) and five of the sergeants. Wallace assumed command. The Battery also came under fire from enemy aircraft and small arms fire from the ground increased.

Eventually only Wallace and twelve men remained. They fought on for two hours, engaging targets at 100–450m, including a party of Germans at Gonnelieu cemetery. By then Wallace had only five men (Sergeant W Howard, Bombardiers F Gould and W Coyles, and Gunners J Mantle and A Burgess – all awarded the DCM for this action) and two guns remaining. These were run out of their pits with their trails close together to allow them to be swung to cover the front and flanks. The Germans were to the front, rear and right flank. Running from one gun to the other they kept both in action, firing in three directions. They covered other battery positions and assisted the remnants of 35th Brigade to hold out. The enemy closed to 135m, but the gunners maintained their fire to protect the infantry in Green Switch and prevented the enemy from crossing the Cambrai road and gaining the high ground to the north. The other three 63rd Brigade RFA batteries supported C/63rd Battery and enabled it to achieve its objective.

With almost no ammunition left, Wallace prepared to carry on the fight by hand. After being in action for eight hours, reinforcements from 60th Brigade (20th Division) arrived from the north via Gin Avenue and the guns were saved. Wallace and his exhausted men had no ammunition, so they recovered the sights and breechblocks from the guns before pulling back with their wounded. The guns were recovered a few days later by 9th Division. Green Switch was relieved by elements of the Guards Division about 2 p.m.

On the left of 12th Division, 37th Brigade held the line with 6th Royal West Kent on the left and 7th East Surrey on the right, in contact with 8th Royal Fusiliers (36th Brigade). 6th Buffs was in support at Pam Pam Farm. The first attack at 6.50 a.m. came from the north. It passed west of Lateau Wood, cutting between the front line and supports to reach Pam Pam Farm at 7.30 a.m., where it was held by 6th Buffs. The second attack came from the east. It drove in the front line and passed south of Lateau Wood to reach Pavé Farm about 7.35 a.m. It was checked by fire from HQ 37th Brigade details in a sunken road 550m northwest of the Farm. At 7.50 a.m. 6th Buffs counterattacked and retook Pam Pam Farm. It was driven out later and retook it again, but was eventually forced to fall back to a line 450m to the west, where it was joined by surviving companies of 6th Royal West Kent and 7th East Surrey from the front line. This line was held until 2 p.m. when the Germans brought up minenwerfers. It fell back another 450m to the west in contact with 8th Royal Fusiliers. At 7 p.m. the remnants of 37th Brigade formed a composite battalion and held the line until relieved on the night of 1st/2nd December.

At 10.15 a.m., 5th Cavalry Brigade (2nd Cavalry Division) was ordered to secure Revlon Ridge. By 12.40 p.m., thirty-six tanks of 2nd Tank Brigade were moving towards Gouzeaucourt and around 1 p.m., twenty-seven tanks of 1st Tank Brigade were also advancing. Meanwhile, about 12 p.m., 1st Guards Brigade advanced towards Gouzeaucourt, but due to confusion the other brigades did not come into action all day. The advance swept up 20th Hussars and some sappers and pioneers holding the line west of Gouzeaucourt. By 1.30 p.m. the village had been retaken and the gunners were able to bring their guns back into action. By the time the tanks arrived the fight was over.

60th Brigade pushed the enemy back from Villers-Plouich, stabilised the line south of the Gouzeaucourt–Cambrai road and also stabilised the front south of la Vacquerie. By noon the enemy advance was threatening 20th Division's left flank and 59th Brigade on the right was almost destroyed by a sudden enemy onslaught. A line was established in the Hindenburg support system and, despite repeated attacks, the enemy failed to advance further. 61st Brigade's front was overrun and the survivors fell back on a reserve position east of the Hindenburg support system, where touch was made with 59th Brigade on the right and 29th Division on the left. 20th Division had suffered a heavy defeat, but it had started the day in a poor defensive position and its reserve brigade (60th), which could have restored the situation, was diverted to the south. Having retreated to Welsh Ridge, the combined force of infantry and artillery firepower diverted the enemy thrust northwards into the right of 29th Division.

29th Division's front beyond the St Quentin Canal was held by 86th and 87th Brigades. 87th Brigade on the left covered from the Masnières–Cambrai road to Château Talma, north of Marcoing. 86th Brigade's HQ was on the main road 200m north of the canal bridge in Masnières. 16th Middlesex was on the Brigade's right at Mon Plaisir Farm and the canal lock bridge. It was commanded by Lieutenant Colonel J Forbes-Robertson (Bar to the DSO for this action), who was awarded the VC for his actions in April 1918. 1st Lancashire Fusiliers was on the left, with its left on the Masnières–Cambrai road. 2nd Royal Fusiliers was in support on the eastern edge of Masnières and the Royal Guernsey Light Infantry was in reserve at the

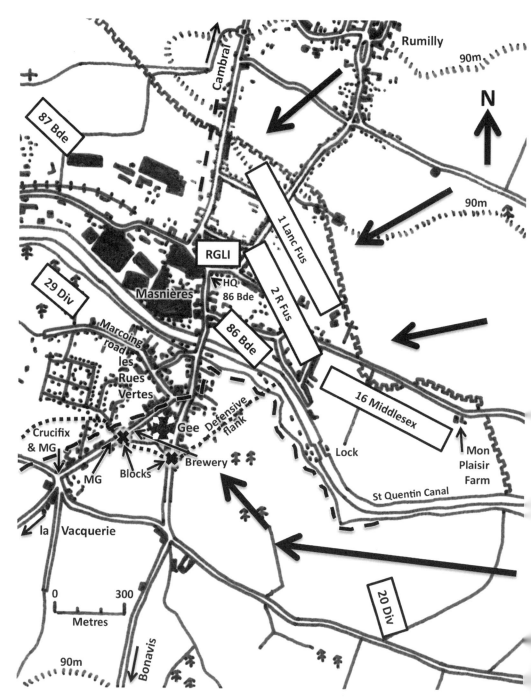

Approach Masnières from the south on the D644 from Bonavis. Go straight on at the crossroads and 300m beyond is the site of one of Robert Gee's roadblocks. At the traffic lights turn left into Rue Verte and immediately left again into Rue du Calvaire. The former brewery is 200m along this road on the left side.

church. Les Rues Vertes to the south of the canal was split by the 29th/20th Division boundary and was not held. The village contained 86th Brigade's ammunition and bomb dump on the La Vacquerie road.

The enemy bombarded the area from 7 a.m. and by 8.40 a.m. the forward battalions were under attack. Despite suffering heavy casualties, the Germans secured Mon Plaisir Farm and advanced south of the canal to enter the south of les Rues Vertes unopposed. **Captain Robert Gee**, the Staff Captain responsible for the dump, was informed by Brigade HQ of the collapse of 20th Division's flank and was ordered to establish a defensive flank in the village. Gee sent a message to warn 497th Field Company RE but the majority had already been captured. Then the telephone line to Brigade HQ was cut by shellfire.

The Brigade Commander, Brigadier General GRH Cheape, sent two Royal Guernsey Light Infantry companies to assist in les Rues Vertes. Gee did not know this and made plans for the force at his disposal, which consisted of Captain Loseby of the Lancashire Fusiliers and twelve signallers and orderlies. Gee sent Loseby and six men to gain touch with 16th Middlesex at the lock while he resolved to clear the village with the rest. He was particularly concerned to prevent the dump falling into enemy hands.

Gee's tiny force ran into strong German parties advancing along the La Vacquerie road. While one man went back for a Lewis gun, he sent two men across the street to engage the enemy while the other two went into the houses to throw out material to form a barricade. One man was killed crossing the road, but the fire of the remainder surprised the Germans and they hesitated, allowing time for a rough barricade to be thrown up. A few minutes later the Lewis gun arrived, but they could not find a position for it to fire over the barricade. Gee ordered the gunner to blow a hole in a feather bed, which he had previously asserted was absolutely bulletproof.

The Germans almost enveloped Masnières and les Rues Vertes was in danger of being overrun from two directions. If it fell the troops north of the canal would be cut off. With the barricade established Gee determined to get into the dump, which was the second house beyond the barricade. Hearing a noise behind he turned and bashed a man over the head with his stick, flooring him. He then climbed the wall into the dump and found both dump men dead and the quartermaster sergeant was missing. Gee was seized by two Germans, but killed one by driving the stump of his broken iron-shod stick into the man's stomach and he then tried to throttle the other. A desperate struggle followed until the man he had just knocked out by mistake arrived and shot the German through the head.

On the way back to the barricade the other soldier was shot dead. Thirty to forty Royal Guernsey Light Infantry reinforcements arrived. Gee sent some to assist Loseby's party and set the rest to work building another barricade, while he led his original party to the dump to load up with grenades. This party cleared the enemy on the eastern side of the street before switching over to clear the opposite side. A few minutes later the two Royal Guernsey Light Infantry companies arrived. Now with a

Site of the roadblock across the Bonavis road looking, from the German side.

reasonably sized force Gee was able to establish a line on the edge of the orchard at the southern end of the village. He linked up with Loseby, established posts on the canal bridges, set up another barricade across the southern end of the Bonavis road and also sent a bombing party to clear the houses along the Marcoing road.

As the action was going well, Gee turned his attention to supplying ammunition and bombs to the troops north of the canal and at the bridges. Once a flow was in motion he resolved to remove the last German foothold in the village at the brewery. He formed a bombing party and moved into the orchard east of the brewery. Some bombs were held in position against the wall and a hole was blown. Gee passed through into the brewery yard where some doctors from 89th Field Ambulance informed him that the Germans had just left, taking a hundred sapper prisoners with them. Gee ran into the road where a barricade had been established to see if they had halted the Germans, but the subaltern in charge had pulled back the post and did not engage the enemy for fear of hitting the British prisoners.

Gee moved the post forward to secure the southwest corner of the village and then set off to see what the Germans were up to. He observed them digging in 100m south of the village with a machine gun on the la Vacquerie road. Gee brought up a Stokes trench mortar and, when it fired a wildly inaccurate round as a distraction, he and an orderly rushed the machine gun from a flank. The orderly was shot, one of four with Gee to suffer this fate that day. Gee rushed the position alone, shot the eight gunners with his two revolvers and then turned the gun on its previous owners. The enemy was driven out of the position, which was consolidated.

Looking southwest along the la Vacquerie road. The brewery stood behind the white gates on the immediate left.

The machine gun post rushed by Robert Gee and his orderly was just beyond this crossroads at the small bus shelter on the right.

From the crucifix looking northeast along the la Vacquerie road into Robert Gee's position. The corner house was behind the wall on the left.

Later the troops came under fire from another machine gun in a corner house near the crucifix, as well as from numerous snipers. Gee was forced into the cover of a shellhole for a while, but realised that it was essential to silence the machine gun before last light. He made a dash for the barricade and as he jumped it a sniper hit him in the knee. He refused to have the wound dressed until he was satisfied with the organisation of the defence. Gee had a Stokes mortar brought up to silence the machine gun.

When the Brigade Commander heard that Gee was wounded, he sent a relief, but Gee insisted on taking him round the whole perimeter to formally hand over the defence before he went back to Brigade HQ to make his report. Once the wound had been dressed the Brigadier ordered Gee back to Marcoing for treatment, but on the way he was challenged by a German sentry and had to swim the canal to escape.

Elsewhere a strong enemy attack at 9 a.m. was beaten off by 1st Lancashire Fusiliers. Three more attacks later in the morning also failed. At 10 a.m. a single machine-gun of 86th Machine Gun Company killed or wounded every man and horse of a German gun battery. Gee's actions saved 86th Brigade from being cut off and destroyed and slowed the whole German advance. At the end of the day the Brigade's line was intact. A defensive flank had been established from the lock to les Rues Vertes and on to the canal bank where it joined 87th Brigade.

87th Brigade's reserve established a position south of Marcoing Copse and the divisional commander (de Lisle) ordered 88th Brigade to assemble south of Marcoing. The Germans were driven back with heavy casualties. A new line was established and the ground lost on the southern bank was recovered. Touch was made with 86th Brigade at les Rues Vertes and with 20th Division on the right.

In IV Corps' area the Germans did not try to achieve surprise, indeed it would have been impossible, with the British overlooking the open country between Bourlon and Inchy. The enemy shelled the area from dawn onwards and the British artillery joined in almost immediately, concentrating on counter-battery work. At 8.50 a.m. the enemy artillery concentrated its fire on the front positions.

On the right 59th Division's front was held by 176th Brigade. 2/6th North Staffordshire was on the left, on the edge of Bourlon Wood, supported by 2/6th South Staffordshire. 2/5th North Staffordshire was on the right, near Cantaing, with 2/5th South Staffordshire in support. To the left was 47th Division and on the right in front of Marcoing was 6th Division (III Corps). The line formed an

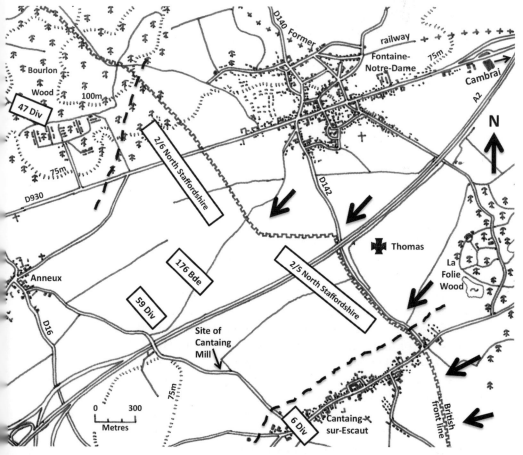

In Fontaine-Notre-Dame turn off the D930 Bapaume – Cambrai road southwards towards Cantaing on the D142. Go under the A2 autoroute and about 350m beyond park on the left where a parallel track heads back towards the autoroute. Follow it northwards to the fence and turn right along the parallel track with the autoroute for 250m. John Thomas's VC action was in the field to the right in line with the church in Cantaing. When last visited the field was being used to grow high quality turf, so best keep off it!

exposed salient and, although outside the area of the main attack, the Germans resolved to squeeze it out. The first attack at 7 a.m. came with little warning, and almost no artillery preparation, but was well supported by aircraft. At 7.30 a.m., an attack against the right of 59th Division and the left of 6th Division was twice defeated by rifle fire. The main concentration was against 6th Division but the line held. However, the situation remained obscure and 177th Brigade was sent to take over the defence of Flesquières. At 8.15 a.m. the Germans began shelling the whole of 2/5th North Staffordshire's position. The Battalion HQ was in Cantaing Mill, which was burnt down and an ammunition dump was destroyed. This bombardment went on until 3.30 p.m.

Around 11 a.m. **Lance Corporal John Thomas** of 2/5th North Staffordshire saw the enemy preparing for another assault. On his own initiative and with a comrade he went forward to make a close reconnaissance. In full view of the enemy they ran forward 200m, but on the way his comrade was shot. Thomas went on alone and reached some trees, which he crawled around and then on for another 135m. He shot three snipers and observed a large dugout used by the enemy to concentrate their troops. They came out in threes and fours and Thomas waited until they were twenty metres away before opening fire. He remained out until 3.30 p.m. On returning he brought back valuable information on enemy dispositions so that when the attack came it was broken up by the artillery.

On the left of 176th Brigade the Germans shelled Bourlon Wood all day. At 10 p.m. the barrage intensified, with gas shells mixed in with the HE, and went on until about 4 a.m. the following day. The two battalions on the left of 176th Brigade suffered about 350 casualties, but the Germans made no attempt to attack.

47th Division, holding Bourlon Wood and the high ground to the west, was shelled heavily. On the left, 140th Brigade was not in close contact with 2nd Division and after 2 p.m. the Germans got around this flank. A renewed frontal

From the south looking north over the autoroute (not visible) towards Fontaine-Notre-Dame.

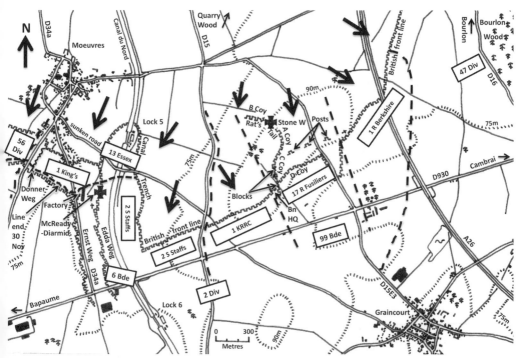

2nd Division on 30th November 1917. To get close to the site of Walter Stone's VC action, cross the Canal du Nord on the D930 towards Cambrai. After two kilometres turn left into a minor road and follow it uphill for 900m to the crest. Stop here and look to the left (southwest). The Rat's Tail ran between here and the prominent copse. It used to be possible to get much closer to the site of Walter Stone's VC action but the area south of the copse has been turned over to breeding game birds and there is no longer any access to the edge of the copse. To overlook Allastair McReady-Diarmid's VC action site, approach Moeuvres from the south along the D34a by turning off the main D930 Bapaume – Cambrai road. Edda Weg ran parallel with the D34a about halfway between it and the Canal du Nord. Continue into the village and take the first right along the sunken road to reach the canal bridge for an elevated view of the Edda Weg area.

attack drove the British off the crest and the right formed a defensive flank facing west. Counterattacks regained some ground, but not the crest. Although the salient was held it was untenable and on 4th December it was decided to withdraw.

2nd Division held the front between Bourlon Wood and Moeuvres with 99th Brigade on the right and 6th Brigade on the left. The troops were already very tired due to spending the previous three days in movement and reliefs. The enemy was seen concentrating for the attack and the artillery and machine guns inflicted heavy losses on them as they emerged from Quarry Wood and entered Moeuvres. Despite losses, the Germans came on. On the right of 99th Brigade, 1st Royal Berkshire lost four advanced posts, but enfilade fire from 47th Division helped restore the situation and reinforcements came up in case a counterattack was required.

In the centre of 99th Brigade, 17th Royal Fusiliers (attached from 5th Brigade) was holding its frontage of 550m and a 900m long sap, the Rat's Tail, which ran out at right angles to the front line. It was part of the original Hindenburg Support Line and had a commanding view of the surrounding country. D Company held the main line and the other three companies were in the Rat's Tail – B Company at the northern end, A Company in the centre and C Company in the south. The CO, Lieutenant Colonel Spencer Vaughan Percy Weston, was unhappy with the arrangements when he took over from 1st King's Royal Rifle Corps on the night of 28th/29th November. The companies in the Rat's Tail were 'in the air' and there was no depth or a reserve. As a result two platoons of B Company were held at Battalion HQ as a reserve and two platoons of C Company were positioned 100m to the rear

Taken in May 2001 after a particularly wet spring. This was one of a number of dugouts that collapsed under the weight of water at the northern end of the Rat's Tail. The fact that they survived for so long is testament to the skill of the German engineers who built them.

of the right of D Company to support that flank. 1st King's Royal Rifle Corps had attacked just before 17th Royal Fusiliers took over and formed three posts forward of the main line. They were held by one and a half platoons of D Company.

When the enemy guns opened fire at 9 a.m. the CO rang B Company to find out what was happening, but the line was dead. **Captain Walter Stone**, commanding A Company in the sap also overlooked the enemy. He reported to the CO that the enemy was advancing in large numbers along the whole divisional front towards the southeast. Unable to contact the artillery the CO rang HQ 99th Brigade and was told that the artillery had already been informed. It was clear that the Rat's Tail was untenable and the Brigade Commander gave authority to pull back and hold the main line. Before this could be done the Battalion was involved in close fighting.

At 9.30 a.m., A Company was ordered to withdraw to the centre of the main line, leaving one platoon as a rearguard. B Company was to go to the left, in touch with 1st King's Royal Rifle Corps, while the RSM and a party of 10th Duke of Cornwall's Light Infantry (Pioneers) and some men from C Company established a block 200m north of the junction of the Rat's Tail with the front line. The block was to be held at all cost. The rest of C Company was sent to the right in touch with 1st Royal Berkshire. The CO ordered Stone to pass on the order to B Company since its telephone line had been cut.

Stone informed the CO that the advancing enemy had disappeared into dead ground 725–900m north of the end of the Rat's Tail. He then organised the withdrawal of his Company and remained with the rearguard platoon. No sooner had the withdrawal commenced than the enemy closed on his position. He calmly stood on the parapet with a telephone sending back much valuable information. The enemy came on in droves and the first line was shot down, as was the second. The divisional artillery ranged onto the enemy and held the attack long enough for the main position to be occupied. However, in the meantime the rearguard was surrounded and was attacked from east, north and west simultaneously. By 10.30 a.m. almost 300m of the northern end of the Rat's Tail had been lost and the rearguard was destroyed fighting to the last. Stone was killed by a shot through the head. Had it not been for his sacrifice and that of Lieutenant Solomon Benzecry (MID for this action – commemorated on Cambrai Memorial) and the rearguard, the rest of the Battalion would have been unable to reform and the enemy would almost certainly have overrun the main line.

The Rat's Tail was evacuated down to the C Company block, which was reported lost just after 11 a.m. when it ran out of bombs. The RSM had established another block at the junction of the Rat's Tail with the main line. When a runner brought the CO news of Stone's death, he was unsure if the rearguard had done its job. The CO sent two platoons of D Company to hold a line 275–350m in front of the main line in order to buy more time. On the left a company of 1st King's Royal Rifle Corps was reported to have been pushed back. As a result, CO 17th Royal Fusiliers sent all available men from Battalion HQ to form a defensive flank from there to the road.

From the minor road looking southwest over the D930 and the Canal du Nord. The Rat's Tail ran between the camera and the copse and then downhill towards the building on the extreme left on the D930.

He also positioned a sergeant to shoot anyone who fell back along this trench and prepared to destroy his maps and papers. At this critical moment supplies of bombs and ammunition arrived. A bombing party drove the Germans back 200m to the block in the Rat's Tail. The flanking companies reported that they were in contact with neighbouring units. Two of the three advanced posts were lost, but 17th Royal Fusiliers' main line was never broken and the casualties inflicted on the enemy were enormous. The men were in fine spirits, although ammunition resupply remained a problem.

On the left of the Brigade, 1st King's Royal Rifle Corps drove off every attempt to close with it. At 11.25 a.m. the enemy launched another attack on 99th Brigade. Penetration of 1st Royal Berkshire's position was restored by a counterattack, aided by a company of 23rd Royal Fusiliers. Another attack at 12.10 p.m. was broken up by artillery but, when 47th Division's left flank collapsed around 2.30 p.m., some 1st Royal Berkshire posts on the right flank were overrun.

At 3.40 p.m. another large attack was repulsed by a Brigade machine gun team and the Rat's Tail block party firing into the enemy flank. The block was commanded by Lieutenant Forbes Menzies, who positioned snipers to pick off any enemy who showed themselves. They eventually accounted for the German leader and the attacks petered out. The final attack in this area came at 4.25 p.m., when the Germans tried to overcome the block held by 17th Royal Fusiliers. They were seen assembling in the Rat's Tail and on the right and the artillery broke them up. 17th Royal Fusiliers was relieved by 24th Royal Fusiliers at 10 p.m. Its casualties were thirty-three killed, 119 wounded and forty-one missing.

On the left, 6th Brigade was also hard pressed. Shelling of battery positions and the rear areas commenced at 7.30 a.m. and at 8.30 a.m. the enemy was seen massing to the north. At 9.20 a.m. the Germans began advancing south of Quarry Wood towards the canal and this quickly extended across the whole Brigade frontage. At 9.50 a.m. the SOS signal was sent up on the left. Shelling was heavy and there were many casualties, but initially the attack fell on 56th Division on the left and 6th Brigade's fire was directed to that flank to support it.

In the centre of 6th Brigade, 13th Essex was forced back from Canal Trench at Lock 5. Just before 10 a.m. the sunken road was attacked and the German broke in. Despite enormous casualties being inflicted on them, they reached close to Battalion HQ and the ruined factory by 11 a.m. A company cut off west of the Canal fought to the end. The enemy was driven back elsewhere with heavy casualties and by 5 p.m. the right flank was secure, but Lock 5 and the canal crossing to the south of it were lost. The Germans tried repeatedly to make progress east and west of the canal but were held by 13th Essex, supported by 2nd South Staffordshire. Attempts during the night to try to link up with the lost company and regain Lock 5 came to nothing. Two runners were sent from the company at about 4 p.m. to say it would fight to the end. It did. During the night 13th Essex was relieved by 22nd Royal Fusiliers.

West of the Canal, 1st King's in the old Hindenburg Line support trench was attacked at 10.25 a.m. from Moeuvres and the left flank. The enemy made an entry in 56th Division's area and a protective flank was formed by B Company, 1st King's. However, it was overwhelmed and the enemy penetrated almost to the southern end of Donner Weg, threatening Battalion HQ in the support line (former Hindenburg Line front line). After heavy fighting, a bombing attack succeeded in driving the Germans back along Donner Weg and establishing a block there. It was then held against many attacks.

A German attack between Donner Weg and Edda Weg was halted with heavy losses by small arms fire. Some survivors took cover in shell holes and sniped at the defenders until they were cleared out at bayonet point. At 10.20 a.m. a German bombing attack came within fifty metres of the support line before it was driven back to 130m short of the front line. Bombing attacks continued throughout the day along Donner Weg and Edda Weg.

17th Middlesex was in support west of the Canal du Nord. A and C Companies were in dugouts south of the Bapaume–Cambrai road, with D Company in dugouts to the rear and B Company in reserve in dugouts near Lock 6. At 9 a.m. the companies were warned to move at a moment's notice, each man in light kit carrying two grenades. A Company was the first to be called forward to support 1st King's. Its place was taken by D Company and B Company moved forward into D Company's old dugouts. C Company then moved up to support 1st Kings,

The area in which 17th Middlesex operated in support of 1st King's from the south.

which was under heavy attack and its left company was badly knocked about. The enemy penetrated down the trenches almost as far as the Bapaume–Cambrai road. However a counterattack by D Company, led by **Captain Allastair McReady-Diarmid**, drove them back 300m and took twenty-seven prisoners.

By 2 p.m. D Company was established 450m southwest of Lock 5, but could advance no further due to a lack of bombs and a mass of uncut wire. B Company was just to the south. Meanwhile A and C Companies had helped 1st King's to prevent a breakthrough and limited the enemy gains to a few hundred metres of front line trench.

At 9 p.m. B Company relieved D Company and was ordered to press on to the sunken road south of Moeuvres and Lock 5, that was reported to be held by a 13th Essex company. The CO of 1st King's took command of the whole front west of the canal (1st King's on the left and 17th Middlesex on the right) with the intention of recapturing the enemy gains, but the attempt did not succeed. During the night the enemy bombed down both sides of the Canal du Nord and the trenches of the Hindenburg Line to the west, but were driven off.

The same area as the previous view from the canal bridge looking south.

At 5 a.m. C Company, 17th Middlesex halted a heavy attack down Edda Weg and at 8 a.m. the enemy launched a series of heavy bombing attacks along the whole front west of the canal. B Company was hit badly and ran out of bombs. The enemy advanced 275m and threatened HQ 1st King's. A Company, 17th Middlesex halted the advance with its Lewis guns but not before B Company had been utterly exhausted and left without any officers.

McReady-Diarmid realised the seriousness of the situation. Calling for volunteers and collecting plenty of bombs, he led the attack along Edda Weg, throwing bombs as he went. The enemy was pushed out of all their gains but, just as he gained the objective, McReady-Diarmid was killed by an enemy bomb. Ninety-four enemy casualties were attributed to his bomb throwing, of which sixty-seven were killed. In 1966 former 42627 Sergeant Ernest Crook DCM, who was with McReady-Diarmid throughout this action, claimed that he was 'two-thirds cut', i.e. drunk, at the time. Whether true or not, it does not detract from McReady-Diarmid's outstanding and sustained bravery in clearing Edda Weg against the odds.

During the next night B and D Companies were relieved by 2nd Highland Light Infantry (attached from 5th Brigade) and moved back to support trenches west of

A similar view in May 2001 after very heavy spring rains. Note the two dark patches in the field, which are collapsed dugouts along the course of Edda Weg.

the canal near the Bapaume–Cambrai road. A Company, still attached to 1st King's, recaptured 275m of Ernst Weg before moving back into support of 2nd Highland Light Infantry. C Company remained in support of 1st King's until relieved in the early hours of 1st December and returned to dugouts south of the Bapaume–Cambrai road. Elsewhere 6th Brigade beat off other attacks and by 5 p.m. on the 2nd the front was again secure. 6th Brigade's casualties were 1,077, of which 17th Middlesex suffered 178.

At the end of the day the extent of the enemy attacks was still not clear to the high command, but it was apparent that III Corps and the right of VII Corps had suffered the worst of the day's fighting. Reserves were being rushed to the area, but at the expense of troops destined for Italy. French units were stood by to assist in case they were needed on the right flank. Orders were issued to III and VII Corps to attack early on 1st December to forestall the expected resumption of the enemy attack at dawn; a tall order without fresh troops.

1st December

The night of 30th November/1st December was a frantic time for both sides. As the Germans reorganised to resume their attack, the British prepared for a desperate counterattack. The British attack, which coincided with the first trace of dawn at 6.30 a.m., was made from south to north by 4th Cavalry Division, 5th Cavalry Division (with 8th (Lucknow) Cavalry Brigade of 4th Cavalry Division attached), and the Guards Division (III Corps). The attackers had little idea about the location of the forward troops of 55th Division, through whom they had to pass, nor of the enemy and his strength.

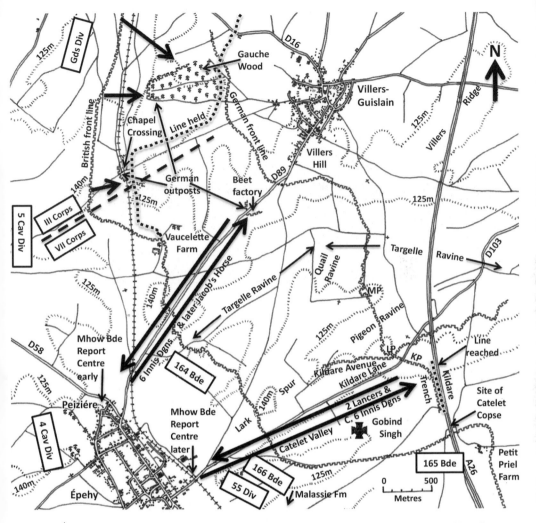

Leave Épehy in a northeasterly direction on the D103 towards Honnecourt. Cross the former railway line where the Brigade report centre was set up later in the day and continue east for 1,300m to a left turn. Stop here to look over Catelet Valley to the south along which Gobind Singh galloped with his messages.

4th Cavalry Division's attack was to be made mounted by 5th (Mhow) Cavalry Brigade galloping along Targelle Ravine, south of Villers Hill, to establish a defensive flank facing south and southeast. 6th Inniskilling Dragoons was then to skirt the Ravine on the west and ride onto Villers Ridge. The Brigade was ready at 6.30 a.m. but there was a delay while lances were brought forward by cart, during which the regiments suffered casualties from artillery. The supporting tanks also failed to arrive.

At 8 a.m. news arrived of the failure of 8th (Lucknow) Cavalry Brigade in 5th Cavalry Division. The Cavalry Corps Commander, Lieutenant General Sir Charles Kavanagh, grew impatient when he learned that the 5th (Mhow) Cavalry Brigade had not left its start positions. He ordered the mounted attack to go ahead immediately in the hope that it would also assist 8th (Lucknow) Cavalry Brigade to get ahead. There was no time to coordinate artillery arrangements with 55th Division and at 9 a.m. the advance commenced, supported only by 4th Cavalry Division's horse artillery. 2nd Lancers left Épehy at 9.35 a.m. by the southern exit under artillery fire, followed by C Squadron, 6th Inniskilling Dragoons to the left rear and a section of 11th Machine Gun Squadron (four guns). They crossed the railway and rode down Catelet Valley, intending to turn north and gain Targelle, Quail and Pigeon Ravines from the east. Instead they came under machine gun fire on either side of the valley and from Kildare Trench, which barred the way forward.

The charge continued, some horses jumped the wire in front of Kildare Trench and others found gaps. The CO of 2nd Lancers, Lieutenant Colonel Henry Hamilton Fryers Turner was killed (Tincourt New British Cemetery), but the defenders fled. Lieutenant Neville Harris Broadway (Cambrai Memorial) led a few men after the retreating Germans. He killed two Germans with his sword before he was shot by a German officer, who had one hand raised in surrender but kept a revolver in the other behind his back. The German officer was immediately killed by a lance thrust from another cavalryman. A number of other enemy were cut down by the pursuing horsemen before they reined in. Enemy fire prevented further advance. The cavalry occupied Kildare Trench and Post and the horses were huddled into the cover of the sunken Kildare Lane, while others were sent back. A defensive line was organised with, from the south D, A, B and C Squadrons, 2nd Lancers, then C Squadron, 6th Inniskilling Dragoons. Two machine guns were placed on both flanks, one facing forward and other to the rear. On the right, D Squadron, 2nd Lancers pushed out a post and gained contact with 1/6th King's (165th Brigade, 55th Division), which facilitated the resupply of ammunition and the evacuation of the wounded.

On the left, C Squadron, 6th Inniskilling Dragoons in Kildare Post drove off a number of counterattacks. An attack from Kildare Avenue, a communications trench running along Lark Spur, to the left rear of the Post, was crushed by a squadron of

From the ridge line south of Catelet Valley looking northeast.

2nd Lancers that moved out to meet it. This allowed 1/6th King's (165th Brigade, 55th Division) on the other flank to establish a post in Catelet Copse.

As soon as 2nd Lancers advanced, the rest of 6th Inniskilling Dragoons left Peiziére on the Villers Guislain road with the aim of gaining Villers Ridge. The leading squadron was followed by a section of 11th Machine Gun Squadron, then the other two squadrons, with a RE field troop in the rear. They crossed the railway line and for about 900m the ground was good going for cavalry, but beyond the western end of Targelle Ravine there was no cover. The leading squadron and machine gun section lost heavily to German machine guns. However, they reached the beet factory, where the survivors were surrounded and few returned. The HQ and remaining squadrons wheeled back to Peiziére.

To the 5th (Mhow) Cavalry Brigade commander it appeared that 2nd Lancers and C Squadron, 6th Inniskilling Dragoons had reached Pigeon Ravine. At 10.15 a.m. he sent two squadrons of 38th Central India Horse forward on foot along the southern slope of Lark Spur. They were checked by fire from Limerick Post. The other two squadrons, on a more southerly route by road, did no better.

A message from 2nd Lancers had to get to HQ 5th (Mhow) Cavalry Brigade to ensure that the commander was aware of the true situation. The distance was about 2,500m, mostly under enemy observation and fire. Volunteers were called for and Sowar Jot Ram and **Lance Dafadar (Lance Corporal) Gobind Singh** came forward. They were given identical messages and set off at a gallop, Jot Ram to the right and Gobind Singh to the left. Jot Ram was shot down and killed as he passed Limerick Post (Neuve Chapelle Memorial), whilst Gobind Singh managed to cover half a mile before his horse was killed by machine gun fire. He lay still until he believed that he was no longer being watched, then rolled, crawled and ran, diving to the ground as shots passed close to him. He reached Brigade HQ at 10.50 a.m.

The brigade commander composed a message, wanting to know if 2nd Lancers could connect with the infantry and hold out. Gobind Singh, with the message and a fresh horse, set off along the higher ground to the south of the valley. His horse

was shot down, but he managed to reach the Regiment by a sunken road. A reply to the commander's question had to be taken to Brigade HQ and Gobind Singh again volunteered. He was rejected initially because it was felt that he had done enough. However, he reasoned that it made sense for him to take the message, as he knew the ground better than anyone else. He set off, riding through the barrage, but halfway through Épehy his horse was killed by machine gun fire. He again avoided injury and reached Brigade HQ at Peizière at 11.55 a.m. The message reported that the Regiment was connected with the infantry on its right flank, but an enemy machine gun on the left meant that flank was in the air and the Germans were attacking from the left rear. Gobind Singh offered to return with another message but was firmly refused. By then he had covered about 7,500m under constant heavy fire to deliver the three messages.

Communications with 2nd Lancers was established by signal lamp at 12.45 p.m. but attempts to send forward more machine guns failed. At 3 p.m. 2nd Lancers reported the location of its line and two German strongpoints. Its left was still in the air and an enemy attack was developing from that flank.

Under the impression that 2nd Lancers was at Pigeon Ravine, HQ VII Corps urged 55th Division to make every effort to seize the line of posts (Kildare, Limerick, Meath) under cover of the cavalry attack on Villers Hill. At 1 p.m. an attempt by 1/5th King's (166th Brigade) to seize the line Meath–Catelet, reinforced by two dismounted squadrons of 38th Central India Horse, was stopped in its tracks by a hail of fire from front and flank. 4th Cavalry Division was ordered to make a fresh attack and 8th (Lucknow) Cavalry Brigade was returned to it. It was to attack the beet factory from

From the railway crossing southeast of Épehy looking along the D103 towards Honnecourt. This is where 5th (Mhow) Cavalry Brigade's report centre was located later in the day. Catelet Valley, along which Gobind Singh galloped three times, is to the right of the road and Lark Spur is to the left.

the west from the area of Vaucelette Farm, while 5th (Mhow) Cavalry Brigade attacked dismounted from the south. 5th Cavalry Division planned to attack at 3 p.m. and 4th Cavalry Division decided to comply. In preparation, VII Corps' heavy artillery was to bombard the objective, while the horse artillery brigade engaged machine posts in the area. However, 5th (Mhow) Cavalry Brigade had too few troops remaining for another attack, just two weak squadrons of 6th Inniskilling Dragoons, a squadron of 38th Central India Horse and two machine guns.

At 3 p.m. Jacob's Horse (8th (Lucknow) Cavalry Brigade) advanced on the beet factory following the road from Peiziére. 6th Inniskilling Dragoons had already failed by this route and the German machine guns were still intact. Little progress was made and heavy casualties were incurred. The Jodhpur Lancers (Cavalry Corps Troops) filled a gap on the left between 36th Jacob's Horse and the Canadian Cavalry Brigade, but no progress was made elsewhere. The overall result of these ill-coordinated attacks by the cavalry, often without tank or adequate artillery support, was that little was accomplished.

In 5th Cavalry Division, 8th (Lucknow) Cavalry Brigade's objective was Villers Guislain, whilst 3rd (Ambala) Cavalry Brigade took advantage of the advancing tanks to move on Gauche Wood. Six tanks allocated to 8th (Lucknow) Cavalry Brigade could not be contacted in time for zero hour, due to a change of plan. The Brigade was led on foot by 36th Jacob's Horse and the Jodhpur Lancers, each with a section of 12th Machine Gun Squadron attached. All the artillery in 5th Cavalry Division was allocated to support the 3rd (Ambala) Cavalry Brigade, so the 8th (Lucknow) Cavalry Brigade set off supported only by twelve guns of 12th Machine Gun Squadron. At 6.50 a.m. 36th Jacob's Horse, about 230 rifles strong, was hit by heavy machine gun fire from Chapel Crossing and posts between there and the beet factory. Efforts to get forward along the railway failed and the survivors were pinned down.

On the left, the tanks supporting 3rd (Ambala) Cavalry Brigade were late and lost direction, but the Brigade was joined by tanks in support of the 8th (Lucknow) Cavalry Brigade instead and pressed on towards Gauche Wood. The other tanks rectified their navigational error and cruised along the west and south of the Wood to engage the German machine guns and generally assist 1st Guards Brigade in the close fighting. Two counterattacks from the right were repulsed and three field guns were captured. Few Guards officers had escaped injury and the cavalry officers rendered great service in consolidating the position.

The dismounted Canadian Cavalry Brigade reached the southeast corner of Gauche Wood, taken in the morning by 3rd (Ambala) Cavalry Brigade and the right battalion of 1st Guards Brigade (2nd Grenadier Guards). Chapel Crossing was taken at 3.30 p.m. and, after repulsing a counterattack from the direction of the beet factory at 4.30 p.m., the Canadians established themselves beyond the railway north of Vaucelette Farm.

HQ VII Corps ordered 55th Division to be relieved by 21st Division between Malassis Farm and Vaucelette Farm, including relieving the cavalry units. 2nd

Lancers made a difficult withdrawal after dark. About 170 horses were in the sunken lane but, due to the shape of the ground, only one could be led out at a time to the south. The withdrawal was covered by C Squadron, 6th Inniskilling Dragoons following which 5th (Mhow) Cavalry Brigade went into reserve, having suffered 126 casualties.

The Guards Division's objective was Gauche Wood–Quentin Ridge–Gonnelieu. 1st Guards Brigade on the right had twenty tanks of H Battalion and 3rd Guards Brigade on the left had thirty-seven tanks of D and E Battalions. 1st Guards Brigade advanced from the railway southeast of Gouzeaucourt to secure Gauche Wood to Quentin Mill. 2nd Grenadier Guards on the right had 900m of open ground to cross, which was covered 'as fast as their legs could carry them'. This tactic worked and there were few casualties until reaching the northern edge of the Wood. Twelve tanks that had been delayed in crossing a sunken road joined the fight. Two counterattacks from the right were repulsed but several tanks were knocked out by the German artillery. 18th Lancers (3rd (Ambala) Cavalry Brigade) assisted in the fight. Three tanks were knocked out trying to move into Villers-Guislain and at 1.20 p.m. the remaining tanks withdrew from action. However, Gauche Wood was secured. On the left, 3rd Coldstream Guards secured the crest of Quentin Ridge as far as the Mill, assisted by four tanks, all of which were hit by direct fire or ditched. About 11 a.m. a company of the Brigade reserve secured the left flank.

On the left of the Guards Division, 3rd Guards Brigade was to continue the capture of the Ridge north of the Mill and take Gonnelieu. 1st Welsh Guards was on the right, 4th Grenadier Guards on the left and 1st Grenadier Guards was in support to protect the left flank. 2nd Scots Guards was already on the high ground on the left about Villers-Plouich. 1st Welsh Guards set off without tank support, having failed to make contact in the dark. Reaching the crest of the Ridge, the two leading companies came under terrific fire from machine guns in the old British Green Switch trench. The survivors were forced to take cover until one of the tanks arrived. It traversed Green Switch with fire, forcing the enemy to surrender. 1st Welsh Guards swept forward, collected about 300 prisoners and began digging in beyond the crest.

4th Grenadier Guards spent the previous night dug in on the railway line. It was to take Gonnelieu without tank support, led by No.2 Company on the right and No.3 Company on the left. No.4 Company was in support and No.1 Company was in reserve. At 6.30 a.m. the Battalion passed through the remnants of 6th Oxfordshire & Buckinghamshire Light Infantry (60th Brigade, 20th Division), which had made an abortive attack the previous night, and advanced up the gentle slope in full view of the enemy. Despite being crowded with Germans, few British shells landed in the village. Machine gun fire was terrific, but the line never faltered. No.2 Company on the right swung too far right and ran into fire from the Germans in front of 1st Welsh Guards, losing many men, including most of its officers. No.3 Company on the left reached the road leading to la Vacquerie and paused to allow

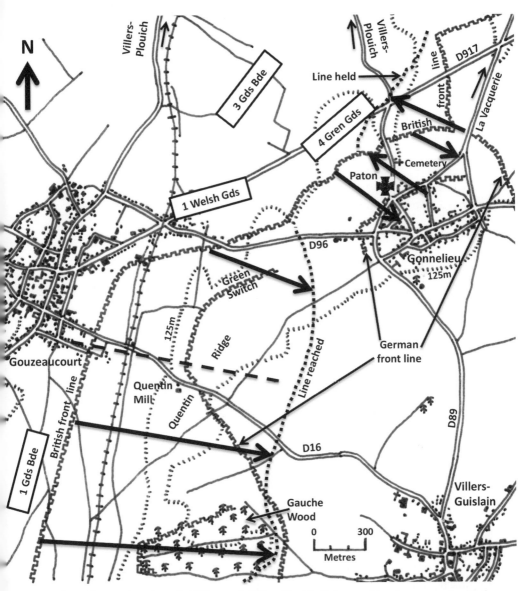

Leave Gonnelieu northwards on the D89 towards Villers-Plouich. Before reaching the crossroads with the D917, stop on the right, where there are a few places to pull over safely for a few minutes. The axis of the 4th Grenadier Guards attack was from the D917 towards the cemetery.

No.4 Company to catch up, then continued to fight its way into the outskirts of Gonnelieu. It came up against a large body of enemy assembling to resume their own attack. The cemetery north of the village was taken, but the Germans reacted quickly and forced 4th Grenadier Guards back. The survivors rallied with their support and reserve companies.

Captain George Paton, commanding No.4 Company in support, established a line in a trench in front of Gonnelieu, but to his left he saw a mixture of troops

From the D917 looking along the axis of the attack by 4th Grenadier Guards. George Paton was active throughout this area.

wavering in the face of the enemy counterattack. He leaped out of the trench and ran over the open ground with bullets kicking up earth all around him. He moved from trench to trench in full view of the enemy machine gunners, encouraging men from various units and steadying those who had lost their officers. He adjusted their dispositions and personally removed some of the wounded, being the last to leave the village. Paton readjusted the line again and held it against four counterattacks, each time springing on top of the parapet to lead the resistance; he was eventually mortally wounded.

The right of the Battalion linked up with 1st Welsh Guards and the Germans were prevented from advancing against Gouzeaucourt and Villers-Plouich, but the British attack had been entirely futile. Even if 4th Grenadier Guards had taken the village, it could not have been held due to the failure on either flank. At the end of the day 4th Grenadier Guards held the face of a salient, with 1st Grenadier Guards holding the northern flank and 1st Welsh Guards the southern. The Battalion held this position until relieved by 2nd Scots Guards on 2nd December. It suffered 204 casualties, including the CO, Lieutenant Colonel Viscount Gort, who was awarded the VC in 1918.

Further north 16th Brigade offered stout resistance, but weight of numbers forced it back. The Germans reached a communication trench behind the old British front line, where they were struck in the flank by 1st Grenadier Guards (3rd Guards Brigade). A new line was established, having given up the awkward salient held the previous night, but the enemy made no further progress in this area.

86th Brigade (29th Division) beat the enemy back with heavy losses, but was so weak that it had to be reinforced to avoid being overrun. That night 86th Brigade withdrew and, by 4 a.m. on 2nd December, a new front had been established by

87th and 88th Brigades between Marcoing and Masnières. 6th Division beat off an attack with little difficulty. Fighting continued in 6th Brigade's area (2nd Division) and enemy gains were restored by counterattacks. Attacks elsewhere were beaten off and by 5 p.m. the front was once again secure.

3rd December

2nd December was comparatively quiet following two days of strenuous fighting. Small-scale operations took place around la Vacquerie and the Germans made some gains. 29th Division's position beyond the St Quentin Canal remained precarious and 16th Brigade (6th Division) moved to cover its rear on Highland Ridge. Meanwhile V Corps took over IV Corps' front. The line was breached in Bourlon Wood but was restored by a counterattack. In the evening 47th Division recovered the position lost west of Bourlon Wood on 30th November.

3rd December marked the end of the German counterstroke, but not before some heavy fighting took place. La Vacquerie fell at 8.25 a.m. and at 10.30 a.m. the salient held by 29th Division and 16th Brigade came under heavy bombardment. Despite heavy casualties, the attack was halted south of the canal. North of the canal, where 87th Brigade had been replaced by 16th Brigade, 14th Durham Light Infantry (attached from 18th Brigade) was on the right, with its right flank on the canal. 1st King's Shropshire Light Infantry was on the left. 14th Durham Light Infantry had three companies in the line. The left and centre companies were in reasonably good trenches, but A Company on the right was in a shallow, poorly sited ditch. Work continued to improve the trench but there was no wire in front.

The first attack at 10.30 a.m. was repulsed by small arms fire, except on the right, where A Company was driven out of its incomplete trench. **Captain Arthur**

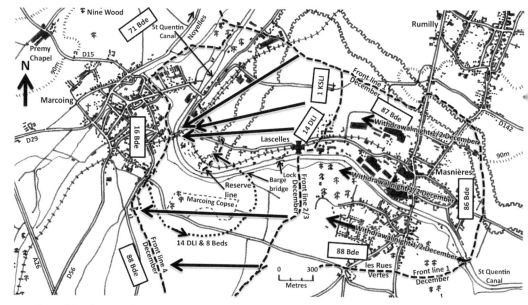

Leave Masnières on the D56 Marcoing road and pass some large storage silos on the left. Continue for 300m and turn left into the track leading to the canal lock (Ecluse de Bracheux). Park just off the track and walk eastwards along the former railway line (now a cycle path) for ten metres to see the area held by Arthur Lascelles' A Company.

Lascelles was hit but refused to have his wound dressed. He jumped on to the parapet and, with the twelve survivors of his Company, rushed the enemy under heavy machine gun fire. They pushed back about sixty Germans and saved a critical situation, but the Germans attacked again at 11.30 a.m. A Company was again ejected from its trench and several prisoners were taken, including Lascelles. The Germans secured the lock house and set up a machine gun, which caused heavy casualties to the reserve company when it counterattacked. Despite these losses, the Germans

The line held by Arthur Lascelles and A Company, 14th Durham Light Infantry on the morning of 3rd December 1917.

were forced out of the trench. A third attack was made at 12.15 p.m. against the whole frontage of 14th Durham Light Infantry and 1st King's Shropshire Light Infantry. This resulted in a confused struggle, during which Lascelles escaped, but with no artillery support the right flank remained open and a block had to be established.

Lascelles received two more wounds, but rallied and encouraged his men to meet the next German attack at 12.45 p.m. His leadership at this critical moment was invaluable. The Germans pressed on regardless of losses and penetrated the left of 1st King's Shropshire Light Infantry and both flanks of 14th Durham Light Infantry, which was almost surrounded. Both battalions fought their way back over the canal railway bridge and took up an outpost line in the east of Marcoing. Having reorganised in a sunken road, eighty to one hundred men from 14th Durham Light Infantry went to support 29th Division covering the south of Marcoing, by forming a line along the ridge south of Marcoing Copse. 88th Brigade counterattacked south of the Canal, but 14th Durham Light Infantry's line held and it was not required to assist.

A company of 8th Bedfordshire arrived to support 14th Durham Light Infantry at 3.45 p.m. Fifteen minutes later the Battalion re-crossed the canal by a barge bridge. There was fierce fighting on the railway but the old reserve line was retaken, together with some prisoners. Another company of 8th Bedfordshire arrived and allowed the small force to expand its holdings to include the railway bridge. The enemy continued to press strong bombing attacks on the right and the British had no grenades with which to reply. The line held but there was nothing to be gained by remaining there.

29th Division's position was still far from secure. 88th Brigade was reinforced by 16th Brigade and 71st Brigade established a line from Noyelles to Nine Wood facing Marcoing. Two battalions also dug in on Premy Ridge and Flesquières Ridge. That night all troops were withdrawn to the west of the canal. 14th Durham Light Infantry withdrew in good order at 1.10 a.m. to the Hindenburg Support Line

and in the early hours the canal bridges were blown. Ironically the withdrawal was conducted without loss but 14th Durham Light Infantry had already suffered 274 casualties out of the 450 men who went into the action.

6th December

While the fighting continued around Cambrai, Haig was considering a withdrawal. His troops were exhausted and he knew the Germans would launch a powerful offensive in the spring. The BEF needed to winter in secure positions where it stood the best chance of containing the German onslaught. At Cambrai a withdrawal was planned in two phases, including an overnight halt in an intermediate position to allow work to continue on a new main line.

On 4th December the new line was occupied by reserve troops. It ran along the old Hindenburg support system from south of Marcoing to Hughes Trench, east of the Canal du Nord, then west to join the old British line on the spur northeast of Demicourt. That night batteries were withdrawn behind the intermediate position and by 3 a.m. the infantry main bodies were also behind the line. The withdrawal was almost unhindered. The Germans spent until 3 p.m. on the 5th bombarding the positions the British had evacuated the previous night. Later, German patrols re-established contact with the British and by nightfall they were lined up about 550m from the covering position.

The withdrawal was completed the next night with some difficulty due to German pressure. By the morning of 7th December the new line was fully occupied, but a great deal of work was required to transform it into a strong defensive position. It was largely based upon the old German line facing southwest, which had to be reversed to face in the opposite direction.

Although fighting died down after 4th December, the Germans continued to try to improve their positions around la Vacquerie. At 10 a.m. on the 5th, following an intense bombardment, they attacked 182nd Brigade along Ostrich Avenue. No ground was lost initially and at 1.30 p.m. another attack was driven off. However, a renewed onslaught at 2 p.m. seized Ostrich Avenue and bombers pressed up the Hindenburg front and support lines.

109th Brigade was in the process of taking over the front when this attack occurred. 9th Royal Inniskilling Fusiliers was on the right and 10th Royal Inniskilling Fusiliers was on the left, with 14th Royal Irish Rifles in support and 11th Royal Inniskilling Fusiliers in reserve. No.10 Platoon, 9th Royal Inniskilling Fusiliers, held the front line, but in the support line the survivors of 2/7th Royal Warwickshire were pushed back. Two sections of No.10 Platoon reinforced 2/7th Royal Warwickshire and the enemy was driven out but the Germans remained in possession of the Hindenburg front system to almost the crest of the ridge. By 2.30 p.m. it was quiet again.

At 3 p.m., Nos 2 and 4 Companies moved forward to reinforce the other companies of 9th Inniskilling Fusiliers. At 4 p.m. the Battalion took over 200m of trench with

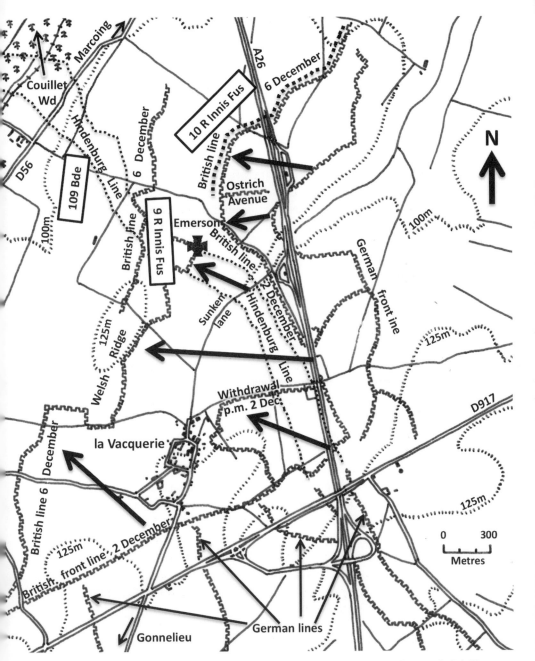

Leave Villers-Plouich on the D56 towards Marcoing. After 1,600m there are some buildings on the left. Turn right onto a track and go to the top of the hill. Park where the tarmac gives out to a grassy track. Walk on for 200m where the track bends first right then left. At the second bend stop and look right. About 200m in this direction, almost in line with the church in la Vacquereie on the skyline 1,400m away, is the approximate site of James Emerson's VC action.

The area held by 9th Royal Inniskilling Fusiliers on 6th December 1917. The location of James Emerson's VC action is approximate. Precise locations for the various units involved are unclear in the various war diaries and accounts. Even the Official History is vague on the actual frontages held by the brigades involved.

No.3 Company on the right and No.2 Company on the left, commanded by **Second Lieutenant James Emerson**. Nos 1 and 4 Companies were in support respectively. That night 109th Brigade took over most of the front from 182nd Brigade.

Fighting on 6th December was confined to 9th Inniskilling Fusiliers' front, which included the Hindenburg front system and Ostrich Avenue. At 6.30 a.m. the Battalion, together with a 14th Royal Irish Rifles platoon (Brigade support) and the remnants of two 2/7th Royal Warwickshire companies in support, recaptured 200m of the lost trench and secured nine prisoners. However, they could not hold it against a counterattack at 10 a.m., which came in from a sunken road on the flank. The fighting swayed back and forth, during which 109th Brigade was without artillery support.

Although he was already wounded in the hand and the head (helmet torn by a grenade splinter), Emerson led his Company to repel the enemy bombers and cleared 350m of trench. When attacked again he sprang from the trench and, with only eight men, met the attack in the open. Having killed many of the enemy, they took six prisoners. He remained with his Company for the next three hours, refusing to go to the dressing station as the other officers were all casualties. During this time he drove off repeated bombing attacks. The Germans attacked in superior numbers and again he went forward to repel them in hand to hand fighting. After pushing the enemy back one hundred metres he was mortally wounded by a sniper, one of fifty-four casualties suffered by the Battalion that day.

That evening at 8 p.m. the Battalion was relieved by 11th Royal Inniskilling Fusiliers and moved to Couillet Wood. On 7th December, in the final act in the Battle of Cambrai, the Germans were finally driven out by 11th Royal Inniskilling Fusiliers.

Chapter Three

Local Operations Winter 1917–18

3 December 1917

313 Pte Henry Nicholas, 1st Canterbury (2nd New Zealand Brigade, New Zealand Division), Polderhoek, Belgium

At the end of the Third Battle of Ypres the Germans held Polderhoek Spur and Château, despite three efforts being made to take it. The position enfiladed the forward trenches about Cameron Covert and Reutel and commanded the approaches to the sector. A combined attack to seize the Spur, and Gheluvelt to the south, was considered but in the end the operation was confined to Polderhoek. The frontage was about 350m wide with the right boundary being on a tower like pillbox known as Jericho and the left boundary on an old German shelter named Joppa. An advance of 550m would push the front line far enough down the reverse slope to deny the Germans observation over the British lines. The area was on the boundary of IX and II ANZAC Corps. As the main problems were suffered by the ANZACs, an attack by the New Zealand Division was proposed. If successful the captured ground would be handed over to IX Corps to the south.

There were two options for the attack: take the Château (essentially a pile of bricks in a shattered wood) from the northern flank and rear by advancing over the Reutelbeek; or a frontal attack along the Spur. Despite the advantages offered by a flanking attack, in this instance there were some distinct disadvantages. The troops would be very exposed while crossing the Reutelbeek valley, which was an all but impassable morass. The supporting artillery would find it difficult to fire in enfilade and there was no satisfactory assembly position for the assault troops. Conversely there were good assembly trenches for a frontal attack and the barrage would be far more effective. Accordingly a frontal attack was approved.

During a snowstorm on 25th November, 2nd Canterbury (2nd New Zealand Brigade) took over the area between the Scherriabeek and Reutelbeek from IX Corps. Additional assembly trenches were dug as extensions of the support system, whose construction was already in progress. The extra activity did not attract undue attention. The first heavy artillery concentration was fired on 28th November and during the day the forward trenches were thinned out to avoid casualties during German retaliation. Wire was also cut and the results were checked by patrols. The single duckboard approach (Polderhoek Track) was improved and extended.

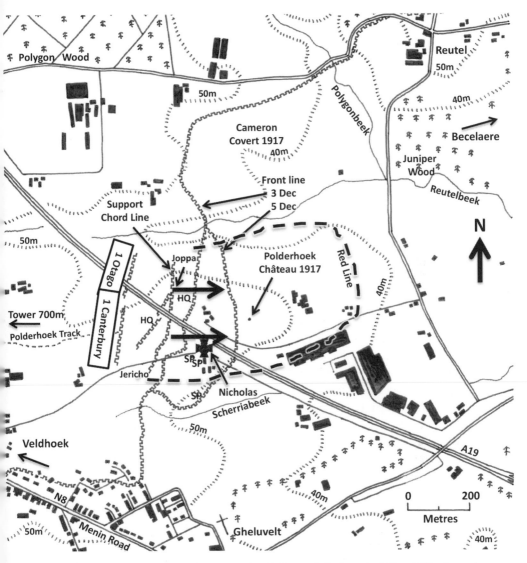

Drive along the N8 from Ypres towards Menen. Pass Bellewaerde Park on the left and 500m beyond go round the right hand bend. After two kilometres turn left in Veldhoek into Polygonestraat and after 150m turn right into Poezelhoekstraat. Follow it for about 400m, passing a farm on the left. Stop shortly after the buildings but be careful parking off the road. There are a number of suitable pull-ins on hard standing but between them are some fearsome ditches. The 1st Canterbury attack started in the field to the left of the road here and headed towards the buildings just before the autoroute. Nicholas' VC action was on the corner of the road where it swings right to run parallel with the autoroute. SP = strongpoint.

Engineering material and ammunition was quietly accumulated in the forward trenches. The Germans in the Château attempted raids on 26th and 30th November, both of which were repulsed.

The attack was set for 3rd December. 1st Canterbury on the right and 1st Otago on the left were selected and trained on replica ground west of Ypres, but this was disrupted by poor weather and congestion with other units. Parties were allocated to clear each pillbox and dugout. Reconnaissance parties also viewed the ground from 2nd Canterbury's positions and Cameron Covert. The assault troops moved into the trenches on 1st and 2nd December, taking over from 2nd Canterbury. The front line was held by the support companies and the reserve was found by 2nd Otago. Consideration was given to coordinating the operation with a dawn attack by II and VIII Corps east of Passchendaele. However, the New Zealanders preferred to attack at noon in the hope of surprising the defenders, the majority of whom would be sheltering below ground during daylight.

Enemy positions at Becelaere and Gheluvelt were to be masked by smoke and gas bombardments. Three field artillery brigades were allocated for the supporting barrage, which would start with the attack at zero hour in order to give no prior warning. A barrage of 18 Pounders was to precede the infantry attack. About 150m in front of it was to be another barrage of 18 Pounders and 4.5″ Howitzers. The artillery would also fire to the flanks, including some IX Corps guns to extend the covering barrage to the south to Gheluvelt and the Menin Road. To the north the enemy outposts would also be kept under fire. There were two machine gun barrages to help neutralise the German trenches and approaches. Five of the new 6″ Mortars at Reutel were to fire gas shells to neutralise machine gun posts around Juniper Wood.

The attack plan was simple. Each battalion would be led by two companies, each one hundred strong. The leading two platoons in each company, forming the first wave, would advance from the Support Chord Line to an intermediate objective (Red Dotted Line) about fifty metres beyond the Chateau. The second wave, consisting of the other two platoons in each company, following fifty metres behind, was to go on to the final objective (Red Line). On the right this coincided with the

Much of the 1st Canterbury and most of the 1st Otago start line is in the dead ground along which the A19 autoroute runs across the picture from left to right. Henry Nicholas' VC action was at the far end of Poezelhoekstraat, where it reaches the tall poplar trees.

Red Dotted Line, but on the left was 275m further on. The final objective would be marked by the left hand gun in each supporting battery firing smoke shells for five minutes.

The boundary between the battalions was an east–west line just south of the Château. Half of the Lewis guns in the assault were to be taken forward wrapped in waterproof sheets, to be used only when absolutely necessary to keep them free of mud. As the assault waves went forward, the support companies were to move forward to occupy the front line and be ready to meet counterattacks. Reserve companies were kept well back, ready to move forward to take over the gains and consolidate them, probably after dark. Eight machine guns of the Brigade Machine Gun Company were involved, two in the front line, two in the support line and two allocated to each assault battalion for covering fire during consolidation.

The Château was in 1st Otago's area, but 1st Canterbury faced a series of pillbox strongpoints, including those at the stables and the manager's house. Two light trench mortars were allocated to 1st Canterbury to deal with these positions. As the advance progressed 1st Canterbury was to form a protective flank to the south, overlooking the Scherriabeek and Gheluvelt. A special party was detailed to capture one particular pillbox and shell hole strongpoint just south of the Red Line. Both battalions were to establish a series of strongpoints on the final objective. Great efforts were made to ensure that the Germans did not suspect anything, including the assault troops hiding under waterproof sheets from dawn to prevent them being seen from enemy aircraft.

At zero hour the attack immediately ran into the British barrage and there were casualties, particularly in the left company of 1st Otago, but also some on the left of 1st Canterbury. The barrage was erratic and at least one battery on the left of 1st Canterbury was firing short throughout the operation. However, the assault pressed on, crossed the front line and found the wire was cut, but the Germans were not

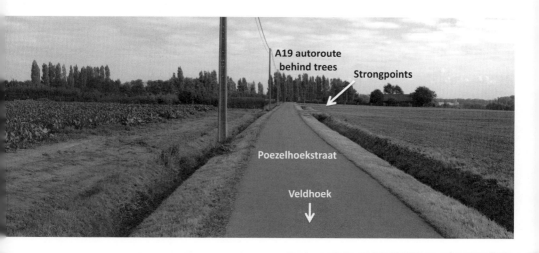

caught in their dugouts as was hoped. The pillboxes were manned and the sentries were vigilant. Machine guns opened fire and the German artillery joined in after a few minutes. Due to the proximity of the trenches, the Germans did not risk hitting their own lines, which meant that the assembly positions escaped attention and instead the German gunners concentrated on the duckboard track and Veldhoek.

1st Canterbury attacked with 12th (Nelson) Company on the right and 1st (Canterbury) Company on the left. 12th Company was to form the defensive flank and 1st Company was to seize the rest of the Battalion's objective. 13th Company was in support in Timaru (or Derelict) Trench (assumed to be one of the lines marked on the map, but it is unclear which one) and the support line. 2nd (South Canterbury) Company was the reserve at the Tower. The attack strength of the Battalion was 458.

Immediately after zero hour 12th Company ran into machine gun fire from a ruined pillbox and dugout about ninety metres east of the front line and just north of the road running along the south of the Château. The company commander, Captain George Herbert Gray (MC for this action), and Lance Corporal Harry Waterworth Minnis (MM for this action) led a handful of men and captured the gun and eight prisoners. Minnis was killed and is commemorated on the Buttes New British Cemetery (New Zealand) Memorial, Polygon Wood. The Company was then able to continue but under increasingly heavy fire, including from Gheluvelt Ridge. A strong westerly wind dissipated the smoke and the barrage was unable to subdue the enfilade fire.

An enemy strongpoint manned by sixteen Germans with a machine gun offered stubborn resistance. A section commander and several men were killed attempting to attack it. **Private Henry Nicholas** MM was in a Lewis gun section on the

Reverse of the previous picture looking along Poezelhoekstraat towards Veldhoek. The autoroute is beyond the trees on the right. Henry Nicholas' VC action was about where the gate stands. Two of the strongpoints were in the field just left of the road.

defensive right flank. He rushed forward, followed twenty-five metres behind by the rest of the section, and reached the enemy parapet before the Germans could react. He shot the enemy platoon commander dead from point blank range then leapt down, bayoneted some of the garrison and flung grenades along a sap after some others. He thereby killed the whole garrison except for four wounded men, whom he took prisoner.

Despite this success the company had lost heavily. Although it managed to get a little further forward, it was held up by another strong pillbox south of the Château on the southern edge of the road. Posts were established on the south side of the road to protect the right flank and small arms fire dealt effectively with at least one enemy machine gun post. The reserve company was brought forward to Jericho. When the advance had reached its limit, Nicholas collected ammunition under heavy fire.

1st Company on the left also advanced under heavy fire and early in the attack lost many experienced officers and NCOs. The Company was held up about seventy metres short of a pillbox, which was about the same distance south of the Château. It was then under fire from the Château and the two pillboxes.

About 1 p.m. the CO sent forward two sections of 13th Company to assist 1st and 12th Companies. They were met with heavy fire, lost many men and were unable to help. Shortly afterwards Battalion HQ was hit by heavy shelling, which cut the telephone lines, so the CO moved to 1st Otago's HQ to resume command. At 1.30 p.m. he sent a complete platoon of 13th Company forward, but it was also unable to make any impression. By this time the creeping barrage had been lost and the German machine gunners were able to fire without interference. Captain Gray came back to the front line at great risk to confer with the CO. Gray had been blown up twice and was shaken, but his report was of great value in clarifying the situation. The CO ordered him to hold where he was and to take advantage of any opportunity to advance. He also ordered the reserve company forward to the Chord Line.

1st Otago received valuable support from machine guns on the left flank, which dispersed enemy parties on the Becelaere road. The medium mortars fired 850 rounds and drew heavy enemy artillery fire, resulting in one mortar being destroyed and another damaged. 1st Otago was less affected by fire from Gheluvelt and made good progress at first in capturing a pillbox. Then the Battalion was held up by fire from the Château about 135m from the objective. Supporting troops sent up to assist made no difference.

Both battalions had lost about half their strength, including many officers and senior NCOs. Momentum was lost and the attackers dug in where they were. Although the objective was not reached, a commanding view into the Scherriabeek valley had been gained. About 2.30 p.m. a concentration of the enemy was detected in the valley and a light trench mortar was moved to Jericho. It opened rapid fire to disperse the enemy force and most of the survivors were dealt with by 12th Company's small arms fire. Enemy reinforcements to one of the pillboxes about

4.30 p.m. were caught by Lewis guns. At 5.40 p.m. orders came from Brigade HQ to consolidate the ground taken.

Tentative plans to renew the attack after dark came to nothing as there were no troops to carry it out without leaving the front line unmanned. It was also a bright moonlit night, which would have favoured the defenders, who had been reinforced at dusk. On 4th December an enemy counterattack force spotted astride the Becelaere–Ghcluvelt road was dispersed by the artillery. Snipers took a toll of Germans wandering about the Château, who probably did not realise how close the New Zealanders were. The German artillery fired on the old front and support lines intermittently all day. Another German attack at 6 a.m. on the 5th was repulsed by small arms fire and suffered heavy casualties. The assault troops were relieved after dark and the gains were handed over to 2nd Bedfordshire (IX Corps). Nine days after the attack the Germans recovered their losses.

Precise losses for 1st Canterbury in the attack are not available, but during December the Battalion suffered 249 casualties. Most of these would have been in the attack on Polderhoek. Seventy-nine were killed, 165 were wounded and eleven were missing. The attack had encountered resistance that was no stronger than on previous operations and there was no mud or wire to contend with. Analysis concluded it failed because:

Training had been inadequate.
Lack of battle experience amongst the men who replaced casualties during the Third Ypres battles.
Experienced officers and NCOs became casualties early on.
Mutually supporting pillboxes were not affected by the artillery.
The volume of machine gun fire in such a confined area was decisive.
The British barrage falling short did little to get the attack off to a good start.
The smoke barrage identified the limits of the attack to the enemy and the strong wind dispersed it quickly, thus neuralising any beneficial effect.

10–11 December 1917

315 Pte Walter Mills, 1/10th Manchester (126th Brigade, 42nd Division), Givenchy, France

The Givenchy front had not changed significantly since 1915. The area had slipped into the routine of trench warfare, with occasional raids and nightly patrols into no man's land. On 10th December, 126th Brigade relieved 125th Brigade on the 42nd Division front astride the La Bassée Canal. 46th Division was on the right and 127th Brigade was on the left. On the left of 126th Brigade, 1/10th Manchester relieved 1/6th Lancashire Fusiliers at 10.30 a.m. 1/9th Manchester was on the right, 1/5th East Lancashire was in support and 1/4th East Lancashire was in

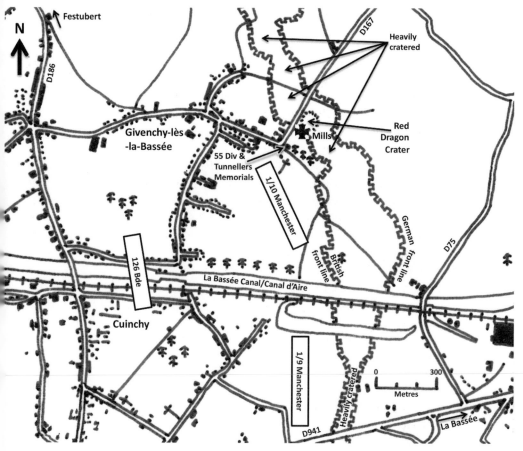

Drive north through Cuinchy on the D186 and cross the La Bassée Canal. Immediately turn right and follow the road parallel with the canal for 600m, where it turns left (north). After another 700m at the crossroads turn right onto the D167. 300m on the road bends round to the left. Turn off half right here into the lane leading to the cemetery and park. There are a number of May–June 1940 CWGC graves within the cemetery and, intriguingly, one Soviet soldier from September 1944. The 55th Division and Tunnellers Memorials are on the corner. Walk northeast from them along the D167 for about 100m but beware of speeding motorists. On the right hand side there is a shallow depression, which is the remains of Red Dragon Crater, the scene of Walter Mills' VC action.

reserve. The entire brigade relief was completed by 2.30 p.m. During the relief **Private Walter Mills** met his younger brother, James, who was serving in 1/6th Lancashire Fusiliers. They exchanged pleasantries and shook hands.

At 1 a.m. on 11th December the centre of 1/10th Manchester's line was bombarded with gas drums. Almost every man in C Company was overcome by fumes in Red Dragon Crater. Those who could struggled to their positions and, although they put up a remarkable fight when the attack came, the gas had done its damage. Gradually the men were overcome and sank into the trench unable to resist further. Walter Mills was one of those who sprang to his post and fought magnificently to save the situation. He was well aware that his own survival lay in not exerting himself but continued throwing bombs alone until the enemy had been

Looking northeast along the D167. The 55th Division and Tunnellers Memorials are behind the camera. The Red Dragon Crater depression is to the right of the road in line with the mast in the distance.

driven off. Only when he was relieved by reinforcements did he fall back into the trench. A company of 1/4th East Lancashire was moved up to reinforce 1/10th Manchester and the line was stabilised again.

Mills died of gas poisoning as he was taken away on a stretcher. Four other men received the MM for their part in this short sharp action. There were seventy-six casualties in 1/10th Manchester, including nine officers.

8th/9th March 1918

316 LCpl Charles Robertson, 10th Royal Fusiliers (111th Brigade, 37th Division), West of Polderhoek Château, Belgium

On 7th March the units holding 37th Division's front were warned that the Germans would attack astride the Menin Road that night. Their aim was to recover the high ground northwest of Gheluvelt lost during the Third Battle of Ypres. 10th Royal Fusiliers was in support to 111th Brigade on the left of the Division. At dawn a preemptive bombardment was fired on the right to which the enemy made no reply. At 6.30 a.m. the German barrage fell and grew in intensity after 9.30 a.m. It went on all day except for a break between at 1 p.m. and 5 p.m.

At 2 p.m., 13th King's Royal Rifle Corps was attacked and D Company, 10th Royal Fusiliers was sent up Polderhoek Track to reinforce the Joppa and Jericho Trench systems. D Company took over Posts 5–10 on the left at 3.30 p.m., while a company and a half of 13th King's Royal Rifle Corps clung to Jericho Trench on the right. At the same time B Company, 10th Royal Fusiliers was moved forward from Nonne Boschen to Jargon Tunnels.

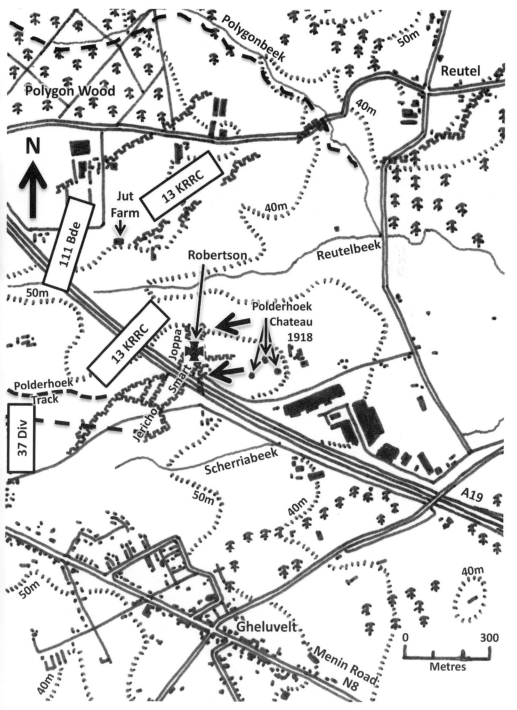

Drive towards Menen from Ypres on the N8. Pass Bellewaerde Park, go round the right hand bend, then turn left into Oude Kortrijkstraat. After 1.6 kms go over the A19 autoroute. Continue with Polygon Wood on the left for just over 500m and turn right. Pass the 'In The Fields' B&B on the right and continue to the end of the track where it turns left to the site of Jut Farm. Park here and look southeast, with the A19 on your right, to the buildings on top of the hill.

Charles Robertson's VC action was on the slope in the centre of the picture, close to the modern buildings.

The Germans advanced down the Reutelbeek valley at 5.45 p.m. under cover of a smoke barrage. At 6 p.m. the British artillery opened fire in response to SOS signals. Despite being met by heroic resistance, at 7.15 p.m. the Germans broke into 13th King's Royal Rifle Corps' lines. The northern part of the system was lost, including the front line and part of Smart Support. B Company, 10th Royal Fusiliers went forward to reinforce the front line and another company was ordered forward from Nonne Boschen.

In D Company, **Lance Corporal Charles Robertson** was in charge of a Lewis gun and found himself and three men almost cut off. He sent two for reinforcements while he remained with the other man. They inflicted heavy casualties on the advancing enemy to their right. Eventually they were surrounded and withdrew ten metres to a new position, where Robertson continued to pour fire into the enemy. They fell back again, this time to a defended post. The enemy pressure did not slacken and Robertson mounted the parapet with his comrade, set up the Lewis gun in a shell hole and opened fire at the Germans pouring over the open and down an adjacent trench. A little later he was severely wounded in the stomach and his comrade was killed, but he continued firing until his ammunition was expended. He managed to crawl back with the Lewis gun.

At 8 p.m. CO 10th Royal Fusiliers was given command of the whole Brigade front south of the Reutelbeek and ordered both companies to counterattack. The situation in Joppa and Jericho Trenches was not clear and only the support company had communications with Battalion HQ in Glencorse Tunnels.

D Company found that the enemy held the whole of Joppa Street and the front line northwards to a point about fifty metres beyond No.5 Post. B Company bombed along Joppa Street and Smart Support, but was unable to establish itself at the junction of the two trenches. At 12.15 a.m. on 9th March, A and B Companies attacked along the line of posts, Smart Support and up the duckboard track. B Company reached the junction of the track and Smart Support, where a strongpoint was established. Smart Support was made good by A Company but bombs ran out and the attack stalled.

A third attack at dawn fought along Joppa Street, supported by Lewis guns on the flanks. A relay was established to ensure a continuous supply of bombs. The enemy was forced to run towards Polderhoek Château and by 6.45 a.m. the original positions had been re-established. Shortly afterwards an intense bombardment fell on the trenches and the enemy made their way back under cover of smoke. This attack was repulsed by 10th Royal Fusiliers and the position was consolidated. The fighting cost the Battalion sixty-eight casualties.

Soon after the position was reorganised and 10th Royal Fusiliers took over the whole front south of the Reutelbeek. There were two companies forward, one in support at the château east of Inverness Copse and another in reserve in Jargon Tunnels. 13th King's Royal Rifle Corps held the sector on the Brigade left. 111th Brigade suffered twenty-five killed, 106 wounded and eight missing in this action. A Polish prisoner taken on 19th March estimated that the Germans suffered 120 casualties.

Polderhoek Château before the war.

Chapter Four

First Battles of the Somme 1918 – Battle of St Quentin

21st March 1918

317 Gnr Charles Stone, C/83rd Brigade RFA (18th Division), Benay, France

318 2Lt Edmund De Wind, 15th Royal Irish Rifles (107th Brigade, 36th Division), Grougies, France

319 Lt Col Wilfrith Elstob, 16th Manchester (90th Brigade, 30th Division), Francilly-Selency, France

320 2Lt John Buchan, 8th Argyll & Sutherland Highlanders (183rd Brigade, 61st Division), East of Marteville, France

321 Lt Allan Ker, Gordon Highlanders att'd 61st Battalion Machine Gun Corps (61st Division), Near St Quentin, France

322 LCpl John Sayer, 8th Queen's (Royal West Surrey) (17th Brigade, 24th Division), Le Verguier, France

323 Capt Manley James, 8th Gloucestershire (57th Brigade, 19th Division), Doignies & Velu Wood, France

On 3rd December 1917 hostilities were suspended between Germany and Russia, allowing Germany to transfer forces to the Western Front. Previously there had been 151 German divisions there, but by the end of March 1918 the Germans had 195 divisions, giving them a superiority of 200,000 troops. The Allies faced other problems, including the U-boat campaign in the Atlantic that had resulted in huge shipping losses, and a manpower crisis. It was in their interests to await the build up of American strength for the main effort in 1919. In the meantime they formed a Supreme War Council to monitor all theatres of operations and coordinate the overall conduct of the war.

By the end of 1917 the BEF's sixty-two divisions (fifty-seven infantry and five cavalry) could no longer maintain their strength with the flow of replacements from England. The situation was not helped by having to send five divisions to Italy, replace six French divisions in Flanders and extend its front southwards. Lloyd George sent minimal drafts and the Army was given a low priority behind the Royal Navy, air forces, shipbuilding, other military industry and food production. Of the 615,000 men demanded by the BEF for 1918 only 100,000 were available. A

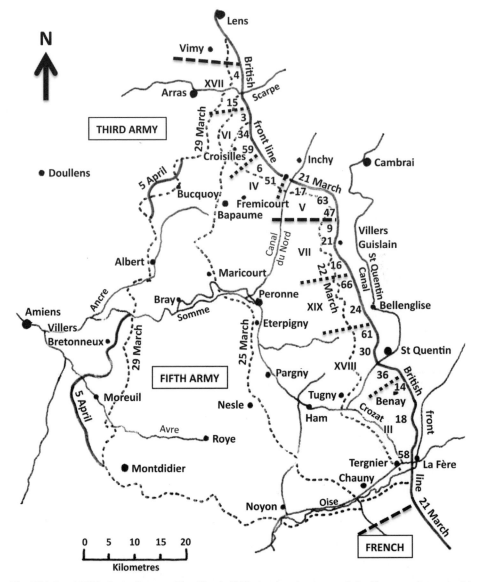

The Third and Fifth Army front on 21st March 1918 showing the stages of the German advance to 5th April. This book only cover the events to the end of the Battle of St Quentin on 23rd March. British corps and divisions are as at dawn on 21st March.

drastic solution was required. The number of battalions in each infantry division was reduced from thirteen to ten. Each brigade lost a battalion. This required a huge reorganisation when the BEF should have been concentrating on meeting the German offensive. The details were settled by 18th January; 115 battalions were to be disbanded, thirty-eight were amalgamated and seven were converted to pioneers. Surplus infantry were formed into entrenching battalions to work on defences until required to replace battle casualties. The re-organisation necessitated the movement of battalions throughout the BEF and took until 4th March to complete. Dominion divisions were unaffected.

The BEF had been on the offensive for two years and the positions it held were where advances had halted, rather than the best for defensive purposes. The troops were also untrained in defensive operations. With the enormous amount of defensive work and training to carry out, troops out of the line had little rest. A German attack towards the English Channel presented the gravest threat to the British and consequently this area was strengthened at the expense of the area to the south that had been recently taken over from the French. By 23rd February it was apparent that the enemy had gone onto the defensive as far south as Lille, indicating that the offensive would strike Third or Fifth Army. Arrangements were made for assistance from the French, either to take over part of the front or to counterattack.

Three defensive zones were constructed: Forward, Battle and Rear. The Forward Zone, the existing front system, was to be held by one third of the available troops. It was not continuous but, where it was held, tended to be arranged in the usual three lines. Its purpose was to break up attacks and cause delay. The forward line was a series of isolated posts, the second was a line of connected posts, while the third consisted of a series of company or half company redoubts. All posts were sited to dominate ground by fire rather than by occupation.

A few miles behind in the Battle Zone three lines of resistance were constructed as defended localities with all round fields of fire. This was where the enemy attack was to be repulsed. If local counterattacks failed, corps or even army reserves would be committed. Four to eight miles behind was the Rear Zone, effectively a second defensive position, but due to the shortage of labour it was afforded the lowest priority. When the offensive opened the Forward Zone was well constructed and the Battle Zone was in fair condition. In Third Army's area some work had been completed on the Rear Zone but when Fifth Army took over from the French nothing had been done. Haig deliberately held this sector weaker than elsewhere in order to draw in the German attack. There was more ground to trade and it also diverted German attention from Flanders and the shortest route to the Channel ports.

The Germans prepared for a number of separate offensives; George 1 near Armentieres, George 2 near Ypres, Mars near Arras and Michael around St Quentin. Ludendorff reasoned that in March it was too wet for George 1 and 2, Mars was difficult with the British holding Vimy Ridge and therefore the initial offensive would be Michael, followed a few days later by the southern part of Mars south of the Scarpe. He approved the offensive on 21st January when he was sure that hostilities had ceased with Russia. The intention was to break into the British line as far north as Ytres and then swing northwest to the line Albert–Arras, rolling up the British front in the process. Ultimately it was designed to knock the British out of the war. The Germans allocated sixty-three divisions for the attack, in addition to eleven holding the line. Although their numbers appeared to be overwhelming, the Germans faced huge logistical problems. They were particularly short of vehicles and fuel and horses and fodder. In addition, the offensive launched on 21st

March had to cross the area devastated in the 1916 Somme battles and during their withdrawal to the Hindenburg Line in 1917.

Fifth Army held a front of forty-two miles on the right of the British line, although ten miles was covered by the Oise marshland. To defend this sector, General Sir Hubert de la Poer Gough had four corps consisting of twelve infantry and three cavalry divisions, plus three tank battalions; eleven of the infantry divisions were in the line. They faced forty-three German divisions. In view of the ground and the assessment of the enemy's intentions, Gough held the right lightly, resulting in III Corps being allocated seventeen miles of the total frontage.

To the north, Third Army had a front of twenty-eight miles and four corps consisting of fourteen infantry divisions, to defend it. Four of these divisions were in reserve. There were also four tank battalions. The length of front could be reduced by three miles in the event of an attack by abandoning the Flesquieres salient. As only part of the Third Army front was attacked, six British faced nineteen German divisions, resulting in a greater density of troops than in Fifth Army.

The only general reserves were two GHQ divisions behind each of the BEF Armies. The Germans managed to achieve air superiority, massing 730 aircraft opposite Third and Fifth Armies to face 579 British machines. They also had massive superiority in guns – 6,608 to 2,686. The battleground was chalk uplands with broad open valleys in some areas and narrow steep-sided re-entrants in others. Two canals traversed the area; the Crozat–St Quentin Canal and the unfinished Canal du Nord. In addition, the Oise and Somme rivers had been canalised through wide marshy valleys, creating considerable obstacles.

The final German preparations were carried out with all precautions. Movement took place at night and the assault troops were kept well back from the front until the last moment. The attacking units (stormtroops) were instructed to advance where resistance was weakest. On 19th March British intelligence discovered the precise time and place of the offensive, but this advantage was reduced when fog and mist formed on the evening of 20th March. It thickened throughout the night and patrols discovered many gaps cut in the German wire. The British artillery began firing at 3.30 a.m., while the St Quentin front was flooded with gas from pre-positioned cylinders.

The German bombardment opened at 4.40 a.m. along the whole Fifth Army front and against three of Third Army's corps. Within a short time most of the carefully buried signal cables to the Forward Zone had been cut and artillery positions were saturated with gas. The move into Battle Zone positions was badly disrupted by having to wear gas masks on a particularly dark night. The fog persisted longest in the south near the Oise valley, where it did not clear until 1 p.m. With communications cut and wearing gas masks, commanders were effectively blinded to what was happening around them. In general the Forward Zone was overrun in the first rush, although stiff resistance was offered in places. Those posts and redoubts holding out were left for later parties of troops to deal with,

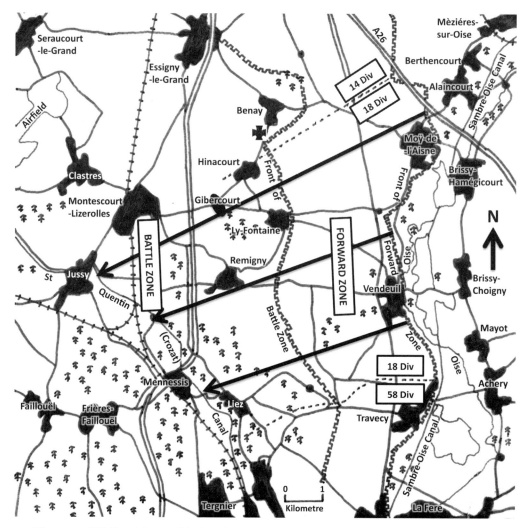

The centre of III Corps' front on 21st March.

while the leading stormtroops swept on to the Battle Zone. The fighting quickly degenerated into a series of isolated battalion actions for the British. The fog meant that cooperation between artillery and RFC was not possible.

On the right of Fifth Army was III Corps, with 58th Division holding the right flank, 18th Division in the centre and 14th Division on the left. The three miles of front south of the Oise and the two miles of the valley itself were not attacked, but 173rd Brigade's (58th Division) three miles of front north of the river, encountered German infantry as early as 6.10 a.m. Despite the time of year the river valley was almost dry and the Germans lowered the level of the Canal so that it presented almost no obstacle. The defenders gave a good account of themselves and those that fell back did so in good order. At 2 p.m. the Battle Zone north of the Oise was attacked and although penetrations were made the Germans did not pass through.

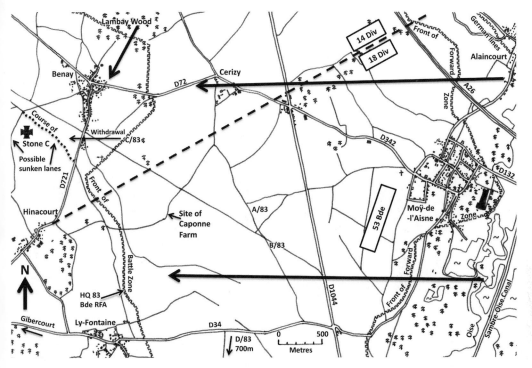

Leave Benay on the D721 towards Hinacourt. Just before the calvary turn right onto a track and follow it for about 600m to the crosstracks. Look southeast. This is the line of one of the former sunken lanes. Most of the sunken lanes south of Benay have since been filled in and ploughed over. Return to the cavalry and turn left this time, following the road to the village cemetery, which contains a number of French military burials from 1914, 1917 and 1918. Look around the hedge surrounding the cemetery to the left of the gate towards the copse where C/83rd Battery was sited early on 21st March. The withdrawal took place across the fields between the cemetery and the village towards the Benay-Hinacourt road (D721).

The Germans also gained no initial success against 18th Division. They gained the canal north of Travecy at 7.15 a.m., but made no progress for some hours. Many posts held out well into the day and some until the evening of the 22nd. However, by 10.30 a.m. considerable numbers of Germans had emerged from the Forward Zone and overran much of the field artillery.

83rd Brigade RFA was supporting 53rd Brigade (18th Division) when at 11.15 a.m. the forward guns of C Battery, southeast of Benay, were threatened with being overrun. Captain LM Haybittel ordered the breach blocks removed from the two forward 18 Pounders and the crews fell back to the next gun position about 400m behind. All made it back except Lieutenant Patterson and three gunners. Captain Haybittel shot one of the Germans taking Patterson away as a prisoner. The second position also had to be abandoned when the Germans attacked from the direction of Lambay Wood. The breach blocks were removed and the detachments fell back to a sunken lane between Benay and Hinacourt, which they held with small arms for an hour.

Just before this withdrawal, **Gunner Charles Stone** had been sent to the rear with a message, but returned voluntarily to assist in holding the sunken

C/83rd Battery's original position was to the left of the copse in the centre. Benay is off to the left of picture. The hedge on the right is the northern boundary of Benay cemetery.

lane. During the withdrawal he lay in the open about a hundred metres from the Germans. Despite the heavy machine gun fire, he calmly shot down a number of the enemy as they tried to rush the position. He had already worked his gun for six hours previously under heavy gas and high explosive shelling. At 12.45 p.m. the telephone lines were cut and the enemy launched an attack around the rear of the party. Haybittel ordered a withdrawal to the rear gun position, which they reached about 1 p.m. Here the last two guns were fired over open sights, but the position came under fire from a captured 18 Pounder put into use by the enemy. A German aircraft flying overhead signaled for them to surrender; it was ignored.

From the D721 south of Benay looking north. The track on the left was once longer and sunken. The original site for C/83rd Battery was on the right, near the cemetery.

The fight continued into the afternoon, with Stone positioned alone on the right flank to keep the enemy at bay as they tried to outflank the guns. On one occasion they succeeded in breaking through. Despite the heavy machine gun fire, Stone charged and killed them one by one, thus saving the guns. At 8 p.m., No.2 Gun became inoperative after seventeen hours of continuous use. Spent cases from the last gun had to be ejected by a ramrod down the barrel. Haybittel ordered it to be rendered unusable by removing the wheel retaining pins. The survivors then retired in pairs and met up 275m to the rear behind some freshly erected barbed wire. The withdrawal was covered by Lieutenant Jackson and six men, including Stone. They captured a German machine gun and its crew of four who had reached the rear of Haybittel's position in the gathering gloom. One of the Germans was chased by Stone for a hundred metres before he caught him. In addition to Stone's VC, Captain Haybittel received the DSO, Lieutenant Jackson the MC and 11297 Gunner Walter William Lugg the MM.

Pressure was maintained on 18th Division. The left was forced back due to the fall of Benay and Essigny. Hinacourt, at the rear of the Battle Zone, fell, but the enemy did not advance further and this flank was reinforced by the divisional reserve between Ly Fontaine and Gibercourt about 5 p.m. The Corps reserve (54th Brigade) also moved forward to cover this area at 6.45 p.m. Late in the day 18th Division fell back over the Crozat Canal, but in general the front held.

14th Division had no natural obstacle to its front and the centre and left took the brunt of the attack. Within an hour the battle was effectively over in the Forward Zone. The Battle Zone lay on a flat plateau falling away gently at the rear to the Crozat Canal. At 11 a.m. the enemy attacked the right of 14th Division and, by avoiding heavy resistance and under cover of the fog, took Benay about noon. The attack spread north and the majority of the plateau was lost by 2 p.m. Local reserves held the rear of the Zone and Corps reserves were called forward. Entrenching battalions were sent to the crossings over the Crozat Canal and 5th Cavalry Brigade

extended the Ly Fontaine–Gibercourt line held by 18th Division, but by 5.30 p.m. the defenders had been pushed out of the Battle Zone almost everywhere. III Corps withdrew during the night and by 6 a.m. on 22nd March was behind the Crozat Canal. By 2 a.m. most of the bridges had been blown and the rest followed by 9 a.m., leaving a few passable on foot only.

XVIII Corps held a front of nine miles astride the Somme valley. The Forward Zone was exposed and the Battle Zone lacked depth but was hidden on reverse slopes. Numerous valleys offered covered approaches at night or in fog. The Forward Zone consisted of fourteen redoubts behind the first line of outposts and formed the main line of resistance. Faced by the rapid advance of fourteen German divisions, resistance evaporated; only a quarter of the troops in the outpost line got away.

On the right the attack fell on 36th Division at 9.40 a.m. All three brigades were in the line – 108th on the right, 107th in the centre and 109th on the left. The outposts were overrun, although a few held out until the afternoon. By 10 a.m. the line of redoubts had been reached. Because of the fog the artillery did not fire the pre-arranged protective barrage. The first redoubt fell around noon and the rest followed in quick succession, except for two that held out until late afternoon. One of these, Boadicea Redoubt, held by 2nd Royal Inniskilling Fusiliers (109th Brigade) near the western end of the line, fell after a negotiated surrender at 5.30 p.m. The other was Racecourse Redoubt, astride the railway south of Grugies in 107th Brigade's area.

In 107th Brigade the Forward Zone was held by 15th Royal Irish Rifles, the Battle Zone by 1st Royal Irish Rifles and 2nd Royal Irish Rifles was in reserve. In the Forward Zone the outpost line and line of resistance were held by two companies with ten machine guns from B Company, 36th Battalion MGC and two Stokes 3″ mortars of 107th Trench Mortar Battery attached. Racecourse Redoubt was held by another company with two Newton 6″ mortars of Y/36th Medium Trench Mortar Battery attached. The fourth company was for local counterattacks. Each of the eight platoons in the outpost line and line of resistance held a strongpoint. Their tasks were to keep the enemy under observation (very difficult that morning with the fog), patrol no man's land, give warning of an attack and to disorganise it to allow time for the Battle Zone positions to be manned.

Racecourse Redoubt was to be held to the last in common with the orders for all the redoubts. It was held by Battalion HQ and D Company, 15th Royal Irish Rifles. Battalion HQ was in a dugout in the railway cutting. The bombardment fell from 4.15 a.m. onwards in this area and the order to man battle stations was issued to units by HQ 107th Brigade at 4.50 a.m. By 7.30 a.m. all line communications forward and rearwards from the Redoubt had failed. Visual signaling was impossible due to the fog. The main German attack materialised from the right flank and came in behind the line of resistance.

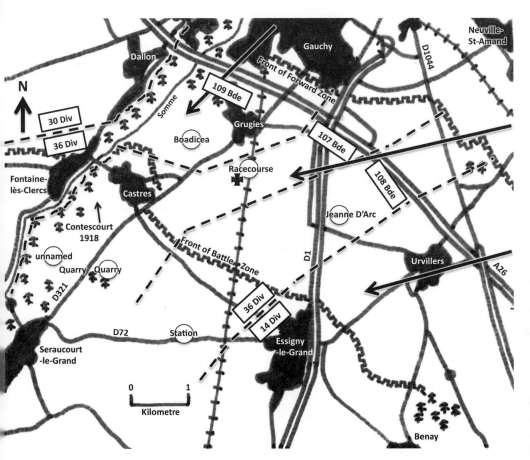

N

30 Div

36 Div

109 Bde

107 Bde

108 Bde

Dallon

Gauchy

Neuville-
St-Amand

D1044

Somme

Front of Forward Zone

Grugies

Boadicea

Racecourse

Fontaine-
lès-Clercs

Castres

Jeanne D'Arc

Contescourt
1918

unnamed

Quarry Quarry

Front of Battle Zone

D1

Urvillers

A26

D321

D72

Station

36 Div

14 Div

Seraucourt
-le-Grand

Essigny
-le-Grand

Benay

0   1
Kilometre

36th Division's front, showing the relative positions of the redoubts.

A runner from HQ 15th Royal Irish Rifles delivered a message to Brigade HQ at 9.50 a.m. It had taken almost two hours to get through. At that time there was very heavy shelling and some casualties had been incurred. Outposts were watching various lines of approach, but the fog was still very thick.

At 10.15 a.m. the outposts were driven in to the Redoubt and by 10.30 a.m. heavy fighting was going on around it. The fog did not clear until 11.30 a.m. The two platoons on the left were overrun, leaving only Contescourt Alley communication trench to the railway cutting in the Battalion's hands. The position was engaged by flamethrowers four times before they were knocked out by the Adjutant, Captain John Hazelton Stewart MC, with rifle grenades (DSO for this action). The position was constantly machine gunned and mortared. Several attacks were launched over the open and along trenches. After each unsuccessful attempt the Germans withdrew and the position was bombarded prior to a fresh attack. The final stand was made between Contescourt Alley and the railway cutting.

Second Lieutenant Edmund De Wind was wounded twice but stuck to his post for seven hours. With 15/1044 Corporal Samuel Getgood and 15/12170 Lance Corporal Charles Hubert Walker MM (both awarded the DCM and MID for this

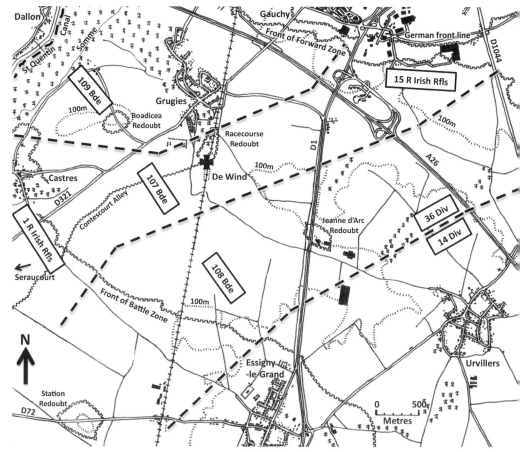

Approach Grugies from the southwest on the D321 from Castres. Pass the town sign on the right, take the third right after it and immediately after turning take the right fork up the hill. As you pass a large farm complex (Ferme de Grugies) on the right, Racecourse Redoubt is on the left but continue to follow the track under the railway. Continue for 600m then turn left and follow the line of wind turbines to turbine VDM4, where there is plenty of room to park on hard standing. Look west from here to overlook Racecourse Redoubt, which straddled the railway line, and beyond to Boadicea Redoubt.

From the base of wind turbine VDM4 looking west overlooking Racecourse Redoubt.

From the top of the railway underpass looking north through the centre of Racecourse Redoubt. 15th Royal Irish Rifles' Battalion HQ was in a dugout in this cutting.

action), he forced the enemy out of Contescourt Alley. Twice they left the trenches and walked along the top, clearing the enemy with their rifles and rifle grenades. Walker was wounded. Around 12.30 p.m. a plane flew low overhead and they signaled to it with flares. At the same time they saw Boadicea Redoubt to the west signalling to the plane so they knew that it still held on. However, the enemy could be seen moving about Jeanne d'Arc Redoubt to the east. At 1.30 p.m. the Adjutant sent off pigeons with the latest information. One arrived at Brigade HQ at 1.45 p.m. At that time the central keep of Racecourse Redoubt was holding, as was the railway cutting, but

casualties had been heavy. The CO wanted to hold until dark and then slip away, but the whole rear area was already swarming with Germans. De Wind continued to repel attack after attack until he was mortally wounded in the afternoon.

About 4 p.m. the enemy brought up two minenwerfen and began to systematically blow in the remaining trenches. The situation was hopeless and at 5.28 p.m. the CO surrendered. The Redoubt had resisted the attacks of one battalion throughout and a second later in the day. Only fifty men walked away, including those attached from the Brigade Trench Mortar Battery and the Machine Gun Company. 15th Royal Irish Rifles had ceased to exist. Almost every man had been killed, wounded or was taken prisoner. Total casualties are difficult to calculate as there was no one left to complete the war diary, except for the rear details and those left out of battle. At least seventy-four were killed on 21st March or over the next few days. Twenty-three more died in captivity. Getgood and Walker were taken prisoner and repatriated in December 1918. Getgood emigrated to America. Walker served in the Royal Irish Constabulary and then became a civil servant.

Meanwhile other Germans swept past either side of Racecourse Redoubt and at 12.30 p.m. the Brigade Intelligence Officer reported that an attack was developing on the Battle Zone. A company of the reserve battalion was sent to reinforce Quarry Redoubt. By 12.50 p.m. the counterattack company in the Battle Zone was moving forward. It retook the lost trench of the Battle Zone east of the Grugies–Seraucourt-le-Grand road but the Germans came on again and took the trench back. The company took up positions southeast of Contescourt. At 1 p.m. the remainder of 2nd Royal Irish Rifles in reserve was pulled back south of the Seraucourt-le-Grand–Essigny road. At 2.45 p.m. one of its companies occupied the unnamed redoubt northwest of the Quarry and at 3 p.m. another company was deployed in the gap between Quarry and Station Redoubts. At 6.30 p.m. a company of 2nd Royal Irish Rifles counterattacked from the Quarry into Contescourt, which had been occupied by the Germans. However, the supporting artillery was not able to suppress the enemy machine guns and the counterattack failed with heavy losses.

36th Division's ability to hold on in the Somme valley depended upon its neighbours holding the high ground on either side. When 14th Division lost the Essigny plateau on the right flank, the writing was on the wall. Touch with 14th Division was lost and not regained until 23rd March. Although penetrations into the Battle Zone were largely contained by 36th Division, its position became increasingly untenable. During the night the Division withdrew behind the Somme and a two-mile gap between it and 14th Division was filled by 61st Brigade (20th Division). The new 107th Brigade line was held by 1st and 2nd Royal Irish Rifles with a combined strength of only eleven officers, 520 other ranks, three machine guns and a Stokes 3″ mortar. The enemy followed close behind and some of the bridges had to be blown in the face of direct attack but none was lost.

The situation was similar in 30th Division's area. The forward defences were overrun quickly but the line of redoubts resisted for a time. In 21st Brigade on the right, L'Epine de Dallon Redoubt, held by 2nd Wiltshire, resisted until 2.30 p.m.

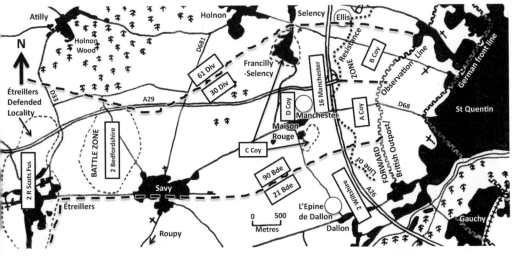

30th Division's sector to the west of St Quentin.

On the left, 90th Brigade had 16th Manchester, commanded by **Lieutenant Colonel Wilfrith Elstob**, in the Forward Zone, which included Manchester Hill and Redoubt. 2nd Bedfordshire was in the Battle Zone with 2nd Royal Scots Fusiliers in the Étreillers Defended Locality behind.

16th Manchester had been in the area since 23rd February and had dug many of the Hill's defences and rehearsed its defence frequently. The Hill offered excellent observation, including a concrete artillery observation bunker, and strong defensive positions. It also had deep dugouts and thick belts of wire in front. The Battalion took over the Hill from 17th Manchester on 18th March. Although it had a strength of 740 all ranks, HQ 90th Brigade limited each battalion going into action to twenty-one officers and 620 other ranks. The position was strengthened by four Vickers machine guns (90th Brigade Machine-Gun Company), four Stokes mortars (90th Brigade Trench Mortar Battery) and two 6″ Mortars in Brown Quarry, behind the Hill.

Late on the afternoon of 20th March mist began to develop and by 9 p.m. it was thick fog. Patrols captured a number of prisoners who were anxious to be taken to the rear; it was clear that an attack was imminent. Elstob made it abundantly clear in his final briefing before going into the line that there was to be no retreat. Pointing to Manchester Hill on the map he announced, *Here we fight and here we die.*

On the morning of 21st March, A Company was right forward and B Company left forward. C Company was split, with two platoons on the left and right to act as counterattack forces. D Company held Manchester Hill. Battalion Headquarters was established in Brown Quarry, with a forward Battle HQ at the junction of Havre Trench and the communication trench running out of Brown Quarry.

In the early hours events happened in rapid succession. A patrol left No.2 Post at 2 a.m. and found no enemy activity. At 2.30 a.m. the British artillery began firing at known enemy locations. When the enemy barrage opened at 4.30 a.m. it cut off a platoon patrol in no man's land. At 4.48 a.m. the order went out to man battle

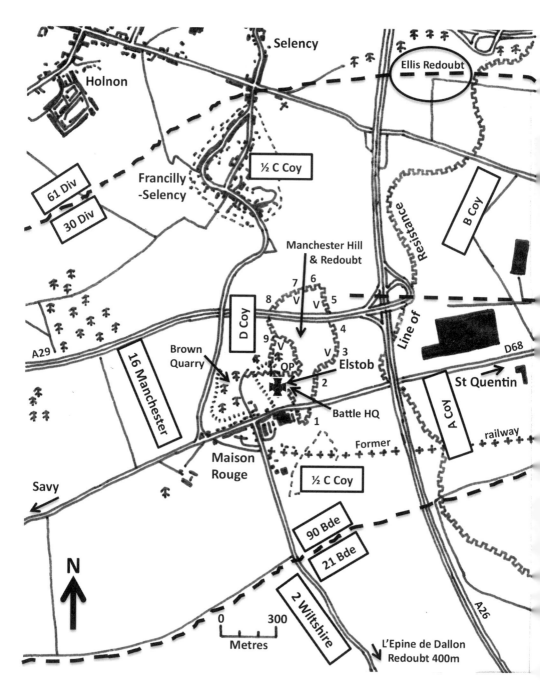

Details of the Manchester Hill position. Leave St Quentin on the D68 towards Savy. Pass under the A26 autoroute and after 250m turn right into a parallel track with the road. Follow it for 200m until just before it rejoins the D68. This was the forward edge of Manchester Redoubt in the vicinity of Post 1. The numbers 1–9 indicate the posts and V = Vickers machine gun positions.

From Post 1 looking into Manchester Redoubt. Wilfrith Elstob's Battle HQ was in the centre of this view, about halfway along the tree line.

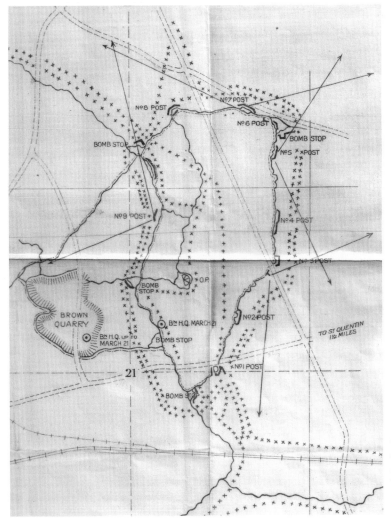

Contemporary sketch of Manchester Hill, showing details of the Vickers machine gun positions and their arcs of fire.

stations. Just before 5 a.m. the British artillery began firing just in front of the line of outposts in the Forward Zone. A few minutes later it shifted to in front of the line of resistance in the Forward Zone. At 7 a.m. the platoon in no man's land began to make its way back through the, by then, empty outpost line before being halted by the British barrage.

On Manchester Hill gas shells began falling at 5.38 a.m. and at dawn visibility was fifty metres at best. Elstob visited the right forward positions in the early morning gloom and on his return to the Redoubt moved to his Battle HQ. This occurred just as the telephone lines to the forward companies were cut by shellfire. At 8.50 a.m. the gas cleared from the hill to be replaced by a high explosive barrage.

In this area the Germans attacked early to take advantage of the fog, which neutralised most of the carefully prepared defences. As another British barrage began falling at 9.30 a.m., runners arrived at the Battle HQ to report that the Forward Zone was being overwhelmed. Ten minutes later the flanks of the Redoubt came under small arms fire and by 10.00 a.m. the defence was only being maintained by determined counterattacks. An hour later the fog began to lift, revealing the enemy advancing towards Francilly-Selency to the north and on the St Quentin–Savy road to the south. Elstob phoned this news to HQ 90th Brigade and the SOS barrage was laid down around the Redoubt, which caught some A and B Company men hanging on in the line of resistance. A Company was virtually wiped out and a little later B Company was taken in the rear by the advancing enemy. D Company and Battalion HQ on the Hill were then isolated and surrounded.

SOS signals were not observed by the British artillery and for a time the Vickers were also not in action. The Germans were held by rifle fire but began to make progress along Havre Trench from the Savy–St Quentin road. Elstob established a block, which he clung to determinedly with his revolver and grenades, and held off six successive attacks. During a short respite, whilst the enemy bombarded the

The rear of Manchester Hill from just south of the A29 autoroute on the Maison Rouge – Francilly-Selency road.

position, he reorganised the defence and repulsed an attack from the direction of No.2 Post. In this fight he assisted the defenders with a rifle and was injured by a grenade splinter. After the wound had been dressed by the MO, Elstob returned to organise the defence once again. As ammunition ran low he was seen running across the Quarry with boxes of grenades and ammunition, and at one time was blown five metres by an exploding shell. He was wounded twice more before 2 p.m. but continued to encourage his men. Artillery support died away as the gunners pulled back from Holnon Wood to avoid being overwhelmed. Despite the determined resistance, the first German troops reached the Battle Zone about noon.

The patrol platoon saw heavy fighting on the Hill as it fought its way back to Francilly-Selency around 2 p.m. Soon after the enemy broke into Brown Quarry and brought up field guns only fifty metres from the final rallying point at the Battle HQ. Elstob made his last call to Brigade HQ at 3.22 p.m. Shortly afterwards he rose to throw a grenade and was shot dead. As his Adjutant, Captain Norman Sharples (Pozières Memorial), tried to pull him back into the trench he too was killed. The survivors surrendered around 4.30 p.m. when their ammunition ran out. The Battalion suffered a total of 575 casualties. Of the 168 men in the Redoubt only seventeen came away unscathed. The day's entry in the Battalion War Diary was written by a second lieutenant, which says it all. The survivors made their way to the north of Étreillers to Villers-St-Christophe. It was entirely due to the determined defence of redoubts such as Manchester Hill that the enemy only reached as far as Savy that day.

The two redoubts to the north put up an excellent fight into the late afternoon. At 2 p.m. the Germans had not penetrated into the Battle Zone but, to the south, by 6.30 p.m. they had gained a foothold in Roupy and made a few penetrations into the Battle Zone. By the time the fighting died down around 10 p.m. these were the only penetrations they had to show for the day.

61st Division had all three brigades in the line: 182nd on the right, 184th in the centre and 183rd on the left next to 72nd Brigade (24th Division). 183rd Brigade's position had to be maintained or the whole Holnon plateau position could be turned. 1/5th Gordon Highlanders was in the Forward Zone, 1/8th Argyll & Sutherland Highlanders was in the Battle Zone and 9th Royal Scots was in the Holnon rear defences. 2/4th Royal Berkshire (184th Brigade) was the reserve.

The night before the battle the officers of 1/8th Argyll & Sutherland Highlanders held a dinner in their huts and had just gone to bed when the bombardment started at 4.30 a.m. The order to man battle station positions went out from Brigade HQ, with the last unit being informed by 5.15 a.m. 1/8th Argyll & Sutherland Highlanders' positions were occupied by 6.45 a.m. but a number of C Company officers were wounded when their hut was hit before setting off. This Company was the most forward and exposed. The Battalion suffered forty casualties just moving to its positions.

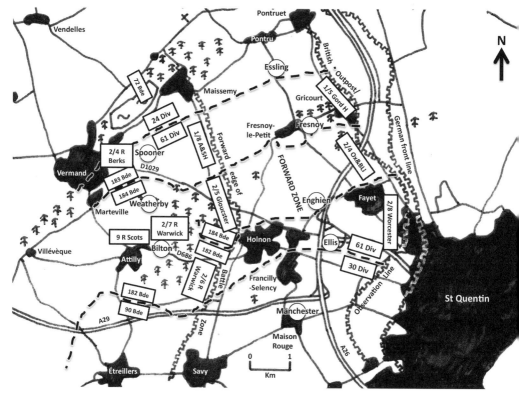

61st Division's positions on 21st March 1918. The main redoubts are shown as circles.

There was a complete absence of information about what was happening on the left, so 1/5th Gordon Highlanders in the Forward Zone was ordered to push out patrols in that direction. The Battalion was also ordered to push patrols well forward through the thick fog, in order to find out what the enemy intended. At 5.30 a.m. 1/5th Gordon Highlanders reported there had been no attack but gas shelling was very heavy. At 5.55 a.m. Divisional HQ reported that 184th Brigade was evacuating Enghien Redoubt on account of the gas concentration there. On the left 72nd Brigade was out of contact with its right battalion and the Left Group of 61st Division's artillery was cut off from all of its batteries due to the telephone cables being disrupted by the shelling.

By 10.30 a.m. 1/5th Gordon Highlander's left flank was being turned from the valley south of Essling Redoubt in 72nd Brigade's area. At 11.05 a.m. 184th Brigade reported that pressure had increased on Enghien Redoubt to the south, which was by then surrounded but holding out. By 11.20 a.m. Fresnoy Redoubt was under pressure on both flanks but also holding. Information from HQ 72nd Brigade indicated that it was moving three companies to gain touch with the left flank of 1/8th Argyll & Sutherland Highlanders in the Battle Zone. By 12.30 p.m. Fresnoy Redoubt was completely surrounded, including the Battalion HQ. CO 1/5th Gordon Highlanders believed he could not hold much longer. The brigade commander urged him to hang on until dark and then to fight his way back. The

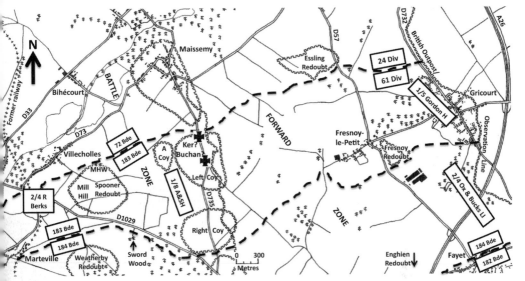

Leave Maissemy on the D735 southwards. The road climbs a long hill and there is a slight bend to the right near the top. 200m beyond is a pull in on the right. This is the left edge of 1/8th Argyll & Sutherland Highlanders' left company position. The forward trench of the Battle Zone ran parallel with the road on the far side of it. A similar view from the centre of the company's position can be had 300m further on, where there is a track running off to the left and a pair of prominent trees on the right. The marked VC sites for Buchan and Ker are not definitive as no accounts are specific about where the actions took place. MHW = Mount Huette Wood.

brigade commander also ordered the artillery to come back onto the Redoubt barrage to support 1/5th Gordon Highlanders more effectively.

1/8th Argyll & Sutherland Highlanders' forward defences on the right of the Battle Zone were lost at 3 p.m. and communication with Fresnoy Redoubt failed. Two platoon posts continued to be held in the right forward redoubt, but the other two platoon posts were occupied by the Germans. A Company, 1/8th Argyll & Sutherland Highlanders and 478th Field Company RE counterattacked to eject the enemy and bombing parties were organised. 478th Field Company was withdrawn from the A Company Redoubt after dark and was replaced by a platoon of 1/5th Duke of Cornwall's Light Infantry (Pioneers).

The left 1/8th Argyll & Sutherland Highlanders' company position was lost about 3 p.m. and telephone contact with HQ 1/5th Gordon Highlanders in Fresnoy Redoubt ceased about the same time. The situation was critical. At 4.30 p.m., 2/4th Royal Berkshire in reserve launched a counterattack under cover of a smoke barrage to regain the forward positions in the Battle Zone. Four machine guns were deployed to cover the left flank. Although the attack began well the CO, Lieutenant Colonel John Dimmer VC, was killed. On the left the 1/8th Argyll & Sutherland Highlanders' counterattack company (A) trenches were regained and Spooner Redoubt on Mill Hill was retained. However, the forward trenches of the Battle Zone could not be regained due to a German attack from Maissemy. When the counterattack broke down about 6 p.m. the brigade commander decided not to

From the left of 1/8th Argyll & Sutherland Highlanders' position looking east. The forward trenches of the Battle Zone ran parallel with this road 100–150m on the far side. The fields of fire from here are excellent, but the trenches would have been very exposed on this forward slope.

attack over the open again. Instead bombing parties were ordered to press on and try to regain the lost trenches. A 2/4th Royal Berkshire company remained with A Company, 1/8th Argyll & Sutherland Highlanders in the left rear redoubt of the Battle Zone. Another 2/4th Royal Berkshire company joined the 1/8th Argyll & Sutherland Highlanders company in Spooner Redoubt, where the Battalion HQ was located. The remainder of 2/4th Royal Berkshire formed a reserve at Brigade HQ in the railway cutting east of Marteville. 1/8th Argyll & Sutherland Highlanders held its positions for the rest of the day.

At the end of the day the whole of the forward edge of 61st Division's Battle Zone was being held, except on the far left of 183rd Brigade. A few defenders of the three redoubts in the Forward Zone managed to get back during the night but the vast majority of the three forward battalions was lost.

Second Lieutenant John Buchan was wounded early on in the battle but refused to leave. He continually visited his posts, which suffered heavy casualties, encouraging and cheering the men. When the enemy closed in later and the position came under machine gun fire, Buchan continued to move around disregarding his personal safety. He was injured again and a little later noticed the enemy were about to encircle his position from the right flank. As he prepared to fight his platoon out, the Germans called upon him to surrender. He replied, *to hell with surrender*, shot the leading German and drove off the attack. He and his men fought back to the support line of the forward position, where he held out until dusk. All the time he refused to have his wounds tended. During the evening the troops to the left withdrew unexpectedly and left Buchan isolated. He received no order to withdraw and remained in this position. It is unclear precisely where this took place but it is understood to have been in the forward left company's position.

Attacks on Spooner Redoubt during the night were repulsed. A company of 1/5th Duke of Cornwall's Light Infantry (minus a platoon) filled the gap between

Spooner Redoubt and Sword Wood on the Brigade's right flank. The four machine guns, deployed earlier to support the counterattack, were withdrawn from Mill Hill to the high ground east of Brigade HQ to cover from Maissemy round to Sword Wood. Some guns of the Left Group of 61st Division's artillery, which had to be abandoned during the day near Mount Huette Wood, were recovered during the night, covered by parties from 1/8th Argyll & Sutherland Highlanders. Contact was also re-established with some of the batteries.

1/8th Argyll & Sutherland Highlanders held its positions early on 22nd March and several attacks on Mill Hill were thrown back. At 10 a.m., 24th Division on the left began to withdraw and the Brigade reserve (2/4th Royal Berkshire) moved to cover that flank. When the flanks began to give way at 2 p.m., withdrawal by 183rd Brigade commenced to the reserve line west of Villévèque. During this operation Buchan's position was overwhelmed and he was never seen again. 1/8th Argyll & Sutherland Highlanders suffered 292 casualties (forty-two killed, 106 wounded and 144 missing).

61st Battalion MGC was involved fully in the action. A group of twelve machine guns was in the Forward Zone, a second group was in the rear of the front system with twenty guns and the largest group was in the Battle Zone with twenty-four guns. Tactical command of individual guns devolved to the respective Brigade HQ.

When the enemy penetrated 61st Division's flank, **Lieutenant Allan Ker**, with one Vickers machine gun, engaged them as they advanced through dead ground. The attack was held up with many casualties. Ker sent a message to HQ 61st Battalion MGC that he intended to fight it out with his small party until he could be relieved by a counterattack. This he did until his ammunition ran out and he was attacked from behind. When the Vickers was destroyed Ker and his team drove off several attacks using only their revolvers. The wounded were gathered into a small shelter and the rest resolved to fight it out to the last. In one of the hand-to-hand encounters a German rifle was taken and put to use. After ten hours of fighting, lack of food, gas poisoning and tending the wounded, Ker was exhausted but refused to give up. When the ammunition was gone the position was rushed and overwhelmed but the determined defence had held up five hundred Germans for three hours. Ker was taken prisoner.

The precise location of Ker's VC action is not known. It may have been in the Forward Zone on the left flank of the Division. However, from the description of the action it seems more likely that it was on the left flank of 1/8th Argyll & Sutherland Highlanders' left company position in the Battle Zone, close to where Buchan earned his Cross. This is also where a single Vickers machine gun was sited but, it has to be pointed out, there were five other single Vickers positions in 183rd Brigade's Forward and Battle Zones, in addition to nine pairs or larger clusters.

XIX Corps' front along the Omignon valley was held by 24th Division on the right and 66th Division on the left. In the south no man's land was 900m wide and the front was held by a series of isolated posts. In the north no man's land was narrow and the front consisted of the more familiar three lines of trenches. The Battle Zone front line was reasonably well constructed but the other lines were only partly dug.

On the right of 24th Division, in 72nd Brigade's area, the enemy swept on to reach the Battle Zone by 11 a.m. The Division's southern flank was threatened and reserves had to be rushed to halt the flood. Further north, around le Verguier, determined resistance and heavy fire halted the Germans short of the Battle Zone. Here they made no progress until well into the afternoon.

17th Brigade, on the left of 24th Division, was holding the line from near Watling Street to the Priel Farm Posts, with 199th Brigade (66th Division) on its left. 17th Brigade had two battalions forward. 3rd Rifle Brigade was on the right and 8th Queen's was on the left, with its A and C Companies in the front line, right and left respectively. 8th Queen's had relieved 1st Royal Fusiliers late on 18th March and the latter was in reserve at Vendelles. As it took over the line, 8th Queen's noticed considerable movement behind the enemy lines.

On 21st March the bombardment commenced at 4.40 a.m. and fell well to the rear of the forward companies. By 5.40 a.m. all units in 17th Brigade had been notified to move to their designated alarm positions. By 7 a.m. all of 8th Queen's telephone links had been cut and Battalion HQ moved to the lane leading to Vendelles. However, around that time patrols reported nothing unusual. At 9.25 a.m. Brigade HQ ordered the forward battalions to send out listening patrols to give advanced warning of an attack. Just before 11 a.m. Brigade HQ began to receive reports of attacks from flanking formations. As a result, at 11.25 a.m. the forward battalions were ordered to send out officers' patrols to ascertain the situation. At 11.50 a.m. Brigade HQ learned that 72nd Brigade's front at Mareval and Pontru Trenches had fallen and the enemy was advancing south of Cooker Quarry. Twenty-five minutes later 3rd Rifle Brigade reported Dragoon Post and the high ground at Ascension Farm had been lost. With the extensive Vickers and Lewis machine gun defences rendered just about useless by the fog, the Germans swept on through the outpost line and reached the Cooker Trench – Dean Trench position. These trenches were

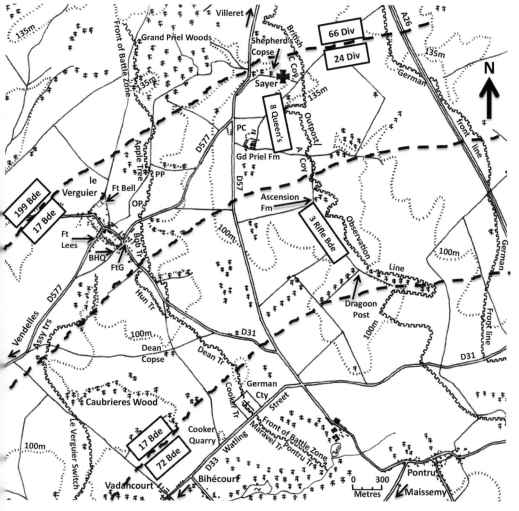

24th Division's front on 21st March. Sayer's VC action was on the left boundary with 66th Division. PC = Priel Crater, FtG = Fort Greathead, OP = Orchard Post and PP = Prieumel Post.

not in the best position and construction was incomplete. They fell quickly except at Cooker Quarry, which held out until 6.30 p.m., inflicting severe losses on the enemy. The left of 3rd Rifle Brigade, held by A Company reinforced by D Company, rallied just west of Dean Copse. It fell back gradually, delaying the enemy advance with great skill.

On the right of 8th Queen's the first that HQ A Company in Priel Crater knew of the attack was at 10.30 a.m., when soldiers from C Company's right post arrived at Company HQ. They were closely followed by Germans from the direction of Grand Priel Farm. Heavy rifle fire was opened and many casualties were inflicted on the advancing Germans, who then attacked from the southwest from west of the Priel Crater Road. A Company came under heavy machine gun fire from the north, resulting in many casualties. It was surrounded as the Germans infiltrated between

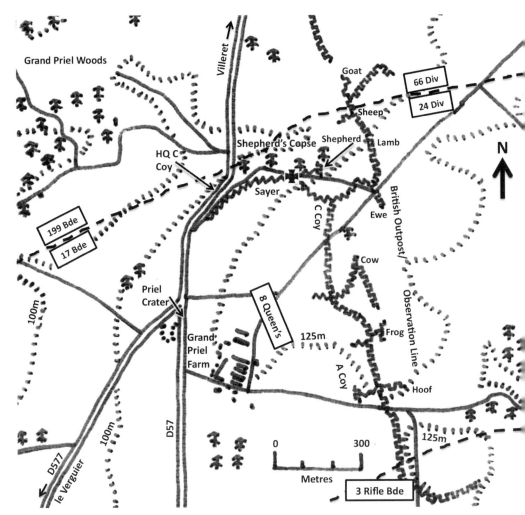

Drive through le Verguier on the D577 northeastwards towards Villeret. At the junction with the D57 go straight over onto a track, with le Grand Priel Farm on the right. After 300m, at the t-junction turn left for 500m, passing a clump of trees on the right. Stop 100m beyond the trees. Shepherd's Copse is on the left just under 200m away. Ewe was in the field to the right. The track that used to run from this point along the southern edge of Shepherd's Copse appears to have been ploughed over but is shown on the map in case it is reinstated. The site of Sayer's VC action can be reached by walking along the tree line from the D57 but the path has been lost. If you wish to do this there is enough room to pull a car off the D57 at the western end of the Copse just before it goes around the right hand corner.

A and C Companies and cut off retreat. After a fierce fight, the few survivors of A Company tried to reach their Company HQ but met a large enemy force coming down the valley west of Priel Crater. Instead they fought their way back to Orchard Post and the southern end of Apple Tree Walk, northeast of le Verguier.

In C Company, **Lance Corporal John Sayer** was in charge of a small party returning to Company HQ at Shepherd's Copse. In this area the Germans attacked around 10 a.m. and, because of the mist, managed to get within thirty metres

Shepherd's Copse from the southeast.

before being discovered. Near Shepherd's Copse, Sayer's platoon, commanded by Lieutenant Claude Lorraine Piesse, numbered only twenty-two men and was poorly equipped and supplied. It was also split between three posts.

Sayer arrived at Piesse's Post (one NCO and four men) just as the Germans attacked from both sides. Sayer seized the junction of two communications trenches about twenty metres southeast of the post that commanded the approaches from the east. He fought off a number of attacks over two hours without assistance. The Germans broke into the trench several times, but each time Sayer repelled them with his rifle and bayonet; he killed at least nine according to Piesse and probably more. During the whole period he was fully exposed to fire. To add to his difficulties, the enemy was able to get close enough along one communication trench to throw bombs without being seen. Loss of this position would have allowed the enemy to enfilade another fire bay and probably lead to the fall of the whole platoon position. Sayer inspired all in the post and made skilful use of fire to hold on but at midday, with three-quarters of the garrison casualties and the fog lifting, the enemy made a final rush and secured the position. Five wounded men were taken away, including Sayer and Piesse. Sayer's leg was amputated by German doctors but to no avail, as he died at Le Cateau on 18th April. Piesse survived and made the initial VC recommendation on 24th February 1919 after being released from captivity.

The remnants of C Company struggled back to the village. From 11 a.m. onwards the enemy began penetrating the Battle Zone. 8th Queen's was attacked from both flanks and the front simultaneously but held out around le Verguier, in no small part due to Sayer delaying the enemy assault. Efforts to take the village were thwarted and the Germans tried to turn it by attacks from north and south.

Shepherd's Copse on the left. Sayer's VC action was in the centre of the picture. The clump of trees on the track to the east of the Copse can just be seen on the right.

At 12.30 p.m. 1st Royal Fusiliers was ordered to move to assembly trenches southwest of le Verguier to prepare for a counterattack on the village. By then the enemy had advanced through Maissemy in 72nd Brigade's area and was moving on Villecholles. Due to a breakthrough in Dean Trench in 3rd Rifle Brigade's area, 8th Queens was ordered to form a flank from Hun Trench, southeast of le Verguier, to the Battalion HQ in the sunken road just south of Fort Greathead. On the left of 17th Brigade, 199th Brigade had lost Grand Priel Woods, resulting in le Verguier also being threatened from the north.

Shepherd's Copse from the D57.

At 1.05 p.m. 1st Royal Fusiliers sent a company to garrison le Verguier Switch southwest of Caubrières Wood where the situation was unclear. 3rd Rifle Brigade was being hard pressed on both flanks at Cooker Quarry and west of Dean Copse. At 1.25 p.m. a company of 12th Sherwood Foresters (Pioneers) was sent to reinforce 1st Royal Fusiliers for a counterattack. Three extra machine guns were sent to protect the right flank but it was clear that 3rd Rifle Brigade's situation was worsening. Its positions could not be held much longer and the brigade commander made arrangements for le Verguier Switch to be held from le Verguier to Bihécourt. Two squadrons, each of seven enemy aircraft, spotted for the artillery and strafed troops on the ground from 4.30 p.m. until dark. Enemy field guns also moved to within 900m of 3rd Rifle Brigade.

At 3.45 p.m. 8th Queen's reported the enemy had reached the sunken road just over a kilometre north-northeast of le Verguier. The Battalion held a line facing north from Fort Bell to Orchard Post. At 5 p.m. two dismounted regiments of 1st Cavalry Division were allocated to 17th Brigade. One was placed in support behind 3rd Rifle Brigade and the other was held in reserve with Brigade HQ. At 6.40 p.m. the garrison of Cooker Quarry was ordered to gain contact with 72nd Brigade and man the Vadencourt defences north of Watling Street.

8th Queen's held two strongpoints (Forts Lees and Greathead), on the southwestern outskirts of le Verguier, against repeated attacks. By 7.35 p.m. the Battalion was being attacked from north and south and at 8 p.m. Prieumel Post was lost. As the enemy was north and west of le Verguier, the brigade commander decided not to counterattack as regaining it would merely create an isolated post that could not be held.

At 3.30 a.m. on the 22nd Bob Trench was lost. Fort Greathead was penetrated but restored by a counterattack. At 7 a.m. an attack against the Battalion HQ was driven off by cooks and orderlies. The enemy got into Fort Lees at 9 a.m. but was driven out by a party under Captain Layton. The Germans worked their way to the west of the Fort and were driven back by Lewis gun fire. However by 10 a.m. they had captured Forts Lees and Greathead. Battalion HQ in le Verguier fell soon afterwards. With the remnants of the Battalion all but surrounded the CO, Lieutenant Colonel Hugh Chevalier Piers, withdrew the survivors to trenches west of the le Verguier–Vendelles road. A retirement down the Vendelles road was ordered, covered by a Lewis gun, the thick fog and 1st Royal Fusiliers. Only one casualty was sustained in this move. When le Verguier fell, the brigade commander realised that the enemy was threatening to envelop his positions from the left rear. He therefore ordered a withdrawal to commence. By the time that 8th Queen's arrived at Montecourt, it numbered just eleven officers and 150 other ranks.

In 66th Division the story was much the same. After hard fighting the Germans reached the Jeancourt–Hargicourt road, before outrunning their artillery support. The left flank was turned, which added to XIX Corps' problems, with both flanks then under threat. By 2 p.m. the Corps front was a salient with resistance continuing at le Verguier and both flanks slipping back. On the left, Templeux le Guerard fell around 5.30 p.m. but the enemy was halted west of the village.

VII Corps' front, running along a narrow ridge, was the line held at the end of the Battle of Cambrai. The Forward Zone was narrow and consisted of only one trench but was well provided with machine guns and strongpoints. The Battle Zone consisted of two continuous trenches with two intermediate trenches between and the defended localities of Ronssoy-Lempire and Épehy. The German attack fell against the whole Corps front except on the extreme left.

On the right, 16th Division's Forward Zone was quickly rolled up and the Battle Zone in front of Ronssoy was attacked at about 9.30 a.m. By 10.30 a.m. the whole Battle Zone front was engaged. The Division was forced back and joined 21st Division in the defence of Épehy. A gap was filled by the reserve brigade of 21st Division throwing back a defensive flank from Épehy towards Ste Emilie. This was filled in the evening by 39th Division (GHQ Reserve). The rear of the Battle Zone was held, while behind it the remainder of 39th Division dug in on a switch line.

In the centre, 21st Division was attacked from 7 a.m. onwards. The Forward Zone had little depth in which to absorb attacks but, despite this, the enemy was delayed in closing up to the Battle Zone until noon. At the end of the day the Division held the line from Épehy to Chapel Hill. The right flank had to be extended to keep touch with 16th Division and in compensation for this 9th Division took over Chapel Hill.

On the right, 9th Division's right flank at Gauche Wood fell at noon. However, the enemy was unable to advance further due to defensive lines to the west and fire from the area not attacked to the north. The rest of the Division's front held all day but the decision to abandon the Flesquières Salient by V Corps (Third Army) to the north meant 9th Division had to conform. By morning the line held ran along the rear of the Forward Zone.

In summary, by 11 a.m. the Germans had closed up to the Battle Zone, except in 24th Division's area. Damage to communications rendered the British artillery largely ineffective but the lifting of the fog allowed for some assistance from the surviving guns. By mid-afternoon it was clear to General Gough that, although his troops were holding, a breakthrough would occur unless he received substantial reinforcements. In the meantime he resolved to delay by every means and slip away at night to resume the fight in the morning. News was received that the enemy had broken in north of the Flesquières Salient in Third Army's area, thus threatening VII Corps. It was also known that fresh enemy divisions were surging forward. Accordingly III Corps was ordered to withdraw behind the Crozat Canal and XVIII Corps was to bend back its front to comply. XIX Corps was to bend back its left to maintain contact with VII Corps, while that formation did the same to remain in contact with the right of Third Army. At the end of the day Fifth Army was badly battered and had lost many guns and men but there had been no breakthrough.

In Third Army's area the Germans aimed to pinch out the Flesquières Salient from the flanks. The main weight of the attack fell on IV and VI Corps. The

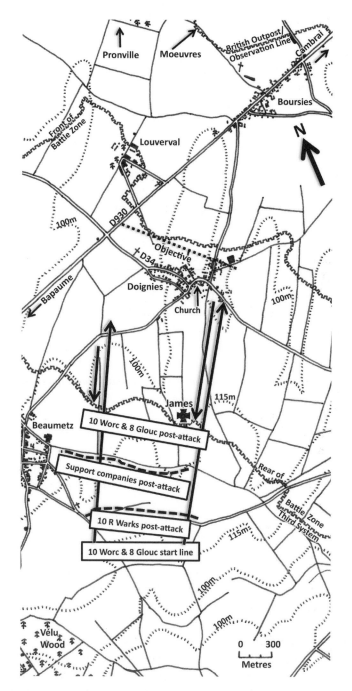

The 57th Brigade attack on the evening of 21st March. Leave Beaumetz to the southeast on the unclassified road to Hermies. Pass Beaumetz Cross Roads Cemetery on the left and 250m beyond the road swings to the left. Continue for 1,600m to a cross tracks and turn left. After 100m the track crosses the old railway line. Park here and walk northwest for 600m to the top of the rise. Look north (right) towards Doignies and the direction of 8th Gloucestershire's attack on 21st March. The second part of Manley James' VC action on 23rd March was approximately 400m along this line (refer to the map for Julien Gribble for dispositions that day). Without wading through muddy fields and/or crops it is difficult to get any closer.

remaining sixteen miles of the Army's front was engaged by artillery and minor attacks to tie down the reserves. The main attack on the seven miles of front from Boursies to Bullecourt was delivered at 9.40 a.m. In some areas the fog lifted by 10 a.m. but such was the weight of the bombardment that few escaped from the front line.

In IV Corps the enemy broke into the front in two places. The first was in the centre of 51st Division on the right, in the valley running southwest from Moeuvres to Louverval. The other was on the left, in the adjacent valley south of Pronville, on the right of 6th Division. The penetration in 6th Division swung behind the rear of 153rd Brigade (51st Division) and the two penetrations then linked up to advance along the intervening spur. Soon after 11 a.m. Louverval was taken in a simultaneous attack from the northwest, north and northeast.

The German penetration into the centre of 51st Division was extended. By 10.40 a.m. Boursies had fallen but the enemy was prevented from going further by a switch line. By 11 a.m. the troops in the Battle Zone were heavily engaged. The enemy swept on in close formation and suffered heavy casualties but captured Doignies by 2 p.m. By this time most of the Battle Zone, from the left boundary to the Cambrai–Bapaume road, had fallen but the right still held the original front line. The Beaumetz–Morchies Line was held firmly by divisional reserves and help was on hand from 19th and 25th Divisions. After 3 p.m. the enemy made no further progress although attacks and counterattacks swayed back and forth all afternoon.

57th Brigade (19th Division) had been stood to since 6.30 a.m. At 11.15 a.m. B Company, 19th Machine Gun Battalion was attached to it and at 12 p.m. the Brigade moved to assembly positions southwest of Vélu. At 2 p.m. a company of 10th Royal Warwickshire formed four widely dispersed platoon posts along a ridge northeast of Vélu and was reinforced with a section of machine guns. At 3 p.m. orders came through to move to positions southeast of Beaumetz-lès-Cambrai in preparation for

The ground over which 10th Worcestershire and 8th Gloucestershire attacked on the evening of 21st March. The second part of Manley James' VC action on 23rd March was approximately 400m into the fields in line with Doignies. Refer to the map for Julian Gribble for the dispositions that day. Without wading through muddy fields and/or crops it is difficult to get any closer.

a counterattack on Doignies. The Brigade was in position by 4.40 p.m. but orders for the counterattack were not received by Brigade HQ until 5.45 p.m. Despite this, the units were briefed by 6.15 p.m., although there was insufficient time to ensure that every man was aware of all aspects of the plan.

The counterattack against Doignies commenced at 7 p.m. with the aim of preventing the enemy getting behind the Flesquières Salient. The start was delayed while artillery was brought into supporting positions. In the event it played no part in the attack and the delay merely allowed the enemy time to consolidate his hold on the objectives. The attack by 8th Gloucestershire on the right, with a company of 8th Tank Battalion attached, and 10th Worcestershire on the left, commenced 1,800m southwest of Doignies. 10th Royal Warwickshire remained in reserve southeast of Beaumetz. Support was provided by the attached machine gun company and two mortars of 57th Brigade Trench Mortar Battery.

The attack set off down the hill towards Doignies with the light fading and mist forming. The tanks led, inflicting heavy casualties, followed by two companies from each infantry battalion. They passed through the forward elements of 51st Division and encountered the enemy in and beyond the third British defence system (rear of Battle Zone). As the outskirts of Doignies were reached, the tanks had to break off the attack due to the onset of darkness. On the right 8th Gloucestershire reached its objective, the church in Doignies, and took twenty-seven prisoners and two machine guns. However, in the dark touch was lost with 10th Worcestershire. The 8th Gloucestershire company commanders (Captains Bowles and **Manley James**) held a hurried conference. In view of the heavy machine gun fire, particularly from the open and exposed right flank, they decided to pull back to a trench in the third system, with advanced posts deployed in front. This trench was already occupied by a few Seaforth Highlanders (51st Division) and offered a suitable defensive position. On the left 10th Worcestershire reached its objective in the sunken Doignies–Beaumetz road but both flanks were exposed. The withdrawal of 8th Gloucestershire on the right compounded the problem on that flank but the Battalion held on.

The attack had been only partially successful. All objectives would have been achieved if a simultaneous counterattack by 51st Division against Louverval on the

left flank had materialised, the attack had started earlier instead of in the gathering gloom of dusk, and there had been time for proper briefings.

Firing soon died away but both Battalions had suffered heavy losses from enemy artillery and machine guns. The other companies of both battalions established themselves in depth in the sunken lane running southwest from Beaumetz. 10th Royal Warwickshire dug in on the high ground behind them, assisted by 94th Field Company RE and a company of 5th South Wales Borderers (Pioneers). The Brigade remained in these positions for the next thirty-six hours.

James was wounded in the neck in the attack, but refused to leave his company and the organisation of the defence took until midnight. Due to a misunderstanding, 8th Gloucestershire attacked Doignies again at 4 a.m. on 22nd March but without success. At 12.45 p.m. 8th Gloucestershire and 10th Worcestershire came under command of HQ 154th Brigade. During the day James and his men repulsed three attacks. At 5 a.m. on 23rd March, 57th Brigade was issued orders for a withdrawal to the Green Line that night. However, prior to this 51st Division was forced to withdraw in the face of overwhelming enemy pressure, commencing at about 10 a.m. This left 8th Gloucestershire and 10th Royal Warwickshire isolated and with their flanks in the air. They held on until 11 a.m., when they were forced to withdraw towards Vélu Wood. 8th Gloucestershire's withdrawal was covered by A Company, commanded by Manley James. It was ordered to hold to the last and it did, inflicting terrible casualties on the enemy as they passed the right flank. This gained sufficient time for the rest of the Battalion to get away and for the withdrawal of guns in the area. During a counterattack to maintain pressure on the enemy, James was wounded in the face by shrapnel and was later shot through the stomach. A Company fought almost to the last man. James was last seen manning a machine gun single-handed before he and the other survivors were overwhelmed. James was picked up by the Germans next day and taken prisoner. By the time 57th Brigade had completed this stage of the withdrawal at midnight on 23rd/24th March, it had suffered 833 casualties, although somewhat ameliorated by 318 reinforcements arriving on the 23rd.

In 6th Division, on the left, the Forward Zone fell quickly and by 10.30 a.m. the Battle Zone was under attack, but held firm until Lagnicourt on the right and Noreuil on the left in 59th Division's area fell. A counterattack restored the situation but the line was pushed back. The right was still in the front of the Battle Zone but was jeopardised by the troubles in 51st Division's area. The left was in the rear of the Battle Zone and the centre was trying to keep touch with both flanks. There was also a gap of over three kilometres on the right, filled by two companies from brigade reserve. After dark the line fell back to the rear of the Battle Zone.

In VI Corps the main attack fell on 59th Division on the right, where the enemy broke through southeast of Bullecourt and took the Noreuil–Bullecourt road. By noon the Germans controlled the Forward Zone completely. Reserves from 40th Division moved forward; 120th Brigade into the third defensive system astride the

Bapaume–Écoust road northwest of Vaulx-Vraucourt; 119th Brigade to hold Henin Hill, and 121st Brigade into the third system from the left of 120th Brigade (Mory–Ecoust road) to the right of 34th Division at St Leger.

At the end of 21st March Third Army still held a significant proportion of the Flesquières Salient. However, further north the majority of IV and VI Corps had been forced to the rear of the Battle Zone. Losses had been heavy and three of the five available reserve divisions had been committed. However, better visibility in this area helped aircraft to assist the artillery. Brigades were down to less than 500 men and some were even lower. The defence of the Flesquières Salient was costly and required a large number of troops. It was therefore decided to withdraw to the Intermediate Line (previously part of the Hindenburg Line), since it was stronger than the Battle Zone. The withdrawal was completed by 6 a.m. on the 22nd with little interference from the enemy.

Overall the British were pleased with their effort on 21st March. They had prevented the enemy from making a breakthrough but the high command realised that, with few reserves against the many available to the Germans, they were not in a good position. Given the length of frontage held and the weakness of the BEF at this time, it is remarkable that so little was lost. Just over 200 kilometres of front was held at the lowest density ever and with only eight reserve divisions. For the first time on the Western Front the defenders were not able to launch a counterstroke.

22nd March 1918

324 2Lt Alfred Herring, ASC att'd 6th Northamptonshire (54th Brigade, 18th Division), Montagne Bridge, France

325 2Lt Cecil Knox, 150th Field Company RE (36th Division), Tugny, France

326 Pte Herbert Columbine, 9th Squadron MGC (9th Cavalry Brigade, 1st Cavalry Division), Hervilly Wood, France

327 Sgt Harold Jackson, 7th East Yorkshire (50th Brigade, 17th Division), Hermies, France

328 Capt Reginald Hayward, 1st Wiltshire (7th Brigade, 25th Division), near Frémicourt, France

329 2Lt Ernest Beal, 13th Yorkshire (121st Brigade, 40th Division), St Leger, France

On 22nd March the Germans concentrated upon gaining crossings over the Crozat Canal and pinching out the Flesquières Salient. The fog cleared more quickly than on the 21st but persisted in the valleys until about 11 a.m. Fifth Army started the day holding four more miles of front than on the 21st but had been reinforced by three dismounted cavalry brigades; there were only two cavalry divisions (less two brigades) in reserve. With little likelihood of French reinforcements, and the prospect of a disaster if he fought where he stood, General Sir Hubert de la Poer Gough elected for a gradual and orderly withdrawal. III Corps in the south was to

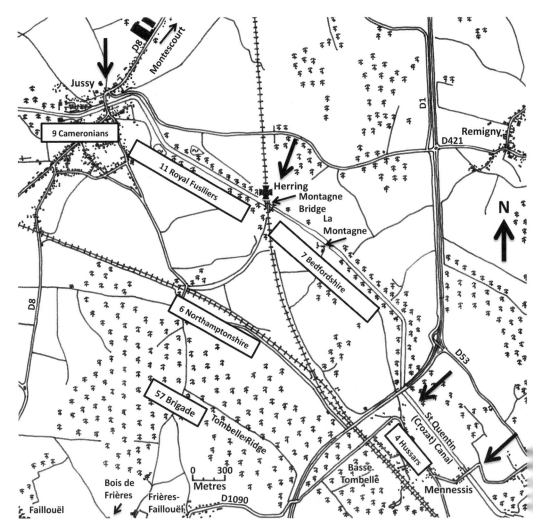

Enter Jussy from the north along the D8 from Montescourt. Just before the main road swings left to cross the canal, take the left turn into Chemin de Remigny. Follow it for 1,600m to the bridge over the railway and continue for 100m, where there is space to park off the road on the left. On the bridge look south along the railway line for 700m to Montagne bridge, which is in line with the gap in the trees, i.e. the line of the canal. To reach the bridge cross the road where you parked and follow the track southwards. It soon joins the railway and runs parallel with it to the canal bank. There used to be a footbridge just east of the railway bridge. The abutment is still there but the bridge has been removed and it is no longer possible to reach the south bank from here. Approaches to the bridge from the south are more difficult and time consuming. Do not be tempted to climb onto the railway embankment as it is a fast electrified line.

stand fast, XVIII Corps was to retire to the Somme, XIX Corps was to hold the Péronne bridgehead and VII Corps the forward portion of the Rear Zone.

In III Corps three divisions and two dismounted brigades were engaged along the Crozat Canal. During the day three more dismounted brigades (3rd Cavalry Division) and 13th Entrenching Battalion reinforced the line. The defences were poorly prepared and the line of the canal prevented patrols warning of the enemy's intentions. Consequently the Germans breached the canal on a two-mile front on the right from Tergnier almost to Liez.

At 8.30 p.m. on 21st March, 54th Brigade (18th Division) was ordered to form a rearguard to cover the retirement of 14th Division over the Crozat Canal. It was then to withdraw over the canal to hold a line between it and the railway embankment. This was achieved soon after midnight. 11th Royal Fusiliers was on the left, in contact with 9th Cameronians (43rd Brigade, 14th Division) on the eastern edge of Jussy. 7th Bedfordshire was on the right, in contact with 16th Lancers near the edge of Mennessis. However 16th Lancers was mixed up with III Corps Reinforcement Training Battalion and some reorganisation was required. 16th Lancers was withdrawn into Brigade reserve in Bois de Tombelle, while III Corps Reinforcement Training Battalion concentrated in front of Mennessis. There was some ambiguity over responsibilities in this area, which resulted in a gap in the line between the right of 7th Bedfordshire and 4th Hussars.

6th Northamptonshire was on the railway embankment in Brigade reserve by 5.30 a.m. At 6 a.m. the brigade commander, Brigadier General LW de V Sadleir-Jackson, conducted a reconnaissance of the whole position and ordered the bridges between Jussy and Mennessis to be destroyed. It was quickly discovered that no preparations for demolition had been carried out. It is understood that the destruction of the bridges in this area was a French responsibility. Whatever the truth, Sadleir-Jackson ordered the sappers to get on with the demolitions and also ordered a further supply of explosives. To allow the work to proceed, the infantry held bridgeheads on the far bank, supported by Lewis guns and Stokes mortars. It was not until 10 a.m. that a small quantity of explosives arrived. Sadleir-Jackson ordered the sappers to concentrate upon the Montagne bridge, which 7th Bedfordshire had tried to destroy with trench mortar bombs, but it was still passable. Despite many efforts by Sadleir-Jackson to get more sapper support from HQ III Corps and HQ 18th Division, little was done. He believed the RE officer sent to destroy the Montagne bridge failed to cooperate fully. With a few exceptions he was also very critical of the support provided by 18th Division Machine Gun Battalion.

From 9 a.m. onwards the Germans brought machine guns and mortars onto the high ground overlooking the canal. Their fire made movement difficult and it was clear that they were preparing to forced the canal crossings, although no attempt was made until later in the day.

At 6 p.m. a heavy artillery and mortar bombardment fell on the whole Brigade front. The assault began at 6.15 p.m. against Jussy and Montagne bridges. At Jussy 9th Cameronians was forced back but a counterattack by the reserve squadron of 5th Lancers restored the line. The Germans were forced back over the Canal.

The Germans succeeded in rushing Montagne bridge. The 7th Bedfordshire company there was driven back. A counterattack by A, C and D Companies, 6th Northamptonshire and the 7th Bedfordshire company drove the Germans back over the canal. The lost ground was recovered at about 6.50 p.m. but with heavy

Looking south from the railway bridge on the Remigny road to Montagne bridge.

casualties. Three enemy machine guns and several prisoners were captured. **Second Lieutenant Alfred Herring** of 6th Northamptonshire was in action for the first time. As the only officer left in the area he went forward to establish a bridgehead with a Lewis gun post on the far bank in front of Montagne bridge.

By 7.30 p.m. the situation on 54th Brigade's front was restored completely. The Brigade reserve was reformed on the railway one kilometre southwest of Montagne bridge. About 8 p.m. it became apparent that orders issued by HQ 3rd Cavalry Brigade for 16th Lancers to hold part of the Mennessis sector had not been received. Consequently there was a gap in the line on the right flank of 54th Brigade. As soon as HQ 3rd Cavalry Brigade was made aware, it found fifty-seven reinforcements from 20th Hussars and the Royal Scots Greys, together with four cavalry machine guns, to fill the gap. During the night 54th Brigade's line was subjected to constant sniper and machine gun fire, including Herring's post at Montagne bridge.

About 9 a.m. on 23rd March it became clear that the Germans had crossed the canal at Jussy and were threatening the left flank of 11th Royal Fusiliers. At 9.15 a.m. Sadleir-Jackson ordered a counterattack by thirty men of the Royal Scots Greys, a platoon of 11th Royal Fusiliers and sixty men from III Corps Reinforcement Training Battalion. They drove the enemy back but casualties were heavy. Patrols found Jussy was held by the Germans and 9th Cameronians had been forced back to the level crossing about 600m south of the village. A detachment of the Northumberland Hussars manning Hotchkiss machine guns was pushed out to cover the left flank, where three guns of 18th Division Machine Gun Battalion had retired unexpectedly.

Meanwhile on the right, 7th Bedfordshire reported that the Germans had crossed the canal at the cemetery northeast of Mennessis. Before midday it became clear that the enemy was pressing forward from Jussy and Mennessis. At 11.55 a.m. 200 men from the Royal Canadian Dragoons arrived. Half were sent to prolong the left of 11th Royal Fusiliers and gain contact with 9th Cameronians, which had been forced back again. The other half was sent to the right flank of 7th Bedfordshire to gain touch with 4th Hussars. If it could not, it was to form a defensive flank.

The situation continued to deteriorate. The mist lifted and enemy aircraft were very active. Hostile enfilade machine gun fire was being received from the left. Most of the Brigade was still on the canal line but III Corps Reinforcement Training Battalion had disappeared behind. By 12.15 p.m. it was clear that the enemy was infiltrating around both flanks and had been reported in Bois de Frières. The canal line could not be held any longer. Commander 54th Brigade ordered a retirement to the Tombelle Ridge initially, with each flank being covered by two squadrons of Royal Canadian Dragoons. Although the Canadian cavalry arrived late, it did good work in the retirement. Casualties in 54th Brigade were heavy due to the fog lifting, which allowed clear lines of sight for the German machine gunners. After a very trying day 54th Brigade concentrated at Caillouël. By then 11th Royal Fusiliers was only twenty-seven strong. 6th Northamptonshire and 7th Bedfordshire each had about 200 men. The rest at Caillouël was short-lived as the Brigade took up defensive positions on the high ground north of the town next morning.

At Montage bridge Herring had received orders at 10 a.m. to withdraw to the railway embankment. Having put the captured German machine guns out of action, he pulled his men back. Reaching the embankment, he was informed that the order had been countermanded. By the time he returned, the Germans had set up machine guns on the far bank. Of the fifty men with him, only he and two others reached their former positions. They were too weak to prevent the Germans swarming over Montagne bridge and the canal in boats. Herring's tiny party was surrounded but fought until their ammunition ran out and they were forced to surrender. Soon afterwards Herring was congratulated by the Kaiser in St Quentin on his magnificent fight.

Except for the gap between Tergnier and Liez, the Corps front was maintained throughout 22nd March despite heavy fighting and a number of counterattacks. From midday French reinforcements began to arrive in 58th Division's area on the far right.

In XVIII Corps' area the Germans launched a heavy attack with the main blow falling on the left near the Omignon valley. The withdrawal of III Corps to the Crozat Canal the previous evening forced 36th Division, on the right of XVIII Corps, to swing back in conformity, effectively forming itself into a sharp salient.

61st Brigade (20th Division) was put at 36th Division's disposal and withdrew across the canal to gain touch with III Corps on the right. It was to hold the line of the canal from Avesne to Tugny via Saint-Simon until other brigades had completed their retirement. 108th Brigade to the north held the canal from halfway between Tugny and Artemps to the cemetery in Happencourt. From there north to Le

Montagne bridge from the north bank of the St Quentin (Crozat) Canal.

Hamel was held by 107th Brigade. The line was extended by 9th Royal Inniskilling Fusiliers to the original Battle Zone defences, which were still held by 1st Royal Inniskilling Fusiliers. The withdrawal to these positions commenced at 10.30 p.m. on the 21st.

When the German offensive opened the engineers of 36th Division received the order *Man Battle Stations*. This was the signal to prepare the bridges over the St Quentin Canal for demolition. The bridges were divided into groups, with sections of engineers allocated to each. 121st Field Company was located in Grand Seraucourt and Le Hamel. A section under Second Lieutenant Isaac TV Norman (killed on 28th March 1918 and buried in Namps-au-Val British Cemetery – I A 17) prepared the group of six bridges there. 150th Field Company, split between Le Hamel and Marsh Farm, 600m southeast of Saint-Simon, had the majority of the demolition tasks. Half a section under Lieutenant William MW Brunyate (MID for this action and MC for an action on 19th October 1918) was allocated the Artemps group of four bridges. The group of thirteen bridges (one 'railway', ten road and two foot) around Tugny was allocated to one and a half sections under **Lieutenant Cecil Knox**. Lieutenant John B Stapylton-Smith (MC for this action) and another section had the group of twelve bridges around Saint-Simon and Avesne. 122nd Field Company was deployed further forward.

The bridges had already been assessed and had been divided into four types of construction:

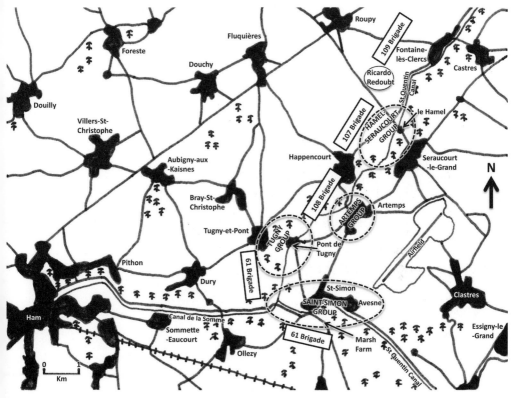

36th Division's sector, with 61st Brigade (20th Division) attached, along the St Quentin Canal, showing the various groups of bridges to be destroyed by the sappers.

> Steel lattice and plate girder.
> Wooden trestle and pile.
> Pontoon.
> Pile foot bridges.

The first three types were to be destroyed by guncotton charges and the latter by ammonal tubes. Charges specific to each demolition were assembled in special boxes stored near the site and given unique numbers and/or letters. Pre-fabricated boxes for the explosives to slip into were fitted precisely where each charge was to be laid and marked with the number/letter of the charge. Electrical exploders were to be used, backed up by time and safety fuses.

The pontoon wagons of all three field companies and bridging equipment allocated by the Chief Engineer of XVIII Corps were parked at Ollezy, in case they were needed urgently to build more crossings for the withdrawal. The majority of the field companies were withdrawn during the night to Pithon, about four kilometres behind the Canal. Despite the existing bridges being readied for destruction, some construction continued to allow the troops to fall back. A footbridge near Saint-Simon was completed by two sections of 122nd Field Company at 9 p.m. on the

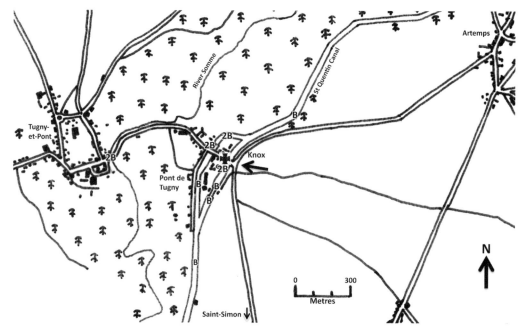

Pont de Tugny. There are plenty of places to park, particularly on the east side of the bridge. B = one of the twelve bridges in the Tugny group in March 1918.

21st. Lieutenant Benson was sent by the CRE to the bridge groups to ensure that they were not blown prematurely.

Pontoon and foot bridges were destroyed at Fontaine le Clercs just after noon. These bridges had been damaged by enemy shelling previously. The main demolitions commenced at 10.15 p.m. on 21st March. 121st Field Company destroyed the Hamel-Seraucourt group by 4 a.m. on the 22nd. The Artemps group followed at 6 a.m., the Tugny group at 9.30 a.m. and the Saint-Simon group shortly after 10 a.m. The demolition parties then rejoined their units at Pithon. 121st Field Company was ordered to take over the bridges along the Canal de la Somme from Ham to Ollezy.

Although all the bridges over the St Quentin Canal were destroyed successfully, it was often a near run thing in the presence of the enemy. The first indication that Knox had that the bridges were to be blown was when wreckage from the Artemps bridges drifted downstream. He immediately commenced his task and a number of the Tugny group of bridges had to be destroyed under machine gun fire. At Tugny itself the Germans were advancing on the main girder bridge when the fuse junction failed. Knox rushed forward under heavy fire just as the enemy reached the bridge. He tore away the time fuse and clambered under the framework to light the instantaneous fuse. The bridge was destroyed and miraculously Knox was unhurt. He also managed to destroy the other twelve bridges entrusted to him.

Attacks against the north face of 36th Division's salient failed to dislodge the Ulstermen until a retirement was forced to Ricardo Redoubt. Having forced 36th Division back at Fontaine, the enemy then threatened the Division's flank along the

The bridge destroyed by Cecil Knox from the east (German) bank of the canal.

Somme. 107th and 109th Brigades gradually withdrew to the Green Line between Happencourt and Fluquières, assisted by the resistance of Ricardo Redoubt. The Green Line was already held by 60th Brigade (20th Division). Further south between Saint-Simon and Happencourt, 108th and 61st Brigades remained in position.

Tugny bridge from the 'home' bank.

The post-WW1 Tugny bridge, which was replaced by the current structure recently.

30th Division lost Roupy and Savy and at 2 p.m. the front line of the Battle Zone fell. Despite six counterattacks, the garrison fell back on Stevens Redoubt north of Étreillers. By 5 p.m. the Division was on and behind the Green Line. To conform 61st Division conducted a costly withdrawal and by 5 p.m. one of its brigades was on the Green Line but there were no trenches there. By early evening the whole of XVIII Corps, less 108th Brigade on the extreme right, had pulled back from the front of the Battle Zone to the Green Line. The corps commander realised he could not hold there for long as the line was not prepared for defence. Accordingly he issued orders to withdraw behind the Somme that night. 20th Division acted as rearguard while two entrenching battalions commenced digging the new line. 36th and 30th Divisions pulled back with little interference and most of the bridges over the Somme were blown by 10 a.m. on the 23rd. 61st Division was pressed all the way and its last units did not cross the Somme until 6 a.m. on the 23rd. At the end of the withdrawal and reorganisation, 36th Division (with 61st Brigade attached) held the Somme from the III Corps boundary to Ham, 30th Division held from Ham to Canizy and 20th Division from there to Béthencourt. 61st Division was in reserve.

XIX Corps' front was held by 66th and 24th Divisions in a series of re-entrants and salients across the Battle Zone. 1st and part of 2nd Dismounted Brigades were intermingled with the infantry. 9th Dismounted Brigade was in reserve behind 66th Division at Hervilly and Roisel. The remainder of 2nd Dismounted Brigade was at Le Mesnil. 50th Division had two brigades on the Green Line and the third was in the Cologne valley. 5th Tank Battalion was at Nobescourt Farm and the heavy artillery had been reinforced during the night. The Corps was in good shape and a fighting withdrawal was ordered to the Green Line, when the defenders were in

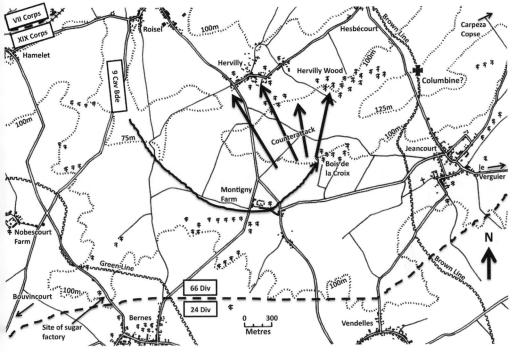

Drive south through Hesbécourt on the D6E. At the t-junction at the southern end of the village turn left then right and follow this lane to the top of the hill, where there is space to pull over on the right side. The Brown Line ran parallel with this lane about 100m on the eastern side. This seems to be the most likely location for Columbine's VC action but is not the only contender.

danger of being overrun. 24th Division was attacked from 4 a.m. and held its own until pressure on both flanks led to a retirement to the Green Line, commencing at 12 p.m. Rear parties held on until 2 p.m. while three bridges over the Omignon were blown to avoid being surprised from the right flank due to the withdrawal of 61st Division.

On 21st March 9th Cavalry Brigade had assembled at the divisional rendezvous south of Aix Farm, southwest of Bernes. Shortly afterwards it was ordered to hold the Brown Line near Hervilly Wood, with a view to advancing later. C Squadron, 8th Hussars garrisoned Upstart Redoubt, east of Hervilly, but was withdrawn after dark. 15th Hussars and four guns of the Brigade Machine Gun Squadron reported to HQ 197th Brigade at Roisel, while the remainder of 9th Cavalry Brigade was in reserve in the valley west of Hervilly.

During the night shelling forced Brigade HQ to move from Hervilly to Montigny Farm. The horses were sent back to Bernes. At 1 a.m. on the 22nd the dismounted brigade, including 9th Squadron MGC, moved up to Montigny Farm. From there the Squadron's horses were also sent back to Bernes, less the pack animals carrying the machine guns. At 2.10 a.m. orders came through for the Brigade to advance towards Jeancourt. It was also to be prepared to support the Brown Line and Carpeza Copse. If Upstart Redoubt had been lost it was to be retaken. At 3 a.m.,

From the top of the hill southeast of Hesbécourt overlooking the Brown Line in the most likely location for Columbine's VC action.

8th and 19th Hussars, all under Lieutenant Colonel Guy Macaulay Mort (DSO for this action), moved to Bois de la Croix (Cross Wood), west of Jeancourt, with eight guns of the Machine Gun Squadron. Six supporting tanks arrived there at 8 a.m. Shortly afterwards two of the machine guns were detached with an escort of twenty men of C Squadron, 8th Hussars to hold the eastern exit of Jeancourt towards Le Verguier. At 9 a.m. heavy shelling of Cross Wood forced the cavalry to fall back just to the west of it.

At 8.30 a.m. it was reported that the Germans had seized Hervilly and were advancing southwards towards Montigny Farm. Mort was ordered to confirm the report and, if the enemy was found there, to counterattack at once. Patrols quickly established that the Germans were in possession of Hervilly. Mort formed up his troops astride the Hervilly road and they moved off in cooperation with three of the tanks, supported by the Machine Gun Squadron. 15th and 19th Hussars headed for the village, while 8th Hussars went for the high ground to the south of it. The counterattack was successful, the village was entered without opposition and Hervilly Wood was occupied. A potentially critical situation had been averted.

From the Hesbécourt – Hervilly road north of Hervillly Wood showing the route of the counterattack on the village.

One of the Machine Gun Squadron guns was in a post forward of the main line unprotected by wire. The enemy approached suddenly and having gained advantageous positions on either side inflicted heavy casualties on the defenders, including the exposed machine gun team. **Private Herbert Columbine** raced forward through the enemy fire, followed by a few comrades, and took command of the gun. Despite every enemy machine gun in range firing at them, and almost totally unprotected by sandbags and wire, they managed to keep the gun in action from 9 a.m. until 1 p.m. Attack after attack was driven back. The Germans all but surrounded the post but a small gap was held open to allow ammunition to be brought up. Columbine remained throughout, except when dodging bullets to get more ammunition. The post was then attacked by a low-flying aircraft, allowing the enemy to get into the trench on either side of Columbine's position. Seeing that it was no longer tenable, Columbine sent his two assistants back, *Save yourselves; I'll carry on*. Reluctantly they realised that it was pointless sacrificing three lives and dashed back to the main position.

For the last hour Columbine fought alone and drove off eight separate attacks, despite being bombed by German infantry from both flanks. He inflicted heavy casualties and eventually the enemy backed off and brought in several aircraft. Most were engaged by British machines but one peeled off to attack Columbine's position. One account says that Columbine was last seen elevating his gun to engage

the aircraft until he was blown up by a falling bomb. Other accounts say the aircraft diverted his attention, allowing the enemy to get closer to him on either flank and blow him up with a grenade. Whatever the truth, his sacrifice gave his comrades four precious hours in which to prepare for the German attack on the main position.

The situation to the north remained obscure and the infantry was seen falling back on the high ground towards Roisel. Large numbers of Germans then advanced against Hervilly and the Wood. Sergeant B Neville returned to report that the posts under Lieutenant MR Russell of 8th Hussars had been driven out of the Brown Line and only two survivors returned. At 12.15 p.m. orders were received for the Brigade to pull back to the Green Line from the sugar factory near Bernes to Nobescourt Farm. On being relieved on the Green Line by 66th Division about 5 p.m., 9th Cavalry Brigade rejoined its horses at Bouvincourt and, once mounted again, moved back to Ennemain.

It is unclear precisely where Columbine's VC action took place. The Squadron war diary states that one machine gun was lost after the whole team had been killed or wounded, except for two men who put it out of action. This does not tally completely with Columbine's story but it is perhaps significant that only two men returned. No location is given for this incident. Another machine gun was destroyed by shellfire but the evidence suggests that Columbine's gun was knocked out by grenades, or possibly an aircraft bomb. Both these guns were lost during or after the counterattack on Hervilly and it is known that Columbine was in action against German attacks from 9 a.m., i.e. an hour before Hervilly fell to the British attack. Taking everything into account, it seems most likely that the action took place in the Brown Line. It is possible that he was part of Lieutenant Russell's party as only two men returned from it and this tallies exactly with the accounts of Columbine's VC action. However, it also cannot be ruled out that Columbine was with the small party sent to the east of Jeancourt.

VII Corps' right was attacked and pushed back at 7 a.m. 16th Division held off five attacks until the enemy infiltrated into the rear area and forced it to retire at 11.10 a.m. In 21st Division the enemy attacked the front of the Battle Zone and broke into the southern end of Épehy at 8 a.m. The Division started to retire at 12.15 p.m. and the village fell at 1 p.m. after a fierce struggle. 9th Division was only attacked heavily on the right flank. The enemy took Chapel Hill but was prevented from going further. By 2 p.m. 16th Division was pulling back to the Green Line, 21st Division was on the rear boundary of the Battle Zone and 9th Division continued the line before it swung back to the front of the Battle Zone. At 8.50 p.m. the whole of VII Corps was ordered to withdraw to the Green Line, by which time many elements had already been forced back there.

In summary, by nightfall in Fifth Army, III and XVIII Corps were on the Crozat Canal and the Somme, XIX Corps was not in contact with its neighbours and was still east of the Somme. Only VII Corps was still holding its section of the Green Line.

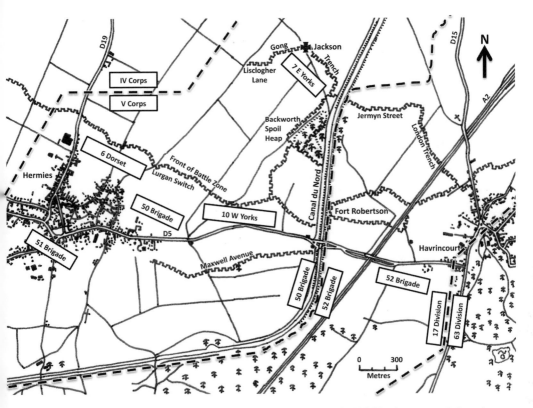

Drive through Hermies, where there is a shop and cafés, easterly on the D5 Havrincourt road. Pass the church on the left and after 350m at a crossroads turn left into Rue Neuve. Stay on this road as it winds through housing and eventually becomes a track. Follow it for 2,200m until it peters out. Look right along the rough track. Gong Trench, the front line, was just beyond the clump of bushes. The same point can be reached by continuing along the Havrincourt road until just before the bridge over the impressive Canal du Nord cutting. Turn left here and follow the track parallel with the cutting for one kilometre, where there is a track branching off to the left. It can be driven but it is rough in places and it is recommended to park and walk the 550m to the site of Harold Jackson's VC action instead.

To the north Third Army's situation was not as critical as Fifth Army's due to having double the number of troops per mile of front. Only two of the four Corps had been attacked and only three divisions had been driven back to the rear of the Battle Zone. Despite V Corps withdrawing 1,800m in the Flesquières Salient, it was still in an extremely exposed situation on the morning of the 22nd.

V Corps had 47th, 63rd and 17th Divisions in line, with 2nd Division behind. Despite enemy pressure to pinch out the Flesquières Salient, Third Army did not want to give up the Cambrai gains easily. About 11 a.m. 47th and 63rd Divisions were attacked. When 9th Division (VII Corps) retired on the right, 2nd Division extended the right flank near Equancourt. The whole salient was in danger from this direction as the retirement of Fifth Army had increased the southern flank by 7,300m. Another attack on 47th Division at 7 p.m. was repulsed.

During the night 17th Division pulled back to conform to the movements of flanking formations. The line to be held was astride the Canal du Nord and consisted of the outer defences of Hermies and Havrincourt, with Fort Robertson on the eastern canal bank. On the right of the Canal was 52nd Brigade. On the left was 50th Brigade, with 10th West Yorkshire on the right and 6th Dorset on the left in Lurgan Avenue (Lurgan Switch on trench maps), the front of the Battle Zone. An exposed outpost line ran along London Trench and Jermyn Street in 52nd Brigade's area, then crossed the Canal into 50th Brigade's area along Gong Trench and Lisclogher Lane to the sunken road running southwest to Hermies, which was held by 51st Brigade. The outpost line in 50th Brigade was held by 7th East Yorkshire around Backworth Spoil Heap on the west bank of the canal.

The movement of troops was completed about 5 a.m. and soon after 7 a.m. the Germans began probing forward into the abandoned British positions. At 8 a.m. an intense bombardment on Hermies commenced and lasted for about three hours. While the enemy preparatory bombardment was falling on the front line, **Sergeant Harold Jackson** in C Company, 7th East Yorkshire, volunteered to go out on a daylight patrol. He crept out of the comparative safety of the trench, identified the enemy and returned with valuable information about their concentrations. The first attack east of the Canal at 9.30 a.m. amounted to little more than a strong patrol. The fog had dispersed by 10 a.m. and a strong attack developed around 10.15 a.m. It was pressed with great tenacity, supported by flamethrowers, and was only repulsed after some of the enemy had penetrated the outpost line.

Attacks then developed west of the Canal, in particular against Gong Trench near the canal bank. D Company, 7th East Yorkshire performed particularly well in holding off the enemy and inflicting severe losses. When the enemy penetrated Gong Trench, Jackson held an important bombing stop. In a single-handed counterattack he vigorously bombed them back into the open. Later he stalked a German machine gun and put the whole crew out of action with grenades. Heavy artillery and machine gun fire brought the enemy to a standstill.

Other attacks were made with the intention of isolating V Corps in the Flesquières Salient and 17th Division was under pressure all afternoon between Havrincourt

The section of Gong Trench where Harold Jackson's VC action took place.

and Hermies. 5th Brigade (2nd Division) was allocated to secure the left flank as the enemy's main effort was directed against the left of the salient in 51st Division's area (IV Corps). When 51st Division was forced back, it exposed 17th Division's left flank about Hermies, which was attacked from 11 a.m. 17th Division could no longer hold its position, despite a magnificent defence.

At 1.15 p.m. Third Army ordered V Corps to withdraw to the front line of the Battle Zone during the night. However, VII Corps on the right had withdrawn to the Green Line and IV Corps on the left had been forced out of the Battle Zone, which meant that V Corps would still be in a salient. Accordingly, at 7 p.m. V Corps was ordered to retire to the Metz Switch and Metz–Équancourt Switch, while the left kept in touch with the defenders of Hermies.

In accordance with orders received at 2 p.m., 7th East Yorkshire fell back to Maxwell Avenue between the Canal du Nord and Hermies. This position was held throughout the night. Jackson continued to fight with great gallantry for the next seven days. On 31st March, northeast of Albert, close to Bouzincourt Ridge CWGC Cemetery, he took command of his company, after all the officers had become casualties, and led it in an attack to regain some posts lost a few days previously. The attack failed and later, when ordered, he withdrew under heavy fire into a new defensive position. Having achieved that, he went back into the open repeatedly to bring in badly wounded men under murderous fire.

IV Corps faced eight enemy divisions with eight weak brigades, backed by four others. Attacks began at 7 a.m. and made little progress for some hours but, when ammunition ran short in the afternoon, gaps appeared. A break of almost ten kilometres opened between Beaumetz and Mory, threatening Bapaume. The extreme right was under pressure due to the attack on Hermies in V Corps' area and reinforcements had to fill the gap. Elsewhere the enemy got to within 800m of Vaulx and the line west of Vaulx Wood was driven in. The left flank was also forced back and at 6.30 p.m. the enemy gained Vaulx-Vraucourt. Further east the troops held out until 2 p.m., when they were forced back to the Morchies-Vaulx line, where the enemy was checked with severely heavy casualties. The Germans

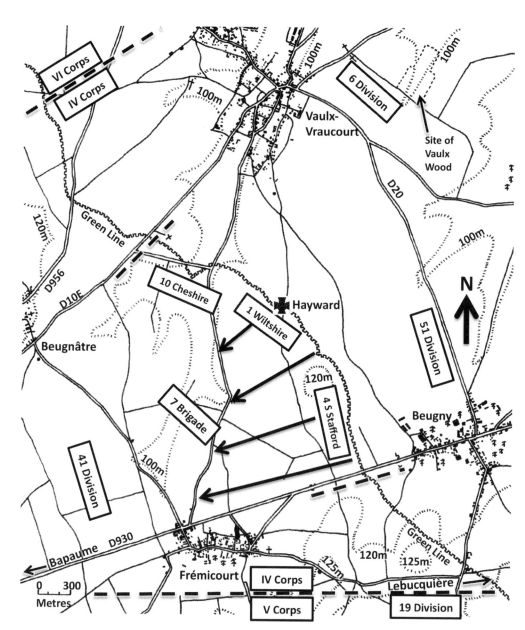

In Vaulx-Vraucourt follow the track that leads to the water tower south of the village. Continue south and at the track junction take the right fork and follow it for almost 900m. This is where the centre of 1st Wiltshire's line crossed the track. Not all formations are shown as there were numerous moves over the days that 1st Wiltshire was in position northeast of Frémicourt. 7th Brigade's front is shown in detail and the first part of the withdrawal on 24th March.

were also halted between Morchies and Vaulx-Vraucourt by 2nd Tank Battalion. No further advance was made on that flank. Touch with V Corps on the right was lost late in the afternoon and by the end of the day the enemy had made gains of up to two and a half kilometres. Although IV Corps had suffered badly, no reserves had been expended except for the tanks.

1st Wiltshire started 21st March in Corps reserve with the rest of 7th Brigade (25th Division) at Achiet le Grand. At 4.40 a.m. the village was hit by long-range heavy shells and at 5 a.m. the Brigade was put on immediate notice to move. However, it was not until 11.30 a.m. that it starting moving to the Bihucourt area to occupy camps vacated by 75th Brigade (25th Division). En route the order was changed to proceed to Frémicourt to take over accommodation vacated by 74th Brigade (also 25th Division). 7th Brigade was ordered not to pass through Bapaume on the way. Frémicourt was reached at 8 p.m. and an hour later the Brigade deployed to the northeast, where it took up positions in the Army (Green) Line) under command of 51st Division. Its right boundary was the Frémicourt–Beugny road and the left was on the Beugnâtre–Vaulx-Vraucourt road (exclusive). On the right was 4th South Staffordshire, with 1st Wiltshire in the centre and 10th Cheshire on the left. Twelve guns of 25th Machine Gun Battalion were in support as were four trench mortars. Another four trench mortars were kept in reserve. The line was found to be wired in front but only partially dug. The Brigade set about working on the defences, with the priority being to establish platoon posts with supporting posts behind them, rather than a continuous line. This resulted in two companies per battalion being forward and two in support. Two 25th Division engineer field companies and two companies of 6th South Wales Borderers (Pioneers) were working on the left up to the left IV Corps boundary. Meanwhile 75th Brigade came under orders of 6th Division and 74th Brigade came under 51st Division.

By 7.30 a.m. on 22nd March the shelling was continuous and the first enemy attacks started. Vaulx Wood fell and the Corps Line (rear of Battle Zone) to the front was broken, resulting in 75th Brigade's portion of the Army Line becoming the front line. **Captain Reginald Hayward** in 1st Wiltshire was buried, wounded in the head and deafened by shellfire during the day but insisted on staying with his company. In complete contrast, HQ 7th Brigade's war diary describes the day in the Army Line as quiet. 41st Division took over command of the rear zone in the morning and 7th Brigade came under its command. The Brigade was due to be relieved that night by 123rd Brigade (41st Division) but due to the deteriorating tactical situation this did not occur.

Early on 23rd March 7th Brigade's front was subjected to a heavy barrage and three attacks took place, two in the morning and another in the afternoon. All were repulsed. The first attack fell mainly on the left of 1st Wiltshire and the whole frontage of 10th Cheshire. The second attack was against the frontage of both battalions, but again made no progress, despite inflicting heavy casualties on the defenders. During the day the Germans did make progress on the right, where 124th Brigade (41st Division) was pushed out of Lebucquière and the factory east of Beugny. 123rd Brigade north of Beugny was forced to pull back to conform with the movements of the left of 19th Division on the right flank. It was to take over 7th Brigade's front in contact with 124th Brigade on its left, while 4th South Staffordshire's line on the right of 7th Brigade was to be taken over by 58th Brigade

The main part of Reginald Hayward's VC action took place in almost featureless terrain between Frémicourt and Vaulx-Vraucourt.

on the left of 19th Division. This changed later, with 58th Brigade taking over the right of 4th South Staffordshire's front and 123rd Brigade taking over the rest to the boundary with 1st Wiltshire. 4th South Staffordshire then went into Brigade reserve about 900m behind 1st Wiltshire and 10th Cheshire.

On the night of 23rd/24th and during the day on the 24th the Germans took advantage of dead ground to mass as close as possible to the British wire. Numerous artillery targets were presented but for an unknown reason the British guns did not take full advantage of these opportunities. Although the Germans attacked strongly to the north and south of 7th Brigade, no attack took place on the Brigade's front. There was heavy hostile shelling instead. Hayward's arm was shattered but he remained in command, encouraging his men.

At 3 p.m. on 24th March 7th Brigade was ordered to pull back, in conjunction with the brigades to north and south, as part of a general withdrawal by V and IV Corps. The first move by 7th Brigade was made with 123rd Brigade on the right and consisted of the line wheeling back to the right to reach the Frémicourt–Vaulx-Vraucourt road, which was held already by 4th South Staffordshire. The withdrawal was conducted under heavy machine gun fire, with the Germans following close behind. Having withdrawn, 7th Brigade was ordered to the Achiet-le-Petit area and reverted to the command of 25th Division.

At 6.30 a.m. on 25th March 7th Brigade was ordered to hold a new line southeast of Logeast Wood and west of Achiet-le-Grand, with 74th Brigade on the right and 75th Brigade on the left. This line was to be held at all costs if troops further forward were forced back through it. An extra one hundred rounds of ammunition was carried by every man. However, later in the morning orders arrived for all three brigades to withdraw to a position of readiness near Bucquoy. Two hours later 25th Division was ordered to the area north of Gommecourt, where it arrived at 4 a.m. on 26th March.

Throughout this period Hayward continued to set up defensive positions and encourage his men until he was wounded for a third time, on this occasion in the

head. He collapsed from exhaustion and was evacuated with other casualties on the night of 25th March. For three days he had moved around his positions in the open, concentrating on reorganising the defences and encouraging his men, rather than on his own safety. It was entirely due to his efforts that the enemy failed to take the trench system in his area.

As a result of the previous day's fighting VI Corps had swung back its left flank. 40th Division was on the Green Line and had lost Mory. 34th Division was in the rear of the Battle Zone and 3rd Division was still in the Forward Zone. The Corps was generally in good condition and during the day the Guards Division was allocated from XVII Corps. 31st Division was also moving up.

40th Division was in GHQ Reserve behind VI Corps when the offensive commenced. At noon on 21st March 121st Brigade was ordered to move immediately to Hamelincourt. Interestingly, 13th Yorkshire at Hendecourt-les-Ransart received the order to move at 9 a.m., whereas the Brigade HQ does not appear to have received it for another three hours. As the battalions began to arrive at Hamelincourt at 3.30 p.m. they were sent to occupy the rear trench of the third system (rear of Battle Zone) between the Mory–Écoust road and St Léger, with 12th Suffolk on the right, 13th Yorkshire on the left and 20th Middlesex in support in an assembly area southwest of St Léger.

13th Yorkshire was up to strength, having been reinforced recently. It was to extend northwards to the southeast corner of St Léger. Once the rear trench had been occupied every effort was to be made to occupy the front trench. On the right of 121st Brigade was 120th Brigade and 34th Division was on the left. Earlier 177th Brigade had counterattacked and partially restored the line but the precise situation in the third system was obscure. While 121st Brigade held the third system, the remnants of 176th and 178th Brigades were to hold the Green (Army) Line in support some distance to the west, while 177th Brigade held the rear of the third system behind 120th Brigade.

In 121st Brigade, 12th Suffolk established itself in the third system as far north as Banks Wood without difficulty. However, the Germans were holding the line to

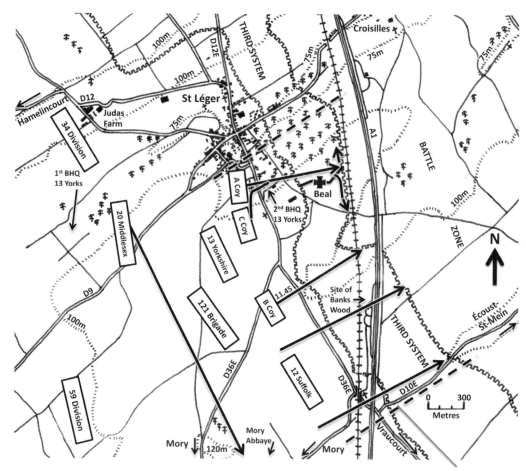

Drive through St Léger southwards on the D36E2. As you emerge from the trees about 100m before Mory Street Military Cemetery turn sharp left into the sunken lane. This is where 13th Yorkshire's Battalion HQ was established on the evening of 22nd March. Follow the lane round to the right and go up the hill to the barn on the right. Park there and look over the fields to the northeast, where Ernest Beal was in action.

the north and the Battalion had to establish a defensive flank as no contact was made with 13th Yorkshire.

Preceded by patrols to the front and on the flanks, 13th Yorkshire had advanced from the northeast of Hamelincourt towards St Leger. On arrival Battalion HQ was established 800m south of Judas Farm. At about 5 p.m. A Company on the left reported that St Léger was still occupied by enemy patrols, which were driven back into the village. Elements of 34th Division were holding the cemetery in the village while trying to recover two heavy howitzers. A Company was ordered to hold the east of the village and cover the withdrawal of the guns, which was accomplished successfully. Meanwhile C Company on the right reported that the front line was held by enemy machine gun posts. Brigade HQ ordered the Battalion to clear up the situation, replace the 34th Division units and to gain contact with 12th Suffolk. In the evening Battalion HQ moved to the sunken road just south of St Léger and

From Mory Street Military Cemetery looking northeast.

efforts were made to close the gap between the Battalion and 12th Suffolk. At 1 a.m. on 22nd March 20th Middlesex moved to another assembly area north of Mory Abbaye.

Elsewhere the situation was not as bleak and, despite desperate fighting, the rear system in the Battle Zone was still held at nightfall. At 6 p.m. 34th Division still held the left half of the Forward Zone but on the right the front swept back to meet 59th Division at the rear of the Battle Zone. Behind this flank the pioneer battalion and some engineers held the unfinished trench of the Green Line. Only raids were launched against 3rd Division on the left on the morning of the 22nd. However, about 3 p.m. the right brigade was attacked, as was the left flank of 34th Division. The front line was lost but the support trench held.

During the night of 21st/22nd March 40th Division redirected 119th Brigade from Hénin Hill in support of 34th Division, to hold a support line running south from west of Hill Copse covering Ervillers in support of 120th and 121st Brigades. During the night 13th Yorkshire was unable to clear the enemy south of St Léger and make contact with 12th Suffolk. Early on the morning of 22nd March two companies of 13th Yorkshire advanced again. A Company was to take the enemy line on the left and C Company on the right. A Company led along a communication trench until a machine gun was encountered. The companies halted while **Second Lieutenant Ernest Beal** and a Lewis gun team went forward. Beal's party totaled no more than twelve men. He was aware of the dangers of a gap opening between his company and the unit on the left. He advanced along the trench until challenged by a German machine gunner. Beal then sprang forward, shot the whole gun team with his revolver and captured the gun. He continued the advance and repeated this three more times, bringing back four machine guns and one prisoner.

A Company occupied the enemy front line from the southeast corner of St Léger Wood for 230m to the south. C Company attempted to work along the same trench

From the barn looking northeast. Ernest Beal advanced along this communication trench to overcome four machine gun teams.

to the right but was halted by machine guns. At 7 a.m. two platoons of D Company took the trench, killing twenty enemy and capturing seven machine guns in the process. A few minutes later the Germans counterattacked and all the gains were lost, except at the junction with 34th Division, where they were repulsed. A properly organised counterattack by 13th Yorkshire, with artillery support, was launched at 11.45 a.m. B Company attacked from the southwest along a re-entrant. While the short preparatory bombardment was being fired, B Company covered 650m of open ground and was only fifty metres from the trench when it lifted. The Company successfully ejected the Germans and linked up with 12th Suffolk at Banks Wood, taking eight machine guns in the process.

Almost immediately the enemy counterattacked and regained some of the losses. Both battalions were forced to form defensive flanks but maintained contact in the rear trench of the third system. About the same time 20th Middlesex moved to support 120th Brigade on the right and at 2.30 p.m. 120th and 121st Brigade HQs pulled back to Béhagnies. At 3 p.m. 13th Yorkshire reported that the enemy was massing to the front again and enemy aircraft were very active.

That evening Beal was informed that one of his men, who had been wounded in the attack, was lying in the open close to an enemy machine gun. He went forward alone under heavy fire and brought the man in on his back. As he neared his own lines a shell exploded nearby and fragments cut into him. He managed to get the man to safety before losing consciousness and died later from the effect of his wounds. At 6 p.m. the Germans bombarded 121st Brigade's line heavily. The situation in the formations to right and left was also deteriorating and a withdrawal became inevitable. B Company just managed to get away before being surrounded. By the time 121st Brigade came out of action on 27th March it had suffered 828 casualties, including 268 in 13th Yorkshire.

There was very little activity in XVII Corps' area. Despite withdrawals further south, there was no desire to give up ground since Monchy-le-Preux offered

Communication trench

Front trench of third system

excellent observation over the whole of the German territory. However, at 8.30 p.m. HQ Third Army decided that 3rd Division (VI Corps) had to pull back to conform with movements further south. XVII Corps had to comply and at 9.30 p.m. orders were sent out to withdraw and abandon Monchy.

At 11.30 p.m. GHQ ordered Third and Fifth Armies to remain in touch in view of the strong enemy thrust at the junction point, which threatened the Flesquières Salient. Shortly afterwards Third Army ordered V Corps to make the third withdrawal of the day to the Green Line (Metz and Équancourt Switches), while IV Corps complied on the left. All Corps were ordered to start work on the Red Line, the rear line of the uncompleted Rear Zone.

23rd March 1918

330 Capt Christopher Bushell, 7th Queen's (Royal West Surrey) (55th Brigade, 18th Division), West of St Quentin Canal, France

331 Lt Col Frank Roberts, 1st Worcestershire (24th Brigade, 8th Division), Pargny, France

332 Capt Julian Gribble, 10th Royal Warwickshire (57th Brigade, 19th Division), Beaumetz, France

By dawn on 23rd March Fifth Army was holding a front of sixty-five kilometres. General Gough intended that the Green Line, running north as a continuation of the Crozat Canal from its junction with the Somme, would form the new Fifth Army front. However, XVIII Corps and part of XIX Corps had already fallen back beyond it. Only III and VII Corps, on the right and left flanks respectively, were still on the Green Line.

III Corps had a front of fourteen kilometres. On the right it had been forced back from the Crozat Canal but behind this sector the French 125th Division was beginning to arrive. The canal bank was still held from Liez northwards to the boundary with XVIII Corps. III Corps had only one fresh brigade (54th Brigade,

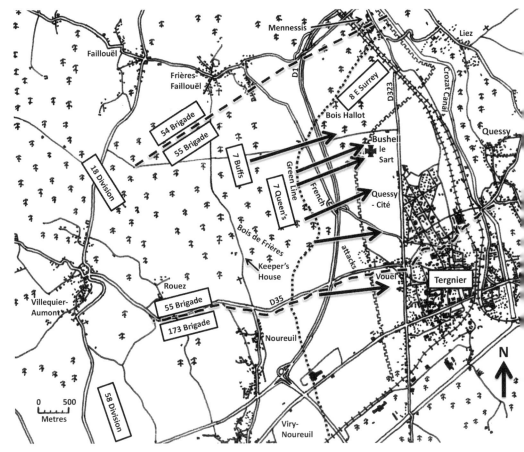

Drive southwards on the D323 from Mennessis towards Tergnier. The ground rises before reaching the outskirts of Tergnier and there is a barn on the right. Just beyond it a track leads to the woods on the right. Park here and look up the slope towards Tergnier. The high ground half right is le Sart. Bushell's VC action was in line with the storage tanks and pylon on the edge of the wood. Be aware that Tergnier is ever expanding and when you visit there may be new roads and buildings in the area. It is possible to follow the track to the edge of the wood and then turn left to the storage tanks for a better view. The track is a little rough in places but passable for cars.

From the barn on the D323 looking southwest along the axis of 7th Queen's advance to the high ground at le Sart.

18th Division) and gaps in the line were filled by dismounted cavalry, entrenching battalions, a signals school and a number of other hastily formed units. Fortunately the artillery had no shortage of ammunition.

On III Corps' right the French Sixth Army ordered its 125th Division to counterattack to regain Tergnier and re-establish the line along the Crozat Canal. At 7 a.m., after an hour's bombardment by French and British artillery, four French battalions attacked through the British lines. Two battalions were directed against Tergnier and two against the high ground at le Sart, west of Quessy. 55th Brigade (18th Division) was to protect the left of the latter two battalions. The commander of 55th Brigade committed two companies of 7th Queen's to this task. From the time that orders were given to the attack commencing, there was little time for preparations. At the same time two companies of 7th East Kent on the left were to push up to the southern end of Bois Hallot to fill a gap that existed between 7th Queen's and 8th East Surrey.

The French faced a difficult task, having not seen the ground before and having to assemble in the dark. There was also a thick mist over the area. However, they attacked with great courage. Tergnier was almost reached before the Germans recovered. On the left the attack was stopped by a hail of machine gun fire and the French commander was hit.

Lieutenant Colonel Christopher Bushell, commanding 7th Queen's, took command of the French left and his own companies and led them forward under heavy fire. Thick fog caused some to lose direction, but gallant efforts by runners brought them back onto the correct line. Bushell was severely wounded by a bullet grazing his head, but continued to rally the troops and lead them. Although little progress could be made, Bushell's example kept the assault troops on a firm line. When he was sure the line was holding, Bushell reported to the Brigade commander in Rouez. After his head had been bandaged he could not be prevented from returning to his Battalion.

Around 10 a.m., after several attempts to get forward, the French attack broke down when they ran out of ammunition (each man went into action with only

Reverse of the previous view from the storage tanks at le Sart.

thirty-five rounds). They fell back through the British lines, thus masking their fire as the Germans followed close behind. The line was only held with some difficulty.

Further north the Germans attacked the rest of 55th Brigade on the right of 18th Division. 54th Brigade was on the left and 53rd Brigade was in reserve. The situation was very confused. The relief of 4th Hussars (4th Dismounted Brigade) by 7th Queen's, and 12th Entrenching Battalion by 8th East Surrey, had not been completed. There was also thick fog. The arrival of two companies of 7th East Kent, to fill the gap between the two forward battalions, added another complication.

Covered by the fog, an intense barrage and heavy machine gun fire, the Germans crossed the canal in small parties between Liez and Mennessis. The attack on 8th East Surrey and 12th Entrenching Battalion on the left started about 9.30 a.m. Fighting was intense and the two units were gradually forced back to the southwest. They were at the western edge of Frières Wood at 1 p.m. and reached the Noureuil–Frières-Faillouël road at about 4 p.m. with a company of 8th East Sussex (Pioneers) to the left rear. Beyond the left flank was in the air. Meanwhile elements of the Canadian Cavalry Brigade filled a gap on the right between 8th East Surrey and 7th East Kent.

About 10 a.m. the Germans broke in on the left flank of 7th Queen's and the French. During the withdrawal, 7th Queens fell back in good order covered by field guns firing over open sights south of Hallot Wood and east of Frières-Faillouël. It held the western edge of the Noureuil–Frières-Faillouël road through Frières Wood. In spite of his wound, Bushell continued to encourage his men until he fainted from exhaustion for a second time and was carried away.

The situation on 55th Brigade's front was obscure when the French general commanding 125th Division on the right and the commander of 53rd Brigade

arrived at HQ 55th Brigade. The three commanders decided upon a plan of action, based on the information they had. The French were to send two battalions to take up positions on the Noureuil–Frières-Faillouël road within Frières Wood. 53rd Brigade was to send 10th Essex to counterattack towards Mon de Garde (Keeper's House) to re-establish the position in the southeast of Frières Wood.

The attack by 10th Essex did not take place as the troops became disorganised and could not be extricated from the crowd of other British and French troops. Instead the Battalion extended the line to the south, but there were plenty of troops in this area to hold it anyway.

About 11.30 a.m. the French battalions that had advanced on Tergnier earlier began to fall back through the British line. Another French battalion, sent to fill the gap between the two earlier attacks, was overwhelmed and 173rd Brigade (58th Division) on the right was forced back. By 2 p.m. all units had retired three kilometres to a new line along the Noureuil–Frières-Faillouël road through Frières Wood. This included 7th Dismounted Brigade, which had moved up to Frières Wood under command of 55th Brigade. Later all units along the Noureuil–Frières-Faillouël road withdrew another 550m to get off the exposed crest.

A stand was made on the new line, supported by 10th Essex and later by some French armoured cars. However, when the flank was turned about 5 p.m. the troops began to fall back. The 9th Cuirassiers (French 1st Dismounted Cavalry Division) attempted to counterattack the southern part of Frières Wood. However, with no artillery support and under heavy machine gun fire, it was driven back, along with the British troops in the area, to the new line being dug by the French 125th Division between Viry Noureuil and Villequier Aumont. 6th Dismounted Brigade was forced to abandon Noureuil about 5 p.m. and an hour later it was ordered to withdraw through the French. 173rd Brigade also withdrew into support.

On the left of III Corps the Germans crossed the canal in thick fog and took Jussy. By the afternoon 14th Division had been driven back to behind Flavy and was later forced back through the French 9th Division. The last elements of 18th Division pulled back from the canal and by 1.30 p.m. all units were in their new positions. 4th and 5th Dismounted Brigades also fell back, exposing the left flank of other brigades and a withdrawal was ordered at 4 p.m. By nightfall the French had taken over the whole III Corps front, except south of the Oise, which was still held by 58th Division, and where 14th Division was mixed with the French 9th Division. 18th Division fell back to reserve positions northwest of Chauny; 55th Brigade at Béthancourt, 54th Brigade at Caillouël and 53rd Brigade at Commenchon.

Reports that the Germans had crossed the Somme to the north caused XVIII Corps to reinforce its left with an ad hoc collection of cavalry, infantry reinforcements and Lewis guns from No.3 Balloon Company. The Germans forced the Somme at Ham and many British troops were overrun during the withdrawal. The Germans also crossed at Pithon, driving a wedge between 30th and 36th Divisions and threatening the flank of III Corps.

At dawn XIX Corps held a line five miles in advance of the Somme with 24th and 50th Divisions. The river was held by 66th Division and 9th, 1st and 2nd Dismounted Brigades. 8th Division was arriving from GHQ Reserve to fill the gap between the Corps' right and the left of XVIII Corps at Béthencourt. News that XVIII Corps was retiring behind the Somme meant that 24th and 50th Divisions had to withdraw from their exposed positions. This was completed by 3 p.m.

Pending the arrival of 8th Division, 9th Dismounted Brigade was responsible for the crossing at Pargny and 2nd Dismounted Brigade for that at Béthencourt. The last units of 24th Division arrived at Pargny just as the enemy worked round the open right flank. This was in spite of 9th Dismounted Brigade and 1st Worcestershire (24th Brigade, 8th Division) advancing over the river to cover the withdrawal (see below). Many troops were trapped when the bridges were destroyed. The remnants of 24th Division went into reserve.

50th Division vacated the Green Line in the night and got away without interference in the mist. The withdrawal continued with the enemy hard on the Division's heals. At Brie a newly arrived battalion of 8th Division helped to hold a bridge to allow transport to get away. By 3 p.m. 50th Division was over the Somme and the bridges were destroyed. Despite its units being fragmented, the Division went back into the line until relieved by 8th Division.

8th Division had been in GHQ Reserve when the offensive commenced. 24th Brigade entrained at St Omer, the first train departing at 6 a.m. on 22nd March and arriving at Nesle about 6 p.m. The Brigade expected to march to Athies, where it was to be billeted in reserve, but on arrival it was instructed by HQ XIX Corps to take up positions on the Somme. 24th Brigade was allocated the sector from Pargny to St Christ. On the left 23rd Brigade, in the St Christ–Éterpigny sector, relieved

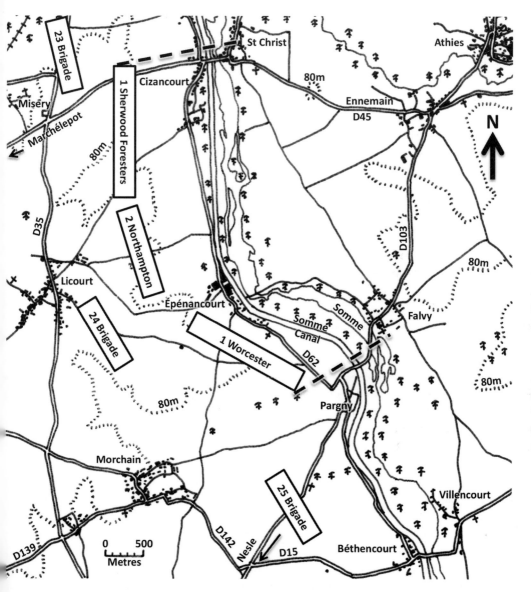

24th Brigade's extended positions west of the Somme on 22nd/23rd March.

50th Division at 5 p.m. On the right 25th Brigade relieved 2nd Cavalry Brigade in the evening, establishing contact with XVIII Corps at Béthencourt.

When 1st Worcestershire (24th Brigade) arrived at Nesle Station at 2.30 a.m. on the 23rd, it was ahead of HQs 8th Division and 24th Brigade. There were no instructions but the RTO had a telegraph order for 8th Division to take up positions along the Somme, from Béthencourt to Brie. Fifth Army was pulling back in some disarray and the precise location of the enemy was not known. However, the Germans could not be far away as firing could be heard in the distance. Marching off in the darkness, the three battalions of 24th Brigade went to their positions. 1st

Worcestershire was on the right, northwest of Pargny. 2nd Northamptonshire was in the centre and 1st Sherwood Foresters was on the left as far as St Christ. The battalions were stretched. Those on the right and left had all four companies in the line and each company had only one platoon in support. 25th Brigade, on the right, had not arrived when 24th Brigade took up its positions and so 1st Worcestershire's line was extended to cover Pargny bridge.

The troops dug in above the river as the sound of gunfire from the east moved ever closer. Troops from 25th Brigade continued the line to the right of 1st Worcestershire, while the roads to the front became congested with retreating troops and civilians. Early on the 23rd it was confirmed that the line held by 24th Brigade would become the new front when the troops in front had passed through. About noon 1st Sherwood Foresters extended its front on the left to cover the St Christ crossing. 1st Worcestershire handed over Pargny bridge to 2nd Rifle Brigade (25th Brigade).

Also around noon **Lieutenant Colonel Frank Roberts**, commanding 1st Worcestershire, took A and B Companies across the river to establish a covering position on the high ground east of Falvy. The exhausted, but well ordered, troops of 50th Division began to pass through from 2 p.m. onwards. They reformed behind 8th Division in a supporting position. The withdrawal was completed about 4 p.m.

The Germans were hard on the heels of the rearguard. Roberts held them long enough for the rearguard to make a clean break and get back over the river. He then withdrew his men and the bridges along the whole front of 24th Brigade were blown. However, it was discovered that the charges had not been powerful enough. Most bridges were not destroyed completely and were still passable. The Germans brought up field batteries and trench mortars, which were quickly into action. During the night the Germans made repeated, but unsuccessful, attempts to cross the river. Those who reached the western bank were either killed or captured.

1st Worcestershire spent an interrupted night occupying posts along the river from Pargny to Épénancourt. However, it was too stretched to cover the whole front properly. At 8 p.m. Roberts left his HQ dugout, on the sunken road just south of Épénancourt, to tour his posts from north to south. On arrival at a post 550m north of Pargny he learned that the enemy had taken the village. It was clear that 2nd Rifle Brigade, on the right, must have moved back and the bridge was still passable. The enemy had to be stopped or the whole Brigade line would be rolled up.

Within twenty minutes Roberts had assembled a reserve of forty-five men. He moved by covered approaches west of the village and then along a sunken road to the crossroads at the western exit. In the cover of a ruined cottage he whispered his orders. The enemy was in vastly superior numbers, so success depended on surprise. He decided to launch a determined attack straight down the village main street, while smaller parties of ten men worked their way down the outside of the houses to cut off escapers.

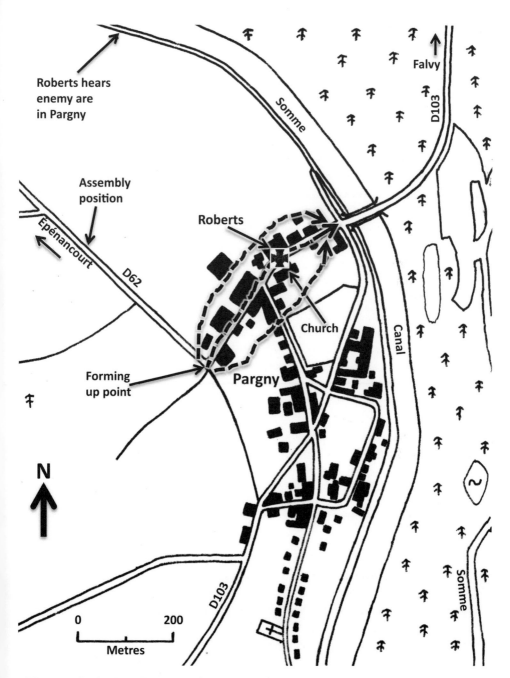

The route taken by Frank Roberts in his audacious counterattack at Pargay.

The party set off at about 9 p.m. For the first one hundred metres they advanced quietly in single file either side of the road. The enemy opened fire but their response was confused and haphazard. Many Germans fled towards the bridge and Robert's party charged, firing as they went and bayoneting anything that moved. By

The main features around Pargny that were involved in the counterattack.

The forming up point for the counterattack from where the three groups set off.

By the time Frank Roberts' small assault party reached this point they were all shouting and screaming to create the impression of a much larger force as they charged on towards the church.

Having secured the church and graveyard, Frank Roberts continued the assault to the bridge over the Somme Canal in the distance.

the time they reached the church they were all shouting and screaming to create the impression of a larger party. The whole village was in uproar, with Germans fleeing for the bridge or surrendering. A hard fight took place amongst the gravestones in the churchyard. Having cleared it, and taken a short rest, they pressed on to the bridge. About eighty enemy were killed and twenty prisoners and six machine guns were taken. The audacious attack succeeded because the superior enemy force was off guard, having taken the village with ease.

Despite this success, by dawn the Battalion was in a precarious situation. On the left of 24th Brigade, 1st Sherwood Foresters was having difficulty holding the onslaught at St Christ, while on the right the retreat had left the enemy free to cross the river at Béthencourt and enter Morchain. They were almost behind 1st Worcestershire. Roberts swung back his right flank to face southeast from the high ground behind Épénancourt. The flank was extended by a platoon of 2nd Northamptonshire. Robert's men swept the advancing Germans with fire on the open ground north of Morchain for several hours. Eventually they were forced to withdraw to conform to the rearward movement of the troops on the right. The Battalion was reinforced by another platoon of 2nd Northamptonshire. The two right companies of 2nd Northamptonshire conformed to 1st Worcestershire's movements. A new Brigade line was established from St Christ for about 1,800m along the Somme, then southwest to a point about 1,350m south-southeast of Licourt, where it was in contact with 25th Brigade.

24th Brigade held this position until early on the 25th. 1st Sherwood Foresters on the left resisted every German attempt to force crossings over the Somme, but it was not enough for the Brigade to remain in position. Preparations had been made to counterattack at 9 a.m. with the troops on the right, in order to regain the line of the Somme. However, when the right withdrew it was impossible for 24th Brigade to deliver the counterattack in isolation. The Brigade's line was untenable and the right flank was forced to pull back. By then the Germans were threatening to work around both flanks and the whole Brigade withdrew by short stages to the line of the railway embankment behind Marchélepot. 1st Worcestershire fell back there through Licourt.

66th Division was not disturbed until noon when the withdrawal of VII Corps on the left caused all available machine guns to be rushed to that flank. After 50th Division withdrew, the bridges over the Somme were blown except for one, which remained open to allow 16th Division (VII Corps) to cross.

VII Corps began the day holding the Green Line from Hamel to Équancourt. The withdrawal of XIX Corps the previous night exposed the right flank but VII Corps pulled back without much trouble. In the early morning VII Corps learned that XIX Corps had been ordered to withdraw behind the Somme and had no alternative other than to conform. At dawn on the 24th, VII Corps was in touch with the right of XIX Corps but was still out of contact with V Corps on the left.

During the day Fifth Army retreated four to six miles. Although the river positions in the centre held, it was unlikely that the flanks would continue to do so, although reinforcements were arriving. All divisions were severely under strength and almost all the reserves had been used at least once. The troops were in poor condition and rear details, divisional troops and even non-combatant troops were in the line.

Third Army began the day with V Corps, on the right, hanging on to the Flesquières Salient. As a result of the withdrawal of neighbouring corps, V Corps withdrew to the Green Line at 9.30 a.m. 47th Division's rearguard held the Germans until 11 a.m. but then the line of the retirement diverted to the northwest. This resulted in the gap between Fifth and Third Armies widening to five kilometres. 63rd and 17th Divisions reached the Green Line, where 2nd Division was already in position. 47th Division was forced back from the Green Line, leaving 63rd Division's right flank open. 17th Division occupied the Red Line by 6 a.m. and 51st Brigade filled the gap between Fifth and Third Armies. Despite this the situation was still perilous. The troops were utterly exhausted and there was confusion as they tried to find their units.

IV Corps evacuated the Battle Zone early on 23rd March, except for near the junction with V Corps. The Green Line was held by 19th and 41st Divisions, while 51st Division fell back through it, keeping pace with 17th Division (V Corps) on the right. 51st Division was to make its way to Bancourt behind the Green Line, giving up 57th Brigade (19th Division) and 74th Brigade (25th Division) on the way. Then

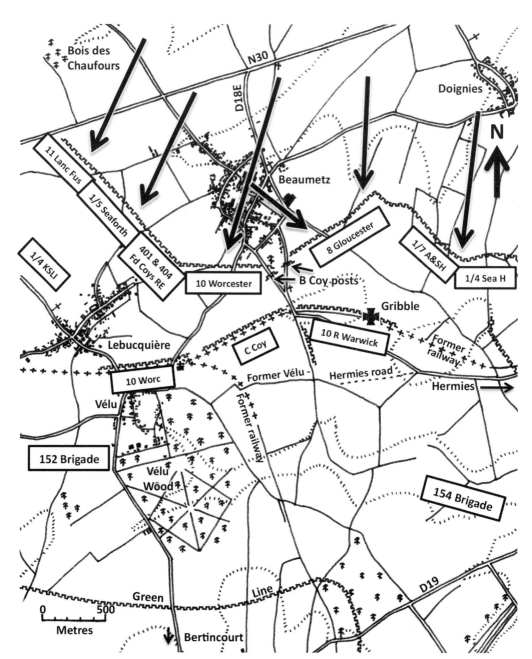

Leave Beaumetz to the southeast on the unclassified road to Hermies. Pass Beaumetz Cross Roads Cemetery on the left and 200m beyond turn left onto the old railway line and park. 10th Royal Warwickshire held the line of the railway. Walk east for 550m to the site of Julian Gribble's VC action. Alternatively view the same area from the position for Manley James.

preparations were to be made to extend the Corps frontage northwards to relieve VI Corps of a division's frontage.

Before these plans could be put into effect, 51st Division was attacked at 5.30 a.m. but the enemy was driven back by 11th Lancashire Fusiliers (74th Brigade, 25th Division) northwest of Beaumetz. The whole IV Corps front was attacked at 7 a.m. 152nd Brigade drove the enemy off three times. However, the Germans gained a little ground in the northern valley (Chaufours Wood) and enfiladed the line to left and right. 11th Lancashire Fusiliers was forced back through 1/4th King's Shropshire Light Infantry (19th Division). By 10 a.m. the Germans had reached the western edge of Lebucquière, forcing 152nd Brigade to begin pulling back towards Vélu Wood. Lebucquière was then occupied by the enemy.

10th Royal Warwickshire and 8th Gloucestershire (both 57th Brigade, 19th Division) were attached to 154th Brigade (51st Division) from 12.45 p.m. on 22nd March. At 5 a.m. on 23rd March, 57th Brigade was issued orders for a withdrawal to the Green Line that night. However, at 9.30 a.m. 154th Brigade was attacked as the fighting spread southwestwards. 51st Division was forced to withdraw in the face of overwhelming enemy pressure, commencing about 10 a.m. The right of 154th Brigade (1/4th Seaforth Highlanders and 1/7th Argyll and Sutherland Highlanders) held on initially, although isolated by the retirement of 17th Division (V Corps) on the right. It eventually fell back to rejoin 51st Division early on the 24th.

The retirement of 154th Brigade left 8th Gloucestershire and 10th Royal Warwickshire isolated, with their flanks in the air. They held on until 11 a.m., when 8th Gloucestershire and 10th Worcestershire (57th Brigade attached to 152nd Brigade), on its left, were forced to commence withdrawing towards Vélu Wood. They fell back through or past the left flank of 10th Royal Warwickshire. 8th Gloucestershire's withdrawal to the railway was covered by A Company, commanded by Manley James. His part in this action is related in the account of the fighting on 21st March.

10th Royal Warwickshire had occupied the line of the Vélu–Hermies railway late on 21st March. Very early on the 23rd, B Company on the left extended this flank by deploying two platoon posts to block the southeastern exits from Beaumetz. The Germans opened a heavy bombardment until just before 10 a.m., when 800–900 enemy debouched from the south and east of Beaumetz. About the same time the British close support artillery was pulled back, somewhat prematurely in the circumstances. C Company, 10th Royal Warwickshire threw a flank back along the railway, which 10th Worcestershire prolonged westwards to the south of Lebucquière. 8th Gloucestershire fell back south of Vélu Wood and covered the withdrawal of the artillery. By 12.30 p.m. the enemy was streaming into Vélu Wood and soon afterwards also appeared between 10th Royal Warwickshire and Hermies.

When 10th Royal Warwickshire began to fall back, **Captain Julian Gribble**, commanding D Company on the right, was unaware that a retirement had been

The line held by Julian Gribble on the Vélu–Hermies railway.

ordered until he realised that the troops on his right had gone. He sent a message to the company to his left rear that he intended to fight it out, at about the same time as the rest of the Battalion was driven off the ridge towards the Vélu–Hermies road. Gribble stopped all attempts by the advancing Germans to master the ridge at a critical time in the withdrawal, inflicting enormous casualties on them. He was seen fighting to the last, emptying his revolver into the surging mass, until he was wounded, overwhelmed and taken prisoner. His resistance allowed 57th Brigade to get away, as well as the garrison of Hermies and three batteries of field artillery. Gribble died in captivity two weeks after the Armistice.

By 1.30 p.m. 10th Royal Warwickshire had been forced south to the Vélu–Hermies road. German attempts to debouch from Vélu Wood were frustrated by small arms fire, assisted by sections of 51st and 19th Machine Gun Battalions, thus averting a potential disaster. However, the Germans reached the southern end of Vélu Wood in the rear of 57th Brigade and 10th Royal Warwickshire came under heavy fire from the eastern edge.

At 2.50 p.m. a message to withdraw got through via 2nd Oxfordshire & Buckinghamshire Light Infantry (2nd Division, V Corps). From 3 p.m. the Green Line to the rear was to be the front line. The remnants of 8th Gloucestershire and 10th Royal Warwickshire fell back in good order through the Green Line. 10th Royal Warwickshire withdrew south along the railway to Bertincourt, where it held positions east and south of the village. Later contact was broken and the Battalion marched to Bancourt, arriving at 7 p.m., where 57th Brigade reassembled behind 2nd Division. By the time 57th Brigade had completed this stage of the withdrawal at midnight on 23rd/24th March, it had suffered 833 casualties, although somewhat ameliorated by 318 reinforcements arriving on the 23rd. 10th Royal Warwickshire's share of the casualties was 321 (thirty-five killed, 200 wounded and eighty-six missing, some of whom were also known to be wounded).

Early on the 24th, IV Corps issued orders for 19th and 41st Divisions to hold the Green Line. 51st Division was to be ready to support the right and hold two miles

of the Red Line, while 6th Division remained in reserve. 25th Division established itself on the high ground near Sapignies. To the north, VI Corps had a relatively quiet day on 23rd March, except for the loss of Mory during the night of 22nd/23rd March. At the end of the day Third Army held the Green Line except for 3,600m on the right and around Mory.

Pétain and Haig met at 4 p.m. and agreed that all troops between the Oise and Péronne would come under French command. With no reinforcements received from home, Haig had to find reserves from within the BEF. The northern armies, having been relieved of some of the line in Flanders, gave up six divisions (in addition to 42nd and 62nd), which were put under Lieutenant General Sir Thomas Morland's command to man the Purple Line. A GHQ Line was also set up eight miles west of the Purple Line. In the next few weeks over 8,000 kilometres of trenches were dug, protected by 23,500 tons of barbed wire. Even the old Boulogne–Calais–Dunkirk Line, set up in 1915, was included in case the British were forced back on the Channel ports.

Biographies

SECOND LIEUTENANT ERNEST FREDERICK BEAL
13th Battalion, Alexandra, Princess of Wales's Own (Yorkshire Regiment)

Ernest Beal was born at 148 Lewes Road, Brighton, Sussex on 27th January 1883. His father, John James William Beal (27th August 1854–2nd March 1942), was a stationer's assistant in 1871 living with his parents. He married Jane 'Jennie' Stillman née Dowsing (1855–22nd March 1927) on 20th January 1876 at St Mary, Bryanston Square, Marylebone, London. She was born at Ipswich, Suffolk. By 1881 he was a wholesale and retail stationer, bookseller and newsagent and they were living at 148 Lewes Road, Brighton. They were still there in 1911 but by 1918 had moved to 55 East Street, Brighton. Jennie died at 89 Beaconsfield Villas, Brighton, leaving £1,930/4/7 to her husband and sons John, Harold and Richard. John was living at Brendon, North Lane, Rustington, Sussex at the time of his death there, leaving effects valued at £181/9/3. Ernest had six siblings:

Ernest's parents were married at St Mary's, Bryanston Square. The church was built in 1823–24.

- Jane Emily Beal (1877–23rd December 1966) married Ernest Walter Greenwood (1877–1960) in 1903. He was a dairyman in 1911 and they were living at 92 Lewes Road, Brighton. They were living at 9 Rugby Road, Brighton in 1960. He died at 3 Harrington Road, Brighton, leaving £1,047/16/10 to his widow. She was still living at Rugby Road when she died in 1966, leaving effects valued at £7,031. They had a son, Ernest Robert Greenwood, in 1908.
- John James Beal (1878–18th November 1938) was a stationer's foreman in 1901 living with his parents. He married Adela Maud Clarke (born c.1877) in 1904. She was born at Mile End, London. By 1911 John was a stationer's assistant and they were living at 330

Ditchling Road, Preston, Sussex. He served during the Great War as a private in 17th Essex. He was living at Springfield, Onslow Road, Hove when he died at Hove Hospital, Sackville Road, Sussex leaving £1,910/0/5 to his brothers Richard and Harold.

* George William Beal (1881–85).
* Grace Ethel Beal (1885–1911) died at the London Hospital, Whitechapel, London, leaving £89/15/- to her father.
* Harold Robert Beal (2nd May 1887– 5th January 1976), a commercial traveller, married Ellen Mary Davis

The Beals were living on East Street, Brighton in 1918.

(1886–9th March 1964) at Lewes Road Congregational Church, Brighton on 8th June 1911. They lived at Wymondley, 1 Ferndale Road, Hove. He enlisted on 10th December 1915 (26204) and transferred to the Reserve next day. He was described as 5' 6½" tall, weighing 127 lbs and his religious denomination was Congregationalist. He was mobilised on 25th May 1916 and joined 22nd King's Royal Rifle Corps with service reckoning from 29th May. Appointed unpaid lance corporal on 21st July 1916 and was posted to C Company, 110 Training Reserve Battalion (TR 13/29471) on 1st September. He was promoted lance corporal on 25th September and was posted to No.4 Officer Cadet Battalion, 9 Alfred Street, Oxford on 4th November 1916. On 1st March 1917 he was commissioned in 5th King's Royal Rifle Corps. He received a gunshot wound to the left leg on 21st November, embarked at Le Havre on 29th November and arrived in Southampton the next day for treatment at 4th London General Hospital. A medical board there on 25th January 1918 found him unfit for General Service. On 14th March a medical board at Devonport Military Hospital granted him three weeks leave

to 4th April, following which he was fit for General Service. He was demobilised from 11th King's Royal Rifle Corps on 28th January 1919 and relinquished his commission on 1st September 1921. Harold and Ellen lived at Barnehurst, Meadway, Rustington, Sussex and he was a company director in the family firm of stationers in Brighton. Ernest's VC passed to him on the death of his father. They were living at Brendon,

Beaconsfield Villas, Brighton.

North Lane, Rustington, Sussex at the time of her death there, leaving effects valued at £756. He was living at Rosemary Mount, 147 Chesswood Road, Worthing at the time of his death there, leaving effects valued at £38,423.

- Richard Wilfred Beal (1889–25th January 1963) was an assistant in his father's business in 1911. He married Muriel Kitching Moon (22nd July 1891–1976) in 1913 at Steyning, Sussex. He was a company director in the family firm of stationers in Brighton and they lived at 43 Little Paddocks, Ferring-by-Sea, Sussex. He died at 42 Shelley Road, Worthing, leaving £1,661/8/1- to his two sons – John Malcolm Beal 1915 and Richard Ernest Beal 1919.

Ernest's paternal grandfather, John Beal (c.1832–22nd August 1911), a master stationer, married Eliza née Hider (1831–57) in 1853. In addition to John they had another son – George Robert Beal (1856–75). John was living with his two sons at Wellington Terrace, Brighton in 1861. He married Mary Lightfoot (c.1834–1862) in late 1861 at Rye, Kent. They had a daughter, Mary Alice Naomi Beal, in 1862 but she and her mother died during the birth. John married Mary's sister, Jemima Lightfoot (1842–17th January 1928), but no marriage record has been found. By 1871 John was employing eight men and fifteen boys. The family was living at 148 Lewes Road, Brighton. They had moved to 5 Wellington Road by 1881, to Apsley Lodge by 1891and 16 Wellington Road by 1901, all in Brighton. They were living at Thorpdale, Cuckfield, Sussex at the time of his death, leaving effects valued at £32. Jemima was living at Oak Lea, Plumpton, Sussex at the time of her death there, leaving effects valued at £4,661/1/5. John and Jemima had four children:

- Mary Beal (born 1866) married Frank Arthur Davis (1863–1926), an ironmonger, in 1886. They were living at 89 Beaconsfield Villas, Brighton in 1911 and he died there, leaving effects valued at £5,457/12/6. They had two children – Kathleen 'Queenie' Helen M Davis 1887 and Dorothy May Davis 1894.
- Katharine Beal (1868–14th June 1954) married Arthur Edward Saunders (1863–1936) in 1889. He was a builder's merchant manager in 1891 and they were living at 152 Lewes Road, Brighton, two doors away from her mother. They were living at 10 Florence Road, Brighton in 1901 and 1911. He died there, leaving effects valued at £37,422/18/1. She was living at 53 Montefiore Road, Hove, Sussex at the time of her death there, leaving effects valued at £3,981. They had two children but only one survived infancy:
  - Alan Arthur Saunders (1892–1957) served as a major in the Royal Engineers during the Great War and was awarded the OBE for valuable services, LG 1st January 1919. He married Florence Edith Nye (1890–1974) in 1915. Alan made his first-class debut for Sussex against Hampshire in the 1922 County Championship and made twelve appearances for the county. He was knighted, LG 1st January 1949. They lived at Whiteleaf, Dyke Road, Hove, Sussex.

- Richard Beal (born 1871).
- Helen (1872–17th November 1960) married Frederick Robert McLaren (1865–1956) in 1901 at Brighton. He was an omnibus proprietor and they were living at Cuckfield, Sussex in 1911. They were living at Goughs, Frostenden, Wangford Beccles, Suffolk at the time of his death, leaving effects valued at £1,263/2/6. She was still living there at the time of her death at Gorleston Nursing Home, Marine Parade, Gorleston, leaving effects valued at £7,999/3/2. They had a son, Alan Robert McLaren, in 1902.

His maternal grandfather is not known. His maternal grandmother, Charity Emma Dowsing (1837–13th June 1915) was born at St Nicholas, Ipswich, Suffolk. She was living with her parents on Whitton Road, Ipswich in 1851. Charity married William Sicklemore (1843–19th April 1924) in 1874 at Hastings, Sussex. He was a muffin and crumpet maker and they were living at 42 Middle Street, Brighton in 1881. William Coles (born 1868), an errand boy born in Brighton, was living with them, described as William's son. By 1891 they had moved to 38 Middle Street, Brighton and were still there in 1901. She died there, leaving effects valued at £416/16/ , and he died there, leaving effects valued at £447/19/8.

Ernest was educated at Brighton Grammar School and was an officer in the Brighton Boy's Brigade, receiving the annual efficiency award. He was employed as a stationer's assistant with his father. On 22nd September 1914 he enlisted in 2/1st Sussex Yeomanry (2005). He was promoted lance corporal 30th October 1914, corporal 26th January 1915 and sergeant 11th June 1915. He transferred to 1/1st Sussex Yeomanry on 10th September and left Britain on 24th September 1915. From 7th October he served at Gallipoli and then Egypt before France. On 3rd January 1917, 1/1st Sussex Yeomanry became 16th (Sussex Yeomanry) Battalion, Royal Sussex Regiment (320206). He transferred to 4th Reserve Battalion on 17th April and joined No.16 Officer Cadet Battalion, Rhyl on 7th June. Ernest was commissioned in 3rd Yorkshire on 26th September 1917 and joined 13th Battalion in France in October.

Brighton Grammar School originated as Brighton Proprietary Grammar and Commercial School in 1859 at Lancaster House, Grand Parade. It became Brighton, Hove and Sussex Grammar School and opened on its present site in 1913. During the Great War it was used as a military hospital, as seen in this view. It became Brighton, Hove and Sussex Sixth Form College in 1975 and has about 2,800 students. Former pupils include:

- Jamie Theakston, television presenter.
- Sir Walter Adams CMG OBE, Director of the London School of Economics 1967–74.
- Sir Charles Cochran, theatre producer.
- Michael Fabricant, Conservative MP.
- Rear Admiral John Lippiet CB CBE, Chief Executive of the Mary Rose Trust.
- Leonard Martin, Chairman of UNESCO 1976–78.

Ernest is commemorated on the Arras Memorial (bottom left) as is fellow Yorkshire Regiment VC, David Hirsch (top left). Another eleven VCs are commemorated on the Arras Memorial and the colocated Flying Services Memorial.

The Arras Memorial stands at the entrance to Faubourg d'Amiens Cemetery. It commemorates 34,848 soldiers of the British, South African and New Zealand forces with no known grave, who died between the spring of 1916 and 7th August 1918. Most of those commemorated died during the Battle of Arras April–May 1917 and during the German spring offensives in 1918. The Memorial was designed by Sir Edwin Lutyens and the sculpture is by Sir William Reid Dick. The Arras Memorial and Flying Services Memorial were dedicated on 31st July 1932 by Marshal of the Royal Air Force Lord Trenchard, commander of the RFC on the Western Front 1915–17. The ceremony had been scheduled for May but French President JA Paul Doumer was shot in Paris on 6th May and died the following day. As a mark of respect the ceremony was postponed for two months. The Flying Services Memorial commemorates 990 airmen who died on active service on the Western Front and have no known grave (Memorials to Valour).

Awarded the VC for his actions at St Léger, France on 21st/22nd March 1918, LG 4th June 1918. He died of wounds received during the VC action on 22nd March 1918 and is commemorated on the Arras Memorial (Bay 5). The VC was presented to his parents by the King in the quadrangle outside Buckingham Palace on 3rd July 1918. They were accompanied by Ernest's fiancée, Miss May Florence Bundy (9th January 1891–April 1981) of 37 Crescent Road, Brighton. She was a clerk at a stationer's in 1911. Probate was granted to his brothers, John and Harold. Ernest left £2,234/7/8. He is commemorated in a number of other places:

- Ernest Beal VC Watch – awarded annually by the Brighton Hove & District Battalion, Boys' Brigade, to the outstanding Boy.
- EF Beal VC Award presented annually to a member of Brighton Hove and Sussex Grammar School for outstanding qualities of fortitude, determination and unselfish devotion. In 1975 the School became Brighton Hove and Sussex Sixth Form College and its annual 'Education for Life Awards' include two Beal Awards. 'Consideration of Oneself' recognises a student who has overcome some difficulty whilst at the College. 'Consideration of Others' recognises a student who has spent a significant portion of their time helping others while undertaking their studies.
- Brighton War Memorial, Old Steine Gardens, St James Street, Brighton, Sussex.

Brighton War Memorial commemorates 2,597 men and three women who died in the Great War. Just the surnames and initials are recorded. The design is in the form of a Roman water garden. It was unveiled by Admiral David Beatty, 1st Earl Beatty, Commander-in-Chief of the Grand Fleet during the Great War. The names of the dead are also recorded in two books of remembrance in the Parish Church of St Peter. They were displayed until 1992 when they were withdrawn because of vandalism but are available on application to the Church authorities.

- Roll of Honour in the Hall of Honour at Brighton Hove & Sussex Sixth Form College, formerly Brighton Grammar School.
- A Department for Communities and Local Government commemorative VC paving stone was dedicated at Brighton War Memorial, Old Steine Gardens, Brighton on 16th March 2018 to mark the centenary of his award.

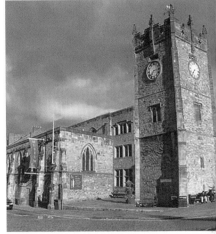

The Green Howards Regimental Museum is housed in the former Trinity Church in the market place at Richmond, North Yorkshire. The Green Howards amalgamated with the other two Yorkshire infantry regiments to form The Yorkshire Regiment in 2006. Until then the Green Howards was one of only five infantry regiments never to have been amalgamated. Coincidentally the Green Howards had been the Yorkshire Regiment until the 1920s. The Museum was founded in 1938 and moved to its present location in 1973.

In addition to the VC he was awarded the 1914–15 Star, British War Medal 1914–20 and Victory Medal 1914–19. The trio was issued to May Bundy. The VC passed to his brother Harold on the death of his father. The VC was presented on permanent loan to the Green Howards by Harold in 1964. May loaned the trio to the Green Howards Museum to join the VC. In July 1973 Harold and May donated the VC group to the Regiment. The VC is held by the Green Howards Museum, Trinity Church Square, Richmond, Yorkshire.

May never married and was living at 2 Southdown Place, Southdown Road, Brighton at the time of her death there on 3rd April 1981, leaving effects valued at £36,935.

SECOND LIEUTENANT JOHN CRAWFORD BUCHAN
1/7th attached 1/8th Battalion, Princess Louises's (Argyll & Sutherland Highlanders)

John Buchan was born at 9 King Street, Alloa, Clackmannanshire, Scotland on 10th October 1892. His father, David Buchan (1856–4th June 1926) was born at Barony, Glasgow, Lanarkshire. He was a newspaper reporter, living at Back o'Dykes, Alloa with his parents in 1881, and was later editor of the *Alloa Advertiser*. David married Margaret (known as Mary) McGregor née Crawford (17th June 1856–14th April 1907), on 27th July 1883 at Alloa, Clackmannanshire, where she was born. In 1881 she was a housemaid at Alloa House, home of Walker Henry Erskine, Earl of Mar & Kellie DL JP. They were living in Alloa at 7 Mar Place by 1888, at 9 King Street by 1901 and at 5 Kellie Place by 1911 (James Lennox Dawson VC's family was living at No.11). David's address was Candle Street when he claimed his son's medals in February 1922, but he died at 5 Kellie Place in 1926. John had six siblings:

- Margaret 'Meg' Ann Taylor Buchan (31st March 1884–27th October 1942) helped to look after the family following the death of her mother in 1907. She worked for the Red Cross during the Great War. Meg was engaged but her fiancée drowned in a bath after inhaling toxic fumes at work. She was a hospital collector at the time of her death at her sister Jessie's home at 162 Beechwood Drive, Glasgow, Lanarkshire. Her normal residence was 5 Kellie Place, Alloa.
- David Buchan (28th September 1886–9th April 1917) was educated at St Andrews University, Fife where he was a cadet in the UOTC. He was living at 17 Arlington Street, Charing Cross, Glasgow when he applied for a commission

The Buchan family lived in Mar Place, Alloa in the 1880s.

Kellie Place, Alloa, where John Buchan's family was living at No.5 in 1911 and the family of James Lennox Dawson VC was living at No.11.

James Lennox Dawson (1891–1967) was born at Tillicoultry, Clackmannanshire. By 1911 his family was living at 11 Kellie Place, Alloa. He attended Alloa Academy at the same time as John Buchan. James was a science teacher in Govan and enlisted in 5th Cameronians on 28th November 1914. He served in France with 1/5th Battalion and transferred to the Special Brigade Royal Engineers on 19th July 1915. He was awarded the VC for his actions at the Hohenzollern Redoubt, near Loos, France on 13th October 1915. James was later commissioned and was demobilised on 1st February 1919. He served again in the Army Educational Corps from 11th December 1920 and transferred to the Indian Army on 30th May 1921, and in 1931 transferred to the Indian Army Ordnance Corps. In 1941 he became a vehicle liaison officer with the India Supply Commission in North America until 1946. After independence in 1947 he remained in India for some time to assist the Indian Army. On retirement on 26th March 1948, he was granted the rank of honorary colonel.

Before she married, John's mother was a housemaid in the residence of Walter Henry Erskine, Earl of Mar and Kellie (1839–88). He succeeded as 13th Earl of Kellie on his father's death in 1872. He also became 11th Earl of Mar in 1875 in the seventh creation of the title. However, concurrently John Goodeve-Erskine was 27th Earl of Mar in its first creation, meaning there were two Earls of Mar. Walter was Grand Master Mason of the Grand Lodge of Scotland 1882–85, an appointment held by the future King George VI in 1936–37. He married Mary Anne Forbes (1838–1927) in 1853 and they had nine children, including Walter John Francis Erskine, 12th Earl of Mar and 14th Earl of Kellie (1865–1955).

on 13th January 1915. In his medical examination he was described as 5′ 3½″ tall and weighed 113 lbs. He was commissioned in 11th Gordon Highlanders on 29th June 1915 but served with 1st Battalion in France. David was killed in action on 9th April 1917 and is commemorated on the Arras Memorial, France (Bays 8 & 9).

• Robert Mackenzie Crawford Buchan (17th June 1888–15th May 1935) was educated at Alloa Academy and served his apprenticeship with Charles Thomson,

Alloa Town Clerk. He qualified as a law agent at Edinburgh University and was fluent in several languages. He volunteered for service at the outbreak of the Great War but was rejected. Instead he was appointed Secretary to Sir Horace Rombold, Ambassador to the British Legation, Berne, Switzerland. He also served with the British Legation in Warsaw, Poland and entered the Consular Service in 1919. Robert married Garnet Longsdon Jerrard (1892–1967) in 1919. They married abroad but she was born at Camberwell, London and died at Blackpool, Lancashire. His appointments included:

- ° Vice Consul in Tripoli, Libya.
- ° Vice Consul Upper Silesia, Poland.
- ° Consul for the States of Maryland, Virginia and West Virginia, USA from 19th May 1927, residing at Baltimore.
- ° Consul at Danzig, Poland from 1st November 1933.
- ° Consul General at Amsterdam, Netherlands, where he died at his residence at 21 Bachstraat in 1935.

• Norman William Buchan (15th January 1894–1964) was very shortsighted and failed to pass the medical requirements for active service. He remained in Scotland, working for his father on the *Alloa Advertiser*.

• Francis Hall Buchan (24th May 1897–7th August 1918) was a reporter. He attested on 6th December 1915, described as 5′ 3″ tall and weighed 101 lbs. He transferred to the Reserve the same day. He was originally intended for the Royal Engineers and then the Army Ordnance Corps before 2/7th Argyll & Sutherland Highlanders (5431 later 277232). He was mobilised on 10th May 1916 and transferred to the Reserve the same day but was mobilised again on 23rd May 1916 to served in 2/7th Argyll & Sutherland Highlanders' signal section at Norwich, Norfolk. He moved to Taverham, Norfolk on 10th July 1917 to join 2/6th Argyll & Sutherland Highlanders. He applied for a commission on 24th January 1917, described as 5′ 5″ tall and weighing 120 lbs, and joined No.12 Officer Cadet Battalion at Newmarket, Suffolk on 7th September. He was commissioned into 5th (Reserve) Battalion, Rifle Brigade on 14th January 1918. He was serving with 11th Battalion when he died of wounds at 62nd Field Ambulance on 7th August 1918 and is buried in Sucrerie Cemetery, Ablain-St Nazaire, France (IV E 7).

Francis Hall Buchan's grave in Sucrerie Cemetery, Ablain-St Nazaire.

• Jessie Crawford Buchan (6th November 1890– 14th August 1962) married Captain Frederick Proudfoot (1894–1949), 9th Black Watch, in June 1918. Frederick was an electrical engineer of 12 Bank Street, Alloa. He enlisted in 7th Argyll & Sutherland Highlanders (1326) at Alloa on 9th February 1911, described as 5′ 4″ tall. He was promoted lance corporal on 21st February and corporal on 18th April 1913. On 5th August 1914 he was embodied and was promoted lance sergeant on 14th September. Frederick embarked at Southampton on 15th December 1914 and was appointed acting sergeant on 4th January 1915. On 25th April he received gunshot wounds to the head and elbow and was treated at 3rd General Hospital, Le Tréport until being evacuated to Britain on 5th May. He applied for a commission on 25th September and was commissioned in 11th (Reserve) Battalion, Black Watch on 21st October 1915. On 9th April 1917 he received a bayonet wound to the right foot and embarked at Calais for Dover on 13th April for treatment at No.2 Western General Hospital, Manchester next day. A medical board on 17th April found him unfit and he was granted leave to 9th May and then reported to 3rd Reserve Battalion at Nigg, Ross-shire. A medical board at Stirling Military Hospital on 14th May found him fit for General Service. On 12th May 1918 he was kicked by a horse on Vimy Ridge resulting in a lacerated wound to the forehead. He was evacuated to Britain on 6th June (Calais to Dover) because the hospital at Étaples was being moved there. He had surgery at Worsley Hall Hospital and was then treated at No.2 Western General Hospital, Manchester. A medical board there on 14th June granted him leave to 5th July, when he joined 3rd Reserve Battalion at the Curragh. Frederick was demobilised on 26th February 1919 from No.1 Dispersal Unit, Georgetown, Paisley. Jessie and Frederick were living at 50 Park Road, West Glasgow in September 1920. They later lived at 162 Beechwood Drive, Jordanhill, Glasgow and had two children:

- ° June Margaret Proudfoot (1920–2003) was a schoolteacher when she married Captain James Mays Fowler RAMC (1920–79) in 1947 in Hillhead, Glasgow. They had two daughters – Pamela Mays Fowler 1948 and Valerie Mays Fowler 1951. James was granted a Regular Army Emergency Commission in the RAMC as a lieutenant on 26th August 1944 and was promoted war substantive captain on 26th August 1945. He was released from service by August 1947.
- ° Frederick Buchan Proudfoot (5th May 1924–2012) was a medical practitioner. He married Elizabeth McGruther Miller (1925–2007) in Glasgow in 1948. She was also a medical practitioner. They had five children – Michael Crawford Proudfoot 1950, Jennifer Margaret Proudfoot 1952, Janice Allan Proudfoot 1955, Susan Elizabeth Proudfoot 1959 and David James Proudfoot 1960.

John's paternal grandfather, David Buchan (14th May 1813–8th April 1878), a carpenter and joiner, married Ann née Taylor (18th July 1819–29th September 1899). In addition to David, they had another son, William Taylor Buchan (born 1858), who worked for the *Alloa Advertiser* as a journalist and took over as the editor and proprietor from his older brother David.

His maternal grandfather, Robert Crawford (11th August 1827–20th April 1909), a wool spinner, married Janet née Hall (died 4th September 1859), on 24th September 1853 at Tillicoultry, Perthshire. They lived at 4 High Street and in addition to Margaret they had two other children:

• Mary Crawford (born c.1855) was an assistant confectioner.
• Janet Hall Crawford (3rd July 1858–9th March 1927), a darner in a factory, married Bentley Shaw (c.1853–4th June 1939), a foreman cloth finisher, in July 1885 at Dennistoun, Glasgow, Lanarkshire. Bentley was born at Tillicoultry, Perthshire and Janet was living at 16 Ochil Street there at the time of her marriage. She died at 19 Kerse Road, Throsk, Stirlingshire.

Robert married Amelia Coutts (9th October 1838–26th October 1924), a power loom weaver, on 24th June 1864 at his home at 39 High Street, Tillicoultry. She was born at Dollar, Clackmannanshire. They were living at Clackmannan in 1881, at Gabbeston, Alloa in 1891 and at 15 Kellie Place, Alloa by 1901. Robert and Amelia had a son, John Crawford, in 1873 at Sauchie, Stirlingshire. He was a law apprentice in 1891. Robert was a confectioner when he died at 15 Kellie Place, Alloa. Amelia died at 16 Newmains Road, Renfrew.

John's maternal grandfather's second wife, Amelia Coutts (1838–1924), was born at Dollar, Clackmannanshire. In the background are the Ochil Hills where John used to ski.

John was educated at Alloa Academy until September 1909, at the same time as James Lennox Dawson VC. He was employed as a solicitor's clerk by Charles Thomson, Alloa Town Clerk and later as a reporter on the *Alloa Advertiser*, which was co-owned by his father and uncle, William Taylor Buchan. He played rugby, mountaineered, skied in the Ochil Hills, worked at the Scottish YMCA Summer Camp during his holidays and wrote articles on climbing and the outdoors for *The Scotsman*. John was also a linguist, musician and a ventriloquist, using 'Johnny' and 'Sammy' at numerous local venues in Alloa. While having a tooth extracted he felt the dentist was taking too long and used his ventriloquist skills to throw his voice

Alloa Academy is now a state funded comprehensive school. It moved to its current location at the end of 2008. The old building seen here in the Claremont area was built in 1859 and opened by Queen Victoria. It was demolished in 2010. In addition to its two VCs, the school has a number of noteworthy alumni. These include Baron Charles Forte, founder of the Trust House Forte hotel group and William McEwan, the brewer and Liberal politician.

to another part of the room shouting, *Hurry up!* The dentist looked round in surprise and, when John left him after the operation, was still wondering where the voice had come from.

When war broke out John was on holiday in the Alpine resort of Leysin, Switzerland. He was unable to return to the United Kingdom for a year and worked as an interpreter and clerk in a local hotel until he received the papers necessary to journey home via France. It was reported that he was a pacifist initially.

John enlisted in 3/3rd Lowland Field Ambulance RAMC on 12th August 1915 (2284) and was based at Kingsmeadows Camp, Peebles. He applied for a commission in 3/7th Argyll

Leysin, in the Vaudoises Alps area of Switzerland, is close to Montreux at the eastern end of Lake Geneva, near the French border. At the time John was there it was known for its sanatoriums for tuberculosis. Today it is a year-round venue for mountain sports and activities.

& Sutherland Highlanders on 10th August 1916 and in his medical examination was described as 5' 5½" tall and weighing 143 lbs. He was granted leave from 30th September and reported to No.10 Officer Cadet Battalion at Gailes, Ayrshire on 5th October 1916. He was commissioned into the 5th (Reserve) Battalion (which by then included 3/7th Battalion) on 25th January 1917. He went to France on 4th October 1917. **Awarded the VC for his actions east of Marteville, France on 21st/22nd March 1918, LG 22nd May 1918.**

John was killed during his VC action near Marteville, France on 22nd March 1918 and was buried by the Germans in Roisel Communal Cemetery. He was initially posted as missing but on 27th November 1918 the War Office accepted that he had died. His remains were moved later to Roisel Communal Cemetery Extension (II 1 6).

He is commemorated in a number of other places:

- War Memorial, Church Street, Alloa, Clackmannanshire.
- Plaque at Clackmannan County Cricket Club, Alloa, commemorating twenty-nine members who died during the Great War. His brothers, David and Francis, are also named. The plaque was unveiled by Provost Mitchell on 30th April 1922.

John Buchan's grave in Roisel Communal Cemetery Extension.

Alloa War Memorial was dedicated on 28th September 1924 by Field Marshal Earl Haig, former commander of the British Expeditionary Force. He is standing to the right of the memorial. The names of the dead are recorded on the panels at the rear.

The Argyll & Sutherland Highlanders Museum in Stirling Castle, where John Buchan's VC is held.

- A Department for Communities and Local Government commemorative VC paving stone was dedicated at the Boer War Memorial, junction between Ludgate and Claremont, Alloa on 23rd March 2018 to mark the centenary of his award.
- Plaque in Alloa Museum with a copy of the picture that recreates *To Hell with Surrender*.

As John never married, the VC was presented to his father by the King at Buckingham Palace on 3rd March 1920. In addition to the VC he was awarded the British War Medal 1914–20 and Victory Medal 1914–19. His medals were donated to the Regiment at Stirling Castle by his niece, Mrs J Fowler, in early 2001. The VC is held by the Argyll & Sutherland Highlanders Museum, Stirling Castle.

LIEUTENANT COLONEL CHRISTOPHER BUSHELL
7th Battalion, The Queen's (Royal West Surrey Regiment)

Christopher Bushell was born at Hinderton Lodge, Little Neston, Cheshire on 31st October 1887. He was known as Kit. His father, Reginald Bushell FRAS (18th August 1842–11th November 1904), was a partner in the Liverpool firm of Bushell Bros and Co, wine merchants and shippers, on Castle Street. He married Caroline née Hope (27th April 1855–18th August 1941) on 3rd April 1883 at Kensington, London. She was living at 6 Addison Road, Kensington at the time and he was living at Oakhill,

Neston, Cheshire. By 1887 they were living at 26 North John Street, Liverpool. He was a member of the Mersey Docks and Harbour Board and a JP for Cheshire. They were living at Hinderton Lodge, Little Neston, Wirral, Cheshire when he died there, leaving effects valued at £62,702/10/7. By 1911 Caroline had moved to 59 Kensington Court, London. She later lived at Hillside, Granville Road, St Margaret's-at-Cliffe, Dover, Kent and 20 Castle Street, Liverpool, Lancashire. She died at Eccleston Rectory, Chester leaving effects valued at £8,587/16/1. Christopher had two siblings:

Little Neston, Cheshire. Hinderton Lodge no longer exists but the site on Cedar Grove is close to Bushell Road.

• Arthur Reginald Bushell (8th July 1884–28th August 1924) emigrated to New Zealand and became a sheep farmer at Fairlie, South Island. He enlisted in the New Zealand Army Service Corps on 8th February 1915 (5/207), described as 6′ 3″ tall, weighing 176 lbs, with fair complexion, grey eyes, brown hair and his religious denomination was Church of England. He was commissioned on 10th February 1915 and departed

Christopher's family was living at 26 North John Street, Liverpool in 1887 (Rightmove).

New Zealand on 17th April in command of a transport section in No.4 Company NZASC, 4th Reinforcements. He was promoted lieutenant on 14th September and served at Gallipoli from 13th November until the evacuation as acting Adjutant, Anzac Divisional Train. Returning to Egypt he was posted to the New Zealand Army Ordnance Corps at Moascar Garrison, Ismailia on 14th January 1916 as acting Deputy Assistant Director of Ordnance Services. He returned to No.4 Company on 4th February and embarked for France on 9th April, where he attended a course on transport duties at Le Havre 22nd May–15th June. Arthur was detached on billeting duties on 13th August and transferred to HQ Company on 16th September. A short attachment to 1st NZ Field Butchery was

By 1911 Christopher's mother, Caroline, was living at 59 Kensington Court, London.

followed by posting to No.4 Depot Unit of Supply on 15th October. He assumed command of the unit on 16th December. However, he was not recommended for a command in the field due to lack of decisiveness. Arthur was promoted captain on 23rd February 1917 and was mentioned in Field Marshal Sir Haig's Despatch of 7th November 1917 (LG 28th December 1917). On 5th February 1918 he returned to the strength of No.4 Company. He was granted leave in England 17th February–3rd March 1919 and returned to Britain on 4th April with A Group NZEF at Sling Camp, Bulford, Wiltshire. He sailed for New Zealand aboard HMNZT *Maunganui* on 17th May, arriving on 23rd June. He applied for a permanent commission in the New Zealand Army but it was not granted. Arthur was struck off strength on 21st July 1919 and retained the rank of captain in the Reserve of Officers. He returned to farming at Korari Downs, Canterbury. Arthur committed suicide on 28th August 1924 at Christchurch.

• Lilian Hope Bushell (22nd July 1885–13th March 1964) married Reverend Canon Douglas Waller Hobson (c.1875–26th December 1950) on 10th April 1911 at St Dunstan and All Saints, Stepney, London. He was born on the Isle of Man. They lived at Greenfields, Odiham, Hampshire. When he died he left effects valued at £10,241/9/5 to his widow. When she died at Marley House Nursing Home, Haslemere, Surrey she left effects valued at £138,955.

Christopher's paternal grandfather, also Christopher Bushell (1810–18th February 1887), was born at Chatham, Kent. He married Catharine Anne Sellars (1810–36) on 2nd September 1833 at Westow, Yorkshire and they had a son, Christopher Percy Bushell (22nd August 1834–1855). Christopher senior married Margaret Smith née Easton (c.1820–10th January 1906) on 23rd October 1838 at Edinburgh, Midlothian. She was born at Berwick-upon-Tweed, Northumberland. In 1861 Christopher was a landed proprietor and wine merchant and they were living at Hinderton Hall, Little Neston, Wirral, Cheshire. He also owned New Hall Farm, Neston, (c.300 acres) which he let to tenant farmers. He was a Conservative member of the Municipal Council in Liverpool and was elected inaugural chairman of the Liverpool School Board. He promoted the Liverpool Council of Education and was chairman from its formation in 1874 until his death. He was also one of the principal promoters of Liverpool University College and was named a vice-president in the Royal Charter of Incorporation. He was also a member of the Liverpool Cathedral Committee and a JP. In 1851 Margaret was living with her children at St Anne's Crescent, Garston, Lancashire. In 1871 she was living at 2 Gambier Drive, Liverpool. Her husband was not part of the household in either census return. He died at Bowdon Vicarage, Park Road, Bowdon, Cheshire, home of Archdeacon Arthur Gore and his wife Ellen, Christopher Bushell's niece. In addition to Reginald they had eleven other children:

• Charles John Bushell (17th December 1839–12th November 1909) married Katherine Ann Torr (c.1848–9th May 1913) in 1871. She was born at Eastham, Cheshire. They lived at Woodlands, Bromborough, Cheshire and he worked at

Exchange Buildings, Liverpool. They had seven children – Christopher Torr Bushell 1872, Edith Margaret D Bushell 1874, Charles Hubert Bushell 1879, Harold Edgar Bushell 1880, Oliver Wyndham Bushell 1883, Godfrey Maurice Bushell 1884 and Bernard William Torr Bushell 1886. When Charles died he left effects valued at £45,037/5/9 and Katherine left £1,014/18/4.

James (later Sir James) Rankin married Christopher's aunt, Anne Laura Bushell.

- Margaret Ann Bushell (c.1841–69) never married.
- Anne Laura Bushell (1843–22nd June 1920) married James (later Sir James) Rankin (1843–17th April 1915) on 12th January 1865. He served as a major in the Royal Artillery and was a senior partner of the family timber and shipbuilding company of Pollok, Gilmour & Co. He was MP for Leominster 1880–1906 and 1910–12 and was also DL and JP. On 20th June 1898 he was created 1st Baronet Bryngwyn. They were living at 35 Ennismore Gardens, Westminster, London in 1881. By 1891 they had moved to Bryngwyn, Much Dewchurch, Hereford. They had nine children – Annie Beatrice Rankin 1866, Margaret Ethel Rankin 1869, Robert Rankin 1870, James Reginald Lea Rankin 1871, Charles Herbert Rankin 1873, Mary Sybil Rankin 1875, Edwyn Christopher Rankin 1879, Veronica Rankin 1881 and Robert Rankin c.1884. Sir James left effects valued at £336,031/10/7 and Dame Annie left £10,170/10/6.
- Marion 'Maria' Bushell (c.1846–29th November 1901) married George Harris Lea (2nd April 1843–3rd May 1915) on 25th February 1873. George had married Mary Inglis Futvoye (died 1867) in 1864 and they had two children – Gertrude Mary Lea 1865 and Harold Futvoye Lea 1867 (later CMG DSO). George was a JP, DL (Herefordshire) and County Court Judge for Herefordshire and Shropshire. George and Marion were living at Broadlands, Hereford at the time of her death at 3 Nottingham Place, London, leaving effects valued at £1,904/13/3. George died at Broadlands leaving effects valued at £41,455/6/10. They had six children – Ethel Marion Lea 1873, George Percy Lea 1875, Gerald Ernest Lea 1877, Ida Margaret Lea 1880, Edith Brenda Lea 1883 and Ronald Sydney Harris Lea 1890. Gerald was commissioned in the Cameronians (Scottish Rifles) on 10th June 1895 and transferred to 2nd Worcestershire on 15th May 1897. He married Brenda Wadworth (1885–1962) in August 1912 and they had a daughter, Marigold Geraldine Lea, in 1914. Gerald was a captain when he died on active service on 16th September 1914 (Vendresse British Cemetery, Aisne, France – III C 2).
- Helen M Bushell (c.1848–1921) never married.
- Alfred Bushell (born c.1850).
- Catherine Smith Bushell (c.1851–21st January 1904) married James Maclean Graham (1852–2nd February 1923) in 1876. They were living at Ashton House, Leighton Road, Neston, Cheshire in 1901 and at 3 King's Buildings, Chester

at the time of her death. She left effects valued at £1,762/12/8. He was living at Ty Coch, Mold, Flintshire at the time of his death, leaving effects valued at £3,114/7/2. They had three children – Sybil Margaret Graham 1880, Duncan Maclean Graham 1882 and Arthur Graham 1886.

- Arthur Bushell (c.1853–5th July 1879).
- Herbert Smith Bushell (c.1857–30th October 1910) was a banker's clerk in 1881. He was living at 26a West Street, Brighton, Sussex at the time of his death, leaving effects valued at £80/1/1.
- Frederick Edwin Bushell (18th February 1859–9th November 1928) was an articled clerk in 1881. He became a barrister and was living at 3 Palmeira Square, Hove, Sussex at the time of his death at 74 Tisbury Road, Hove, leaving effects valued at £108,005/15/1.
- Harold Bushell (c.1859–1932) was an articled clerk merchant in 1881. He was living at 51 Old Sleine, Brighton in 1911.

His maternal grandfather, Thomas Arthur Hope (5th August 1817–7th May 1897), was born at Everton, Lancashire. His first wife, Ann Hodgkinson (born c.1817) was born at Clayton-le-Moors, Lancashire. Thomas married Christopher's grandmother, Emily Hird née Jones (28th December 1818–27th September 1887) in 1839. Thomas was a landowner and they were living at Holly Street, West Derby, Lancashire in 1851. By 1861 they had moved to Stanton Hall, Lower Bebington, Cheshire. In 1881 they were at 2 Great Cumberland Place, Marylebone and at 14 Airlie Gardens, Kensington in 1891. Emily died there, leaving effects valued at £2410. Thomas also died there, leaving an estate valued at £177,496/9/11 to his sons, Charles and Collingwood, and son-in-law Reginald Bushell. In addition to Caroline, Thomas and Emily had thirteen other children, of whom eleven are known:

- Samuel Thomas Hope (11th October 1840–18th January 1906) married Henriette Clemence/Clementine Daumas (c.1845–98). She was born in Basutoland, South Africa. He was an underwriter and ship owner in 1871 and they were living at Beacon Tree House, Victoria Road, Sefton, Lancashire. By 1881 they had moved to Stanton Hall, Lower Bebington, Cheshire. In 1891 they were at Les Douvres, St Martin, Guernsey, Channel Islands and were still there in 1901. They had seven children – Reginald Arthur Hope 1867, Rebekah Clemence Eugenie Hope 1868, Margaret Francoise Hope 1870, Miriam Adeline Hope 1871, Gertrude Hope 1873, Emily Colani Hope 1875 and Cecilia Daumas Hope 1879.
- Rebekah Bateman Hope (1842–15th August 1924) married Henry Richard Pinker (January 1849–2nd

Christopher's maternal grandparents were living at 14 Airlie Gardens, Kensington in 1891.

August 1927), a sculptor, in 1893 at Kensington. He was born at Brighton, Sussex and later changed his name to Hope-Pinker. He had married Ann Elizabeth Prodgger (1849–81) in 1873 and had four children – Elizabeth Ann Pinker 1874, Mary Edith Pinker 1875, Henry George Pinker 1876 and Richard Edgar Pinker 1879. Henry and Rebekah lived at Pilgroves, Brasted Chart, Kent. Rebekah died at Trinity Nursing Home, Falkland Park, Torquay, Devon, leaving £6,418/15/- to her husband and daughters Mary Greg and Augusta Shand. He died at his home at Pilgroves, leaving £2,447/11/4 to Elizabeth Ann Pinker, spinster.

Christopher's aunt, Rebekah Bateman Hope, married Henry Richard Hope-Pinker, a highly regarded Victorian portrait sculptor. He is best known for his statues of Charles Darwin at Oxford University of Natural History and WE Forster in Victoria Embankment Gardens. He also produced statues of Queen Victoria at George Town in Demerara, Henry Fawcett in Salisbury market place and Lord Reay in India.

- Emily Hope (22nd August 1844–29th September 1880) married Reverend Walter Harper (12th January 1848–6th January 1930) on 13th July 1875, registered at Wirral, Cheshire. He was born at Christchurch, New Zealand and was educated there at Christ's College, Christchurch and Trinity College, Oxford, England. He was ordained deacon by the Bishop of Chester in 1873 and priest in 1874. He was Curate of Belington, Cheshire 1873–75, Vicar of Ellesmere, Canterbury, NZ 1876–82, Vicar of St Michael's, Christchurch 1882–93, Principal Upper Department of Christ's College, Christchurch 1893–1906, Dean of Christchurch 1901, Fellow of Christ's College and a member of the Board of Governors of Canterbury College. She died at Southbridge, Canterbury, New Zealand. Walter lived at 229 Armagh Street, Christchurch. They had three children – Maurice Cecil Harper 1876, Ethel Hope Harper 1879 and Emily Harper 1880.
- William Hope (1846–6th January 1933) married Georgiana Catherine Squarey (7th September 1849–14th October 1944) on 6th December 1870 at Bebington, Cheshire. They lived at Riverside, West Kirby, Cheshire. In 1911 he was managing director of a waterworks and blast furnace engineering firm and they were living at Heath Hays, Woodchurch Road, Birkenhead. When he died he left £12,332/6/1. William and Georgiana had seven children – Alaric Hope 1871, Godfrey Tucker Hope 1873, Margery Hope 1875, Norah Hope 1876, Basil Hope 1877, Geoffrey Dodleston Hope 1880 and Brian Hope 1882.
- Harriett Selina Hope (1847–6th December 1937) never married. She was living at 26 St Mary Abbots Court, Kensington, London at the time of her death, leaving effects valued at £3,677.
- Mary Hope (1st March 1850–15th September 1949) married Thomas Tylston Greg MA FSA (29th November 1858–18th September 1920), a barrister, in 1895 at Kensington, London. He was a collector of English pottery and maintained the

Christopher's aunt, Mary Hope, married Thomas Tylston Greg, who wrote *A Contribution to the History of English Pottery* and *Through a Glass Lightly: Confession of a Reluctant Water Drinker.*

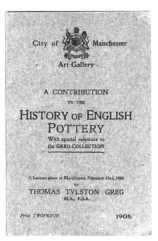

Greg Collection, Westmill Museum, Hertfordshire. He also wrote *A Contribution to the History of English Pottery* and *Through a Glass Lightly: Confession of a Reluctant Water Drinker.* They lived at Coles, Buntingford, Hertfordshire. He died at Empire Nursing Home, London, leaving £123,208/12/5. She was living at Alpha, Greenleighs, Sedgley, Staffordshire at the time of her death, leaving £34,906/16/11.

• Augusta Hope (1852–8th October 1944) married Robert Fielden (22nd November 1823–20th September 1874) in 1873 at Kensington. They had a daughter, Mary Fielden, in 1874. Augusta married William Henry 'Harry' Richmond MA (1857–9th December 1944) in 1882 at Leominster, Herefordshire. Harry was a schoolmaster, born at West Cranleigh, Surrey. They were living at Ipswich, Suffolk in 1891 and at Bank House, Kingsland, Shrewsbury, Shropshire in 1901. Harry was visiting his sister-in-law, Caroline Bushell (née Hope), at 59 Kensington Court, London at the time of the 1911 Census. They were living at The Rectory, Saham Toney, Norfolk at the time of her death, leaving effects valued at £5,118/4/-. Harry died there two months later, leaving effects valued at £6,026/9/9. Augusta and Harry had two children – Hope Richmond 1883 and Maurice Hope Richmond 1885.

• Arthur Hope (26th September 1853–1st April 1935) was educated at Rugby School and worked for six years in Liverpool with cotton brokers, west coast merchants and underwriters. He travelled extensively during this time and was in Boston and Chicago at the time of the great fires in both cities. He emigrated to New Zealand in 1876 aboard SS *Waipa*, arriving at Canterbury. He studied pastoral care at Longbeach Station for eleven months before returning to England aboard SS *Hereford*. He travelled through Russia and returned to New Zealand at the end of 1878. He joined Andrew Grant on Rangitata Island and in 1880 they purchased Richmond Station, Mackenzie County, of 36,000 acres and later expanded it to 87,000 acres with 24,000 sheep. Arthur married Frances Emily Tripp (24th March 1861–12th December 1950) on 25th July 1882 at St Thomas,

Woodbury, Geraldine. She was born at Bishop's Court, Christchurch, New Zealand. Andrew Grant sold his share of Richmond Station to VF Musgrave. In 1888 Arthur and Musgrave lost 10,000 sheep from a flock of 18,000 due to adverse winter conditions. Arthur bought out Musgrave and in 1895 he lost 21,000 sheep from a flock of 24.000, again due to a heavy winter. He travelled to England in 1897 and sold Richmond Station in 1899, returning to New Zealand in 1903. He was a member of South Canterbury Acclimatisation Society, Mackenzie County Council and was a lay member of Synod for Timaru. He was living at Tumanako, 101 Wai-iti Road, Timaru at the time of his death, leaving effects valued at £36,672/7/4. Frances also died at Timaru. Arthur and Frances had seven children – Henry Norman Hope 1883, Edith Mary Hope 1884, Owen Morley Hope 1886, Selwyn Peter Hope 1889, Roma Hope 1890, Frances Vera Hope 1898 and Arthur Howard Hope 1903.

- Charles Edward Hope (1856–20th July 1934) was a land agent living at 101 Leadenhall Street, London in 1887. He married Annie Dunbar Trotter (1860–14th March 1916) on 11th July 1893 at Westminster, London. She was born at Lincoln. They lived at Bank House, Burton, Cheshire and also at 20 Castle Street, Liverpool. When she died, she left £7,111/2/6 to her husband. He died at Bank House, leaving effects valued at £153,825/0/3.
- Collingwood Hope (1858–5th May 1949), a barrister, married Alice Thérèse Dale (January 1864–20th January 1925) in 1887. He was appointed King's Counsel (LG 1st February 1901), Recorder of the Borough of Bolton on 10th October 1903 (LG 13th October 1903), Chairman Essex Appeal Tribunal and CBE (LG 7th January 1918). They were living at The Grange, Chislehurst, Kent in 1901 and at Crix, Hatfield Peverel, Essex in 1911. He died there, leaving £74,479/19/9. They had six children – Joyce Hope 1889, Rhoda Hope 1892, Therese Mary Hope 1895, Patience Winifred Hope 1896, Evelyn Hope 1898 and Kenneth Collingwood Hope 1901.
- Bateman Hope (27th September 1865–30th December 1943), a farmer, married Caroline Margaret Tufnell (1860–14th June 1957) on 28th October 1890 at Great Waltham, Essex, where she was born. They were living at Blunts Hall, Witham, Essex in 1891 and at Tofts, Little Baddow, Essex in 1901 and Kilderry, Hatfield Peverel, Essex in 1911. They emigrated to Canada in August 1921 and settled at Jaynes Road, Duncan, Vancouver, British Columbia. They had at least three children – Margaret Irene Hope 1891, Geoffrey Bateman Hope 1893 and Sylvia Eleanor Murray Hope 1896.

Christopher was educated at:

- Moorland House, Heswall, Cheshire.
- Rugby School 1901–06.
- Corpus Christi College, Oxford 1906–09 (BA 1909), where he was captain of his college boat and rowed at the Henley Regatta.

Rugby is one of the oldest independent schools in Britain, founded in 1567 and reformed by Thomas Arnold as Headmaster 1828–41. It is one of the original seven English public schools, defined by the Public Schools Act 1868. The school was the birthplace of Rugby football, although the legend of William Webb Ellis is believed to be a myth, generated many years later. Thomas Hughes based *Tom Brown's Schooldays* on his experiences at Rugby. The inventor of Australian Rules Football, Tom Wills, also attended the school. Other famous alumni include:

- Field Marshal Sir Archibald Cassels GCB KBE DSO, Chief of the General Staff.
- General Sir Ivor Maxse KCB CVO DSO, who commanded XVIII Corps on the Western Front, gaining a reputation for innovation and training.
- Lieutenant General Arthur Percival CB DSO OBE MC OStJ DL, GOC Malaya, who surrendered Singapore to the Japanese in 1942.
- Lieutenant Commander Robert Selby Armitage was awarded the George Cross and George Medal for bomb disposal during the Second World War.
- Maurice, 1st Baron Hankey GCB GCMG GCVO PC, Secretary to the Committee of Imperial Defence and first Cabinet Secretary during the Great War.
- William Temple, an influential radical thinker was Rugby's headmaster before becoming Bishop of Manchester 1921–29, Archbishop of York 1929–42 and Archbishop of Canterbury 1942–44.
- Rupert Brooke, the war poet.
- Sir Salman Rushdie, author, essayist and Booker Prize winner.
- Charles Lutwidge Dodgson (Lewis Carroll) author of *Alice's Adventures in Wonderland*.
- Robert Hardy, actor and expert on the English longbow.
- Anthony Quayle, actor.
- Frederick Courteney Selous, explorer, hunter and conservationist in Africa.
- Neville Chamberlain, Prime Minister at the outbreak of the Second World War.
- Chris Brasher, Olympic gold medalist in 1956 and pace setter when Roger Bannister broke the four-minute mile.

Moorland House, Heswall, Cheshire.

Corpus Christi College, founded in 1517, is the twelfth oldest college in Oxford and one of the smallest, with about 350 undergraduate and graduate students. Thomas Arnold, headmaster of Rugby School 1828–41, was a student there as were the Miliband brothers. David Miliband was Foreign Secretary 2007–10 and Ed Miliband was leader of the Labour Party 2010–15.

He became a solicitor in Liverpool and was called to the Bar (Inner Temple) in 1912. He was commissioned in the Royal West Surrey Regiment Special Reserve on 8th May 1912 and was mobilised on 8th August 1914. He went to France on 13th August with 1st Battalion and was wounded on the Aisne on 14th September. He was promoted lieutenant on 20th November.

On 24th August 1915 Christopher married Rachel Edith Florence née Lambert (1892–9th February 1965) at East Ashford, Kent. The officiating vicar was his brother-in-law, Reverend Canon Douglas Waller Hobson. She was born at Sunderland and was living at Boughton Aluph, Kent. They lived for a short while with his mother at Hillside, Granville Road, St Margaret's-at-Cliffe, Dover, Kent.

They had a daughter, Elisabeth 'Betsy' Hope Bushell (15th June 1916–2002), born at Ashford, Kent. She married Alexander MacLehose (20th December 1904–1989) on 11th January 1938 at Bridge, Kent. He was born in Glasgow, Lanarkshire, Scotland. They lived at Lockerley Vicarage, Romsey, Hampshire. His brother, James Colin MacLehose (1897–1917), died whilst serving as a second lieutenant in 16th Rifle Brigade on 14th February 1917 (Brandhoek Military Cemetery, Belgium – II K 15). Elisabeth and Alexander had six children:

St Margaret's-at-Cliffe, where Christopher's mother was living in 1916.

- Andrew MacLehose (born March 1939) was a teacher in Australia for two years at Timbertop Geelong Grammar School, Victoria. He then moved to United World College of the Atlantic Limited, St Donats Castle, Llantwit Major, Glamorgan in 1960 and was appointed a director in 2004. He married Heather J Fauset in 1966 and they had two children – Laura Jayne MacLehose 1969 and Harriet Gail MacLehose 1976.
- Christopher Colin MacLehose (born July 1940 in Glasgow) was educated at Shrewsbury School and Oxford University. He worked as a journalist on the Glasgow Herald. Later he worked in the editorial office of the family printing firm by day and freelanced in the evenings for The Herald writing reviews and obituaries. He was literary editor of The Scotsman 1964–67 then moved to London, where he was an editor at Cresset Press. He was editorial director of Chatto & Windus 1972–79 and then editor-in-chief of William Collins 1979–84. He took charge of Harvill House Publishing 1984–94 and was Director of Harvill Press 1995–2006. Christopher founded MacLehose Press Ltd, Arundel House, 3 Westbourne Road, London and was appointed Director on 13th October 2009. In 2006 he received the London Book Fair Lifetime Achievement Award for International Publishing and was created CBE for services to the publishing industry in 2011. In 2016 he

was awarded the Benson Medal by the Royal Society of Literature. Christopher married Koukla Dourange in April 1985 and they had two children – Timothy Andre MacLehose and Leopold Alexander MacLehose. Koukla's grandfather was General Foch's interpreter during the Armistice negotiations.

- Diana MacLehose (April 1943–August 1998) was part of a group of British volunteers working in a school for Tibetan refugees at Mussoorie, India. She met Baljit 'Bal) Singh Malik (July 1939–February 2017) and they married in 1967. Bal was born into a wealthy family and was educated at Doon School, Dehra Dun and the School of Oriental and African Studies, University of London. They had a daughter, Sonya Malik. Bal married Kamla Bhasin, a feminist and peace activist, and they had a daughter, Meeto Malik, who died in 2006.
- David MacLehose (born 1948) was a director of John Muir Trust, Tower House, Station Road, Pitlochry, Perthshire 2011–17. He married Anne Meldrum Kennedy (born 1953) in 1992 and they lived at Over Kinfauns Farm, Church Road, Kinfauns, Perthshire and 9 Colenhaugh, Stormontfield, Perthshire.
- Timothy Alexander MacLehose (May 1950–September 1971) was living at Lockerley Vicarage, Romsey, Hampshire at the time of his death.
- Julia Elisabeth MacLehose (born April 1954).

Rachel's father, Reverend Edgar Lambert MA (21st November 1858–13th May 1949), was born at Hull, Yorkshire. He married Nora née Taylor (1866–1947) in 1889 at Guisborough, Yorkshire. She was born in Middlesbrough, Yorkshire. They were at Toxteth Park, Liverpool in 1901 and later at Wye Vicarage, Kent. They were living at Abernchaf, Abersoch, Pwllheli, Caernarvonshire in 1911 by when he was a canon. He was living at 3 Balfour Court, Folkestone, Kent at the time of his death at 10 Clifton Crescent, Folkestone, leaving effects valued at £11,594/6/7. In addition to Rachel they had six other children:

- Joseph Edgar Hugo Lambert (1890–1974), a civil servant, married Mildred Mason (1902–69) in 1925 at Canterbury, Kent. She was born at Blean, Kent. He was commissioned in the Royal Garrison Artillery on 19th July 1912. He was awarded the MC serving as a temporary captain with the King's African Rifles, LG 27th July 1918. Joseph served in the Kenya Administrative Service in a variety of appointments: District Commissioner, Wajir District, Northern Frontier Province 13th April 1929; District Officer in Kiambu District, Central Province 1st July 1934; Fort Hall District, Central Province 17th March 1938; and Mombasa District, Coast Province 28th March 1941. They were living at 1A King George Avenue, Petersfield, Hampshire at the time of her death, leaving effects valued at £22,200. He was living at Heath Hall, 8 Platts Lane, Hampstead, London at the time of his death, leaving effects valued at £7,191. They had at least two children – Christopher Hugo Lambert 1927 and Richard E Lambert 1929.
- Hilda Elizabeth Lambert (1894–1970) married Norman Guinness Wale (1892–1983) in 1919 at East Ashford, Kent. He was born at Croydon, Surrey. They were

living at 49 Lower Ashley Road, New Milton, Hampshire at the time of her death. They had twins – David G Wale and George D Wale in 1922.

- Harold Lambert, born and died 1901.
- Denis Malet Lambert (twin with Roger) (born 8th January 1904) served in the Royal Navy. He was appointed midshipman on 7th June 1922 (confirmed 10th January 1924) and acting sub lieutenant on 8th January 1925. He was promoted sub lieutenant 4th March 1926 and lieutenant 18th April 1928. Between 21st May 1923 and 16th August 1925 he served on HMS *King George V*, *Wolfhound*, *Vivid* and *Royal Sovereign*. He attended gunnery, torpedo and signalling courses at HMS *Vivid*, *Defiance* and *Victory* 13th November 1926–21st January 1927 and was graded average. Between 22nd January and 5th November 1927 he served on HMS *Vivacious*, *Viceroy* and *Wakeful*. Denis resigned on 4th February 1929 and transferred to the Royal Naval Reserve. He became a fruit farmer and married Elizabeth Ursula Cadbury (1906–) in 1929 in Birmingham, Warwickshire. She was born at King's Norton, Worcestershire, daughter of George Cadbury (1839–1922) and Elizabeth Mary Taylor (1858–1951) of the Cadbury's chocolate family. They had two daughters – Cicely C Lambert 1930 and Elizabeth A Lambert 1933. Denis was recalled as a temporary lieutenant RNR on 29th January 1940 and was promoted temporary lieutenant commander on 25th September 1943. He was awarded the DSC in the King's Birthday Honours for outstanding zeal, patience and cheerfulness and for never failing to set an example of wholehearted devotion to duty, without which the high tradition of the Royal Navy could not have been upheld, LG 11th June 1942. He was serving on the frigate HMS *Zanzibar* in February 1945.

George Cadbury was the third son of John Cadbury, who founded the Cadbury cocoa and chocolate company. George and his brother Richard took over the family business in 1861. They opened a new factory south of Birmingham in 1879. Through concern for the quality of life of their employees, they built Bournville village to house them. George was against the imperialistic policy of the Balfour government and was opposed to the Boer War, so he bought the *Daily News* to campaign against the war and sweatshop labour and for old age pensions. George Cadbury also donated many buildings and land to Birmingham and elsewhere.

- Roger Tuke Lambert (twin with Denis) (born 8th January 1904) married Jean Isobel Graham (born 1905) in 1931 at West Ashford, Kent. They moved to Kenya and he served in the Kenya Administrative Service in a variety of appointments: Magistrate 2nd Class in June 1929 with power to hold a Subordinate Court whilst Assistant District Commissioner, Machakos Ukamba Province; District Officer, Kajiado District 7th January 1933; District Commissioner, Kisumu-Londiani District, Nyanza Province 26th

January 1938; Magistrate 1st Class in June 1941 with power to hold a Subordinate Court in North Kavirondo whilst District Commissioner, Kakamega; and District Commissioner, Baringo District, Rift Valley Province 27th October 1941.

• Eric Stephen Lambert (1905–84) was a steel works manager living at 84 Bouverie Road West, Folkestone, Kent in 1929. He gained the Royal Aero Club Aviator's Certificate No.8808 flying a De Havilland Moth 85hp Cirrus Mk II at Cinque Ports Flying Club, Lympne, Kent on 18th September 1929. He was commissioned as a pilot officer in the General Duties Branch, Auxiliary Air Force in 605 (County of Warwick) Squadron, was promoted flying officer on 13th July 1931 and resigned his commission on 2nd December 1933. Eric married Irene EM Evrall (born 1917) in 1939 at Coventry, Warwickshire.

Christopher was promoted captain on 6th October 1915. He was appointed ADC to GOC 33rd Division 15th October 1915–June 1916 and returned to France in November 1915. He was appointed Staff Captain, HQ 100th Brigade on 10th August 1916. Later he was successively a company commander, second-in-command and CO of his Battalion. **He was mentioned in General Sir Douglas Haig's Despatch of 13th November 1916, LG 4th January 1917.** In December 1916 he was appointed CO 7th Queen's and acting lieutenant colonel on 16th January 1917. He was promoted major on 21st August 1917 and was a French liaison officer November–December 1917. **He was mentioned in Field Marshal Sir Douglas Haig's Despatch of 7th November 1917, LG 18th December 1917.** Appointed temporary lieutenant colonel 21st September 1917. **Awarded the DSO for gallantry and devotion to duty on many occasions, LG 1st January 1918. Awarded the VC for his actions north of Tergnier, France on 23rd March 1918, LG 3rd May 1918.**

The VC was presented by the King at Buckingham Palace on 11th May 1918. He returned to France on 22nd May 1918 and was killed in action at Cloncurry Trench, Corbie Road, south of Morlencourt, France on 8th August 1918. He is buried in Querrieu British Cemetery, France (I E 6). He is commemorated in a number of other places:

• Bushell Road, Neston, Cheshire.
• Christopher Bushell Road, Ashford, Kent.
• Christopher Bushell Prize for history founded in 1928 and awarded annually by Corpus Christi College, Oxford.
• St Margaret of Antioch War Memorial, St Margaret's-at-Cliffe, Kent. The original memorial was destroyed by enemy action during the Second World War and a replacement was erected.
• War memorial at St Gregory & St Martin's Church, Wye, Kent and on a bronze plaque in the church.

Christopher Bushell's grave in Querrieu British Cemetery.

The war memorial at St Margaret of
Antioch, St Margaret's-at-Cliffe.

Christopher Bushell's memorial plaque at St Mary and St
Helen, Neston, Cheshire.

- War memorial and plaque at the parish church of St Mary and St Helen, Neston, Cheshire.
- An oak chair in his honour was donated to the Chapel of the Queen's Royal Surrey Regiment in Guildford Cathedral, Surrey by Colonel RG Clarke CMG DSO MBE.
- War memorial of Corpus Christi College, Oxford.
- War memorial in the chapel at Rugby School, Warwickshire.
- Rugby School VC and GC Memorial dedicated in 2017.
- A plaque to his wife mentions him at St Mary the Virgin Church, Bishopbourne, Kent.
- The Department for Communities and Local Government decided to provide a commemorative paving stone at the birthplace of every Great War Victoria Cross receipient in the United Kingdom. Christophers' stone is the be dedicated at Neston Town Hall on 23rd March 2018 to mark the centenary of his award.

Rugby School war memorial. Christopher Bushell's name
is fourth from the bottom in the third column from the
left.

When Christopher died, Rachel was living at the Vicarage, Wye, Kent. In his will dated 6th September 1915 at Fort Darland, Chatham, Kent he left everything to his widow, effects valued at £919/13/10. Rachel was people's warden of Bishopbourne, Kent for twenty-five years and the Women's Voluntary Service County Borough Organiser, Canterbury and was awarded the MBE (LG 1st January 1960). She was living at 11d The Precincts, Canterbury at the time of her death in 1965 at Kent and Canterbury Hospital. She left effects valued at £1,807 to her daughter.

In addition to the VC and DSO he was awarded the 1914 Star with Mons clasp, British War Medal 1914–20 and Victory Medal 1914–19 with Mentioned-in-Despatches Oakleaf. The VC was donated to the Queen's Royal West Surrey Museum by members of his family on 27th April 2003. The VC is held by the Surrey Infantry Museum (East Surrey and Queen's Royal Surrey Regiments), which used to be at Clandon Park, Guildford, Surrey until it was severely damaged by fire on 30th April 2015. Fortunately all VC groups held by the Museum were stored in a bank. The National Trust plans to rebuild the house but the Surrey Infantry Museum will not return following the renovation and a new museum will have to be found.

L/6657 PRIVATE GEORGE WILLIAM BURDETT CLARE
5th (Royal Irish) Lancers

George Clare was born at Prospect Place, St Ives, Huntingdonshire on 18th May 1889. He was known as Donkey, Needle or Billy. His father, George William Clare (1865–1946), was born at Chatteris, Cambridgeshire. He was a printer's apprentice in 1881 living with his parents at Wellington Lane, St Ives. He married Rhoda Mehetabel Martha née May (1861–1949), born at Hemingford, Huntingdonshire, in 1888 at Peterborough, Northamptonshire. Her birth was registered at St Ives in the 4th quarter of 1863. In 1939 her date of birth

High Street, Chatteris.

Wickham Lane, Plumstead where the Clare family was living in 1911.

was recorded as 28th October 1861 and when she died in 1949 she was registered as eighty-eight years old, also indicating birth in 1861. By 1891 he was a printer/compositor and they were living at 1 Belle Vue Terrace, Plumstead, London. For an unknown reason, before 1901 George changed his surname to Howe, but most of his children were born as Clare. In 1901 they were living at 61 Cedar Grove, Greenwich, London and in 1911 at 28 Woodview Terrace, Wickham Lane, Plumstead. He later reverted to Clare. George was a patient in the Ely Institution (Public Assistance Institution), Cambridge Road, Ely in 1939. Rhoda was living at 6 Princess Terrace, South Cambridge at the time. George junior had six siblings:

- Claude Emerson/Emmerson Clare (1890–1964) served during the Great War and was gassed. He married Ellen Eileen (c.1895–1995), but no details of the marriage have been found.
- Edith 'Cis' May Clare (c.1894–1961) appeared as Clara Edith Clare in the 1901 Census and as Edith May in the 1911 Census. She worked as a cook in London and died unmarried.
- Dora 'Dolly' Clare (c.1896–1919) appeared as Dorah Howe in the 1901 Census and as Dorah Clare in the 1911 Census, when she was living with her brother William at Anchor Street, Chatteris. She died following complications with the birth of her son, Douglas Edward Howe Clare, in 1919. Her death was registered as Dora K Howe. Douglas was raised by his grandparents and was employed at Spicers Ltd. He enlisted in the Royal Armoured Corps (409111) on 7th September 1936 and was attached to the Queen's Bays

George's nephew, Sergeant Douglas Edward Howe Clare, is buried in Tobruk War Cemetery, Libya.

(2nd Dragoon Guards) as a sergeant when he was killed at Tobruk, Libya on 14th June 1942 (Tobruk War Cemetery – 1 H 29).
- Donald Hill Clare (1901–79) married Isabella Hannah Delo (1900–79) in 1924 at Canterbury, Kent. He joined the Cambridgeshire Regiment with his brother-in-law, Ken Richard Fuller, and was a company sergeant major when they sailed for the Middle East in December 1941. The ship was diverted to Singapore, arriving in February 1942, just in time to be captured when the island surrendered to the Japanese. They were prisoners of war until repatriated in late 1945. They had four children – Barbara May Caroline Clare 1926, Joyce Doris Edith Clare 1927, Brian William Clare 1931 and Keith Clare 1942.
- John 'Jack' Cyril Clare (1903–78) changed his surname to Howe. He married Elsie Nora Page (1906–90) in 1932 at Luton, Bedfordshire. He was an assistant manager in retail clothing in 1939 and they were living at 102 Ashburnham Road, Luton. He was also a Special Constable in the Bedfordshire Police (No.231). They had a daughter, Maureen J Howe, in 1936.

- Rhoda Irene 'Rene' Clare (1907–59) was registered as Howe at birth, but had changed her maiden name to Clare by the time she married Kenny Richard Fuller (1904–90) in 1924 at Linton, Cambridgeshire. He joined the Cambridgeshire Regiment with his brother-in-law, Donald Hill Clare (see above). Rhoda and Kenny had eight children – Iris Maureen Fuller 1925, Dora Edith Anne Fuller 1926, Gaynor I Fuller 1928, Frances Clare Fuller 1930, Ivy R Fuller 1932, Miriam D Fuller 1938, Kenneth Richard George Fuller 1940 and Martin J Fuller 1949. Iris' first husband, David Royston Phillips (1917–2009), was captured during the Battle of Crete in 1941 and was interned in Poland. Kenny married secondly, Rose Chapman (1910–90), in 1961.

George's paternal grandfather, George Emerson Clears (1838–1902), born at Louth, Lincolnshire, was a turner and engine fitter. In 1841 he was living at Newmarket and Quarry, Louth, in 1851 at Long Lane, Louth and in 1861 at Quarry, Louth. He changed his name to Clare after 1861. George married Emma Comfort née Hill (1842–1912), but no record of their marriage has been found. In 1851 she was living at Hive End, Chatteris with her mother and sisters. She was a seamstress in 1861 still living at Hive End. George

Louth, Lincolnshire, where George's paternal grandfather, George Emerson Clears, was born.

and Emma were living at Wellington Lane, St Ives in 1871 and moved to Anchor Street, Chatteris between 1891 and 1901. They adopted Mary Ann Smith (born 1885) before 1901.

His maternal grandfather, William May (c.1818–1906) was a waterman. He married Frances née Mayes (c.1822–91) in 1844. By 1851 they were living at 17 Victoria Terrace, Hemingford Grey, Huntingdonshire. In 1871 she was living there with four of her children, but there was no mention of her husband. By 1881 William was the foreman of the coal wharf at St Andrew the Less, Cambridge and the family was living at Hills Road, Avenue Coal, Wharf Cottage. In 1901 he was a lock keeper living with his single daughters, Joanna and Hephzibah, at The Slaunch, St Ives, Huntingdonshire. In addition to Rhoda they had twelve other children:

- Possibly Edward William May (1844–45).
- Susanna May (born and died 1845).
- William George May (1848–1854).
- Frances Susanna May (born 1850).
- Maud Mary May (1851–1922) never married.
- Sarah Melinda May (1853–1922) married Samuel Collings (1850–1935) in 1876. His birth was registered as Samuel Collins. He was a college waiter and

she was a bell maker college [sic] in 1881 and they were living at 14 Malcolm Street, Cambridge. By 1901 they had moved to 11 Benson Street, Chesterton, Cambridgeshire. They had at least four children – Alfred Ernest T Collings 1876, Samuel H Collings 1879, Frederick H Collings 1882 and Frances Emma M Collings 1891.

- Joannah Sylvanus May (1854–1945). Her middle name has also been seen as Salvinus. In 1901 she was a housekeeper for her father. She married Edward Jonas Andrews (1843–1917), a beating (sic) engineer in a paper mill, in 1909. Edward had married Frances Rowlinson (1845–76) in 1863 and they had five children – William Rowlinson Andrews 1865, Edward Andrews 1867, Charles Jonas Andrews 1870, Albert Andrews 1872 and Henry Andrews 1874. He then married Eliza Nottage (1836–1907) in 1877 and they had an adopted daughter, Edith Bridge (born c.1887). Edward and Joannah were living at Princes Terrace, Sawston in 1911.
- Joseph William John May (born 1855) was a shoemaker's apprentice in 1871 and a steamboat engine driver in 1881, when he was recorded as Thomas in the Census. He married Emily Hand (born 1859) in 1883.
- Hephzibah Mahala May (1857–1931) was a domestic servant in 1901. By 1911 she was a housekeeper for Arthur J Chater at Broadway House, Bourn, Cambridgeshire. She never married.
- Possibly twins Elizabeth and Zachariah (born and died 1858).
- Kedar William Hammaway May (1860–1913) was a railway carman in 1881 and a railway points shunter in 1891. He married Alice Allen (1864–1932) in 1889. They were living at 8 Bread Street, Fletton, Huntingdonshire in 1891. By 1901 they had moved to 43 Orchard Street, Fletton. They were still there in 1911, when he was recorded as William. They had four children – Maud Alice May 1890, George Burdett May 1892, William Allen May 1894 and Ernest May 1897.

George was brought up by his grandparents, George and Emma Clare, in Anchor Street, Chatteris. He was educated at Chatteris Church School and sang regularly in church services and at local concerts. George began working for a land surveyor and then for Reuben Shank, a builder, as his pony and cart driver. By 1911 George was a groom, working for Mr Hazeldine, a veterinary surgeon, and was living with his sister, Dorah, at Anchor Street, Chatteris.

George served in the Chatteris Troop, Bedfordshire Yeomanry for eight years and registered for the National Reserve on 29th January 1914. He was mobilised when war broke out to the Remounts Department and transferred later to 5th Lancers, probably before going to France on 4th December 1914. **Awarded the VC for his actions at Bourlon Wood, France on 28th/29th November 1917, LG 11th January 1918.** He was killed during his VC action and is commemorated on the Cambrai Memorial (Panel 1). As he never married, the VC was presented to his parents by the King at Buckingham Palace on 2nd March 1918. George is commemorated in a number of other places:

George Clare's Memorial Plaque. These were issued after the war to the next-of-kin of service personnel who died as a result of the war. The plaques were made of bronze and were known as the 'Dead Man's Penny' or 'Death Penny'. They were produced at the Memorial Plaque Factory in Church Road, Acton, London until December 1920 when production shifted to the Royal Arsenal, Woolwich. Plaques were issued with a commemorative scroll and a letter from the King (Chatteris Community Archive).

A troop of Bedfordshire Yeomanry before the First World War.

George Clare's name on the Cambrai Memorial.

George's memorial window in the Lady Chapel of St Peter's and St Paul's Church (Chatteris Community Archive).

- Clare Street (formerly Anchor Street), Chatteris, Cambridgeshire.
- George Clare Surgery, Chatteris, Cambridgeshire, opened in 2005.
- Memorial window in the Lady Chapel, St Peter's and St Paul's Church, Market Hill, Chatteris, Cambridgeshire, where he was a chorister as a boy. The window was paid for by public subscription and was dedicated on 4th September 1918.
- Chatteris War Memorial, outside St Peter's and St Paul's Church, unveiled in 1920 by the Lord Lieutenant of Cambridgeshire.
- The Department for Communities and Local Government decided to provide a commemorative paving

St Peter's and St Paul's Church, Market Hill, Chatteris, Cambridgeshire.

stone at the birthplace of every Great War Victoria Cross recipient in the United Kingdom. George's stone was dedicated at Chatteris War Memorial, Parish Church of St Peter & St Paul, Market Hill, Chatteris, Cambridgeshire on 28th November 2017 to mark the centenary of his award.

In addition to the VC he was awarded the 1914–15 Star, British War Medal 1914–20 and Victory Medal 1914–19. His VC is understood to have been sold to an English collector before passing to Dwight L Thomson, 601 North Street, Hamilton, Ohio, USA. It was purchased by Spink & Son, who sold it to Major General AC Shortt, of Hayward's Heath, Sussex. He sold it to 16th/5th The Queen's Royal Lancers for £550 in 1961. The campaign medals passed to George's cousin, Martha Samson (née Smith), and were reunited with the VC when they were presented to the Regiment by the family. The VC was held by the Queen's Royal Lancers Museum, Belvoir Castle, near Grantham, Lincolnshire until the Castle became unavailable. The VC was in storage until the Queen's Royal Lancers and Nottinghamshire Yeomanry Museum at Thoresby Courtyard, Thoresby Park, Ollerton, Nottinghamshire opened in 2011.

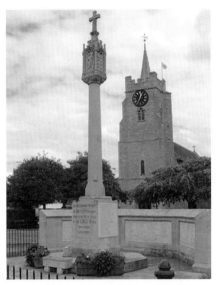

Chatteris War Memorial (Memorials to Valour).

The Queen's Royal Lancers and Nottinghamshire Yeomanry Museum at Thoresby Courtyard, Thoresby Park, Ollerton (QRLNY Museum).

50720 PRIVATE HERBERT GEORGE COLUMBINE
9th Squadron Machine Gun Corps

Herbert Columbine was born at Penge, South London on 28th November 1893. His father, Herbert Edward Columbine (1865–11th July 1900), appears as Edmund in the 1871 Census, living with his parents. He married Emma Jane née Royal (1855–1945) in 1893 at Thetford, Norfolk. She was born at Brandon, Suffolk. Herbert served during the Second Boer War as a private in 2nd Lincolnshire (748) and was killed in action at Zillikat's Nek, South Africa. Emma left Walton-on-the-Naze,

Essex for London after her husband's death as she had no family connections there. In 1901 she was a furniture dealer living with her only son at 44 Anerley Road, Penge, Surrey. By 1911 she was living alone at 33 Crescent Road, Walton-on-the-Naze, on small private means and needlework. She refused to accept the Army pension to which she was entitled after her husband's death. The people of Walton set up a street collection and raised £312/9/2, which she exchanged for War Bonds.

Herbert's paternal grandfather, Mark Columbine (c.1834–July 1900), was a tailor. He married Sarah née Clarke (c.1836–1918) at Shoreditch, London in 1858. His surname was registered as Colyonbine. They were living at 3 Barnsbury Park, Islington, London in 1861, at 88 Offord Road, Finsbury, London in 1871 and later at 23 Montrell Road, Streatham, London. Sarah was living with her daughters, Rose and Louisa, at 14 Paragon, Streatham, London in 1881. They were visitors in the home of William Caulier Sherriff, an unmarried accountant aged 50, born at Kington, Hertfordshire. In 1871 he was lodging with the family and was an unemployed upholsterer. In 1901 she was living as head of household at 21 Montrell Road, Streatham with daughters Florence, Louise, Emily and Rose, plus a boarder, Frederick William Clements, aged 37, born in Sussex. William Sherriff was boarding next door at 23 Montrell Road, living on own means. William died there

Anerley Road, Penge about the time that Emma and Herbert lived there.

Penge High Street.

Crescent Road, Walton-on-the-Naze.

on 9th January 1917, leaving effects valued at £126/9/- to Susan Elizabeth Sherriff, spinster. Sarah died at 23 Montrell Road on 17th October 1918, leaving effects valued at £469/13/6 to her unmarried daughters, Florence and Louise. In addition to Herbert, Mark and Sarah had seven other children:

- Mark William Columbine (1859–21st February 1928) married Grace Musgrave (born 1861) in 1879. He was a manufacturing jeweler. In the 1891 Census he was recorded as William Columbine and they were living at 129 Highbury Quadrangle, Islington. He was living at 5 Palmeira Square, Hove, Sussex at the time of his death, leaving effects valued at £43,486/5/6. He was recorded as Mark William or Lewis William Columbine on his probate document. Mark and Grace had three children – Sidney William Columbine 1879, Leonard Arthur W Columbine 1883 and William Herbert Columbine 1886.

Herbert's uncle, Mark William Columbine, was living on Palmeira Square, Hove, Sussex at the time of his death. His jewellery business was very successful as his effects were valued at £43,486, about £2.5M today.

- Alice Ann Columbine (1863–72).
- Sarah Emily Columbine (1867–1938) never married and was living at 23 Montrell Road, Streatham at the time of her death there on 21st May 1938, leaving effects valued at £1,108/11/8 to her sisters Florence and Louise.
- Louise Columbine (born c.1868) was aged three in the 1871 Census with her parents and siblings but no birth or death records have been found. It is assumed that she did not survive infancy as another Louise was born in 1873 – see below.
- Florence 'Flora' Mary Columbine (1869–24th December 1947) never married. She was living at 23 Montrell Road, Streatham at the time of her death. Probate records her death in December 1948.
- Rose Beatrice Columbine (1871–9th April 1953) was living at 76 Peckham Road, Camberwell, London when she married Edward Savage (1875–1954) on 8th June 1904 at Camberwell Parish Church. He was an engineer for a timber merchant in 1911 and they were living at 76 Upland Road, East Dulwich, London.
- Louise Mary Columbine (1873–1957) never married. When she was in hospital in 1955 the doctors felt that the sight of her nephew's VC might help her condition. Frinton and Walton Council sent it to her by post, together with newspaper cuttings kept with the medal. The Council even returned the 2/- postal order she sent to cover the cost of postage.

His maternal grandfather, Robert Royal (c.1816–67), was born at Weeting, Norfolk. His year of birth ranges from c.1812 to 1819 in the various census returns. He married Harriet née Smith (c.1823–1911) on 8th April 1844 at St Peter, Brandon, Suffolk. She was born at Swaffham, Norfolk. He was an agricultural labourer in 1851 and they were living at Back Lane, Swaffham, Norfolk. By 1861 he was a maltster's labourer and they were living at Church Walk, Brandon, Suffolk. In 1891 she was a provision dealer, living with her daughters Charlotte and Emma at 48 Ernest Street, Norwood, London. In addition to Emma they had six other children:

Herbert's maternal grandparents married at St Peter, Brandon, Suffolk in 1844. There was a church there when the Domesday Book was compiled but the earliest parts of the current church date from the late 13th century. It was added to in the late 14th and 16th centuries and was restored in 1842 and 1873, so that much of the fabric is now Victorian (Geograph).

- Henry Royal (1847–1919) worked variously as a farm labourer, general labourer, porter and a labourer in a gas factory. He married Elizabeth Hart (1847–1931) in 1872 at Guisborough, Yorkshire. She was born at Thetford, Norfolk. They were living at 7a Sleaford Street, Battersea, London in 1891, at 5 Sleaford Street, Battersea in 1901 and at 54 Stewarts Road, Battersea in 1911. They had eight children including – Harry Royal 1875, Edwin Ernest Royal 1880, Emma Jane Ruth Royal 1882, Robert Charles Royal 1884, James William Royal 1885, Frank Royal 1887 and Sarah Royal c.1888.
- Anna Maria Royal (twin with Harriet) (1848–1934) never married.
- Harriet Ruth Royal (twin with Anna) (1848–1947) never married.
- Charlotte Elizabeth Royal (1852–1945) never married.
- Robert Royal (1857–94) was a stoker in 1891 and a patient at District South Western Hospitals, Lambeth.
- Drucilla Royal (c.1861–1950) was a housemaid at 29 Alfred Place West, Kensington, London in 1881. She married Garrett Dundon (c.1853–1928) in 1881. He was born at Cork, Ireland. They had seven children – Mary Margaret Dundon 1884, William Garrett Dundon 1890, Ruth Dundon 1892, Annie Dundon 1895, Charlotte Catherine A Dundon 1900, Drucilla Minnie Dundon 1902 and Kathleen Emma Dundon 1904.

Herbert was educated at Melvin Road Council School, Penge. He enlisted at Colchester in 19th (Queen Alexandra's Own Royal) Hussars (5780) in 1911 and went to France on 23rd August 1914 with the Regiment's machine gun detachment. He transferred to the Machine Gun Corps on 27th June 1916. **Awarded the VC for his actions at Hervilly Wood, France on 22nd March 1918, LG 3rd May 1918.**

He was killed during the VC action and is commemorated on the Pozières Memorial (Panels 93/94). As Herbert never married, the VC was presented to his mother by the King in the quadrangle at Buckingham Palace on 22nd June 1918. Herbert is commemorated in a number of other places:

Herbert Columbine's name on the Pozières Memorial, bottom of the middle column.

- A bronze bust, erected on The Esplanade, Walton-on-the-Naze, Essex, was unveiled by Lord Byng, former Commander of Third Army, in 1920. It was vandalised several times in the 1970s and was moved to the Memorial Gardens, close to the town's war memorial on Walton and Church Roads. The bust was stolen in 1990 and a replica was produced but the original was then found.
- Columbine Centre, Walton-on-the-Naze, Essex opened in March 1993, where the original bronze bust is now located.
- Columbine Gardens, Walton-on-the-Naze.
- War Memorial, Memorial Gardens, Walton Road, Walton-on-the-Naze.
- Bronze statue, by John Doubleday, was unveiled by Field Marshal Lord Guthrie on the seafront at Walton-on-the-Naze on 1st August 2014. The Columbine Statue Fund was initiated by Michael Turner several years previously but unfortunately he did not survive to see the project come to fruition. The Patron of the Columbine Statue Fund was Dame Judi Dench.
- Plaque at Ashworth Barracks Museum, Doncaster, South Yorkshire unveiled by Lord Lieutenant Andrew Coombe on 22nd June 2015.
- Memorial at All Saints Garrison Church, Aldershot, Hampshire.
- Department for Communities and Local Government commemorative VC paving stones were dedicated at Penge War Memorial, High Street, Bromley and at his statue on the seafront at Walton-on-the-Naze on 22nd March 2018 to mark the centenary of his award.

Walton-on-the-Naze War Memorial. Herbert's name is about halfway down the left column of the upper panel.

The statue of Herbert Columbine dedicated in August 2014

In addition to the VC he was awarded the 1914 Star with 'Mons' clasp, British War Medal 1914–20 and Victory

Medal 1914–19. The VC is held by the Royal British Legion (Walton-on-the-Naze & District), Vicarage Lane, Walton-on-the-Naze, Essex. His medals are currently displayed at the Essex Regiment Museum, Chelmsford.

SECOND LIEUTENANT EDMUND DE WIND
15th Battalion, The Royal Irish Rifles

Edmund De Wind was born at Kinvara, Killinchy Road, Comber, Co Down, Ireland on 11th December 1883. His surname has also been seen as De Wind and DeWind. His father, Arthur Hughes De Wind (10th March 1837– 22nd February 1917), was born at Malacca, Malaya. He completed studies at a private school in London, gained a degree in civil engineering from London University in 1860 and was then employed as an assistant engineer on the London and North Eastern Railway. He married Margaret Jane née Stone (8th March 1841–8th April 1922) on 12th April 1863 at St Mary's Parish Church, Comber. Shortly afterwards they moved to Singapore, where he was Commissioner of Public and Municipal Works until 1872. Arthur was Chief Engineer and Permanent Way Inspector of the Belfast & County Down Railway March 1876–December 1877, when he resigned having incurred the Board's displeasure with his report into an accident at Downpatrick. He then set up a private practice as an architect and land surveyor, which he continued until his death. He was also the organist and

The square at Comber. The town is the birthplace of Thomas Andrews (1873–1912), managing director and head of the drafting department of Harland and Wolff in Belfast. He was in charge of designing RMS *Titanic* and was on board for her maiden voyage. When the ship hit an iceberg on 14th April 1912 he died with 1,513 others and his body was not recovered.

St Mary's Parish Church, Comber is on the site of a Cistercian Abbey built in 1199. The present church dates from 1840 and was extended in 1912 and 2008.

choirmaster at Comber Parish Church for forty years. In 1901 the family was living at Castle Street, Comber and at Kinvara, Killinchy Road, Comber from 1909. By 1911 he was living with his daughter Florence at The Square, Comber, Co Down and Margaret was living with her daughter, Louise Margaret, at Town Parks, Comber. The family also lived at Hill View 1874–86, Uraghamore 1886–1903, 32–32a Bridge Street and 31 Castle Street, all in Comber. Edmund had seven siblings:

- Arthur Adrian De Wind (c.1864–4th February 1908) was an engineer who emigrated to India and became a tea planter at Dibrugarh, Assam, where he also hunted big game. He died a bachelor of yellow fever at Bhamum Gardens, Upper Assam.
- Catherine Anne De Wind (1865–1948) married James Graham Allen (died 1924) of The Square, Comber. There were no children.
- Louise Margaret De Wind (c.1870–27th May 1917).
- Alice Maud De Wind (3rd November 1873–7th November 1947) was a bookkeeper in 1901, living with her father at Castle Street, Comber. She was living at Town Parks, Comber in 1911.
- Norman De Wind (24th January 1875–18th February 1974) worked for the Belfast Banking Co in Armagh and Belfast until 1896 and then for his brother-in-law, James Allen, who had a mechanical engineering firm in Comber. Norman emigrated to America in 1907 and worked as a design engineer and inventor in Chicago, Illinois, initially to design a petrol powered motor road roller for Austin Manufacturing Co. He was general sales manager for several companies – Austin May & Co, Mussen's of Montreal, Canada 1921–24 and Parsons Engineering Company's Eastern Sales Manager and Vice President 1927. He married Ethel Andrews (1876–1976) on 30th December 1909 at Comber, Co Down. Ethel was cousin of Thomas Andrews, Managing Director of Harland & Wolff shipyard in Belfast, who supervised the design and construction of RMS *Titanic* and went down with the ship when it sank on its maiden voyage in April 1912. Other relatives were prominent in Ulster politics. They were living at 110 Pricefield Road, Toronto, Ontario in 1918 and are also known to have lived at Aurora, Illinois, USA. She was living at 11 Whittlesey Avenue, New Milford, Connecticut, USA in 1976. Norman and Ethel had two sons:
    ◦ Norman 'Norrie' John Stone De Wind (1912–2012) was born at Chicago. He was christened in October 1912 and the ceremony was attended by his uncle Edmund, who travelled from Edmonton, and his aunt Edith, who travelled from Ireland. Norman was educated at Trinity College School, Port Hope, Ontario 1929–30, Grinnell College, Iowa, USA and then studied architecture at Harvard. He married Helen Susan Rogers (1915–2003) in 1939. He was an architect in 1947 and they lived in Alexandria, Virginia, USA and also at Pittsburgh, Pennsylvania, USA. They had two children – Robin Heid De Wind and Jo Ann De Wind.

° Adrian William Andrews De Wind (1913–2009) was educated at the Sorbonne, Paris, France and graduated from Harvard University, Cambridge, Massachusetts, USA as a Bachelor of Laws (LLB) in 1937. He married Joan Elizabeth Mosenthal (1915–97) in 1941. They lived in Manhattan, New York, USA and had four children – Adrian William Andrews De Wind, John De Wind, Barbara De Wind and Susan De Wind.

• Florence Madeline De Wind (born 12th May 1877) travelled to Canada in October 1914 to marry George WJ O'Meara of Killinchy Rectory. George had gone ahead to buy land at Wainwright, Alberta. Florence stayed with her brother, Edmund, in the same boarding house in Edmonton until 2nd November, when they travelled to Wainwright for the wedding, at which Edmund gave her away. Florence and George lived at Wainwright before settling in Lethbridge, Alberta. Florence planted grain to support the war effort and worked for health and welfare charities, including the Independent Daughters of Empire on behalf of veterans' children and orphans and the Nursing Mission Board to provide public health training at a local school of nursing. They had three children – Isobel Florence O'Meara, Margaret Wingfield O'Meara and Edmund W Burton O'Meara.

• Edith Caroline De Wind (c.1879– 24th December 1955) was born in India according to the 1911 Census of Ireland. She qualified as a nurse, King's College Hospital (certificate) December 1894–December 1897 and worked at Birmingham General Hospital February 1898–July 1900. Thereafter she was a private nurse. In 1901 she was living with her father at Castle Street, Comber. She also lived at 62 Ladbroke Grove, Notting Hill Gate. Edith volunteered for the Friend's Ambulance Unit in France, formed by Quakers but including non-Quaker volunteers. She arrived in France on 11th November 1914 and was a sister at the Unit's hospital at Villa St Pierre, Malo-les Bains. The hospital closed in July 1915 due to patients being directed to larger hospitals in the area. Edith transferred to No.3 British Red Cross Hospital in Abbeville, where she was appointed matron. When the hospital

Malacca (now Melaka) was one of the earliest Malay sultanates. It was conquered by the Portuguese in 1511. In 1641 the Dutch defeated the Portuguese and ruled Malacca until ceding it to the British in 1824 in exchange for Bencoolen on Sumatra. It was ruled by the British East India Company and later as a Crown Colony. Malacca formed part of the Straits Settlements, which also included Singapore and Penang. In 1946 it became part of the Malayan Union, which in 1948 became the Federation of Malaya. It became independent on 31st August 1957 and in 1963 became Malaysia with the merger of Malaya with Sabah, Sarawak and Singapore. Malacca was designated a UNESCO World Heritage Site in 2008.

closed in January 1916 Edith returned to Comber, where she was engaged in local efforts to support soldiers. She was awarded the Royal Red Cross in addition to the usual trio of campaign medals. After the war Edith was President of the Comber British Legion and devoted herself to the welfare of ex-service men. She worked for other charitable causes through Comber Parish Church and the Comber District Nursing Society. Having emigrated to Canada in April 1952, she returned to live at 71 Eglantine Avenue, Belfast in August 1954 and died at No.74.

Edmund's paternal grandfather, Johannes Bartholomew De Wind, was the son of JB De Wind, who was Governor of Malacca, Malaya before the Dutch ceded it to the British. Johannes was a planter in Malacca. He married Lily Maria (also known as Elizabeth). In addition to Arthur they had at least ten other children, all born in Malacca:

- Catherine Maria De Wind (born c.1821) married Lieutenant Hay Ferrier (1811–54), 48th Madras Native Infantry, in 1838 at Christ Church, Malacca. Hay was born in Edinburgh, Scotland and was appointed Assistant to the Governor of the Eastern Settlements in 1839. He was granted local rank of major on 20th June 1854, but died on 24th July at Peringit, Malacca. They had seven children – Louis John George Ferrier 1840, Hay Arthur Ferrier 1842, Alexander Walter Ferrier, George Henry Ferrier 1847, Adrian Norman Ferrier 1849, Charles David Ferrier 1850 and James Archibald Ferrier 1854.
- Charlotta Lubertha De Wind (born 1824) married Willem Fredrik Baumgarten (born 1815) in 1852.
- Henry De Wind (died 1828).
- Eliza Clementina De Wind (died 1828).
- Bartholomew Lubert De Wind (born and died 1827).
- Lily Maria De Wind (born and died 1828).
- Rozalie Catherine De Wind (born and died 1831).
- Edmund Robert De Wind (born 1836).
- Lily Ann De Wind (born 1838).
- Johannes Bartholomeus De Wind (1839–91), known as John Bartholomew De Wind, married Eliza Jones (c.1852–1947) in 1880 at Hackney, London. He was a retired government officer at the time of the 1881 Census, living with his wife and sister-in-law, Emma L Jones, at 43 Windmill Road, Edmonton. Eliza was living with her children at 169 Ladbroke Street, Kensington in 1891. They had five children – Lillie Maria De Wind 1881, John Bartholomew De Wind 1883, Angelique Edith De Wind 1886, Gertrude Beatrice De Wind 1889 and Louis De Wind 1891.

His maternal grandfather, Guy Stone (1808–62) married Anne née Graham (1810–87). He was a member of the committee that met at the Donegal Arms Hotel, Belfast to promote approval for the construction of the Belfast & County Down Railway to Parliament. He later served as the Company Chairman. In addition to Margaret they had five other children:

- Anne Stone (1831–1910).
- Frances Elizabeth Stone (1834–1903).
- Mary Stone (1837–1906).
- Catherine Stone (1843–59).
- Samuel Stone (1846–1921).

Edmund was educated privately at home by a governess, Miss Riddel, and then at Campbell College, Belfast May 1895–December 1900. Although he was quite delicate, he was a keen sportsman, participating in hockey, cricket (North Down Cricket Club), badmington, tennis, fishing, golf, shooting and sailing on Strangford Lough. He was initially employed as a Bank of Ireland clerk in Belfast and Cavan. In Cavan he was close to Mary 'Mollie' Emily Robinson, daughter of William J Robinson, a solicitor in Boyle, Co Roscommon. On 1st November 1911 he emigrated to Canada, travelling on SS *Royal George* from Bristol to Montreal. Edmund was employed by the Bank of Commerce and worked at the Toronto, Yorkton, Humboldt and Edmonton branches, the latter as chief accountant. He enlisted in 2nd Regiment of Queen's Own Rifles of Canada, Canada's oldest active militia unit, on 15th April 1912 but had to resign on 12th September when he transferred to Yorkton with the Bank. He also made small investments in real estate and stocks and became Chief Warden at All Saints Episcopal Cathedral, Edmonton. While in Canada Edmund took a keen interest in the Ulster Volunteer Force.

Edmund De Wind in his Legion of Frontiersmen uniform. The Legion was a paramilitary group formed in Britain in 1905 by Roger Pocock, a former North-West Mounted Police constable and veteran of the Boer War. It was a field intelligence corps with headquarters in London and branches throughout the empire to prepare patriots for war and foster vigilance in peacetime. During the Great War its members filled the ranks of a number of Canadian battalions, the Newfoundland Regiment and 25th Royal Fusiliers. Various groups still exist but the Legion never gained official recognition.

When war broke out Edmund served in the Legion of Frontiersmen until 16th November 1914 when he enlisted in 31st Battalion (Calgary Regiment) CEF at Edmonton, Alberta (79152). He was described as 5′ 6″ tall, weighing 140 lbs, with medium complexion, dark blue eyes, dark brown hair (slightly grey) and his religious denomination was Church of England. The Battalion formed at Calgary in the Horse Show Buildings and trained there until 12th May 1915 when it entrained for Quebec. The Battalion sailed for England aboard RMS *Carpathia* on 17th May (forty officers and 1,033 men) and SS *Northland* on 29th May (one officer and eighty-nine men). Separate documents in Edmund's service record indicate he was aboard both ships and it has not been possible to resolve this. The Battalion was posted to Shorncliffe, Kent for training, the main party arriving there on 29th May and

Campbell College was founded in 1894 with a bequest from Henry James Campbell, who made his fortune in the linen trade. In 1935 the gate lodge was the scene of a gun battle between the IRA and RUC, when the former attempted to secure the arms in the OTC armoury. Edmund de Wind was one of 134 former students who died in the First World War. The author CS Lewis attended the school for two months. William John English VC (1882–1941) was also educated at the College.

SS *Zeeland*, launched in 1900, was built for the International Mercantile Marine Co. Her maiden voyage was from Antwerp to New York on 13th April 1901. Her name was Dutch, but as it sounded German it was changed during the war to SS *Northland*. She served as a troopship for a while as HMT *Northland*, but reverted to *Zeeland* after the war and was renamed SS *Minnesota*. She sailed primarily for Red Star Line, but was also chartered to White Star Line, International Navigation Co, American Line, and Atlantic Transport Line, all subsidiaries of the International Mercantile Marine Co. Her last voyage was in September 1929 and she was scrapped in 1930.

the smaller party on *Northland* on 12th June. The Battalion was located in various camps, including Dibgate, Lydd, Beachborough and Otterpool. On 30th July Edmund was absent for over thirteen hours from Otterpool and forfeited two days' pay. The Battalion was inspected by the King on 2nd September. Edmund embarked for France on 15th September. He was a member of the Machine Gun Section by then or shortly afterwards.

Edmund saw action at Ypres, the St Eloi craters in April 1916 and at Courcelette on the Somme in September. In May 1916 he attended training on the

The Edmonton branch of the Bank of Commerce.

Lewis gun as the heavy machine guns had been transferred to the Brigade Machine Gun Company. He was admitted to a field ambulance for treatment after the battle of Courcelette. He was in the machine gun section of C Company at the time but the nature of his wound is not known. He went on eight days leave to Ireland in the autumn of 1916.

On 11th December 1916 Edmund applied for a commission in 20th Royal Irish Rifles, by when he was 5′ 8½″ tall and weighed 150 lbs. On 20th March 1917 he was posted to 21st Canadian Reserve Battalion, Alberta Regiment Depot, Bramshott. Whilst there he appears to have been taken ill as he was at the Canadian Casualty Assembly Centre on 21st April and the British Hospital, Bramshott on 31st May. On 6th June he joined No.17 Officer Cadet Battalion, Kinmel Park, Rhyl, Wales. Edmund

The First World War camp at Bramshott.

was discharged to a commission from No.2 Canadian Discharge Depot, London on 25th September, described as 5′ 8″ tall, with fresh complexion, blue eyes, brown hair and his religious denomination was Church of Ireland.

Edmund was commissioned into 17th (Reserve) Battalion, Royal Irish Rifles at Dundalk, Ireland on 26th September 1917. He and Mollie agreed to marry and he modified his will on 26th November 1917 to refer to her as his fiancée and to leave her and his unmarried sisters, Edith and Alice, equal portions of his estate. He was posted to 3rd (Reserve) Battalion, Belfast in December 1917 before returning to the front to join 15th Battalion. Awarded the VC for his actions at Racecourse Redoubt, near Grugies, France on 21st March 1918, LG 15th May 1919. He was killed during his VC action and is commemorated on the Pozières Memorial (Panel 74). It is understood that he had applied to return to the Canadian Army just before his death. The delay between the VC action and gazette date is due to the CO of the Battalion, Lieutenant Colonel Claud George Cole-Hamilton DSO, being a prisoner and unable to make the recommendation until his return from captivity. Edmund never married, although he was engaged at the time of his death.

Edmund de Wind's name on the Pozieres Memorial, bottom left.

On 21st August 1918 Private Alfred Wright, D Company, 15th Royal Irish Rifles, made a statement to the Red Cross, witnessed by the commandant of his prisoner of war camp. He stated that about noon on 21st March he had witnessed Edmund with his platoon when a mortar bomb landed and killed him instantly. Wright stated that Second Lieutenant Hilder was also a witness but he did not know where he was being held prisoner. This information reached the War Office via the Red Cross in Copenhagen. Based on Wright's evidence and the lapse of time, the War Office accepted that death had occurred on 21st March 1918 and this was communicated to Edmund's mother by letter on 30th September 1918. In the meantime she had received the news from the Red Cross in Geneva in a letter dated 19th August.

The VC was presented to his mother by the King at Buckingham Palace on 28th June 1919. He left effects valued at £1,020/15/7 in his will dated 26th November 1917, which was administered by his brother, Norman, and sister, Catherine. Mollie was badly affected by Edmund's death. She became a companion helper in Dublin and later in Belfast. Edmund is commemorated in a number of other places:

Comber War Memorial.

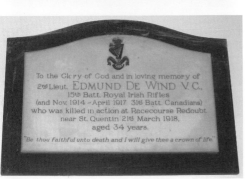

The two memorial plaques in St Mary's Church, Comber.

The captured German gun in the town square of Comber being prepared for removal for scrap in the Second World War.

- Comber, Co Down, Northern Ireland:
  - ° War Memorial.
  - ° De Wind Drive.
  - ° Edmund De Wind VC House, Andrews Memorial Primary School.
  - ° A captured German gun in the town square, a memorial to Edmund, was scrapped in the Second World War and the commemorative plaque is now in the porch of St Mary's Church of Ireland Parish Church.
  - ° Memorial in St Mary's Church of Ireland Parish Church.
  - ° Ulster History Circle Blue Plaque on his former home dedicated in 2007.
  - ° His picture is on the standard of Loyal Orange Lodge 100, Comber Ulster Defenders.
  - ° A Department for Communities and Local Government commemorative VC paving stone was dedicated at The Square, Comber on 21st March 2018 to mark the centenary of his award.

The standard of Loyal Orange Lodge 100 with the image of Edmund de Wind in the lower centre.

- Belfast, Northern Ireland:
  - ° Named at the foot of a pillar at the west front door of St Anne's Cathedral, Belfast.
  - ° War Memorial, memorial plaque and photograph at Campbell College.
- VC memorial stone at Ulster Tower, Thiepval, France.
- Alberta, Canada:
  - ° Mount De Wind at the head of the Little Berland River, in the Berland Range of Willmore Wilderness Park, north of Jasper National Park.
  - ° Canadian Bank of Commerce Memorial and Book of Remembrance in the Canadian Imperial Bank of Commerce, Edmonton.
  - ° Memorial at All Saints Cathedral, Edmonton.

Campbell College War Memorial.

Mount De Wind.

- Named on a Victoria Cross obelisk to all Canadian VCs at Military Heritage Park, Barrie, Ontario dedicated by The Princess Royal on 22nd October 2013.
- Named on one of eleven plaques honouring 175 men from overseas awarded the VC for the Great War. The plaques were unveiled by the Senior Minister of State at the Foreign & Commonwealth Office and Minister for Faith and Communities, Baroness Warsi, at a reception at Lancaster House, London on 26th June 2014

The Canadian Bank of Commerce War Memorial in the Canadian Imperial Bank of Commerce, Edmonton.

attended by The Duke of Kent and relatives of the VC recipients. The Canadian plaque was unveiled outside the British High Commission in Elgin Street, Ottawa on 10th November 2014 by The Princess Royal in the presence of British High Commissioner Howard Drake, Canadian Minister of Veterans Affairs Julian Fantino and Canadian Chief of the Defence Staff General Thomas J Lawson.
- York Cemetery VC Memorial, West Don River Valley, Toronto, Canada dedicated on 25th June 2017.
- Canadian Book of Remembrance.
- Two 49 cents postage stamps in honour of the 94 Canadian VC winners were issued by Canada Post on 21st October 2004 on the 150th Anniversary of the first Canadian VC's action, Alexander Roberts Dunn VC.

In addition to the VC he was awarded the 1914–15 Star, British War Medal 1914–20 and Victory Medal 1914–19. The VC is held privately.

LIEUTENANT COLONEL NEVILLE BOWES ELLIOTT-COOPER
8th Battalion, The Royal Fusiliers (City of London Regiment)

Neville Elliott-Cooper was born at 81 Lancaster Gate, London on 22nd January 1889. His father, Robert (later Sir) Elliott-Cooper KCB M.Inst.CE VD FRGS (29th January 1845–16th February 1942) was living with his mother and sister, Isabella, at a lodging house at 16 Little Woodhouse, Leeds in 1861. He was educated at Leeds Grammar School, studied civil engineering under John Fraser M.Inst. CE and worked with him as Resident Engineer on the construction of railways in Yorkshire until November 1874. Robert was commissioned as a lieutenant in 1st

Yorkshire Artillery Corps on 27th September 1870 and was promoted captain on 5th June 1875 and major on 16th April 1879. He resigned his commission on 27th February 1886, retaining the rank of major. In 1874 he was living in Leeds when he and Francis Campin took out Patent No.1893 for the invention of 'improvements in apparatus for locking railway signals and switches and for locking railway signals and gates at level crossings'. He was in India to inspect engineering works November 1874–May 1875. In June 1876 he went into practice as a civil engineer (railway builder) at Westminster, London. On 10th January 1878 Robert married Fanny née Leetham (21st April 1857–1948) at Christchurch, Hampshire. They were living at 37 Kensington Park Gardens, Kensington, London in 1881. Robert constructed railways and other engineering works in England, the Crown Colonies and South Africa. He travelled professionally throughout Europe, Asia Minor, Egypt, India, South Africa and the West Indies. He held numerous appointments:

Neville's father, Sir Robert Elliott-Cooper KCB.

- Tax Commissioner Westminster 9th August 1899.
- Lieutenant Colonel Engineer & Railway Volunteer Staff Corps 6th January 1900 (Volunteer Officers' Decoration 15th November 1904), transferred to the newly formed Territorial Force on 1st April 1908, Honorary Colonel and Commandant of the Corps 27th July 1912 and resigned his commission on 21st March 1914, retaining his rank.
- Crown Agent Engineer for the Construction of Railways in British West Africa 1907.
- Consultant Engineer for Nigeria & Gold Coast Colonies 1908–16.
- Chairman of the Committee of the Engineering Standards Association on Steel Bridges 1911–28.
- President of the Institution of Civil Engineers November 1912–November 1913 and of the Smeatonian Society of Civil Engineers 1923.
- Member of the Advisory Board of the Science Museum 1912, India Office Committee for appointments in the Public Works Department and State

Kensington Park Gardens, London where the Elliott-Cooper family was living in 1881.

Railways, General Board of the National Physical Laboratory, London County Council Tribunal of Appeal (Building Act) 1914, Committee on the Deterioration of Structures Exposed to Sea Action 1916, Government Mining Sub-Committee 1919 and British Standards Committee for the use of Portland Cement 1919.
- Consulting Engineer Regent's Canal and Dock Co (later Grand Union Canal).
- Chairman of the War Office Committee of Institute of Civil Engineers and of the War Office Committee for Hutted Camps 1919 (Knight Commander of the Order of the Bath, LG 1st January 1919).
- Technical Adviser to the Treasury to supervise payments to contractors under the Trades Facilities Act 1925.
- Planned the widening of Knowle Lock on the Birmingham & Warwick Canal in the 1930s.

They were living at 81 Lancaster Gate, Paddington by 1885, at Sladeland House, Kirdford, Billingshurst, Sussex in 1907 and at Bentworth Hall, Alton, Hampshire in 1911. After the war he was living at 44 Prince's Gate, London. Robert was a member of the Athenaeum and Hurlingham clubs. He was living at Knapwood House, Knaphill, Woking, Surrey at the time of his death there on 16th February 1942, leaving effects valued at £74,495/19/2. Neville had five siblings:

- Evelyn Gladys Elliott-Cooper (1878–1953) married Edward George Cowan (1869–1949) in 1921. They lived at 52 Eresby House, Rutland Gardens, London.
- Gilbert D'Arcy Elliott-Cooper (1880–1922) was educated at Eton College 1893–97. Commissioned in the Royal Fusiliers on 15th February 1899, transferred to the Lancashire Fusiliers 6th March 1900 and was promoted lieutenant on 13th July 1901. He was appointed adjutant on 25th March 1907 and in 1911 he was on the staff of HQ Straits Settlement in Singapore as ADC. In the same HQ was Frederick William Lumsden, who was awarded the VC in 1917. Gilbert served during the Great War, reaching the rank of major. He was severely wounded on 13th August 1915 and never fully recovered. He married Margaret Charlotte Dann (1888–1981) in 1917. They reportedly had a child, but no details have been found. Gilbert died as a result of the wounds he received on 7th March 1922. He was living at 4 Elmsleigh Park, Paignton, Devon at the time and left effects valued at £5,097/2/2. Margaret married Gilbert William Coventry (1868–1947) in 1923. Gilbert had previously married Georgina Blanche Bluett (c.1873–

Bentworth Hall, Alton, Hampshire, home to the Elliott-Coopers in 1911.

1922) in 1902 and they had five children – William George Coventry 1903, Cecil Dick Bluett Coventry 1905, Charles Henry Gerald Coventry 1906, Arthur John Clifford Coventry 1909 and Gilbert Hugo Gordon Coventry 1911. Gilbert and Margaret had a daughter, Anne Coventry, in 1931. Margaret was living at The Croft, 22 College Road, Newton Abbot, Devon at the time of her death on 9th January 1981, leaving effects valued at £16,078.

• Malcolm Elliott-Cooper (1881–1875) was educated at Eton College (Eton College Rifle Volunteers 1899–1900) and King's College, Cambridge (MA AMICE) (Cambridge University Rifle Volunteers, Mounted Infantry Section 1900–03). He held a variety of civil engineering appointments with a number of railway companies. He was Assistant under Resident Engineer on the Shireoaks, Laughton and Maltby Railway August 1905–January 1906, then worked at the Great Central Railway Locomotive Shops, Tuxford, Nottinghamshire January–May 1906, before being engaged on the contractor's engineering staff during the construction of Immingham Dock and Railway June 1906–August 1908. In August 1908 he became the Assistant Engineer on the Bengal-Nagpur Railway in India until September 1911 and was also a member of the Bengal-Nagpur Railway Rifle Volunteers 1908–11 (Arthur Martin-Leake VC was a surgeon lieutenant in the unit from April 1905). He returned to Britain as Resident Engineer on the Mansfield Railway January 1912–May 1913 and while there married Florence E Qu'horn (1894–1979) in

1913. He returned to India as Resident Engineer on the Great Indian Peninsula Railway. He was in charge of maintenance and construction on eighty-four miles of double and sixty-eight miles of single track, including the construction of bridges and staff quarters from September 1913 until September 1916. He was also a second lieutenant in the Great Indian Peninsula Railway Rifle Volunteers 1915–16. Malcolm applied for a British Army commission on 8th December 1916. He was described as 5' 8½" tall and weighed 133 lbs. He was commissioned in the Royal Engineers, Railway Companies on 18th December 1916 and was appointed acting captain on 27th October 1918. He was demobilised on 3rd May 1919 and relinquished his commission on 1st September 1921. Malcolm died on 11th August 1975 at Cranford Lodge Nursing Home, 36 St Catherine's Road, Southbourne, Bournemouth, Dorset, leaving effects valued at £66,956. Malcolm and Florence had two sons:

The Brookwood 1939–1945 Memorial commemorates those who died in the Norway campaign, on raids into occupied Europe, at sea, in aerial combat or working behind enemy lines with underground movements. Inset is Peter Douglas Elliott-Cooper's name.

° Peter Douglas Elliott-Cooper (1917–42) trained at the Royal Military College, Sandhurst, was commissioned in 1st Royal Fusiliers (74609) on 27th January 1938 and was promoted lieutenant on 1st January 1941. He died on 12th September 1942 and is commemorated on the Brookwood 1939–1945 Memorial, Surrey. It is believed he was aboard the troopship RMS *Laconia*, when she was torpedoed and sunk off West Africa by U-*156*.

° Michael Bowes Elliott-Cooper (1927–2008) was an engineer. He was living at 12 Haytor Grove, Newton Abbot, Devon at the time of his death.

• Millicent Elliott-Cooper (1882–1973) was a spinster living at 14 Dalmeny Road, Southbourne, Bournemouth, Hampshire at the time of her death on 21st December 1973, leaving effects valued at £60,135.

• Vera Elliott-Cooper (1885–1949) was a visitor at the home of Charles H Palmer (of Huntley & Palmers Biscuits) at Bozedown House, Whitchurch, Oxfordshire in 1911. She served as a nurse with the British Committee French Red Cross October 1915–November 1918 and was awarded the British War and Victory Medals. She was a spinster living at 18 Mortlake Road, Kew, Surrey at the time of her death there on 22nd October 1949, leaving effects valued at £42,014/10/.

Neville's paternal great-grandfather, Captain John Elliott RN, as a midshipman sailed with Captain James Cook (1728–79) on HMS *Resolution* during his second voyage to the Pacific Ocean. Cook, pictured here, mapped Newfoundland before making three voyages to the Pacific, during which he made the first European visit to the east coast of Australia and the Hawaiian Islands (Nathaniel Dance-Holland).

Neville's paternal grandfather, Robert Cooper (c.1809–60), born at York, married Louisa Lucretia née Elliott (c.1802–85), born at Ripon, Yorkshire. He was a land agent in 1841 and they were living at Buslingthorpe Lane, Leeds, Yorkshire. By 1851 he was a stockbroker and they were living at 31 South Grove, Camberwell, Surrey. In 1861 Louisa was described as a 'proprietor of houses and fundholder'. She was the daughter of Captain John Elliott RN (1759–1834) of Elliott House, Ripon who, as a midshipman, sailed with Captain James Cook on HMS *Resolution* during his second voyage around the world. She was living at Coppice, Nottingham at the time of her death on 28th September 1885. In addition to Robert they had two other children:

HMS *Resolution* by another member of the crew, Henry Roberts.

- Isabella Mary Cooper (1840–1925) was a Sister of Mercy at All Hallows Mission, 127–129 Union Street, St Saviours, London in 1881 and at Victoria Place, Southwark, London in 1901. She died at The House of Mercy, Clewer, Berkshire on 21st May 1925, leaving effects valued at £2,844/17/9.
- Maria Jane Cooper (born 1843).

His maternal grandfather, William Leetham (1823–75), born at St Mary's, Bishopshill, York, married Sarah née Cordukes (c.1824–1902), born at York, in 1849. He was a steam ship owner in 1861 and they were living at 27 Lister Street, Hull, Yorkshire. By 1871 they had moved to Crown Terrace, North Myton, Hull. He died on 14th January 1875 at Nervi, Italy and is buried in the English Cemetery, within Staglieno Cemetery, Genoa. Sarah was living with her daughter, Marian, and daughter-in-law, Selina, at Museum Street Club Chambers, York in 1881. In addition to Fanny they had seven other children:

- William Henry Leetham (1850–53).
- Emily Leetham (1851–81) married Reverend Henry David Jones (1842–1925) in 1871. In 1881 he was Curate of St John's Church, Hastings, Sussex and was living at Finley House, Brittany Road, Hastings. They had three children – Mary Gertrude Jones 1872, Emily Beatrice Jones 1877 and Robert Leetham Jones 1878. Henry was living at The Chantry, Chichester, Sussex at the time of his death on 26th April 1925, leaving effects valued at £26,552/2/2.
- Walter Leetham (1853–80) was an underwriter at Lloyd's of London. He married Selina Turner Prynn (1856–97) in 1877. They were living at 57 Addison Road, Kensington at the time of his death on 27th June 1880. She married James Jackson Gawith (1850–90) in 1883. They were living at 222 Harrow Road, Paddington by 1889 and also had a property at 15 Vicarage Villas, Neasden, London.
- John Leetham (1855–79) died on 29 January 1879 at Abu Simbel, Upper Egypt.
- Arthur (later Sir Arthur) Leetham (1859–1933) was commissioned in 13th Hussars on 17th April 1880. Promoted lieutenant 23rd March 1881, captain 13th Hussars 9th September 1885, captain (honorary major) Royal Monmouthshire, Royal Engineers (Militia) 3rd September 1898 and major 18th October 1902. He married Louisa Caroline Shakespear (1865–1951) in 1888. In 1901 they were living at 92 Mount Street, St George, Hanover Square, London and at 100 Park Street, St George, Hanover Square in 1911. Later they lived at 65 Albert Hall Mansions, Kensington. He was appointed Honorary Lieutenant Colonel, Monmouthshire Royal Engineers Militia and Secretary of the Royal United Service Institution. He was awarded the CMG and KCVO on 12th February 1914. On 15th September 1914 he was attached to the office of the Secretary of State for War, David Lloyd George MP, as a lieutenant colonel, late Royal Monmouthshire RE and was graded as a staff captain. Later, when Lord Derby was Secretary of State for War, Arthur was attached to the office of the Permanent-Under Secretary of State for War, Sir

Reginald Herbert Brade KCB, as a staff captain and is shown as such in the Army List until September 1919. Louisa was living at 16 Hans Road, Kensington at the time of her death.

- Marian Leetham (1861–1950) married Douglas Clarke (born c.1852), a retired tea planter, in 1896. They were living at 37 Cromwell Road, Kensington in 1901.
- William Leetham (1864–1906) was commissioned as a lieutenant in 5th Dragoons on 7th February 1885 and was promoted captain on 25th April 1893. He married Ida Gordon (1865–1953) in 1896. They lived at Kingsclear, Camberley, Surrey and had a son, William Ian Leetham, in 1898. When William died on 27th November 1906, he left £41,980/9/7 to his widow. Ida married Kenneth Walker (1874–1947) in 1909. They were living at Tegfynydd Llanfallteg, Pembrokeshire in 1911. By 1947 they were living at Boulston Manor, Boulston, Haverfordwest, Pembrokeshire. William died at the County Hospital, Haverfordwest on 5th July 1947, leaving effects valued at £87,978/16/2.

Neville was educated at Eton College, Berkshire September 1901–1907, in Mr HM Macnaghten's House. He was a member of 2nd Buckinghamshire (Eton College) Rifle Volunteer Corps. He trained at the Royal Military College, Sandhurst and was commissioned in 3rd Royal Fusiliers on 9th October 1908. He served in South Africa, Mauritius and India. Promoted lieutenant 7th February 1912 and captain 19th March 1915. He went to France with 8th Battalion in May 1915 and was appointed acting major in 9th Battalion on 4th September 1915. **Awarded the MC for his actions on 2nd March 1916 at the Hohenzollern Redoubt, Hulluch, France during an attack by a company each of 8th and 9th Battalions on the Chord. Seven mines were exploded and the craters were occupied. He commanded C Company 9th Battalion, taking Craters A, 1 and 2 and the crater in the Triangle, LG 15th April 1916.**

The Royal Military College was established in 1802 in Great Marlow to train gentleman cadets for the infantry and cavalry of the British Army and the Presidency armies in India. In 1812 the College moved to purpose-built buildings at Sandhurst, Berkshire. In 1947 it became The Royal Military Academy, having merged with the Royal Military Academy, Woolwich when the latter closed. It continues to train officers for all arms and services of the British Army to this day.

On 9th July 1916 he was appointed CO 8th Battalion as an acting lieutenant colonel. **Awarded the DSO for his actions at Roeux on 3rd May 1917 for reorganising and rallying his Battalion at a critical moment after suffering heavy casualties. He also led a patrol of twenty men under heavy fire and returned with twenty prisoners and valuable information, LG 18th July 1917.** Corporal George Jarratt in the same Battalion was awarded the VC for this action. During the night the remnants of 8th and 9th Battalions amalgamated under Neville's command. **Awarded the VC for his actions east of La Vacquerie, near Cambrai, France on 30th November 1917, LG 13th February 1918. Mentioned in Sir Douglas Haig's Despatch dated 7th November 1917, LG 18th December 1917.**

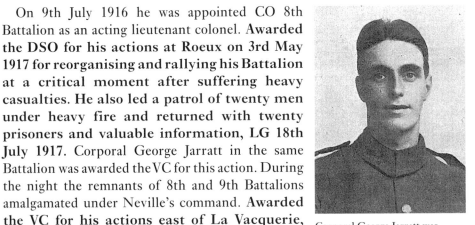

Corporal George Jarratt was serving under Neville Elliott-Cooper's command, when he was awarded the VC for his actions on 3rd May 1917.

Neville was wounded in the right thigh and was taken prisoner during his VC action. He died of wounds at No.1 Reserve Prisoner of War Camp Lazarette, Hanover on 11th February 1918. News of his death was received through a British Red Cross, Copenhagen telegram to the Central Prisoners of War Committee, London on 4th March. He was buried at Limmer, Hanover and his body was later moved to Hamburg Cemetery, Ohlsdorf 1914–1918, Germany (V A 16), one of three CWGC plots in Hamburg Ohlsdorf Cemetery (Friedhof Ohlsdorf), the largest non-military cemetery in the world. His estate was valued at £5,455/16/3. He is commemorated in a number of other places:

- War memorial and a personal memorial plaque in the south aisle of Ripon Cathedral, Yorkshire.
- St Mary's War Memorial, Bentworth, Hampshire.

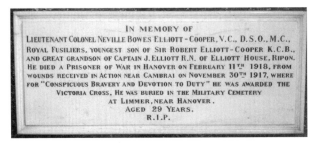

IN MEMORY OF
LIEUTENANT COLONEL NEVILLE BOWES ELLIOTT-COOPER, V.C., D.S.O., M.C.,
ROYAL FUSILIERS, YOUNGEST SON OF SIR ROBERT ELLIOTT-COOPER K.C.B.,
AND GREAT GRANDSON OF CAPTAIN J. ELLIOTT R.N. OF ELLIOTT HOUSE, RIPON.
HE DIED A PRISONER OF WAR IN HANOVER ON FEBRUARY 11TH 1918, FROM
WOUNDS RECEIVED IN ACTION NEAR CAMBRAI ON NOVEMBER 30TH 1917, WHERE
FOR "CONSPICUOUS BRAVERY AND DEVOTION TO DUTY" HE WAS AWARDED THE
VICTORIA CROSS, HE WAS BURIED IN THE MILITARY CEMETERY
AT LIMMER, NEAR HANOVER.
AGED 29 YEARS.
R.I.P.

Neville's memorial plaque in Ripon Cathedral.

Neville Elliott-Cooper's grave in Hamburg Cemetery, Ohlsdorf.

St Mary's War Memorial at Bentworth is in front of the church tower.

Eton College War Memorial (Memorials to Valour).

The Royal Fusiliers Museum within the Tower of London.

The memorial to Neville and Gilbert Elliott-Cooper at Eton College (Memorials to Valour).

- Oak panel war memorial inside St Marks Church, Farnborough, Hampshire.
- Four memorials at Eton College – the War Memorial, the 'For Valour' Memorial unveiled by the Queen on 27th May 2010, a memorial to him and his brother, Gilbert, and the Macnaghten House memorial.
- Royal Fusiliers panel in the Royal Memorial Chapel, Sandhurst, Surrey.

The 1914–15 Star was awarded to members of British and Imperial forces who served in any theatre during the First World War during 1914 and 1915. It was always awarded with the British War Medal and Victory Medal, to form the 'Pip, Squeak and Wilfred' trio. There were a number of exceptions to the award, the main one being those awarded the 1914 Star. 2,366,000 medals were awarded.

- The Department for Communities and Local Government decided to provide commemorative paving stores at the birthplace of every Great War Victoria Cross recipient in the United Kingdom. A commemorative store for Neville was dedicated at Victoria Embankment Gardens, Ministry of Defence, Whitehall, London on 23rd November 2017 to mark the centenary of his award.

Neville's VC was presented to his parents by the King at Buckingham Palace on 25th May 1918. In addition to the VC, DSO and MC he was awarded the 1914–15 Star, British War Medal 1914–20 and Victory Medal 1914–19 with Mentioned-in-Despatches Oakleaf. The VC, DSO and MC and his bronze memorial plaque were presented to the Royal Fusiliers Museum in 1973 by his family. His other medals are in private hands. In 1992 they were offered to the Regiment with a copy of the VC and what were claimed to be the original DSO and MC for £3,450. The VC is held by the Royal Fusiliers Museum at the Tower of London.

LIEUTENANT COLONEL WILFRITH ELSTOB
16th Battalion, The Manchester Regiment

Wilfrith Elstob was born at Chichester, Sussex on 8th September 1888. His father, John George Elstob (1856–6th October 1926), was born at Houghton Le Spring, Co Durham. He was curate of St Mary's, Barnsley Parish Church, Yorkshire 1879–82 and in 1881 he was boarding at 37 Victoria Crescent there. He married Frances Alice née Chamberlain (1849–30th June 1912), born at Worcester, in 1883 at Wakefield, Yorkshire. In 1881 Frances was living

St Mary's, where Wilfrith's father was curate, is the main church of Barnsley. Its foundations date back to the 8th century and the tower is 15th century, but the main body of the church was built in the 19th century, taking its current shape by 1870.

Chichester Cathedral, Sussex.

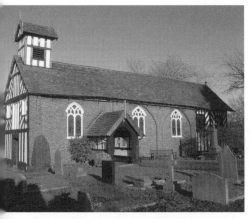

Wilfrith's father was vicar of All Saints for many years. Although in Siddington, it is the Parish Church of Siddington with Capesthorne. Records of a chapel at Siddington go back to 1337, but the current building was consecrated in 1521. Originally timber framed, by 1815 the walls were bulging and had to be strengthened by being enclosed in brick. Major restoration work was carried out in 1853 and 1894.

as head of household at 1 Churchfield, Barnsley. John held a number of other appointments:

Chaplain in Ealing 1882–85.
Priest-vicar at Chichester Cathedral, Sussex 1885–September 1888.
Vicar of All Saints, Capesthorne with Siddington, near Macclesfield, living at Fanshawe Vicarage by 1891 and was still there in 1911.
Rural Dean of Macclesfield 1904–12.
Honorary Canon of Chester 1911.

John left effects valued at £1,682/2/5 and Frances left effects valued at £2,075/5/8. Wilfrith had three brothers:

• Noel Chamberlain Elstob (1884–13th December 1963) married Jessie Urwick (1866–1946) in 1912 at Upton, Worcestershire. Noel was a schoolmaster at Capesthorpe, Monmouth when he was commissioned in 2nd Monmouthshire on 1st January 1915 and was appointed temporary captain on 19th June 1915 with a provisional battalion. He was restored to the establishment on 29th January 1917, relinquishing temporary captain. Promoted lieutenant 20th June 1917 with precedence from 16th March 1917, later backdated to 1st June 1916. Appointed acting captain whilst commanding a company from 20th July 1917 until 18th January 1919. He was diagnosed with pyrexia of unknown origin at Ypres on 30th July 1917 while serving with 1/2nd Monmouthshire and was evacuated to Britain on 12th August. He was treated at 1st Western General Hospital, Liverpool and Park Hall Camp, Oswestry. A series of medical boards found him unfit for service due to heart murmurs but he had recovered by 11th February 1918. In July 1918 he was commanding the Returned Expeditionary Force Company, 2nd (Reserve) Monmouthshire at Kinmel Park and he was demobilised on 18th January 1919. Noel was Headmaster of Monmouth School 1941–46. They lived at Capesthorne, Dixon Road, Monmouth. When Jessie died she left effects valued at £4,045/4/-. By 1959 Noel was a solicitor with Vizard & Son at Monmouth. He left effects valued at £11,983.

- Eric Bramley Elstob (2nd August 1885–15th May 1949) joined the Royal Navy on 15th July 1903 and was appointed clerk on 15th July 1904. He was appointed assistant paymaster on 2nd August 1906. He was promoted lieutenant commander and paymaster on 2nd August 1910 and staff paymaster on 2nd August 1918. Eric was awarded the OBE for valuable services as Secretary to Rear Admiral Cecil F Dampier CMG when he was Rear Admiral commanding 3rd Battle Squadron, Admiral Superintendent Dover and Rear Admiral Controlled Minefields (LG 21st June 1919). Promoted paymaster lieutenant commander 15th January 1920 and paymaster captain 30th June 1935. He served on various ships and shore establishments including HMS *Ariadne*, *New Zealand*, *Prometheus*, *Suffolk*, *Queen*, *Pembroke*, *Wildfire*, *Hermes*, *Vernon*, *Victory*, *Hibernia*, *President* and *Arrogant*, as well as the RN College Dartmouth. He represented the Royal Navy in two first class cricket matches in 1913 and 1923 and retired in 1940. Eric married Ivy Renée (also seen as Rosine) Turner (1897–6th September 1942) at Holy Trinity, Ryde, Isle of Wight on 6th July 1915. His father and brother Auberon took part in the ceremony. They had three children:

  ° Ianthe Elstob (1917–2001) married Captain John Patrick Carswell (1918–97) at Delhi, India in September 1944. Visitors to the family home included DH Lawrence and Katherine Mansfield. John's mother, Catherine, was very close to DH Lawrence and after his death in 1930 she sold hundreds of his personal letters to pay for John's education at Merchant Taylors' School and St John's College, Oxford. John was commissioned in the South Lancashire Regiment (180370) on 29th March 1941 and was promoted war substantive lieutenant on 29th September 1942. He served in India and was released from service by October 1946. Thereafter he held a number of prominent civil service and other appointments: Joint Secretary to the Committee on Economic and Financial Problems of Provision for Old Age (Phillips Committee) 1953–54; Principal Private Secretary to Minister of Pensions and National Insurance 1955–56; HM Treasury 1961–64; Under-Secretary, Office of Lord President of the Council and Minister for Science 1964; Under-Secretary, Department of Education and Science and Ministry of Health 1964–74; Secretary, University Grants Committee 1974–77 (CB 1977); Secretary, British Academy 1978–83 (Emeritus); Honorary Research Fellow, Department of History, University College, London 1983–97; Life Member of the Institute of Historical Research, University of London from 1984; Fellow of the Royal Society of Literature 1984; and Chairman for two years of the Heath and Old Hampstead Society, one of the oldest preservation societies in the country, and became its vice president. His publications include: *The Prospector* 1950; *The Old Cause* 1954; *The South Sea Bubble* 1960, *The Diary and Political Papers of George Bubb Dodington* (with LA Dralle) 1965; *The Civil Servant and his World* 1966; *The Descent on England* 1969; *From Revolution to Revolution: English Society 1688–1776* in 1973; *Lives and Letters* 1978; *The Exile: a memoir of Ivy Litvinov* 1983; *Government and the Universities in Britain: Programme and Performance 1960–1980* in 1986; *The Porcupine: a life of Algernon Sidney* 1989; and *The Saving of Kenwood and the Northern Heights* 1992. Ianthe and Sheila Jones formed the National Committee for the Abolition of Nuclear Tests in 1957, which with other organisations and individuals merged into the Campaign for Nuclear Disarmament. Ianthe and John had two children – Catherine D Carswell 1946 and Harriet U Carswell 1950.

○ Wilfrith FC Elstob (born 1918) married Elizabeth AE Davidson in 1940. They had two children – Richard A Elstob 1947 and Alan C Elstob 1948. Wilfrith married Dora M Etholen (née Norwood) (born 1922) in 1961. Dora had married Alec Nicholas Etholen (1911–83) in 1943. Alec was commissioned in the Intelligence Corps on 8th February 1942 (226343) and was promoted war substantive lieutenant on 1st October 1942. He transferred to the Gordon Highlanders as a lieutenant on 11th April 1945 and was released from service by June 1946.

○ Philip Jasper Chamberlain Elstob (1922–79) suffered from a mental condition and was admitted to Borocourt Hospital, Wyfold, near Reading, Berkshire where he died on 21st December 1979, leaving effects valued at £11,327.

Eric and Ivy divorced in 1929. He married Signe Mathilda Olsson (also seen as Ohlsson) in 1937 at Marylebone, London. She was the daughter of Carl Olsson of Ystad, Sweden. Eric left effects valued at £3,391/14/9 in his will. Signe was a physiotherapist running a practice from her home at 13 St James Square, Bath, Somerset, supplementing her wage with hospital employment, before moving to Erik Dahlbergregatan 1.5, 21148 Malmo, Sweden. She died there in November 1968 leaving an estate valued at £17,587 in England. Eric and Signe had a son:

○ Eric Carl Elstob (1943–2003) was educated at Hawtreys in Wiltshire, Marlborough College and Queen's College Oxford. In 1965 he joined Foreign & Colonial Management in London. By 1969 he was a director and until 1995 was a joint manager of the Foreign & Colonial Investment Trust. He was heavily involved in the restoration of Christ Church, Spitalfields, East London from 1976 as treasurer, then chairman in 1996 and president in 2002. He wrote *Sweden: a traveller's history* in 1979 and *Travels in a Europe Restored 1989–1995* in 1997. In honour of his mother he founded the Signe Trust to help the young, the arts and the artisan. He was also treasurer to the Worshipful Company of Parish Clerks and a trustee of St Andrew's,

Holborn. He travelled widely for business and pleasure with his companion, Eva-Lena Ruhnbro.

Ivy married Joseph Irving Davis (1889–1967) in 1941. He was a Cambridge classical scholar and became a bookseller in partnership with Giuseppe Orioli of Florence in 1911, with branches in Florence and London. Joseph became the sole proprietor in the early 1930s, specialising in early Italian, medical and scientific books. He organised an exhibition of Italian books for the National Book League in 1955 for which he was decorated by the Italian Government. During the Spanish Civil War he drove an old saloon car filled with medical supplies over the Pyrenees to Barcelona. Ivy died at her home at Berrin's Hill, Ipsden, Oxfordshire in September 1942. Joseph was living at 20 New End, Hampstead at the time of his death in May 1967, leaving £54,742 to his stepdaughter, Ianthe Carswell.

• Auberon Elstob (1890–1961) served with the YMCA in France in 1916. He was Curate of St Paul, Helsby 1914–17 and Hoylake 1919–23. He was commissioned as a Church of England Chaplain to the Forces 4th Class on 25th February 1918 and appears in the Army List until June 1920. Various appointments followed – Vicar of Goostrey 1923–29, Vicar of St James, Prestbury 1929–36, Rector of Heswall 1936–52 and Rector of Claverton 1952–56. Auberon married Katharine Mary Lowndes (1899–1972) in 1924. She was the daughter of Reverend Ernest Campbell Lowndes (1859–1908) of St Oswald's Vicarage, Chester. They had a daughter, Aileen F Elstob (born 1925) who married Geoffrey S Davy (born 1927) in 1959 and they had a son, Robert G Davy, in 1961.

Wilfrith's paternal grandfather, George Elstob (c.1816–90), was born at Houghton-le-Spring, Co Durham. He married Mary Ann née Jackson (c.1819–1906), born at Esh, Co Durham, in 1845. In 1861 George was a joiner employing one apprentice and the family was living at Sunderland Street, Houghton-le-Spring. By 1871 he was employing a man and a boy. In addition to John they had three other children:

• Jane Elstob (1846–1920) was a dressmaker, living with her parents in 1871 and 1881 and as head at 64 Sunderland Street, Houghton-le-Spring in 1911. She never married.

• Thomas Jackson Elstob (1848–1918) was a joiner, employing two men and a boy in 1871, whilst living with his parents. He married Dorothy Ann Bellerby (1855–87) in 1883 and they had a daughter, Mary Bellerby Elstob in 1884. Thomas was boarding with his sister Jane in 1911.

Wilfrith's paternal grandparents were living on Sunderland Street, Houghton-le-Spring in the 1860s and 1870s.

- Ann or Annie Elizabeth Elstob (1850–1940) was a dressmaker. She was living with her parents in 1871 and 1881 and with her sister Jane in 1911. She never married.

His maternal grandfather, Humphrey Chamberlain (c.1825–92), was born at Bredicot, Worcestershire. He married Frances née Barlow (c.1821–78) in 1845 at St James the Less, Bredicot. He was a farmer of 170 acres in 1851, living with his family at Claines, Worcestershire. Humphrey married Mary Ann Barlow (born c.1830) in 1880 at Lambeth, London. By 1891 they were living at 45 Victoria Road, Barnsley, Yorkshire, by

Wilfrith's maternal grandparents married at St James the Less, Bredicot, Worcestershire in 1845. The church dates back to c.1300 and was fully restored in 1843 when the bellcote was added.

when he was a brick and carbon manufacturer. He died at Barnsley leaving effects valued at £14,071/6/6. In addition to Frances, Humphrey and Frances had two other children:

- Agnes Chamberlain (1847–1927) married Thomas Taylor (1822–1900) in 1867. Thomas had married Jemima Atkinson (1825–64) in 1847 and they had ten children – Louisa Mary Taylor 1848, Thomas Edward Taylor 1849, John Windle Taylor 1850, Ernest Taylor 1852, Francis Taylor 1854, Josephine Taylor 1855, Eleanor Taylor 1857, Amy Taylor 1859, Philip Arnold Taylor 1860 and Evangeline Taylor 1863. Thomas was an attorney/solicitor, County Coroner for Yorkshire and Coroner for the Honour of Pontefract 1852–1900. He died at 36 Bond Street, Wakefield leaving effects valued at £4,243/9/10. Agnes left effects valued at £3,256. Thomas and Agnes had two children – Agnes M Taylor 1870 and Humphrey Taylor 1876.
- William Barnes Chamberlain (1851–1927) was educated at St John's College, Cambridge (BA 1882) and was appointed Curate at Ossett, Yorkshire. He was consular chaplain at Montevideo, Uruguay in 1887. He was living at 18 Pembridge Square, Bayswater, London at the time of his death in Kensington, London leaving effects valued at £7,909/7/5.

Wilfrith began his education at Ryles Preparatory School, Alderley Edge, Cheshire 1894–98, where he formed a lifelong friendship with Hubert Worthington. He was then educated at Christ's Hospital School, London 1898–1905, which moved to Horsham in 1902. At Christ's he was a monitor of Coleridge B House, a lance corporal in the OTC and played for the first XV. At Manchester University he

Christ's Hospital was established as a school in 1552 by King Edward VI at Newgate Street, London, on the site of a Grey Friars friary. There was a preparatory school in Hertford and supplementary schools at Ware and Broxbourne. However, in 1902 they relocated to the current school site at Horsham, West Sussex. A railway station was built adjacent to the site and a girls' school was founded in Hertford when the boys moved to Horsham. The girls' school was incorporated into the Horsham site in 1985. Wilfrith is one of four VCs and two GCs who were educated at Christ's. The others are Edward Baxter VC, Charles Green GC, Joshua Leakey VC, Henry Pitcher VC and Laurence Sinclair GC. Famous alumni include:

- Poets/authors Edmund Blunden and Samuel Taylor Coleridge.
- Conductor Sir Colin Davis.
- Journalist, author and broadcaster Bernard Levin.
- Barnes Wallis, scientist and inventor famous for the bouncing bombs of the Second World War.

graduated BA in 1909 and gained a teaching diploma in 1910. At 6′ 1″ tall he was known as 'Big Ben' or 'Bindy'. Having taught for a year at the Lycée at Beauvais, he attended the Sorbonne in Paris for another year before being appointed senior French master at Merchiston Castle Preparatory School, Edinburgh in October 1912.

The Army came to Larkhill in 1899 when a tented camp was established for units to train on Salisbury Plain during the summer. The area was particularly suitable for artillery units. In 1914 the first hutted camps were built and during the Great war there were thirty-four battalion sized camps at Larkhill. A light military railway was built to connect the camp to the Amesbury–Bulford Line, which also served the airfields at Stonehenge and Lake until lifted in the early 1920s. Many divisions completed their training at Larkhill prior to embarking for operational theatres. After the war Larkhill became almost exclusively for artillery use and the School of Artillery (later Royal School of Artillery) was established there in 1919. More permanent buildings were established in the inter-war years, including a hospital, married quarters, NAAFI, messes and churches. The first British military airfield was set up at Larkhill in 1910 and the Military Aeroplane Trials were conducted there in August 1912. The airfield closed in 1914 and was soon covered by the hutted camps, but the original hangers survive.

Hubert Worthington (1886–1963) was born into a family of architects and he worked with Edwin Lutyens 1912–14. During the war he served in 16th Manchester as a company commander alongside Wilfrith Elstob, his old school friend. Hubert was severely wounded on 1st July 1916 and rejoined his half brother Percy in the family business in 1919. In 1929 he was appointed Slade Lecturer in architecture at Oxford and designed many buildings for the University as well as conducting restorations on others. In 1943 he was appointed principal architect for Egypt and North Africa by the Imperial (later Commonwealth) War Graves Commission and designed the cemeteries at El Alamein and Heliopolis. His major post war rebuilding project was the Inns of Court in London, which was carried out with TW Sutcliffe and Sir Edward Maufe, cousin of Great War VC Thomas Harold Broadbent Maufe. Hubert also repaired the Blitz damaged Manchester Cathedral, work that was not completed until 1955. He was knighted in 1949. He was also vice president of the Royal Institute of British Architects 1943–45, a member of the Royal Fine Arts Commission 1945–50, an associate member of the Royal Academy 1945 and an Academician of the Society in 1955. Hubert's brother, Lieutenant Colonel Claude Swanwick Worthington DSO TD, 6th Manchester, had already served at Gallipoli and in Egypt when he took command of 5th Dorsetshire on 8th April 1918. On 3rd October he was seriously wounded during heavy shelling of the front line while supervising consolidation and died of his wounds on 14th October (Mont Huon Military Cemetery, Le Tréport – VIII J 14). Claude was awarded a posthumous bar to his DSO.

Wilfrith applied for a commission in 6th Manchester on 16th August 1914, but for an unknown reason his papers were returned by the War Office. He enlisted in one of the Royal Fusiliers Public Schools Battalion on 19th September and was about to join it at Epsom, when he again applied for a commission, prompted by his school friend Hubert Worthington. As a result he was commissioned in 16th Manchester on 3rd October. He was lean, lithe and athletic. Wilfrith trained with A Company at Heaton Park, Manchester, where he captained the Battalion's officers' tug-of-war team at the Brigade Sports Competition on 21st April 1915. The Battalion won the championship cup. On 24th April the Battalion moved to Grantham, Lincolnshire, where the whole of the newly formed 30th Division, commanded by Major General William Fry CB CVO, was based at Belton Park. While there field training included trench digging and routine at Willoughby Park, route marches up to twenty-eight miles, live firing and mock assaults. Promoted captain 3rd May. The Battalion moved to Larkhill Camp on Salisbury Plain on 7th September for a final period of training, rounded off with field days, brigade & divisional exercises and firing the new Part III Army Musketry course, in which the Battalion came first in the Brigade. The final inspection, prior to 30th Division's deployment overseas, was on 4th November by Lord Derby on behalf of King George V, who had suffered an accident in France.

Early on the morning of 6th November, the Battalion marched from Larkhill to entrain at Amesbury for Folkestone, where it embarked for Boulogne, France, arriving on 9th November. Wilfrith was 2IC of A Company under Hubert Worthington. The Battalion arrived at Hèbuterne on 7th December, where it suffered its first casualties to heavy enemy shelling along the main street. The companies were paired off for initiation into trench warfare with more experienced troops of the Gloucestershire and Worcestershire Regiments. The Battalion took over trenches at Maricourt from 1st Devonshire on 5th January 1916 and relieved 15th Royal Warwickshire in the front line on 6th January. From January to July 1916, except for short spells of training behind the lines, 16th Battalion followed the usual rotation through front line, support and reserve in the trenches. In March Wilfrith was appointed commander of D Company.

A battalion of the London Regiment at Amesbury station in 1908. The scene as 16th Manchester entrained there on 6th November 1915 would have been very similar. The London & South Western Railway opened the Amesbury & Military Camp Light Railway branch line in 1902 and extended it to Bulford and Bulford Camp in 1906. During the Great War a branch was added to serve Larkhill and nearby camps, Fargo Hospital and the airfields at Stonehenge and Lake. Passenger services ceased in 1952 and goods traffic in 1963 when the track was lifted. The site of Amesbury station is now occupied by a supermarket.

On 1st July 1916 the Battalion took part in its first significant action on the Somme, in the capture of Montauban. It advanced with 17th Manchester and suffered heavy casualties from a machine gun behind the old German frontline, which was eventually dealt with by a Lewis gun crew. The objective was reached and German artillery in Caterpillar Valley was overrun, but at the end of the action the Battalion numbered just 300 men. Wilfrith was wounded in the neck but, having been bandaged with a sergeant's handkerchief, continued to command his company. Hubert Worthington, commanding A Company, was badly wounded and evacuated to Britain. On 9th July the 17th Battalion retired to Bernafay Wood following a severe mauling

The Military Cross was created on 28th December 1914 for officers of the rank of captain and below and warrant officers. In August 1916 bars were awarded for further acts of gallantry. In 1931 the MC was extended to majors and to members of the RAF for ground actions. In the 1993 honours review the Military Medal for other ranks was discontinued and the MC became the third level decoration for all ranks of the British Armed Forces for acts of gallantry on land.

on the eastern edge of Trônes Wood. 16th Battalion was ordered to gain the southern part of the Wood and cover the left of the Royal Scots Fusiliers in Maltz Horn Trench. This was accomplished, the enemy was outflanked and the Battalion dug in about fifty metres from the southwestern edge of the Wood. Wilfrith was wounded again in this action and the Battalion suffered a total of 219 casualties. **Awarded the MC for his part in the attack on Montauban on 1st July and for operations in Trônes Wood 8th–11th July, LG 1st January 1917.**

Wilfrith was appointed second in command of the Battalion on 10th July and was promoted major on 1st August. On 13th October the CO, Lieutenant Colonel Hubert Knox, was killed by a shell and Wilfrith was promoted lieutenant colonel next day and assumed command. The Battalion was involved in the Battle of Arras from 10th April 1917 and suffered severe casualties. On the night of 27th/28th July he led a large reconnaissance patrol near Zillebeke, Belgium, consisting of his company commanders and representatives from each of the Battalion's sections. He penetrated the enemy's forward support trenches and returned with valuable intelligence about the ground over which they would advance on 31st July. **For his devotion to duty and leadership he was awarded the DSO, LG 1st January 1918.** The attack commenced at 3.50 a.m. and the Battalion gained all objectives in the first hour. Wilfrith went forward to assess the situation and found a confusion of mixed up units under heavy machine gun and sniper fire. He reorganised the men and moved them forward in small parties to mop up enemy resistance. **Mentioned in Field Marshal Sir Douglas Haig's Despatch dated 7th November 1917, LG 21st December 1917.**

Early in January 1918 Wilfrith returned to Britain for leave, during which he played rugby. Returning to France, he captained a Divisional football team against a French XI in Paris in February. He also captained the Divisional rugby XV against a French side in Paris a few weeks before his final action. **Awarded the VC for his actions at Manchester Redoubt, near St Quentin, France on 21st March 1918, LG 9th June 1919.** He was killed during his VC action and is commemorated on the Pozières Memorial (Panels 64–67). He left effects valued at £1,833/15/9. A

Wilfrith's name on the Pozières Memorial. Captain Sharples is bottom middle.

memorial service was held at Manchester Cathedral for 16th Manchester on 15th April 1918.

A number of members of 16th Manchester, who were taken prisoner around Manchester Hill, made statements later in 1918 to confirm Wilfrith's death:

26th June – 54946 Private WE Smith stated he had been killed by a bomb.

24th July – 7396 Sergeant Samuel Banks, who knew Wilfrith well, was imprisoned at Bayreuth and confirmed he had seen him dead with wounds in his neck, head and left arm.

30th July – 6962 CSM J Brown at the POW camp at Meschede confirmed the death.

6th August – Lieutenant Clarke and 11465 Corporal E Bamber at the POW Camp Chemnitz confirmed they had seen his body.

In February 1921 former Warrant Officer J Franklin, 2nd Bedfordshire, who was part of a burial party while a prisoner, claimed to have buried Wilfrith and Captain Norman Sharples about 180m in front of Battalion Headquarters near a Vickers post. Both had been shot and were surrounded by Mills bombs ready for throwing. Post war Hubert Worthington went to France to try to find Wilfrith's body and again in May 1919. **Mentioned in Field Marshal Sir Douglas Haig's Despatch dated 8th November 1918, LG 28th December 1918.**

As Wilfrith never married, the VC was presented to his father by the King at Buckingham Palace on 26th July 1919. He is commemorated in a number of places:

• Named on War Memorials at:
     Park Green, Macclesfield, Cheshire.
     Town Hall, Macclesfield, Cheshire.
     St Michael's and All Angels Church, Market Place, Macclesfield, Cheshire.
     Manchester University.
     Merchiston Castle School, Edinburgh, Scotland.
     Ryleys School, Alderley Edge, Cheshire.
     Christ's Hospital School, Horsham, West Sussex.
     All Saints Church, Siddington, Cheshire window and plaque.
     Chichester War Memorial, Litten Gardens, St Pancras Road, Chichester, West Sussex.

Macclesfield War Memorial was designed by John Millard of the Manchester School of Art. It includes a statue of Britannia laying a crown of laurels on the body of a soldier who had died from gassing. Although somewhat controversial at the time, the design was accepted and it was dedicated by the Mayor of Macclesfield on 21st September 1921 in front of a crowd of 20,000 people.

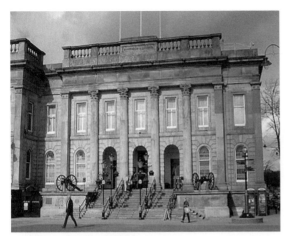

Museum of the Manchester Regiment at Ashton-under-Lyne Town Hall.

Manchester University War Memorial in the quadrangle of the John Owens Building on Oxford Road. The bottom panel commemorates the 512 former members of the University who died in the Great War and the top panel the 157 who died in the Second World War.

- Memorial board and Elstob Dormitory, Merchiston Castle School, Colinton Road, Edinburgh, Scotland.
- Elstob House and painted inscription in the dining hall of Ryleys School, Ryleys Lane, Alderley Edge, Cheshire.
- Elstob Leadership Prize, Christ's Hospital CCF, Horsham, West Sussex, to encourage and reward leadership is awarded annually to the member of Great Erasmus (Year 11) who most exhibits the potential to lead others. It was first presented on 30th May 2013.
- Book of Remembrance of the Manchester and King's Regiments in Manchester Cathedral.
- A Department for Communities and Local Government commemorative VC paving stone is to be dedicated at Litten Gardens, St Pancras Road, Chichester on 11th November 2018 to mark the centenary of his award.

In addition to the VC, DSO and MC he was awarded the 1914–15 Star, British War Medal 1914–20 and Victory Medal 1914–19. The VC is owned by Christ's Hospital School, Horsham. On 21st March 1993 it was transferred on long loan to the Museum of the Manchester Regiment, Ashton-under-Lyne Town Hall.

Memorial window and plaque to Wilfrith in All Saints Church, Siddington, where his father was the vicar for many years.

SECOND LIEUTENANT JAMES SAMUEL EMERSON
12th attached 9th Battalion, The Royal Inniskilling Fusiliers

James Emerson was born at Collon, Drogheda, Co Louth, Ireland on 3rd August 1895, although in his application for a commission he gave his year of birth as 1896. His father, John Emerson (1844–1915), an estate officer of the Collon Estate, married Ellen née Wallace (1851–1925) c.1872 at Collon. They lived at Seven Oaks, Drogheda Street, Collon. James had six brothers:

- William Alexander Wallace Emerson (born 10th February 1880) was an Excise Officer in 1911, living with his wife Eleanor (born c.1884) in Co Cork. He also lived at one time at Palace Row, Armagh, Co Armagh and later served as an Indian Revenue Officer. He was living at 9 Woodford Terrace, Armagh in July 1918.
- John Emerson (born c.1883) was a land agent's clerk in 1901. By 1911 he was an estate agent on the Collon Estate before moving to Greystones, Co Wicklow, where he managed the La Touche estate.
- Herbert Gordon Emerson (5th February 1885–12th March 1923) was a carpenter and emigrated to Canada in 1906. He lived at 126 5th Avenue East, Calgary, Alberta. He cut off half of three fingers and the thumb of his left hand in an accident with a mechanical saw, but still managed to enlist in the Canadian Forestry Corps (883756) on 26th October 1916 and served as a lance corporal with 35th Company, 187th (Central Alberta) Battalion. He was described as 5' 5" tall, with fresh complexion, blue eyes, light brown hair and his religious denomination was Church of England. The Battalion embarked on RMS *Olympic* at Halifax on 20th December 1916 and disembarked in England on 26th December. A draft of 354 men went to 202nd Battalion and the remainder of 187th Battalion was absorbed by 21st Canadian Reserve Battalion on 20th February 1917. Herbert returned to Canada after the war and worked for the Canadian Pacific Railway, but died of peritonitis at Calgary, Alberta in 1923.
- Egerton 'Teb' Arthur Emerson (c.1887–1962) enlisted in 2nd Connaught Rangers (8742) on 8th March 1906 at Dundalk. He was posted to Renmore Barracks, Galway and subsequently assigned to 1st Battalion at Mullingar. The Battalion sailed for Southampton on 11th March 1907 and then to Malta aboard HMT *Braemar*, arriving on 23rd March, where it was based at Verdala Barracks, St George's Barracks, Pembroke Camp and Melliha Camp at various times. Whilst at Marsa on 15th April, the Battalion was inspected by King Edward VII. It sailed for India aboard TS *Rewa* on 23rd February 1908, disembarking at Karachi on 11th

March, and was stationed at Dagshai, Umballa and Ferozepore. He attained 1st, 2nd and 3rd Certificates of Education and was promoted lance corporal. The Battalion took part in the Delhi Durbar in December 1911. Teb became a military clerk and was posted to Dublin as temporary sergeant in October 1912. He transferred to the Army Reserve in 1913 but was mobilised on 4th August 1914 and was posted to Renmore Barracks, Galway before transferring to 2nd Battalion three days later at Aldershot, Hampshire. He went to France on 14th August and was in action at Le Grand Fayt when the Battalion was overrun. Six officers and 280 men were posted missing, most of them had been taken prisoner. He was held at Kuepgefangenen-lager, Guben, Brandenburg on the German/Polish border until being repatriated at the end of the war. Teb was discharged to the Class Z Reserve on 3rd April 1919 and took up a temporary position in the Department of Social Welfare. He was living at 26 Chelmsford Road, Ranelagh, Dublin at

James' brother, Egerton 'Teb' Arthur Emerson.

the time of his marriage to Constance Faiers (c.1890–1974), a bookkeeper, in August 1919 at Christ Church, Leeson Park, Dublin. She was living nearby at 18 Ranelagh Avenue. Teb served in the Fórsa Cosanta Áitiúil, training recruits throughout the Second World War. Teb and Constance lived at St Peter's Close, Drogheda and they had three children – John Frederick Wallace Emerson 1920, Vera Constance Emerson and Dorothy Emerson 1927. John was a lieutenant in 26th (Dublin) County Boys' Brigade. He enlisted in the Royal Air Force (1795670) and served during the Second World War as a sergeant flight engineer in 106 Squadron on Lancaster bombers. He took part in a number of operational sorties in late 1944 including to Nuremberg 19th October, mine laying in the Kattegat 24th October, Bergen U-boat pens 29th October, a daylight raid on German defences on Walcheren 31st October and Landbergen, North Rhine – Westphalia on 21st November. Returning from a night raid on the German Baltic fleet at Gdynia in the early hours of 16th December his Lancaster was attacked by a Ju88, piloted by Major Werner Houses Mann, and crashed near Anholt Island in the Kattegat. His body was washed ashore on 6th March 1945 and is buried in Anholt Cemetery, Denmark.

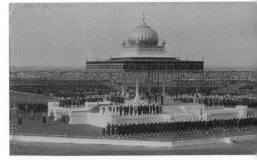

Egerton Emerson's Battalion took part in the Delhi Durbar in December 1911.

- Evelyn Francis Emerson (1889–1968) was a farmer in 1911 and married Frances Mary Magill (born c.1892). They had a son, Lennox Campbell Noel Emerson, in 1923. Frances' two brothers, William John Magill (c.1893–1918) and Samuel Richard Magill (born 1898), enlisted in the South Irish Horse, which by September 1917 had dismounted and become 7th (South Irish Horse) Battalion, Royal Irish Regiment. Samuel survived the war and emigrated to Australia, serving in the Army there as a bombardier 31st March 1942–19th October 1945. William was a sergeant when he was killed at Ronssoy, France on 21st March 1918 (Pozières Memorial – Panel 30/31).

James' nephew, Sergeant John Frederick Wallace Emerson, was killed returning from a raid on Gdynia on 16th December 1944.

- Alfred Henry Emerson (born c.1892) was a commercial clerk, living at 19 Harrington Road, St Kevins, Dublin and served as a private in the RASC (T4/124270). He married Edith Scott Ruttle (born c.1891), a bank clerk, in November 1919 at the Church of St John, Brixton, London. She was living at 12 Barrington Road, Brixton at the time of her marriage. He was later the manager of Piggot's Music Shop at 112 Grafton Street, Dublin.

James' paternal grandfather, also James Samuel Emerson (1816–97) married Margaret (1822–1919) c.1843. She was living with her son John and his wife Ellen in 1911.

Dundalk Grammar School was founded in 1739 as a Charter School and in 1835 became the Dundalk Educational Institution. Having been in abeyance during the Great War, it was revived in 1921 as Dundalk Grammar School. The school is rooted in the Anglican tradition, but is now multi-denominational. A second VC was educated there, William David Kenny.

Wellington Barracks, Dublin. The site was first used for a prison, commenced in 1813. In 1887 it was transferred to the War Department and Wellington Barracks was completed in November 1893. On 15th April 1922 it was handed over to the Irish Free State and renamed Griffith Barracks. In 1991 the site was handed over to the Office of Public Works and is now Griffith College and Griffith Barracks National School.

James was educated at Erasmus Smith School in Collon, Dundalk Educational Institute in Co Louth and at Mountjoy Secondary School in Parnell Square, Dublin, Ireland as a boarder. He was employed as a clerk. James enlisted in 3rd Royal Irish Rifles (3/14430) on 15th September 1914 and was described as 5′ 3½″ tall, weighing 115 lbs, with fresh complexion, blue eyes, brown hair and his religious denomination was Church of England. His teeth were in very poor condition and remedial action had to be taken. He carried out basic training at Kinnegar Camp, Holywood, Co Down and later moved to Wellington Barracks, Dublin and subsequently to Portobello Barracks in the city. He went to France to join the 2nd Battalion on 14th April 1915 as a machine gunner.

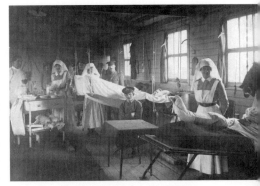

No.3 Canadian General Hospital was the first hospital unit created by a university (McGill) during the war. It mobilised in Montreal on 5th March 1915 under Colonel HS Birkett, McGill's Dean of Medicine 1914–21 and, after a short period in England, moved to France on 16th June and opened at Dannes-Camiers on 19th June. From 6th January 1916 onwards it was in the old Jesuit College at Boulogne. Lieutenant Colonel John McCrae, who wrote *In Flanders Fields*, was involved in setting it up (McGill University).

James was badly wounded by gunshots to his wrist and right foot at Hooge, near Ypres, Belgium on 25th September and was treated at 8th Field Ambulance and 3rd Canadian General Hospital before being evacuated to England via Dieppe on 29th September. He was treated at the Royal Infirmary in Sheffield and King George V Hospital in Dublin 4th–25th January 1916, followed by Temple Hill Auxiliary Hospital, Blackrock, Dublin and Holywood Convalescent Hospital until 7th April. The first phalanx of the big toe was removed on 12th January as it was necrotic. While in hospital he was on the strength of the Depot until posted to 3rd (Reserve) Battalion at Londonderry, Ireland on 2nd January. His return to duty in Dublin coincided with the Easter Rising on Monday 24th April. His section was assigned to guard the Bank of Ireland on College Green. Promoted unpaid lance corporal on 20th May and paid on 28th June. He returned to France, embarking on SS *Viper* at Southampton on 29th June, and arriving at 36th Infantry Base Depot, Harfleur, Le Havre the following day. He joined 9th Royal

Sheffield Royal Infirmary opened in 1792 as Sheffield General Infirmary and was renamed Royal Infirmary in 1897. It closed in the 1980s. The author's grandmother was a nurse there. An innovative octagonal outpatients department was built in 1884, lit by a cupola, and a nurses' home was added in 1897. The site is now used by a supermarket and an insurance company.

Irish Rifles at Beaumont Hamel on the Somme on 13th July, serving in B Company, having been appointed acting corporal on 3rd July.

On 11th December 1916 James applied for a commission. On 8th February 1917 he returned to England to attend officer training at No.8 Officer Cadet Battalion, Lichfield, Staffordshire from 7th April. He was commissioned in 12th (Reserve) Battalion, Royal Inniskilling Fusiliers on 1st August 1917 and was attached to the 9th Battalion in France. **Awarded the VC for his actions north of La Vacquerie, France on 6th December 1917, LG 13th February 1918.** He died of wounds shortly after the VC action near La Vacquerie on 6th December 1917. Despite this his grave could not be identified after the war and he is commemorated on the Cambrai Memorial (Panels 5/6). A medical officer, Captain Thomas William Gerald Johnson MC, who was with him when he died, wrote to his mother:

King George V Hospital was founded as a military medical facility in 1909. When it transferred to the Irish Free State in 1922, it was named after St Bricín, a 7th century Irish surgeon. It remains a military hospital.

SS *Viper* was built at Govan in 1906. With three steam turbines powering triple screws, she had a top speed of 22 knots. She operated on the Ardrossan–Belfast route until 1914 and then served as a troop carrier in the English Channel. Post war there was a decline in trade due to the unrest in Ireland and she was sold to the Isle of Man Steam Packet Co and renamed *Snaefell*.

Bank of Ireland on College Green, Dublin and James Emerson (front row left) with members of his section in 1916.

He had had his steel helmet torn with a bullet and been hit in the hand, but refused to leave his men. An enemy sniper eventually shot him, and before he passed away he asked me to write to you and let you know that he did his duty. We all miss him very much, and his place will never be filled in the battalion, as far as I am personally concerned. His death was very quiet,

James Emerson's name on the Cambrai Memorial.

and he suffered very little pain and the padre and myself were with him in his last moments. We lost a lot of fine officers the same day, and, believe me, my heart is torn for every one of their parents.

James is commemorated in a number of other places:

- Cambrai Company, Army Foundation College, Harrogate comprises six platoons named after VC winners in the Battle of Cambrai, including 8 (Emerson VC) Platoon.
- Family headstone in Collon, Co Louth.
- Collon War Memorial.
- War Memorial in Mary Street, Drogheda, Co Louth, Ireland.
- Plaque at Mount Temple School, Dublin.
- Royal Irish Regiment (27th (Inniskilling), 83rd, 87th and Ulster Defence Regiments) VC Memorial in St Anne's Cathedral, Belfast, Northern Ireland.
- One of nine VCs named on the 36th (Ulster) Division memorial stone at Ulster Tower, Thiepval, France dedicated on 1st July 1991 by the Royal Irish Rangers.
- The Department for Communities and Local Government decided to provide a commemorative paving stone at the birthplace of every Great War Victoria Cross recipient in the United Kingdom. A commemorative stone for James was dedicated at the Cross of Sacrifice, Glasnevin Cemetery, Dublin, Ireland on 11th November 2017 to mark the centenary of his award.

Collon War Memorial with James Emerson's name on the forward face.

The Royal Irish Regiment VC Memorial in St Anne's Cathedral, Belfast (Memorials to Valour).

Whitworth Hall, on the left, in Laurence Street, Drogheda was built in 1865 by Benjamin Whitworth MP as a community centre. It passed into private ownership in the 1970's. It its time it has been a cinema, theatre, music hall, dance hall and a venue for boxing and wrestling tournaments.

James' friend, Private William George Abraham's grave in Écoivres Military Cemetery, Mont St Eloi.

James made a will while a soldier, leaving any property found on his body to his mate, 3/14434 Private William George Abraham, 2nd Royal Irish Rifles Machine-Gun Section …. *as he already knows.* William was born at Collon c.1896 and the service numbers of the two men are only four apart, so they probably enlisted on the same day. By the time the will had to be enacted, Abraham was a lance corporal and had transferred to 74th Brigade Machine Gun Company (18119). He was killed in action on 21st May 1916 (Écoivres Military Cemetery, Mont St Eloi, France – II B 4). James Emerson's effects therefore reverted to his family. As he never married, the VC was presented to his mother by Brigadier General George W Hacket-Pain CB (later KBE) at Whitworth Hall, Drogheda on 3rd April 1918.

Memorial to the nine VCs of 36th (Ulster) Division at Ulster Tower, Thiepval, France.

In addition to the VC he was awarded the 1914–15 Star, British War Medal 1914–20 and Victory Medal 1914–19. The VC is held privately.

CAPTAIN ROBERT GEE
2nd Battalion, The Royal Fusiliers (City of London Regiment) attached HQ 86th Brigade

Robert Gee was born on 7th May 1876 at 29 Metcalf Street, Leicester St Margaret, Leicestershire. His father, also Robert Gee (19th June 1830–27th November 1875), a framework knitter, married Amy née Foulds (c.1835–1st May 1885), also a framework knitter, on 29th October 1854 at St Mary's Parish Church, Anstey, Leicestershire. Amy was a seamer of cotton stockings in 1861 and they were living at 35 The Square, Hathern, Leicestershire. They had moved to 29 Metcalf Street, Leicester by 1871. Robert senior died of pneumonia in Leicester Infirmary five months before Robert junior was born. Robert junior had at least eight siblings:

- William Gee (1854–1919) was a shoe/boot finisher. He appeared in court in November 1884 for being drunk and disorderly in Willow Street, Leicester and assaulting Sergeant Johnson of the Leicester City Police. He was found guilty and fined £1 or 14 days' hard labour. William married Ann Heathcote (1863–1906), but no record has been found. They were living at 18 Bremen Street, Hackney, London in 1891 and 16 West Side, Hackney by 1901. William was living with his children at 111 Glyn Road, Clapton, London in 1911. They had six children – Amy Gee 1888, Thomas Gee 1890, William Gee 1892 (served during the Great War), Amy Elizabeth Gee 1895, Annie Gee 1898 and Robert Gee 1902.

Robert Gee's parents married at St Mary's Parish Church, Anstey in October 1854. The church is of Norman origin, but was extensively rebuilt in 1845–46.

- Thomas Gee (1858–61).
- Ellen Rebecca Gee (1859–1940, known as Rebecca, was a machine hand in 1871. She married Mezzino Sanders (1857–1918), a carter, in 1879. She was a shoe machinist in 1891 and they were living at 13 Milne Street, Leicester. By 1901 they were living at 58 Stoughton Street, Leicester. By 1911 he was a boot maker and they were living at 38 Sparkenoe Street, Leicester. They had three children – John Robert Sanders 1880, William Mezzino Sanders 1881 and Amy Blanche Sanders 1883. William was a shoe laster in 1901 and emigrated to Canada, where he married Annie Sophia Pickford (born c.1883) in 1906 at Halifax, Nova Scotia. He served in the Militia and transferred to the Canadian Expeditionary Force (1274694) on 22nd June 1918. At the time he was a shoemaker living at Main Road, Eastern Passage, Halifax, Nova Scotia. He declared previous service in 1st Leicestershire RHA (TF), Canadian Royal Garrison Artillery and 63rd Regiment (Halifax Rifles) from 1st March 1916. He was described as 5' 10½" tall, weighing 160 lbs, with grey eyes and his religious denomination was Methodist. He was serving with Hugonias Battery, Halifax in December 1918. William and Annie had a son, Wilfred M Sanders in 1907.

The Le Touret Memorial where Arthur William Linney is commemorated.

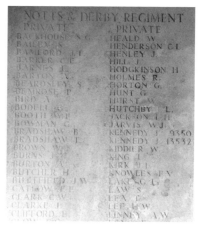

Arthur Linney's name on the Le Touret Memorial is bottom right.

- Lois Elizabeth Gee (c.1860–1945) married Arthur William Linney (1861–1931) in 1879. They lived at 42 Montrose Road, Old Aylestone, Leicester and had five children – Arthur William Linney 1881, Albert Edward Linney 1883, Amy Elizabeth Linney 1888, Ethel May Linney 1891 and Ellen Rebecca Linney 1900. Arthur junior served as a private in 1st Sherwood Foresters (4932) and was killed in action on 13th March 1915 at Neuve Chapelle (Le Touret Memorial, France – Panel 26/27). Private Jacob Rivers was awarded the VC for the same action.
- Amy Laura Gee (born 1863) was a shoe hand in 1881.
- Ellen 'Polly' Gee (born 1867) was a domestic servant in 1881.
- Jane Gee (born c.1872).
- Mary Ann Gee (1873–1937) married William Watt (1876–1909) in 1898 and they moved to Derbyshire. He was born in Scotland and was a watch and clock maker. They had two daughters – Alexa Alice Watt 1905 and Jessie Lois Watt 1908. After William died, Mary emigrated to Australia with her daughters and died on 11th July 1937 at North Fitzroy, Victoria.
- He may also have had a brother named Arthur and a sister named Sarah.

Robert's paternal grandfather, William Gee (born c.1783), a framework knitter, married Rebecca née Geary (c.1787–1857) on 12th December 1808 at Anstey. In addition to Robert they had at least six other children:

- Robert Gee (born c.1809). He is assumed to have died before 1830, when the VC's father was born.

- Thomas Gee (c.1814–91) married Sophia Cufflin (c.1803–79) in 1839. They had three children – Elizabeth Cufflin Gee 1841, Lois Gee 1843 and William Gee 1847.
- James Gee (born c.1821) was living with his mother and stepfather in 1841.
- Samuel Gee (born c.1826) was living with his mother and stepfather in 1841.
- Isaac Gee (born c.1827) was living with his mother and stepfather in 1841.
- Sarah Gee (born c.1829) was living with his mother and stepfather in 1841 and was a handloom weaver in 1851.

It is assumed that William died before 1836 as Rebecca married John Kelham (c.1787–1856), a framework knitter, on 4th April 1836 at Anstey. He had married Sarah Pearson (1788–1829) in 1810 at Thornton, Leicestershire and they had six children – Elizabeth Kelham 1818, Joseph Kelham 1820, James Kelham 1821, Samuel Kelham 1826, Isaac Kelham 1827 and Sarah Kelham 1829. John and Rebecca were living at Stanton-under-Bardon in 1841 and 1851. In the latter year he was a cotton handloom weaver and she was a tanner of hose cotton. They had a daughter, Ellen, born c.1838 at Markfield, Leicestershire.

Robert's maternal grandparents lived on Bag Lane, Derby.

His maternal grandfather, John Foulds (20th May 1813–1890), a stonecutter, married Eleanor née Geary (c.1818–44) on 8th February 1836 at Anstey, Leicester. They were living with his parents at Newtown Linford, Leicestershire in 1841. John married Ann Hopkinson (c.1826–98), a lace mender, in 1854 at Nottingham. They were living at Radford Grove, Radford in 1861, at 10 Bag Lane, Court 5, Derby in 1871 and by 1881 had moved to 43 Bag Lane (now East Street). They had four children:

- Fanny Ann Foulds (born 1854), a silk mender, married John Clarke (born 1852) in 1878. In 1881 she was living with her parents and sons Ezra and John, who were recorded as Foulds by mistake. Her husband was elsewhere. By 1911 he was a clerk with a railway company and they were living at 10 Plashet Road, Plaistow, London. They had six children – Ezra Clarke 1878, John Clarke 1880, Hilda Clarke 1885, Alexander Clarke 1887, Leslie Clarke 1890 and Fanny Clarke 1895.
- Martha Foulds (born 1860) was a confectioner in 1881 boarding at 6 Brook Street, Derby. She married John Wade (born c.1855) in 1882 at Derby. He was a general labourer in 1881 lodging at 6 Brook Street, Derby. They had five children – Fanny

Wade 1884, John William Wade 1886, Robert Wade 1888, Florence Annie Wade 1890 and Martha Wade 1895.

- Mary Foulds (1862–1928) married John Spratt (1864–1942) in 1887. In 1901 he was a fruiterer and they were living at 19 Ramilies Road, Toxteth Park, Lancashire. By 1911 they were living at 11 Lennox Avenue, Liscard, Cheshire. They had six children including – John William Spratt 1889, Lilian Spratt 1890, Emily Spratt 1891, Albert Spratt 1893, Margery Spratt 1897 and Muriel Marian Spratt 1898.

- William Foulds (c.1866–1934) was a light porter in 1881. He married Annie Sutcliffe (1867–1944) in 1889 at Nottingham. They were living at 25 Dale Road, Derby in 1901 when he was a commercial traveller. They had three children – William S Foulds 1891, Albert J Foulds 1894 and Arthur P Foulds 1896.

Cottage No.7 at the Countesthorpe Cottage Homes, where Robert lived. The Cottage Homes were a progressive way of looking after orphans and poor children, providing parental care, stability, education and preparation for work. The Cottages were run by Mr and Mrs William Harrison, Superintendent and Matron respectively, and each cottage had a house mother. The future Private William Buckingham VC was admitted to Cottage No.6 in July 1892, shortly after Robert Gee left (Derek Seaton).

Following the death of his parents, Robert was brought up initially by his eldest married sister, Elizabeth, but he proved too difficult for her. He was put in the Leicester Union Workhouse on 20th July 1887 and moved to the Countesthorpe Cottage Homes on 5th August. 1887. William Buckingham VC was also brought up there. Robert was educated at Aylestone, Leicester and then at the Cottage Homes. He was apprenticed to Robert Austin, a shoemaker, of 15 Crown Street, Leicester on 8th March 1890 but did not get on with Austin and on 30th March 1892 he was readmitted to Leicester Workhouse. On 2nd May he was apprenticed to Joseph Charles Shaw & Co, art metal workers, of Carlton Street, Leicester. He lived with the Shaws and got on with them but in 1893 the firm closed before he completed his apprenticeship.

Robert tried to enlist in 6th Dragoon Guards but was rejected and enlisted in 4th (Queen's Own) Hussars (3498) on 8th

Robert was cared for in the Leicester Union Workhouse in July and August 1887 and March– May 1892.

April 1893, joining at Colchester on 14th April. He was described as 5′ 6¼″ tall, weighing 133 lbs, with fresh complexion, dark brown eyes, dark brown hair and his religious denomination was 'Other Protestant'. Much of the information he gave on enlistment was false, probably because he was under age. He gave his next of kin as a cousin, Fred Geary, and his date of birth as 8th March 1875. He deserted on 18th October and re-enlisted in the Royal Fusiliers (4821) the following day under the assumed name of Sydney Evershed. He gave his parents as Arthur and Sarah Evershed of Albert Villas, Richmond Road, Aylestone Park, Leicester and declared siblings William, Arthur and Sarah. The real Arthur Evershed was Secretary of the Harborough Liberal Association and lived at Albert Villas, Wigston Road, Clarendon Park, Leicester, close to his former employer, Joseph Shaw. Robert was described as 5′ 6¼″ tall, weighed 142 lbs, with fresh complexion, hazel eyes, brown hair and his religious denomination was Presbyterian. He joined the 2nd Battalion in Guernsey on 9th December and was awarded the Third Class Education Certificate on 24th January 1894.

His former service in 4th Hussars was discovered and he was imprisoned on 2nd July 1894 for fraudulent enlistment and forfeited his previous service of 256 days, which was later restored due to his subsequent good conduct. He was released on 13th August and continued serving with the Battalion in Guernsey, Dover and Woolwich. Robert was awarded the Second Class Education Certificate on 18th October 1895 and was promoted lance corporal on 1st January 1896. He was awarded the Musketry Drill Certificate on 13th February 1896 and was granted Good Conduct Pay @ 1d per day on 13th August. He was posted to the 1st Battalion and served in the East Indies from 25th November 1896. On 23rd February 1898 at Mhow he declared he had enlisted under the false name as Sydney Evershed and reverted to Robert Gee. Promoted corporal on 20th August 1898, passed Transport Duties on 24th August 1899 and was granted Good Conduct Pay @ 2d per day on 19th October. On 7th February 1900 he signed on to complete twelve years service. On 15th March 1900 he was posted to 4th Battalion in

Robert married Elizabeth Dixon at Salem Baptist Church, Folkestone, Kent on 8th March 1902. It was funded largely by Samuel (later Sir Samuel) Morton Peto (1809–89), one of the great railway contractors of the Victorian era, responsible for laying about 750 miles of track in England and another 2,300 miles globally. His company built Nelson's Column, the Reform Club and Houses of Parliament in London. He was a MP for more than twenty years, but resigned in 1866, having been declared insolvent. The church has been taken over by a pub chain and is named *The Samuel Peto*.

Britain and was promoted sergeant on 1st August while stationed at Shorncliffe. He excelled at hockey and cross-country running.

On 8th March 1902 Robert married Elizabeth Dixon (1873–1960) at Salem Baptist Church, Folkestone, Kent. She was born at Sydenham, London and they met while she was visiting her sister in Folkestone. They had two daughters:

• Edith Tanycastell (also seen as Tannycastle) Gee (7th December 1902–29th December 1998), born at 103 Samuel Street, Woolwich, London, married Douglas William Harrison (1900–91) on 7th June 1924 at All Saints Church, Twickenham, Middlesex. He was the youngest son of William and Sarah Jane Harrison, superintendent and matron of Countesthorpe Homes. Douglas's brother, Norman Cyril John Harrison, a farm labourer, enlisted on 15th November 1915 at Leicester and was attested at Newcastle upon Tyne on 5th May 1916 at No.1 Depot RFA. He was described as 5′ 9″ tall and weighed 132 lbs. He subsequently served in 21st Reserve Battalion, Lancashire Fusiliers (26658), 72nd Training Reserve Battalion (36060) and the East Lancashire Regiment (34644). He went to France on 7th October 1916 and transferred to 18th Manchester on 22nd October 1916. Norman died of gas poisoniong on 13th June 1917 (Hop Store Cemetery, Ypres, Belgium – I B 43). Edith and Douglas had a son, Robert Norman Harrison (1925–2016).

• Amy Tanycastell Gee (24th (also seen as 14th) May 1905–25th June 1969), born at Dublin, Ireland, trained as a nurse at St George's Hospital in London and later worked in private nursing. She had a daughter, Margaret Elizabeth Gee, in 1931 at Blean, Kent. Amy married Francis Joseph Andrews (1855–1942) in 1936 at Blean. He had married Isabel Goodman (1856–1936) in 1891. They had no children. Francis was the secretary of a limited company in 1911 and was living at 1 Lathbury Road, Oxford. Amy was living at 14 Fitzroy Road, Tankerton, Whitstable, Kent in 1950. She changed Margaret's name to Andrews by Deed Poll on 5th June 1950 (LG 30th June 1950). Amy married Herbert H Green in 1966 at Bridge.

Elizabeth's father, Peter Dixon (1842–1909), was born at Brampton, Huntingdonshire. He married Eliza née Roberts (c.1843–1933), born at Bangor, North Wales, in 1865 at Hackney, London. He was a gardener in 1881 and they were living at

Robert's daughter, Amy, trained as a nurse at St George's Hospital, London. The original Lanesborough House, built in 1719 by Viscount Lanesborough, was replaced by this 350-bed facility completed in 1844, at Hyde Park Corner. By 1980 the hospital had moved to Tooting and the building is now the Lanesborough Hotel, one of the most exclusive in London.

Longfellow Road, Cheam, Surrey. By 1891 they had moved to 135 Wellfield Road, Streatham, London. She was living at 112 Wellfield Road by 1915. In addition to Elizabeth they had six other children:

- Kate Dixon (1867–1956), a dressmaker in 1901, married Frederick Lincoln (1863–1941) in 1904. They had two children – Horace Frederick Lincoln 1906 and Elizabeth Amelia Lincoln 1908.
- Bathsheba Dixon (1871–73).
- Robert Henry Dixon (born 1876) was a port errand boy in 1891 and a florist/gardener in 1901.
- Louisa Dixon (1877–83).
- George Dixon (born 1880) was a railway porter in 1901. He married Eleanor Ruth Bye (1883–1961) in 1902 at Lambeth, London. They had two children – Kate Louisa Dixon 1903 and Frederick George Dixon 1907. By 1911 he was a roadman with the borough council and they were living at 172 Wellfield Road, Streatham.
- Frederick Charles Dixon (1882–1915) was a night washer on the tramways in 1901. He married Florence Catherine Ellis (1889–1976) in 1908 at Dartford, Kent. They had two daughters – Violet Catherine Dixon 1909 and Doris Elizabeth Dixon 1910. They were living at 25 Wingfield Place, Halfway Street, Sidcup, Kent in 1915. Frederick served as a sergeant in 12th Rifle Brigade (S/123) and died of wounds on 9 September 1915 (Boulogne Eastern Cemetery, France – VIII B 77).

Robert's wife encouraged him to study while serving to make up for his lost education as a child. He was promoted colour sergeant on 4th March 1904 and was awarded the First Class Education Certificate on 28th March and Class 1 Service Pay on 1st April. On 13th May he signed on to complete twenty-one years service and was posted to Portobello Barracks, Dublin, Ireland. He attended a course at the School of Musketry, commencing on 12th December 1905. On a battalion march on 21st

Portobello Barracks was constructed between 1810 and 1815, originally for cavalry, and was expanded during the 19th century. On independence in 1922 the Barracks became the National Army HQ under Michael Collins. In 1952 it was renamed Cathal Brugha Barracks, after a leader of the 1916 rising who died during the Civil War. It is currently the HQ of 2nd Brigade and houses a number of units.

June 1906 he turned his left leg on a stone and damaged his knee. While taking drill on 27th November the knee gave out again and he was in hospital for three weeks.

On 15th February 1907 Robert was posted to the Regimental Depot, Hounslow, Middlesex. He suffered from heart trouble in 1908, but remained with O Company, 6th (Reserve) Battalion as the pay sergeant at Hounslow. He passed Map Reading on 31st March 1908 and was appointed orderly room sergeant on 8th November. While at Hounslow he learned to ride with the cavalry regiment based there. On 16th December CO 6th Battalion applied for Robert to be retained with the Battalion for another year. He passed Composition on 25th March 1909 and was posted to 4th Battalion on 2nd October 1909 but returned to 6th Battalion on 8th November.

Robert was appointed regimental quartermaster sergeant on 1st January 1911. He was living with his family at 162 Wellington Road South, Hounslow in 1911. Robert was awarded the Long Service & Good Conduct Medal in November 1912 and on 15th April 1914 was permitted to continue his service beyond twenty-one years. He was still serving with 6th (Reserve) Battalion when war broke out and moved with it to Dover as an instructor. He was promoted warrant officer class 2 on 29th January 1915 and studied military history to become a lecturer on the subject. Robert sailed with 2nd Battalion for Egypt and arrived in Alexandria, Egypt on 29th March.

Robert was commissioned on 21st May 1915 and was loaned a sword by Lieutenant Colonel SF Legge, 1st Dragoon Guards. The irony of this was not lost on Robert, having been rejected by the Dragoon Guards when he tried to enlist in 1893. He served at Gallipoli from August 1915 and was in command of a company in 2nd Battalion from 5th September. Appointed acting captain 27th September. On 26th November a violent storm flooded the trenches at Suvla Bay. Several men were drowned, others were shot by Turkish snipers as they scrambled for safety and some died of exposure. Only twenty-seven men remained in the line with ten working rifles. The Battalion was withdrawn from Suvla to Cape Helles on 16th December from where it was evacuated on 5th January 1916, arriving at Alexandria, Egypt on 8th January on HT *Caledonia*. He was appointed acting staff captain, HQ 86th Brigade in Suez on 2nd February and staff captain from 15th March.

The Brigade left Port Tewfik for France on RMS *Alaunia* on 14th March and he was promoted lieutenant on 21st March. **Awarded the MC for his actions at Beaumont Hamel on 1st July 1916 when he cheered his men on in full view of the enemy until wounded in the thigh, but refused to retire and continued to urged them on until he was blown into the air by a shell and carried away semi-conscious, LG 22nd September 1916.** He was evacuated to England on 4th July with a thigh wound and shell shock on SS *St David*, arriving at Southampton. A medical board on 20th July found him unfit for General Service and Home Service for four months and for Light Duties for three months. While on sick leave at 20 St Andrew's Terrace, Dover until 19th October, he learned French. A medical board on 24th October found him unfit for General Service for four months and Home Service for two months, but fit for Light Duties in an office. As a result he was appointed as extra assistant to the Officer in Charge, Records Cork, Ireland on 2nd December. However, a medical board on 12th December found him fit for General Service and he was subsequently ordered to report to 5th Battalion.

Robert returned to France in February 1917, served in HQ 29th Division until 24th June and returned to HQ 86th Brigade as staff captain. He was appointed temporary captain next day until 1st May 1918. He was wounded near Ypres

Robert moved from Egypt to France aboard RMS *Alaunia* (13,405 tons), a Cunard Line ship built in 1913, sister to RMS *Andania* and *Aurania*. When war broke out she was requisitioned as a troopship and was widely employed in the role bringing Canadian troops to Europe, supporting the Gallipoli campaign, carrying troops to Bombay and returning to the North Atlantic route in 1916. On 19th October 1916, outbound for New York from London, she struck a mine in the English Channel laid by UC-16 and sank off Hastings, Sussex with the loss of two crewmen. Cunard named another vessel RMS *Alaunia*, which was in service 1925–57.

on 13th August and was treated at 88th Field Ambulance before returning to the Brigade HQ on 31st August. Robert was temporary ADC to the Prince of Wales when he visited the front in the autumn. He was granted leave in Britain 19th–27th October. **Mentioned in Field Marshal Sir Douglas Haig's Despatch dated 7th November 1917, LG 11th December 1917.**

Awarded the VC for his actions at Les Rues Vertes, Masnières, France on 30th November 1917, 11th January 1918. He was treated at 37th Field Ambulance on 1st December for a gunshot wound to his right knee and next day was admitted to 3rd General Hospital from 12 Ambulance Train. Having been released on 7th December he was admitted to 89th Field Ambulance on 12th December and 6th Stationary Hospital next day with the same knee wound. Robert returned to duty on 19th December. The VC was presented by the King at Buckingham Palace on 23rd February 1918. On 5th April he was admitted to 89th Field Ambulance and No.3 Australian Casualty Clearing Station with chronic gastritis. Next day he was transferred to the British Red Cross Hospital and was evacuated to England on 8th April on HMHS *Cambria* suffering from neurasthenia. Medical boards on 17th April, 23rd May and 8th August found him unfit for service. After the first board he was in hospital, after the second he was in an officers' convalescent hospital and after the third he was recommended for three weeks leave to 29th August. Staff pay ceased on 5th July.

At a reception in Leicester on 11th July he was presented with a gold watch and chain by the Mayor. He was accompanied by his wife, who was presented a gold brooch, and daughter Edith. That afternoon he visited Countesthorpe

The recommendation for Robert Gee's VC raised by Brigadier General GRH Cheape, commanding 86th Brigade, and supported by Major General Beauvoir de Lisle, commanding 29th Division. Ronald Cheape married Margaret Ismay, daughter of Joseph Bruce Ismay of the White Star Line, who survived the *Titanic* disaster in 1912. Ronald Cheape's sister, Catherine, was not so lucky, as she perished in sinking of the *Empress of Ireland* in 1914. Ronald's brother, Hugh Annesley Gray-Cheape, led the last British cavalry charge against guns in the Sinai Desert on 8th November 1917.

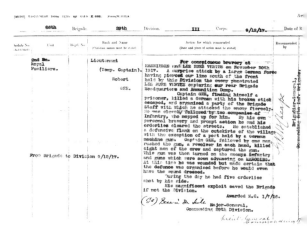

Cottage Homes for the annual sports day. Superintendent and Matron Harrison had lost their elder son, Norman Cyril John Harrison, to gas poisoning at Ypres in July 1917. The younger son, Douglas William Harrison, met Edith and they married six years later.

On 4th September 1918 Robert was admitted to Gray's Inn, presumably to study law, and was living at 254 Link Road, London at the time. However, he was appointed Staff Captain, Tees Garrison, Middlesbrough on 12th September 1918 and continued lecturing in military history, including during visits to public schools. A medical board on 19th January 1919 found him fit for service and on 7th February

The grave of 41591 Private Norman Cyril John Harrison, 18th Manchester, son of William and Sarah Jane Harrison of the Cottages Homes at Countesthorpe.

he was promoted captain and transferred to the Queen's Own (Royal West Kent Regiment). On 4th April he was admitted to hospital with a duodenal ulcer but continued to receive pay at staff rates until 20th May, having joined the Regiment at Catterick on 19th May. A medical board on 10th June at Prince of Wales Hospital, London found him unfit for service for three months and recommended two months convalescence at home. Leave was granted until 12th August at 254 Link Road, London. A medical board on 19th August also found him unfit for three months and he was sent to Sir Ernest Cassel's Convalescent Home, Sandacres, Parkstone, Dorset. The next medical board on 27th October found him unfit for service for a further three months and special leave was recommended to 26th January 1920. However, a medical board on 29th January found him unfit for a further three months and an extension of special leave was recommended. On 8th March 1920 he transferred to the Reserve due to ill health and was paid a gratuity of £1,500 and pension of £150 per year.

Robert attended the VC Garden Party at Buckingham Palace on 26th June 1920 and was a member of the Honour Guard at the burial of the Unknown Warrior at Westminster Abbey on 11th November. He ceased to belong to the Reserve of Officers on 8th May 1925. Robert and Elizabeth were living at 7 Manor Road, Twickenham, Surrey in 1921. He unveiled the Ratcliffe-on-the-Wreake war memorial in Leicestershire on 19th February, was present at the unveiling of Countesthorpe War Memorial by the Duke of York (future King George VI) in November and unveiled Swithland War Memorial in Leicestershire in December.

Robert was Initiated as a Freemason into the Roll Call Lodge (No.2523) meeting at Hounslow, Middlesex on 13th June 1907. He Passed to the Second Degree on 13th September and was Raised to the sublime degree of a Master Mason on 14th November. On 12th October 1916 he was appointed Senior Warden and was later elected to the Chair, being Installed on 10th October 1918. He was a founder member of Alma Lodge (No.3534) in 1911 and was appointed Junior Warden on 17th September 1913 and Senior Warden on 18th September 1918. In 1921 he was appointed Assistant Grand Sword Bearer, but resigned all Masonic memberships in Britain when he went to Australia, where he was active in a Western Australian lodge.

James Ramsay MacDonald 1866–1937 was the first Labour Prime Minister in 1924. With Keir Hardie and Arthur Henderson, he was one of the principal founders of the Labour Party. He entered Parliament in 1906 and was the Chairman of the Parliamentary Party 1911–14. He opposed the war and lost his seat in 1918. He lost to Robert Gee in 1921 but was elected in 1922. His first Labour government in 1924 only lasted nine months. When returned to power in 1929 it was overwhelmed by the crisis created by the Depression. In 1931 he formed a National Government and as a result was expelled from the Labour Party. He stood down as Prime Minister in 1935, but remained in the Cabinet and died in 1937, still an MP.

After the war Robert turned to politics, standing as the Coalition (National Democratic and Labour Party) Candidate for Consett, Co Durham in the General Election on 14th December 1918. He came second by only 293 votes to the Liberal candidate, Aneurin Williams, the sitting member since 1914. However, in a by-election on 2nd March 1921 he became the Coalition MP for East Woolwich, London, defeating Ramsay MacDonald, future leader of the Labour Party and Prime Minister in 1924 and 1929–35, by 683 votes. Robert had a celebratory breakfast with Prime Minister David Lloyd George on 5th March and took his seat in the Commons on 7th March. He was elected Treasurer of the House of Commons British Legion branch in May 1922. However, his tenure was short as he lost his seat in the General Election on 15th November 1922 to the Labour candidate, Henry Snell, by 3,906 votes.

Robert was the unsuccessful Conservative candidate in a by-election at East Newcastle upon Tyne on 11th January 1923, coming third to the Labour candidate, Arthur Henderson. He was also unsuccessful in the General Election on 6th December 1923, standing for Bishop Auckland, Co Durham, again being beaten into third place by the Labour candidate, Benjamin Charles Spoor. However, he was successful in the General Election on 29th October 1924, when he was elected Conservative MP for Bosworth, Leicestershire, beating the Liberal candidate by 358 votes. Robert became an Honorary Freeman of the City of Leicester on 22nd July 1925.

An action was brought against him by Lord Lambourne, Chairman of the Council of the Royal Society for the Prevention of Cruelty to Animals. The RSPCA had been collecting evidence to halt the export of old horses to Europe for slaughter. Robert made comments to a Departmental Committee appointed to inquire into the export, which the RSPCA knew to be untrue. Robert later withdrew the remarks, although at the time he was convinced that the allegations were true.

Robert collapsed during a lengthy session in the House of Commons as a result of overwork and his war wounds. He also had a seizure at Leicester station in January 1926. It was rumoured that he was considering resigning his seat and spent three months in France resting. Soon afterwards he was granted a year's leave of absence from the Commons and decided to go to Australia for a prolonged rest, leaving his wife and family in England. He sailed on SS *Ormonde* and disembarked at Fremantle for treatment. He officially ceased to be a MP on 31st May 1927, when he was appointed Crown Steward and Bailiff of the Manor of Northstead, effectively the same as applying for the Chiltern Hundreds. Elizabeth moved to 14 Fitzroy Road, Tankerton, Kent, where she remained until her death on 7th November 1960, leaving effects valued at £2,120/16/7 to her daughter Amy.

Robert purchased 1,600 acres at Mendel Estate, Mullewa, about 300 miles from Perth, Western Australia on 13th September 1926 and named it *Cambrai*. He farmed it with former Sergeant Frederick Hills, Royal Fusiliers and initially the venture went well and his health improved. However, the economic crisis of 1929 caused wheat prices to slump and small farms were particularly hard hit. Robert ceased farming in 1934, almost bankrupt, but with just enough money to find board accommodation before purchasing a small cottage about twenty miles east of Perth. He secured temporary employment with Boan's Ltd, the Perth department store, at Christmas 1937. When the chairman, Frank Boan, heard there was a VC working for the company in a temporary capacity he created the position of Staff Welfare Officer, which Robert applied for successfully in 1940. He held this position until his retirement in 1951. In 1953 he was appointed Commissioner of Declarations, Western Australia.

Robert settled with Joan, born c.1886 in England, at Cambrai Farm, Mendel Estate, Mullewa, Western Australia and later at Dunmuvin, Orange Road,

Work on RMS *Ormonde* (14,853 tons) for the Orient Steam Navigation Company commenced in 1913, but was suspended when war broke out. The demand for troop transports meant the project was revived and she was finished in 1917 as a basic troopship. She carried troops from Australia to Europe and later operated in the Mediterranean. She was attacked three times by U-boats, but survived. In 1919 she was refitted as a passenger liner on the UK – Suez – Australia route. Her first commercial voyage commenced on 15th November 1919 from London to Brisbane. In 1922 she was used on the first cruises to Norway and in 1923 was converted from coal to oil. In the Second World War she was requisitioned again as a troopship. She assist in the withdrawal from Narvik, Norway in May 1940 and the following month embarked elements of the BEF from St Nazaire, France. In July she landed part of the Iceland garrison. In November 1942 *Ormonde* landed troops in North Africa during Operation Torch and in July 1943 in Sicily during Operation Husky. In 1945 she landed troops in Malaya and repatriated POWs from Burma. She steamed over 300,000 miles and transported more than 120,000 troops before returning to commercial service in 1947 on the Europe – Australia route. She was chartered by the Ministry of Transport to operate emigrant voyages to Australia with a capacity of 1,052 passengers. On 10th October 1947 she departed London as the first liner to make the voyage under the joint agreement between the British and Australian Governments. She made a total of seventeen such voyages. In March 1950 she helped evacuate Dutch citizens from Indonesia and that November moved New Zealand troops to Korea. She was broken up at Troon in 1953.

When Robert went to Australia, Elizabeth moved to Fitzroy Road, Tankerton, Kent.

Boan's department store, founded by brothers Harry and Benjamin Boan, operated in Perth from 1895 to 1986 (William E Fretwell).

Darlington, Western Australia. They had a daughter. On the outbreak of war in 1939, Robert tried to enlist in the Australian Volunteer Defence Corps. He falsified his age by ten years, but was rejected on medical grounds. Robert had served with many Jews in the Royal Fusiliers and took an interest in Jewish affairs thereafter. He was appointed Vice President of the Western Australia Council of Jewish Affairs in 1944 and in 1951 became a life member and Patron of the Western Australia Jewish Ex-Servicemen's Association. When he returned to Britain in 1956 he was appointed honorary life vice-president of the Leicester Branch of the Association of Jewish Ex-Servicemen.

Robert travelled with twelve other VCs from Western Australia and Victoria on RMS *Orcades*, to attend the VC Centenary Celebrations at Hyde Park, London on 26th June 1956. The liner docked at Tilbury on 4th June and he was met at St Pancras by his grandson, Robert N Harrison, and was later reunited with his daughter, Edith, and her husband Douglas Harrison in Leicester. Robert attended a reunion of surviving holders of the Freedom of Leicester on 19th June. He departed England on 17th July 1956 never to return.

RMS *Orcades* was the Orient Line's third ship of that name. Her maiden voyage from Tilbury to Australia commenced on 14th December 1948. In 1955 she began a world service westwards, departing London to New Zealand and Australia via the Panama Canal and returning to Britain via the Suez Canal. During the November 1956 Olympic Games in Melbourne she was used as an accommodation ship. She sailed her last cruises in 1972 and was broken up in 1973.

Robert was admitted to the Home of Peace, Thomas Street, Subiaco, Perth, Western Australia on 30th January 1960 and died there on 2nd August 1960. He was cremated at Karrakatta Crematorium, Perth and his ashes were scattered in Rose Garden P. He is commemorated in a number of other places:

Robert Gee in April 1956.

- Memorial fountain at the War Veterans' Home, Mount Lawley, Perth, dedicated on 11th March 1961 by Bishop CL Riley. It was provided by the staff and executive of his former employer, Boan's Ltd. The fountain was later damaged by the bore water used in the project and had to be removed. The plaque was placed in the rotunda in the gardens of the Home.
- Memorial paving stone unveiled outside Freemason's Hall, Covent Garden, London on 25th April 2017 by The Duke of Kent to sixty-four Freemasons awarded the VC in the Great War.
- The Department for Communities & Local Government decided to provide commemorative paving stones at the birthplace of every Great War Victoria Cross recipient in the United Kingdom. A commemorative stone for Robert was dedicated at Leicester Town Hall Square on 30th November 2017 to mark the centenary of his award.

The Army Long Service and Good Conduct Medal, instituted in 1830, was replaced by the Medal for Long Service and Good Conduct (Military) in 1930. It was initially awarded to soldiers after twenty-one years of service in the infantry or twenty-four in the cavalry. In 1870 the qualifying period was reduced to eighteen years of irreproachable service. A recipient subsequently awarded the Meritorious Service Medal had to stop wearing the Army Long Service and Good Conduct Medal. In 1916 a new ribbon was introduced to distinguish it from the Victoria Cross. It remained crimson, but was edged with white bands. For an unknown reason the ribbon of Robert Gee's Long Service and Good Conduct Medal in the Royal Fusiliers Museum is the 1916 version, although he was awarded the Medal in 1912.

Joan moved to 119 Causeway Flats, Adelaide Terrace, Perth, Western Australia after Robert's death. In addition to the VC and MC he was awarded the 1914–15 Star, British War Medal 1914–20, Victory Medal 1914–19 with Mentioned-in-Despatches Oakleaf, Army Long Service & Good Conduct Medal, Edward VII Coronation Medal 1902, George VI Coronation Medal 1937 and Elizabeth II Coronation Medal 1953. His medals were donated by his wife and handed over to the Regimental Secretary at the Royal Fusiliers City of London Headquarters at the Tower of London in May 1960 by his daughter, Edith Harrison. The VC is held by the Royal Fusiliers Museum at the Tower of London.

2008 LANCE DAFADAR GOBIND SINGH
28th Light Cavalry, attached 2nd Lancers (Gardner's Horse)

Gobind Singh (also seen as Gobind Singh Rathore) was born on 7th December 1887 at Damoi, Nagaur, Rajputana, India. Nothing is known of his parents, but he had at least one brother, Amar Singh, who enlisted in the Jodhpur Lancers with Gobind in 1910 and volunteered for service with the Indian Expeditionary Force at the outbreak of the Great War. However, Amar was persuaded to remain in India to help look after the family. He married, had at least one son, Tez Singh, and died before 1947.

Gobind wanted to study but his village had no school and it is understood that he may have been admitted to one of the predecessor schools to Chopasni School at Jodhpur, founded by Maharajah Sir Pratap Singh. He enlisted in the Jodhpur Lancers in 1910 and transferred later to 28th Light Cavalry. In 1914 he went to France with the Indian Expeditionary

The Jodhpur Lancers has the reputation of being the most aristocratic unit in India. The Regiment formed in 1888 under the Imperial Service Troops scheme established to train some Indian princely states forces to the standard of the Indian Army. The Jodhpur Lancers served in the 3rd China War (Boxer Rebellion) in 1900. On the outbreak of the Great War His Highness Maharajah Sir Pratap Singh of Jodhpur placed the Regiment at the disposal of the Crown for Imperial Service overseas. The Jodhpur Lancers went to France with the Maharajah as its commander. As part of the Lucknow Cavalry Brigade the Jodhpur Lancers was also in action on 1st December 1917, albeit a little distance to the north of 2nd Lancers and Gobind Singh. That day the Regiment took part in a dismounted attack on Villers Ridge. However, the artillery support was weak and, despite a dashing advance, the attack was unsuccessful in the face of overwhelming enemy firepower. On 11th May

1918 the Regiment was assigned to the Imperial Service Cavalry Brigade in Palestine, where it was very active until the armistice with Turkey. (Cecil Lawson)

Force and was attached to 2nd Lancers (Gardner's Horse). **Awarded the VC for his actions east of Épehy, France on 1st December 1917, LG 11th January 1918.** The VC was presented by the King at Buckingham Palace on 6th February 1918. Following the ceremony he was the guest of honour at a reception with two distinguished Indian cavalry officers – General Sir Garrett O'Moore Creagh VC, formerly Commander-in-Chief India, and Lieutenant General Sir Pratap Singh, who was a member of the same tribe as Gobind Singh. During the reception Gobind was presented with a piece of silver plate and a gold watch.

After the war Gobind gained authority to study up to class five education certificate. He married Jattal Kanwar and they had a son, Ganga Singh Rathore (1937–99), who also served in 2nd Lancers. He commanded successively B Squadron, then the Regiment and later an infantry and armoured brigades. Ganga married Kamal Kanwar and they had two sons:

• Colonel Rajinder Singh Rathore, who also joined 2nd Lancers. In 2016 he was serving with 52nd Infantry Brigade.
• Colonel Narpat Singh Rathore, who retired to Jaipur.

Gobind was promoted through the ranks of 28th Light Cavalry and was eventually commissioned and rose to risaldar (captain). He was still serving in 1934 and when he retired was granted a hundred acres in Punjab. When India was partitioned in 1947 upon independence, his land was in Pakistan. His nephew, Tez Singh, petitioned

28th Light Cavalry traces its history back to 1784, when a cavalry force was hired from the Nawab of Arcot by the East India Company. Having mutinied over pay, the regiments involved were disbanded and volunteers from them formed 2nd Madras Cavalry, which later became 3rd Madras Native Cavalry. It fought in the Third Mysore War 1790 against Tipu Sultan, the Fourth Mysore War 1799 and the Pindari War 1817, following which it was renamed 3rd Madras Light Cavalry. It took part in several minor operations against the southern Mahrattas in 1844–55 and a detachment fought with the Deccan Horse during the Indian Mutiny in 1857. In 1891 the Regiment converted to lancers and become 3rd Regiment of Madras Lancers, changing to 28th Light Cavalry in 1903. When the Great War broke out the Regiment was in 4th (Quetta) Division. At that time it was composed of four squadrons, one each of Madras and Dekhani Mussulmans, Punjabi Mussulmans, Rajputana Rajputs and Jats. In July 1915 two squadrons were sent to Persia, mounted on camels, to stop German agents

getting to Afghanistan. The rest of the Regiment followed in November. In May 1918 the Regiment was sent to Trans-Caspasia to assist the White Russians, returning to Persia in April 1919. It returned to India (Lucknow) in February 1920. In 1921 it left Lucknow for Dera Ismail Khan on the North West Frontier. The following year it was renamed 7th Light Cavalry. Postings to Bolarum, Sialkot, Jullunder, Loralai and back to Bolarum followed in the 1920s and 1930s. The Regiment was one of the first two to receive newly commissioned Indian officers, initially from Sandhurst but from 1932 from the Indian Military Academy, Dehradun. By September 1939 sixteen of the Regiment's twenty-two officers were Indian. At the outbreak of the Second World War the Regiment was in 4th (Secunderabad) Cavalry Brigade. Conversion to armour began in 1940 and the Regiment joined 254th Indian Tank Brigade in November 1941. By April 1943 it was equipped with Stuart tanks and fought at Imphal and in Burma. In August 1945 it joined the British Indian Division for service in the occupation forces in Japan until returning to India in August 1947. Following independence it played a key role in operations in Jammu and Kashmir.

the Indian government to give the family an equal measure of land in Rajasthan. Gobind Singh died at Nagaur, Rajputana (now Rajasthan) on 9th December 1942. He was cremated at Damoi, Nagaur and is commemorated in a number of places:

- The Commonwealth Memorial Gates on Constitution Hill, London, commemorate the armed forces of the British Empire that served Britain in the World Wars from the Indian subcontinent, Africa and the Caribbean. The memorial was inaugurated on 6th November 2002 by the Queen in her Golden Jubilee year. The ceiling of a memorial pavilion on the Green Park side of the Gates lists the names of seventy-four VC and GC recipients – twenty-three First World War VCs, thirty-nine VC recipients from the Second World War and twelve GCs.

Gardener's Horse was raised by William Gardner in 1809 and saw action in the Nepal War 1815. The Regiment went through a number of name changes – 2nd (Gardner's) Local Horse 1823, 2nd Irregular Cavalry 1840, 2nd Regiment of Bengal Cavalry 1861, 2nd Regiment of Bengal Lancers 1890, 2nd Bengal Lancers 1901, 2nd Lancers (Gardner's Horse) 1903, 2nd/4th Cavalry April 1922, 2nd Lancers (Gardner's Horse) July 1922, 2nd Royal Lancers (Gardner's Horse) 1935 and following Partition back to 2nd Lancers (Gardner's Horse). In 1914 it went to France in 5th (Mhow) Cavalry Brigade. In February 1918 it moved to Egypt, joining 10th Cavalry Brigade, 4th Cavalry Division, Desert Mounted Corps. At the Battle of Megiddo in Palestine in

May 1918 the Regiment charged and broke the Ottoman line defending the Jezreel Valley. In the Second World War it served in the Western Desert in 3rd Indian Motor Brigade, which was overrun by the Italian Ariete Armoured Division on 27th May 1942. 2nd Royal Lancers moved to Haifa, Palestine in July and overland to Sahneh, Persia in August to join 31st Indian Armoured Division. In November it moved to Shaibah near Basra, Iraq and returned to India in January 1943 to convert to armoured cars. After a number of moves within India the Regiment was posted to the frontier at Kohat in October 1944. In 1946 the Regiment went to Malaya and in 1956 became a tank regiment. The Regiment continues to celebrate Cambrai Day on 1st December. This 1920 painting by Thomas Flowerday Clarke is entitled *The second ride of Lance Dafadar Gobind Singh VC.*

General Sir Garrett O'Moore Creagh VC GCB GCSI (1848–1923), born in Co Clare, Ireland, was the son of Captain James Creagh RN. He was commissioned in 95th (Derbyshire) Regiment from Sandhurst in 1869 and was posted to India, where in 1870 he transferred to the Indian Army. He was awarded the VC for his actions on 22nd April 1879 at Kam Dakka during the Second Anglo–Afghan War. O'Moore Creagh commanded the Merwara Battalion 1882–86 and 29th Bombay Infantry from 1890. He commanded the Indian contingent in the Boxer Rebellion in China in 1900 and was appointed to command the entire force in 1901. He was knighted (KCB) in 1904 and in 1909 succeeded Lord Kitchener as Commander-in-Chief India, an appointment he held until retiring in 1914. Douglas Haig served as his Chief of General Staff 1909–12. During the Great War he was the military advisor to the Central Association of Volunteer Training Corps. With EM Humphris he published *The Victoria Cross 1856–1920 – A Complete Record of the Recipients of the Victoria Cross from its Institution in 1856, to the 29th October 1920* and *The Distinguished Service Order, 1886–1923: A Complete Record of the Recipients of the Distinguished Service Order, 1886–1923.*

Lieutenant General Sir Pratap Singh GCB GCSI GCVO (1845–1922), third son of the Maharaja of Jodhpur, Takht Singh, was commissioned in the Jodhpur Risalda in 1878. He served during the Second Afghan War in 1879 (MID) and was wounded in the Tirah Campaign in 1898. Pratap Singh commanded the Jodhpur contingent during the Boxer Rebellion 1900 and rose through the ranks to lieutenant general in 1916. He was also Chief Minister for Jodhpur 1878–95. He served as regent after his brother's death for his nephew and heir to the Jodhpur throne 1895–98, for his grandnephew 1911–18 and for his second grandnephew 1918–22. Pratap Singh was also Maharajah of Idar from 1902 until he abdicated in 1911. He was close to Queen Victoria and served as ADC to the future Edward VII from 1887 and continued through his reign until 1910. Although aged seventy when the Great War broke out, he accompanied the Regiment to France. After the funeral service for Lord Roberts he drove the ambulance carrying the coffin in freezing conditions for two hours to Boulogne without the protection of a windshield or greatcoat. Pratap Singh later accompanied the Regiment to Palestine.

- Named on one of eleven plaques honouring 175 men from overseas awarded the VC for the Great War. The plaques were unveiled by the Senior Minister of State at the Foreign & Commonwealth Office and Minister for Faith and Communities, Baroness Warsi, at a reception at Lancaster House, London on 26th June 2014 attended by The Duke of Kent and relatives of the VC recipients. The Indian plaque is mounted in New Delhi.
- The Secretary of State for Communities and Local Government, Eric Pickles MP announced that Victoria Cross recipients from the Great War would have commemorative paving stones laid in their birthplace as a lasting legacy of local heroes within communities. The stones would be laid on or close to the 100th

The Commonwealth Memorial Gates on Constitution Hill, London, with the memorial pavilion on the right.

The ceiling of the memorial pavilion with the names of seventy-four VC and GC recipients from India, Africa and the Caribbean. Gobind Singh's name is fourth from the bottom.

The 145 commemorative paving stones for Great War VCs born in Australia, Belgium, Canada, China, Denmark, Egypt, France, Germany, India, Iraq, Japan, Nepal, Netherlands, New Zealand, Pakistan, South Africa, Sri Lanka, Ukraine and United States of America at the National Memorial Arboretum, Alrewas, Staffordshire. Inset – Gobind Singh's paving stone.

anniversary of their VC actions. For the 145 VCs born in Australia, Belgium, Canada, China, Denmark, Egypt, France, Germany, India, Iraq, Japan, Nepal, Netherlands, New Zealand, Pakistan, Sri Lanka, South Africa, Ukraine and United States of America, individual commemorative stones were unveiled at the National Memorial Arboretum, Alrewas, Staffordshire by Prime Minister David Cameron MP and Sergeant Johnson Beharry VC on 5th March 2015.

In addition to the VC he was awarded the 1914–15 Star, British War Medal 1914–20, Victory Medal 1914–19 and George VI Coronation Medal 1937. The VC was presented to 2nd Lancers (Gardner's Horse), Indian Army by his son, Brigadier Ganga Singh, and is currently held by the Regiment.

681886 SERGEANT CYRIL EDWARD GOURLEY
D Battery, 276th (West Lancashire) Brigade, Royal Field Artillery

Cyril Gourley was born at 6 Victoria Park, Wavertree, Liverpool, Lancashire on 19th January 1893. His father, Galbraith Gourley (1865–21st November 1938), was born at Irvinestown, Co Fermanagh, Ireland. He moved to Liverpool with his brother, John, in 1889 and opened a provision store at his home at 55 Earle Road. Galbraith married Martha Ann 'Cissie' née Ashcroft (1866–1955) on 16th March 1891 at West Derby, Liverpool. She was born at Wavertree, Liverpool and was educated privately at a boarding school in Tattenhall, Cheshire. They had moved to 6 Victoria Park, Wavertree by 1893. Galbraith

went into partnership with his brother, John, establishing Gourley Brothers Ltd, wholesale provision merchants at 43 Lawrence Road. The business prospered and they expanded into another six stores in the Smithdown Road area. They had a warehouse in Dove Street. In 1899 the family moved to 23 North Road, West Kirby and by 1901 they were at Arncliffe House, 39 Westbourne Road, West Kirby. In 1925 they moved to Hill Close, School Lane, off Column Road, Grange, West Kirby. When he died, Galbraith left effects valued at £14,671/10/4. In 1952 Martha moved to Grayswood House, Grayswood, Haslemere, Surrey with her children Eunice, Irvine and Cyril. Cyril had five siblings:

23 North Road, West Kirby, where the Gourley family lived at the turn of the 19th century, was later the home of Emily Shaw (1882–1915), only child of George Henry and Jane Shaw. Emily was returning from Winnipeg, Canada as a 2nd Class passenger on RMS *Lusitania* when the ship was sunk by U-*20* on 7th May 1915. She was one of 1,198 passengers and crew who lost their lives out of a total of 1,962 aboard (Wordpress).

- Irvine Galbraith Gourley (1891–1972) was a university student in 1911. He enlisted in 4th West Lancashire (Howitzer) Brigade RFA (TF) (retitled 278th Brigade RFA on 15th May 1916) on 12th May 1914 (296861 and 690309) with his brother Cyril and served with the unit in France as a signaller. He married Mary Kennedy in 1932 at Ormskirk, Lancashire. In 1938 he was a building surveyor.
- Reginald Leslie Gourley (1895–1979) was apprenticed to a surveyor in 1911. He married Violet Elsie Rigby (1893–1976) in 1920 and they were living at Tranmere, Cheshire in 1943. They had two children:
  - ° John Galbraith Gourley (1922–43) served as a flight sergeant in 279 Squadron RAF (Air Sea Rescue) (1288466) at Bircham Newton, Norfolk. On 24th August 1943 a distress signal was received from a Stirling (BF522) of 218 (Gold Coast) Squadron RAF based at Downham Market, Norfolk on the return journey from a 727 aircraft raid on Berlin. It had been attacked by a German night fighter and crashed into the sea off the island of Sylt. A Stirling of 149 Squadron spotted a dinghy and it and another Stirling circled it and called for assistance. At 2.15 p.m. two Hudsons (OS-H and OS-R) of 279 Squadron took off from Bircham Newton and reached the dinghy two hours later. A lifeboat was dropped and the men in the dinghy scrambled aboard before two German BF 110 fighters attacked the Hudsons. OS-H was damaged and OS-R was shot down. The German aircraft also attacked the lifeboat, which sank with the loss of all five aboard. John Gourley was in Hudson OS-R and he and the rest of the crew were lost (Flying Officer Alan Owen Whapham, Pilot Officer Douglas Cameron Neil and Flight Sergeant Ellis Lister Pennington). They are commemorated on the Runneymede Memorial, Surrey. The crew of the downed Stirling (one of fifty-six heavy bombers lost on that raid) also perished. Two were washed ashore in Denmark, where

they are buried (Sergeants George Arthur McArthur and Keith Robson) and the other five are also commemorated on the Runneymede Memorial (Pilot Officer William Martin RCAF, Sergeant Evan Robert Lowe, Flying Officer Leslie James De'Ath, Flight Sergeant James Cassidy and Sergeant Herbert Taylor.
  ° Maureen E Gourley (born 1933).
* Eunice Evelyn Gourley (1896–1983).
* Roland Stanley Gourley (1898–1986) served as a Gunner (188176 & 200884) with Base Details RFA and later with the RGA. He was awarded the British War and Victory Medals.
* Alfred Dudley Gourley (1900–70) worked for Frisby Dyke Co, Lord Street, Liverpool as an apprentice draper, but one of his enlistment documents states that he was an agricultural worker. He was called up into the King's (Liverpool) Regiment (29465) on 28th February 1918 at Seaforth, described as 5′ 9″ tall. He was posted to 53rd (Young Soldier) Battalion at Kinmel Park the same day and to 51st (Graduated) Battalion on 3rd May. On 21st August he was posted to the Infantry Base Depot in France and transferred to 8th King's Own (Royal Lancaster Regiment) on 25th August. On 1st October he received a gunshot wound to the back/chest and was admitted to 20th General Hospital at Camiers next day. He was evacuated to Britain and treated at Queen Mary Military Hospital, Whalley from 12th October 1918 until 22nd February 1919 and also at Townley's Military Hospital, Bolton. On

The Hudson was an American built light bomber and reconnaissance aircraft built for the RAF. It was the first significant aircraft order for the Lockheed Aircraft Corporation. Hudsons were used throughout the Second World War, mainly by RAF Coastal Command, but also by the RCAF, RAAF, USAAF and US Navy. By the start of the war seventy-eight Hudsons were in service. Due to US neutrality until December 1941, completed aircraft were flown to the US-Canadian border and towed over it on their landing wheels. They were then dismantled for transportation as deck cargo to Britain, where the Boulton Paul turret was installed. On 8th October 1939 a Hudson over Jutland was the first aircraft operating from Britain to shoot down an enemy aircraft. On 27th August 1941, a Hudson of 269 Squadron damaged U-*570* off Iceland, which surrendered and was salvaged by the Royal Navy. Hudsons were also operated by RAF Special Duties squadrons for clandestine operations in Europe and Burma.

4th March he was posted to 3rd Battalion and 1st Battalion on 26th July. Alfred was treated for gonorrhoea at New Bridge Street Military Hospital, Manchester (a specialist venereal disease hospital) from 13th November until 1st March 1920 and then transferred to Kinmel Park. A medical examination at Dublin on 17th March found he was less than 20% disabled. He was discharged on demobilisation on 23rd April 1920 and was awarded a provisional pension of 5/6 per week plus a £30 gratuity. Alfred married Dorothy Walmsley Dales (1916–2000) in 1939 in Bombay, India. She was born at Leeds, Yorkshire. Alfred became a company director of Lever Brothers in 1948. They later lived at Wildwoods, Sandy

Lane, Gillitts, Natal, South Africa. He died at Durban, KwaZulu, Natal and some time thereafter Dorothy returned to Britain. She died in July 2000 at Sutton Scotney, Hampshire. They had three children including David Gourley born in 1940 in India and Adrian N Gourley born in 1944 in Bournemouth.

The Air Forces Memorial, or Runnymede Memorial, near Egham, Surrey was dedicated in 1953 to commemorate 20,456 airmen and women who were lost on operations during the Second World War and have no known grave.

Cyril's paternal grandfather, Irvine Gourley, farmed thirty acres along the Fermanagh-Tyrone border. He married Margaret née Richie and in addition to Galbraith they had two other children:

• James Gourley (born c.1861) married Isabella Swanston (born c.1863) of Creevehill, Co Fermanagh. They had seven children – Irvine Gourley c.1884, Lizzie Gourley c.1886, Ida May Gourley c.1888, James Gourley c.1890, Margaret E Gourley 1893, Isabel Gourley c.1896 and Redvers Gourley.
• John Gourley (c.1863–1934) went to Liverpool with his brother, Galbraith, in 1889. He married Emily Wright (c.1869–1952) in 1891 at Toxteth Park, Liverpool. They were living at 49 Lawrence Street, Liverpool in 1891. By 1911 they were living at 10 Hawarden Avenue, Liverpool. They had six children including – Florence May Gourley 1893, Gertrude Lilian Gourley 1894, Doris Emily I Gourley 1900, Norman Ritchie 1902 and Margery Louise Gourley 1906.

His maternal grandfather, Edward Ashcroft (1814–94), born at Wavertree, Lancashire, married Eunice Ann née Barnett (c.1837–1917), born at Much Dewchurch, Herefordshire, in 1863 at Hereford. They lived at Ivy Farm/Cottage, 12 Prince Alfred Road, Wavertree. He was a farmer of sixty-five acres in 1871 and had increased it to seventy-six acres by 1881. In the census that year, she was recorded as Louisa A Ashcroft. In 1891 they were living at Ivy Farm on Prince Alfred Road. By 1901 she was living with her sons, James and Frederick, at Stoney Cottage, Clieves Hills, Aughton, near Ormskirk, Lancashire. All three were market gardeners. In addition to Martha they had six other children:

• John Ashcroft (born 1864) was a farm servant in 1881 living with his parents.
• Emily Elizabeth Ashcroft (1868–1935) was recorded as Emma in the 1871 Census. She was a governess in 1891 living with her parents. Emily married Arthur Edward Kingsley (1866–1954), a bookkeeper with the harbour board, in 1894. They were living at Clieves Hill, Aughton in 1911 and at 20 Rock Lane West, Rock Ferry,

Birkenhead, Cheshire in 1915. They had five children – Arthur Reginald Kingsley 1895, Emily Marjory Kingsley 1897, Doris Margaret Kingsley 1899, Geoffrey Barrett Kingsley 1902 and Charles Eric Barrett Kingsley 1905. Arthur Reginald Kingsley served as a private in 1/10th King's (3943). He enlisted on 5th November 1914 and was described as a clerk, 5′ 9¼″ tall and weighing 140 lbs. He went to France on 23rd January 1915 and was employed with the Divisional Sanitary Squad 9th April–6th May. He was admitted to 8 Casualty Clearing Station at Bailleul on 31st May with gastritis, transferred to Boulogne on 5th July and 9th General Hospital at Rouen on 18th July. On 8th August he transferred to England on HMHS *St George* with influenza. Arthur returned to France, embarking at Southampton on 9th June 1916 and disembarking at Le Havre the following day. He rejoined his unit on 20th June and was listed as missing in action on 9th August. He died while a prisoner of war on 17th August 1916 and is buried in St Souplet British Cemetery, France (II AA 22).

Arthur Reginald Kingsley's grave in St Souplet British Cemetery.

• James Barnett Ashcroft (1870–1923) was a farmer in 1891 living with his parents.
• Alfred Edward Ashcroft (1873–86).
• Frederick Charles Ashcroft (1876–1955) was a grocer's apprentice in 1891 living with his parents. He was a farm worker at Shave Hall Farm, Flixton, Lancashire at the time of his marriage to Sarah Cooper (1894–1958) in 1928. They were living at 25 Alderley Road, Flixton when he died in February 1955. They had three children – Cyril Ashcroft 1929, Douglas Ashcroft 1931 and Roy Ashcroft 1934.
• George Henry Ashcroft (1878–1936).

Cyril was educated at Calday Grange Grammar School, Wirral, Cheshire, where he won the Edward Rathbone Scholarship to Liverpool University in 1910. Calday Grange was also attended by actor Daniel Craig, who played James Bond in several films, and Philip May, husband of British Prime Minister Theresa May. Geoffrey Anketell Studdert Kennedy, known as 'Woodbine Willy' during the First World War, taught at the school 1905–07. Cyril was recorded as a draper's apprentice in the 1911 Census. He became the first student at Liverpool University to graduate as a Bachelor of Commercial Science in 1913, gaining distinctions in Economics, French and Commerce. Cyril was then employed by Alfred Holt and Co, owners of the Blue Funnel Line, as a clerk in the shipping office.

On 12th May 1914 Cyril enlisted in 8th Lancashire Battery, 4th West Lancashire (Howitzer) Brigade RFA (TF) (4630 later 681886) for four years. He was mobilised on 4th August and trained in the Sevenoaks and Canterbury areas in Kent. He was promoted bombardier on 19th January 1915 and went to France on 28th September. Many units in 55th (West Lancashire) Division were sent to reinforce other formations and Cyril's unit served initially with 2nd Canadian Division in the Kemmel area south of Ypres. 55th Division had reformed by 27th January 1916 in France with all its former units rejoining. His unit was in the Hallencourt area, east of Albert, in January 1916 and moved to Arras in February.

On 31st March he relinquished the appointment of pay accountant for 7th Battery and next day transferred to the Brigade Ammunition Column. He was granted eight days leave in England from 2nd May and on his return transferred to Brigade HQ on 19th May. On 4th June near Ficheux, France, shells from his unit fell short amongst men of 1/5th King's in the early stages of a trench raid. Later Private Arthur Herbert Procter, a stretcher-bearer, spotted two wounded men in full view of

The University of Liverpool was founded as a college in 1881 and in 1903 it gained its royal charter as one of the six original red brick universities. It was the world's first university to establish departments in oceanography, civic design, architecture and biochemistry. In 2006 it established an independent university in China. Famous alumni include Dame Stella Rimington, head of MI5, the actress Patricia Routledge and the television news presenter Jon Snow. The university has produced nine Nobel Prize winners.

the enemy. He went out to them under heavy fire, dragged them into cover, bandaged their wounds and made them as comfortable as possible before dashing back to arrange for them to be recovered that night. Arthur Procter was awarded the VC.

On 20th July 1916 the batteries transferred to the Somme and were in continuous action for over two months. He qualified for Class 1 Proficiency Pay on 4th August. Cyril was promoted sergeant on 10th August and transferred the same day to 275th Brigade RFA and to D/276th Battery on 10th October. In June 1917 he was involved in the Battle of Messines. **Awarded the MM for his actions near Ypres on 24th July when a barrage was being fired. A German 5.9″ shell hit the ammunition dump alongside his gun pit and set it on fire. He immediately began removing adjoining ammunition, including gas shells, and confined the effects of the fire. He had just retired from the**

Arthur Herbert Procter was awarded the VC for his actions on 4th June 1916 near Ficheux, France. He became a vicar after the war.

dump when the burning ammunition exploded. His courageous action saved the guns, hundreds of shells and many lives had the whole dump exploded, LG 17th September 1917. Cyril was granted ten days leave in England from 14th October.

Awarded the VC for his actions at Little Priel Farm, east of Épehy, France on 30th November 1917, LG 13th February 1918. His application for a commission on 11th February 1918 was endorsed by the divisional commander on 23rd March. Cyril was described as 5′ 10″ tall and weighed 154 lbs. His leave to England commencing on 27th February was extended to 17th March to allow him to attend the investiture. A civic reception was planned for 2nd March in Hoylake and West Kirby, but Cyril did not turn up. He was known to be shy and the reception was rescheduled for 5th March. Accompanied by his parents and sister, Eunice, he was honoured at Liverpool University by the Vice Chancellor, Sir Alfred Dale, and the student body. He declined an invitation to speak and was carried shoulder high from the hall by the students and sent on his way for a meeting with the Lord Mayor. Thereafter he was known as the 'bashful hero' by the local press. The MM was presented by Brigadier General Edwards, commanding Mersey Defences, at Liverpool on 13th March. The VC was presented by the King at Buckingham Palace on 16th March.

Cyril was commissioned in the RFA on 5th June for service with 55th Division Artillery (D/276th Brigade RFA). He was admitted to 2/1st Wessex Field Ambulance with not yet diagnosed pyrexia on 13th June. On 16th June he moved to 34th Field Ambulance with debility and influenza and rejoined his unit on 3rd July. He attended a gunnery course in the field 17th July–9th August and was granted fourteen days leave in England from 3rd October. Cyril transferred to C/276th Brigade RFA on 5th May 1919 and was appointed acting captain on 19th May. He returned to Britain on 20th June and was demobilised with the cadre of C/276th Battery on 30th June. He appears in the Army List until April 1920 and relinquished his commission on 10th September 1921.

From 11th August 1919 Cyril was employed in the export department of Lever Brothers (later Unilever), Liverpool until retiring on 31st March 1958. He spent many years in the Balkans, Central and South America and the Mediterranean developing the company's trade. When King George V and Queen Mary visited Liverpool on 19th July 1924 for the consecration of the new Cathedral, they also reviewed 55th (West Lancashire) Territorial Division at Wavertree Playground. Cyril was one of nine VCs presented to Their Majesties. One of the others was Arthur Procter.

During the Second World War Cyril was an ARP Warden in Liverpool. When he retired, he was presented with a silver salver and two decanters. Mr Morrell, a director of Unilever, spoke of Cyril's *quiet, gentle courteousness and his readiness to do all he could for other people. In fact he was a jolly good man to have beside you when you were in trouble….* Cyril then moved to Grayswood, near Haslemere, Surrey to live with his mother and sister. Cyril Gourley died at Grayswood on 31st January 1982 and is buried in the family grave at Grange Cemetery, West Kirby, Liverpool (F 17).

Wavertree Playground, where King George
V reviewed 55th (West Lancashire) Territorial
Division on 19th July 1924 and was introduced to
Cyril Gourley.

Lever Brothers offices at Port Sunlight. Lever
Brothers was founded in 1885 by brothers William
Hesketh Lever (1851–1925) and James Darcy Lever
(1854–1916). They started with their father's small
grocery business and went into the soap business
in 1885, buying a small soap works in Warrington.
They then teamed up with a chemist, William Hough
Watson, who invented a new process to produce
soap, using glycerin and vegetable oils rather than
tallow. This became 'Sunlight Soap' and the business
expanded, so larger premises were built at what
became Port Sunlight. Lever Brothers took an interest
in the welfare of its employees and the model village
of Port Sunlight was developed between 1888 and
1914 to accommodate the company's staff. Other
products were developed such as 'Lifebuoy', 'Lux'
and 'Vim'. Subsidiary companies were set up in
the United States, Switzerland, Canada, Australia,
Germany and elsewhere to create a global industrial
empire. By late 1929, when the company merged with
the Dutch margarine manufacturer Unie to become
Unilever, it employed 250,000 people and was the
largest company in Britain.

He is commemorated in a number of
other places:

- Cyril Edward Gourley VC Scholarship,
  founded on 30th September 1919,
  awarded annually for undergraduate
  study at the University of Liverpool
  by candidates educated at Calday
  Grange Grammar School, West Kirby
  Grammar School for Girls or whose
  parents or guardians resided within
  the former Hoylake and West Kirby
  Urban District Council.
- Gourleys Lane, off Column Road,
  Grange, West Kirby (previously
  School Lane), was named after his
  death. He had been approached to
  approve the change during his lifetime, but declined politely.
- Gourley Road, Liverpool, Lancashire.
- A memorial unveiled by the Mayor of Wirral at 208 Air Defence Battery, 103
  (Lancashire Artillery Volunteers) Air Defence Regiment RA in Liverpool in 1983.
- Royal Artillery VC Memorial in the ruins of St George's Chapel, the former
  Garrison Church at Woolwich, which was reduced to a roofless shell by a V1 in
  1944.
- A memorial to Captain Noel Chavasse VC & Bar MC, unveiled in Abercromby
  Square, Liverpool in July 2008, opposite No.19, where the Chavasse family lived
  and close to No.13, where Ernest Alexander's VC father lived. The names of

St George's Chapel, the Woolwich Garrison Church, before it was destroyed by a V1 in the Second World War. The Royal Artillery VC Memorial is on the curved wall behind the altar.

Cyril Gourley is buried with his parents in the family grave in Grange Cemetery, West Kirby.

The memorial to Captain Noel Chavasse VC & Bar MC in Abercromby Square, Liverpool, which also commemorates fifteen other VCs associated with Liverpool, including Cyril Gourley.

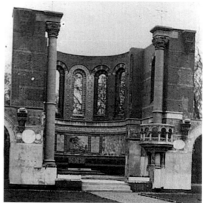

The remains of St George's Chapel.

fifteen other VCs associated with Liverpool are also inscribed on the memorial, including Cyril Gourley.

- Victoria Cross Memorial, Wallasey Town Hall, Wirral.
- Wirral VC Memorial at the Birkenhead War Memorial, Hamilton Square, Birkenhead.
- The Department for Communities and Local Government decided to provide a commemorative paving stone at the birthplace of every Great War Victoria Cross recipient in the United Kingdom. A commemorative stone for Cyril was dedicated at Liverpool Parish Church of Our Lady and St Nicholas, Chapel

Birkenhead War Memorial. The Wirral VC memorial is on one of the surrounding kerb stones.

Street, Liverpool, Merseyside on 30th November 2017 to mark the centenary of his award.

- The Royal Artillery VC Memorial in the Royal Artillery Centenary Chapel and Cloister, Larkhill, Wiltshire unveiled by Queen Elizabeth II on 26th May 2016.

In addition to the VC and MM he was awarded the 1914–15 Star, British War Medal 1914–20, Victory Medal 1914–19, George VI Coronation Medal 1937, Elizabeth II Coronation Medal 1953 and Elizabeth II Silver Jubilee Medal 1977. The VC is held by the Royal Artillery Museum.

The King George VI Coronation Medal celebrated his coronation in 1937. Until 1977 the British government decided how many commemorative medals were to be produced and allocated a proportion to Commonwealth countries and dependencies. In this case 90,279 medals were awarded, including 6,887 to Australia and 10,089 to Canada.

CAPTAIN JULIAN ROYDS GRIBBLE
1st attached 10th Battalion, The Royal Warwickshire Regiment

Julian Gribble was born at 24 Lennox Gardens, London on 5th January 1897. His father was a lifelong friend of the Byng family and Julian may have been named after Julian Byng, later Viscount Byng of Vimy. Julian's father, George James Gribble (2nd July 1846–16th June 1927) was educated at Harrow School and joined Messrs Cook, Son and Co as a warehouse man. In 1871 he was a clerk to a warehouseman, living with his parents, and in 1881 was living at 24 Marine Parade, Brighton, Sussex. He married Norah née Royds (5th April 1859–8th March 1923), born at Coddington, Cheshire, on 27th July 1881 at Chester. She was visiting Kimbolton Lodge, Bedford at the time of the 1881 Census and was recorded as an artist with her brother Edmund. George eventually became a partner and subsequently a director when the firm converted to a limited company in 1920. He was an art connoisseur and collected oriental china, snuffboxes and other *objets d'art*. The family was living at Henlow Grange, near Hitchin, Hertfordshire in 1901 and at Biddesden House, near Andover, Hampshire in 1911. The family owned a number of other properties – 34 Eaton Square, London and Kingston Russell House, Dorchester, Dorset. George was a JP and High Sheriff of Bedfordshire in 1897. He was also a keen yachtsman and a member of the Royal Yacht Squadron, owning two schooners, *Softwing* and *Medora*.

Lennox Gardens, where Julian was born in January 1897.

Her son, Philip, described Norah as a marvelously beautiful woman, with golden-red hair and almost violet eyes. She was self-centred, artistic, intellectual and convinced that her family was beyond reproach. As much as her family loved her it was only when she left the house that they could relax. She was active in local government but religion dominated her life. She wrote several books on religion, including *My Way Out*, published by a close friend, John Murray. She also wrote poetry and was a competent portrait painter having studied at the Slade School of Fine Art. She claimed that her family was descended from King Edward III. Julian had five siblings:

• Phyllis Gribble (1882–1958) married Wolverley Attwood Fordham (9th September 1859–24th February 1921) on 28th April 1903 at Biggleswade, Bedfordshire. He was a director of Fordham Brewery at Ashwell, Hertfordshire and played first class cricket for Wellington, New Zealand during the 1877–78 season. During the Great War they offered

It is understood that Julian was named after Julian Byng, later Field Marshal 1st Viscount Byng of Vimy (1862–1935). During the Great War he saw service in France with the BEF in 1914 and at Gallipoli in 1915, commanding XI Corps. Back on the Western Front he commanded the Canadian Corps at Vimy Ridge and later Third Army. He was Governor General of Canada 1921–26.

Henlow Grange is now a spa resort.

Biddesden House (Grade 1 listed). In 1693 the estate was bought by General John Richmond Webb, who served under Marlborough at Blenheim 1703, Ramilles 1706, Oudenaarde 1708 and Wynendaele 1708. On his retirement he built Biddesden House, replacing an earlier manor. The estate was owned by the Webb family until the 1780s, then the Everett family owned it until 1908, after which it had several owners. In 1931 it was bought by Bryan Walter Guinness, who became the 2nd Lord Moyne in 1944 when his father, Resident Minister in the Middle East, was assassinated by a Jewish terrorist gang in Cairo. Bryan Guinness was an heir to the Guinness brewing fortune. In 1929 he married Diana, one of the Mitford sisters. He had two sons with her but they divorced in 1933, when she left him for the British fascist leader, Sir Oswald Mosley. In 1936 Bryan married Elisabeth Nelson, of the Nelson publishing family, and they had nine children. Biddesden is still in the family and is a horse stud farm.

Kingston Russell House takes the second part of its name from the Russell family, who were granted the manor for their services to the King, probably John. Sir Theobald Russell (1301–40) was an ancestor of John Russell, 1st Earl of Bedford. Around 1640 part of the manor came into the possession of the Michel family, who partly rebuilt the house as it appears today. During the 1760s the house was let to Admiral Sir Thomas Hardy, whose son was Nelson's flag captain at Trafalgar. Before 1861 the Dukes of Bedford bought Kingston Russell for a second time. When Lord John Russell (1792–1878), the Liberal statesman, was raised to the peerage on 30th July 1861, he chose the title Earl Russell of Kingston Russell. Bertrand Russell was the third Earl. By the early 20th century the house was dilapidated and was sold in 1913 to George Gribble. He demolished a stub wing from the older Tudor building and extended and built new wings at either end of the original structure. He also laid out the gardens. The Gribbles no longer own the house, which is still in private ownership.

their house, The Bury, at Ashwell as a convalescent home. They played a key role in the construction of Ashwell War Memorial. There were no children. Wolverley left effects valued at £71,015/15/11 when he died and she left £103,913/9/-.

- Leslie Grace Gribble (1883–20th September 1913) married Hugh Exton Seebohm (5th April 1867–1946) on 28th January 1904 at Henlow Church, near Hitchin, Hertfordshire. Hugh was educated at Rugby School, Cambridge University and became a banker. They lived at Poynder's End, Hitchin. In September 1913 they returned from holiday in Brittany, France when she was suddenly taken ill and died later in the morning. They had four children:
  ° Derrick Seebohm (14th January 1907–1981).
  ° Frederic Seebohm (twin with George) (18th January 1909–15th December 1990) was educated at Trinity College, Cambridge and joined Barclays Bank. He married Evangeline Hurst (19th September 1909–28th December 1990) on 9th April 1932 registered at Finsbury, London. Frederic served in the Royal Artillery, rising to lieutenant colonel, and was MID and awarded the TD. After the war he became director of the main board and in 1951 was made a member of the bank's overseas board. In 1965 he became chairman of Barclays Bank International. He chaired the Committee on Local Authority Personal Social Services, whose December 1965 report recommended establishing unified social services within each major local authority. He was chairman of the Overseas Development Institute, the 3i Group and the Joseph Rowntree Memorial Trust. He was president of the National Institute for Social Work, the Royal African Society and Age Concern and a governor of the London School of Economics and Haileybury & Imperial Service College. Frederic was knighted in 1970 and was created Baron Seebohm of Hertford on 28th April 1972. He was High Sheriff of Hertfordshire 1970–71. Frederic died in a road accident and Evangeline as a result of it less than two weeks later. They had three children – Richard H Seebohm 1933, Victoria Seebohm 1937 and Caroline Seebohm 1940.
  ° George Seebohm (twin with Frederic) (18th January 1909–4th September 1993) was a stockbroker working with Gordon L Jacob and later with James Capel. He was commissioned in the Hertfordshire and Bedfordshire Yeomanry during the Second World War and was captured by the Japanese in the fall of Singapore. He contracted multiple diseases before he was repatriated but left the ship at Lisbon and was cared for by relatives, Alfred and Audley Seebohm. He married Lavender J Strickland (1922–90) in 1946 at Fakenham, Norfolk. She was the daughter of General Sir Edward Peter Strickland KCB KBE CMG DSO (1869–1951) and Barbara Ffolkes (1884–1977). They had three children – Philippa J Seebohm 1948, Edward H Seebohm 1951 and Patience R Seebohm 1953. George was a Member of the London Stock Exchange in 1958. The marriage ended in divorce. George lived at Chesfield, near Stevenage, Hertfordshire and collected paintings and sculpture. He adopted

John David Gathorne-Hardy was educated at Eton College and
the Royal Military Academy, Woolwich. He was Parliamentary
Private Secretary to the First Commissioner of Works 1927–28,
Alderman of London County Council 1928–33, Alderman of
East Suffolk County Council, Deputy Lieutenant of Suffolk
and JP Suffolk. He was Honorary Air Commodore of No.3169
(Suffolk) Fighter Control Unit RAAF 1950–61, Treasurer and
Vice-President of the Linnean Society 1958 and Trustee of
the British Museum 1964–73. He received the KStJ and CBE
(1955).

the ruined church of St Ethelreda near his
home and spent many hours renovating it,
including installing a statue of St Ethelreda
by his friend Mary Spencer-Watson. He
was living at Chesfield Park, Graveley at
the time of his death, leaving effects valued at £2,116,291. Lavender married
Frank Charles L Broadribb (1917–92) in 1969.

° Fidelity Seebohm (5th July 1912–25th March 2009) married John David
   Gathorne-Hardy (15th April 1900–22nd November 1978.), on 26th July 1932
   in London. He became the 4th Earl of Cranbrook and 4th Baron Medway
   of Hemsted Park on 23rd December 1915. John had married Bridget Cicely
   D'Oyly Carte (1908–85) in October 1926, daughter of Rupert D'Oyly Carte
   (1876–1948) and Lady Dorothy Milner Gathorne-Hardy. The marriage
   ended in divorce in 1931. John and Fidelity lived at Great Glemham House,
   Saxmundham, Suffolk and she served as JP for Suffolk from 1943 (OBE
   1972). She was living at Red House
   Farm, Great Glemham in 2003. John and
   Fidelity had five children – Gathorne
   Gathorne-Hardy 1933, Juliet Gathorne-
   Hardy 1934, Catherine Sophia Gathorne-
   Hardy 1936, Christina Gathorne-Hardy
   1940 and Hugh Gathorne-Hardy 1942.

• Hugh Exton Seebohm married Marjorie Lyall
  (née Burton) (1879–1968), Philip Gribble's

Bridget Cicely D'Oyly Carte was the granddaughter of
impresario Richard D'Oyly Carte. After her father's death in
1948 she inherited the D'Oyly Carte Opera Company, which
performed and controlled the copyrights of Gilbert & Sullivan
productions, and the Savoy Hotel. She also undertook child
welfare work. In 1972 she founded the D'Oyly Carte Charitable
Trust to support charitable causes in the arts, medical welfare
and the environment. She was created DBE in 1975. She had
no children or surviving siblings and when she died she was the
end of her family line.

mother-in-law, in 1933 at St George, Hanover Square, London. There were no children. Marjorie had married Charles George Lyall (1871–1914), at Eastgate, Lincoln in April 1898. He was commissioned in the Lincolnshire Regiment in July 1892 and served in Malta 1895–96, on the Nile Expedition in Egypt August–November 1898, including at the Battle of Khartoum, and in the Second Boer War in South Africa from 4th January 1900, during which he was in action at Orange Free State, Paardeberg, Poplar Grove, Karee Siding, Vet and Zand Rivers, Transvaal and Pretoria. He was promoted captain and retired to the Reserve of Officers in 1907. Marjorie and Charles were living at The Cottage, Tangley and Vernham Dean, near Andover, Hampshire in 1911 before moving to The Laurels, Alton Road, Roehampton, London. Charles was recalled at the outbreak of the Great War and was assigned to 1st Lincolnshire. He went to France on 10th October 1914 and was killed in action during the Battle of La Bassée on 18th October. It is known that he was buried at La Cliqueterie Farm but his body was never recovered and he is commemorated on the Le Touret Memorial, France (Panel 8). He left effects valued at £8,588/9/4. Charles and Marjorie had three children, including Joyce Lyall 1903 and John David Lyall 1905.

• Norah Le Grand Gribble (29th December 1885–12th March 1977) is recorded as Barbara in her son Anthony's entry in the Commonwealth War Graves Commission records. She married Eustace Hill (30th April 1869–21st October 1946) in 1913 at Pewsey, Wiltshire. His mother, Marianne, was Julian Gribble's paternal aunt. Eustace was commissioned in the Essex Yeomanry in 1901 and was promoted captain on 8th May 1905 and major on 17th June 1912. He served during the Great War and was MID and awarded the DSO (LG 3rd June 1918) and TD (LG 15th July 1919). He was promoted lieutenant colonel commanding the Essex Yeomanry on 8th May 1920 and brevet colonel on 8th May 1924. He

Charles George Lyall is commemorated on the Le Touret Memorial.

last appears in the Army List in January 1927. Eustace was DL Essex (LG 5th June 1924), Sheriff for the County of Essex (LG 19th March 1926) and Director of The Australian Estates Co Ltd from about 1930. He died at Redlands Grange, Ashwell, Baldock, Hertfordshire, leaving effects valued at £12,005/0/8. She also died there, leaving effects valued at £37,839. They had five children:

Anthony Eustace Hill.

° Anthony Eustace Hill (1914–12th November 1942) enlisted in the RAFVR, was promoted to sergeant (740153) and transferred to the Reserve. He was commissioned as a pilot officer on probation on 29th March 1939 (72992), rank confirmed 29th March 1940 and was promoted flying officer on 3rd September 1940 and flight lieutenant on 3rd September 1941. On 5th December 1941, flying Spitfire PR.IV R7044, he took the famous photographs that first identified the German *Würzburg* radar system on the cliffs at Bruneval in northern France. This led to the Bruneval Raid on 27th/28th February 1942, in which a small parachute force landed close by, captured the radar and returned with it by sea to Britain. As an acting squadron leader, and first CO of the newly formed 543 Squadron, he carried out a dangerous photo-reconnaissance mission. On 17th October 1942 Bomber Command hit the Schneider Works at Le Creusot and Tony Hill flew over the area next day to photograph the damage but his camera failed. He went over the target again on 19th October and was shot down and seriously injured. He died in a German hospital a few weeks later and is buried in Dijon (Les Pejoces) Communal Cemetery, France, the only Second World War serviceman buried there. Tony was awarded the DFC (LG 27th May 1941), Bar to the DFC (LG 10th March 1942), MID (LG 11th Jun 1942), DSO (LG 31st July 1942) and MID (LG 1st January 1943). He is named on the Ashwell War Memorial.

One of the photographs Tony Hill brought back from overflying Bruneval on 5th December 1941. The camera was mounted behind the pilot and looked out obliquely. As low-level photography runs had to be made at high speed in order to avoid flak, it took enormous skill and cool nerves to take pictures such as these.

○ Jean Eustace Hill (twin with Cynthia) (born 1916).

○ Cynthia Eustace Hill (twin with Jean) (born 1916) married Daniel Gurney Sheppard (born 1909) in 1936. He was the son of Lieutenant Colonel Samuel Gurney Sheppard. They had four children – Michael G Sheppard 1938, Jonathon E Sheppard 1941, Susan G Sheppard 1943 and Richard A Sheppard 1950.

○ Timothy Julian Eustace Hill (born 1918), known as Julian, joined the Royal Australian Air Force, was promoted to sergeant and served with 10 Squadron RAAF. On 19th June 1941 he was aboard Short Sunderland X-8274 from 119 Squadron RAF flying from RAF Mount Batten, Plymouth, Devon for Gibraltar with a full crew and passengers. The aircraft developed engine trouble off the Spanish coast and crashed into the Atlantic about 160 kms northwest of Cape Finistere. Ten crewmen died (seven RAF, one RAAF and two Forces Aeriennes Françaises Libres). The other five aboard survived and were taken prisoner, including Julian.

○ Daphne Vivian Eustace Hill (born 1920).

• Vivien Massie Gribble (born 1888–6th February 1932) married Douglas Doyle Jones (3rd December 1886–10th November 1980), a barrister, in 1919 at St George, Hanover Square. They lived at Valley Farm, Higham near Hadleigh, Suffolk, having given up his practice to look after his estate. In 1935 he planted the Jubilee Wood to celebrate George V's Silver Jubilee and also painted. She died at Valley Farm, leaving effects valued at £15,132/7/2. He died at Ipswich, leaving effects valued at £331,540. They had a daughter:

○ Daphne Christobel Jones (15th July 1927–16th February 2008) married William Victor Marno (26th November 1925–2002) on 15th July 1952 at Samford, Suffolk. William was an officer cadet (14691990) and was commissioned in the Royal Regiment of Artillery on 9th December 1945 (362014). He was promoted lieutenant before resigned his commission on 11th August 1951. They had four children – Madeleine Sarah Doyle Marno 1954, Denise Barbara Marno 1955, Alison Jane Marno 1958 and Nicholas Douglas Doyle Marno 1961. The marriage ended in divorce in 1968. Daphne married Anthony N Warner in 1971. William married Hazel Dorothy Buckle (née Westley) (born 1941) in January 1969. Hazel had married John A Buckle in 1963 but it ended in divorce. William and Hazel had two children – Lowri Marno 1973 and Zoe Selena Marno 1977. The marriage ended in divorce in 1979. William married Claire Linette Mordaunt in 1983.

• Philip le Grand Gribble (6th May 1891–23rd February 1976) was commissioned in the Hampshire Yeomanry (Carabineers) on 23rd February 1910. He was commissioned again in 1st Hampshire Yeomanry on 6th September 1914 as a lieutenant. He was appointed flight commander in the RFC on 30th April 1916 and was promoted captain on 1st June. In 1917 he was appointed GSO2 but was declared unfit for service on 12th June 1917 and permanently unfit as a pilot or observer on 11th September 1917. Further periods of similar restrictions followed between 20th November 1917 and 21st February 1918. He last appears in the Army List in December 1918. Philip relinquished his commission on account of ill health and retained the rank of honorary captain on 19th April 1919 but was granted the rank of acting major on 16th July 1919. He was in partnership with the Government of Southern Rhodesia, having initiated a successful tobacco sales promotion in the UK 1927–35. He received a Regular Army Emergency Commission on 30th September 1939 and was appointed Press Censor with the British Expeditionary Force in France in November 1939. On 1st March 1940 he was appointed Army Intelligence Liaison Officer on the staff of the Air Officer Commander-in-Chief, British Air Force in France (GSO3 Specially Employed). Philip was promoted war substantive lieutenant and temporary captain on 1st June 1940. He was transferred to the Unemployed List on 15th March 1948 and last appears in the Army List in August 1948. He was a director of various companies, the military critic of the *News Chronicle* 1941–52 and a successful horse breeder. He wrote *Diary of a Staff Officer* 1941 and his autobiography, *Off The Cuff*, in 1964. His father remarked to Philip that he was leaving an extra £100,000 to his daughters as, *... you will never need the money. You make it too easily*. Philip had an eventful private life, with four wives:

- He married Hon Mary Morwenna Bolitho McNeill (1888–14th September 1924) on 15th June 1915 at Holy Trinity Church, Sloane Square, Chelsea, London. She was the daughter of Ronald John McNeill (1861–1934). Philip and Mary lived at 26 Chapel Street, Belgrave Square, London.
- His second marriage was to Marjorie Joyce Lyall on 21st July 1925 at Holy Trinity Church, Roehampton, London. She was the daughter of Captain George Charles Lyall and Marjorie Burton (see

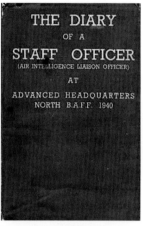

Diary of a Staff Officer was published by Methuen in 1941.

Ronald John McNeill DL JP, barrister, assistant editor of *St James's Gazette* 1899 and editor 1900–04, assistant editor *Encyclopaedia Britannica* 1906–10 and Unionist MP for St Augustine's, Kent 1911–18 and Canterbury 1918–27. He was Under-Secretary of State for Foreign Affairs 1922–24 and 1924–25 under Lord Curzon, a Privy Counsellor from 16th January 1924, Financial Secretary to the Treasury 1925–27, Chancellor of the Duchy of Lancaster with a seat in Cabinet 1927–29 (raised to the peerage as Baron Cushendun of Cushendun, Co Antrim, Ireland on 7th November 1927), acting Foreign Secretary 1928 and was twice chief British representative to the League of Nations. He retired in 1929 (Bassano).

Julian's sister Leslie Grace Gribble below). Philip had an affair with Anthea Mary Sholl (née Hunt), wife of Thomas H Sholl, during the summer of 1934. Sholl sought the dissolution of his marriage on the grounds of her infidelity and Philip, who did not contest the action, was ordered to pay the sum of £5,000 on 21st March 1935 after a decree nisi. Joyce was living at Kent House, Harting, Petersfield, Hampshire in 1950. Joyce and Philip had three children:

- Phillida Mary Royds Gribble (24th April 1926–10th October 1930).
- Felicity Jane Gribble (born 1929) married David Hamilton Gault born 1928) in July 1950 at Harting, near Petersfield. They had five children – Annabel S Gault 1952, Katherine JH Gault 1954, Charles LH Gault 1955, William PH Gault 1958 and Richard JH Gault 1962.
- David JC Gribble (1932). His birth was slow, so Philip and Joyce hired a taxi and drove around a badly-surfaced square at high speed to induce the birth. He married Angela K Davies (1941–66) in 1961 at Weston-super-Mare, Somerset. They had two children – Emma L Gribble 1962 and Nathaniel S Gribble 1964. David married Rosemary L Lewis in 1967 at Lewes, Sussex and they had a son, Toby Peter Gribble, in 1968.

° Philip's third marriage was to Anthea Mary Sholl (née Hunt) (c.1911–1957) in 1935. The marriage ended in divorce. Anthea married Patrick Arthur Bronte Branwell (1904–64) in 1946 at Westminster.

° Philip's fourth marriage was to Aylmer Jean Philippa Eveleigh (née MacFarlane) in 1946 at Westminster, London. She was known as Jean and was the widow of Captain Brian Downing Eveleigh (1918–44), whom she married in 1941. Brian was serving in C Squadron, 16th/5th Lancers (85589) when he died on active service on 28th May 1944 (Cassino War Cemetery, Italy – I F 20). Brian and Jean had a daughter, Amanda Jane Eveleigh, in 1942. Philip purchased Wamil Hall, near Mildenhall, Suffolk, in May 1948, which burned down in February 1958. He and Jean were living at 36 South Street, London in 1950. He left effects valued at £7,157. Jean married Patrick Massey in 1978. Philip and Jean had a son:

- Aylmer P Gribble (born 1948) married Elizabeth Evan-Jones in March 1970 at St Michael's, Chester Square, London.

Julian's paternal grandfather, Thomas Gribble (c.1823–18th September 1871) married Mary Ann née Cook (c.1821–30th January 1882), on 19th September 1839 at St Mark's, Kennington, London. She was born at Tooting, London and was distantly related to brothers Euston and Reginald Sartorius, both awarded the VC. He was a Portugal merchant in 1851 and they were living at 9 Craven Hill, Paddington, London. By 1861 he was a fundholder and they were living at 125 Marine Parade, Brighton, Sussex. He had retired by 1871 and they were living at Frenches, Reigate, Surrey. Mary was a fundholder living with her daughter Amy at 38 Hyde Park Gardens, Paddington, London in 1881. Her nephew, Lieutenant Colonel Edwin Berkeley Cook, son of Major EA Cook, 11th Hussars of Roydon Hall, Tonbridge, died while commanding 1st Life Guards on 4th November 1914 (East Peckham (St Michael) Churchyard, Kent). She was living at Bohun Lodge, East Barnet, Hertfordshire at the time of her death, leaving effects valued at £5,321/4/11. In addition to George they had ten other children:

Wamil Hall, near Mildenhall, purchased by Julian's brother, Philip, in 1948, suffered a catastrophic fire in 1958.

- Marianne Gribble (1842–2nd March 1921) married James Duke Hill (11th May 1834–29th September 1901) on 22nd June 1863 at Harrow St Mary, Middlesex. She was living at Terlings Park, Harlow, Essex in 1918. She was living at 4 Onslow Gardens, London at the time of her death, leaving effects valued at £28,581/7/5. They had eight children – Marion Elizabeth Hill 1864,

Julian's paternal grandparents were living at 9 Craven Hill, Paddington in 1851 (Cavendish Rowe).

St Mark's Church, Kennington was built in 1824 on the old gallows corner of Kennington Common, one of four 'Waterloo' churches built after the defeat of Napoleon. Each was named after one of the four gospel writers – St Mark's Kennington, St John's Waterloo, St Luke's Norwood and St Matthew's Brixton. From 1879 to 1889, the Vicar was the Reverend Henry Montgomery (1847–1932), later Bishop of Tasmania and father of Field Marshal Viscount Bernard Law Montgomery, who was born in Kennington. St Mark's Montgomery Hall is named after him. St Mark's suffered serious damage in the Blitz and was to be demolished, but the restored church reopened in 1960. The First World War Memorial in the front of the church includes the name of George Jarratt VC.

Reginald Duke Hill 1866, James William Hill 1868, Eustace Hill 1869, Leslie Noel Hill 1873, George Bernard Hill 1875, Ronald Cholmeley Hill 1877 and Dorothy Margaret Hill 1883.

- John Charles Gribble (1844–8th June 1901) never married and was living at 12 Park Road, Richmond, Surrey at the time of his death, leaving effects valued at £28,230/18/-.
- Eliza Jane Gribble (1848–58).
- Emily Gribble (1849–1933) married Singer Barclay (c.1833–2nd January 1924), a wine merchant, on 28th July 1880 at St James, Paddington. He was born at Wickham Market, Suffolk. They were living at Bohun, Weston-under-Penyard, Herefordshire in 1901. When he died there he left effects valued at £31,906/7/10.
- Helen Beatrice Gribble (1851–9th October 1946) appears as Ellen in the 1871 Census, living with her parents, and as Grace in 1881, by when she was a fundholder, living with her brother George. She married James William Langworthy (1827–96), a barrister, in 1891. He married Emily Sarah Markby (died 1886) in 1863 at Maidstone, Kent and they had five children – Emily Langworthy 1865, William S Langworthy 1866, John D Langworthy 1868, Richard Langworthy 1869 and Dorothy Langworthy 1870. Helen was living with her aunt, Caroline Louisa Byng, at Great Culverden, Tunbridge Wells, Kent in 1901. She was living at Fairfield, Wadhurst, Sussex at the time of her death, leaving effects valued at £60,273/6/1.
- Caroline Florence Gribble (1853–66).
- Katherine Constance Gribble (1855–3rd February 1936) was living with her brother George in 1881. She married David Miller Barbour (29th December 1841–12th February 1928) on 21st March 1883 at Malabar Hill, Bombay, India. He was born at Omagh, Co Tyrone, Ireland and was educated at Queen's College, Belfast. He went to India in 1863 and served in Lower Bengal until becoming Under Secretary of the Financial Department, Government of India in 1872. Other appointments followed – Accountant-General of Bengal, Secretary to the Government of Bengal Revenue Department 1882, Member of the Bengal Legislative Council 1882, Secretary to the Government of India Financial Department 1882, member of the Royal Commission in England on gold and silver 1886, Financial Member of the Supreme Council 1888–93, Indian Currency Commission 1898 and was also a member and chairman of several Royal Commissions and Committees on currency and finance. Awarded CSI 1887, KCSI 1889 and KCMG 1899. He published *The Theory of Bimetallism*. They were living at Tiltwood, Crawley Down, Sussex at the time of his death, leaving effects valued at £70,503/2/3. She was living at Ensham, Groombridge, Sussex at the time of her death, leaving effects valued at £27,000/11/3. They had four children – Ralph Henry Barbour 1883, Kenneth Durand Barbour 1885, Catherine Margaret Barbour 1887 and David Nevill Barbour 1895.
- Eleanor Byng Gribble (1856–3rd March 1931) appears as Ellen A in the 1871 Census and was living with her brother George in 1881. She married George

Somes Layard (4th February 1857–30th May 1925) on 8th October 1885 in London. He was born at Clifton, Gloucestershire. They were living at 31 South Street, Thurloe Square, London and at Bulls Cliff, Felixstowe in 1919. Later she was living at 12 Guessens Road, Welwyn Garden City, Hertfordshire. She died at 12 Rue St Cloud, Clamart, Hauts de Seine, France, leaving effects valued at £3,426/9/4. They had four children – Nancy Layard 1886, George Anthony Layard 1888, John Willoughby Layard 1891 and Peter Clement Layard 1896. Peter was commissioned on 27th November 1914 in 4th Suffolk, went to France on 9th January 1916 and was seconded to trench mortar batteries on 30th April. He was wounded on 18th June and evacuated to Britain on 22nd June. He was serving with 2/5th Battalion when he was killed in action on 23rd August 1918 at Gommecourt, France (Douchy-Les-Ayette British Cemetery – II J 3). He died intestate and letters of administration were issued to his father on 25th January 1919. He left effects valued at £203/10/-. His letters were published in *Peter Clement Layard – Extracts From His Letters* by Forgotten Books.

- Henry Cholmeley Gribble (1858–28th August 1882) was commissioned in 3rd (The Prince of Wales) Dragoon Guards on 11th May 1878 and was promoted lieutenant on 26th May 1879. He was killed during the midnight charge at Kassassin, Egypt. He left effects valued at £11,543/1/3.
- Amy Bruce Gribble (1860–25th February 1936) was living with her mother in 1881. She married Frederick Charles Coxhead (10th October 1848–12th November 1940), a barrister, in 1888 at Kensington. They were living at 47 Russell Square, St George Bloomsbury, London in 1881 and at 7 Essex Villas, Kensington in 1901. He died at Fulmer Grange Nursing Home, Farnham Royal, Buckinghamshire. They had three children – Maurice Edward Coxhead 1889, Olive Lydia Coxhead 1892 and Henry Jessop Coxhead 1893. Maurice died on active service as a major with 9th Royal Fusiliers on 3rd May 1917 (Faubourg D'Amiens Cemetery, Arras, France – IV G 14).

His maternal grandfather, Francis Coulman Royds MA (24th October 1825–20th September 1913) was born at Brereton, Cheshire. His sister, Anne Mary Royds, married John Herbert Jones, brother of Alfred Stowell Jones VC. Francis married Cornelia Frances née Blomfield (6th July 1829–12th December 1919) on 13th January 1852 at Stevenage, Hertfordshire. Her brother, Rear Admiral Sir Richard Massie Blomfield KCB, served throughout the Crimean War and the Egyptian War 1882. Francis was Rector of Codrington and Honorary Canon of Chester Cathedral. They lived at 34 Eaton Square, London and at Kingston Russell House, Dorchester, Dorset. By 1911 they were living at Bryngolen, Penmaenmawr, Conway, Caernarvonshire. He died there leaving effects valued at £13,041/15/-. She died at Conway, Caernarvonshire leaving effects valued at £4,165/10/9. In addition to Norah they had nine other children:

- Alice Mary Royds (3rd January 1853–29th March 1926) married Reverend John Aneurin Howell (October 1853–19th April 1909) on 10th March 1883 at Chester, Cheshire. He was born at Llangan, Glamorgan, son of Reverend David Howell, Vicar of Wrexham. John was Vicar of Dwygfylchi, Glamorgan 1881–96 and St Bede, Hartington Road, Toxteth Park, Lancashire 1895–1909. He died at Paddington, London leaving effects valued at £226/11/6. Alice was living with her parents in 1911. She died at Outram Lodge, Llandrillo, Rhos, Colwyn Bay, Denbighshire, leaving effects valued at £4,815/17/5. They had three children – Hugh Aneurin Howell 1885, Francis David B Howell 1887 and John Aldersey Howell 1888.
- Frances Royds (9th February 1854–8th March 1903) never married.
- Ellen Hester Royds (October 1855–11th May 1928) lived at 12 Buckingham Avenue, Sefton Park, Liverpool, Lancashire and died there unmarried, leaving effects valued at £114/12/11.
- Frank Massie Royds (born 14th November 1856–1st March 1884). He entered the Royal Navy on 15th July 1870 and was promoted acting sub-lieutenant on 18th July 1876 and lieutenant on 23rd June 1880. He served aboard HMS *Volage*, *Excellent* December 1876, Royal Naval College March 1877, *Duke of Wellington* 8th November 1877, *Agincourt*, *Achilles* 28th November 1877 and *Bacchante* 15th July 1879. Princes George and Albert also served aboard *Bacchante* September 1879–August 1882. Frank was serving on HMS *Carysfort* at Suez and took part in the Anglo-Egyptian War 1882. He commanded a detachment of the Naval Brigade attached to 2nd Infantry Brigade in the expedition from Trinkitat and was wounded at El Teb, Sudan on 29th February 1884. His position was taken by Lieutenant Arthur Knyvet Wilson RN, who was awarded the VC for his part in the action. Frank died of his wounds on 1st March and was buried in the Red Sea the following day.
- Edith Royds (1st January 1858–20th January 1943) married Archibald Peyton Skipwith (1853–27th December 1883) on 3rd June 1880 at Coddington. He died at Melbourne, Australia leaving effects valued at £8,144/13/7. She was living at 22 Belgrave Road, London at the time. They had two children – Frank Peyton Skipwith (28th February 1881–25th September 1915) and Norah Skipwith (1882–1959). Their son, Frank, served as a private in the RAMC March 1901–November 1902 and as a private in the Cape Mounted Riflemen from January 1903. He was living at 5 Old Bond Street, London when he applied for a commission on 24th September 1914, described as 5′ 10¼″ tall and weighing 169½ lbs. He was appointed temporary captain Royal Scots Fusiliers on 27th October 1914 and temporary major 9th July 1915. He married Hon Bridget Vera Byng (born 11th November 1882) on 9th November 1909 at St Peter, Pimlico and they had two children – Nannette Elizabeth Skipwith 1910 and Cynthia Skipwith 1912. He was serving with 7th Battalion when he was killed in action on 25th September 1915 (Loos Memorial, France – Panels 46–49). His name is recorded incorrectly

as Frank Peyton Skipworth by the Commonwealth War Graves Commission. His executor was his wife and his affairs were dealt with by Messrs Royds Rawstone, a company in which his uncle Edmund was a partner. He left £6,004/11/1 in his will dated 10th June 1915. On 31st August 1916 the War Office accepted that he was dead and informed his wife, who was living at 82 Grayton Road, Harrow. When she married WG Cardew on 22nd February 1919, her widow's pension of £140 p.a. was cancelled. She was living at The Park House, Killiney, Co Dublin. Edith married Reginald Curtis Toogood (1856–1939) on 21st January 1888 at St George, Hanover Square, London. He served in 21st Foot, 3rd Royal Scots Fusiliers and the Ayr Militia. He was commissioned as a lieutenant on 22nd March 1877 and was promoted captain on 2nd June 1885 and major on 26th May 1886. He served in the Sudan 1884–85 and the Burma Expedition 1886–87 where he was Mentioned in Despatches. Edith was living at Low Wood, Winthorpe, Newark at the time of her death, leaving effects valued at £4,032/7/9.

- Edmund Royds (6th July 1860–31st March 1946) was educated at Haileybury and became a solicitor in 1882. He married Rachel Louisa Fane (30th January 1869–18th December 1943) on 21st May 1889 at Newark, Nottinghamshire. She was the daughter of Colonel Francis Augustus and Augusta Fane. Edmund became a partner in Royds, Rawstone & Co, of 46 Bedford Square, London (many members of the family used the company for their legal affairs). He was also a director of the Lukwah Tea Company and the Life Association of Scotland. He was commissioned in the Lincolnshire Yeomanry on 27th May 1903 and was promoted lieutenant 30th April 1904, captain 6th November 1908 and major 19th August 1910. Edmund was embodied on 5th August 1914 and transferred to the Territorial Force Reserve on 15th June 1917. He was appointed lieutenant colonel and Colonel Commandant Lincoln Volunteer Corps the same day until 30th March 1920. He was employed in the Air Ministry from 4th July 1918 and relinquished his commission in the Territorial Force Reserve on 30th September 1921, retaining the rank of major/honorary lieutenant colonel. Edmund was MP for Sleaford and later Stamford, Lincolnshire 1910–18 and was Chairman of the Land Union's Legal Committee. He was also Chairman of the Lincolnshire Chamber of Agriculture. He purchased Stubton Hall, Fenton Road, Stubton, Lincolnshire, in 1918. He was awarded the OBE (LG 3rd June 1919), and was appointed DL Lincolnshire 1922, High Sheriff of Lincolnshire 1931 and was knighted in the King's Birthday Honours in 1939 (invested at St James's Palace on 17th July 1939). He enjoyed fox hunting and the Belvoir Hunt met regularly at Stubton Hall in the 1920s and 1930s. They had two children – Anthony Fane Royds 1890 and Jasper Francis Royds 1896. Sub-Lieutenant Jasper Francis Royds died on 9th November 1917, while serving on the depot ship HMS *Arrogant*.

- Mary Royds (1862–7th November 1945) married Charles Stewart Carlisle (1844–25th March 1914) in 1882 at Chester. He was a JP for the County of Cheshire and an East Indies and South America merchant. They were living at The Grange, North Rode, Cheshire in 1891 and at Brookside, Ryleys Lane, Alderley Edge, Cheshire by 1901. He died at Macclesfield, Cheshire, leaving effects valued at £10,401/0/6. She died at Bucklow, Cheshire leaving effects valued at £5,143/14/-. They had four children – George Blomfield Carlisle 1883, Evelyn Rose Carlisle 1885, Philip Edmund Carlisle 1890 and Geoffrey Townsend Carlisle 1899.

- Evelyn (1863–15th June 1952) married Hugh Aldersey JP (1858–4th April 1931) in 1888 at Chester. They were living at The Crooke, Aldersey, Cheshire in 1891 and at Aldersey Hall, Aldersey in 1901. He left effects valued at £3,856/16/3. She was living at The Beeches, Winslade Road, Sidmouth, Devonshire at the time of her death, leaving effects valued at £1,445/18/10. They had three sons:
  - ° Hugh Aldersey (28th December 1888–10th March 1918) was commissioned on 1st February 1911 in 1st Cheshire Yeomanry and resigned on 4th October 1913. He was commissioned in the Cheshire Yeomanry on 26th August 1914 and was promoted temporary lieutenant on 9th June 1915. He was serving in 10th (Shropshire and Cheshire Yeomanry) Battalion, King's Shropshire Light Infantry when he was killed in action as a captain on 10th March 1918 (Jerusalem War Cemetery, Israel and Palestine – A 67). He died intestate and letters of administration were issued to his father on 20th November 1918. He left £1,441/5/5.
  - ° Ralph Aldersey (20th March 1890–12th December 1971) was commissioned in 3rd Cheshire on 15th August 1914 and was promoted lieutenant on 7th October 1915. He was appointed Land Tax Commissioner for the County of Lincoln with the City and County of the City of Lincoln on 2nd August 1927. He lived at Fenton Old Hall, Coddington and was living at The Crook, Aldersey, Cheshire at the time of his death.
  - ° Mark Aldersey (28th October 1897–1st November 1917) suffered a knee injury in October 1914 resulting in the cartilage being removed. His OTC report noted a keen but rather feeble personality. He applied for a commission on 26th August 1915, described as 5' 11" tall and weighing 130 lbs. His report prior to attending the Royal Military College noted that he was not a leader and was about equal to the average. He served in 1st Cheshire and left the unit with muscular strain of the right leg/synervitis of the knee on 23rd September 1916. He was treated at 2nd Red Cross Hospital. Having embarked on HMHS *Aberdonian* on 25th September at Rouen, he disembarked at Southampton on 27th September and was treated at 3rd Southern General Hospital, Oxford. A medical board there on 3rd October found him unfit for General Service and granted him leave until 13th November. A medical board at Chester Military Hospital on 18th November found him unfit for General Service for one month but fit for Home Service and he joined 3rd Reserve Battalion on 22nd November. A medical board at 4 St James Road, Liverpool on 18th December found him

fit for General Service. He suffered a severe contusion of the left foot on 29th May 1917 and was admitted to 14th General Hospital, Wimereux next day. He embarked at Boulogne on HMHS *St Denis* for Dover on 1st June 1917, arriving the following day. He was treated at 4th Southern General Hospital, Plymouth from 3rd June. A medical board there on 16th July found him unfit for General Service for four months and on 9th August for one month. A medical board at the Command Depot, Sutton Coldfield on 28th August found him fit for General Service and recommended leave until 18th September. Another medical board at 4 St James Road, Liverpool on 17th October examined him for an undescended left testicle but found him fit for General Service. He was killed in action on 1st November 1917 (Tyne Cot Memorial, Belgium – Panels 61–63). He died intestate and letters of administration were issued to his father on 6th April 1918. He left effects valued at £193/9/8.

- Agatha Royds (15th June 1865–27th October 1938) married James Steuart (7th September 1860–27th September 1938) in 1890 at St George, Hanover Square. He was born in Edinburgh, Midlothian and was a Writer to the Signet. They were living at 10 Rothesay Terrace, Edinburgh, Midlothian in 1901 and later at 25 Rutland Street, Edinburgh. They also lived at Highways, Dover Park Drive, Roehampton, London. They had a daughter, Sylvia Steuart, in 1893.

Julian was educated privately until September 1908, then at Hillside Preparatory School, Godalming until July 1910 and at Eton College September 1910–December 1914, where he was a good all-rounder with an interest in art and music. He applied for a commission on 18th September 1914, described as 6' 2¼" tall and weighing 174 lbs. He entered the Royal Military College, Sandhurst in December 1914 and was commissioned in the Royal Warwickshire Regiment on 15th May 1915. He was posted to the 3rd Reserve Battalion at Albany Barracks, Parkhurst, Isle of Wight. He broke his right metatarsus on 10th August while bathing and a medical board on 31st August found him unfit for service for six weeks. He was granted leave until 15th October and a medical board at Parkhurst Military Hospital on 20th October found him fit for General Service. He was promoted lieutenant on 1st January 1916 and went to France on 21st May. He suffered a severe attack of pyrexia on 2nd October and was admitted to a casualty clearing station at Corbie and then 20th General Hospital at Camiers. On 13th October he embarked on HMHS *St Andrew* at Calais and disembarked next day at Dover. A medical board at 2nd Western General Hospital, Manchester on 18th October found him unfit for service for one month and granted him leave until 17th November. A medical board at Dorchester Military Hospital on 17th November found him fit for General Service. He returned to France on 5th December from 3rd Reserve Battalion on the Isle of Wight. He was promoted acting captain on 20th December 1916 and temporary captain on 23rd March 1917. A medical board at Boulogne on 10th April found him unfit for service for three weeks due to debility and he was recommended for three weeks leave in Britain. He was fit to rejoin his unit on 2nd May.

Awarded the VC for his actions on Beaumetz – Hermies Ridge, France on 23rd March 1918, LG 28th June 1918. During the action he received a scalp wound, fell unconscious and his comrades left him for dead but he was subsequently taken prisoner. He was treated at Hameln Hospital from 20th April, which came under the officers' prisoner of war camp at Karlsruhe. He was later a prisoner at Mainz, Germany, where he learned that he had been awarded the VC and was carried around the prison camp on the shoulders of his comrades. He died in captivity at the Royal Fortress Hospital (also seen as No.16 Hospital), Mainz of Spanish flu and pneumonia on 25th November 1918. On 6th February 1919 the War Office informed his father that his death had been accepted. He died intestate and his father was granted letters of administration on 7th February 1920. He left effects valued at £834/2/2. Julian was originally buried in Mainz Military Cemetery in the grounds of Mainz Zitadelle but his remains were later moved to Niederzwehren Cemetery, Kassel, Germany (III F 4).

His mother visited his grave on 6th November 1919 and described it as being in an ivy covered garden with a green marble headstone. Her son Philip recalled his mother's grief over the loss of Julian:

Hillside Preparatory School, Godalming was in a large 19th century house that had previously been a hydropathic establishment, for the treatment of acute and chronic diseases. It was later a guest house/hotel. The school opened in 1872 and by 1891 there were thirty-five boarders. Aldous Huxley was a boarder from 1903 and John Gielgud from January 1912. Hillside was demolished in the 1970s and was replaced by housing.

Eton College in Berkshire was founded by King Henry VI in 1440. It has produced nineteen British Prime Ministers, the latest being David Cameron. Numerous members of the Royal Family have been educated there, including Princes William and Harry. Other notable Old Etonians include Aldous Huxley, George Orwell, Ian Fleming, Beau Brummell, John Maynard Keynes, Ranulph Fiennes, Bear Grylls and Hubert Parry. The College has produced numerous TV presenters and actors, including Ludovic Kennedy, Eddie Redmayne, Damian Lewis, Hugh Lawrie, and Michael Bentine. Thirty-seven Old Etonians have been awarded the VC, the largest number for any school.

....My mother was broken hearted. She went into a spiritual decline and never recovered a balanced view of life. The early death of my sister Lesley after a few years of marriage had much affected my mother. She believed that Lesley's death was due to carelessness and she brooded over this loss. Julian's death, again, as she thought, due to neglect, seemed to break down her final defences. She was the victim of regret and mourning throughout the remainder of her not very long life. I took my mother to Germany to view my brother's grave early in 1919. We stayed in Cologne and then in Mainz. It was bitter weather. The ground was covered in snow when we arrived at the cemetery, and my poor mother kneeled at the grave and wept. She scraped away the snow with her bare hands and kissed the ground, gathering earth and leaves in her fingers as if these were part of her son. I stood beside her. I was inexperienced in the depths of emotional abandon and of utter soul-destroying misery; that was what I looked down on, and, I am ashamed to say, thought it an uncontrolled reaction. Visited by the same sense of loss not so many years later, I came to understand and respect my mother's uninhibited demonstration of grief.

HMHS St Andrew was operated by Great Western Railways between Fishguard in Wales and Rosslare in Ireland. It was one of the first ships to be taken over in 1914 and was fitted out as a hospital ship. She was in use until 29th May 1919 when she returned to her normal service and was renamed *Fishguard* in 1932. A year later she was sold for scrap.

Julian Gribble's grave in Niederzwehren Cemetery, Kassel, Germany (VConline).

The Zitadelle in Mainz, Germany was used as a prisoner of war camp in both world wars.

Before her own death in 1923, Norah produced *The Book of Julian*, a biography of her son, including all the letters he wrote to her from prep school days to the time he was a prisoner. Julian is commemorated in a number of other places:

- Named on the Regimental panels in the Royal Memorial Chapel, Royal Military Academy, Sandhurst, Surrey.
- Named on the brass war memorial plaque at St Peter's Church, Long Bredy, Dorset.
- Memorial window and a plaque at St Martin's Church, Preston, Hertfordshire.
- Eton College Cloisters *For Valour* Memorial, unveiled by the Queen on 27th May 2010.
- Named on the War Memorial, Eton College, Windsor, Berkshire.
- Long Bredy village hall, built in 1920 for George and Norah Gribble, is dedicated to the memory of their son and the other six men of the village who died in the Great War.
- A Department for Communities and Local Government commemorative VC paving stone was dedicated at Sloane Square War Memorial, Kensington on 23rd March 2018 to mark the centenary of his award.

Julian never married. The VC was presented to his father by Brigadier General LD Jackson, Commanding No.3 Area, Southern Command at the family home, Kingston Russell House, Dorchester, on 15th September 1919.

In addition to the VC he was awarded the British War Medal 1914–20 and Victory Medal 1914–19. His original VC and medals were destroyed in a fire at his brother Philip's home at Wamil Hall, near Mildenhall, Suffolk in February 1958. In his autobiography, *Off The Cuff*, Philip stated, … *Every record in my possession, from family photograph albums to my diary of events during my ten years as military commentator to The News Chronicle, was cindered in a fire at my country home in February 1958.* A replica VC is held by the Royal Warwickshire Regiment Museum, Warwick. There is no record that a duplicate VC was requested or issued.

CAPTAIN REGINALD FREDERICK JOHNSON HAYWARD
1st Battalion, The Duke of Edinburgh's (Wiltshire Regiment)

Reginald Hayward was born at Beersheba Post, Swartberg, East Griqualand, South Africa on 17th June 1891. His father, Frederick Joachim (also seen as Joakim and Johnson) Hayward (1864–12th November 1918) was born at Presteigne, Radnorshire. He was known as 'Bull' due to his size. He moved to North Adelaide, South Australia, where he was a sheep farmer and was declared insolvent in November 1890. He moved to South Africa, where he was more successful and built

a large house at Swartberg with tennis court, swimming pool and library. Frederick was well known for his hospitality and ran an illicit still to produce copious amounts of liquor. The Cape Mounted Riflemen hoped to catch him in the act of distilling and stationed an officer behind a large rock to watch the premises. Frederick heard about this and in response organised a shooting party, with the rock being the target. Frederick married Gertrude Sarah Ann née Harris (c.1863–12th October 1929) on 15th February 1890 in Adelaide, South Australia. Gertrude died at her home farm at Ben Lomond, Umzimkulu, South Africa. Reginald had two siblings:

- Victor Cyril Hayward had a son, Michael Redvers Hayward, who married Janet and became an Anglican priest at St Luke Parish, Swartberg, Kokstad, KwaZulu-Natal, South Africa. Victor died in South Africa in 1945.
- Dorothy Maud Hayward (born c.1894 at Griqualand) married RG or RD Wilsdon.

Presteigne, where Reginald's father was born, was the county town of Radnorshire, but is now is Powys, close to the border with England. In the 13th and 14th centuries the town was devastated by the Black Death and the Owain Glyndwr rebellion. A thriving cloth industry in Tudor times was destroyed by Black Death epidemics in three successive generations. By the end of the 19th century the administrative centre for Radnorshire had moved to Llandrindod Wells.

Reginald's paternal grandfather, Johnson Frederic Hayward (5th September 1822–8th April 1912), was born at Uley, Gloucestershire. He arrived in Australia in March 1847 and became a sheep farmer. He married Ellen Margaret née Litchfield (13th December 1844–22nd February 1925) on 12th January 1864 at Walkerville, South Australia. She was born at South Adelaide, Australia, daughter of Captain Charles William Litchfield (1802–50) and Ellen Munro (1818–1908). They returned to Britain in 1864 and were living at Alkalm Mansion, Frampton, Gloucestershire in 1871, where he farmed sheep. By 1881 they had moved to Aroona (named after his station in South Australia), Limpley Stoke, Bradford on Avon, Wiltshire and were still there in 1911. He was known locally as Squire Hayward and was churchwarden of St Mary's Church for nineteen years. When he died Johnson left effects valued at £11,895/19/8. When Ellen died she

Reginald's paternal grandparents lived at Aroona in Limpley Stoke from the 1870s for the rest of their lives.

left effects valued at £32,548/17/10. In addition to Frederick they had ten other children:

- Charles Wiltens Andrée A Hayward (21st July 1866–10th August 1950) was born at Presteigne, Herefordshire. He was educated at Exeter College, Oxford (BA 1888) and was called to the Bar (Inner Temple) in 1890. After working in South Africa he moved to the Western Australia goldfields. He married Elizabeth Maria Dunn on 7th November 1900 at Perth, Western Australia. Charles was a journalist with the *Geraldton Express* (sub-editor 1896–98 and 1905–06) and *Geraldton Guardian*. From 1898 he edited the *Murchison Advocate* and the *Kalgoorlie Sun* 1901–02. He also wrote for the *Kalgoorlie Miner*, the Perth *Sunday Times* (1902–04 and 1906 onwards) and the *Sydney Bulletin* from 1922. He published a book of verses, *Along the Road to Cue* in 1897, about his experiences in the goldfields. He was living at 116 Spencer Road, Cremorne, Sydney, New South Wales at the time of his death, leaving effects valued at £7,481/3/11. Charles and Elizabeth had three children – Adrian Meredith Hayward 1902, Lucy Andrée Hayward 1904 and Hubert Thyne Hayward 1909.
- Ellen 'Nellie' Munro Hayward (1868–27th June 1958) was living with her parents in 1911 and never married. She was living at Watergate, Monkton Combe, Somerset at the time of her death.
- Anna Maria Catherina Hayward (1871–1961) married Charles Edward Stewart Flemming (1863–1951) in 1892 at Bradford on Avon. He was a surgeon in 1901 and they were living at 4 Kingston Road, Bradford on Avon. By 1911 they had moved to 3 Kingston Road. They had three children – Thomas Frederick S Flemming 1893, Charles Cecil Flemming 1894 and Arthur Adrian Greig Flemming 1902.
- Jacob Scott Hayward (born 1873) is understood to have died in 1907.
- Arthur Edward Hayward (1875–31st August 1916) was a labourer when he enlisted in 16th Australian Infantry Battalion AIF at Geraldton, Western Australia on 13th August 1915 (3916). He was described as 6′ tall, weighing 190 lbs, with fresh complexion, blue eyes, light brown hair and his religious denomination was Roman Catholic. He sailed for Egypt aboard HMAT A31 *Ajana* from Fremantle on 22nd December. Arthur was admitted to 4th Auxiliary Hospital, Abbassia with measles on 18th February 1916 and was

Reginald's uncle, Charles Wiltens Andrée A Hayward, was a journalist on a number of publications, including the *Sydney Bulletin*. He lived at 116 Spencer Road, Cremorne, Sydney, New South Wales.

The Villers-Bretonneux Memorial where Reginald's uncle, Arthur Edward Hayward, is commemorated. The views from the tower over the surrounding battlefields are stunning.

discharged to No.4 Training Battalion, Zeitoun on 6th March. He rejoined 16th Battalion at Tel-el-Kebir next day and arrived at Marseille, France aboard HMT *Canada* on 9th June. Arthur was reported missing in action on 31st August, later changed to killed in action at Mouquet Farm. He is commemorated on the Villers-Bretonneux Memorial, France.

- Adrian Lemmers Hayward (1877–30th August 1951) emigrated to Australia and married Mary Elizabeth Allender (c.1897–9th October 1968) in 1915 at Northampton, Western Australia. Adrian was a farmer at Roslyn Farm, Geraldton in 1916. Depending upon sources they had between six and twelve children including – John Frederick Hayward 1915, Margaret Ann Hayward 1917, Norman Hayward 1917, Arthur Edward Hayward 1919, Adrian Augustus Hayward 1921, Dorothy Nancy Hayward 1923 and possibly Elle Mary Hayward 1925, Mavis J Hayward 1927 and Phyllis N Hayward 1929.

- Maud Elizabeth Hayward (1880–1964) married Dr Rupert Edward Moorhead (1875–15th February 1939), a physician, in 1906. He was born on Mauritius. They were living at Batheaston, Somerset in 1911. They were living at 1 Circus Mansions, Bath, Somerset at the time of his death, leaving effects valued at £4,395/8/-.

- Cyril Albertus Hayward (6th March 1882–1949) was a second engineer in the Merchant Service in 1911. He joined the Royal Navy on 5th August 1916 and was described as 6' 1" tall, with grey hair, fresh complexion and a tattoo of a dragon on his left forearm. He served aboard HMS *Pembroke II* on three occasions and also on *Humber*, *Grafton*, *Diligence* and *Pekin*. He was demobilised on 8th December 1919. Cyril married Kathleen Mary Barnard (1894–1933) on 24th April 1915 at St John, Kingston upon Thames, Surrey. She died at Hammam, Tunisia. They had eight children – Kathleen Margaret Joan Hayward 1915, Cyril Frederick Norman Hayward 1917, Diana Catarina Hayward 1919, André L Hayward 1920, Charles William Arthur Hayward 1922, Habib Bryan Hayward 1925, Zohra Elizabeth Hayward 1927 and Raouf Paul Hayward 1933.

- Hubert Martinus Hayward (1885–20th March 1942) married Cecily Margaret Joan Davies (5th May 1890–1978) on 25th April 1916 at Stonehouse, Gloucestershire. She was a private secretary and they lived at Pearcroft Cottage, Stonehouse. They had a son, Martinus Peter Jenner Hayward, in 1918. Cecily was living at Haywards End, Stonehouse at the time of her death.

• Dorothy 'Doss' Mary Hayward (5th July 1887–6th March 1976) married Frederick William Gordon Smith (1885–11th October 1935) in 1916. In 1908 he was an engineer sub-lieutenant (1st February 1908) on HMS *Suffolk* and was serving on HMS *Minotaur* on the China Station in 1911. Promoted engineer lieutenant commander on 1st February 1916. He was stationed at Auckland, New Zealand in 1928 and sailed for Honolulu, Hawaii on 24th October 1928 aboard RMS *Niagara* and on to San Francisco, USA on 7th November aboard SS *Matosonia*. He was serving as an engineer captain in the Engineer-in-Chief's Department, living at 13 Portland Place, Edgbaston, Birmingham at the time of his death at Queen's Hospital, Birmingham, leaving effects valued at £4,575/6/11. Probate was granted to his brother-in-law, Inman Harry Harvey (1876–1961), husband of Florence Mildred Smith (1882–1978). Dorothy was living at Tyndale, Dovers Park, Bathford, Somerset at the time of her death.

Reginald's maternal grandparents were William Henry Harris (born c.1831) and possibly Mary Ann née Calton (c.1841–1919), who married on 28th May 1859 at Queenstown, Adelaide, South Australia.

Reginald was educated at Hilton College, Natal, where he was RSM of the cadet unit and represented the school at rugby and cricket in 1907–08. He joined Durban Wanderers Rugby Club and in 1911 played in the Inter-Provincial Currie Cup competition, the Springbok trials and represented Natal against England. Of the twenty-five players in the Natal squad, six were killed in the Great War, one received the MC and another was Mentioned, in addition to Hayward's VC. Reginald attended Durban Business College 1909–10 and, after moving to England in May 1912, the Royal College of Veterinary Surgeons. In England he played for Rosslyn Park, captained the Royal College of Veterinary Surgeons XV in 1914–15 and also represented Middlesex.

Reginald was commissioned in 6th Wiltshire on 29th September 1914 and was promoted lieutenant on 24th December. He transferred to 1st Battalion in March 1915 and went to France on 18th July. On 27th February 1916 he received a Regular Commission with seniority backdated to 29th June 1915. The Battalion war diary for 7th July 1916 records that he was slightly wounded in the hand but remained at his post, where he was afterwards killed (sic). **Awarded the MC for his conspicuous gallantry and initiative on the Somme, possibly at Stuff Redoubt in October 1916, LG 4th June 1917.** He was evacuated to Britain where a piece of shrapnel was removed from his eye. He was admitted to hospital sick on 3rd December 1916. He was appointed acting captain 19th December 1916–14th September 1919 and was promoted lieutenant on 22nd December 1916. **Awarded a Bar to the MC for his actions at Messines on 7th June 1917 – although wounded in two places he led his company with great dash to its objective, setting a splendid example to**

Hilton College is a non-denominational private boys' boarding school, modeled on the English public school system. It was founded in 1872 by Gould Arthur Lucas and Reverend William Orde Newnham. Nearby Michaelhouse is the only other full boarding single-sex boys' school in South Africa and the two schools have developed a friendly rivalry, particularly in the rugby field. Their first match was in 1904 and is now the oldest continuous rugby fixture in KwaZulu-Natal. Gould Arthur Lucas went to South Africa in 1851 as a lieutenant in the 73rd Foot and was one of only three officers to survive the sinking of HMS *Birkenhead* in 1852. In 1878 the school was taken over by Henry Vaughan Ellis, a Rugby old boy, who did much to adopt the English public school model. The Hilton College Guard, a mounted unit, was established in 1872 and was only disbanded in the mid-1980s, by then the oldest cadet corps in South Africa. Hilton has produced over twenty Rhodes scholars and has a student exchange programme with Eton and Harrow as well as other schools in England, Scotland, Germany, Australia and the USA.

his men. **He was the only company officer left and it was owing to his gallant leadership that his company captured five machine guns and fifty prisoners, LG 16th August 1917.** The Battalion war diary for 9th June records that he was wounded but remained at duty in the trenches at Wulverghem. He was acting CO in early 1918, while the CO commanded the Brigade.

Awarded the VC for his actions near Frémicourt, France on 21st/22nd March 1918, LG 24th April 1918. He was evacuated to Britain on 2nd April 1918. The VC was presented by the King at Buckingham Palace on 24th October 1918. Reginald joined the 1st Battalion on 1st May 1919 and was the Adjutant 14th September 1919–13th September 1922. He served at Royal Barracks, Dublin and later in Egypt and Palestine. Promoted captain 21st September 1927 and retired on 4th April 1935 to the Reserve of Officers with seniority from 27th December 1924.

Reginald was employed in the BBC Publications Department. He married Linda Agnes Bowen (1915–2nd August 1970) on 9th July 1938 at Christ Church, Burbage, Buxton, Derbyshire. She was born at Chapel-en-le-Frith, Derbyshire. There were no children.

Linda's father, Charles Brice Bowen (1874–1st June 1950) was born at Barton-upon-Irwell, Lancashire, eldest son of Herbert Blane Bowen (1839–97) and Laura Agnes Brice (1851–1926), of Ollerenshaw Hall, Chapel-en-le-Frith. Charles was

Built in 1701–02 in the Arbour Hill area of Dublin and extended in the late 18th and 19th centuries, The Barracks, later Royal Barracks, became Collins Barracks (after Michael Collins, first CinC of the Free State) when it was handed over to the Irish Free State in 1922. Occupied by military forces for almost three centuries, they were the oldest continuously occupied barracks in the world. Wolfe Tone, one of the leaders in the 1798 rebellion was held prisoner, tried and convicted of treason there. In the 19th century the barracks held up to 1,500 troops. During the 1916 Easter Rising, 10th Royal Dublin Fusiliers deployed from Royal Barracks to fight the Irish Citizen Army and Irish Volunteers. After seventy-five years of occupation by the Irish Army, 5th Infantry Battalion marched out for the last time in 1997 to make way for the National Museum of Ireland – Decorative Arts and History. The barrack buildings have been used in a number of films and television productions, including *Michael Collins* and *Ripper Street*.

an apprentice at a calico printing works in 1891. He married Jane 'Jean' McGuffie (born 1877) in 1902 and they had a daughter:

• Laura Catherine Bowen (born 1906) is believed to have married Alan Cecil Clackson (1906–74) in 1930 at Kensington, London and they had four children – Peter A Clackson 1932, Laura J Clackson 1937, Sarah C Clackson 1939 and Richard AP Clackson 1947.

Charles' and Jane's marriage ended in divorce in 1912. He married Linda's mother, Linda Redenta Eugenie née D'Amato (17th September 1891–1977), in 1913 at Fulham. Linda senior was born there, the daughter of Carlo Dance D'Amato (1864–1953), an Italian flautist from Naples, and Natalia Fischer (1861–1951), who was born at Trieste, Austria. Linda was a violinist in 1911, living

The parish church of Christ Church in Burbage, Buxton, where Reginald and Linda married in 1938, was built in 1861 and extended thirty years later.

with her parents at 113 Edith Road, West Kensington, London. Charles was a partner in Herbert Blane Bowen, cotton goods merchants trading at 33 Chorlton Street, Manchester, with Laura Agnes Bowen and Bertram Herbert Bowen. The company was dissolved by mutual consent on 30th June 1917. He was living at Lower Eaves, Chapel-en-le-Frith at the time of his death at Westminster Hospital, London, leaving effects valued at £11,730/9/-. In addition to Linda, he and Linda senior had two other children:

Linda's parents lived at Lower Eaves, Chapel-en-le-Frith.

- Charles Earle Bowen (1916–1st October 1940) was commissioned as an acting pilot officer (39488) in the RAF. He was confirmed in the rank on 21st December 1937 and was promoted flying officer 21st July 1939 and flight lieutenant 3rd September 1940. During the Battle of Britain Charles was serving in 607 Squadron at RAF Tangmere. On 26th September 1940 he was flying Hawker Hurricane I 'P5205', when he bailed out over Merlins Farm, Calthorpe, Isle of Wight, Hampshire. He was killed in action on 1st October when his Hawker Hurricane I 'P2900' was shot down by a Messerschmitt Bf 110 at 10.50 a.m. over the Isle of Wight. He is commemorated on the Runnymede Memorial, Surrey (Panel 4).
- Godfrey V Bowen (29th April 1919–1939).

On 24th August 1939 Reginald was recalled as a major in the RASC, with seniority from 9th July 1938, and served with Anti-Aircraft Command until 1945. He was appointed temporary lieutenant colonel on 18th April 1945. Between 1945 and 1947 he was commandant of prisoner of war camps and retired as honorary

607 Squadron pilots with a Hawker Hurricane fighter at RAF Tangmere.

Reginald's brother-in-law, Charles Earle Bowen, is commemorated on the Runnymede Memorial, Surrey.

The Hurlingham Club during a polo match in 1939. The Club was formed in 1869. The Prince of Wales, the future Edward VII, was an early patron, and ensured the club's status and notability from the outset. In 1873 the Club published the rules of polo, which are still followed to this day. In 1886, the first international polo match between England and the United States was held there, as were the polo matches during the 1908 Summer Olympics. Other sports played at the club include golf, croquet, lawn tennis, cricket, bowls, squash and swimming, both indoor and outdoor. There is currently a thirty-year waiting list for membership.

Reginald Hayward later in life.

lieutenant colonel on 9th July 1947. He was then London Area Manager of the BBC Publications Department 1947–June 1951 and Games Manager of the Hurlingham Club in London 1952–67.

Reginald attended the VC Garden Party at Buckingham Palace on 26th June 1920, the VC Dinner at the Royal Gallery of the House of Lords, London on 9th November 1929, the Victory Day Celebration Dinner & Reception at The Dorchester, London on 8th June 1946, the VC Centenary Celebrations at Hyde Park, London on 26th June 1956 and the first six biannual VC & GC Association Reunions at the Café Royal, London between July 1958 and July 1968. He died at 7 Ormonde Gate, Chelsea, London on 17th January 1970 and was cremated at Putney Vale Crematorium, Wandsworth, where his ashes were scattered opposite Panel 13 in the Garden of Remembrance. He is commemorated in a number of other places:

Reginald's ashes were scattered in this area in the Garden of Remembrance at Putney Vale Crematorium (Memorials to Valour).

- Hayward Avenue, Putney Vale Cemetery, named in 1997 by Wandsworth Borough Council. Six other roads and paths at Putney Vale Cemetery are also named after VC recipients buried, cremated or commemorated there:
    ° Alexander Way – Ernest Alexander VC CB CMG.
    ° Boulter's Path – William Boulter VC.
    ° Greenwood Road – Harry Greenwood VC DSO & Bar OBE MC.
    ° Paton's Path – George Paton VC MC.
    ° Richard's Way – Alfred Richards VC.
    ° Schofield Road – Harry Schofield VC.
- RFJ Hayward VC Memorial Prize for Form 5 geography awarded annually by Hilton College, Hilton, KwaZulu-Natal.
- Hayward Care Centre, Corn Croft Lane, off Horton Road, Devizes, Wiltshire.
- Display at the Royal British Legion, Endless Street, Salisbury, Wiltshire.
- Memorial in St Mary's Church, Limpley Stoke, near Bradford on Avon, Wiltshire.

- Named on one of eleven plaques honouring 175 men from overseas awarded the VC for the Great War. The plaques were unveiled by the Senior Minister of State at the Foreign & Commonwealth Office and Minister for Faith and Communities, Baroness Warsi, at a reception at Lancaster House, London on 26th June 2014 attended by The Duke of Kent and relatives of the VC recipients. The South African plaque is at the Castle of Good Hope, Cape Town.

Reginald is commemorated in the Church of St Mary the Virgin at Limpley Stoke. The church dates from the 10th century and was originally dedicated to the Wiltshire Saint Edith of Wilton. After 500 years it was rededicated to St Mary.

- The Secretary of State for Communities and Local Government, Eric Pickles MP announced that Victoria Cross recipients from the Great War would have commemorative paving stones laid in their birthplace as a lasting legacy of local heroes within communities. The stones would be laid on or close to the 100th anniversary of their VC actions. For the 145 VCs born in Australia, Belgium, Canada, China, Denmark, Egypt, France, Germany, India, Iraq, Japan, Nepal, Netherlands, New Zealand, Pakistan, South Africa, Sri Lanka, Ukraine and United States of

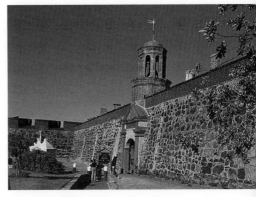

The Castle of Good Hope, Cape Town.

The Queen Elizabeth II Coronation Medal. A total of 138,214 medals were awarded, including 11,561 to Australians and 12,500 to Canadians. The medals were issued without inscription, except for thirty-seven issued to the successful British Mount Everest Expedition, which were engraved 'MOUNT EVEREST EXPEDITION' on the rim.

The Efficiency Decoration was instituted in 1930 for part-time officers of the Territorial Army of the United Kingdom and of the Auxiliary Military Forces of the British Dominions, Colonies and Protectorates and India after twenty years efficient service as a thoroughly capable officer. It superseded a number of awards, including the Volunteer Officers' Decoration and the Territorial Decoration. In 1949 the qualifying service was reduced to twelve years of commissioned service. A clasp was awarded for each further period of six years of qualifying service. In the Commonwealth it has been superseded by national decorations in Canada, South Africa and Australia. In the United Kingdom it was superseded by the Volunteer Reserves Service Medal in 1999. New Zealand continues to award the Efficiency Decoration.

America, individual commemorative stones were unveiled at the National Memorial Arboretum, Alrewas, Staffordshire by Prime Minister David Cameron MP and Sergeant Johnson Beharry VC on 5th March 2015.

Linda was living at Flat 1, 2 Ormonde Gate, London at the time of her death in August 1970. In addition to the VC and MC & Bar he was awarded the 1914–15 Star, British War Medal 1914–20, Victory Medal 1914–19, Defence Medal, War Medal 1939–45, George VI Coronation Medal 1937, Elizabeth II Coronation Medal 1953 and Efficiency Decoration (Territorial). The VC is held by The Rifles (Berkshire & Wiltshire) Museum, 58 The Close, Salisbury, Wiltshire.

SECOND LIEUTENANT ALFRED CECIL HERRING
Army Service Corps att'd 6th Battalion, The Northamptonshire Regiment

Alfred Herring was born at 53 The Avenue, Bruce Grove, Tottenham, Middlesex on 26th October 1888. His father, George Edward Herring (c.1853–10th January 1943), was born at Tendring, Essex. He married Cecilia Emily née Lewis (1861–1924) in 1882. She was born at Acton, Middlesex. George was a solicitor's clerk in 1891 and they were living at 53 The Avenue, Tottenham. By 1901 they had moved to 5 Victoria Terrace, Tottenham. In 1911 they were living at 143 Fox Lane, Palmers Green, Edmonton, Middlesex, by when he was a solicitor's managing clerk. Alfred had three siblings:

- George Herbert Herring (1884–2nd August 1961) was a commercial clerk in 1901. By 1911 he was a clerk to a wholesale stationer. He was serving as a sergeant in the Royal Buckinghamshire Hussars at Yeomanry House, Buckingham when he married Ida Minnie Ward (born 1888), a schoolteacher, on 22nd April 1916 at Christ Church, Southgate, London. In 1911 she was living with her parents at 27 Broomfield Avenue, Palmers Green, London and at 77 Derwent Road, Palmers Green at the time of her marriage.

Tendring village, where Alfred's father was born.

He was living at 36 Oakfield Road, Southgate, Middlesex at the time of his death. They had two children:
  - David A Herring (born 1920) married Alice F Sturmey (born 1920) in 1940 at Edmonton. They had a son, Nigel D Herring, in 1951.
  - Nancy W Herring (born 1922) married Humphrey Dean in 1955 at Wood Green. This appears to have been her second marriage as the registration in 1955 also recorded her as Nancy W O'Connell. Humphrey and Nancy had five children – Steven J Dean 1955, Michael W Dean 1956, Jane E Dean 1958, Catherine Dean 1961 and Richard J Dean 1963. The birth of a Robin D O'Connell was registered in 1946 at St Neots, Huntingdonshire to an O'Connell/Herring marriage but no marriage record has been found.
- Eleanor Cecilia Herring (1885–1947) was a pupil teacher in 1901 and a schoolteacher in 1911. She married Benjamin Pratt George (1875–1928) in late

1911 at Edmonton. They were living at 142 Fox Lane, Palmers Green, Southgate, Middlesex at the time of their deaths. They had two children:

  ° Marjorie F George (born 1912) married Edward George Sidney Jackson (born 1905), an accountant, in 1933. Edward married Lucie EF Pidgeon in 1952 and they had two sons – Richard CE Pidgeon 1956 and Stephen GL Pidgeon 1957.

  ° Daphne H George (born 1920) married Arthur Ronald Midgley (1908–72) in 1941. They were living at The Manor House, Thrapston, Northamptonshire at the time of his death. They had three children – twins Andrew M and Simon G Midgley 1943 and Sarah Midgley 1946.

• Winifred Herring (1896–1966) married Thomas Steel Vandy (1892–1975), a civil engineer, in 1924. He was living with his parents at 305 Victoria Park Road, South Hackney in 1911. He was living at 7 Benhale Close, Green Lane, Stanmore, Middlesex at the time of his death. They had a daughter, Mary C Vandy, in 1930.

Alfred's paternal grandfather, Abel Herring (born c.1807) was born at White Colne, Essex. He married Eliza née Meadows (c.1811–74), born at Barningham, Suffolk, on 18th May 1830 at Ashen, Essex. By 1861 he was a groom and they were living at Tendring, Essex. By 1871 he was an unemployed gatekeeper and they were living at 18 St James Street, Islington, London. He may have died in 1875. In addition to George they had nine other children:

• Abel Herring (c.1831–1910), a boot maker, married Julia Maria Garner (c.1835–1924) in 1856 at East London. They were living at 148 Lever Street, St Luke's, London in 1871. They had eight children – Julia Eliza Herring 1859, Thomas Abel Herring 1861, Alice Willindia Herring 1863, Emily Rose Herring 1865, George Parker Herring 1867, Minnie Herring 1870, Robert Herring 1872 and Frederick William Herring 1874.

Barningham in Suffolk is where Alfred's paternal grandmother was born c.1811. It was recorded in the Domesday Book with a population of thirty-six. James Fison founded what became the Fisons pharmaceutical company in the flourmill and bakery in the late 18th century.

• Eliza Herring (born c.1833).
• William Herring (c.1834–99) married Eleanor Reeves (c.1834–1905) in 1860 at West London. She was born at Grittleton, Wiltshire. In 1861 he was a valet for Sir Charles Robert Rowley at Tendring Hall, Stoke by Nayland, Suffolk. His family was living with his parents at Tendring, Essex. William was still at Tendring Hall in 1871 and by 1881 his wife had joined him there as a housemaid. By 1891 he was a stationer and they were living at Church Street, Stoke by Nayland. They had at least one child, Emma Eliza Herring, in 1860.

- Walter Herring (c.1837–75) married Martha Bennell (c.1829–96) in November 1860 at St James, Paddington, London. He was a warehouse porter in 1871 and they were living at Haverstock Street, Finsbury, London. They had two children – Emily Eliza Herring 1862 and Walter Edward Herring 1864.
- Mary Ann Herring (born c.1840).
- Emily Herring (1842–1916) married William Bragg (c.1822–71), a domestic servant coachman, in 1861. They were living at Weeley Road, Tendring in 1871. In 1881 Emily was a housemaid for William D Johnson, a hall porter, at 4 Craig's Court, St Martin in the Fields, London. She married Samuel Goodhall (born 1843) in 1889 at St George, Hanover Square, London. He was born at Birstall, Dewsbury, Yorkshire and was a mule spinner when he enlisted

Alfred's uncle, William Herring, was a valet at Tendring Hall, Stoke by Nayland, Suffolk in the 1860s, 70s and 80s. William and Beatrix de Tendring were given a grant for a fair and market in the manor of Stoke in 1303 and the estate remained in the family until 1421, when it passed to the Dukes of Norfolk. By 1750 the estate had been purchased by Admiral Sir William Rowley. His son, Sir Joshua Rowley, who inherited in 1768, commissioned the building of a new mansion. It was demolished in 1955 except for the entrance portico seen in this view.

in 2nd Life Guards (162) on 10th May 1860, described as almost 6′ 2½″ tall, with fair complexion, grey eyes and light hair. On 29th September 1867 he married Joanna Foster (1837–88) at Trinity Church, St Marylebone. Samuel was promoted corporal of horse on 1st April 1868 and re-engaged at Windsor to compete twenty-one years on 31st August 1870. He was stationed at the Cavalry Barracks, Clewer, Berkshire in 1871. Samuel was awarded Good Conduct Pay on 12th May 1863, 1868, 1872 and 1876 and the Good Conduct Medal on 1st May 1879. On being discharged on 20th June 1882 his character was assessed as Very Good. Samuel and Joanna had four children, including Robert Frederick S Goodhall 1872, Maude Mary Goodhall 1875 and Blanche Beatrice Goodhall 1877. Joanna died at 3 Brougham Villas, Brougham Road, Acton, London on 3rd April 1888. Samuel and Emily were living there in 1891 and at 19 Brougham Road, Acton, London in 1901 and 1911. The death of a Samuel Goodhall, aged 74, was registered in 1920 at Brentford, Middlesex.
- John Herring (1845–1926) was a stud groom for Sir Charles Robert Rowley at Tendring Hall, Stoke by Nayland in 1861 and 1871. He married Susannah Howard (1849–1913) in August 1881 at All Saints, Edmonton, Middlesex. She was born at Little Bentley, Essex, registered as Susan. They were living at Symington Street, Harpenden, Hertfordshire in 1911. He was living at The Ridge, Luton Road, Harpenden at the time of his death. They had four children – John William Herring 1885, Susan Eliza Herring 1886, Edith Mary Herring 1888 and George Howard Herring 1891.

- Rose Herring (1848–1916) married George Singleton (1853–98), a domestic coachman groom, in March 1885 at All Hallows, Tottenham, London. He was born at Swanmore, Hampshire. They were living at Cross Lane, Halsall, Lancashire in 1891. She was a cook working for the Reverend Ernest A Waller at The Rectory, Church Road, Little Packington, Warwickshire in 1901. Rose married Joseph Lindfield Peckham (c.1838–1915), a carpenter, in 1905 at Steyning, Sussex. He was born at Arundel, Sussex. They were living at 12 Myrtle Terrace, Lancing, Sussex in 1911. There were no children.
- Robert Herring (born 1850) is believed to have died before 1871.

His maternal grandfather, Thomas Lewis (born c.1840), married Elizabeth née Wilson (born 1841) in 1861. He was born at Shrewsbury, Shropshire and she at Wadenhoe, Northamptonshire. He was a coachman (domestic) in 1871 and they were living at Barwith, Studham, Hertfordshire. By 1881 he was working for the Earl of Harrington at Elvaston Castle, Elvaston, Derbyshire. By 1891 they had moved to 10 Lennox Mews, Chelsea, London and to the stables at Silwood Park, Sunninghill, Berkshire by 1901. Thomas died before 1911 (possibly in 1905 at Camberwell), by when Elizabeth was living at 54 Russell Road, Bowes Park, Southgate, Middlesex with her sister Lucy Bate (born 1844), also a widow. In addition to Cecilia they had a son:

- Henry Evelyn Lewis (1864–1945), a cabinetmaker in 1891, was working at Bunker Hill Lodge, Norton, Nottinghamshire by 1901. He married Sophia Elizabeth Schwer (1861–1945) in 1891 at Poplar, London. Her father was German and her mother was British. They died when she was five and she was brought up by an uncle named Cooper in Southampton. She was living with her children at 58 Hillier Road, Wandsworth, London in 1901 and Henry had joined the family there by 1911. They had two sons – Frank Wilson Lewis (1892–1912) and Harry Arnold Lewis (1895–1988). By 1918 Henry was a sub-manager in an aircraft construction works. Their son Harry gained an international cap for netball, won many medals for swimming and played for Croydon FC. He was a shipping clerk and enlisted on 7th November 1914, serving in France for twenty-seven months with the infantry and latterly as a pioneer (193001) with the Special Factory Section, Special Brigade Royal Engineers, engaged in producing phosgene gas at a manufacturing plant near Calais. He applied for a commission

Wadenhoe, Northamptonshire, the birthplace of Alfred's maternal grandmother in 1841.

Elvaston Castle in Derbyshire, where Alfred's maternal grandfather worked for the Earl of Harrington in the 1880s. The estate was held by Shelford Priory until the Dissolution of the Monasteries, when it was sold to Sir Michael Rampton. The manor house was built in 1633 and was redesigned and extended in the early 19th century for the 3rd Earl of Harrington. In the Second World War a teacher training college in Derby was evacuated there and remained until 1947. Thereafter the castle has been mostly empty and has steadily

deteriorated. Since 2008 it has been on the Buildings at Risk Register. In 1969 Elvaston was used in Ken Russell's film of DH Lawrence's novel *Women in Love*.

in the RFC and returned to Britain on 31st January 1918. His mother was found wandering in London by the Metropolitan Police on 19th January, claiming that Harry had stabbed her with a bayonet. She was found to be insane and removed to Cane Hill Asylum/Mental Hospital, Coulsdon, Surrey. She had been affected by the death of her eldest son when he drowned in a boating accident in 1912. Learning that her only surviving son was going to join the RFC seems to have driven her to insanity. While Harry was training with No.2 RFC Cadet Wing, Cadet Brigade, Royal Victoria Hotel, St Leonards on Sea, Hastings enquiries were conducted by MI5 into his mother's father, although he had been dead for many decades. Harry's desire to serve on Home Defence duties due to his mother's condition was supported by GOC Cadet Brigade. Harry was commissioned on 6th March 1918. He was an editor in 1945.

Alfred was educated at Tottenham County Grammar School, where he was captain of the cricket and football teams and was a member of the King's Royal Rifle Corps Cadets March–September 1906. He served his articles with Daniel Steuart Fripp FCA and qualified as a chartered accountant in December 1912.

Alfred's maternal grandfather worked at the stables of Silwood Park around the turn of the 19th century. The original manor was replaced about 1788 by a Georgian mansion, which in turn was replaced by the present mansion in 1878. During the Second World War Silwood Park was converted into a convalescent home for airmen. In 1947 it was purchased by Imperial College, London.

In December 1914 he was appointed to the Army Pay Department and served as Acting Paymaster, Army Pay Depot, Chatham. He enlisted on 10th December 1915 (S4/217103) and transferred to the Army Reserve next day. Alfred was mobilised on 1st September 1916 and was commissioned in the Army Service Corps on 26th October. He went to France on 1st November, where he was employed in supply duties at Le Havre and later with Deputy Assistant Director Supplies and Transport GHQ 2nd Echelon for railhead staff duties. He left France on 31st August 1917 and joined No.1 School of Instruction, Brocton Camp, Cannock Chase, Staffordshire on 8th September. He was attached on the strength of 6th Northamptonshire from the same date.

Awarded the VC for his actions at Jussy and Montagne Bridge, Crozat Canal, near Remigny, France on 23rd/24th March 1918, LG 7th June 1918. This was his first engagement. Having been taken prisoner on 24th March, he was presented to the Kaiser at St Quentin, who shook his hand and congratulated him on his fine fight.

Alfred was promoted lieutenant on 26th April 1918. The VC ribbon was presented by Brigadier General Edward Henry Charles Patrick Bellingham DSO CMG, Senior British Officer at the POW Camp, Graudanz, Western Prussia (now Grudziadz, Poland), on 18th August 1918. After the presentation the German officers were the first to offer their congratulations. According to Lieutenant Douglas W Milne, 7th Gordon Highlanders, *The German of those days always had admiration for a good soldier, whether friend or enemy*.

Alfred was released on 14th December and was repatriated on 18th December

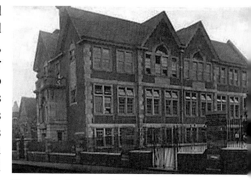

Tottenham Grammar School dates back to 1456. In 1631 a legacy left by Sarah, Duchess of Somerset was used to extend the schoolhouse and provide free education to poor children. In 1882 pupils from the school and St John's Presbyterian School formed Hotspur FC, which subsequently became Tottenham Hotspur FC. In 1910 most of the old school was demolished and replaced with a new building. However, due to increasing pupil numbers in February 1938 a new site opened on Creighton Road, near White Hart Lane, by Middlesex County Council for 450 boys. During the Blitz the school was evacuated to Chelmsford. On 15th March 1945 a V2 landed on the corner of White Hart Lane and Queen Street, killing two boys and seriously injuring another. The school was expanded in 1960 to accept 700 boys and in 1967 it merged with Rowland Hill Secondary Modern School to form the comprehensive Somerset School. Due to falling numbers the school closed in 1988 and the site has been redeveloped for housing.

Brocton and Rugeley Camps on Cannock Chase, Staffordshire were constructed on the estate of Lord Lichfield in 1914. The camps eventually held 40,000 men at any time and were used to train about 500,000 men. The camps had all their own facilities – churches, post offices, bakery, amenity huts and a theatre.

1918, following which he was granted two months leave. He was seconded to the Corps of Military Accountants as Accountant 3rd Class to work as a group accountant with the Cost Accounting Committee, War Office on 19th November 1919. Appointed temporary major on 27th January 1919. The VC was presented by the King at Buckingham Palace on 15th February 1919. Alfred was a member of the VC Guard at the Interment of the Unknown Warrior on 11th November 1920. He relinquished his commission on 1st February 1922 and retained the rank of major.

Alfred Herring married Winifred Ethel née Frankland (1888–1968) at St Barnabus Church, North Dulwich in February 1922. They were living at 52 Melbury Court, Kensington in 1944 and later at 143 Fox Lane, Palmers Green, London. They had four children:

- Joyce F Herring (born 1923) married Edward P Shaw in 1943 at Westminster, London. It is understood that he was born on 17th July 1915 at Portage, South Bend, Indiana, USA.
- Sheila Victoria Herring (born 1924) served as a leading aircraftswoman in the Women's Auxiliary Air Force during the Second World War. She married Donald Leatham (1916–77) in 1944 at Cheltenham, Gloucestershire. He was living at 16 Inglewood Avenue, Heatherside, Camberley, Surrey at the time of his death. They had four children – Gay A Leatham 1947, Deidre A Leatham 1950, David A Leatham 1952 and Jane W Leatham 1958. Sheila married David J Blissett (1921–73) in 1971 at Merton, Greater London.
- Anthony Edward Herring (born 1925) became a stockbroker and a member of the London Stock Exchange after service in the RAF. He married Margery A Bremridge in 1951 and they lived at Green Dene, East Horsley, Surrey. They had four children – Sally A Herring 1955, John A Herring 1958, Peter R Herring 1962 and Andrew C Herring 1964.
- Jean M Herring (born 1928) married Robin Dick Pearson Triefus (1922–83) in 1950 at Chelsea, London. He was a company director in 1966. He was living at The Dewar House, Breech Lane, Walton-on-the-Hill, Tadworth, Surrey at the time of his death. They had four children – Graham P Triefus 1952, Colin F Triefus 1953, Fiona C Triefus 1956 and Robert L Triefus 1961.

Winifred's father, Edward James Frankland (1862–1940), married Mary Matilda née Taylor (1862–1902) in 1885 at Camberwell, London. She was born at Southampton, Hampshire. He was a commercial traveller in 1891, visiting at 9 Arkwright Street, Nottingham. She was living with her children at 54 St Marys Road, Camberwell in 1901. In addition to Winifred they had two other children:

- Edward Percy Frankland (1886–1935) was a commercial traveller in 1911, living with his father and stepmother. He attested in 5th City of London Rifles (394) on 3rd September 1914, described as 5′ 8″ tall. He served in France from 4th November 1914, embarking at Southampton, but suffered from bronchitis on

16th December and was evacuated on HMHS *Gloucester Castle* on 28th December. He transferred to 3/5th Battalion on 10th May 1915 and was attached to 107th Provisional Battalion on 27th November and detached to HAC Detachment Depot on 12th January 1917, then transferred to the Middlesex Regiment on 31st March. He married Marie Lilian Elizabeth Gurney (1895–1977) at St Michael's, Pimlico on 12th April 1917. They lived at 2 Purcell Mansions, Queen's Gardens, West Kensington. Edward transferred to the Labour Corps on 27th April and to 32nd London on 3rd July. On 3rd December he was admitted to 334th (London) Field Ambulance with stricture of the urethra and was treated at Colchester Military Hospital until 1st January 1918. He transferred to 2/1st Surrey Yeomanry (46577) on 7th February and was admitted to Ipswich Military Hospital 21st-25th February with stricture of the urethra and again 15th April–2nd May. From then until 5th June he was treated for gonorrhoea. Treatment for stricture of the urethra continued at 1st Eastern General Hospital, Cambridge 5th June–22nd July and in Ireland 26th July–7th September. Edward was discharged from Canterbury on 20th November 1918, no longer fit for war service. His address was 2 Ludgate Circus, London. They were living at 59 Millway, Mill Hill, Hendon, Middlesex at the time of his death on 29th December 1935 at University College Hospital, Gower Street, London. She was living at Park Lodge, 6 Victoria Drive, London at the time of her death.

• Sidney James Frankland (born 1890) was a commercial traveller in 1911, living with his father and stepmother. He enlisted in 21st London (800) on 22nd February 1909, described as 5′ 5″ tall and was a jeweller's accountant for Messrs Elkington, Regent Street, London. He was discharged on 18th March 1912, being unable to attend drills and camps, and paid £2 to leave prior to the end of his four-year engagement. He is understood to have married Alice/Gladys Harris in 1916.

Edward James Frankland married Edith Marian Edwards (c.1871–1944) in 1903 at Croydon, Surrey. He was a general merchant in 1911 and they were living at Llanberis, High Street, Dulwich Village. They were living at Temperley, Bromley Road, Beckenham, Kent at the time of their deaths. They recorded the birth of a child in the 1911 Census who was not with them. However, in that Census Winifred was boarding at The Towers Private Hotel, Southcliffe, Great Clacton, Essex with the six-year old child below:

• Cyril Edward Frankland (2nd June 1904–1970), birth registered at Camberwell, London, married Phyllis Mary Hewett (1906–61) in 1929 at Camberwell. They separated and she may have remarried. Cyril married Doris Eveline Hill (1912–62) in 1946. They were both company directors in 1958, living at Frankland House, Buyers Lane, South Godstone, Surrey. Cyril married Joan Rymer in 1964 at Cirencester, Gloucestershire.

Alfred became a partner in Evans, Fripp, Deed & Co, Chartered Accountant 1920–25 and in Laing & Cruikshank, a Moorgate stockbroking firm 1925–61. He was a member of the London Stock Exchange from May 1925 and was also a director of George W King Ltd, Safeguard Industrial Developments Ltd, Austin Motor Co and other companies. Alfred attended the VC Garden Party at Buckingham Palace on 26th June 1920, the VC Dinner at the Royal Gallery of the House of Lords, London on 9th November 1929, the VC Centenary Celebrations at Hyde Park, London on 26th June 1956 and the third VC & GC Association Reunion at the Café Royal, London on 18th July 1962.

The Towers Private Hotel, Southcliffe, Great Clacton, Essex, where Winifred was staying at the time of the 1911 Census. The building has since been divided into apartments.

He was living at Oatlands Park Hotel, Weybridge, Surrey when he died at Ascot Nursing Home, Sunningdale, Berkshire on 10th August 1966. He was cremated at St John's Crematorium, Woking, where his ashes were scattered in Chaucer South Area in the Garden of Remembrance. He is commemorated in a number of other places:

Alfred Herring's final resting place.

• Herring Troop, 96 (The Duke of Gloucester) Squadron, Royal Logistic Corps, 1 Army Training Regiment, Pirbright, Surrey.
• The Alfred Herring Public House, 316–322 Green Lanes, Palmers Green, London.
• *Alfred Herring V.C.* a range safety craft (61 tons) built in 1978 (Pennant Y02) was operated by 18 Maritime Squadron RCT at the Royal Artillery Missile Range, Outer Hebrides. It

The Alfred Herring pub in Palmers Green.

transferred to the Royal Maritime Auxiliary Service in 1988 and was renamed RSC *Petard* in 1991. It was operated by Smit International (Scotland) as a range safety craft under MOD contract from 1995 based at Pembroke Dock. She was sold in 2004 to Izax Offshore as MV *Petard*, based at Maryport, Cumbria as an offshore workboat and safety vessel.

- Portrait in the Army Reserve Centre, London Road, Peterborough, Northamptonshire headquarters of 158 Regiment RLC.
- A Department for Communities and Local Government commemorative VC paving stone was dedicated at Tottenham War Memorial at the junction of Tottenham High Road and Town Hall Approach on 23rd March 2018 to mark the centenary of his award.

In addition to the VC he was awarded the British War Medal 1914–20, Victory Medal 1914–19, George VI Coronation Medal 1937 and Elizabeth II Coronation Medal 1953. The VC is held by the HQ Royal Logistic Corps Officers' Mess, Princess Royal Barracks, Deepcut, Camberley, Surrey.

18474 SERGEANT HAROLD JACKSON
7th Battalion, The East Yorkshire Regiment

Harold Jackson was born at Allandales, Kirton, near Boston, Lincolnshire on 2nd June 1892. He was known as Chummy. His father, Thomas Boardman Jackson (1849–1933), was born at Bicker, Lincolnshire. At the time of the 1871 Census he was a farm servant working for his future father-in-law at Frampton Marsh. He married Mary Ann née Stevenson (1854–1904), registered in the 2nd quarter of 1871, at Boston. His name was recorded as Thomas Boardman. Thomas was described variously as a farm or agricultural labourer. In 1881 they were living at Kirton.

By 1891 they had moved to Medlam Bank North, West Fen, Spilsby and by 1901 at Bishops Hill, Kirton. Thomas was a road foreman in 1911 and was living with his daughter, Mary Ann Searby and her family at Kirton. Harold had nine siblings:

- Eliza Boardman Jackson (born 1872 as Eliza Ann J Boardman) married George Beaumont Winn Bland, as Eliza Jackson Boardman (1875–1943), in 1896. She was living with her parents at Bishops Hill, Kirton in 1901. Eliza married John Thomas Humphreys (1882–1947) in 1908 at Nottingham. He was a taxicab proprietor in 1911 and they were living at 184 Trent Boulevard, Bridgford, Nottingham. George married Emma Elizabeth Ingram (1889–1950) in 1913 at Peterborough, Northamptonshire.

- Elizabeth Ann Boardman Jackson (born 4th December 1874) was a domestic servant working for a farmer at Holbeach, Lincolnshire at the time of the 1891 Census.
- Thomas Robert Jackson (9th December 1876–9th June 1946), an agricultural labourer, was living at Carrington, Lincolnshire in 1891. He married Elsie Hayward (10th February 1887–17th February 1931) in 1913 at Grimsby, Lincolnshire. She was born at Islington, London. Thomas served in 8th Hussars during the Great War and was badly gassed. They had a son, Thomas Jackson, in 1911. Both Elsie and Thomas were living in Manchester when they died.
- Mary Ann Jackson (1880–1955) married John Robert Searby (1875–1941) in 1900 in Manchester. John was a general labourer in 1911 and they were living at Kirton. Mary Ann was living at 5 Cheshire Road, Bowes Park, Wood Green, London in 1918. They had three children – Doris Mary Searby 1905, Stanley Robert Searby 1909 and Mabel F Searby 1911.
- William Jackson (born c.1882) was an agricultural labourer in 1901. He served in the Machine Gun Corps during the Great War.
- Jesse Jackson (1884–93).
- George Henry J Jackson (23rd December 1885–1974) was an agricultural labourer in 1901.
- Florence Jackson (1889–1961) married her cousin, Thomas Boardman Jackson, in 1907 at Edmonton, Middlesex. He was a printing machine minder in 1901 living with his paternal uncle, Joseph Robert Jackson. They were living at 86 Palmer Road, New Southgate, Middlesex in 1911. He was living at 5 Cheshire Road, London at the time of his death. They had three children – Clarence Boardman Jackson 1907, Florence Margaret Jackson 1908 and Mary Kathleen Jackson 1910.
- James Henry 'Harry' Jackson (born c.1891) married Minnie Poole in 1909 at York. He is reported to have been awarded the DCM during the Great War.

Harold's paternal grandfather, Thomas Jackson (c.1822–99), born at Donington, Lincolnshire, was an agricultural labourer. He married Elizabeth née Boardman (c.1825–93) on 10th July 1848 at Bicker, Lincolnshire. She was born at Gosberton, Lincolnshire. They were living at Chapel Yard, Bicker in 1851. By 1861 he was a road labourer. In 1891 he was an agricultural labourer and they were living at Willington Road, Kirton. Elizabeth had a son, William Armstrong Boardman (1845–1913). He was a bricklayer and married Mary Ann Sivill (1842–1921) in 1867 at Guisborough, Yorkshire. They had two children – Elizabeth Boardman 1869 and Florence Boardman 1879. They were living at 111 Longside Lane, Bradford in 1911. In addition to Thomas junior, Thomas and Elizabeth had five other children:

- Elizabeth Sophia Jackson (1851–1931) married Sneddle Nelson (1843–1912) on 26th July 1868 at Kirton in Holland, Lincolnshire. They had a daughter, Elizabeth Eliza Nelson, in 1869.
- Sarah Ann Jackson (born 1856).

- Joseph Robert Jackson (1858–1935), a bricklayer, married Elizabeth Bennett (born c.1861) in 1882 at Bethnal Green, London. She was born at Boston. They were living at 22 Avondale Terrace, Palmers Green Road, Southgate, London in 1901. They had six children – Joseph R Jackson 1883, Frank W Jackson 1885, Jesse Jackson 1888, Frederick T Jackson 1893, Margaret G Jackson 1895 and Percy Jackson 1897.

Harold's grandfather, Thomas Jackson, was born at Donington, Lincolnshire about 1822.

- Mary Emma Jackson (1861–93), a domestic servant, had a son, Thomas Boardman Jackson, born on 3rd July 1880 in Boston Union Workhouse on Skirbeck Road. The father's name was not recorded. Mary and Thomas were living with her father in 1881. Thomas was still living with his grandparents in 1891. By 1901 Thomas was living with his uncle, Joseph Robert Jackson. He married his cousin in 1907 (see the VC's sister Florence Jackson above). Mary married Edward Rowe Faulkner (1847–1941), a carpenter, in 1882 at Boston. He was born at South Somercoates, Lincolnshire. They had a son, John William Faulkner, in 1887. Edward emigrated to Australia and died at Melbourne, Victoria.

Harold's grandmother, Elizabeth Boardman, was born at Gosberton, Lincolnshire about 1825.

- Jesse Macham Jackson (1863–1918) was a carpenter living with his parents in 1891. In 1911 he was a general labourer living with his niece, Mary Ann Searby, and family at Kirton.

His maternal grandfather, William Stevenson (c.1826–1908), an agricultural labourer, married Elizabeth Ann née Allen (c.1833–1885) in 1848. They lived at Frampton, Lincolnshire. In 1861 they

Thomas and Elizabeth Jackson were living at Willington Road, Kirton in 1891.

were living at Skeldy Broad, Kirton. By 1871 he was a farm bailiff and they were living at Frampton Marsh. In 1881 he was again an agricultural labourer living at Frampton. In addition to Mary they had eight other children:

- William Allen Stevenson (1851–78) was a farm labourer in 1871.
- Elizabeth Ann Stevenson (born 1856).
- Susannah Stevenson (1858–1935) married James Cook Elding (1843–1936), a gardener, in 1874. They were living at Spalding Road, Wyberton, Lincolnshire in 1881, at Turnpike, Wyberton in 1891 and at 33 Tower Street, Boston in 1911. They had six children – Mary Elizabeth Elding 1875, James Elding 1878, Arthur Elding 1879, Alice Elding 1881, Clara Elding 1886 and Mabel Elding 1889.
- Allen Stevenson (1861–12th November 1926), an agricultural labourer, married Elizabeth Spice (1861–92) in 1886. They were living at Tilton Lane, Wyberton in 1891. He was a foreman on a farm in 1911, living at Fishmere End Road, Sutterton, Lincolnshire. He was living at Bellwater Farm, Eastville, Lincolnshire at the time of his death, leaving effects valued at £154/14/4. They had a son, John George Stevenson, in 1888.
- Hephzibah Ann Stevenson (1862–1900) married Robert Pearson (1856–83), an agricultural labourer, in 1880. They were living with her parents at Frampton in 1881. They had two children – Rose Pearson 1881 and Robert Pearson 1883. In 1891 Hephzibah was recorded as a housekeeper for William Westmoreland at Kirton Holme Road, Kirton and had three more daughters – Gertrude Pearson 1887, Ada Pearson 1889 and Laura Pearson 1893. Hephzibah married William Westmoreland (1862–1922), an agricultural labourer, in 1893. They had three children – Lily Westmoreland 1895, William Westmoreland 1898 and Georgiana Westmoreland 1899. William was living with his children and stepchildren at Kirton End in 1901 and at Sea Bank, Kirton in 1911.
- George Frederick Stevenson (1865–22nd February 1930), a farm foreman, married Harriet Stevenson (c.1864–3rd December 1938) in 1891. They were living at Main Road, Deeping St Nicholas, Lincolnshire in 1901. He was a farm foreman in 1911 and they were living at Goose Hill Farm, Deeping St Nicholas, Lincolnshire. They were living at King Street, Kirton when he died there, leaving effects valued at £3,377/8/4. She was living at Ticehurst, Willington Road, Kirton at the time of her death. They had an adopted daughter, Margret 'Daisy' Stevenson, born in 1901.
- Rosie Ann S Stevenson (born 1867).
- Sarah Ann Stevenson (1870–1947) married George Handson (1859–1943) an agricultural labourer, in 1886. He was born at Derby Alford, Lincolnshire. They were living at Kirton End, Lincolnshire in 1891. They had six children – George H Handson 1887, Richard A Handson 1888, Elizabeth Julia Handson 1891, Daisy Handson 1894, Arthur Handson 1897 and Willie Handson 1900.

Harold was educated at Kirton village school and was well known as an amateur boxer. He also attended Kirton Church Sunday School and received a Queen Victoria 'Memorial Edition' Bible in January 1902. He received another Bible signed by the Vicar of Kirton in 1918. Harold was employed as a drayman by Messrs Tunnard

Bros in Kirton. He moved to Nottingham in 1912, where he worked on the railway and later as a Messrs McAlpine bricklayer.

Harold enlisted in 18th (Queen Mary's Own) Hussars on 14th April 1915 (19897) and joined at the Depot at Scarborough next day. He transferred to 3rd East Yorkshire on 2nd June 1915 and went to France on 16th July to join 1st Battalion. He was awarded fourteen days' Field Punishment No.2 on 8th August. He transferred to 7th Battalion and received a gunshot wound to the right forearm at Bazentin on 14th July 1916. Having been treated at 6th General Hospital, Rouen from 17th July he was evacuated to Britain on the 19th. He was held on the strength of 3rd Battalion while recovering. Promoted lance corporal on 27th February 1917 and returned to France on 4th April, rejoining 7th Battalion next day. He was admitted to 20th General Hospital, Camiers with scabies on 23rd April transferred to 37th Infantry Base Depot, Etaples on 29th April and returned to his unit on 11th May. He was promoted corporal on 23rd August.

Awarded the VC for his actions at Hermies, France on 22nd/23rd March 1918, LG 8th May 1918. Promoted sergeant on 20th April and was presented with the VC ribbon by Commander V

20th General Hospital was at Camiers from May 1915 until April 1919.

Harold Jackson's grave in AIF Burial Ground, Grass Lane, Flers, France. His remains were not identified until 1927.

Kirton War Memorial (Peter O'Connor) and the panel bearing Harold Jackson's name (John Emerson).

Harold is also commemorated on the Wood Green War Memorial, probably because his sister, Mary Ann Searby, lived there and his sister, Florence Jackson, lived in the area (Philafrenzy).

The East Yorkshire Regiment Great War Memorial in Beverley Minster. Harold's named is on Panel 15c.

Corps, Lieutenant General Cameron Deane Shute, on 18th May 1918. The VC was presented by the King at Buckingham Palace on 26th June 1918. He was given a hero's welcome in Kirton after the investiture and was presented with a gold half-hunter pocket watch. The watch was sold at auction at Lockdales auctioneers of Ipswich on 28th January 2007 for £823.

Harold was killed in action near Stuff Redoubt and Mouquet Farm, France on 24th August 1918 and was buried in a battlefield cemetery north of Thiepval. In 1919, when graves were being concentrated into formal cemeteries, no trace of his body was found in the marked grave. A temporary memorial cross was erected in Mill Road Cemetery No.2 (now Mill Road Cemetery). In 1927 further information came to light and his

Harold Jackson's medals and bronze Memorial Plaque. The Plaque was issued to the next-of-kin of all British and Empire service personnel who died as a result of the war (1,355,000 plaques were issued). They were popularly known as the 'Dead Man's Penny' because of the similarity with the smaller penny coin. The design resulted from a public competition in which there were over 800 entries. The competition was won by the sculptor Edward Carter Preston, under the pseudonym *Pyramus*. The plaques were issued in a pack with a commemorative scroll and a letter from the King, although in some cases the letter and scroll were sent separately.

remains were identified amongst twelve other bodies and they were reburied in AIF Burial Ground, Grass Lane, Flers, France (XV A 21/30). He is commemorated in a number of other places:

• Jackson Drive, Kirton, Lincolnshire.
• Kirton War Memorial, Lincolnshire.
• War Memorial at High Road, Wood Green, London.
• Regimental War Memorial, Beverley Minster, East Yorkshire.

In addition to the VC he was awarded the 1914–15 Star, British War Medal 1914–20 and Victory Medal 1914–19. His sister, Mary, had the VC after his death. She loaned it to her father who wore it to a Buckingham Palace garden party. It was discovered after his death and returned to Mary. After she died in 1955 it passed to her daughter, Mabel F Scuffham of 154 Sleaford Road, Boston. The medals were sold at Sotheby's for £10,450 on 11th May 1989 and are held privately.

CAPTAIN MANLEY ANGELL JAMES
8th Battalion, The Gloucestershire Regiment

Manley James was born at 140 High Street, Odiham, Hampshire on 12th July 1896. His father, John Angell James MRCS LRCP (21st January 1864–22nd January 1953), was medical assistant and surgical assistant at the General Hospital, Birmingham and later house surgeon at Queen's Hospital, Birmingham. He was commissioned as a surgeon lieutenant serving with 1st Volunteer Battalion, Hampshire Regiment on 22nd May 1901 and was promoted surgeon captain on 18th July 1904. John married Emily Cormell née Ashwin (1862–7th October 1958) at St James's Church, Alveston, Warwickshire on 9th August 1893. They were living at 140 High Street, Odiham, Hampshire in 1901, at 43 Nevil Road, Bishopston, Bristol, Gloucestershire by 1911 and later at Dusk, 31 Elmlea Avenue, Stoke Bishop, Bristol. Manley had four siblings:

• Margaret Angell James (9th October 1894–16th January 1987) never married.
• Kathleen Angell James (17th November 1898–11th September 1981) married John Elling Collier (1894–1966) on 21st September 1926. They were living at Severn Lodge, The Avenue, Sneyd Park, Totnes, Devon when John died.
• John 'Jack' Angell James CBE MB BS MBChB MD FRCS FRCP FRSocMed (23rd August 1901–19th June 2002) married Evelyn Miriam Everard (1905–98) on 28th June 1930 at St Martin, Birmingham. They had three children:

140 High Street, Odiham, where Manley was born. There is an Odiham Society Blue Plaque to the right of the entrance.

Work on Birmingham General Hospital stopped through lack of funds in 1766 and much of the cost was raised by the Birmingham Triennial Music Festival, first held in September 1768. The hospital opened in September 1779 with forty beds and extensions were added in 1790, 1857 and 1880, increasing capacity to 235 beds. In 1897 it moved to Steelhouse Lane and the building of a larger facility commenced in 1934. Neville Chamberlain was one of the fundraisers, even while serving as Prime Minister. Until 1964 the hospital was also a training centre for nurses. The General closed in the mid-1990s but became part of the Birmingham Children's Hospital.

St James's church, where Manley's parents married in 1893, was built in 1839 as Alveston expanded. The chancel, vestry and Lady Chapel were added in 1879.

The James family was living at 43 Nevil Road, Bishopston, Bristol by 1911. The building is now a medical practice.

- ○ Roger Everard Angell James (born 1932) married Mary J Neale (born 1937) in 1960. They had two children – Ruth Miriam Angell James 1967 and John Benjamin Angell James 1971.
- ○ Rosemary D Angell James (1935–81) married Ian Fergie-Woods (born 1931) in 1957. They had five children – Jonathan J Angell Fergie-Woods 1958, Juliet M Angell Fergie-Woods 1960, Rupert C Angell Fergie-Woods 1961, Elisabeth RA Fergie-Woods 1963 and Sarah Louise Angell Fergie-Woods 1966.
- ○ Jennifer E Angell James (born 1937).

John held a series of appointments prior to the Second World War:

House Surgeon and House Physician in Ear, Nose and Throat, Gynaecology and
Ophthalmology Departments, Bristol Royal Infirmary.
Clinical Assistant, Golden Square Throat Hospital, London.
House Physician, West London Hospital 1924–28.
Honorary ENT Registrar, Bristol Royal Infirmary 1928–29.
Honorary ENT Surgeon, Bristol Children's Hospital 1928–48.
Clinical Tutor, University of Bristol 1928–55.
Honorary Assistant ENT Surgeon later Honorary ENT Surgeon, Bristol Royal
Infirmary 1929–48.

John was commissioned as a lieutenant in the Royal Army Medical Corps on 27th
June 1942 and was promoted war substantive captain and temporary major on
25th October 1942. He served in North Africa, Italy and the Middle East and was
Advisor in Otorhinolaryngology in the Middle East Force in 1945. After the war he
held a number of other appointments:

Consultant ENT Surgeon, Bristol Children's Hospital 1948–66.
Consultant Otologist and Consultant ENT Surgeon, United Bristol Hospitals
1948–66.
Lecturer and Head of Department of Otorhinolaryngology, University of Bristol
1955–66.
Hunterian Professor, Royal College of Surgeons 1962.
Semon Lecturer in Laryngology, University of London 1965.

On retiring from the National Health Service in 1966 he practiced privately at
Litfield House, Clifton Down and at Sundayshill House, Falfield, Gloucestershire.
In the 1960s he introduced two new operations – transethmoidal hypophysectomy
and an operation to relieve Ménière's disease. In addition to his many other duties
he was Chairman of the Editorial Committee of Clinical Otolaryngology and a
member of the section of laryngology of the Royal Society of Medicine (President
1955), the British Association of Otorhinolaryngologyists (President 1966–69), the
Otolaryngological Research Society (President 1978) and from 1948 the Collegium
Oto-Rhino-Laryngologicum Amicitiae Sacrum (Councillor 1966–74 and President
1974). Aside from his surgical career, John kept pigs and cows, exhibiting his prize
heifers at the Bath and West Show and travelling the county with his prize bull. He
won the Silver Medal at the International Dairy Event, Stoneleigh Park in 1974 for
his calf and lamb resuscitator. He changed his name to John Angell-James by Deed
Poll on 2nd November 1972. John was appointed CBE (LG 10th June 1967) and
was made Honorary FRCSE in 1971 and Honorary FRSM in 1976.

- Frances Isabel Finetta James (23rd July 1905–1995) married Charles Edward Kirwan Bagot (1895–1976), born at Curraghmore, Athleague, Co Roscommon, Ireland, on 2nd November 1928. He served in the Special Reserve 4th February 1915–2nd October 1916 and was in France from 12th October 1915. He was commissioned in the Connaught Rangers on 6th November 1915 and promoted lieutenant on 1st July 1917. Charles was twice Mentioned in Despatches (LG 4th January and 25th May 1917) and was awarded the Military Cross (LG 1st January 1918). He transferred to the Gloucestershire Regiment as a lieutenant with seniority from 29th July 1922 and was promoted captain on 6th August 1925. He was appointed adjutant 2nd July 1926–1st July 1929 and served as a staff officer 1st class in India 20th March 1936–14th March 1937. Promoted major 1st August 1938, acting lieutenant colonel 27th June 1941 and lieutenant colonel 2nd September 1944. He retired on 22nd March 1947. Frances and Charles had two children:
  - ° Charles Christopher Neville Bagot (born 1930) married Jennifer Muriel Massey Sumner (born 1938) in 1964 and they had four children – Sarah Finetta Bagot 1966, Alexandra Muriel Bagot 1967, Vanessa Caroline Bagot 1969 and Charles Richard Milo Bagot 1973. Jennifer's father, William Donald Massey Sumner, was MP for Orpington 1955–62. Charles senior was granted an Emergency Commission in the Royal Artillery on 18th February 1949 (22048896 later 400290), which he relinquished on 18th April 1953. He became a shipping executive. They lived at Parkhurst, Bois Lane, Chesham Bois, Amersham, Buckinghamshire.
  - ° Finetta Veronica Angell Bagot (born 1933) married Richard Wallace Paul Mellish (1923–2008), son of Edward Noel Mellish VC MC, in 1956. Richard qualified as a doctor and was commissioned as a flying officer (Emergency) in the RAFVR Medical Branch on 16th May 1946 (202757). He served on the Isle of Man and in India January 1946–May 1948 and was promoted flight lieutenant on 16th May 1947. Richard and Finetta emigrated to the USA where he became a paediatrician. They lived at 123 Spartina Court, Kiawah Island, South Carolina and at 1421 Spear Street, Burlington, Chittenden, Vermont. They had three children – Martin Christopher Bagot Mellish 1957, Nicholas Charles Mellish 1961 and Fiona Molesworth Mellish 1964.

Manley's paternal grandfather, John Angell James (6th September 1825–25th December 1870), was a land surveyor in 1851 at East Stoke, Dorset and also owned Bridge Town Farm, Old Stratford, Warwickshire, of 400 acres. He married Margaret Mary née Burbury (c.1832–1912) in 1863 at Warwick. In 1871 she was a farmer at Bridge Town Farm, Old Stratford employing three men, two boys and three women. In addition to John they had three other children:

- Frederick James James (born 1866).
- Herbert Henry James (1867–1956), a mechanical engineer, married Laura Brind Waldron (1876–1953) in 1908 at Frome, Somerset. Her father, Thomas White Waldron (1835–1903), had extensive financial interests in Argentina. By 1911 Herbert was a superintendent testing engines and they were living at 3 Morton Terrace, Gainsborough, Lincolnshire. They later lived at 58 Norfolk Road, Littlehampton, Sussex. Herbert and Laura had three children – Muriel Noreen James 1910, Robert Brian James 1912 and Nancy Brind James 1918. Robert was commissioned in the Essex Regiment on 1st September 1932 (53746) and was promoted lieutenant 1st September 1935, acting captain 3rd September 1939, temporary captain 3rd December 1939, captain 1st September 1940, acting major 10th November 1940, temporary major 10th February 1941, temporary lieutenant colonel and war substantive major 4th May 1943. He served in Palestine 1936–39 (medal and clasp). Robert was appointed adjutant 22nd January–9th November 1940 and GSO1 (Research) at the School of Infantry, Barnard Castle on 4th May 1943. He was a lieutenant colonel commanding 5th East Yorkshire when he was killed in action on 3rd August 1944 (Hottot-les-Bagues War Cemetery, France – VII A 9). Robert was awarded the DSO and Mention in Despatches (both LG 19th August 1941), and a bar to the DSO (LG 1st June 1943).
- Robert Blake James MRCS LRCP (1869–1953) was known as Seamus. After qualifying he was a ship's doctor for a year, travelling to the Far East including Hong Kong and China. He joined Dr Richard Barker's medical practice at Hungerford in 1898, becoming a full partner in 1904. Robert married Margaret 'Daisy' Clara Waldron (1878–1955) in 1903. She was the younger sister of Laura Brind Waldron who married Robert's brother, Herbert. They lived at Church Street, Hungerford before moving to Manor House, Hungerford following the death of Dr Barker in 1910. They were living at Riverside, Hungerford when Robert died and Daisy was living at The Pillars, High Street, Hungerford at the time of her death. They had three children – Thomas Eric Blake James 1904, Norah Brind Blake James 1907 and Agnita Margaret Blake James 1918. Agnita married Roger Seaward Brennan (1917–44) in 1941. He was commissioned in the Wiltshire Regiment (121218) on 25th February 1940 and was promoted war substantive lieutenant 25th August 1941, temporary captain 3rd April 1942 and acting major 14th December 1943. He was killed in action on 9th June 1944 (Ranville War Cemetery, France – IV F 5). Agnita married Francis HP Barber in 1946.

His maternal grandfather, Manley Cormell Ashwin (c.1827–10th October 1908), married Susannah née Holyoake (c.1831–1909) in 1857 at Alcester, Warwickshire. He was a farmer and merchant at Crop Hill Farm, Old Stratford, Warwickshire (105 acres), employing four men and two boys in 1881. In addition to Emily they had five other children:

- Anne Frances 'Fanny' Ashwin (born 1858).
- Isabel Mary Ashwin (1860–18th February 1956) married Herbert Broad (1865–1949), a coal and corn merchant, in 1901. They were living at Welcombe Road, Stratford upon Avon in 1911.
- Manley Holyoake Ashwin (born and died 1865).
- Manley Horton Ashwin (1869–1952) was a merchant in 1911 living with his sisters Frances and Alice at Fiddington, Stratford-upon-Avon. He married Joan Winifred Devereux Hickman (1898–1980) in March 1918 at St Philip, Kensington,

Manley's maternal grandparents married at Alcester, Warwickshire in 1857.

London. They had three children – Janet Ashwin 1923, Mary Joy Ashwin 1924 and Manley 'Michael' Devereux Ashwin 1926. She was living at 10 Westhope Avenue, Copthorne, Shrewsbury, Shropshire at the time of her death.
- Alice Maud Ashwin (1872–1939) never married. She was living at Fernlea, 96 Maidenhead Road, Stratford-upon-Avon when she died on 21st June 1939, leaving effects valued at £2,147/11/8 to her sisters, Frances, Isabel and Emily.

Bristol Grammar School was founded in 1532 by Robert and Nicholas Thorne, one of the new schools founded after Henry VIII's dissolution of the monasteries. It closed in 1844 but reopened in January 1848. By 1870 the buildings were dilapidated and poorly located for most pupils. In 1879 the first buildings in Tyndalls Park were opened and were expanded later. A preparatory school opened in 1900. The school became a direct grant grammar school in 1946 and became independent when direct grants were abolished in the 1970s. The school was also attended by fellow VC Frederick Lumsden. Other notable alumni include:
    William Gregor (1761–1817), who discovered titanium.
    Charles Kingsley (1819–1875), novelist.
    Sir Allen Lane (1902–70), founder of Penguin Books.
    Timothy West (born 1934), actor.
    Michelle Goodman (born 1976), first female RAF officer to be awarded the DFC.

Manley was educated at Robert May's Grammar School, Odiham, Hampshire (also attended by William Robert Fountaine Addison VC) and Bristol Grammar School 1906–14, where he was a sergeant in the OTC. He gained a place for medical training at Bristol University in the autumn of 1914 but did not take it up due to the war. Manley was an all round sportsman, playing cricket, hockey and rugby.

On 1st December 1914 Manley was commissioned in 8th Gloucestershire and was promoted temporary lieutenant on 28th June 1915. He went to France commanding the Lewis gun detachment on 19th July 1915. Although wounded, he took part in the capture of La Boisselle on 3rd July 1916. As a result of this action his CO, Adrian Carton de Wiart, was awarded the VC. Manley was evacuated to England on 4th July and returned to France on 19th December, where he was attached to HQ 57th Brigade. In February 1917 he returned to the Battalion and was wounded by shrapnel. On 22nd February he was promoted temporary captain and was **Mentioned in Field Marshal Sir Douglas Haig's Despatch dated 9th April 1917, LG 22nd May 1917.**

Manley returned to the Battalion again in June 1917. **Awarded the MC for his actions on 9th-10th July 1917 near Wytschaete and Messines. That night he was commanding A Company with the mission of capturing Druid's Farm. He took up a forward position under heavy enemy artillery fire in order to assess the progress of the advance. He later went forward again and assisted in the capture of a strongpoint. He rallied disorganised troops, led them to their position and finally carried out a reconnaissance of the whole line under heavy shell and rifle fire enabling him to send a vital situation report to his CO, LG 17th September 1917.**

Lieutenant Colonel Adrian Paul Ghislain Carton de Wiart was Manley's CO in July 1916. De Wiart was a remarkable character. Born in Brussels, Belgium on 5th May 1880, he fought with the British in in the Second Boer War and was commissioned into 4th Dragoon Guards in 1901. He lost an eye in action in Somaliland in November 1914 and his left hand near Ypres in April 1915. With an eye patch and a hook for a hand he became the model for Evelyn Waugh's character Brigadier Ben Ritchie-Hook in the *Sword of Honour* trilogy. After the war de Wiart headed the British Military Mission to Poland and he settled there when he retired in 1923. In the early days of the Second World War he again headed the Mission to Poland and managed to escape through Romania. He commanded the Central Norwegian Expeditionary Force in April and May 1940 and extracted his force with great skill. On 6th April 1941, he was appointed to the Military Mission to Yugoslavia, but the Wellington bomber carrying him crashed in the sea off Libya and he had to swim ashore, where he was captured by the Italians. He attempted to escape a number of times and on one occasion eluded capture for eight days. In August 1943 he was released by the Italians to help negotiate the Italian surrender. Churchill then appointed him Head of the Special Military Mission to Nationalist Chinese leader Chiang-Kai-Shek. He retired on 4th October 1947, having risen from private to lieutenant general, the greatest rank difference of any VC recipient. Ian Fleming, author of the James Bond books, said of him, *one arm, one eye and, rather more surprisingly only one Victoria Cross.*

Following a counterattack on 27th/28th July, the divisional commander, Major General Tom Bridges, awarded A Company the 'Butterfly Badge' (19th Division's emblem) to be worn on the right sleeve. During the entire war this honour was awarded to only one other unit, a section of the Royal Engineers.

The site of Druid's Farm.

Awarded the VC for his actions near Vélu Wood, France on 21st-23rd March 1918, LG 28th June 1918. During this action he was wounded in the neck, jaw, shoulder and stomach and was taken prisoner. He was treated in hospitals in Valenciennes and Stralkowo Camp near Posen and was then held in camps at Rastatt and Schwerdintz in Silesia. Manley was repatriated on 25th December 1918. The VC was presented by the King at Buckingham Palace on 22nd February 1919 and he was demobilised on 28th October 1919.

On 11th December 1920 Manley joined 1st Gloucestershire as a regular lieutenant with seniority from 1st July 1917. He served in Silesia with the Army of Occupation in 1922 and at Cologne in 1923. He was promoted captain on 27th May 1925 and was

Manley outside Buckingham Palace on the day of his VC investiture.

appointed adjutant of the 1st Battalion 12th December 1925–14th December 1928. During this period he played rugby union for Clifton and Bristol and cricket for the Bristol Nomads.

Manley James married Noreen Cooper (1st September 1898–August 1994), born at Sale, Cheshire, on 28th April 1928 at Bristol. They had a son, Peter Manley James (born 5th October 1930), who was commissioned in the Gloucestershire Regiment (418300) on 3rd August 1951. He carried the Regiment's old

The Gloucestershire Regiment rugby team, winners of the Aldershot Cup 1925–26. Manley is seated third from left in the middle row. Third from the right standing in the back row is Second Lieutenant James Carne, who was awarded the VC in Korea in 1951.

Colour when the new Colour was presented on parade in April 1952. Peter was promoted lieutenant on 3rd August 1953 but was forced to retire on 8th June 1954 due to a knee injury. He married Jane McCormack (born 1935) in 1958. Peter was Director of Personnel at Honeywell Integrated Pension Scheme Trustee Limited 31st December 1992–1st July 1994. Peter and Jane had two children – Jeremy M James 1961 and Edward J James 1965.

Noreen's father, Thomas Brammall Cooper (1870–1947), a civil engineer and contractor, married Kathleen Clara née Murphy (1872–1937), born in Dublin, Ireland, in 1896 at Chorlton, Lancashire. In 1911 they were living at 68 Oakfield Road, Clifton, Bristol. In addition to Noreen they had two other children:

• Morley Holland Cooper (1897–1971) married Winifred 'Winkle' Ruth Laws (1905–98) in 1931 at Axbridge, Somerset. She was born in Cardiff, Glamorgan. They lived at Beachcroft, Beach Bitton, Bristol and had a son, Jonathan B Cooper, in 1934.
• John Brian Cooper (born 1901).

Manley served in Egypt with the 1st Battalion 1928–30, then at the Depot in Bristol and attended the Staff College in 1932. He was a company commander in 1933 and was appointed GSO2 Weapon Training, HQ Aldershot Command 21st November 1934–8th December 1936 and Brigade Major 13th Infantry Brigade 9th December 1936–9th January 1939. He was promoted major 25th December 1936, brevet lieutenant colonel 1st July 1938 and lieutenant colonel to command 2nd Royal Sussex in Belfast on 10th January 1939. Other appointments followed – GSO1 HQ 54th Infantry Division 22nd March–17th July 1940 (home defence duties), Brigadier General Staff HQ VIII Corps 19th July 1940–18th February 1941 (also home defence) and Commander 128th (Hampshire) Infantry Brigade (43rd (Western) Division) 19th February 1941–20th September 1943. In the latter appointment he succeeded Brigadier Frederick 'Boy' Browning, who later commanded I Airborne Corps in Operation Market-Garden in September 1944. Manley took the Brigade to North Africa with First Army in Operation Torch. Awarded the DSO for his actions on 26th February 1943 in halting an enemy attack northeast of Beja, Tunisia, 5th August 1943. Mentioned in Despatches, LG 5th August 1943. His Brigade landed with 46th Division at Salerno, Italy in September 1943 and Manley was badly wounded in the leg after four days' fighting. He continued in command until after a visit by General Alexander and was then evacuated in a hospital ship to Egypt.

Having recovered, he was appointed Brigadier Infantry, Middle East Force 3rd December 1943–6 July 1944, then Brigadier Royal Armoured Corps, Eastern Command 27th July–8th August 1944, Brigadier General Staff (Training), Home Forces 9th August 1944–15th July 1945 and Commander 140th Infantry Brigade 24th July–5th October 1945. During the war he had numerous, often overlapping, promotions – acting colonel 22nd March–21st September 1940, acting brigadier

The Staff College Camberley grew out of the Senior Department of the Royal Military College formed in 1802. In 1858 the Senior Department became the Staff College and in 1870 it separated from the Royal Military College. Except for during the two world wars, it operated until 1997, when it merged with its Royal Navy and Royal Air Force equivalent colleges to form the Joint Services Command and Staff College.

The HQ Aldershot Command building was completed in 1895. In August 1914 the BEF's I Corps was based on Aldershot Command under Lieutenant General Sir Douglas Haig. Similarly, in 1939 GOCinC Aldershot Command, Sir John Dill, became GOC I Corps in the BEF sent to France. From 1968, HQ South East District was at Aldershot and was renamed Southern District in 1992 and HQ 4th Division in 1995. Three VCs have been GOC Aldershot Command – Evelyn Wood, Redvers Buller and Dudley Johnson (Reg Davis).

19th July 1940–18th February 1941, temporary colonel 22nd September 1940–11th December 1941, temporary brigadier 19th January 1941–6th July 1944, colonel 12th December 1941 (seniority from 1st July 1941) and temporary brigadier 27th July 1944–30th June 1948.

In October 1945 Manley was appointed Senior RAF Regiment Officer at Air HQ, British Air Forces of Occupation (Germany) until 10th October 1948. He was promoted brigadier on 1st July 1948 and was appointed Director of Ground Defence, Department of the Chief of the Air Staff, Air Ministry on 11th October 1948. The post was retitled Commandant General RAF Regiment and Inspector of Ground Combat Training on 19th October. Manley retired on 1st March 1951. He and Noreen settled at 101 Passage Road, Westbury-on-Trym, Gloucestershire.

Lieutenant General Sir Frederick 'Boy' Browning GCVO KBE DSO (1896–1965), known as the 'father of British airborne forces'. During the planning for Operation Market-Garden he is reputed to have said, *I think we might be going a bridge too far*. Boy served in the Grenadier Guards in the First World War and was awarded the DSO. In 1932 he competed in the Winter Olympics bobsleigh. Boy married the author Daphne du Maurier.

The Bristol Aeroplane Company started life as the British and Colonial Aeroplane Company. It produced numerous aircraft types, including the Boxkite, Bristol Fighter, Scout, Beaufighter, Blenheim, Britannia and the Sycamore and Belvedere helicopters, in addition to a number of famous engines, such as the Hercules, Pegasus and Olympus. The Bristol Type 223 was developed with French Sud Aviation's Super-Caravelle to produce the Concorde supersonic airliner. In 1956 the company split into Bristol Aircraft and Bristol Aero Engines. In 1959, Bristol Aircraft merged with several other British aircraft companies to form British Aircraft Corporation. BAC in turn merged into the nationalised British Aerospace, which later became BAE Systems, with a continuing presence at the Filton site.

Manley in later life.

Manley was employed by the Bristol Aeroplane Company Ltd at Filton near Bristol as Works Defence Officer 1951–61. **Awarded the MBE for his work there, LG 12th June 1958.** Appointed DL Gloucestershire 28th December 1956 and Avon 1st April 1974 and was an Associate Fellow of the Institute of Civil Defence. Manley attended the VC Garden Party at Buckingham Palace on 26th June 1920, the VC Centenary Celebrations at Hyde Park, London on 26th June 1956 and all VC & GC Association Reunions between 1958 and 1974, except for 1968.

Manley played a full part in Bristol life, being very active in the affairs of Bristol Grammar School, the Regimental Association (Chairman of Bristol Branch 1967) and the 8th Battalion Old Comrades' Association. He was elected President of the Shakespeare Club of Bristol in 1965, named after the pub in which its members (former officers of the three services), held their meetings.

Manley James Close, Odiham, Hampshire.

The Distinguished Service Order was instituted by Queen Victoria on 6th September 1886. It is usually awarded to majors (or equivalent) or above but was occasionally awarded to valorous junior officers. There were 8,981 awards in the Great War. The order recognised meritorious or distinguished service in war. Prior to 1943 the order could only be given to someone mentioned in despatches. Since 1993 the order has been restricted solely to distinguished service and not for gallantry. The Conspicuous Gallantry Cross was introduced at the same time as the second highest award for gallantry. Although the DSO is now open to all ranks it has yet (2017) to be awarded to a non-commissioned rank.

The Civil Defence Long Service Medal was instituted by Queen Elizabeth II in March 1961 to be awarded for fifteen years continuous service in organisations such as the Auxiliiary Fire Service, National Hospital Service Reserve, UK Warning and Monitoring Organisation and Civil Defence Corps. It was extended in 1965 to Civil Defence personnel in Gibraltar, Hong Kong, Malta, the Channel Islands and the Isle of Man.

Manley James died at his home at 101 Passage Road, Westbury-on-Trym on 23rd September 1975 and was cremated at Canford Crematorium, Bristol, where his ashes were scattered in Memorial Bed 12 in the Shrubberies. He is commemorated in a number of places:

- Manley James Close and Addison Gardens in Odiham, Hampshire built in the 1980s were named in honour of the two VCs of Robert May's Grammar School.
- Odiham Society Blue Plaque on his house at 140 High Street, Odiham, Hampshire dedicated on 11th May 2013.

In addition to the VC, DSO, MBE and MC he was awarded the 1914–15 Star, British War Medal 1914–20, Victory Medal 1914–19 with Mentioned-in-Despatches

Oakleaf, 1939–45 Star, Africa Star with 1st Army clasp, Italy Star, Defence Medal, War Medal 1939–45, George VI Coronation Medal 1937, Elizabeth II Coronation Medal 1953 and Civil Defence Long Service Medal. The medals were stolen from his home on 11th October 1971 and he offered a reward of £100. The medals were recovered and the thief was apprehended and sentenced to six years' imprisonment. The medals were sold at Christie's on 21st October 1991 for £37,400 to Lord Michael Ashcroft. They are held by The Michael Ashcroft Trust, the holding institution for the Lord Ashcroft Victoria Cross Collection, and are displayed in the Imperial War Museum's Lord Ashcroft Gallery.

LIEUTENANT ALLAN EBENEZER KER
3rd Battalion, The Gordon Highlanders attached 61st Battalion Machine Gun Corps

Allan Ker was born at 16 Findhorn Place, Edinburgh, Midlothian, Scotland on 5th March 1883. His father, Robert Darling Ker (15th January 1853–24th April 1940), was a solicitor and notary public, who was living at 10 Moston Terrace, Edinburgh in April 1882. He was a partner in the legal firm of Messrs Ker & Winchester and was admitted to the Society of Writers to the Signet in 1886, serving as Writer to Queen Victoria's Signet. Robert married Johanna 'Joan' née Johnston (18th November 1853–8th May 1931) at St Abbs, Russell Place, Trinity, North Leith on 20th April 1882. They were living at Westgrove, Ferry Road, Edinburgh in 1891 and by 1901 had moved to 4 Wardie Road, Edinburgh. Allan had three siblings:

* John Stanley Ker (28th July 1890–1975), a stockbroker, married Margaret Mavis Scott Paterson (1901–78) on 19th February 1935 at Calcutta, India.
* Hilda Margaret Hume Ker (13th April 1886–28th March 1964) married Alfred Ebenezer Spence Thomson (1880–1950), a solicitor and notary public, on 26th July 1911. They had a son, Geoffrey Ker Thomson (1914–2000), who was a law apprentice. Geoffrey was a sergeant in the Royal Artillery in 1939 and received a Regular Army Emergency Commission in the Royal Artillery on 7th September 1940. He was promoted war substantive lieutenant on 7th March 1942 and temporary captain on 28th March 1944. He transferred to the Reserve in late 1946. By 1950 he was a solicitor. He married Mary Kennedy Cuthbert (born 1915) in 1939 and they had a son, Derek Spence Thomson, in 1940. The marriage ended in divorce. Geoffrey married Margaret Monica Grosvenor Guthrie née Stewart (1912–96) in 1950 and they had a son, Barry Grosvenor Thomson, in

1952. Margaret's previous marriage to John Graeme Robert Guthrie (1911–53) in 1936 also ended in divorce. John Guthrie married Phyllis M Stansbury in 1944 and served as an officer in 2nd Lothians Border Yeomanry RAC (88954) and 16th/5th Lancers, rising to lieutenant colonel. He died on 8th January 1953 at Malta and is buried in Imtarfa Military Cemetery (1 1A 12).

Findhorn Place, Edinburgh, where Allan Ker was born.

• Gertrude Theodora Ker (2nd May 1888– 29th November 1968) married Ebenezer Proudfoot Flint (1887–1936) at St Abbs, Russell Place, Trinity, North Leith on 31st August 1921. He was a spice and sugar merchant of Primrose Villa, Primrose Bank Road, Leith. They had two children:
  ° Doris Marjorie Johnston Flint (30th September 1922–1999).
  ° Gordon Douglas Flint (13th January 1927–2003).

The Ker family was living on Wardie Road in 1901.

Allan's paternal grandfather, Robert Darling Ker (c1818–31st March 1890), married Ann née Hume (21st August 1826–21st February 1884) on 9th June 1848 at St Cuthbert's, Edinburgh. She was born at Kelso, Roxburghshire, daughter of Alexander Hume, a landscape painter, and Ann Drysdale. Robert was a wholesale corn and coal merchant and army contractor in 1861. By 1881 he was a colliery insurance and shipping agent and they were living at St Leonards House, 32 St Leonards Street, Edinburgh. Robert married Matilda Godfrey in 1885 at Kensington, London. In addition to the VC's father, Robert and Ann had eight other children:

The Society of Writers to Her Majesty's Signet of Scottish solicitors dates back to 1594. Originally Writers (Scottish solicitors) had special privileges in drawing up documents that required to be signeted. They were exempt from taxation, military service and had rights of audience before the bar of the College of Justice but all of those privileges are long gone. The Society is now an independent, non-regulatory association of solicitors. The Keeper of the Signet is a ceremonial appointment.

- Thomas Ker (13th May 1849–1929), a civil engineer, married Martha 'Minnie' Grange Rait (1852–1940) in 1883, probably in India. They had eight children born in India – Evelyn Minnie Ker c.1883, Robert Gordon Ker 1885, Edith Constance Ker 1886, Stanley Darling Ker 1888, Edward Cameron Ker 1888, Mary Geraldine Ker 1890, Dorothea Hume Ker 1893 and Thomas D Ker 1894. She was living with her children at Airlie, Bexhill-on-Sea, Sussex in 1901. The family was living at Trewithian, Hadlow Road, Sidcup, Kent in 1911. They later settled at The Beeches, Beech Avenue, Sanderstead, Surrey.
- Ann Drysdale Ker (1st June 1851–1928) married Robert Alexander Rait (c.1850–1944) a wallpaper merchant's clerk in 1882. They were living at 56a Haverstock Hill, St Pancras, London in 1901 and Church Gate, Thorpe-le-Soken, Yorkshire in 1911. He was living at 23 Maxwell Road, Southsea, Hampshire at the time of his death.
- Alexander Hume Ker (23rd November 1856–26th October 1874).

Allan's paternal grandparents married at St Cuthbert's below Edinburgh Castle. A church has stood on the site since 850. As the parish boundary includes the Castle, there are many soldier graves in the churchyard. Numerous extensions and alterations have been added to the church over the centuries. It closed in 1969 and was used for storage by the University of Edinburgh until being converted into a Greek Orthodox Church. One of the stained glass windows, depicting David and Goliath, is by Tiffany Glass Co of New York. In 1863 the churchyard was closed by order of the Medical Officer of Health as it was full. The church authorities refused to comply as burials were an important source of income. As a result in 1873 the church was taken to court for *permitting a nuisance to exist under the Public Health Act 1867, being offensive and injurious to health*. A number of peers and other notable people are buried there, including:

John Napier 1550–1617, inventor of logarithms.
Reverend David Williamson 1636–1706 was ousted in 1665 as a Covenanter, served on the rebel side, was restored as minister of St Cuthberts in 1689 and became Moderator of the General Assembly of the Church of Scotland in 1702.
Thomson Bonar 1739–1814, cofounder of the *Encyclopaedia Britannica*.
Alexander Nasmyth 1758–1840, artist, architect and inventor known for his painting of Robert Burns.
Thomas De Quincey 1785–1859, author of *Confessions of an English Opium-Eater*, influenced many later authors, including Edgar Allan Poe.
William Borthwick Johnstone 1804–65, first Keeper of the National Gallery of Scotland.
The heart of Canadian physician, educator, sculptor, athlete, soldier and scouter, Robert Tait McKenzie. During the war he developed methods and inventions to restore and rehabilitate wounded soldiers that laid the foundations for modern physiotherapy. One of his famous sculptures is the Scots American War Memorial in Edinburgh.

- George Darling Ker (17th June 1858–11th February 1920) married Alice Mary Eliza Bentley (c.1853–1919) on 28th October 1882. They had a daughter, Ethel Ker, in 1885. He was living at Elmcroft, Chelston, Torquay, Devon at the time of his death, leaving effects valued at £6,408/18/10.
- Frances Elizabeth Ker (7th July 1860–1930) was living at 32 Cadzow Drive, Cambuslang, Lanarkshire when she married Dr Godfrey William Simpson (c.1865–1946), a surgeon, on 1st August 1892 at St John's Episcopal Church, Edinburgh. They were living at The Grange, Spencer Park, Wandsworth, London in 1911 and at 82 Northside, Wandsworth at the time of her death. Godfrey was living at 8 St James Road, Tunbridge Wells, Kent at the time of his death, leaving effects valued at £1,422/2/2. They had two children – Sturley Philip Simpson (1896–1966) and Gwynnedd Hume Simpson (1893–1930). Sturley was commissioned in the Bedfordshire Regiment on 20th October 1915 and was attached to the RFC from 19th February 1916. He served in 32 and 60 Squadrons and transferred to the RAF on 1st April 1918. Sturley was posted to No.6 Armoured Car Company on 23rd November 1923 and was awarded the MC (LG 14th May 1926) for valuable and distinguished service on operations in Kurdistan July–October 1924. He was appointed a flight commander in 30 Squadron on 4th February 1925. On 6th February 1926 he was seriously injured in an accident aboard a Bristol Fighter at Heliopolis, Egypt in which Flying Officer Arthur Cleverton Tremellen was killed. He was OC 4 Squadron 29th December 1930–4th October 1933, OC Administrative Wing, No.1 School of Technical Training (Apprentices), RAF Halton 10th February 1935 and OC No.2 (Apprentices) Wing 20th January 1936. Appointed Station Commander RAF Thornaby 28th July 1938 and promoted group captain on 1st November. He was acting air commodore and Air Officer Commanding Air HQ Gibraltar from 16th December 1941, including during the Operation Torch landings in North Africa. Appointed acting air vice marshal on 14th September 1943 and Commander No.18 Group (Reconnaissance), Coastal Command 2nd February 1944–January 1947. He then commanded RAF Northolt and retired as an air vice marshal on 27th March 1947. Sturley married Hilda Marion Drabble (1898–1972) in 1923 at Brentford, Middlesex. They were living at The Cedar Cottage, Bridle Way, Goring, near Reading, Berkshire at the time of their deaths.
- Malcolm Albert Ker (26th December 1863–24th February 1915) was studying medicine at Edinburgh University in 1881 (MB MCh). He was commissioned as a surgeon in the Indian Medical Service on 31st March 1887 and was promoted captain 31st March 1890, major Bengal Establishment 31st March 1899 and lieutenant colonel as MO 2/5th Gurkha Rifles 31st March 1907–28th October 1910. He married Mary Violet D Evans (1878–1953) in 1904 at Brecknock, Wales. They had three children – Iris Ker 1905, Irene Daphne Vida Ker 1907 and John MD Ker 1911. Malcolm was granted one year's leave outside India from 20th March 1913. They were living at Heathgate, Bucklebury, Berkshire at the time of

his death. She was living at Hen Bersondy, Scethrog, Brecknock at the time of her death, leaving effects valued at £15,826/1/8.

- Charlotte Barbara Drysdale Ker (13th August 1864–31st August 1926) married James Greer Silcock (1849–1941), an Indian civil servant, c.1894. They had two children – Phyllis Marjorie Silcock 1895 and Ronald Ker Silcock 1902. They were living at Park House, Warwick Park, Tunbridge Wells, Kent in 1911 and at 36 Landsdowne Road, Tunbridge Wells at the time of her death.
- Leonard Maurice Ker (31st March 1870–1887) lived at 10 Moston Terrace, Edinburgh. He set sail aboard the barque **Zamora** and was listed missing in the Marine Returns from 21st December 1887.

His maternal grandfather, Daniel Johnston (2nd October 1814–28th July 1895), married Margaret née Crawford (c.1818–30th May 1897) in 1845 at West Derby, Liverpool, Lancashire. She was born in Ireland. In 1881 Daniel was a timber merchant and cabinetmaker and they were living at Russell Street, North Leith, Edinburgh. In addition to Johanna they had five other children:

- Robert, born c.1847 at Stirling, died in infancy.
- Edmund Johnston (3rd February 1850–26th October 1905) was a warehouse clerk in 1881.

Edinburgh Academy opened in 1824 as an independent day and boarding school for boys. It became a fully coeducational day school in 2008. The founders aimed to provide a classical education to compete with the English public schools. When authority was granted for the school in 1823, fifteen Directors were elected, comprising the three founders and twelve other luminaries, including Sir Walter Scott. The school has educated several rugby internationals and nine VCs, the highest number of any school in Scotland. Other notable alumni include:

Robert Louis Stevenson 1850–94, writer.
Magnus Magnusson 1929–2007, journalist, writer and television presenter of *Mastermind* for twenty-five years.
Baron Falconer of Thoroton (born 1951), Labour peer, barrister, Lord Chancellor and the first Secretary of State for Constitutional Affairs under Prime Minister Tony Blair in 2003. In 2007 he became the first Secretary of State for Justice.
John Michael Kosterlitz (born 1943), British born Anglo-American physicist, awarded the 2016 Nobel Prize for Physics.

- Thomas Johnston (born 22nd November 1851) was a wholesale ironmonger in 1881.
- Robert Johnston (born 22nd December 1854).
- Margaret Johnston (born 3rd October 1855).

Allan was educated at:

- Edinburgh Academy 1890–99, where he was a member of the OTC. Edinburgh Academy produced eight other VCs – WL Brodie, ED Browne, J Cook, T Cadell, J Dundas, J Hills, ACC Miers and JA Tytler.
- Edinburgh University 1903–08, studying law.

Allan became a member of the Society of Writers to His Majesty's Signet in 1908 and was employed as a solicitor in Edinburgh as an associate with his father. He also served in the Queen's Edinburgh Mounted Infantry, which disbanded in 1908. His cousin, Captain Arthur Milford Gordon Ker, Gordon Highlanders was killed in action on 14th October 1914 (Vieille Chapelle New Military Cemetery, Lacoutre, France – V F 18). Allan travelled to Aberdeen to settle his affairs.

Allan was commissioned on 11th June 1915 and was promoted lieutenant on 1st January 1917. He went to France on 15th May 1917, probably to one of the brigade machine gun companies in 61st Division. **Awarded the VC for his actions near**

Allan's cousin, Arthur Milford Gordon Ker, was born at Simla, India in 1882. His father, Sir Arthur Milford Ker CIE MVO, was the son of General TD Ker. His mother was Constance Mitchell, daughter of Peter Mitchell CIE of Chapslee, Simla. Sir Arthur was a Member of the Council of the Lieutenant Governor of Punjab for making laws and regulations. He was also a Director of the Alliance Bank, India. Arthur junior was embodied in the Militia for 166 days and was then commissioned in the Gordon Highlanders on 10th October 1901. He served towards the end of the South African War (Queen's South Africa Medal with two clasps). Arthur was promoted lieutenant on 21st February 1906, captain on 29th May 1911 and landed at St Nazaire, France with 1st Gordon Highlanders on 12th September 1914. On 14th October the Battalion was in an exposed position when Captain Ker saw good natural cover in front. He turned to his company and said, *Come on men, follow me*. About twenty who heard followed him and after reaching cover a German machine gun began firing. When it slackened Arthur looked over their cover and was shot dead by a bullet through the head. His body was recovered next day. He is buried between two unknown Gordon Highlanders.

St Quentin, France on 21st March 1918, LG 4th September 1919. Allan was taken prisoner the same day and was held at Karlsruhe until July 1918 and then at Beeskow in der Mark. He was secretary and food controller for British officers in both lagers. On 16th December 1918 he was repatriated and was appointed staff captain in the Judge Advocate General's Department in Cologne in 1919. The VC was presented by the King at Buckingham Palace on 26th November 1919.

Allan also served in Greek Macedonia, Serbia, Bulgaria, European Turkey and the Islands of the Aegean Sea after the war. He was appointed temporary captain and staff captain in the War Office 1st April 1920–31st March 1922. Having served in the Special Reserve until 23rd May 1921, he received a Regular Commission in the Gordon Highlanders next day as a captain with seniority from 1st January 1921. Although shown in the Army List against 2nd Gordon Highlanders, he was specially employed elsewhere. He last appears in the Army List in the June-September 1924 edition and he returned to the law. He defended Private Richard Wright, 1st West Yorkshire, in Cologne in 1925. Wright was accused of murdering Lance Corporal FL Whitman, 2nd Cameron Highlanders and Miss Maria Stasiak with a revolver in a lover's tiff on 22nd December 1924. Wright was sentenced to death but it was later commuted to life imprisonment.

Allan Ker married Vera Irene Gordon-Skinner at Grantham, Lincolnshire in 1916 and they had two daughters:

The prisoners of war camp for officers at Karslruhe. Allan was held there until July 1918.

The War Office in Whitehall, London. It stands opposite the Admiralty and is only a short walk from Horse Guards and Downing Street. Construction took five years and it was completed in 1906 at a cost of £1.2M (£140M today). It contains about 1,000 rooms on seven floors and has over four kilometres of corridors. The building was the War Office until 1964 and continued in MOD use as the Old War Office Building until 2014. It was sold in March 2016 for more than £350M for conversion to a luxury hotel and apartments.

- Vera G Ker, birth registered in the 4th quarter of 1916 at Wandsworth, London.
- Adrienne Ann Mary Veronica Carmell, birth registered in the 3rd quarter of 1920 at Wandsworth. She married John Maxwell Linnell (died 2009) and moved to Canada. They had at least two children – Jennifer Linnell and David Linnell.

The lettering on Allan Ker's grave in West Hampstead Cemetery is difficult to read (Memorials to Valour).

The Machine Gun Corps Memorial is on the north side of the traffic island at Hyde Park Corner, close to Wellington Arch. The Royal Artillery, New Zealand and Australian War Memorials are nearby. The MGC memorial was originally erected next to Grosvenor Place near Hyde Park Corner and was dedicated on 10th May 1925 by Field Marshal Prince Arthur, Duke of Connaught and Strathearn. The statue of *The Boy David* is by David Derwent Woods, who enlisted as an orderly in the RAMC in 1915 and designed masks for soldiers with facial disfigurements. In 1945 the memorial was dismantled due to road works and was not reconstructed and rededicated in its present location until 1963.

Their address was 68 Victoria Street, London when he applied for his medals in March 1922. Allan was a member of VC Guard at the Interment of the Unknown Warrior on 11th November 1920. He attended the dedication of the Machine Gun Corps Memorial by the Duke of Connaught at Hyde Park Corner on 10th May 1925. Three fellow VCs also attended – WA White, JRN Graham and AH Cross. Allan attended the VC Garden Party at Buckingham Palace on 26th June 1920, the VC Centenary Celebrations in Hyde Park, London on 26th June 1956 and the first VC Association Reunion at the Café Royal, London on 24th July 1958. He was chairman of the Fifth Army Comrades' Association.

Allan moved to India, where he became a partner in Clarke, Rawlins, Ker and Co, Solicitors of Calcutta. He was suspended from acting in the High Court for a minor rule infringement in 1937. On 29th October 1940 he was recalled as GSO2 in the Directorate of Military Intelligence at the War Office. Appointed temporary major on 29th January 1941 and last appears in the Army List in July 1945. He attended the Potsdam Conference. Awarded the Brazilian Knight of the Order of Military Merit in 1944.

The Brazilian Order of Military Merit (Ordem do Mérito Militar) was established on 11th June 1943. There are five grades to recognise distinguished service and exceptional contributions to Brazil by members the Brazilian Army and the armies of friendly nations. Allan received the fifth grade award. General Dwight D Eisenhower was awarded the highest grade, Grand Cross, in August 1946.

The War Medal 1939–1945, instituted on 16th August 1945, was awarded to subjects of the British Empire and Dominions who served full-time in the armed forces or Merchant Navy for a minimum of twenty-eight days between 3rd September 1939 and 2nd September 1945.

After the war Allan became clerk to the Rent Tribunals for Paddington and Marylebone from 1946. He was living at 24 Fordwych Road, Cricklewood, London when he died at New End Hospital, Hampstead, London on 12th September 1958. He is buried in West Hampstead Cemetery, Fortune Green Road (Q4 7). He left effects valued at £7,228/0/5. A Department for Communities and Local Government commemorative VC paving stone was dedicated at Findhorn Place, Edinburgh in March 2018 to mark the centenary of his award.

In addition to the VC he was awarded the British War Medal 1914–20, Victory Medal 1914–19 with Mentioned-in-Despatches Oakleaf, Defence Medal, War Medal 1939–45, George V Silver Jubilee Medal 1935, George VI Coronation Medal 1937, Elizabeth II Coronation Medal 1953 and the Brazilian Knight of the Order of Military Merit. His medals were sold at auction by Dix Noonan Webb on 12th June 1991 for £15,500 and were purchased by Michael Ashcroft's VC Trust. They are held in the Imperial War Museum's Lord Ashcroft Gallery.

SECOND LIEUTENANT CECIL LEONARD KNOX
150th Field Company, Royal Engineers

Cecil Knox was born at Hinckley Road, Nuneaton, Warwickshire on 9th May 1889. He was known as Dick. His father, James Knox (7th April 1850–23rd July 1931), was born at Dysart, Fife, Scotland. He married Florence Elizabeth née Sadler (1851–1935), in 1877 at St Saviour, London. She was born at Clifton, Bristol, Gloucestershire. James was a civil engineer and founded the Haunchwood Brick and Tile Co in Nuneaton. He was also a director of Arley Colliery Co, Barnstone Cement Co of Nottingham and GW Lewis Ltd, tilemakers of Cannock, as well as

being a local JP. They were living at 6 Attleborough Road, Nuneaton in 1881, at Roseleigh, Hinckley Road, Nuneaton in 1891 and had built The Chase, Higham Lane, Nuneaton by 1901 (now the Chase Hotel). When James died he left effects valued at £317,135/17/11, with probate being granted to his widow and sons Edwin and Thomas. Cecil had eight brothers:

- James Meldrum Knox (10th April 1878–23rd September 1918) was commissioned in 2nd Volunteer Battalion, Royal Warwickshire Regiment on 4th November 1899 and served in the Second Boer War. He was promoted lieutenant 28th November 1900 and captain 23rd August 1905. On 1st April 1908 the unit changed its title to 7th Battalion, Royal Warwickshire Regiment. James married Dorothy Marian Iles (1874–21st February 1955) in 1904 at Watford, Hertfordshire. They lived at Castlemere, Hinckley Road, Nuneaton. James was embodied on 5th August 1914 and was promoted major on 24th October. On 12th May 1916 he was appointed

Cecil's father, James Knox, was born at Dysart, Fife, Scotland.

temporary lieutenant colonel on assuming command of 1/7th Battalion. He received a gunshot wound to the left shoulder on 14th July 1916, embarked on HMHS *St Andrew* at Rouen on 15th July and disembarked at Southampton next day. In addition to his wound, he also had an incontinent bladder, which necessitated wearing a rubber bag. He had suffered similarly four years before but recovered. Medical boards at Caxton Hall, London on 22nd and 25th July 1916 found him unfit for General Service for two and three quarter months and he was granted sick leave to 30th September. A medical board at Warwick Military Hospital found him unfit for General Service for one month on 18th October 1916; the wound had healed but he was still suffering bladder trouble.

The Haunchwood Brick and Tile Works was formed by James Knox and others in 1870. It produced a wide variety of ceramic products and its blue bricks were renowned for their quality. Production ended in 1970 and the chimneys, kilns and buildings were demolished the following year.

However, he was declared fit for General Service by a medical board at the War Office on 27th October and rejoined the Battalion on 24th November 1916. James relinquished temporary lieutenant colonel on 5th July 1917 and was promoted acting lieutenant colonel on 25th July. **Awarded the DSO (LG 1st January 1917). Awarded a Bar to the DSO for conspicuous gallantry and devotion to duty in command of his battalion. He kept touch with the situation until ordered by the division to counterattack when the enemy had broken through. Thanks to his splendid handling of his battalion, this counterattack was decisive, the enemy was at once held up, and after heavy fighting was driven back with severe losses, several**

The Knox family home, The Chase, is now a hotel. The modern picture was taken in the late 1990s.

hundred prisoners being captured and the front line restored (LG 24th September 1918). He was Mentioned in Despatches five times (LG 1st January 1916, 4th January 1917, 18th December 1917, 30th May 1918 & 6th January 1919). James died of wounds sustained on the Asiago plateau in Italy on 23rd September 1918 (Granezza British Cemetery – I E 9). His estate was valued at £3,243/11/9 and was jointly administered by his wife and brother Edwin. She was living at Duncton, 216 Manor Way, Bognor

Cecil's brother, James, is buried in Granezza British Cemetery, Italy.

Regis, Sussex at the time of her death at Chichester Hospital, Sussex. She left effects valued at £21,435/9/3. James and Dorothy had three children:

- ° Dorothy Barbara Knox (1905–39) married Roy Gerard Corcor Brock (1884–1968) in 1928 at Chelsea, London. He was commissioned in the Queen's Own Royal West Kent Regiment on 22nd October 1902, promoted lieutenant on 24th August 1904 and was appointed Adjutant 1st Battalion 1st January 1909–31 December 1911. Having been seconded to the Egyptian Army on 18th January 1912, he was promoted captain on 3rd September 1913, appointed staff captain 3rd June–16th August 1915 and was promoted major on 22nd October 1917. He retired from the Army on 1st February 1921. **Awarded the OBE for valuable services in connection with operations against the Aliab Dinkas in Sudan (LG 17th June 1921).** He was appointed District Commissioner in Bahr-al-Ghazal and Mongalla Provinces, Deputy Governor of Mongalla Province and Governor of Bahr-el-Ghazal 1928–34. During his tenure he abolished the town of Kafia Kingi in Darfur and created the 'Brock Line', a no man's land along the southern border of Darfur and Kordofan. The area remains disputed to this day. **Awarded the Order of the Nile 4th Class (LG 23rd May 1922) and 3rd Class (LG 10th June 1932).** He retired at the end of October 1934. They were living at 75 Ashley Gardens, Westminster when Dorothy died at 20 Devonshire Place, London. He was living at Ryder Street Chambers, 3 Ryder Street, London at the time of his death.
- ° Alexander Meldrum Knox (2nd September 1906–3rd January 1933) was commissioned in the Royal Engineers on 3rd February 1926 and was promoted lieutenant on 3rd February 1929. He was serving at Jhansi, India when he contracted pneumonia and died at the British Military Hospital there. He left effects valued at £8,119/17/10 to his mother.
- ° George Ronald Meldrum Knox (born 19th March 1908) was commissioned as a pilot officer on probation in the RAF on 20th March 1933 and was

confirmed in the rank on 20th March 1934. He was promoted flying officer on 20th September 1934 and transferred to the Class C Reserve on 20th March 1937. He was recall in the Second World War and promoted flight lieutenant in the Administrative & Special Duties Branch on 1st March 1941 and squadron leader on 15th December 1943. He had transferred to the Reserve by July 1946. George married Jean Marcia Leith-Marshall (27th July 1908–13th December 1993) at Watford in 1935. They were registered as George RH Knox and Jeannettie Marcia H Marshall. She was born Jeannettie Marcia Hannah Marshall at 25 Wolseley Road, Southtown, Great Yarmouth to parents Granville George Marshall, a publican, and Ivy formerly Ashby. Jean was previously married to Ewart Vernon Miller (1901–64) in 1926 and had a daughter, Julia, in 1927, believed to be Margaret J Miller. They subsequently divorced and Ewart married again in 1939 (Stella Atkinson) and 1952 (Norah Atkins/McMaster). Jean joined the Auxiliary Territorial Service (ATS) in October 1938, working on kitchen duties. She was commissioned as second subaltern on 30th May 1941 and was appointed commander of 2nd Hertfordshire Company. Promoted senior commandant (major equivalent) and appointed Inspector of ATS with a seat on the ATS Council. Promoted acting chief controller (major general equivalent) and Director ATS on 21st July 1941, becoming the world's youngest general at the time. One of her first actions was to design a new, well fitting uniform for the ATS. Promoted war substantive controller (colonel equivalent) on 21st July 1942 and travelled to Canada in September 1942 to inspect the Canadian Women's Army Corps and assist in its recruiting campaign.

She returned to Britain in November and relinquished her appointment on health grounds on 30th October 1943 (CBE 1st November 1943) and her commission on 12th December 1943. Jean was appointed Managing Director of Peter Jones, Sloane Square, Chelsea, London in 1948 but after six weeks she resigned without explanation. George and Jean divorced and she married Stuart Albert Samuel Montagu (1898–1990), 3rd Baron Swaythling, in August 1945 at Southampton, Hampshire. He had married Mary Violet Levy in 1925 and they had three children (Jean Mary Montagu 1927, David Charles Samuel Montagu 1928 and Anthony Trevor Samuel Montagu 1931) but they divorced

Cecil's nephew, George, married Jean Marcia Leith-Marshall, who was appointed Director of the Auxiliary Territorial Service in July 1941.

in 1942. When Jean died she was living at Terwick Hill House, Rogate, Petersfield, Hampshire and left effects valued at £998,224. George married Diana Mary Gossage née Morgan (1920–2001) in 1949 at Westminster. She had married Terence Leslie Gossage (1918–99) in 1941. Diana married Wing Commander William Reginald Farnes OBE (1915–86) in 1968.

- Edwin 'Teddy' Charles Knox (3rd May 1879–15th July 1977) was a mining engineer at Cinderhill Colliery, near Nottingham and was in charge of sinking the Arley Colliery in 1901–02. He was the manager until it was nationalised and played a significant role in the construction of Arley Colliery village, pithead baths and welfare hall. Edwin married Margaret Ethel Haslam (1887–17th March 1970) in 1910. She was born at East Retford, Nottinghamshire. They were living at Ryder House, Marine Parade, Gorleston, Great Yarmouth, Norfolk at the time of her death on 17 March 1970. They had four children:

    ° Andrew Ian Knox (twin with John) (1912–26th June 1939) married Janet Desborough Burnell (1909–99) in 1937 at Henley, Oxfordshire. Janet was an actress best known for her parts in the films *Henry V* 1944, *It's the Only Way to Go* 1970 and *Invitation to the Wedding* 1983. They were living at Marston Way, 85 Bulkington Road, Nuneaton at the time of his death at Coventry and Warwickshire Hospital resulting from a road traffic accident.

    Janet Burnell played Queen Isabel of France in Laurence Olivier's *Henry V* in 1944.

    ° John I Knox (twin with Andrew) (born 1912).
    ° Anthony Kenneth Knox (1917–2013) married and had two children, Jill Knox and Sally Knox. His second marriage was to Helen H Jones in 1971 at Newtown, Montgomeryshire. He was living at 51 Kighill Lane, Ravenshead, Nottingham at the time of his death in February 2013.
    ° Joan Knox (16th November 1923–4th July 2016) married Howard Roderick Duval (28th October 1907–4th January 2001) at Nuneaton on 12th November 1947. He was born at South River, Parry Sound, Ontario and qualified as a doctor (MD FRCS). He was commissioned in the Royal Army Medical Corps (195203), was promoted lieutenant on 26th June 1941 and rose to lieutenant colonel. Post war he was a consultant surgeon. Joan served in the Auxiliary Territorial Service during the Second World War. They had two sons, Roderick Charles Duval 1950 and Nicolas Kenneth Knox 1958.

- Alexander Knox (3rd December 1880–29th July 1954) was a mariner on a number of merchant ships, including SS *Macquarie, Canova, Irada, Inkum, Indore, Siddons, Phidias, Boswell, Marconi, Hogarth, Raeburn* and *Thespis*. He qualified as second mate on 9th April 1901, first mate on 16th February 1903, provisional master on

13th January 1906 and master on 3rd November 1909. He was a first officer on Gulf Transport Ships and was appointed captain with Lamport and Holt Line. Alexander also served in the Royal Naval Reserve. He was appointed midshipman on 27th February 1899 with seniority from 22nd February. His reserve service was in short periods. He was with HMS *Daedalus* 8th May 1899–31st May 1900, 21st January–17th February 1901, 29th January–4th February 1903, 13th November–3rd December 1905 and 18th January–15th February 1906. He also served with HMS *Eagle* 13th June–10th July 1903, 18th April–12th July 1904, 27th May–16th June 1908, 11th October–1st November 1909 and 29th January–7th April 1910. Alexander was promoted acting sub lieutenant 3rd May 1905 and sub lieutenant 23rd March 1906 with seniority from 2nd May 1905. On 26th August 1914 he was activated at HMS *Pembroke* at Chatham and was posted to HMS *President*, London on 11th September for service as coal agent at Lamlash, Isle of Arran. On 27th October he transferred to HMS *Imperieuse*, a repair ship, for victualling duties. He was promoted acting lieutenant 12th December 1914 and lieutenant 24th April 1915 with seniority from 21st October 1914. A number of appointments followed – HMS *Implacable* 7th September 1915, joining at Malta having travelled on HMS *Terrible*, HMS *Glory* 23rd March 1916, HMS *Excellent* while in hospital 28th April 1916, HMS *Britannia* 6th July 1916 (sunk by UB-*50* off Cape Trafalgar on 9th November with the loss of fifty men), HMS *Excellent* 22nd November 1918, HMS *Malaya* 31st January 1919 and HMS *Excellent* 2nd June 1919. He attended signals and torpedo courses at HMS *Vernon* 8th August–12th September 1919 and was demobilised on 21st November 1919. His reserve service continued with promotion to lieutenant commander on 21st October 1922 and gunnery and torpedo courses at HMS *Vivid* and HMS *Defiance* 6th June–13th July 1923. He was on HMS *Ramillies* 16th–29th July 1923 and retired on 3rd December 1925 in

HMS *Britannia* (17,500 tons), a King Edward VII Class pre-Dreadnought battleship, carried four 12″, four 9.2″, ten 6″, fourteen 12 Pounder, fourteen 3 Pounder guns and five 18″ torpedo tubes. She was commissioning in September 1906 and served in the Atlantic, Channel and Home fleets. When war broke out *Britannia* joined 3rd Battle Squadron in the Grand Fleet and in 1916 was attached to 2nd Detached Squadron in the Adriatic. In 1917 she was assigned to patrol and convoy escort duties in the Atlantic with 9th Cruiser Squadron. On the morning of 9th November 1918 she was torpedoed off Cape Trafalgar by UB-*50*. She listed to port and a few minutes later a second explosion started a fire in a 9.2″ magazine. She sank two and a half hours later. Fifty men died, mainly from toxic smoke from burning cordite, but 712 were rescued, including Alexander Knox.

the rank of commander. Alexander married Doris Webster in 1928 in Liverpool. They were living at 2 Windermere Terrace, Primacy Park, Liverpool and 77 Hillbrook Road, Tooting, London in the late 1920s and early 1930s and settled at Greenbanks, Dawlish Road, Teignmouth, Devon in the late 1940s. They adopted a son, Alexander. David Knox, known as David, who married Jane and died in November 2014.

Andrew Ronald Knox's grave in Albert Communal Cemetery Extension.

- Andrew Ronald Knox (1882–12th December 1915) was a member of Bedford School OTC in 1900. He applied for a commission on 13th October 1915 to utilise his mining skills. His address at the time was Rosemary House, Cannock. He was medically examined, found fit for service at Lichfield Military Hospital and was described as 5′ 11″ tall, weighing 124 lbs, with some problems with varicose veins. He was commissioned on 23rd October in 185th Tunnelling Company RE and was posted to Chatham, Kent on 4th November 1915 to proceed overseas. He was killed on 12th December 1915 (Albert Communal Cemetery Extension – I A 4). His brother, James, attended the funeral.

- Thomas Kenneth Knox (14th February 1884–29th August 1968) served in University Company, 1st Volunteer Battalion, Royal Warwickshire Regiment as a private in 1901 (1903). He was a coalmining engineer working for George Fowler at Cinderhill Colliery, Nottingham for five years and went to Canada about 1909 to become a civil engineer. He was employed by the Edmonton, Dunvegan & British Columbia Railway Company and was appointed assistant manager of Crow's Nest Colliery in the Rocky Mountains. He worked on the Grand Trunk Pacific Railway through the Rockies. Thomas was a member of the Institute of Mining Engineers. He returned to Britain and applied for a commission on 26th April 1915, supported by the Mayor of Nuneaton who recommended service with 216th Fortress Company RE based in Nuneaton. Thomas was commissioned as a temporary lieutenant on 20th May 1915 and went to France about 23rd January 1916. He received a gunshot wound to the scalp at Ypres, Belgium on 15th August 1917 while serving with 122nd Field Company RE. He embarked at Calais and disembarked at Dover on 19th August for treatment in England. A medical board at 3rd London General Hospital, Wandsworth on 4th September declared him fit for General Service after three weeks leave. Promoted acting captain 26th June 1918. Discharged and relinquished his commission on 14th February 1919 from No.1 Dispersal Unit, Chiseldon having served with 121st Field Company RE. Thomas was awarded the MC (LG 3rd June 1918). He was also awarded a Bar to the MC for conspicuous gallantry and devotion to duty under heavy shell and direct machine gun fire during the bridging of the river Lys on 19th October 1918, south of Oyghem. He managed to conceal the whole of his company's bridging equipment in farmhouses close to the river and at dusk rendered valuable assistance in the bridging of the river under heavy shellfire. He set a fine example to those under him (LG 15th February 1919). Thomas became Managing Director of Haunchwood Brick & Tile Co and GW Lewis Tileries and subsequently Chairman of both companies. He was living at Hobble Barn, Sandels Way, Beaconsfield, Buckinghamshire at the time of his death, leaving effects valued at £286,207.

Thomas Kenneth Knox was employed by the Edmonton, Dunvegan & British Columbia Railway Company before his war service in the Royal Engineers. This is the Company's depot at Edmonton, Alberta.

• John Douglas Knox (6th August 1885–October 1987) went to Malaya with the Bertram Rubber Co, becoming general manager of this and other local companies. He married Winifred Kate Elliott (c.1884–1963) in 1914 at Bristol, Gloucestershire. She was born in Guernsey, Channel Islands. On return to Britain John became a director of several rubber companies. She was living at Bertram, Ledborough Lane, Beaconsfield, Buckinghamshire at the time of her death on 24th January 1963 at The Priory, Roehampton, London. They had two daughters:
  ° Elizabeth 'Betty' Knox, believed to have been born in Malaya, married Walter Northcott-Green, a rubber planter in Malaya who was captured by the Japanese and spent time on the Burma railway. Betty and her son James were evacuated to Australia and returned to Britain via America. They were reunited after the war, returned to Malaya and had a second son, Alistair. They subsequently returned to Britain and lived in Old Windsor, Berkshire.
  ° Marjorie 'Joy' Florence Knox (1914–2006), in Malaya. Marjorie married Alastair Bruce Jenkins (c.1911–44) in 1940 at Amersham. Alastair was commissioned in the Royal Artillery on 21st September 1940 and was promoted war substantive lieutenant on 21st March 1942. He was a captain in 89th (2nd Battalion, The Liverpool Scottish) Anti-Tank Regiment RA (149556) when he died on 7th December 1944 (cremated at Putney Vale Crematorium, London and commemorated on Screen Wall Panel 2). Marjorie and Alastair had a daughter, June Helen Jenkins, in 1943. Marjorie married Denis Eley Colquhoun Hayes (1907–98) in 1946 in Bombay, India. He was born at Mafeking, South Africa. She was living at Bertram, Ledborough Lane, Beaconsfield, Buckinghamshire at the time of her death on 24th January 1963 at The Priory, Roehampton, London.

• Archibald Septimus Knox FInstCE MIE (15th September 1887–13th May 1984) was a consultant water engineer in charge of a water-drilling department for the Indian Government by 1914. He married Ellen Muriel Barber (9th October 1890–13th April 1972), known as Muriel, in December 1914 at Bombay and they had a daughter, Margaret Knox c.1917. He applied to join the Army but was rejected because of his protected employment. He subsequently joined the Cawnpore Artillery as a volunteer and transferred to the United Provinces Light Horse Artillery. Archibald spent twenty years in India, Burma and Assam, working for the Public Works Department and as managing director of two engineering contractors, which designed and built mills, factories, water supply installations and the electricity generating station at Cawnpore. On return to England he was a rural district councillor for Meriden and served as a JP. Archibald was in charge of air raid precautions for twenty-four parishes between Birmingham and Coventry during the Second World War. He was a director of Haunchwood Brick & Tile Co and GW Lewis Tileries until 1960. They lived at Rosemary, 2 Sandels Way, Beaconsfield, Buckinghamshire.

• Cedric Knox (20th July 1890–12th April 1959) was a farmer when he enlisted in the Royal Marine Artillery (1545) in London on 15th December 1915. He was described as 5′ 11½″ tall, with fresh complexion, blue eyes and brown hair. He was appointed gunner 2nd class on 21st June 1916 and served with the East African Expeditionary Force 24th June 1916–2nd March 1917. He was appointed gunner on 15th July 1916 and served with the Royal Marine Howitzer Brigade from 11th September 1917. He was awarded the Good Conduct Badge on 15th December 1917 and was demobilised on 27th February 1919, giving his address as Little London Farm, Little Totham, Maldon, Essex. He was living at Laxton House, 138 Cheltenham Road, Evesham, Worcestershire at the time of his death at Evesham Hospital, leaving effects valued at £30,677/3/4.

Cecil's paternal grandfather, Thomas Knox (2nd August 1815–3rd January 1890), was born at Forgan, Fife. He became Chief Engineer to Sir James Brunlees (1816–92), consulting engineer on some of the early railways in Scotland and abroad. Thomas designed Methil Docks at Leven, Fife and was later resident engineer on the Edinburgh, Perth and Dundee Railway. He travelled to Argentina where he estimated for a contract for an early railway system there. He married Janet née Meldrum (born c. 1826 at Scoonie, Fife), in 1847. They lived at St Andrews, Fife and at Mount Pleasant, Dysart, Fife in 1851. He was living at Mertyn House, Hinckley Road, Nuneaton at the time of his death, leaving effects valued at £12,506/18/2. In addition to James they had another son, Andrew Knox (born 1st January 1848 at Markinch, Fife), who emigrated to Australia and became a sheep farmer.

His maternal grandfather, Charles James Sadler (26th February 1817–21st February 1882), was born in Oxford. He was a senior examiner in the Exchequer and Audit Department. He married Elizabeth Sadler née Reed (c.1817–84) in 1840 in Bristol, Gloucestershire. They were living at 41 Wilson Road, Camberwell, Surrey in 1881. In addition to Florence they had four other children:

• Amelia Elizabeth Sadler (born and died 1841).
• Emily Jane Sadler (1844–1920) never married.

- Frederick Charles Sadler (1845–76) married Christina De Wilde Cater (1847–1912) in 1868 at St George Hanover Square, London. They were living at Caroline Place, Larkhall Rise, Clapham, London when he died. She was living at 37 Drakefield Road, Upper Tooting, London at the time of her death. They had a son, Herbert Charles Sadler, in 1872.
- Augustus Henry Sadler (1847–1925) was living at 44 Lincoln's Inn Fields, London in 1882. He was living at High Field, Altoft Gardens, Ventnor, Isle of Wight, Hampshire at the time of his death.

King Edward VI Grammar School dates back to 1552. It was originally fee-paying, with some county council scholarships, until the Education Act 1944, when it became voluntary aided. The grammar school closed in 1974 and became King Edward VI College. Amongst its notable alumni are the aviation pioneer, Geoffrey de Havilland, and the TV and film director, Ken Loach.

Cecil was educated at King Edward VI Grammar School, Nuneaton and Oundle School, Northamptonshire 1902–07. He was articled to a consulting mechanical and electrical engineer in Birmingham for three years and by 1911 was an electrical engineer living with his parents. Cecil moved to Canada, where he was employed

Oundle School was founded as Laxton Grammar School in 1556, although there had been a school on the site since 1485. It was run by the Worshipful Company of Grocers. In 1876 the school split into Laxton Grammar School, to educate local boys, and Oundle School for the sons of gentlemen from further afield. Oundle quickly established itself as one of the leading public schools and gained a reputation for science and engineering education. The school admitted girls from 1990 and in 2000 Oundle School and Laxton School reunited, with Laxton becoming the day house. Oundle is now the third largest independent boarding school in England after

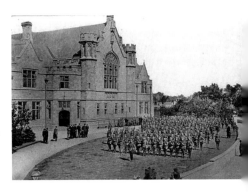

Eton and Millfield. Two other Old Oundelians were awarded the VC – Alan Jerrard and Charles Geoffrey Vickers. Kevin Walton GC DSC taught at the school, as did WG Grace, eldest son of the famous cricketer of the same name. Amongst its other famous alumni are:

Count Manfred Beckett Czernin, Second World War RAF pilot and SOE operative.
Micky Wynn, 7th Baron Newborough, Royal Navy officer, who took part in the raid on St Nazaire in March 1942.
Benjamin Bryant CB DSO DSC, the most successful British submarine ace to survive the Second World War.
Damian Grammaticas, television correspondent.
Cecil Lewis, First World War RFC pilot and co-founder of the BBC.

as Assistant Resident Construction Engineer in Alberta on the Northern Alberta Railway running from Edmonton through Grande Prairie to Dawson Creek.

Cecil returned to Britain to enlist in the Royal Engineers at Birmingham on 9th May 1916 (167488), giving his profession as draughtsman. He was described as 6′ tall, his religious denomination was Church of England and he was deemed to be qualified as a surveyor (cadastral and engineering). While in Birmingham he shared accommodation with Arnold Waters, who was also awarded the VC in 1918. He trained at the Royal Engineers Training Centre, Newark in No.8 Depot Company RE from 28th June and No.5 Depot Company RE from 16th November, followed by posting to 288th Company RE at Buxton on 25th November. Cecil applied for a commission on 29th November 1916 and transferred to the Royal Engineer Cadet Lines, RETC Newark on 12th March 1917. He was commissioned on 2nd June 1917 and went to France immediately, where he took part in the Battle of Messines on 7th June. He joined 150th Field Company on 26th August 1917. Appointed temporary captain in October 1917.

Awarded the VC for his actions at Tugny, France on 22nd March 1918, LG 4th June 1918. The Freedom of Nuneaton was conferred at a ceremony in Riversley Park on 17th July. William Beesley VC was granted the Freedom on the same day. Cecil's wife presented the casket containing the Freeman's Scroll to the Mayor of Nuneaton for safekeeping in 1972. The VC was presented by the King at HQ Second Army at Blendecques, France on 6th August 1918.

Cecil was promoted lieutenant on 2nd December 1918 and relinquished his commission on 14th June 1919, retaining the

Cecil was employed by the Canadian Pacific Railway before the war. The railway was originally built between Eastern Canada and British Columbia between 1881 and 1885 and was Canada's first transcontinental railway.

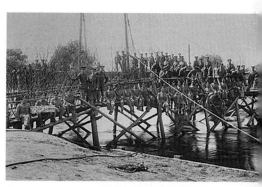

Sappers training at RETC Newark in July 1917.

Cecil Knox receiving the Freedom of Nuneaton on 17th July 1918. William Beesley VC, who was granted the Freedom on the same day, is seated on the right.

Castle Bromwich airfield was used from 1909 onwards. In 1914 it was requisitioned for the RFC and 605 Squadron formed there in October 1926, remaining until 27th August 1939, when it moved to Tangmere. Between the wars the airfield was jointly used by the military and civilian companies. In September 1922 it was used as a staging point for the first round of the King's Cup air race. In 1939 commercial flying moved to a new airfield at Elmdon, which is now Birmingham International Airport. Just prior to the Second World War a shadow factory was built at the airfield and an initial order for one thousand Spitfires was placed in April 1939. Castle Bromwich Aeroplane Factory was the largest of its kind in Britain, covering 345 acres and employed 12,000 people. In March 1940 Vickers-Armstrong took over the running. Almost 12,000 Spitfires were built there, over half of the total number produced. In addition 300 Avro Lancaster bombers were built as well as fifty Seafires. After the war aircraft production was replaced by cars. The airfield closed in 1958 and much of it is now covered by housing.

Cecil Knox receives his VC from the King on 6th August 1918.

rank. He appears in the Army List until June 1920. Cecil went into the family business and became a director of the Haunchwood Company with Kenneth and also of GW Lewis Tileries Ltd. He was the best man at the wedding of Arnold Horace Santo Waters VC DSO MC RE on 27th October 1924. He attended the VC Garden Party at Buckingham Palace on 26th June 1920 and the VC Dinner at the Royal Gallery of the House of Lords, London on 9th November 1929.

Cecil took up flying, qualifying as a pilot in a DH Moth 27/60hp Cirrus at the Midland Aero Club, Castle Bromwich on 4 August 1926. He served in 605 (County of Warwick) (Bombing) Squadron RAAF, Castle Bromwich as a pilot officer from 23rd November 1926. Promoted flying officer on 23rd May 1928 and flight lieutenant on 1st January 1930. Cecil was seriously injured in a parachuting accident while training with the Squadron at Manston in August 1927, which eventually forced him to retire from the RAAF in 1932.

Cecil Knox married Eileen Mary née Baylor (23rd February 1898–2nd January 1990) on 3rd September 1936 at Hungerford, Berkshire. She was born at Eastry, Kent and had married Geoffrey Campbell Bourne (1891–1978), a bank clerk, in 1917 at Ipswich, Suffolk. They had two daughters – Patricia M Bourne 1920 and Felicite A Bourne 1922. Eileen's first marriage ended in divorce. Cecil built their home, Fyves Court, Watling Street, Caldecote, Nuneaton, named after his favourite

De Havilland Moths were a series of light aircraft, sports planes and military trainers designed by Geoffrey de Havilland, who also attended King Edward VI Grammar School in Nuneaton a few years before Cecil Knox. In the late 1920s and 1930s they were the most common civil aircraft flying in Britain.

Cecil was best man to Arnold Horace Santo Waters VC DSO MC RE in October 1924. Arnold was awarded the VC for his action at Ors, France on 4th November 1918.

sport at school. It contained a court with a spectator's gallery on the south side of the house. Cecil and Eileen had a daughter, Katrina 'Kate' Victoria Knox, born on 9th October 1941. She married Nicholas John Collingwood Barling (born 1939) in 1964 at North Cotswold, Gloucestershire. They moved to Devon and had three children – Sophie Victoria Collingwood Barling 1965, Timothy James Collingwood Barling 1967 and Robert Nicholas Collingwood Barling 1971.

Cecil's home, Fyves Court at Caldecote. His ashes were scattered in the grounds.

Eileen's father, Edward Arthur Crampton Baylor (c.1863–1943), a physician and surgeon, was born at Fermoy, Co Cork, Ireland. He married Harriotte Marianne née Lovell (1868–1947) in 1892 at Kensington, London. She was born at Pancras, Middlesex. They were living at Ash, Canterbury, Kent in 1911 and at North Lodge, Angelsea Road, Ipswich by 1914. He was living at Ashurst,

Watling Street, Radlett, Hertfordshire at the time of his death. She was staying at The Desmond Hotel, Leamington Spa, Warwickshire at the time of her death. In addition to Eileen they had two other children:

- Audrey May Baylor (1893–1941) married Ernest Alexander Steward (1885–1963), a tea planter, in August 1920 at All Saints' Church, Ipswich, Suffolk. They had a daughter, Wendy Steward, in 1921. They were living at 17 Brunner Close, Finchley, London in 1930 and at Little Orchard, The Warren, Radlett, Hertfordshire by 1941. He was living at Highbury, Oakridge Avenue, Radlett, Hertfordshire at the time of his death.

- Arthur Edward Lovell Baylor (1895–1989) was educated at St Lawrence College, Ramsgate, Kent, where he was a member of the OTC September 1910–April 1913. He enlisted in G Company, 19th Royal Fusiliers (62), Public Schools Brigade at Westminster, London on 3rd September 1914. He was described as a probationer in a merchant's office, 5′ 6″ tall, weighing 140 lbs, with dark complexion, brown eyes, brown hair and his religious denomination was Church of England. He applied for a commission on 14th December 1914 and was commissioned in the Royal Berkshire Regiment on 16th January 1915. He served in 7th Battalion at Salonika from 16th February 1916, where he suffered heat stroke, malaria and dysentery. Having been admitted to 31 Casualty Clearing Station with diarrhoea on 11th August and to 29th General Hospital with dyspepsia the same day, he sailed for Malta on HMHS *Grantully Castle* on 22nd August, arriving on 25th August. A medical board in Malta on 24th September found him unfit for General Service for three months and leave was granted until 15th December. He embarked on HMHS *Herefordshire* from Malta to Mudros on 30th September 1916 for transfer to HMHS *Aquitania* for England. A medical board on 17th October found him unfit for General Service for three months and two months for Home Service. He joined 3rd Reserve Battalion at Victoria Barracks, Portsmouth, Hampshire on 1st December. Further medical boards followed on 28th December 1916, 26th January 1917, 29th January, 15th March, 14th April, 23rd May, 21st June, 23rd July, 15th August and 10th September, which found him unfit for General Service for periods of four

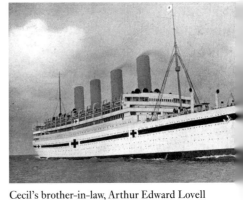

Cecil's brother-in-law, Arthur Edward Lovell Baylor, was evacuated to Britain aboard HMHS *Aquitania*. RMS *Aquitania* was built for Cunard on Clydeside by John Brown and her maiden voyage to New York commenced on 30th May 1914. She was in use for thirty-six years and served in both world wars. The author's grandfather was evacuated from Gallipoli on *Aquitania* a few months later. He awoke in a delirious state to see angels floating above him and thought he was dead, until he realised he was looking at the painted dining room ceiling.

Nuneaton General Hospital, where Cecil Knox died on 4th February 1943.

Nuneaton War Memorial in Riversley Park.

weeks up to six months. He was declared Category A on 10th January 1918. Promoted temporary lieutenant with seniority from 1st July 1917. He was assigned to the Training Reserve on 3rd January and was attached to 52nd (Graduated) Battalion, Devonshire Regiment at Norwich, Norfolk as an acting captain and company commander 8th February–12th September 1919. He was demobilised on 13th September 1919 from Crystal Palace Dispersal Centre, London. On 26th January 1942 he was granted an Emergency Commission in the Burma Reserve of Officers.

Cecil was appointed a company commander in 3rd Warwickshire (Nuneaton) Battalion Home Guard as a major on 1st February 1941. He was later second in command of the Battalion. Cecil Knox died at Nuneaton General Hospital, Warwickshire following a motorcycle accident at 10.30 a.m. at Bucks Hill on 4th February 1943. He skidded on ice travelling at only ten to fifteen miles per hour. The cause of death was concussion and intracranial haemorrhage. He was cremated at Gilroes Crematorium, Leicester following a funeral service at St Peter's Witherley, near Atherstone. His ashes were scattered in the grounds of his home, Fyves Court, Caldecote near Nuneaton. Eileen moved to Broadwell, near Stow-on-the-Wold, Gloucestershire after his death. She was living at Rosemount, Old Exeter Street, Chudleigh, Devon at the time of her death. Cecil is commemorated in a number of other places:

The Special Constabulary Long Service Medal was established on 30th August 1919 to recognise the service of members of the Special Constabulary during the First World War I. Recipients had to serve for nine years, with wartime service counting as triple.

- Knox Crescent, Nicholas Park Estate, Nuneaton, Warwickshire.
- Cecil Leonard Knox Crescent, Gamecock Barracks, Bramcote, Nuneaton.
- Named on a family memorial at Oaston Road Cemetery, Nuneaton, Warwickshire.
- Named on the War Memorial, Riversley Park, Nuneaton.

- Named on a memorial at Ulster Tower near Thiepval, France to 36th Division's VCs.
- Named on the Royal Engineers Honours Board, Royal Engineers Museum, Brompton Barracks, Gillingham, Kent.
- His VC action was featured in Issue No.367 of the Victor Comic, entitled *The Blowing of the Bridge*, dated 2nd March 1968.
- A Department for Communities and Local Government commemorative VC paving stone was dedicated at Riversley Park, Coton Road, Nuneaton on 22nd March 2018 to mark the centenary of his award.

In addition to the VC he was awarded the British War Medal 1914–20, Victory Medal 1914–19, King George VI Coronation Medal 1937 and the Special Constabulary Long Service Medal. The medals are held privately.

CAPTAIN ARTHUR MOORE LASCELLES
3rd attached 14th Battalion, The Durham Light Infantry

Arthur Lascelles was born on 12th October 1880 at Wilby Lodge, Nightingale Lane, Battersea, London. His father, John Lascelles MA JP (22nd June 1849–29th March 1931), was born at Low Hall, Whitehaven, Cumberland. He was educated at Pembroke College, Oxford and was destined for the clergy but decided against it. He married Mary Elizabeth née Cotton (1856–4th November 1917) on 21st April 1879 at St Luke's Church, Oseney Crescent, Kentish Town, London. At the time of the 1871 Census she was living with her sister, Susan, at the Greyhound Hotel, Hereford, which was run

Arthur's parents were married at St Luke's Church, Kentish Town in 1879. The church was built in 1867–69 and is Grade II* listed.

Arthur was born at Wilby Lodge on Nightingale Lane, Battersea.

by her maternal grandmother, Mary Cotton (born c.1810). John and Mary were living at Wilby Lodge, Nightingale Lane, Battersea in 1881 before moving to Llugwy, Pennal, Merionethshire. They moved about 1884 to Penmaen Hall, Dyfi, Merionethshire. In 1911 Mary was living with her daughter Elizabeth at 3/4 Catherine Place, Bath, Somerset and John was living at Pennal, Machynlleth. Following the death of his wife in 1917, John proposed to his kitchen maid, Jane Ellen Davies (born 1897), but she refused. He moved to Milford Hall, Newtown, Montgomeryshire about 1921 and died there in 1931, leaving effects valued at £74,720/12/10. Before they married Mary had a son, Percy St John Lascelles Cotton (1878 -1949), and it seems likely that John was

Arthur's brother, Reginald, died at Cannanore, Madras 1904. Today it is known as Kannur in Kerala state, except for Indian Railways, which still use the anglicised version. The wider urban area has a population of about 1.7 million, of which only 60,000 live in Kannur city. The Portuguese built St Angelo Fort there in 1505. It was captured by the Dutch in 1663, who modernised and extended it. The British captured the area in 1790 and it became a significant military station.

the father. By 1911 Percy was an assistant shipping superintendant, boarding at 37 Talbot Street, Cardiff, Glamorgan. He married Bertha Selby Cousins (1876–1959) in 1914 at Caernarvon, Caernarvonshire. Percy served in the Artists Rifles during the Great War and was employed by Spillers and Bakers of Cardiff in 1918. He was living at 171 Cathedral Road, Cardiff in 1919 and was later appointed a Justice of the Peace. Arthur had two other siblings:

- Reginald George Lascelles (10th March 1883–16th August 1904) was commissioned in 4th Durham Light Infantry (Militia) on 8th June 1900 and was based at Stanhope and Wellington Lines in Aldershot at the time of the 1901 Censes. It is understood that he sailed for South Africa with the 4th Battalion in early January 1902 and was commissioned in 1st Durham Light Infantry on 30th April 1902. Reginald was posted to India with the Battalion and drowned at Cannanore, Madras on 16th August 1904.
- Elizabeth Constance Lascelles (1879 -1971) married Samuel Farrer Godfrey Pallin FRCVS (1878–1930) in 1915 at Machynlleth, Montgomeryshire. Samuel served during the Second Boer War 1901–02 and was awarded the Queen's South Africa Medal with five clasps (Paardeberg, Relief of Kimberley, Tugela Heights, Natal & Cape Colony). He became a civilian veterinary surgeon and worked as such for a year and 290 days before being commissioned as a lieutenant in the Army Veterinary Department (later Army Veterinary Corps and Royal Army Veterinary Corps from November 1918) on 16th May 1903. He was promoted captain on 16th May 1908 and major on 10th July 1915. He went to France on 31st January 1915 and was an Assistant Director of Veterinary Services in Home Forces and in France from 10th April 1915 until 26th June 1917. He left France on

20th November 1917 for Italy and was Assistant Director of Veterinary Services there as an acting lieutenant colonel 25th January 1918–31st March 1919. During the war he was awarded the DSO (LG 1st January 1917) and was Mentioned in Despatches three times (LG 4th January 1917, 13th May 1917 and 30th May 1918). Samuel served on operations in Iraq 1919–20 and was awarded the General Service Medal 1918–62 with Iraq clasp. He was placed on Half Pay due to ill health on 31st March 1928 and retired on 13th July 1929 with the rank of lieutenant colonel. Elizabeth and Samuel had two children – Elaine Mary Elizabeth Pallin 1916 and Farrer John Lascelles Pallin 1923.

Arthur's paternal grandfather, John Lascelles (1798–1889), was born in Dumfriesshire, Scotland, son of General Francis Lascelles of the Dragoon Guards. John was commissioned in the Royal Navy and served aboard HMS *San Josef*, a 114 gun first-rate ship captured from the Spanish in 1797. John was promoted lieutenant on 19th April 1828 and volunteered to go on Half Pay in 1829, although he was promoted commander in 1830. He married Elizabeth née Moore (c.1809–95) on 16th January 1836 at St Nicholas, Whitehaven, Cumberland, where he built and operated a merchant vessel, *Earl of Harewood*. John was offered the position of Harbour Master at Holyhead, Anglesey by the Home Secretary, Sir Robert Peel. He held this appointment for eleven years and during that time they lived on Salt Island. By 1861 they had moved to 9 Frederick Place, Clifton, Bristol and by 1871 to Keynsham Lodge, Cheltenham, Gloucestershire. They also had a home at Low Hall, Cumberland, where John died on 10th October 1889, leaving effects valued at £14,380/12/2. In addition to the VC's father, John and Elizabeth had three other children:

• Edwin Lascelles (c.1838–1923) was educated at Pembroke College, Oxford before being ordained into the Church of England. He married Margaret

HMS *San Josef*, a 114-gun ship of the Spanish Navy captured at the Battle of Cape St Vincent on 14th February 1797, was originally named *San José*. During the battle, HMS *Captain*, commanded by Captain Horatio Nelson, came out of the line to attack the *San Nicolás*. Nelson led his men aboard. Meanwhile *San José* fired on *Captain* and *San Nicolás*, but her rigging became entangled with that of *San Nicolás*. Having secured *San Nicolás*, Nelson led his men aboard *San José* and forced its surrender. The captured ships were renamed HMS *San Josef* and HMS *San Nicolas*. Two other Spanish ships were captured during the battle. In 1801 *San Josef* was Nelson's flagship in the Channel and in 1809 she was the flagship of Admiral John Thomas Duckworth. From 1839 she was used as a gunnery training ship and guard ship at Devonport. She was broken up in 1849. This watercolour shows *San Josef* off Plymouth in 1848 flying the flag of Admiral Sir William Hall Gage, C-in-C Plymouth (William Joy).

Arthur's paternal grandparents were living at 9 Frederick Place, Clifton, Bristol in 1861 (Zoopla).

Salt Island was so named after a sea salt factory located there that ceased production in 1775. The Stanley Sailor's Hospital opened there in 1871 and closed in 1987. The 300m long Admiralty Pier, opened in 1821 and has been used for ferry traffic ever since. Today almost all the island is used for the Dublin ferry terminal and berths. Shown here are the port buildings and clock tower (Arthur Harris).

Bushby   MacKenzie   (c.1836–91) in 1862 at Brighton, Sussex. She was born at Pondicherry, India. They had two children – Edwin John Moore Lascelles 1863 and Alexander Charles Lascelles 1866. Edwin senior was Rector of Newton St Loe, Somerset 1878–1904. He married Helen Hardwick née Eaton (c.1849–7th December 1919) in 1895 at St George, Hanover Square, London. Helen had married Philip Charles Hardwick (1823–92) in 1872 at Bath. They had three children – Helen Julia Hardwick 1873, Philip Edward Hardwick 1875 and Stephen Thomas Hardwick 1876. Stephen Hardwick was commissioned in 4th Middlesex and transferred to

Keynsham Lodge, Cheltenham (Rightmove).

the Royal Field Artillery in June 1899. He served in Egypt and Sinai 1897–98 on survey work. In 1900 February he went to South Africa and took part in the Second Boer War. He was promoted lieutenant in February 1901. On 25th December 1901 he was commanding a pom-pom section at Tweefontein when De Wet's forces attacked. He fired off a few rounds before realising that he was about to be overrun and endeavoured to render the gun useless but was shot through the heart and killed (MID). Philip senior was living at 2 Hereford Gardens, London at the time of his death on 27th January 1892, leaving effects valued

The Greyhound Hotel, Hereford was kept by Arthur's maternal grandmother in 1871 (Herefordshire History).

Hillside (1870–1991) was a preparatory and pre-preparatory school, founded by Reverend Edward Ford, initially for boys, in West Malvern Road near a spring of the same name. The school moved in the 1950s and the original building was divided into private residences.

at £211,316/10/9 (£24M in 2016). Edwin and Helen were living at Rotherfield House, Midhurst, Sussex by 1911 and she died there without further issue, leaving effects valued at £13,479/14/6. Edwin was living at The Grange, Weston Park, Bath, Somerset at the time of his death on 24th December 1923, leaving effects valued at £63,798/19/3 to his son Edwin.

• Elizabeth Jane Lascelles (1840–63).
• Francis John Lascelles (born and died 1843).

His maternal grandfather, James Cotton (c.1830–74), was born at Gloucester. He married Mary née Scattergood (born c.1831 at Leigh, Worcestershire) in 1856 at Abergavenny, Monmouthshire. He was a china dealer at Ross, Herefordshire in 1861. By the 1871 Census he was assistant hotelkeeper at the Greyhound Hotel, Hereford, which was run by his mother, Mary (c.1810–74). His wife, Mary, was not with him. In addition to Mary they had another daughter, Susan Emily (1858–96). She was visiting her sister, Mary, at Wilby Lodge, Nightingale Lane, Battersea at the time of the 1881 Census. Susan died unmarried at Martley, Worcestershire.

Arthur was educated at:

• Hillside School, Malvern.
• Uppingham School May 1895–December 1898.

Uppingham School, founded in 1584, remained small until expanding in the 19th Century. By the 1960s it had 600 pupils. The first girl attended in 1973. In addition to Arthur Lascelles, four other Old Uppinghamians have been awarded the VC – George Maling, Thomas Maufe, John Collings-Wells and Willward Sandys-Clarke. Famous alumni include:

Jonathan Agnew, the BBC's Chief Cricket Correspondent.
Rowan Atkinson, actor and comedian.
Edward Brittain, brother of Vera Brittain, who wrote *Testament of Youth*.
Sir Malcolm Campbell and Donald Campbell, world land and water speed record holders.
Stephen Fry, actor, comedian and writer.
Lieutenant General Sir Brian Horrocks, commander of XXX Corps in the Second World War.
CRW Nevinson, official war artist in both World Wars.
William Henry Pratt, film actor using the stage name Boris Karloff.
John Schlesinger, film director.
Rick Stein, chef, restaurateur and television broadcaster.

- University College of North Wales, Bangor 1899.
- Edinburgh University 1899–1902 studying medicine but did not graduate.

Arthur emigrated to South Africa and enlisted in 1st Cape Mounted Riflemen (17) on 11th August 1902 (it became 1st South African Mounted Infantry on 1st March 1913). He married a South African, Sophia Cassidy (c.1880–16th March 1964), at Idutywa, Transkei on 7th December 1907. They had a son, Reginald George Lascelles (14th September 1908–22nd December 1984), born at Cape Town, South Africa, who was named after his uncle. Reginald was commissioned in the Royal Artillery on 31st January 1929 and was promoted lieutenant on 31st January 1932. In 1933 he was serving in 1st Air Defence Brigade, Blackdown, Hampshire. He was promoted captain 1st August 1938, acting major 22nd April–21st

Arthur attended the University College of North Wales, Bangor (now Bangor University) in 1899. The College is top right. On the left is the North Wales Heroes' Memorial. Above the archway the room is lined with wood panels listing 8,500 people from the region who died on active service during the First World War, including Arthur Lascelles. Prime Minister David Lloyd George was a patron and students at Bangor University helped with fund-raising. The Memorial was opened by the Prince of Wales (later Edward VIII) on 1st November 1923.

July 1941, temporary major 22nd July 1941–7th September 1943, acting lieutenant colonel 8th June–7th September 1943, war substantive major 8th September 1943,

When war broke out in Europe in August 1914 the South African Prime Minister, Louis Botha, informed London that South Africa could defend herself, which allowed Imperial forces to depart for France. South African troops were mobilised along the border with German South West Africa under General Henry Lukin and Lieutenant Colonel Manie Maritz. However, amongst the Boer population there was considerable sympathy for the Germans. Maritz declared the former South African Republic, Orange Free State, Cape Province and Natal free from British control and 12,000 rebels were gathered in what became known as the Boer Revolt or the Maritz Rebellion. The government declared martial law on 14th October 1914 and forces loyal to the government under Generals Botha and Jan Smuts moved against the rebels. Maritz was defeated on 24th October and sought refuge with the Germans. By early February 1915 it was all over and the leading rebels were imprisoned, although they were released two years later. Meanwhile the first attempt to invade German South West Africa from the south failed on 26th September 1914. The Germans launched their own invasion in February 1915 but were prevented from gaining fords over the Orange River. With the homeland secure, Botha began the complete occupation of German territory, invading from north and south. The capital of German South West Africa, Windhuk, fell on 5th May. Having cut the colony in half, Botha divided his forces into four contingents, which moved very rapidly. Smuts landed another force at Luderitzbucht and advanced inland. By the end of May the entire country had been secured. The South African forces had 529 casualties, including 266 killed or died of injury and illness. German casualties totaled 993 of which 103 were killed. South Africa administered the colony under a League of Nations mandate from 1919. When the United Nations succeeded the League in 1946, South Africa refused to give up its mandate when it was revoked by the General Assembly. In 1971 the International Court of Justice opined that South Africa's administration was illegal. Transition to the independent Namibia began in 1988 following agreement by South Africa to withdraw while Soviet and Cuban forces pulled back into southern Angola. The process was supervised by a UN civilian and peacekeeping force.

temporary lieutenant colonel 8th September 1943–30th September 1945 and major on 31st January 1946. He retired as an honorary lieutenant colonel on 24th July 1950. Reginald married Barbara Aylwin Sulivan (1914–2003) in 1933 at St Mark's, Farnborough, Hampshire. The marriage ended in divorce. Reginald married Ethel Geddes Williamson (1911–74) on 15th January 1944 in New Delhi, India. Barbara married Alan A Martin-Jenkins (born 1913) in 1945. Reginald's third marriage was to Joan 'Jill' Wearing (born 1924) in 1951 at Whitehaven, Cumberland. They had two children – Kathryn S Lascelles 1954 and Mark GW Lascelles 1958.

Arthur returned to Britain on leave in 1910 and on his return to South Africa he applied for a commission. He passed the examination in 1912. He served as a quartermaster sergeant during the Maritz Rebellion and the German South West Africa campaign 4th August 1914–9th July 1915. On 10th October he was discharged at his own request from Grootfontein and returned to Britain with his family the following month. He was described as 5′ 9″ tall, with fair complexion, blue eyes and brown hair. They lived at 9 Richmond Road, Olton, Warwickshire and Sophia worked in the canteen of a Midlands munitions factory.

Arthur applied for a commission on 9th December, giving his address as Penmaen, Machynlleth. He was commissioned in 3rd Durham Light Infantry on 28th December 1915 and undertook officer training at Cambridge from 1st January until 3rd February 1916. He then attended a sniper course at Rugby and went to France on 16th July, where he joined 35th Infantry Base Depot and 14th Battalion later the same day. Arthur was wounded by shrapnel in the neck on 18th September 1916 and was treated at 2/2nd London Casualty Clearing Station the same day and at 8th General Hospital, Rouen on 22nd September. He was evacuated to England later that day and whilst being treated was on the strength of 3rd (Reserve) Battalion. Arthur returned to France on 6th February 1917, where he served in 11th Battalion from 18th February until 14th May and then with 14th Battalion from 29th May.

Awarded the MC for his actions on 15th June 1917 in the 15 Bis Sector, Loos. He led a daylight raid of forty all ranks, taking all objectives and five prisoners and killing twenty enemy, before withdrawing without a casualty, LG 1st January 1918. Promoted lieutenant 1st July and was appointed second in command of A Company as acting captain on 20th July 1917. He was admitted to

SS *Ville de Liège* (1,365 tons) entered service in January 1914 for the Ostend–Folkestone service. During the war she was a troop and hospital ship and was involved in the evacuation of Ostend 10th–14th October 1914. In January 1919 she and *Stad Antwerpen* brought Belgian refugees back from Britain. On 11th February 1929 *Ville de Liège* sank on rocks inside Dover harbour but was refloated, repaired and the opportunity was taken to refit her to take cars as well as foot passengers. In June 1940 she carried refugees to Britain. In February 1941 she was taken up by the Royal Navy as the minesweeper depot ship HMS *Ambitious*. In June 1944 she was involved in the Normandy landings and from 19th June was inside the Mulberry harbour at Arromanches directing minelaying and minesweeping operations. After renovation she reopened the Ostend service on 22nd October 1945 and was scrapped in 1950.

Arthur's grave in Dourlers Communal Cemetery Extension (Memorials to Valour).

18th Field Ambulance on 22nd July and to No.42 Casualty Clearing Station with a dislocated knee on 23rd July, returning to the Battalion on 31st July. He was granted leave in England 3rd–13th August and was appointed temporary captain on 19th August. He was also granted leave to attend his mother's funeral 5th–19th November.

Awarded the VC for his actions at Masnières, France on 3rd December 1917, LG 11th January 1918. He was seriously wounded in the head and right arm during the VC action and was treated at 2/1st Midland Field Ambulance and No.48 Casualty Clearing Station before being evacuated to Britain on 12th December on HMHS *Ville de Liège*. Arthur was appointed temporary captain on 6th March 1918 with seniority from 19th August 1917. The VC was presented by the King at Buckingham Palace on 23rd March 1918. Despite being disabled in the right hand he returned to France on 14th October via Folkestone and Boulogne and served with 15th Battalion from 27th October. On 7th November 1918, only four days before the war ended, Arthur was severely wounded at Limont Fontaine, near Maubeuge, France and died later the same day. His body was recovered after the war and lies in Dourlers Communal Cemetery Extension, France (II C 24). He is commemorated in a number of other places:

The Wandsworth VC and GC memorial. Arthur Lascelles' commemorative paving stone is close by (Memorials to Valour).

- Pennal, Gwynedd, Wales – named on the War Memorial, a memorial at St Peter ad Vincula Church and on the family grave in Pennal Cemetery.
- Bangor, Gwynedd – University College of North Wales War Memorial and the North Wales Heroes' Memorial.
- Edinburgh University War Memorial.
- War Memorial, Memorial Gardens, Tywyn, Gwynedd.
- Memorial in St George's Memorial Church, Ieper (Ypres), Belgium dedicated to the 447 old boys of Uppingham School who died in the Great War and the 250 who died in the Second World War.
- Uppingham School, Rutland – War Memorial, Victoria Cross Memorial and a plaque in the dining hall of Uppingham Lower School.
- Memorial at the Union Jack Club, London.

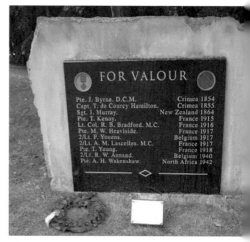

The commemorative stone honouring the eleven Durham Light Infantry soldiers awarded the VC in the grounds of the Durham Light Infantry Museum (Memorials to Valour).

- Memorial outside Wandsworth Town Hall, London to the recipients of the VC and GC who were born, lived, studied, worked or died in the borough.
- A commemorative stone honouring the eleven Durham Light Infantry soldiers awarded the VC was unveiled in the grounds of the Durham Light Infantry Museum on 8th September 2001 by Brigadier Robin MacGregor-Oakford MC. The stone was funded by the Durham Light Infantry veterans' group, 'The Faithful Inkerman Dinner Club'. The ceremony was attended by the Regiment's sole surviving VC holder, Captain Richard Annand.
- Named on one of eleven plaques honouring 175 men from overseas awarded the VC for the Great War. The plaques were unveiled by the Senior Minister of State at the Foreign & Commonwealth Office and Minister for Faith and Communities, Baroness Warsi, at a reception at Lancaster House, London on 26th June 2014 attended by The Duke of Kent and relatives of the VC recipients. The South African plaque is mounted at the Castle of Good Hope, Cape Town.
- The Department for Communities and Local Government decided to provide a commemorative paving stone at the birthplace of every Great War Victoria Cross recipient in the United Kingdom. A commemorative stone for Arthur was dedicated at Wandsworth Town Hall Gardens, London on 22nd April 2017 to mark the centenary of his award.

Administration of his will was granted to his widow in Birmingham on 14th June 1919. He left effects valued at £152/8/8. By the time of his death they had moved to 110 New Avenue, Acocks Green, Birmingham and Sophia moved later to Merionethshire, Wales. She was living at Rickstones, Lower Wokingham Road, Crowthorne, Berkshire at the time of her death, leaving effects valued at £5,785 to her son, Reginald.

In addition to the VC and MC he was awarded the 1914–15 Star (South African issue), British War Medal 1914–20 and Victory Medal 1914–19. The medals were purchased by the Regiment for £18,500 in 1983. The medals were held by the Durham Light Infantry Museum, Aykley Heads, Framwell Gate, Durham until it closed due to funding difficulties. The Durham Light Infantry Medal Collection is on loan to the Palace Green Library, Durham University, Stockton Road, Durham and is not on display but can be accessed by appointment.

Arthur is related to Flight Commander Francis 'Colin' Roy MacKenzie DSO (1892–1917), No.8 (Naval) Squadron RNAS. Arthur's great grandfather, General Francis Lascelles, had a daughter, Maria Lascelles (c.1813–47), who married Alexander L MacKenzie (c.1801–75). One of their children, John Fraser MacKenzie (born 1835), married Julia Margaret Linton (born 1838) and their son, Alexander Linton MacKenzie (1859–1933), married Marion Patrick Kerr (1856–1935), born in Melbourne, Australia. Colin was one of their three children. In addition Alexander and Maria MacKenzie had a daughter, Margaret Bushby MacKenzie, who married Edwin Lascelles, the VC's uncle. Colin was a medical student at Cambridge University in 1911. He was also a surgeon probationer in the Royal Naval Volunteer

Reserve on HMS *Spitfire* when war broke out. On 14th July 1915 he transferred to the RNAS and trained as a pilot at the Royal Naval Flying School at Eastchurch, Isle of Sheppey, gaining his licence on 2nd August. He was appointed flight sub-lieutenant on 21st September with seniority from 14th July, flight lieutenant from 30th June 1916 and flight commander on 31st December 1916. Colin was posted to Eastchurch, No.4 Wing, Dunkirk, back to Eastchurch and then to No.1 Wing. He was admitted to

Flight Commander Colin Roy MacKenzie DSO.

Colin MacKenzie's grave, one of three isolated CWGC burials in Achiet-le-Grand Communal Cemetery, with the Cross of Sacrifice in Achiet-le-Grand Communal Cemetery Extension in the background.

hospital at Malo-les-Bains, Dunkirk on 2nd January 1916. Colin was awarded the DSO (LG 25th October 1916) for an attack on a hostile kite balloon on 11th September. He was awarded the French Croix de Guerre on 17th September 1916 for destroying a hostile kite balloon. He was also twice Mentioned in Despatches. One recommendation was by Vice Admiral Dover for pressing home his part in an air raid on Mariakerke aerodrome on 24th April 1916. Vice Admiral Dover on 7th September noted his successful attack on a hostile kite balloon near Ostend, which fell to the ground in flames despite the number and efficiency of the anti-aircraft guns. The second MID was for his good work with No.8 Squadron while attached to the RFC. On 24th January 1917 he was flying Sopwith Pup (N5198) over Bapaume, heading east in pursuit of an enemy aircraft, when he was shot down by Leutnant von Keudell of Jasta 1 near Bihucourt. He is buried in Achiet-le-Grand Communal Cemetery (Grave 3). Von Keudell was killed on 15th February.

10053 SERGEANT JOHN MCAULAY
1st Battalion, Scots Guards

John McAulay was born at Rossland Place, Kinghorn, Fife, Scotland on 23rd December 1888. The surname has been seen with various spellings including Macaulay. His father, also John McAulay (1857–1918), was born at Cumbernauld, Dunbartonshire. He married Isabella née Stevenson (1863–1941), a farm servant born at Auchenbowie, St Ninians, Stirlingshire, in December 1885 at Plean, Bannockburn, Stirlingshire. They were living at East Plean before moving to Pirnhall Inn, St Ninians by 1901. John was a shale miner in 1888

and a coal miner in 1901. He was living at 4 Gillespie Terrace, Plean, Stirlingshire when he died. John junior had seven siblings:

Pirnhall Inn, St Ninians where the McAulay family lived in the early 1900s.

- Mary Ronald McAulay (1891–1920) died unmarried at 4 Gillespie Terrace, Plean. She had a son, William Rattray McAulay, in 1913.
- David Stevenson McAulay (1893–1969) was a coal miner living at 4 Gillespie Terrace, Plean at the time of his marriage to Jane Dewar (1892–1960), a housekeeper, in 1933 at The Manse, Plean.
- Isabella McAulay (1895–1951) was a fruiterer, living at Cardrowan, Plean.
- Agnes McAulay (1897–1996) was a domestic servant, living at 5 Gillespie Crescent, Plean at the time of her marriage to William Henderson Walls (c.1888–1951), a hairdresser, in 1921 at Pleanholm, Plean. They had a son, Ian Walls, in 1926.
- Margaret Stevenson McAulay (1899–1988) was a domestic servant, living at 2 Golf Place, Troon, Ayrshire at the time of her marriage to Thomas Melrose (c.1895–1957), a chauffeur, in 1927 at Troon, Ayrshire. Thomas later became a fruit salesman. They had two children – Isabella Stevenson Melrose 1930 and Mary Glen Melrose 1933.
- James McAulay (1901–83) married Mary Reynolds (1901–70) in 1933 at Plean.
- Lilias Stevenson McAulay (1904–83) was living at 4 Gillespie Terrace, Plean at the time of her marriage to Malcolm Mckinnon Shaw (1904–90), a coal miner, in 1926 at The Manse, Plean. They lived at 21 Balfour Crescent, Plean and had a daughter, Isabella McAulay Shaw, in 1927.

John's paternal grandfather, Bernard McAulay (c.1837–1912) worked at various times as a limestone worker, railway surface man and quarry labourer. He married Mary née Ronald (c.1835–1914) in 1853 at Airdrie, Lanarkshire. She was born in Co Mayo, Ireland. In addition to John they had nine other children:

- Thomas McAulay (1856–63).
- Ann 'Annie' McAulay (1857–1942), a twin with John, married Patrick Hughes (c.1853–1913) in 1878 at Kilsyth. He was born in Ireland. They had five children – James Hughes 1880, Patrick Hughes 1889, Michael Hughes 1890, Elizabeth Hughes 1891 and Anne Hughes 1900.
- Mary McAulay (born c.1861).
- Anthony McAulay (1862–1940) married Jane Ann Forfar (1869–1951) in 1897. They had a son, Anthony McAulay, in 1898.
- Margaret McAulay (born 1865).
- Agnes McAulay (1867–1955) married Peter Ferguson (c.1855–1940) in 1895. They had six children – Donald Ferguson 1897, Peter Ferguson 1899, Margaret Ferguson 1901, James Ferguson 1905, John Ferguson 1908 and Mary Ferguson 1910.

- Thomas McAulay (1869–1957).
- James McAulay (1871–1947) married Agnes Keir (1873–1911) in 1894 at Sandyknowes, Cumbernauld. They had nine children – Agnes Keir McAulay 1893, Thomas James McAulay 1895, Robert Keir McAulay 1897, Mary McAulay 1899, John McAulay 1900, Susan Robertson McAulay 1901, John McAulay 1904, Agnes Keir McAulay 1906 and James McAulay 1910. James married Isabella Rattray (1890–1951) in 1913 and they had four children – William Rattray McAulay 1913, Helen McIntyre McAulay 1914, Isobella Rattray McAulay 1916 and Janet McAulay 1926.
- Janet McAulay (born 1873) married James Hall in 1895. They had two sons – James Hall 1898 and William Hall 1900.

His maternal grandfather, Nicol Stevenson (c.1829–76), a coal miner, married Elizabeth née Johnston (1833–1908) in 1851. In addition to Isabella they had eleven other children:

- William Stevenson (born 1856), a coal miner, married Janet Bennett (born c.1855) in 1874. They had five children – Nicol Stevenson 1882, William Stevenson 1885, Janet Stevenson 1887, John Stevenson 1889 and Elizabeth Stevenson 1890.
- Margaret Stevenson (born 1856).
- John Stevenson (1858–1922), a coal miner, married Martha Goldie Anderson (1858–1928) in 1891 at Bannockburn.
- Agnes Stevenson (1860–81).
- Nicol Stevenson (1860–1935), a coal miner, married Janet Hutton (1864–1947) in 1885. They had five children – Nicol Stevenson 1886, Ann Stevenson 1888, Lizzie Stevenson 1890, Janet Stevenson 1895 and William Stevenson 1900.
- David Eadie Stevenson (1865–1937), a coal miner, married Margaret Laird (born c.1867) in 1897 at Bannockburn.
- Elizabeth Johnstone Richardson Stevenson (1867–1901).
- George Sneddon Stevenson (1869–1935) was a carter living at Beanmarket Close, Falkirk at the time of his marriage to Janet Docherty (born c.1869), a housekeeper, in December 1891 at Falkirk Parish Church. They were living at 23 Mayfield Street, Glasgow in 1911. He became an inspector with the Glasgow Cleansing Department. They had five children including – George Stevenson c.1897, Nicol Stevenson 1901, Robert Stevenson c.1903 and William Stevenson c.1906.
- Robert Stevenson (born 1871).
- Lilias Stevenson (1873–1938) married James Muir Rollo (1870–1959) in 1894. They had five children – James Muir Rollo 1896, Elizabeth Johnston Stevenson Rollo 1897, Nichol Walter Robert Stevenson Rollo 1900, Lilias Margaret Stevenson Rollo 1902 and Mary Munn Rollo 1905.
- Janet Bennett Stevenson (born 1876).

John was educated at Milton School, East Plean 13th May 1895–29th May 1903. He was employed as a miner at East Plean Colliery before joining the Glasgow Northern Police Force on 27th February 1911. After four weeks training in the muster hall of the Central Police Office, Turnbull Street he was appointed to E (Northern) Division on 27th March. John won the police heavy weight boxing championship 1912. He was a sergeant when war broke out.

Central Police Office, Turnbull Street, Glasgow.

John enlisted in the Scots Guards at Glasgow on 3rd September 1914. He was described as 5′ 9¾″ tall, weighing 200 lbs, with fair complexion, brown eyes, light brown hair and his religious denomination was Presbyterian. He joined the 3rd Battalion at Caterham, Surrey on 5th September and was appointed unpaid lance corporal on 13th November. Promoted lance corporal backdated to 12th November 1914. John arrived in France on 5th January 1915, having embarked at Southampton the previous day to join the 1st Battalion. Appointed acting corporal 25th February–

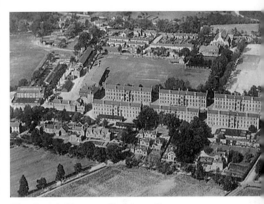

The Guards Depot at Caterham, Surrey.

30th March 1915. He was admitted to a field ambulance on 30th March and to 8th General Hospital at Rouen on 1st April with synovitis. On 3rd April he was evacuated to Britain on SS *Oxfordshire* and was taken on the strength of the 3rd Battalion on 7th April.

On 17th August he embarked at Southampton to return to the 1st Battalion in France. Appointed paid lance corporal on 1st October and acting corporal/acting unpaid lance sergeant on 14th October. Later he was promoted corporal and appointed unpaid lance sergeant and acting sergeant backdated to 1st October. John was granted leave 19th–25th February 1916, was promoted sergeant on 10th July and was awarded Class Pay on 3rd September 1916. **Mentioned in General Sir Douglas Haig's Despatch dated 13th November 1916, LG 4th January 1917.** He attended an infantry training course at Fourth Army School 10th February–18th March 1917 and was granted special leave to Britain 13th–29th April. **Awarded the DCM for his actions near Ypres on 31st July 1917. He cleared two strongly held pillboxes, killing all the occupants and taking charge of his platoon when the officer was killed. Whenever a sniper's post was located he headed for it and accounted for several singlehandedly, LG 17th September 1917.**

SS *Oxfordshire* (8,648 tons) was built in 1912 by Harland & Wolff at Belfast. On 2nd August 1914 she was the first ship to be requisitioned for military service. She was converted into Naval Hospital Ship No.1 with 562 beds and was sent to Scapa Flow on 25th September. She later moved to the English Channel to undertake Army hospital work. In April 1915 she deployed as the base hospital ship at Mudros, where she assisted in the ANZAC withdrawal from Gallipoli. She served in the Persian Gulf and German East Africa during 1916 and in 1918 became a hospital ship in the English Channel. She was decommissioned on 24th March 1919, having made 235 voyages

without a single breakdown and having carried 50,000 wounded, the highest of any hospital ship in the war. On 3rd September 1939 she was requisitioned again and converted into Hospital Ship No. 6 with 500 beds. On 11th November she sailed for Freetown, Sierra Leone as the base hospital ship. In September 1942 she deployed to the Mediterranean. On 29th October 1944 she was damaged by a bomb near miss between Ancona and Bari. That November she went to the Far East and was loaned to the US 7th Fleet during the landings on Okinawa. After the war she repatriated the wounded from Hong Kong and in May 1946 brought home the sick from the Near and Far East. She also repatriated Indian troops from Basra to Bombay, made four North Atlantic crossings with refugees and in 1948 brought home troops from Palestine. On 19th July she was decommissioned having carried 22,321 casualties, again the highest of any hospital ship in the war. That September she was chartered to Jeddah with pilgrims before being refitted. In April 1949 she made her first voyage for the International Refugee Organisation to Australia and in 1950 was used to move troops between Trieste and Port Said. In 1951 she was sold to the Pan-Islamic Steamship Co and was used on the Karachi–Jeddah pilgrim service and later in the year operated between Karachi and Chittagong. She was broken up at Karachi in 1958 after forty-six years of outstanding service.

The DCM was presented by Field Marshal Sir Douglas Haig on 18th August 1917.

Awarded the VC for his actions at Fontaine-Notre-Dame, France on 27th November 1917, LG 11th January 1918. John was granted leave in Britain 6th February–18th March 1918. The VC was presented by the King at Buckingham Palace on 16th March 1918. Appointed acting company sergeant major 9th–23rd April. He was posted to the 3rd Battalion in England on 12th May 1918 as a drill instructor. He was presented with a silver cigarette case by Major The Earl of Stair on behalf of the Sergeants' Mess, Scots Guards at Wellington Barracks, London. Arthur Kinnaird's parents presented him with a clock as a mark of their appreciation for his compassionate act. The

Field Marshal Sir Douglas Haig, Commander of the British Expeditionary Force, presented John McAulay with his DCM in August 1917.

family donated the clock to Glasgow Police Museum in 2007. He also received gifts from his former colleagues in the Police Force and from the people of Plean. John was demobilised to the Class Z Reserve on 25th January 1919.

The Glasgow Royal Maternity Hospital, where John's first wife, Isabella, and baby son, John, died in December 1920, was founded as the Glasgow Lying-in Hospital and Dispensary in Greyfriars Wynd in 1834. By 1860 it had moved to this location at Rottenrow, the name by which it became widely known. By 2001 the fabric of the building had deteriorated and the Hospital moved to a new extension of Glasgow Royal Infirmary. The Rottenrow site was sold to the University of Strathclyde and the building was demolished. The site is now Rottenrow Gardens (Scotsman).

John receives a silver cigarette case from Major The Earl of Stair on behalf of the Sergeants' Mess, Scots Guards at Wellington Barracks, London.

Sergeant John McAuley with a tug of war team at a Blind Veterans UK meeting in 1918. He helped the charity in Regent's Park, coaching physical training, before being demobilised.

John had an affair with Helen Maclean (born c.1890) while he was stationed in London in late 1918. A son, Simon Maclean (24th August 1919–16th January 2007), was born at Hampstead, London. He was placed in a home soon after birth and had no contact with either parent. He changed his surname to Harding and married Joan Clark (born 1920) in 1946. They had a son, Raymond J Harding, in 1947, who became a police sergeant and married Eileen D Gladman (born 1948) in 1969.

John married Isabella Horn (1889–1920), a dressmaker, on 22nd April 1919. She was living at 154 Oxford Street, Glasgow. They lived at 58 Oxford Street, Glasgow. Isabella gave birth to a son, John Harding McAulay, on 25th December 1920 in the Maternity Hospital, Glasgow, but there were complications with the birth and she died on 27th December. Baby John died the next day. Isabella's parents were Gavin Horn, a commercial traveler, and Elizabeth née Perry.

John married Catherine Thomson (c.1890–13th December 1963), a drysalter's assistant of 197 Crown Street, Glasgow, on 1st August 1923 at Abbotsford Parish Church, Glasgow. She was living at 915 Aitkenhead Road, Glasgow at the time of her death at David Elder Infirmary, Glasgow. They had a daughter, Isabella Stevenson McAulay, on 26th October 1924 at 58 Oxford Street, Glasgow. She married Raymond Skea (1932–69) in 1966.

Catherine's father, Alexander Thomson (born c.1853), an engine fitter of 75 Surrey Street, Glasgow, married Agnes née Maxwell (1859–1929), a domestic servant, in 1881. In addition to Catherine they had at least one other daughter, Mina Thomson.

John returned to the Glasgow Police (Northern Division) as a constable on 13th January 1919 (No.125D). He was promoted sergeant on 11th June 1919 and was posted to H (Maryhill) Division, but a

Crown Street, Glasgow where John's second wife, Catherine, was living when they married on 1st August 1923.

few weeks later transferred to D (Southern) Division. He was promoted inspector in the Central Division on 27th September 1922. He transferred to A (Central) Division on 9th June 1926, where he remained for the rest of his service. John was twice commended by the Chief Constable and retired on pension on 31st January 1946.

John attended the VC Garden Party at Buckingham Palace on 26th June 1920. He was a Freemason (Greyfriars Lodge No.1221 and Pilgrim Lodge) from May 1924. He also attended the VC Dinner at the Royal Gallery of the House of Lords, London on 9th November 1929 and the Victory Day Celebration Dinner and Reception at The Dorchester, London on 8th June 1946. He was one of four VCs to attend the funeral of Henry May VC at Riddrie Cemetery, Glasgow, on 26th July 1941. He was presented to King George V and Queen Mary when they visited Scotland on the occasion of the 25th Anniversary Parade for members of the British Legion.

John McAulay died at 915 Aikenhead Road, Burnside, Glasgow on 14th January 1956 and is buried at New Eastwood Cemetery, Glasgow (Section L–V11, Lair 139). He is commemorated in a number of other places:

John McAulay's gravestone in New Eastwood Cemetery, Glasgow.

John McAulay while serving as a sergeant in the Glasgow Police.

The Distinguished Conduct Medal was instituted by Royal Warrant on 4th December 1854 for warrant officers and below for 'distinguished, gallant and good conduct in the field'. It ranked second only to the Victoria Cross and equated to the Distinguished Service Order for officers when awarded for gallantry. It was the first official decoration awarded by the British to recognise acts of individual gallantry in the Army. During the First World War there was concern that the number of medals being awarded would devalue it. As a result the Military Medal was instituted on 25th March 1916, as a lesser award for bravery. Nevertheless 24,591 DCMs were awarded during the First World War plus 472 Bars and nine second Bars. In 1942 other ranks of the Royal Navy and Royal Air Force also became eligible. In 1993 the DCM was discontinued after a major review of the honours system, which removed distinctions of rank in respect of awards for bravery. With the Conspicuous Gallantry Medal and the Distinguished Service Order when awarded for gallantry, these three decorations were replaced by the Conspicuous Gallantry Cross as the second highest award for gallantry for all ranks of all services.

- Cambrai Company, Army Foundation College, Harrogate comprises six platoons named after VC winners in the Battle of Cambrai, including 7 (McAulay VC) Platoon.
- Named on The Household Division (Foot Guards) Honour Roll for the Victoria Cross in the Sergeants' Mess, Wellington Barracks, London.
- Display at the Glasgow Police Museum, 30 Bell Street, Merchant City, Glasgow.
- The Ayrshire poet, Matthew Anderson, wrote a poem in his honour in February 1918.
- The Department for Communities and Local Government decided to provide a commemorative paving stone at the birthplace of every Great War Victoria Cross recipient in the United Kingdom. John's stone was dedicated at the War Memorial, Rossland Place, Kinghorn, Fife, Scotland on 26th November 2017 to mark the centenary of his award.

In addition to the VC and DCM he was awarded the 1914–15 Star, British War Medal 1914–20, Victory Medal 1914–19 with Mentioned-in-Despatches Oakleaf, Defence Medal (1939–45), George V Silver Jubilee Medal 1935, George VI Coronation Medal 1937 and Queen Elizabeth II Coronation Medal 1953. His VC was presented to the Scots Guards in 1964 by his daughter Isabella and is held by RHQ Scots Guards.

240171 LANCE CORPORAL ROBERT GORDON McBEATH
1/5th Battalion, Seaforth Highlanders (Ross-shire Buffs, The Duke of Albany's)

Robert McBeath was born on 5th December 1897 at Fraserburgh as Robert McBeath Murison Shepherd. His mother Williamina née Murison (22nd March 1865–23rd March 1933) married Robert George Shepherd in 1883. She was running a small grocery shop at 54 Mid Street, Fraserburgh in 1891 living with her children Alexander, Isabella, Christina and Henry. Her husband was not with the family.

Robert senior stated on the birth certificate that he was not the father of this child. Williamina had eight children in total, four of them illegitimate. She was unable to look after Robert and he was adopted by Robert MacKenzie (born c.1873 at Kinlochbervie) and his sister Mrs Barbara MacIntosh (born c.1869 as McKenzie). Robert MacKenzie was a gardener in 1911 and Barbara was a fish worker, living at 8 Kinlochbervie.

Williamina was a fish worker (herring) in 1901, living on her own at 27 Hunter's Lane, Fraserburgh (age recorded as thirty-three). Her seven other children were:

Kinlochbervie, Sutherland.

- Alexander Shepherd (born 1885) was under detention on the Empress Industrial School ship on the Clyde In 1901.
- Isabella Wiseman Shepherd (born 1886) married William Mitchell in 1916 at St Mary, Dundee, Angus.
- Christina Cardno Shepherd (1888-1957) married James McKinnon in 1913.
- Henry Fyfe Shepherd (born 1891) emigrated to Canada and is buried at Vancouver, British Columbia.
- James Barrie Murison or Shepherd (born 1894) had his birth certificate changed to name the father as James Barrie of Fraserburgh.

Inshegra School 1879–1970 is now a restaurant and B&B.

- William Murison or Shepherd (born 1900) was adopted by a childless Fraserburgh couple.
- Alister Barrie Murison or Shepherd (1904–06).

Robert's maternal grandfather, William Murison (born 22nd March 1821), a mariner, married Mary Lyons (28th December 1828–1st August 1876) on 8th December 1848 at St Nicholas, Aberdeen. She was a servant living at Grant Street, Cullen in 1841. They were living at Shore Street, Fraserburgh in 1851, when she was a servant working for a grocer and spirit retailer. They had moved to 39 Bread Street, Fraserburgh by 1871. In addition to Williamina they had five other children, all born in Fraserburgh, except Alexander, who was born in Sheffield:

- Alexander (born 8th August 1849) was an apprentice mason in 1871 at Cairnhill, Aberdeenshire.
- Jessie Murison (1853–8th March 1916) married William Rosie (1845–24th January 1928) on 7th November 1872 at Fraserburgh. They were living at 20 High Street, Fraserburgh in 1901. She died there at 90 High Street and he at 92 High Street. They had seven children – James Rosie 1874, Margaret Rosie c.1876, Sarah Rosie 1879, Jessie A Rosie 1883, David Rosie 1886, William Rosie 1889 and Jan Rosie 1893.
- Christian Murison 1857.
- Margaret Murison 1862.
- George Murison (born 2nd August 1869).

Robert was educated at Inshegra School, Kinlochbervie and enlisted underage on 12th August 1914 at Golpsie, Sutherland (758 later 240171). He went to France with the Battalion on 1st May 1915 and was wounded on 16th November 1916. Having been evacuated to Britain, he returned to France on 8th March and was promoted lance corporal on 24th July. **Awarded the VC for his actions at Ribécourt-la-Tour, France on 20th November 1917, LG 11th January 1918.** The VC was presented by the King at Buckingham Palace on 16th February 1918.

Robert travelled home after the investiture but was unable to reach Kinlochbervie due to heavy snow and alighted at Golspie, where 5th Seaforth Highlanders had its pre-war headquarters. He was met at the station by a piper and a reception was held, during which he was presented with an inscribed gold watch, a silver tea service and £367.

Robert McBeath married Barbara née McKay (20th June 1899–23rd September 1946) at St Andrew, Edinburgh on 19th February 1918. She was born at Kinlochbervie as MacKay and was also married under that name. There were no children. Barbara's father, John McKay (1875–1900), a fisherman, married Williamina née Morrison (born 1875 at Kinlochbervie) in 1897 at Fraserburgh. John drowned on 30th March 1900 while fishing with his father off Sheigra, Sutherland. In addition to Barbara they had two other children:

- John McKay (born 1897) married Henrietta Belashmie at Morningside, Edinburgh in 1918 and they had several children including – John McKay 1919, William McKay 1920 and Robert McKay 1922.
- Johan 'Joan' Williamina McKay (1900–86) married John MacKenzie in 1928 and they had a son, William McKay McKenzie in 1935.

Golpsie High Street.

Williamina married Hugh McKay in November 1908 at the United Free Church, Oldshore School, Kinlochbervie and they had at least three children:

- Georgina 'Ina' McKay (born 1909).
- Dolina McKay (born 1910) married Frederick William Cunningham in 1954 at Morningside, Edinburgh.
- William McKay (1914–90).

Golspie station where Robert was greeted by a piper before a reception in the town in February 1918.

Robert was promoted corporal on 25th August 1918 and lance sergeant on 23rd November. He was discharged on 12th or 29th March 1919. He was a Freemason, initiated in St Mary's Caledonian Operative Lodge No.339 in Inverness on 12th July 1919. He was awarded a farm on his return to Scotland by the Duke of Sutherland. However, he didn't settle, sold the farm and emigrated to Canada in August 1919, arriving at Quebec. They moved to Vancouver, where he worked at Coughlan shipyards before joining the British Columbia Provincial Police and later the Vancouver Police Department on 12th August 1921. He attended the VC Garden Party at Buckingham Palace on 26th June 1920. Robert renewed his Masonic connections in Canada and he became an affiliate member of Mount Hermon Lodge No.7 in Vancouver and was Passed on 29th October 1921. On 18th April 1922 he was raised to the sublime degree of a Master Mason and on 18th May 1922 he received his Grand Lodge Diploma from the Grand Lodge of Scotland.

On 9th October 1922 Robert was on patrol with Detective R Quirk on Granville Street, Vancouver

Robert's wife, Barbara.

Coughlan's shipyard at shift change in May 1918. J Coughlan & Sons, steel fabricators, built twenty-one cargo ships for the Imperial Munitions Board at False Creek, Vancouver during the Great War. The yard was dormant soon after the war, but was revived as Hamilton Bridge (Western) Co, which changed name to Western Bridge & Steel Fabrication in 1941, to build cargo ships for the war effort. The old Coughlan shipyard site became the Athlete's Village for the 2010 Winter Olympics.

when they saw a car swerving across the road. Robert stepped into the road and signalled the driver to stop. He attempted to avoid the officers, who jumped onto the car's running boards and succeeded in getting the driver, Fred Deal, to stop. Robert took Deal to a patrol box while Quirk remained with the female passenger, Marjorie Earl. Deal tried to break free and a struggle ensued, described by Quirk, *I heard a sudden roar behind me and saw McBeath and the man struggling. As I went to McBeath's aid I saw the flash of a gun. It was pointed directly at my breast but I swung it aside just as it went off and the bullet passed through my hand. A second shot struck me in the side of the head as I grappled with the man and I fell. There was another shot and McBeath fell on top of me. As I tried to crawl from under McBeath the man who had moved off some distance fired again. I guess that was the bullet that went through the*

Robert in Vancouver Police uniform.

shoulder of my coat. I rolled McBeath on his back and fired. Then I followed him a little way and we again exchanged shots. I could not keep up and went back to McBeath.

Both officers were rushed to St Paul's Hospital, but Robert died shortly after arrival. A witness told police where Deal was hiding and Constable Langham arrested him shortly thereafter. Deal was Earl's driver at the time and she was described as a *middle-aged southern belle gone astray*. In January 1923 Deal was convicted of Robert's murder and the attempted murder of Quirk and sentenced to hang. However, reasonable doubt was cast on the prosecution's case. Deal had been beaten several times while in custody, police witnesses lied in court and there is evidence that McBeath may have targeted Deal and Earl for harassment and possibly violence on the night of the shooting. In addition, the bullet that killed Robert McBeath was fired from a police service revolver. There was a retrial in March 1923 that resulted in Deal being sentenced to life imprisonment, serving sixteen years

The original St Paul's Hospital founded in 1894 was a four-storey wooden building with twenty-five beds. It was run by the Sisters of Providence and opened a school of nursing in 1907. In 1912 the original building was demolished and replaced with the structure shown here to accommodate 200 patients.

The junction of Granville and Davie Streets in Vancouver where the incident that resulted in Robert McBeath's death took place.

in Canada before completing his sentence near his home in Florida, USA.

Robert's funeral was one of the largest ever seen in Vancouver. Thousands of people filed past the open coffin to pay their respects at Vancouver Police Station on 12th October. All stores and banks were closed and thousands of people watched the funeral procession, which took twenty minutes to pass the main Post Office. During the

Marjorie Earl (Vancouver City Archives).

Fred Deal (Vancouver City Archives).

church service Reverend JS Henderson recalled how Robert had won the Victoria Cross and added, *I would that in the solemn atmosphere of this hour we might catch a vision of his great noble spirit, the high purpose and devotion and enthusiasm with which he gave himself to his life's mission. Canada's greatest need is just such men. This brave young officer will not have died in vain if his tragic passing will awaken a new civic spirit in relation to our police force – a new purpose on the part of the authorities to rid this city of that herd of undesirables, who through someone's blunder has made Vancouver its breeding and feeding ground.* There was also a civic funeral under the auspices of Mount Hermon Lodge No.7. The procession, stretching for several blocks, was led by 377 Freemasons, followed by contingents of the Vancouver Police, including the Pipe Band, Vancouver Fire Department, Royal Canadian Mounted Police, Seaforth

Highlanders Regiment, Irish Fusiliers of Canada, British Columbia Electric Railway, Canadian Pacific Railway, hundreds of World War One veterans, members of the Foresters, St Andrew's and Caledonian Societies and bringing up the rear several hundred members of the public. The Mayor of Vancouver, CE Tisdale, who was also Deputy Grand Master of The Grand Lodge of British Columbia, led members of the civil council. Robert was cremated at Mountain View Crematorium, Vancouver and his ashes were interred in Masonic Section 193, Lot 6, where there is now a headstone.

Robert McBeath's memorial headstone at Mountain View Crematorium.

Robert is commemorated in a number of other places:

- *R.G. McBeath VC* – a patrol vessel (8.3 tons) (818067) built in 1994 by Daigle Welding & Marine Ltd, Campbell River, British Columbia for the Vancouver Police Department Marine Squad. It was the primary vessel for patrolling the city's shoreline, marinas and Fraser River. It was withdrawn from service in 2008 and replaced by a new *R.G. McBeath VC* (9.5 tons) (No.832175) built in 2008, also by Daigle Welding & Marine Ltd.
- McBeath Court, Kinlochbevie, Lairg, Sutherland.
- Cambrai Company, Army Foundation College, Harrogate comprises six platoons named after VC winners in the Battle of Cambrai, including 11 (McBeath VC) Platoon.
- Memorial cairn overlooking Loch Innis, at Kinlochbervie, dedicated on 12th September 2009.
- Memorial cairn at the Vancouver Police Tactical Training Centre dedicated on 14th June 2010 to Constable Robert McBeath and other officers killed in the line of duty.
- His picture hangs in the lobby of the Vancouver Police Headquarters.

The Vancouver Police Department's Patrol Vessel *R.G. McBeath VC.*

Barbara returned to Scotland two months after her husband's death and married Robert's friend, Alexander MacDonald (born c.1900), at Anderston, Glasgow in 1924. There were no children.

Memorial cairn at Kinlochbervie (Memorials to Valour).

The Victory Medal (or Inter-Allied Victory Medal) was first proposed by French Marshal Ferdinand Foch as a common award for all the nations allied against the Central Powers. Regardless of nationality, each medal is 36mm in diameter, the ribbon is a double rainbow and the obverse shows winged victory (except Japan and Siam, where winged victory has no relevance). For British Empire forces the medal was issued to all who received the 1914 or 1914–15 Star and to almost all who received the British War Medal. The British alone struck 6,335,000 Victory medals. These three medals were known as Pip, Squeak and Wilfred after a popular newspaper comic strip. To qualify for the Victory Medal recipients had to be mobilised for war service and have entered a theatre of war between 5th August 1914 and 11th November 1918, plus Russia 1919–20 and mine clearance in the North Sea until 30th November 1919. Those Mentioned in Despatches wore an oakleaf on the Victory Medal ribbon, as shown here.

In addition to the VC he was awarded the 1914–15 Star, British War Medal 1914–20 and Victory Medal 1914–19. The VC was presented to the Queen's Own Highlanders Museum by his sister-in-law, Mrs Jean Mackenzie. The VC is held by the Highlanders Museum, Fort George, Ardersier, Inverness-shire.

The inscribed gold watch presented to Robert in February 1918 vanished after his widow returned to Scotland. It is possible that Barbara sold the watch to pay for her passage home. In 2013 an off-duty Vancouver police officer, Don Tymchyshyn, overheard a conversation in a pub in which watch seller, Soren Lyth, talked about an antique watch that once belonged to Robert McBeath VC. The watch had been in the Lyth family for thirty years and had belonged to Soren's father, who had also been a watchmaker. Soren donated the watch to the Vancouver Police Department Museum.

CAPTAIN ALLASTAIR MALCOLM CLUNY MCREADY-DIARMID
4th attached 17th Battalion, The Duke of Cambridge's Own (Middlesex Regiment)

Allastair McReady-Diarmid was born at 8 Grove Road, New Southgate, Southgate, Middlesex on 21st March 1888, registered as Arthur Malcolm Drew and known later as Arthur Malcolm McReady-Drew. His father, Herbert Leslie Drew (1859–1st June 1933), was a clerk in the Higher Division of the Post Office in 1881. He married Fanny Annie née McReady (22nd February 1862–1931) on 20th October 1883 at St Helier, Jersey, Channel

Islands. She was a milliner in 1881, living with her widowed mother. They were living at 100 Sandmere Road, Clapham, London in 1885, at 1 Harold Terrace, Hermitage Road, Tottenham in 1891, at Granville Road, South Mimms, Barnet, Hertfordshire in 1901 and at 71 Goldsmith Avenue, Acton in 1911. By 1901 Fanny was an authoress. Herbert left effects valued at £1,149/18/4. Allastair/Arthur had four siblings:

- Herbert Clive Drew (1884–1968) graduated BSc, emigrated to Australia and became a banker. He married Blanche Havergal Walters (1884–1955) in 1916. They were living at 17 Grandview Grange, Armadale, Victoria in 1919 and at 535 Waverley Road, Malvern East, Victoria in 1949, by when he had changed his name to McReady-Drew. Herbert was living at 410 Wattletree Road, Higgins, Victoria in 1967.
- Harry Dugald Keith Drew (1886–1959) was a 2nd class Civil Service clerk in 1911. He published several articles in the *Journal of the Chemical Society* and also published *Heterocyclic Systems containing Tellurium in the Ring* in 1926.
- Douglas Laurel Drew (27th February 1890–1965) changed his name to McCready Drew. He was educated at Christ's Hospital School (OTC five years) and St John's College, Oxford. On 9th December 1914 he applied for a commission and was commissioned from the Officer Training Corps into the Royal Field Artillery on 28th December. He was described as 5′ 9½″ tall and weighed 154 lbs. He served in 12th Siege Battery RGA and was promoted lieutenant on 20th May 1916. Douglas was posted to 1st Field Survey Group on 28th May 1916 and was appointed acting captain on 4th August 1917 while commanding a sound ranging section attached to a field survey company RE. On 20th November he was posted to 4th Field Survey Company RE. He was admitted to 141st Field Ambulance with pyrexia of unknown origin on 29th October 1918 and discharged from 8th General Hospital on 3rd November to the Cyclist Base Depot. On 5th November he left for GHQ and on 26th November was granted special leave in Britain from 5th Field Survey Battalion RE until 26th December. He was demobilised from No.1 Dispersal Unit, Dover, Kent on 20th January 1919, giving his address as 94 Cambridge Street, Warwick Square, London. He was awarded the MC (LG 3rd June 1919). Douglas was a classics teacher by 1926 and published *The Allegory of the Aenid* in 1927. He applied to rejoin the Army in September 1938 but had no reserve

Allastair's family lived in Sandmere Road, Clapham in 1885.

liability and had exceeded the age limit. He married Jean M Owens in 1955 at Liverpool, Lancashire.
• Valentine Gwendoline McReady Drew (1892–1959) was living as a spinster at Wyches, Deadherne Lane, Chalfont St Giles, Buckinghamshire at the time of her death on 22nd June 1959 at Freeland Hospital, Witney, Oxfordshire. She left effects valued at £8,474/19/3.

Allastair's paternal grandfather, Henry Thomas Drew (c.1830–8th May 1905), was a clerk in the Higher Division of Her Majesty's Customs. He married Kate née Harrington (c.1834–1912) in 1853. They were living at 2 Kenilworth Road, Bethnal Green, London in 1861, at 8 Shaftesbury Terrace, Grove Road, Bethnal Green, London in 1871 and at 2 Gresham Villas, Lower Fore Street, Edmonton, Middlesex in 1881. By 1905 they were living at 1 St Peter's Road, St Leonards-on-Sea, Sussex. Henry left effects valued at £900/3/7. Kate was living with her daughter at 11 St Peters Road, St Leonards-on-Sea in 1911. In addition to Herbert they had three other children:

• Harry Fabino Drew (born 1854).
• Frederick Oscar Drew (1856–13th August 1919), known as Oscar, was a clerk in the Civil Service and worked at one time for the Ministry of Works. He married Theresa Carolina Antonia Ottilia Gibbs née Brévert (born c.1852 at Boulogne, France), known as Antonia, in 1882 at the Strand, London. She had a daughter from her previous marriage born c.1875 in Kent, believed to be Elsa Tula Gibbs. Antonia grew up in England and her family ran a dress shop off Oxford Street, London. She was living as a widow with her brother George and his wife Clementine at 14 Langham Place, Marylebone in 1881. In the 1890s Antonia became one of the first women to be elected to the Fulham Board of Guardians. Oscar was an elected member of Fulham Vestry, predecessor to the London Borough of Fulham, and was on the committee that ran Fulham's first free public library. He was a keen supporter of Fulham Football Club and was involved in funding the Craven Cottage ground and was also the main football correspondent for the *West London and Fulham Times* under the pseudonym Merula. By the time of his death at the East Sussex County Asylum, Hellingly in 1919 they were living at 12 Wellington Road, Hastings, Sussex. He left effects valued at £1,819/13/6 to his widow.
• Kate Maud Drew (1862–1941) died unmarried.

Allastair's paternal grandparents were living on Lower Fore Street, Edmonton in 1881.

Allastair's uncle, Frederick Oscar Drew, was involved in funding Fulham Football Club's Craven Cottage ground. A new 5,000 seat stand on Stevenage Road was built in 1905, designed by Archibald Leitch. At the same time mud banks on the other sides were terraced with crush barriers, which Leitch patented. The Johnny Haynes Stand is now Grade II listed.

His maternal grandfather, Frederick McReady (also seen as Mcready) (born c.1828 at St Helier, Jersey, Channel Islands) married Fanny Susannah née Rapsey (born 1837 at St Helier) on 24th March 1861 at St Saviour, Jersey. At the time she was living with her sister Mary Ann Gibbons and her husband William Gibbons, a brass founder, at 25 Colomberie, St Helier. Frederick was a musician in 1861 when they were living at Belmont Place, St Helier. He was a music teacher in 1871 and they were living at 7 Chevalier Road, St Helier. Frederick died before 1881. Fanny was living with her children at 11B Tunnel Street, St Helier in 1881. By 1891 she was a night nurse, living with her two youngest children at 36 Pier Road, St Helier. In addition to Fanny they had six other children:

- Frederick Edmund McReady (21st September 1864–1937) married Emily Cordelia Hayward (1864–1940) in 1894 at Christchurch, Hampshire. She was born at Sturminster, Dorset. He was a motor trimmer in 1911 and they were living at 18 Aldershot Road, Kilburn, London. She was living at 15 Aldershot Road, Kilburn at the time of her death on 7th October 1940, leaving effects valued at £435/12/7 to her surviving child, Kate. They had three children – Kate Cordelia Macready 1896, Frederick Harry Macready 1900 and Dorothy Kathleen Macready 1901.
- Florence Minnie McReady (born 24th November 1866).
- Lilian Mary McReady (born 5th March 1869).
- Henrietta Blanche McReady (born 11th May 1871).
- Ernest William McReady (28th February 1874–1st April 1938) was a sailor in 1891. He was living at 3 Manor Place, London at the time of his death, leaving effects valued at £4,130/13/1 to his sister, Portia, and Valentine Gwendoline McReady-Drew.
- Portia Henrietta McReady (c.1876–1932) was a dressmaker's apprentice in 1891. She married Harold Eames Leach (1872–1932), an organ builder, c.1904. He was born at Bath, Somerset. They were living at 9 Rockliffe Road, Bath, Somerset

in 1911. Harold left effects valued at £1,296/13/8 to his widow. They had six children – Ernest Macready Leach 1904, William Victor Leach 1906, Colin Kenneth Leach 1907, Arthur Ian Leach 1910, Alan RA Leach 1912 and Portia MA Leach 1914.

Allastair was educated at:

- Queen Elizabeth's Grammar Preparatory School, Barnet April 1897–July 1904.
- Victoria College Jersey for one term in 1904. He was in the OTC.
- Ealing Grammar School.

Allastair never started a particular career and was more an outdoor type than an academic. His parents wanted him to go to Cambridge and then into the clergy, but he planned to travel. Neither plan materialised. He joined London University OTC on the outbreak of war and a medical on 11th December 1914 at Queen Alexandra's Military Hospital, Millbank passed him fit. He was described as 5′ 10½″ tall and weighed 147lbs. Allastair applied for a commission on 13th January 1915 in the name of AM McReady-Drew. His suitability for a commission was confirmed on 5th February and he was commissioned on 10th March in 4th Battalion. He changed name by deed poll to Allastair Malcolm Cluny McReady-Diarmid on 10th September 1915.

Allastair McReady-Diarmid married Hilda née Dainton (26th January 1890–21st July 1981), a nurse, on 20th September 1915 at Dursley, Gloucestershire. They lived at Springfield, Kingshill Road, Dursley and had a daughter, Alizon Hilda McReady-Diarmid (25th May 1917–6th January 1966). Alizon married James M Brown in 1940 and Cecil James Chidgey (1912–76) in 1947. Both marriages failed and there were no children. Cecil had married Winifred HD Weston in 1936 and

The foundation stone of Victoria College was laid on Queen Victoria's birthday, 24th May 1850, with about 12,000 people attending the ceremony. The College opened in September 1852 with ninety-eight pupils. At the time French was the official language in Jersey, but the new college was patterned on the English public school model and English was used from the outset. Queen Victoria visited the College in 1859. In 1901 College House was added to accommodate a small number of boarders (including the author 1968–74). In 1911 the College was expanded with the building of the quadrangle, partly seen on the right of the picture. Between it and the main building on the left is a statue of Sir Galahad, the College's First World War memorial. The College was used by German occupation forces 1940–45 for the Reichsarbeitsdienst and Feldkommandantur. The College now has 500 pupils. College House became part of a new Jersey College for Girls opened in 1999.

married Margaret EB Ratcliffe in 1954. Alizon was living at Hilary, Littlecroft Road, Egham, Surrey at the time of her death at St Peter's Hospital, Chertsey, Surrey leaving effects valued at £4,864.

Hilda's father, George Herbert Dainton (1862–1936), a tinsmith, married Emily née Bye (1860–1939). They were living at Parsonage Street, Dursley in 1887. By 1901 he was running his own business and they were living at Spring Cottage, Dursley. At the time of George's death at Golden Square Hospital, Westminster, London they were living at 13 Dane Road, St Leonards-on-Sea, Sussex. He left effects valued at £380/16/3. Emily died at Buchanan Hospital, St Leonards-on-Sea in 1939, leaving effects valued at £997/14/2. In addition to Hilda they had four other children:

- Percy Reginald Dainton (1884–1963), a tinsmith, married Alice England (1883–1957) in 1909. He was living at 26 Cambridge Avenue, Dursley at the time of his death. They had a son, Harold Percy Dainton, in 1912.
- Charles Edward Dainton (1886–87).
- Eveline/Evelyn Mabel Dainton (born 1887).
- Albert Dainton (born and died 1891).

Allastair was posted to 14th (Reserve) Battalion for training and landed in France on 8th October 1915. He joined 4th Battalion on 15th October. About May 1916 he was blown off a trench fire-step by a shell and continued serving for several weeks until a serious internal injury was discovered. He was sent on leave on 28th May, initially for a week, but this was subsequently extended to 4th September. He was struck off strength 4th Battalion on 23rd June and transferred to 14th (Reserve) Battalion until December 1916. During this time he spent four months in hospital and convalescing. Allastair returned to France on 6th December 1916 and joined 17th Battalion on 23rd June 1917. It is not known what he was doing in the interim. Promoted lieutenant on 1st July 1917 and acted as adjutant for a period in August 1917. He was appointed acting captain on 26th October. **Awarded the VC for his actions at Moeuvres, France on 30th November/1st December 1917, LG 15th March 1918.**

Allastair was killed during his VC action on 1st December 1917 and is commemorated on the Cambrai Memorial (Panel 9). He left effects valued at £213/6/6 to his widow. He is commemorated in a number of other places:

- Diarmid House, Victoria College, Mont Millais, St Helier, Jersey, Channel Islands.

Parsonage Street, Dursley where Hilda's family was living in 1887.

The College's five Houses are named after Old Victorian war heroes. Diarmid House was added in 2002 in the College's 150th year.

Allastair's name on the Cambrai Memorial.

- Victoria College, Jersey War Memorial.
- Dursley War Memorial, Gloucestershire.
- St James the Great Church, Dursley war memorial window.
- The Department for Communities and Local Government decided to provide a commemorative paving stone at the birthplace of every Great War Victoria Cross recipient in the United Kingdom. A commemorative stone for Allastair was dedicated at Grove Road, New Southgate, London on 1st December 2017 to mark the centenary of his award.

After Allastair's death Hilda settled at St Leonards-on-Sea, Sussex where she ran a confectionery business. She did not remarry and later lived at Hillary, Littlecroft Road, Egham, Surrey. She left effects valued at £60,752. Alizon, wearing her father's VC, laid a wreath at the Cenotaph, London on 11th November 1929 with Earl Jellicoe.

Victoria College pupils doffing their boaters to the First World War memorial, topped by a statue of Sir Galahad. Between the wars the actor Kenneth More was a pupil at the College. He got himself into trouble by adorning Sir Galahad with a school scarf.

In addition to the VC Allastair was awarded the 1914–15 Star, British War Medal 1914–20 and Victory Medal 1914–19. The VC was presented to his widow by the King at Buckingham Palace on 20th April 1918. Hilda presented his medals to the Middlesex Regiment in August 1973 and they were held by the Middlesex Regiment Museum at Bruce Castle, Lordship Lane, Tottenham. In 1992 the London Borough of Haringey wanted the rooms for a borough museum and asked the Middlesex Regiment to move elsewhere. As a result the Middlesex Regiment collection, including his medals, moved to the National Army Museum, Chelsea.

Dursley War Memorial is mounted on the gates leading to St James the Great Church. Allastair's name is on the panel on the left.

375499 PRIVATE WALTER MILLS
1/10th Battalion, The Manchester Regiment

Walter Mills was born at 13 Bond Street, Oldham, Lancashire on 21st July 1894. In his unit he was known as Spud. His father, James Mills (1868–1906), married Alice née Finney (c.1869–1916) on 21st April 1888. She was born at St John's, Newfoundland and was a tenter in a cotton factory in 1881, living with her parents at 3 Davison Street, Oldham. Both James and Alice gave their address as 25 Bankside Street, Oldham when they married. James was an iron turner in 1894 and a general labourer iron (driller) in 1901, when they were living at 2 Bond Street, Oldham. They had nine children of whom three did not survive infancy. In 1911 Alice was living at 4 Pernham Street, Oldham. Walter had five brothers:

- Fred Mills (30th May 1888–20th May 1971) married Annie Watson (1890–1960) in September 1907. At the time he was living with his mother at 4 Pernham Street and Annie was living a few doors away at No.10. By 1908 he was a driller and they were living at 1 Miles Street, Huddersfield Road, Oldham. By 1911 they had moved to 46 Newark Street, Oldham. He was a machine driller in a willow-making factory and she was a roving machine tenter in the cotton trade. Fred was later an insurance agent. They were living at 11 Suffolk Road, Blackpool, Lancashire at the time of her death, leaving effects valued at £623/3/4 to her husband. He was living at Seacroft, Hillsborough Road, Ilfracombe, Devon at the time of his death, leaving effects valued at £1,160. They had two daughters – Amy Mills 1908 and Veronica Mills 1926.
- Albert Mills (born c.1893) was a driller in a textile factory in 1911.
- James Mills (born c.1897) was a piecer in a textile factory in 1911. He served as a private in 1/6th Lancashire Fusiliers at Gallipoli, Egypt and in France. He was able to speak briefly with Walter just before the latter's final action.
- Robinson Mills (1898–1918).
- Edward Mills (born 1900) married Annie Heywood in 1925 at Ashton-under-Lyne, Lancashire. They had a son, Gordon Mills, in 1928.

Walter's paternal grandfather, John Mills, was an iron turner, who died before 1888. His maternal grandfather, Moses Finney (c.1831–87), was the son of James Finney (1797–1872) and Alice Woods (1797–1879). James, a weaver by trade, attested on 16th February 1811 in the 25th Regiment aged fourteen. He was discharged on 12th April 1831, unfit for further service, although his conduct was assessed as good and he was an efficient soldier. On discharge he was described as 5′ 7¾″ tall, with sandy hair, grey eyes and swarthy complexion. Moses attested in the 47th Regiment at Manchester, Lancashire on 11th May 1849 (1147) and served in the Mediterranean for five and half years and the Crimea for a year and ten months. He re-engaged at Aldershot on 11th December 1858. He married Mary Elizabeth née Poulter (1841–1913) on 10th June 1861 at St Bridget, Dublin, Ireland. Mary was born at Farnham, Surrey and was previously married to John Creed in 1859. They moved to Canada and he transferred to the Royal Canadian Rifles on 1st April 1863. He completed his service there on 28th April 1870, giving his trade as shoemaker and his intended place of residence as Oldham. During his service he was awarded four Good Conduct Badges (15th August 1857, 17th July 1862, 7th October 1867 and 7th October 1869, forfeited 3rd December 1857 (restored 17th July 1860) and 28th September 1866. His name was entered in the Defaulters' Book on several occasions and he was charged with being absent from barracks 30th September–6th October 1866. He was described as 5′ 9″ tall, with fresh complexion, brown eyes and brown hair when he was discharged at Chichester, Sussex on 2nd August 1870. Moses was a labourer in an iron works in 1871, living at 68 Alfred Street, Oldham, Lancashire and at 3 Davidson Street, Oldham in 1881. In addition to Alice they had five other children:

Walter's mother was born at St John's, Newfoundland.

Oldham just before the Great War.

- Mary Ann Finney (c.1863–1908) was born at Montreal, Canada. She married Wilfred Liley (1860–1918) in 1883 at Oldham. He was an overlooker of machine minders at a cotton mill in 1901 and they were living at 213 Coalshaw Green Road, Chadderton, Lancashire. They had at least three sons – Walter Liley 1886, Albert Liley 1887 and George Liley 1890. The first two did not survive infancy.
- George Henry Finney (1866–1942) was born at St John's, Newfoundland. He married Rachel Ann Goodier (1868–1925) in 1891 at Oldham. In 1911 he was a cotton spinner and they were living at 18 Castleton Street, Werneth, Oldham. They had three children, including Herbert Finney 1895 and Ernest Finney 1897.
- Sarah Ellen Finney (1871–1939), a cardroom hand, married Frank Hall Turner (1871–1933), a piecer, in 1891. At the time he was living at 21 Sussex Street and

she at 4 Hathersage Street, Oldham. He was a machine minder in a cotton mill in 1901 and they were living at 59 Main Road, Oldham. They were still there in 1911. They had six children, including Harold Turner c.1894, Doris Turner c.1899 and Hilda Turner 1904. When he died on 17th January 1937 they were living at 75 Ward Street, Oldham. He left effects valued at £347/15/9 to his widow.

- Alfred Finney (1875–1910) was a cotton spinner in 1901.
- Rebecca Finney (1878–1918) was a cotton card room hand in 1901. She married Joshua Nield (born 1877) in 1902. They had four children – Amos Nield 1905, George Henry Nield 1906, Alice Nield 1907 and Lily Nield 1909. Joshua served as a sergeant in 20th Lancashire Fusiliers (21505) and died on active service on 5th May 1916. He is buried at St Vaast Post Military Cemetery, Richebourg-L'Avoué, France (III D 6).

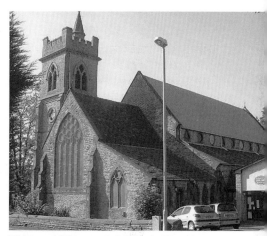

Walter and Ellen married at Christ Church, Chadderton in May 1913 (Mike Berrell).

After the death of Moses, Mary Finney married Richard Marsh in 1893. She was living at 16 Castleton Street, Oldham in 1901.

Walter was employed as a cotton mule piecer and was later a labourer for Eli Lees & Co at Hope Mill, Oldham. He married Ellen née Britt (1894–1974) on 19th May 1913 at Christ Church, Chadderton, Lancashire. Both Walter and Ellen falsely gave their ages as twenty-one and their address as 31 Bredbury Street, Chadderton. It is understood that this was an accommodation address as they were living at 10 Smith Street, Oldham with his mother at the time. Ellen was recorded as a ring spinner in the 1911 Census. They had a daughter, Ellen, born on 13th July 1914 at 35 Fielding Street, Townfield, Oldham.

Ellen's father, Michael Britt (1865–1920), married Mary née Moran (1864–1938) in 1883. His name was registered as Brett. She was born at Walsall, Staffordshire. In 1891 Michael was a cotton card room jobber and they were living at 3 Greenwood Street, Oldham. By 1901 they

Walter and Ellen were living at 10 Smith Street, Oldham when they married.

were living at 1 Hibbert Place, Oldham and at 8 Pernham Street, Oldham by 1911. In addition to Ellen they had six other children:

- Honora Britt (born c.1884) was a ring frame tenter in 1901.
- Mary Ann Britt (c.1886–1960) married Daniel Crabb (1882–1960), a carter, in 1902. They had at least two children – Elizabeth Crabb 1906 and Hilda Crabb 1909. Ellen Crabb born in 1924 is believed to be their child as well.
- James Britt (1888–1948), birth registered as Brett, served as a private in the Lancashire Fusiliers during the Great War. He married Mary E Hudson (1881–1954) in 1915. They had seven children – Thomas Britt 1916, Mary A Britt 1919, James Britt 1924, Joseph Britt 1925, Peter Britt 1927, Margaret Britt 1929 and Dennis Britt 1932.
- Catherine Britt (1891–92).
- John Thomas Britt (1897–1963) served as a private in the West Riding Regiment during the Great War. He married Emily Duffy (1897–1954) in 1919. They had six children – Nellie Britt 1920, Mary Britt 1921, Emily Britt 1922, John T Britt 1924, Nellie Britt 1928 and Lilian Britt 1931.
- Margaret Britt (1901–42) married James William Sutcliffe (1898–1966) in 1921. They had two daughters – Veronica Sutcliffe 1921 and Irene Sutcliffe 1928.

One of the sons was discharged in early 1918, having been severely wounded.

Walter enlisted on 6th September 1914 (2154). He probably served in 2/10th Battalion initially and moved to Egypt about April 1915 to join 1/10th Manchester, which was ordered to Gallipoli on 2nd May. The Battalion embarked on 5th May on SS *Haverford* and SS *Ausonia*. As Walter was in C Company it is likely he was on the latter. C and D Companies landed on W Beach on 9th May and the remainder of the Battalion on 14th May. Walter was wounded in the right eye and also suffered from enteric fever, but it is not known precisely when. The Battalion

Ellen Britt's family lived at 3 Greenwood Street, Oldham seen here on the right.

was evacuated to Mudros on 9th January 1916 and then to Egypt by 17th January. It arrived in Marseille, France on 6th March 1917.

Awarded the VC for his actions at Givenchy, France on 10th/11th December 1917, LG 13th February 1918. He died shortly after his VC action and is buried in Gorre British and Indian Cemetery, near Beuvry, France (V C 2). His brother, James, placed a floral tribute on Walter's grave immediately after the funeral. A few hours before his death Walter wrote to his wife to say he had been granted leave over Christmas. He had only been home on one other occasion during the war. He is commemorated in a number of other places:

- Roll of Honour at Eli Lees Hope Mills, Oldham, which closed in 1992.
- War Memorial, Church Square, Oldham.
- Commemorated with two other Oldham VCs, John Hogan and Thomas Steele, on the Victoria Cross Memorial Plaque, Church Terrace, Oldham, Lancashire dedicated on 4th October 2003.
- Book of Remembrance of the Manchester and King's Regiments in Manchester Cathedral.
- The Department for Communities and Local Government decided to provide commemorative paving stones at the birthplace of every Great War Victoria Cross recipient in the United Kingdom. Walter's commemorative stone was dedicated at St Mary & St Peter Church, Rock Street, Oldham on 11th December 2017 to mark the centenary of his award.

SS *Tortona* (8,153 tons) was launched on 18th August 1909 by Swan, Hunter & Wigham Richardson at Wallsend on Tyne. She was owned by Thomson Line until 1911, when she was sold to Cunard and renamed *Ausonia*. She worked on the London–Southampton–Quebec–Montreal service and was used as a troopship during the war. On 30th May 1918, en route from Montreal to Avonmouth carrying general cargo, she was torpedoed without warning by U-62 about 620 miles from the Fastnet Rock. The U-boat surfaced and shelled the hulk until it sank. Forty-four lives were lost.

The VC was presented to his widow on the steps of 2nd Northern General Hospital (also known as the Orthopaedic Hospital or Beckett Park Hospital), Beckett Park,

Walter Mills' grave in Gorre British and Indian Cemetery (Memorials to Valour).

The dedication of Oldham War Memorial in Church Square.

Leeds by the King on 31st May 1918. Ellen married James William Brown (1899–1970) on 21st August 1920 at St Ann's Roman Catholic Church, Greenacres, Oldham. At the time of their marriage James was an ironworks labourer living at 120 Lees Road, Oldham. She was a cotton ring spinner living at 10 Smith Street, Oldham. By 1934 they were living at 2 Court, 1 Bankhill Street, Oldham. James and Ellen are known to have had at least two children named Margaret and Joseph, but all of the following may be theirs:

The page of the Hope Mills Roll of Honour commemorating Walter Mills.

- Margaret J Brown (born 1921) married Arthur W Newell in 1953.
- James Brown (born 1922).
- Thomas Brown (born and died 1923).
- Joseph Brown (born 1927) attended the unveiling of the plaque to the three Oldham VCs in 2003.
- Clifford Brown (born and died 1928).

Ellen and her daughter were presented to the Prince of Wales at Oldham Athletic Football Ground, Boundary Park on 6th July 1921. Ellen junior presented the Prince with a small blood red rose on behalf of the ex-servicemen of Oldham. The Prince in turn presented her with his buttonhole, which was treasured by the family. Ellen junior was employed as a cotton card room hand and lived with her mother and stepfather at 2 Court, 1 Bankhill Street, Oldham. She died unmarried at Boundary Park Municipal Hospital, Oldham on 5th October 1934 of suppurative meningitis

This picture is understood to be of the investiture at Beckett Park on 31st May 1918. Could the little girl on the right be Walter's daughter, Ellen? The building was constructed in 1912 as a teacher training college. It was used as a military hospital in both world wars, treating 57,200 soldiers in 1914–18 alone. Today it is the James Graham Building, part of Leeds Beckett University.

and chronic mastoiditis. She is buried with her maternal grandparents in Greenacres Cemetery, Oldham (Section D2, Grave 109).

In addition to the VC he was awarded the 1914–15 Star, British War Medal 1914–20 and Victory Medal 1914–19. The VC was pinned to his daughter's burial robe when she was buried in the Britt family plot at Greenacres Cemetery, Oldham (D2 109) in 1934.

24213 PRIVATE HENRY JAMES NICHOLAS
1st Battalion, Canterbury Regiment NZEF

Henry Nicholas was born at Lincoln, New Zealand on 11th June 1891. His father, Richard Henry Nicholas (c.1857–1932), married Hannah née Day (1867–9th July 1932) in 1886. She was born in Abingdon, Berkshire, England and her forename has also been seen as Annie, Anna and Annah. They were living at 35 Berry Street, St Albans, Christchurch, when Henry enlisted and were still there in November 1918. Richard may have moved to Brisbane, Queensland, Australia at some time. Henry had six siblings:

- Frederick Charles Nicholas (1887–1951).
- Alice Jane Nicholas (1888–1958) married Joseph Henry Chapple (1880–1958) in 1923. They had at least one daughter, Judith, who married as Reid.
- Mabel May Nicholas (1890–1946) married Charles Sutton (1876–1965) in 1914. They had at least one son, Leonard Currie Sutton, in 1915.
- Ernest Nicholas (1895–1939) enlisted (12457) on 17th January 1916, described as 5′ 4″ tall, weighing 132 lbs, with dark complexion, blue eyes, brown hair and his religious denomination was Presbyterian. He declared three years previous service in 1st Canterbury Regiment Territorials. He was a painter working for Mr Jackson of Jarvis Quay, Wellington and lived at 73 Webb Street, Wellington. He was posted to F Company, 12th Reinforcements the same day at Trentham. On 23rd February he was admitted to Featherston Military Camp Hospital with measles and was sent on sick leave 7th–13th March. He embarked on SS *Navua* on 5th May and disembarked at Suez, Egypt on 22nd June. He embarked on 26th July at Alexandria on HT *Ivernia* and disembarked at Southampton, England on 7th August. He was posted to 5th Reserve Battalion, 3rd New Zealand Rifle Brigade at Sling Camp, Bulford, Wiltshire the same day. For unseemly conduct (urinating outside his hut) at Sling on 31st March 1917, he was sentenced to 168 hours detention. His movements thereafter are unclear but by 18th January 1918 he was with the Reserve New Zealand Rifle Brigade

Christchurch, New Zealand is the largest city on South Island and the seat of the Canterbury Region. It was first settled by Europeans around 1840 and acquired its name in 1848, probably after Christ Church, Oxford, England. In recent times the city of about 350,000 people suffered a number of earthquakes, the worst on 22nd February 2011, in which 185 people died and hundreds of buildings collapsed or were severely damaged.

St Albans is a large suburb of Christchurch.

at Brocton Camp, Staffordshire and appears to have remained there. On 13th December he was promoted corporal, but reverted to private at his own request on 20th June 1919. He embarked at Liverpool on SS *Somerset* on 2nd July and returned to New Zealand on 20th August. Ernest was discharged at Wellington on 17th September 1919.

* Reginald Armstrong Day Nicholas (1901–52).
* Pearl Hannah Nicholas (born 1906).

Henry's maternal grandfather, Frederick Day (1844–1926) was born at Harwell, Berkshire. He married Lydia née Wright (c.1841–1913), born at Steventon, Berkshire, in 1866. She was living with her mother, Susan Wright, at High Street, Steventon in 1841 and with her mother and stepfather, William Kent, an agricultural labourer, in 1851. At the time of the 1861 Census she was a dressmaker visiting John Higgins, innkeeper, and his wife Martha at The Jolly Sailor, Kingston, Surrey. In 1871 Frederick was an agricultural labourer and they were living at Townsend, Harwell. They emigrated to New Zealand in 1874. In addition to Hannah they had three other children:

* Alfred Day (born 1868).
* John Humphrey Day (1877–1956) married Louisa Porteous (1879–1960) in 1901. Louisa had a daughter, Annie 'Daisy' Porteous, born in 1898. John and Louisa had a son, Reginald Day.
* Frederick Thomas Day (1879–1954) married Alice Maud Robinson (1873–1918) in 1896. They had five children – Harold Frederick Thomas Day 1897, Dorothy

Maud May 1899, Eric Thomas Day 1901, Raymond Charles Day 1902 and Albert Ronald Malcolm Day 1905.

Henry was educated at Christchurch Normal School in Cranmer Square and at Christchurch East School. He was apprenticed as a carpenter to Baker Brothers, Loburn, Christchurch and was well known as an amateur boxer. Later he moved to Queensland, Australia with his schoolmate, Albert, and worked there for four years, living in the Brisbane suburb of Hamilton. He was a member of the Hamilton Wheelers cycling club and the Valley Swimming Club there and was welterweight runner-up in the Queensland Boxing Championship in Brisbane.

When war broke out he went to the recruiting office in Brisbane to enlist but, although physically very sound, was rejected due to a defect with his teeth. He tried twice more but was rejected for the same reason. Henry returned to New Zealand and joined the New Zealand Expeditionary Force on 8th February 1916, giving his religion as Spiritualist. He was assigned to C Company, 13th Reinforcements. He was granted leave in May but overstayed by one day and was docked a day's pay on 13th May.

Henry sailed for Britain on 29th May with 13th Reinforcements on SS *Willochra*. He was taken ill on the voyage and hospitalised for five days in early July. Having disembarked at Devonport, Devon on 26th July, he was posted to 1st Canterbury Company two days later at Sling Camp, Bulford. He went to France on 22nd September and attended machine gun training at Rouen with 1st New Zealand Machine Gun Company on 24th September. He joined 12th (Nelson) Company, 1st Canterbury on 27th October.

On 25th April 1917 Henry was admitted to 7th General Hospital, St Omer, with a slight attack of mumps, and transferred to the Base Depot on 13th May. He was fined 7/6d to replace a pair of trousers, having cut off the legs to make them into shorts. He absented himself from billets on 27th June and was awarded five days' Field Punishment No.2. He was admitted to 2nd New Zealand General Hospital, Walton-on-Thames, Surrey from 8th July until 7th August. On 7th September he was detached to Second Army Rest Camp, Rouen and rejoined his Battalion on 20th

The Normal School, completed in 1874, was one of the most significant Gothic style buildings in the city. In 1878 it was extended to provide a kindergarten and a training department. In 1954 the Normal School was transferred to Elmwood and the old school became the training centre for the Post-Primary Department of Christchurch Teachers' College. In 1970 it moved and the building was neglected until 1981, when it was sold to an investment company and converted into luxury apartments and a restaurant. The building suffered considerable damage in the 2010–11 earthquakes and had to be demolished.

Building of Sling Camp commenced in 1903, but it expanded rapidly once war broke out. By 1916 it had been taken over by New Zealand forces and comprised four main sections – Auckland, Wellington, Otago, and Canterbury Lines. Its main purpose was to train reinforcements and recovering casualties. At the end of the war, there were 4,600 New Zealand troops there and it became a repatriation centre. The men were eager to return home, but no troopships were available due to overuse and strikes. Eventually the men rioted in frustration and in the aftermath they were put to work carving an enormous Kiwi into the chalk hillside in February and March 1919. Although Sling Camp was removed in the 1920s, the Bulford Kiwi remains to this day. It covers 6,100 m2 and is 130m long. In the post-war years the Kiwi Polish Co maintained it and during the Second World War it was covered over to prevent it being used by enemy aircraft as a navigation marker. In 1948 local Boy Scouts removed the covering and added fresh chalk. Military units then took over the maintenance, including the author's own unit, 249th Signal Squadron (AMF(L)), in the 1980s and 90s.

SS *Willochra* (7,784 tons) was launched in Scotland in August 1912 and was completed in February 1913 for the Adelaide Steamship Co. She was used as a troopship during the Great War. In 1919 she was sold to Furness Withy and renamed *Fort Victoria*. She was operated by the Quebec Steamship Co until 1921, then transferred to the Bermuda & West Indies Steamship Co, both companies were owned by Furness Withy. On 18th December 1929, *Fort Victoria* sailed from New York in dense fog, but anchored to await an improvement. She was hit by SS *Algonquin* but all aboard *Fort Victoria* were rescued before she sank.

September. He was attached to Wing Reinforcement Camp, Rouen on 30th September and returned to the Battalion on 25th October.

Awarded the VC for his actions at Polderhoek, Belgium on 3rd December 1917, LG 11th January 1918. He is the only member of the Canterbury Regiment to be awarded the VC. Henry was promoted corporal shortly afterwards and was granted fourteen days' leave in Britain from about 9th December, returning to France on 26th December. He was attached to the Brigade School for training on 7th January 1918 and rejoined the Battalion on 28th January. Henry was promoted lance sergeant on 21st May and sergeant on 18th June. He was granted leave in Britain from 28th June and was admitted to 2nd New Zealand General Hospital, Walton-on-Thames on 8th July with tonsillitis. However, it cannot have been too serious as he was presented with the VC by the King at Buckingham Palace on 10th July. On 7th August he was discharged to the Assistant Provost Marshal London HQ and handed his VC over to the New Zealand Record Office for safekeeping. He joined No.2 Command Depot, Codford, Wiltshire on 22nd August from New Zealand HQ, London and on 2nd September returned to his Battalion in France.

Awarded the MM for his actions on Welsh and Bon Avis Ridges between 28th September and 1st October 1918, exhibiting fearless leadership and contempt of danger during the operations, particularly on 29th September, when, after a successful advance, his company's flank was in the air and the situation was critical. By skilful handling and heroic example, he inspired his men and enabled his half platoon to break an enemy attack by superior numbers, LG 13th March 1919. On 23rd October he was involved in the capture of Beaudignies. Later that day there was a skirmish with a German patrol on the Le Quesnoy Road at one of two bridges across the Ecaillon River. In a brief exchange of fire, Henry was the only New Zealander fatality. The Germans veered off down a side street. He was originally buried in Beaudignies Cemetery, the service being conducted by the Reverend GT Robson, attached to 1st Canterbury. On 29th October his body was reburied with full military honours in Vertigneul Churchyard (Grave 15), Romeries. The ceremony was conducted by the Bishop of Nelson. A letter of sympathy was sent to his father by Lord Liverpool, Governor General of New Zealand, on 14th November 1918. Henry is commemorated in a number of other places:

No.2 New Zealand General Hospital at Mount Felix, Walton-on-Thames, Surrey. At the outbreak of war Sir Thomas MacKenzie, New Zealand High Commissioner in London, and other fellow countrymen formed the New Zealand War Contingent Association to provide comforts for the troops, visit them in hospital, find accommodation for convalescents and keep in touch with the soldiers and their relatives. Meanwhile the War Office requisitioned the Mount Felix estate to house British troops and by November 1914 1,200 were billeted there. In June 1915 it transferred to the New Zealand War Contingent Association as a military hospital with 350 beds. On 3rd August the King, Queen and Prince of Wales visited, speaking to every soldier. In January 1916 five large ward huts were constructed to increase bed capacity to 1,040. More huts were added in October 1916 to provide another 500 beds and the nearby Oatlands Park Hotel was added to further increase accommodation. In 1919 a serious fire destroyed five marquees and a considerable amount of equipment. The number of inmates gradually decreased and the Hospital closed in March 1920, having treated 27,000 patients.

- Nicholas Barracks, Linton Military Camp, near Palmerston North, New Zealand.
- Sergeant Nicholas VC Match – a service rifle match in the Wellington Service Rifle Association's Charles Upham Memorial Championship held annually in January. Ten shots are fired at thirty second intervals in the prone position at 500 yards.
- Nicholas Street, Taradale, Napier, New Zealand.

Henry Nicholas' grave in Vertigneul Churchyard today and with New Zealand soldiers at his graveside in November 1918 (Henry Armytage Sanders).

- Rue Sgt HJ NICHOLAS (VC), Beaudignies, France was dedicated on 25th April 2011. The Mayor of Beaudignies, Raymonde Dramez, officiated and Henry's niece, Judith Reid, represented the family.
- Named on the family headstone in Bromley Cemetery, Christchurch, New Zealand.
- An obelisk surmounted with a sundial in the centre of the War Memorial Wall, Caroline Bay, Timaru bears the names of eleven New Zealand VCs, including Henry Nicholas.
- Named on a memorial to VC winners in Queens Gardens, Dunedin, Otago, New Zealand.
- Victoria Cross winners' memorial dedicated by the Reverend Keith Elliott VC outside the Headquarters of the Dunedin Branch of the Returned Services

The Nicholas family headstone in Bromley Cemetery, Christchurch.

Association and unveiled by Governor General Sir Charles Willoughby Moke Norrie GCMG GCVO CB DSO MC on 29th January 1956, the centenary of the institution of the VC by Queen Victoria. The memorial was later relocated to Anzac Square, near the Cenotaph in Queens Gardens, Dunedin.
- A bronze statue, by Mark Whyte, dedicated at the Park of Remembrance, Christchurch, New Zealand on 7th March 2007. The statue stands on a stone base from Le Quesnoy, France.
- Plaque south of Polygon Wood on Oude Kortrijkstraat near Polderhoek, Belgium dedicated on 14th September 2008. The plaque was erected by the Zonnebeke community and the New Zealand Embassy in Brussels. It overlooks where Henry's VC action took place, about 800m to the southeast.

The sundial at Caroline Bay, Timaru.

The statue of Henry Nicholas in the Park of Remembrance, Christchurch.

- Named on one of eleven plaques honouring 175 men from overseas awarded the VC for the Great War. The plaques were unveiled by the Senior Minister of State at the Foreign & Commonwealth Office and Minister for Faith and Communities, Baroness Warsi, at a reception at Lancaster House, London on 26th June 2014 attended by The Duke of Kent and relatives of the VC recipients. The New Zealand plaque was unveiled on 7th May 2015 at a ceremony attended by Defence Minister Gerry Brownlee and Defence Force Chief Lieutenant General Tim Keating. Corporal Willie Apiata VC read the names of the sixteen men on the plaque, to be mounted on a wall between Parliament and the Cenotaph in Wellington.
- The Secretary of State for Communities and Local Government, Eric Pickles MP announced that Victoria Cross recipients from the Great War would have commemorative paving stones laid in their birthplace as a lasting legacy of local

The plaque, south of Polygon Wood, with Polderhoek in the distance.

Canterbury Museum in Christchurch holds Henry's medals.

The Henry Nicholas 60c stamp issued by New Zealand Post on 14th April 2011.

heroes within communities. The stones would be laid on or close to the 100th anniversary of their VC actions. For the 145 VCs born in Australia, Belgium, Canada, China, Denmark, Egypt, France, Germany, India, Iraq, Japan, Nepal, Netherlands, New Zealand, Pakistan, South Africa, Sri Lanka, Ukraine and United States of America, individual commemorative stones were unveiled at the National Memorial Arboretum, Alrewas, Staffordshire by Prime Minister David Cameron MP and Sergeant Johnson Beharry VC on 5th March 2015.

- An issue of twenty-two 60c stamps by New Zealand Post entitled 'Victoria Cross – the New Zealand Story' honouring New Zealand's twenty-two Victoria Cross holders was issued on 14th April 2011.

The Military Medal was instituted on 25th March 1916 and was the other ranks' equivalent of the Military Cross for officers and warrant officers. It ranked below the Distinguished Conduct Medal and was in use until 1993, when it was replaced by the MC for all ranks. Over 115,000 MMs were awarded during the First World War, plus more than 5,700 bars, 180 second bars and one third bar, to Private Ernest Albert Corey, a stretcher-bearer in 55th Battalion AIF.

In addition to the VC and MM he was awarded the British War Medal 1914–20 and Victory Medal 1914–19. The VC was in safekeeping at the New Zealand Record Office in London and was later posted to his mother in Christchurch, New Zealand, arriving on 30th April 1919. His commemorative scroll was despatched to his father on 27th June 1921 and the remaining medals to his mother on 19th October 1921. His commemorative plaque was despatched to his father on 3rd February 1922 and his certificate on 6th October. His mother presented the VC and MM to Canterbury Museum in 1932. The other medals were presented to the Museum in July 2002, together with other items, including his identity disc, an aluminium ring made from a water bottle, VC citation, a regimental medal for boxing in 1918, pay book, commemorative scroll and plaque, diary and four photographs. The VC is held by Canterbury Museum, Rolleston Avenue, Christchurch, New Zealand.

CAPTAIN GEORGE HENRY TATHAM PATON
4th Battalion, Grenadier Guards

George Paton was born at Ashgrove, Innellan, near Dunoon, Argyllshire, Scotland on 3rd October 1895. His father, George William Paton (14th August 1859–23rd March 1934), was born at 76 Regent Street, Greenock, Renfrewshire and became known as the 'Match King'. He was a commercial clerk in 1881 and a sugar merchant in 1886. On 28th April 1886 he married Henrietta 'Etta' Tatham née Henderson (19th March 1862–4th May 1944), born at Kirkwall & St Ola, Orkney, at 1 George Square, Edinburgh, Midlothian. They were living at Wyndham Road, Innellan in 1891 and at Grove Terrace, High Road, Woodford, Essex in 1911. They also lived at 3 Whitehall Court and 11 Portland Place in London, at Portley, Caterham-on-the-Hill, Surrey and at Wolviston House, Whyteleafe, Surrey. George became Chairman and Managing Director of Bryant & May Ltd of London, Liverpool, Leeds and Glasgow. He was Deputy Chairman and Managing Director of the British Match Corporation Ltd formed in 1927 when Bryant & May combined with J John Masters & Co and the Swedish Match Co. He was knighted (LG 1st January 1930) for public services. His many other appointments included:

• Member – Argyll County Council, Poplar Advisory Committee for Juvenile Employment 1916–18 (chairman 1917), London Advisory Council for Juvenile

George's parents, George William Paton and Henrietta Tatham Henderson, were married in George Square, Edinburgh in 1886.

The Paton family lived at 3 Whitehall Court at some time. The right end of Whitehall Court in this view is the Liberal Club and the left end is the Royal Horseguards Hotel. Between the two, at Nos 3 and 4, are various offices, clubs and residences. Famous residents have included Herbert Kitchener, George Bernard Shaw, HG Wells and Stafford Cripps. The building was HQ of the Secret Intelligence Service (MI6) until the end of the Great War.

The Bryant & May match factory in Bow, East London.

Women making matchboxes in the Bow factory.

Employment, Council of the Industrial Welfare Society and the London Tramway and Omnibus Services' Dispute Court of Enquiry 1924.

- President – Caledonian Society of London 1913–19, United Commercial Travellers' Association of Great Britain and Ireland 1924–25 and Festival President of Royal Commercial Travellers' Schools, Pinner 1924.
- Governor of Coopers' Company's School 1915–22.
- Chairman – Public Health Committee, Cowal District, Argyll 1895–98, St Andrew's Scottish Soldiers' Home, Aldershot, Hampshire and the Administrative Committee of the Match Control Board during the Great War.
- Vice President – Royal Scottish Corporation and Royal Caledonian School (also deputy chairman).

Sir George died aboard the P&O liner RMS *Maloja* whilst returning to London following a holiday on the Riviera. He left effects valued at £204,920/9/7.

RMS *Maloja* acting as flagship for the 1930 Anniversary Day Regatta in Sydney Harbour. The construction of the famous bridge is taking place in the left background. *Maloja* and her sister ship *Mooltan* were ordered by the Peninsula and Oriental Steam Navigation Company in 1918. RMS *Maloja*'s maiden voyage began on 2nd November 1923 and in January 1924 both ships began the fortnightly service between Tilbury and Sydney. In September 1939 *Maloja* was requisitioned by the Admiralty as the armed merchant cruiser, HMS *Maloja*, operating between Shetland and Iceland. On 13th March 1940 she intercepted a German ship claiming to be Japanese. Her crew scuttled her and were picked up before *Maloja* hastened the sinking with her guns. In November 1941 she was converted to a troopship and joined a convoy to Calcutta the next year before taking troops to North Africa after the Operation Torch landings. In January 1947 *Maloja* returned to P&O and was scrapped in 1954.

George junior had two sisters, the youngest of whom, Jessie Brenda Paton, was born on 12th November 1892 and died two days later. His older sister, Agnes Annette Paton (23rd August 1887–7th June 1969) married Charles (later Sir Charles) Ogilvy Rennie (1875–1944), director of a match factory, in 1912 at the Strand, London. They had a son, John 'Jack' Ogilvy Rennie (1914–81), who was educated at Wellington College and Balliol College, Oxford, where he became known as a talented painter, exhibiting at the Royal Academy in 1930 and 1931 and at the Paris Salon in 1932. Having graduated in Modern History in 1935, he joined Kenton & Eckhardt Inc, an advertising agency in New York City. He later joined the British Consulate at Baltimore, Maryland and was appointed Vice-Consul in September 1940. John then transferred to the British Press Service and its successor, the British Information Services, combating German propaganda in the USA. He was head of a section in New York producing radio programmes that promoted the British viewpoint 1942–46. He joined the Information Policy Department of the Foreign Office in January 1946. In March 1949 he returned to the USA as First Secretary (Commercial) in Washington DC and was posted to Warsaw, Poland with similar duties in June 1951. In 1953 he was appointed Head of the Information Research Department and in 1956 chaired a committee established to disseminate British propaganda in the Middle East during the Suez Crisis, for which he was awarded the CMG. In 1958 he became Commercial Minister in Buenos Aires and in Washington in 1960. In 1964 he was appointed Assistant Under-Secretary for the Americas and headed a mission seeking to resolve problems between Guatemala and British Honduras. In 1966 he became Chairman of the Civil Service Commission and later that year was appointed Deputy Under-Secretary for Defence. John was knighted (KCMG) in 1967 and in 1968 replaced Sir Dick White as 'C', head of the Secret Intelligence Service or MI6. In 1971 he agreed to a request from Prime Minister Edward Heath to send a MI6 officer, Frank Steele, to Northern Ireland to make contact with republican paramilitaries. These initial contacts with Gerry Adams and Martin McGuinness created a 'back-channel' of communication and eventually led to the Good Friday Agreement and peace in Northern Ireland. Back in 1938 John had married Anne-Marie Céline Monica Godart (c.1916–64) from Switzerland. Their son, Charles Tatham Ogilvy Rennie (born 1947) married Christine M Gurden (born 1949) in 1971. They were arrested on 15th January 1973 for heroin trafficking from Hong Kong, for which they stood trial at the Old Bailey and were sentenced to a term of imprisonment. As a result of the publicity surrounding the case Sir John offered his resignation, but was refused and served until his scheduled retirement in January 1974, when he was succeeded as head of MI6 by Sir Maurice Oldfield. Following Anne-Marie's death on 30th September 1964, Sir John married Jennifer Margaret Rycroft née Wainwright in July 1966. She had married Lieutenant Julian Miles Wemyss Rycroft RN (1931–55) in August 1954. He was promoted acting sub-Lieutenant on 1st May 1951 while serving on HMS *Ambush* and lieutenant on 16th November 1953 while serving on the submarine

HMS *Sidon*. Julian was the Torpedo Officer on HMS *Sidon* on 16th June 1955 when she moored alongside the depot ship HMS *Maidstone* in Portland harbour. Two 21″ Mk 12 torpedoes, codenamed 'Fancy', were loaded for testing. One of the torpedoes exploded in its torpedo tube, rupturing the two forward most bulkheads. Twelve men were killed and seven others were seriously injured, but the rest of the crew was evacuated before the vessel sank. *Maidstone*'s medical officer, Surgeon Lieutenant Charles Eric Rhodes, went aboard *Sidon* and assisted several survivors but suffocated and was posthumously awarded the Albert Medal. Sir John and Jennifer had two sons – Andrew James Ogilvy Rennie 1968 and David Simon Ogilvy Rennie 1971. David was a columnist on the *London Evening Standard* 1992–96, then *The Daily*

Sir John Ogilvy Rennie, head of the Secret Intelligence Service 1968–74.

Telegraph in London, Sydney, Beijing, Washington and Brussels and from 2007 on *The Economist*, becoming Washington Bureau Chief in 2012. He was also a contributor to *The Spectator* 2006–07 and received the University Association for Contemporary European Studies/Thompson Reuters Reporting Europe Award in 2010.

George's paternal grandfather, Archibald Paton (1819–90), born at Greenock, Renfrewshire, was an accountant living at 76 Regent Street, Greenock in 1857, when he married Agnes née Fyfe (1831–1911) at Loanhead, Lasswade, Midlothian. She

HMS *Sidon* was launched in September 1944, one of the third group of S Class submarines built by Cammell Laird of Birkenhead. Inset right is Surgeon Lieutenant Charles Eric Rhodes, who was awarded the Albert Medal posthumously for attempting to rescue members of *Sidon*'s crew, following the torpedo explosion at Portland on 16th June 1955. Inset left is the HMS *Sidon* memorial, overlooking Portland Harbour.

was born in Edinburgh, Midlothian. By 1881 Archibald was a sugar merchant and foreign produce agent and they were living at 65 Finnart Street, West Greenock, Renfrew. He was later a commission merchant and died at The Ferns, Innellan, Argyll. In addition to George they had four other children:

- Archibald John Paton (1857–1915), a sugar merchant, married Christina Hardie McGavin (born 1862) in 1885 at Greenock.
- Elizabeth Ann Paton (born 1862).
- Camilla Marion Paton (1863–1952) married her cousin, Robert Fussey Fisher (c.1834–91), a wool merchant, in January 1887. Robert had been married to Janet Scott and Eliza Boyd previously, the latter in 1874. Robert was commissioned as a lieutenant in 1st Selkirkshire Rifle Volunteer Corps on 16th December 1870. Robert and Camilla had a daughter, Camilla Myra Fisher, in 1889.
- Agnes Jane Paton (1867–1905) married Daniel Macalister MInstCE (1855–1918), a civil engineer, in 1892. They were living at Overton Cottage, Greenock in 1901 and had a son, Daniel Archibald Patondo Macalister, the same year. Agnes died on 11th July 1905. Daniel was working for the Corporation Water Department, Municipal Buildings, Prospecthill, Greenock in 1912 and married Helen 'Nellie' Murdoch Sorley née MacLean (1867–1930) in 1913. She had married William Sorley in 1888.

His maternal grandfather, Edward Henderson (born 1825), was Surveyor of Taxes Orkney and Shetland when he married Jessie Loutit née Robertson (born 1834 at Dundee, Forfar) in May 1861 at Rosebank, Kirkwall, Orkney. He was a Surveyor of Stamps and Taxes in 1881 and they were living at 28 Warriston Crescent, Edinburgh, Midlothian. By 1894 they were living at 2 Gordon Villas, Enfield, Middlesex. They both died there that February, only three days apart. In addition to Henrietta they had three other children:

- John Robertson Henderson CIE (1863–1925) was a medical practitioner with the Madras Government Civil Service. He married Alice Roberta Sinclair (1868–1915) in Madras, India in 1888. John married Eliza Beatrice Adie (1882–1938) in 1921 at Delting, Shetland Islands. He had been living at 3 Whitehall Court, London. He died on 26th October 1925 at 19 Drumsheugh Gardens, Edinburgh, Midlothian. His usual residence was 14 Murrayfield Avenue, Edinburgh.
- Jane Borwick Henderson (born 1864).

George's maternal grandparents were living at 28 Warriston Crescent, Edinburgh in 1881.

• Grace Johnstone Henderson (1866–29th March 1935) married Ernest Theodore Evans (1860–1940) a draper/shopkeeper, in 1901 at West Derby, Lancashire. He was born at Ludlow, Shropshire and they were living there at 40 Mill Street in 1911. When Grace died at Highgate, London, she left effects valued at £2,240/16/1. Ernest died at 40 Mill Street, Ludlow on 28th June 1940, leaving effects valued at £13,778/10/-. They had two children – Grace Henrietta Tess Evans 1902 and Ernest George Douglas Evans 1904.

George was educated at Rottingdean School in Brighton, Sussex and at Clifton College, Bristol. At Clifton he was a cadet second lieutenant in the College Cadet Force's Engineer Contingent. He completed his education in Germany and

Clifton College about the turn of the 19th century. It was founded in 1862, one of the original twenty-six English public schools, and became noted for its emphasis on science rather than classics. The second highest cricket score ever recorded was made at Clifton by thirteen year old Arthur Collins in June 1899. His 628 not out stood as the world record for 116 years until January 2016 when it was overtaken by Pranav Dhanawade aged fifteen in Mumbai, India, when he scored 1,009. Arthur Collins was killed at Ypres in November 1914 (Ypres (Menin Gate) Memorial). In the Second World War the school was evacuated to Bude to avoid the bombing of Bristol and was then used by a RASC Officer Cadet Training Unit. The US Army took it over as HQ V Corps and then First Army, under General Omar Bradley, prior to the invasion of Normandy. First Army was replaced at Clifton by HQ Ninth Army. The College has seven other VCs in addition to George Paton. Numerous famous alumni include:

Leslie Hore-Belisha, Minister of War 1937–40.
Field Marshal Douglas Haig.
Field Marshal William Birdwood.
Lieutenant General Frederick Morgan, who carried out the initial planning for Operation Overlord.
Hugh Elles, who commanded tank forces in the Great War.
Percy Hobart, famous for his 'funnies' armoured vehicles in the Second World War.
Charles EW Bean, war correspondent and author of *Official History of Australia in the War of 1914–18*.
John Cleese, the comedian famous for *Monty Python*.
Actors Trevor Howard and Sir Michael Redgrave.

was in Austria at the outbreak of war. He enlisted in September 1914 and was commissioned into 2/17th London on 1st October. He was appointed acting captain on 15th August 1915 and promoted lieutenant on 3rd October. George gave his address as 61 Holland Park, London in his application for a commission in the Special Reserve on 25th December 1915. On 28th January 1916 he transferred to the Grenadier Guards with seniority as a lieutenant from 24th November 1915. He went to France on 8th July 1916 and joined No.2 Company, 4th Grenadier Guards on 23rd July. Appointed acting captain again on 4th June 1917. **Awarded the MC for his actions on 31st July 1917 commanding No.4 Company between Boesinghe and Wijdendrift near Ypres. In spite of a heavy barrage he led his Company across the Yser Canal using splendid initiative and sound military judgement to achieve the crossing with only slight loss. The final objective was gained in spite of heavy shell and enfilading machine-gun fire, LG 26th September 1917.**

George Paton's grave in Metz–en–Couture Communal Cemetery British Extension (Memorials to Valour).

Awarded the VC for his actions at Gonnelieu, France on 1st December 1917, LG 13th February 1918. He died as a result of the VC action on 1st December 1917 and was buried in Metz–en–Couture German Cemetery Extension, which was later renamed Metz–en–Couture Communal Cemetery British Extension (II E 24). He left effects valued at £505/8/9. As he never married, the VC and MC were presented to his parents by the King at Buckingham Palace on 2nd March 1918. George is commemorated in a number of other places:

- Named on the family headstone at Putney Vale Cemetery, Kingston Road, South London (Grave 1141 Block AS). In addition Paton's Path is one of seven roads/paths named in 1997 by Wandsworth Borough Council after VCs buried, cremated or commemorated in the Cemetery. The

George is commemorated on the family grave in Putney Vale Cemetery.

other six are – Ernest Alexander, William Boulter, Harry Greenwood, Reginald Hayward, Alfred Richards and Harry Schofield.

- War memorials at:
    - ° Argyll Street, Dunoon, Argyll & Bute.
    - ° Dunoon Grammar School, Dunoon, Argyll & Bute.
    - ° Innellan, Argyll & Bute.
    - ° St Paul's Church, Greenock, Inverclyde.
    - ° Little Hallingbury, Essex.
    - ° St Mary the Virgin Church, Little Hallingbury, Essex.
    - ° St Mary's Church, Bow, East London and in the Book of Remembrance.
    - ° St Andrews Church, Litherland, Liverpool, Merseyside.
    - ° Clifton College, Bristol.
    - ° Army Reserve Centre, Mile End Road, Bow, London.

Innellan War Memorial.

- Bryant & May memorials at Grove Hall Park, Bow, East London and at the Royal British Legion Hall, Litherland, Liverpool, Merseyside.
- Paton Close, Bow, East London.
- Household Division (Foot Guards) Honour Roll for the Victoria Cross in the Sergeants' Mess, Wellington Barracks, London.
- Book of Remembrance, St Columba's Church, Pont Street, Knightsbridge, London.
- The Department for Communities and Local Government decided to provide commemorative paving stones at the birthplace of every Great War Victoria Cross recipient in the United Kingdom. A commemorative stone for George was dedicated at Innellan War Memorial, Shore Road, Innellan, Argyll & Bute on 1st December 2017 to mark the centenary of his award.

The Bryant & May War Memorial at Litherland, Liverpool, Merseyside.

In addition to the VC and MC he was awarded the British War Medal 1914–20 and Victory Medal 1914–19. The VC is held by HQ Grenadier Guards at the Guards Museum, Wellington Barracks, Birdcage Walk, London.

LIEUTENANT COLONEL FRANK CROWTHER ROBERTS
1st Battalion, The Worcestershire Regiment

Frank Roberts was born at Highbury, Middlesex on 2nd June 1891. His father, Reverend Frank Roberts (23rd January 1851–14th July 1934), married Rosa Ellen Carpenter (1855–12th October 1884) on 3rd January 1877 at Newton Abbot, Devon. She was born at Dawlish, Devon. Frank was a draper and mercer in 1881 with a business in Fore Street, Tiverton, Devon, employing nine assistants. After Rosa died he became a deacon at Cullompton Church in 1886 and was then assistant curate to Reverend Francis Barnes, Vicar of Holy Trinity, Plymouth, Devon. He married Francis Barnes' daughter, Sarah Ann Mary née Barnes (1852–1939), at Plymouth, Devon on 21st April 1887. They were living at St John's Vicarage, The Green, Southall, London in 1901 and were still there in 1911. They later moved to 44 Villiers Road, Southall. When he died he left effects valued at £4,524/17/2. Frank junior had two sisters:

Fore Street, Tiverton, where Frank's father had his business in 1881.

- Edith Mary Ambury Roberts (21st April 1888–19th February 1959) married Captain Herbert Rew Carpenter (6th June 1889–11th August 1976) on 19th April 1928 at Tiverton. Herbert was commissioned in 4th Devonshire on 12th February 1913 and was promoted captain on 10th April 1917. He was awarded the Territorial Decoration (LG 26th October 1928) and last appears in the Army List in January 1931. In 1935 he was a coal merchant and they were living at Lower Prescott, Tiverton. By 1959 they were living at 69 Park Road, Uxbridge, Middlesex.
- Rosa Henrietta Ellen Roberts (16th January 1893–5th August 1963) was a spinster, living at 393 Margate Road, Ramsgate, Kent at the time of her death at Hill House Hospital, Minster, Ramsgate.

The Anglican Church of the Holy Trinity was located in Southside Street/Friars Lane, The Barbican, Plymouth. The foundation stone was laid on 26th May 1840. Because of its location, the Church was about twenty-one metres square and the only natural light came from a clerestory roof and three windows at the east end. The Church could seat 1,100 worshippers and was consecrated on 26th August 1842. The Church was destroyed in the bombing of Plymouth in the Second World War, as seen here, and was never rebuilt.

Frank's paternal grandfather, Hugh Badcock Roberts (8th March 1820–18th August 1897), was born at Cheriton Fitzpaine, Devon. He married Mary née Davey (4th April 1818–20th December 1895) on 6th June 1844 at St Peter's, Tiverton. In 1851 he was a farmer of 120 acres employing four labourers at Cadeleigh, Devon and had increased his holding to 360 acres by 1861. By 1881 he was farming 140 acres at Canal Villa, Tiverton, Devon and at Meadhayes Farm, Cadeleigh in 1897. In addition to Frank they had nine other children:

Frank's paternal grandparents married at St Peters, Tiverton in 1844. There was probably a church there in Saxon times, but the first stone church was erected shortly after the Norman Conquest and was consecrated in 1073. The church seen today was almost entirely built in the 15th and 16th centuries. Restorations were undertaken in 1825–29 and 1853–56. The carvings in the Greenway Chapel are regarded as some of the finest of any parish church in England. The organ was built in 1696 by Christian and Bernard Schmidt and rebuilt in 1867. The organist, Samuel Reay, played Mendelssohn's *Wedding March* at St Peter's on 2nd June 1847 at the wedding of Dorothy Carew and Tom Daniel, the first occasion it was performed at any marriage ceremony.

- Hugh Roberts (4th February 1845–8th November 1911), a farm bailiff, married Mary Ann Chanin (14th March 1854–21st December 1911) on 28th April 1880 at Tiverton. He was a farmer of eighty-one acres, employing one man and one boy, in 1881 and they were living at Meadhayes, Cadeleigh, Devon. In 1891 they were living at Franklyns Farm, Poltimore, Devon. By 1901 they were at Elfordleigh Farm, Colebrook, Plympton St Mary and in 1911 they were at 10 South Devon Place, 7 Ridgeway, Plympton. They had two children – Mary Jane Roberts 1881 and Hugh Roberts 1883.
- Mary Roberts (3rd March 1846–1st February 1849).
- Fanny Roberts (11th December 1847–12th December 1848).
- Richard Roberts (2nd May 1849–5th April 1865).
- Sarah Roberts (9th October 1852–26th June 1934) married Thomas Walter Hitt (1845–30th March 1914) in 1874. He was a traveler and they were living at 39 Halesworth Road, Lewisham, London in 1911. When he died there he left effects valued at £2,093/3/3. Sarah was living at 103b Tyrwhitt Road, Brockley, Kent at the time of her death, leaving effects valued at £44/9/7. They had four children

Meadhayes Farm, Cadeleigh, Devon, where Frank's grandparents farmed in the 1890s (Geograph).

– Thomas Walter Roberts Hitt 1875, Mary Frances Hitt 1877, Kathleen Jane Hitt 1879 and Ellen Ruby Hitt 1892.
- Elizabeth Roberts (13th June 1854–9th June 1857).
- Henry Roberts (22nd January 1856–3rd March 1857).
- Michael Roberts (15th -20th June 1858).
- Frances Mary Roberts (22nd February 1864–23rd March 1942) was a spinster, living at 50 St Peter Street, Tiverton at the time of her death, leaving effects valued at £421/16/3.

Frank's maternal grandmother, Eliza Ambury, was born at Brislington, Somerset in 1820.

His maternal grandfather, Reverend Francis Barnes MA (1823–16th April 1905) was born at Bristol, Gloucestershire. He married Eliza née Ambury (1820–81), born at Brislington, Somerset, in 1851 at Bristol. In 1881 he was Vicar of Holy Trinity, Plymouth, Devon and they were living at Trinity Parsonage House, Plymouth St Andrew. He was living at 3 Citadel Terrace, Plymouth at the time of his death there, leaving effects valued at £422/3/4. In addition to Sarah they had six other children:

- Eliza Ambury Nanfan Barnes (1853–1924) was living with her sister Sarah and her family at St John's Vicarage, Southall in 1911. She died a spinster at Brentford, Middlesex.
- Caroline Amy Mountfort Barnes (1855–1932) married John Parr (born 1852) in 1878 at Plymouth. In 1891 he was a clerk in Holy Orders and a schoolmaster and they were living at 21–23 Park Road, Battersea, London. By 1911 he was Rector of Milton Bryant, Bedfordshire. They had five children – Hampden John Parr 1879, Edith Caroline W Parr 1881, Arthur Mountfort Parr 1883, Edward Ambury Parr 1884 and Winifred Amy Parr 1886.
- Fanny Bessie Chambers Barnes (1856–14th August 1888) married John Henry Clarke (28th November 1852–1925), a railway engineer, in 1875 at Plymouth. He was born at Derby. They were living at Cliffe House, Penn Lane, Melbourne, Derbyshire in 1881. They had four children – Alfred Henry T Clarke 1875, Charles Ambury Clarke 1878, Hugh Meredith Clarke 1880 and Alice Mary M Clarke 1881. John married Maud Annie Scudamore in 1893 at Bingham, Nottinghamshire. They were living at Oakfield, Newton Park, Leeds, Yorkshire in 1911. They had seven children – Clarice Maud Clarke 1894, Gertrude Marguerite Clarke 1896, John Bennett Clarke 1897, Arthur Lawrence Clarke 1899, Kathleen Marie Clarke 1901, Francis Leslie Clarke 1904 and Lillian Phyllis Clarke 1907.
- Francis Henry Barnes (1858–1935) married Alice Marie Leonide Boswell (1862–99) in 1881. They had a son, Francis John Barnes in 1882, before emigrating to

Australia. They had another nine children there in Sydney and Ryde, New South Wales – Sydney and Ernest Barnes 1884, Amy A Barnes 1887, Arthur S and Rita M Barnes 1889, Percival and Roy Barnes 1890, Nanfan ME Barnes (also seen as Ernistina Nanfan Barnes) 1894 and Thomas P Barnes 1897. Francis married Alice Gillham in 1908 and they had a son, Henry J Barnes, in 1911.

- Alice Maud Martha Barnes (1861–1959) married William Chester Copleston (c.1843–1929) in 1888. He was born at Trichinopoly, East Indies. He had married Mary Elizabeth Williams (1840–86) in 1873 at Forden, Montgomeryshire and they had a son, Reginald Chester Copleston, in 1881. William was Rector of Willand, Devon. He was boarding at 48 Cotham Road, Bristol, Gloucestershire in 1911. They had six children – Dorothy Ambury Copleston 1890, Hilda Nanfan Copleston 1891, Edith Chester Copleston 1892, Frederick Elford Copleston 1894, Nora May Copleston 1896 and Alice Laura Copleston 1898.
- Edith Blanch Meredith Barnes (1863–77).

Frank was educated at St Lawrence College 1906–09 and the Royal Military College Sandhurst. He was known as 'Culley' to his close friends. He was commissioned on 4th March 1911 and was serving with 1st Battalion in Egypt when war broke out. Promoted lieutenant 8th August 1914 and went to France on 5th November. **Awarded the DSO for his actions on 3rd January 1915 at Neuve Chapelle, France – in a raid with twenty-five men he attacked and captured a German sap head fifty metres in front of our lines. Thirty Germans were bayoneted and the party returned to our lines after only four minutes with only two men missing and one wounded, LG 18th February 1915.** Frank was appointed

St Lawrence College, Ramsgate was founded in 1879 as South Eastern College but the name was changed because of its association with the railway company. The school quickly outgrew its original premises and the main buildings were constructed by 1884. During both world wars the school was evacuated to Chester (1915) and Courteenhall, Northamptonshire (1940). Notable alumni include:

Hubert Broad MBE AFC, Great War RNAS aviator and test pilot, who completed 7,500 flying hours in 200 different types of aircraft.

Sir Conrad Corfield KCIE CSI MC, Chief Advisor in India.

General Lord Richard Dannatt, Chief of the General Staff 2006–09.

Captain David Hart Dyke CBE LVO ADC RN, Captain of HMS *Coventry* during the 1982 Falklands War.

Right Honourable Baron John Stevens, former Commissioner of the Metropolitan Police.

adjutant on 13th March. He was wounded on 9th May and evacuated to Britain on 19th May. He returned to France on 30th June and was promoted captain on 6th August. He continued as adjutant until 12th August 1916 and was then appointed Staff Captain, HQ 23rd Brigade. On 24th October he was appointed Brigade Major, HQ 23rd Brigade, which was commanded by Brigadier GWSG Grogan, who was awarded the VC in May 1918. **Awarded the MC for his actions on 31st July 1917 on Bellewaarde Ridge, Belgium for conducting daring personal reconnaissances under heavy fire, LG 26th September 1917.**

The officers of 1st Battalion, The Worcestershire Regiment in Egypt in 1914. Frank Roberts is in the centre of the rear row. The then Captain George Grogan is second from the left in the front row. Just over two years after this photograph was taken, Grogan was commanding a brigade and Frank Roberts was his brigade major.

Frank was appointed acting lieutenant colonel to command 1st Worcestershire on 24th October 1917. **Awarded the VC for his actions west of the Somme and at Pargny, France on 23rd March 1918, LG 8th May 1918.** He was wounded on 27th March and relinquished command on the 29th March, when he reverted to acting major. He was evacuated to Britain on 1st April. The VC was presented by the King at Buckingham Palace on 1st June. Frank returned to France on 12th June and was appointed acting lieutenant colonel 2nd July 1918–18th April 1919, while commanding a battalion. He was gassed on 1st August on Vimy Ridge.

As a result of his service on the Western Front, he was **Mentioned in Despatches six times. Firstly in Field Marshal Sir John French's Despatch dated 14th June 1915 (LG 17th February 1915) and in Field Marshal Sir Douglas Haig's Despatches dated 30th April 1916, 7th November 1917, 7th April 1918, 8th November 1918 and 16th March 1919 (LG respectively**

Bellewaarde Ridge from the PPCLI Memorial looking south. 2nd Northamptonshire (closest to camera) and 1st Worcester emerged from the trees on the right on 31st July 1917 and stormed the top of the rise beyond the Memorial. Captain Thomas Colyer-Fergusson of 2nd Northamptonshire was awarded the VC for his actions here that day, while Frank Roberts received the MC for conducting daring reconnaissances under heavy fire.

15th June 1916, 11th December 1917, 23rd May 1918, 28th December 1918 and 9th July 1919). He was seconded for service in Sudan with the Equatorial Battalion of the Egyptian Army 16th February 1919–25th November 1920 and was appointed brevet major on 3rd June 1919.

The Aliab Dinka, Bor Dinka and Mandari tribes rose in 1919 and attacked the post at Menkamon. Two columns were despatched and the one commanded by Frank Roberts was surprised by the Dinka, who stampeded the carriers and forced a return to Tombe. **Awarded the Egyptian Gold Medal of the Order of Mohammed Ali for operations against the Aliab Dinkas in Mongalla Province 1919–20. It was largely due to his gallantry and disregard of danger, his fine example of coolness, tireless energy and quick grasp of the situation, that the square was so quickly reformed in the action on 8th December 1919, and that the withdrawal to Tombe, which was reached on 13th December, was so successfully carried out without further casualties, Special War Office Gazette Khartoum 7th November 1921. Awarded the OBE for services with the Egyptian Army, LG 17th June 1921. Mentioned in War Office Despatch dated 17th June 1921, LG 17th June 1921.**

Frank attended the Staff College in 1922 and was appointed GSO3 in Egypt 24th January 1923–21st January 1924. He was appointed Brigade Major in Germany 7th April 1925–9th March 1926 and GSO2 South China 10th April 1926–21st April 1928. He transferred to 2nd Royal Warwickshire on promotion to major on 6th July 1927. Frank was attached to the Iraqi Army and took part in operations in South Kurdistan October 1930–May 1931. He was appointed Inspector GSO1 Iraq Army 18th February 1931–2nd October 1932.

On 23rd April 1932, Frank Roberts married Winifred Margaret née Wragg (1892–December 1980) at Swadlincote, Burton upon Trent, Staffordshire. There were no children. Winifred's father, John Downing Wragg (1846–19th February 1917) was born at Wortley, Yorkshire. The Wragg family owned a number of quarries and refractory businesses, producing mouldings for the steel industry. John married Maria née Ronksley (1845–1904) on 4th February 1868 at Ecclesfield Parish Church, Yorkshire. In 1881 he was a brick and tile manufacturer at Winshill, Derbyshire and they were living at 215 Newton Road. By 1911 he had moved to Eureka Lodge, Newhall Road, Swadlincote, Burton upon Trent. He was an alderman and

There may have been a place of worship at Ecclesfield prior to the Norman Conquest but there is no mention of a church in the Domesday Book. The first substantial church was constructed in 1111 and was occupied by monks from Fontenelle Abbey, near Rouen in Normandy. In 1386 Richard II dissolved alien priories and handed over the church to the Carthusians who held it until the Dissolution in the 1530s. At that time the parish was one of the largest in England and had four churchwardens instead of two and this tradition has been retained. The current church dates to 1478–150(but parts of the nave and the main pillars are part of the 12th century building. Most of the decorative pieces and stained glass were smashed in the 1640s. Alexander John Scott, chaplain to Admiral Lord Nelson, who was present at his death at Trafalgar aboard HMS *Victory*, is burie(in the churchyard.

JP. In 1915 he purchased Bretby Park, Burton upon Trent. When he died at Cornwall Street, Birmingham, Warwickshire, he left effects valued at £186,987/1/4 (c.£12M in 2016). In addition to Winifred, John and Maria had nine other children, of whom eight are known:

- Martha Eleanor Wragg (1868–1935) married Septimus Palmer (1858–14th December 1935), a medical practitioner, in 1905. He was born at St Kilda, Victoria, Australia. They were living at Swadlincote, Burton upon Trent in 1911. They both died in London. He was living at 14a Princes Gate Court at the time. They had a daughter, Barbara Winifred Palmer, in 1906.
- Horace Wragg (1869–9th March 1917) married Jeanne Laura ? (c.1875–1967) but no record has been found. They were living at Blake Dene, Parkstone, Dorset at the time of his death, leaving effects valued at £44,164/18/11 (almost £3M in 2016). Jeanne married Frank Percival Hare on 8th November 1920 at Holy Trinity, Brompton, London.
- Emily Wragg (1874–26th April 1968) never married. She lived at Eureka Lodge, Newhall Road, Swadlincote, which she offered for use as a war hospital supply depot during the Second World War. She was living with her sister, Winifred and brother-in-law Frank at Four Winds, Bretby, Derbyshire, when she died, leaving effects valued at £31,397.
- Mary Elizabeth Wragg (1876–1930) never married.
- Jemima Wragg (twin with Herbert) (1878–1922) married William Murthwait How (1873–1957), an architect, in 1906. He was born at Amersham, Buckinghamshire. They had three children – Frederick Murthwait How 1907, Lorna How 1908 and Mima A Howe 1913.
- Herbert Wragg (later Sir Herbert) (twin with Jemima) (1878–13th February 1956) married Fanny Greenwood Sutcliffe (1882–1918) in 1905 at Bradford, Yorkshire. They had six children – John Downing Wragg 1907, Thomas Herbert Sutcliffe Wragg 1914, Eva Ruth Wragg 1915, Frederick Robert Wragg 1916 and twins Francis G and Marguerite Wragg 1918. Fanny died as a result of complications during the birth of the twins. Herbert married Mary Ann Sutcliffe (1878–21st July 1958), his sister-in-law, in 1919 and they had a daughter, Fanny 'Nancy' Greenwood Wragg, in 1920. Herbert was Conservative MP for Belper, Derbyshire 1923–29 and 1931–45 and was appointed Sheriff for Derbyshire in 1930. They were living at Bretby House, Burton upon Trent in 1951 and at 37 East Avenue, Bournemouth, Hampshire in 1956. He died at The Cambridge Nursing Home, Cambridge Road, Bournemouth, leaving effects valued at £66,454/8/11.
- Frederick William Wragg (1882–1st July 1916) was a brick and tile manufacturer in 1911. He was serving as a major in 1/5th Sherwood Foresters when he was killed during the attack on Gommecourt, France (Thiepval Memorial – Pier and face 10C, 10D & 11A). Captain John Leslie Green RAMC, the Battalion MO, was awarded a posthumous VC for his actions that day. Frederick was Mentioned in Despatches.

Frederick Wragg's name, bottom left, on the Thiepval Memorial.

Captain John Leslie Green VC RAMC was MO of 1/5th Sherwood Foresters on 1st July 1916.

• Norman John Wragg (1890–18th July 1916) was an undergraduate at Cambridge in 1911. He was commissioned as a lieutenant in 3rd attached 1st South Staffordshire on 6th August 1914. He received a gunshot wound to the left leg at Bois Grenier on 17th October 1915, embarked at Rouen on 22nd October for Southampton and was admitted to the Royal Victoria Hospital, Netley on 24th October. A medical board there next day found him unfit and granted six weeks leave to 5th December. A medical board at the Military Hospital Lichfield on 7th December found him fit for General Service and he joined 3rd Reserve Battalion on 9th December. Norman received a gunshot wound to the thigh and abdomen at High Wood and was admitted to 8th General Hospital, 28 Route de Neufchatel, Rouen on 16th July 1916. He died there on 18th July and is buried in St Sever Cemetery, Rouen, France (Officers A 3 2). He left effects valued at £3,528/6/3 in his will dated 4th January 1915 to his sisters Emily, Mary and Winifred.

Frank was appointed brevet lieutenant colonel on 6th May 1932 and Inspector GSO1 British Military Mission Iraq Army 3rd October 1932–17th February 1934. **Awarded the Iraqi Order of Al Rafidain 4th Class Military Division, LG 3rd August 1934.** He was appointed GSO2 Northern Ireland District 22nd January 1935–23rd November 1936. On 24th November 1936 he was promoted lieutenant colonel to command 1st Royal Warwickshire until 1938. Appointed brevet colonel 6th May 1932 (seniority from 6th May 1931) and promoted colonel 10th March 1938 (seniority from 1st May 1931). He was specially employed in India as a local brigadier commanding the Poona Independent Brigade 9th April–7th November 1937,

Frank and Winifred Robert's home, Four Winds, Stanhope Bretby.

The Order of Mohammed Ali Gold Medal (Nu'ut al-Muhammad 'Ali) was inaugurated by Sultan Husain Kamil on 14th April 1915 in two classes (First Class in gold and Second Class in silver) for acts of supreme gallantry by officers and men of the Egyptian military forces, regardless of rank or status.

The Khedive's Sudan Medal 1910 was established in 1911 by the Khedivate of Egypt for service in Anglo-Egyptian Sudan, replacing the Khedive's Sudan Medal 1897. In addition to the 'Aliab Dinka' clasp, there were fifteen others. The medal was last awarded in 1926.

while presumably still commanding his Battalion. Appointed Commander Poona Independent Brigade 10th March 1938–31st May 1939 and 48th (South Midlands) Division TA 1st June–18th October 1939. Promoted major general on 13th June 1939 and retired on 16th December. He ceased to belong to the Regular Army Reserve of Officers on 29th April 1942.

After his retirement Frank and Winifred lived at Four Winds, Stanhope Bretby, near Burton upon Trent, Staffordshire. He died there on 12th January 1982. He was cremated at Bretby Crematorium and his ashes were buried in the family grave at St Wystan's Churchyard, Bretby. He left £285,432 gross in his will.

A Department for Communities and Local Government commemorative VC paving stone was dedicated at Islington

The Iraqi Order of the Two Rivers (Wisam Al Rafidain) was awarded by the Kings, and later Presidents, of Iraq from 1922. It was named after the two rivers that flow through the middle of the country, Euphrates and Tigris. The award continued into the 1980s. There were five classes and two divisions (military and civil). Foreign recipients include King George VI, King Hussein of Jordan, Yugoslav President Josip Broz Tito and Marshal of the Royal Air Force Viscount Hugh Trenchard.

Iraqi Active Service Medal.

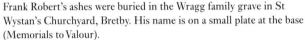

Frank Robert's ashes were buried in the Wragg family grave in St Wystan's Churchyard, Bretby. His name is on a small plate at the base (Memorials to Valour).

Memorial Green, Upper Street on 21st March 2018 to mark the centenary of his award.

In addition to the VC he was awarded the DSO, OBE, MC, 1914 Star with 'Mons' clasp, British War Medal 1914–20, Victory Medal 1914–19 with Mentioned-in-Despatches Oakleaf, War Medal 1939–45, George V Silver Jubilee Medal 1935, George VI Coronation Medal 1937, Elizabeth II Coronation Medal 1953, Elizabeth II Silver Jubilee Medal 1977, Egyptian Order of Mohammed Ali Gold Medal, Khedive's Sudan Medal 1910 with clasp 'Aliab Dinka', Iraqi Order of Al Rafidain 4th Class (Military Division) and Iraqi Active Service Medal. He bequeathed his medals to the Regiment and they are held by the Worcestershire Regimental Museum, City Museum & Art Gallery, Foregate Street, Worcester.

G/58769 LANCE CORPORAL CHARLES GRAHAM ROBERTSON
10th Battalion, The Royal Fusiliers

Charles Robertson was born at The Mill, High Bentham, near Settle, Yorkshire (not Penrith, Cumberland, as is frequently quoted) on 4th July 1879, as Charles Prince Graham. The birth was registered by his mother's brother-in-law, Charles Kirkbride. No details of his father were given. His mother was Eleanor 'Ellen' Graham (1855–1909), a domestic servant. Charles was brought up as Charles Graham Robertson by his aunt and uncle, James Robertson and Catherine née Graham (see below). Ellen was a domestic servant at Lodge Mansion, Penrith, Cumberland in 1871. She married William Frederick Draycott (1859–31st March 1936), a schoolmaster, in 1881 at Rochdale, Lancashire. He was born at Plymouth, Devon. They were living at 15 Ashton Road East, Failsworth, Manchester, Lancashire in 1901 and Frederick was still there in 1911, by when he was a head teacher. William married Florence Dyson in 1914 at Oldham, Lancashire. They were living at 15 Ashton Road East, Failsworth at the time of his death, leaving effects valued at £1,670/4/5 to his widow and daughter. Charles had three half siblings:

- Frederick William Draycott (born 1882) was a process etcher living with his father in 1911.
- Alfred Charles Draycott (1887–25th December 1970) was a farm bailiff in 1911 living at Combrook and Compton Verney, Warwickshire. He married Mabel Eveline Rowlings (1895–1951) in 1943 at Penrith, Cumberland. He was living at 24 Middlegate, Penrith at the time of his death, leaving effects valued at £2,542.
- Eleanor Draycott (1884–22nd February 1963) was living at 24 Middlegate, Penrith at the time of her death at Fairhill Hospital, Penrith, leaving effects valued at £1,824/10/-. She never married.

Charles' maternal grandfather, William Graham (c.1801–75), a farm labourer, was born at Newbiggin, Westmorland. He married Mary (born c.1811 at Beaumont, Cumberland). They were living at Newtown, Rockcliffe, Westlinton in 1841, at Laithes, Unthank in 1851 and at Carlton, Penrith, Cumberland in 1861 and 1871. Mary died before 1871 at Penrith, Cumberland, possibly in 1865. In addition to Ellen they had ten other children:

- Isabella Graham (born c.1833).
- Mary Graham (born c.1835).
- Susan Graham (born c.1836).
- Dorothy Graham (born 1839).
- William Graham (born 1840).
- Mary A Jackson (sic) (born c.1843).
- Elizabeth Graham (born 1845).
- Margaret Graham (born 1847).
- Hannah Graham (1850–1925) had a daughter, Margaret Graham, in 1867. She married Charles Kirkbride (c.1839–1916), a bobbin turner, in 1870. They were living at 17 Millhouses, Bentham, Yorkshire in 1881. By 1901 they were living at 16 Middleton Street, Preston, Lancashire and at 9 Harling Road, Preston by 1911. They had five children – Mary Florence Kirkbride 1871, Katey Kirkbride 1874, Eleanor Kirkbride 1876, Ethel Kirkbride 1881 and Gertrude Kirkbride 1884.

Catherine Graham (1852–1914), a dressmaker, married James Robertson (1855–1951), a clerk at a sawmill, in 1877 at West Derby, Liverpool, Lancashire. They were living at 137 Graham Street, Penrith in 1881 with her nephew, Charles Prince Graham. They moved to Dorking, Surrey in 1885 and were living there at Moleside, Leslie Road in 1891 and 1901. By 1891 Charles' name had changed to Charles Graham Robertson and was recorded as their son in the Census that year. At the time of the 1891 Census James was a sawmill manager, lodging at Fielding Terrace, Altham, Lancashire, while Catherine and Charles were still living at Moleside. Catherine and James had no natural children. By 1901 James was a jobbing carpenter and

When Charles first attended the St Mary the Virgin Church, it was a simple structure constructed of corrugated iron. The current church was designed by Sir Edwin Lutyens in 1903 and is a daughter church of St Martin's, Dorking. Because of its architecture it is Grade II* listed (The Voice of Hassocks).

they were all living at Moleside. By the time of the 1911 Census they were living at River Side, Dorking but James was not present. James and Charles were living at 17 Rothes Road, Dorking in 1925.

Charles was a choirboy at St Mary the Virgin's Church, on the corner of Pixham Lane and Leslie Road, Dorking, Surrey. He worshipped there, on and off, for almost seventy years. Charles was educated at:

• National School, Meeting House Lane, Penrith, Cumberland from c.1883. It was later renamed Beaconside Infants, Hutton Hill.
• Dorking National School, West Street, Surrey, now St Martin's School, Ranmore Road.
• Dorking High School for Boys, possibly in September 1890, now Ashcombe School.

He was employed as a booking clerk by the London, Brighton and South Coast Railway at Box Hill and Burford Bridge Station, Dorking, Surrey, commencing on 7th December 1893. He moved to Ware Station as a clerk with the Great Eastern Railway in July 1900. When war broke out in South Africa he was rejected for service initially for failing the shooting test. He enlisted as a trooper in the Duke of Cambridge's Own Imperial Yeomanry (526 later 33693) at 48 Duke Street, London on 5th February 1901 as Graham Robertson. He was described as 5′ 4″ tall, weighing 146 lbs, with dark complexion, brown hair, dark brown eyes and he had a scar on the right side of his neck. His religious denomination was Church of England and he gave his address as London Road, Ware, Hertfordshire. Charles was assigned to 34th Company (Middlesex) Imperial Yeomanry and sailed for South Africa on

Ware railway station dates from 1843 when the line opened. It is unusual as it has only a single bidirectional platform and track on what is otherwise a double track line.

Box Hill and Burford Bridge Station was constructed at the insistence of Thomas Grissell, who owned Norbury Park, partly to compensate for the railway running across his land. Because of its unique design by Charles Henry Driver, the building is Grade II listed. It is currently a private dwelling and commercial premises. The name of the station has changed many times over the years but in 1893 it was Box Hill and Burford Bridge Station. By 1896 it had changed to plain Box Hill (Ben Brooksbank).

8th March 1901 for training at Maitland Camp, Cape Town. He transferred to 69th Company, 7th Battalion, Imperial Yeomanry and saw action in Cape Colony, Orange Free State and the Transvaal before returning to England on 5th August 1902 for discharge at Aldershot, Hampshire on 11th August.

Charles resumed his job with the Great Eastern Railway, moving to the London offices at Bishopsgate on 12th November 1902 and to Blackwall on 10th October 1903. On 7th September 1915 he enlisted in 10th (Stockbroker's Battalion), Royal Fusiliers (STK 1591) and sailed for France on 19th November. He was in action during the Battle of the Ancre 13th–18th November 1916 and the First Battle of the Scarpe 9th–14th April

Charles was living on London Road, Ware when he enlisted in February 1901.

1917. He was wounded and evacuated to England on 18th April and returned to France on 26th July, where he was temporarily transferred to 4th Royal Fusiliers (9th Brigade, 3rd Division) and was in action near Bapaume before rejoining 10th Battalion on 13th August at Kemmel, southwest of Ypres, Belgium. By then his number had changed to G/58769.

Awarded the MM for his actions on the night of 31st August/1st September 1917 during a raid by three officers and seventy-nine men of D Company one mile east of Oosttaverne

Maitland Camp, Cape Town.

and one mile south of Hollebeke, led by Captain Alexander James Rudolph Frentzel. The raiding party set out at 2.15 a.m. against a series of enemy posts and dugouts. It was a bright moonlit night but despite this they reached their objectives and blew up four dugouts. Some enemy casualties were caused and Second Lieutenant Usher and one other rank were wounded and five other ranks were missing. STK/925 Sergeant E Carter, G/32570 Corporal WH Packham, STK/985 Lance Corporal GJ Graham and 228082 Private EF Meadowcroft were also awarded the MM, LG 2nd November 1917. The MM ribbons were presented to them by the Brigade Commander, Brigadier General CW Compton, on 12th September 1917 at Irish House, east of Kemmel. Charles was promoted lance corporal soon afterwards.

Bishopgate Station was originally named Shoreditch when it opened on 1st July 1840. It became Bishopsgate on 27th July 1846. Lack of capacity led the Great Eastern Railway to build a new terminus at Liverpool Street in 1874. Bishopsgate closed to passenger traffic in November 1875 and was reconstructed to convert it into Bishopsgate goods yard by 1881. A passenger station, Bishopsgate Low Level, was provided on the new route into Liverpool Street. A major fire in December 1964 destroyed the station. It remained derelict until 2003–04, when most of it was demolished except for some Grade II listed structures.

Awarded the VC for his actions west of Polderhoek Chateau, Belgium on 8th/9th March 1918, LG 9th April 1918. Having been seriously wounded during the VC action, he was evacuated to England on 30th March 1918 and admitted to the Ipswich and East Suffolk Hospital, Anglesea Road, Ipswich. The VC was presented by the King at Buckingham Palace on 9th November 1918. He returned to hospital on 11th November and was discharged on 19th December 1918. He received the Silver War Badge (B.228,625) in 1919.

Site of the raid on 31st August/1st September 1917 for which Charles was awarded the MM.

Charles received a number of presentations:

- 7th December 1918 – a case of razors, gold tie ring set with diamonds and a sum of money to buy a bicycle by the Mayor of Ipswich, Mr EC Ransome, at Ipswich Council Chambers.
- 21st December 1918 – Charles agreed to a public collection provided that most of the sum raised went to a charity. He accepted a gold watch and chain from the Chairman of Dorking Council, Mr JB Wilson, at the Red Lion Hotel, Dorking, with congratulatory speeches being made by Lord Ashcombe and Brigadier General Sir George Cockerill, MP for Reigate. Over £100 was donated to charity.
- 30th January 1919 – a gold ring and £110/1/6 at Blackwall Goods Yard, Orchard Street, Poplar by Mr A Bates, the agent at Blackwall and Canning Town.

The Ipswich and East Suffolk Hospital, also known as Anglesea Road Hospital, opened in August 1836. It was extended in 1869 and a children's wing was added in 1875. By 1988 all services had moved to Heath Road and most of the Anglesea Road site was demolished. The original building was converted to a home for the elderly in 1991.

Charles resumed work for Great Eastern Railway. In 1925 he was living with his father at 17 Rothes Road, Dorking. In 1932 he was appointed an assistant canvasser in the London and North Eastern Railway manager's office at 44–47 Bread Street, London. When he retired on 12th August 1939 he was presented with a set of golf clubs and a cheque for a fireside chair by the manager, Percy Syder.

Charles married Doreen Madeline née Gascoigne (14th September 1900–30th April 1987), a railway clerk who worked alongside him, on 13th June 1939. They lived at 5 Longfield Road, Dorking. When she died she left effects valued at £56,221.

Doreen's father, Edwin Percival Gascoigne (1856–1929), was born at Sheffield, Yorkshire. He married Angelina née Devey (1873–1949), born at Tamworth, Staffordshire, in 1900 at Croydon, Surrey. They lived at 133 Southlands Road, Croydon. Edwin was an electrician in 1901 and a coal agent in 1911. In addition to Doreen they had three other children:

Henry Cubitt, 2nd Baron Ashcombe CB TD (1867–1947), was Conservative MP for Reigate 1892–1906 and Lord Lieutenant of Surrey 1905–39. He married Maud Marianne Calvert and they had six sons, three of whom died in the Great War.

- Mary Lyndal Gascoigne (c.1898–1981) married Wainford Richard Ambrose Langhorne (1885–1964), a coffee salesman, in 1925. Ambrose also served in the Royal Fusiliers with Charles. When he died he left effects valued at £9,130 and Mary left £72,756. They had three children – Barbara A Langhorne 1927, Richard G Langhorne 1929 and Lyndal Valerie Langhorne 1938.
- Marjorie Angelina Gascoigne (1904–96) married Edwin Frank Barford (1903–96) in 1929.
- Edwin Percival Gascoigne (1910–12).
- A Department for Communities and Local Government commemorative VC paving stone was dedicated at School Hill, Bentham, Yorkshire on 21st April 2018 to mark the centenary of his award.

Brigadier General Sir George Kynaston Cockerill CB (1867–1957) served in the Queen's Regiment from February 1888 in India and South Africa. He later served in the Royal Warwickshire Regiment and Royal Fusiliers until retiring in 1910. He was British technical delegate at the Hague Conference in 1907. During the war he served as Sub-Director of Military Operations, Deputy Director of Military Intelligence and later Director of Special Intelligence. At the 1918 General Election he was elected unopposed as Conservative MP for Reigate and entered the Commons on 14th December 1918, only a week before the ceremony at the Red Lion Hotel, Dorking. He was an MP until standing down before the General Election on 7th October 1931. He was knighted in 1926.

Charles served in 7th Surrey (Dorking) Battalion, Local Defence Volunteers (later Home Guard) as a sergeant during the Second World War until the Home Guard was stood down on 3rd December 1944. He was very active in the local community, being a member of the British Legion from 1921 and vice president of the Dorking Branch. He was also honorary auditor of Dorking & District Football League Committee, a member of Dorking Football Club (played for 2nd XI), a life member of Dorking Club and a Freemason (initiated in February 1919 in Deanery Lodge No.3071). He sang in St Mary the Virgin Church choir and presented the church with a bound bible in 1951. Charles attended three VC reunions – Garden Party at Buckingham Palace on 26th June 1920, VC Dinner at the Royal Gallery of the House of Lords on 9th November 1929 and the Victory Day Celebration Dinner and Reception at The Dorchester Hotel, London on 8th June 1946.

In 1951 Charles suffered a stroke and was confined to a wheelchair. His health slowly deteriorated and he was admitted to Garth Nursing Home, Horsham Road, Dorking, where he died on 10th May 1954. The cause of death was congestive cardiac failure, auricular fibrillation and arteriosclerosis. He made it known that he did not want a military funeral. The funeral service was held at St Mary the Virgin Church, Pixham Lane and he was buried in Dorking Lawn Cemetery, Reigate Road (Plot 36, Grave 360). Charles is also commemorated:

- On a memorial outside East India Station on the Docklands Light Railway just off Blackwall Way, Poplar, London.
- A small display with his walking stick and some photographs at Dorking Museum, Surrey.

Charles died at Garth Nursing Home, Horsham Road, Dorking in May 1954.

Charles' and Doreen's grave in Dorking Lawn Cemetery.

In addition to the VC and MM he was awarded the Queen's South Africa Medal 1899–1902 with three clasps (Cape Colony, Orange Free State and Transvaal), 1914–15 Star, British War Medal 1914–20,

Victory Medal 1914–19, Defence Medal, George VI Coronation Medal 1937 and Elizabeth II Coronation Medal 1953. His widow presented his medals to the Regiment in 1977. The Queen's South Africa Medal, which was missing, was purchased by the Regiment from CJ and AJ Dixon (Medals & Decorations dealers) of Bridlington, Yorkshire in 1977. The VC is held by the Royal Fusiliers Museum, Tower of London.

The Queen's South Africa Medal was instituted in 1900 for military personnel, civilian officials and war correspondents, who served during the Second Boer War from 11th October 1899 to 31st May 1902. Approximately 178,000 were awarded. There are twenty-six clasps.

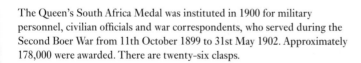

G/14498 LANCE CORPORAL JOHN WILLIAM SAYER
8th Battalion, The Queen's (Royal West Surrey Regiment)

John Sayer was born at 50 Wellington Road, Islington on 12th April 1879. The surname is sometimes seen incorrectly as Sayers. His father, Samuel Sayer (30th October 1850–16th August 1925), married Martha Margaret née Urwin (1847–1919), on 10th April 1875 at Holy Trinity, Newington, London. She also appears in census returns as Margaret M. In 1861 she was a scholar living with her uncle Thomas Phalp, a widowed mason, and his son and daughter at High Marley Hill,

Fellside, Durham. By 1871 she was a machinist living with her mother. Samuel was running Wangye Hall Farm, Iron Yard, Station Road, Chadwell Heath in 1881 but was recorded as a carman when John was born in 1879. By 1891 the family had moved to The Granges, Green Lane, Ilford, Essex. In 1901 they were living at Wangye Farm, Station Road, Ilford. They moved later to Wallwood Street, Chad's Road, Chadwell Heath. When Samuel died he left £5,361/4/2 to his sons Archibald and Albert. John had five siblings:

- Eleanor Mary Sayer (1876–25th August 1958) married Herbert John Little (1872–1944) in 1900. He was a market gardener and they were living at 13 Bennett's Castle Lane, Dagenham, Essex in 1901 and 1911. They were living at Rettendon Place, Rettendon, near Chelmsford, Essex when Herbert died, leaving effects valued at £6,280/0/4. Eleanor left effects valued at £4,707/3/4. They had four children – Herbert John Little 1901, Samuel Frank Little 1903, Winifred Eleanor Little 1907 and Mabel Irene Little 1910.

- Archibald Edmund Sayer (1880–4th May 1931) worked for his father on the family farm. He married Mary Rose Florence Threadgold (1878–1917) in 1905 at Romford, Essex. They were living at 3 Willow Cottages, Chadwell Heath, Essex in 1911. They had three children – Ernest Albert Sayer 1906, Herbert Arthur Sayer 1908 and Lily Ellen Sayer 1909. Archibald married Ada Elizabeth Randall (born 1891) in 1918 at West Ham. Ada was born at Chadwell Heath and in 1911 was a domestic servant in the home of Alfred Richard Ledger, a surveyor, at Glaisdale, Queen's Road, Buckhurst Hill, Essex. They had three children – Frank EH Sayer 1920, Hilda Sayer 1922 and Madge Sayer 1926. They moved into the family home at

Holy Trinity, Southwark (Newington), where John's parents married in April 1875 and his maternal grandparents married in October 1838. The church was so named because the land it is built upon was granted by Trinity House. The foundation stone was laid in June 1823 by the Archbishop of Canterbury and the church was consecrated in December 1824. It suffered some damage during the Second World War and closed in 1961. The church bells were recast and rehung at St Andrew with St Thomas but, when that church closed, the bells were moved to St Peter Walworth. Holy Trinity was declared redundant in 1972 and the parish united with Southwick St Matthew in 1974. In October 1973 the building was devastated by fire and required total reconstruction. In June 1975 an inaugural concert took place in the new hall named after Sir Henry Wood, who helped create the Proms and brought classical music to the general public.

Wangye Hall Farm, Chadwell Heath, Essex following the death of his father in 1925. When Archibald died he left £2,462/10/1 to his widow and son Herbert.

- Albert Henry Sayer (1884–13th June 1953), an elementary schoolmaster, married Caroline Staff (1880–1962) in 1908. They were living at 4 Linwood Terrace, Whalebone Avenue, Chadwell Heath in 1911 before moving to Chivers Farm, Swallows Cross, Brentwood. He left £1,670/4/5 to his widow and she left effects valued at £1,740/14/- to her children, Wilfred and Kathleen. They had five children – Albert Henry Sayer 1910, Wilfred Harold Sayer 1911, Roy Aubrey Sayer 1913, Kathleen Mary Sayer 1915 and Sibyl C Sayer 1919.
- Margaret Isabel Sayer (1887–16th January 1964) never married.
- Annie Gertrude Sayer (1890–1966) was a Civil Service clerk in 1911. She married Arthur Keeling Wray (1888–1918) in 1915. Arthur served as a lance corporal in 2/22nd London (682118) and was killed in action on 9th March 1918 (Jerusalem War Cemetery, Israel – L 19). She was living at Oakhurst, Carron Lane, Midhurst, Sussex when she died on 26th January 1966.

John's paternal grandfather, Edmund Sayer (c.1813–89), an agricultural labourer, married Eleanor née Hooper (c.1819–1903) in 1846. They lived at Heavy Waters Lane, Barking and Chadwell Heath, Essex in 1861 and 1871. By 1881 they had moved to Blue House Farm, Barking. In addition to Samuel they had two daughters:

- Sarah Sayer (born 1853).
- Eliza Sayer (c.1856–1935) married Samuel Gunary (1849–1930), a vegetable jobber, in February 1873. Samuel was an agricultural labourer lodging with Eliza's parents in 1871. They were living at Green Lane, Chadwell Ward in 1881 and at South Hall, Rainham, Essex in 1911. They had eight children – George Gunary 1873, Charles Gunary 1876, Florence Eleanor Gunary 1879, Kate Eliza Gunary 1881, Harry Gunary 1885, Ernest Edmond Gunary 1887, Constance Ivy Gunary 1895 and Stanley Samuel Gunary 1898.

His maternal grandfather, Thomas Edward Urwin (c.1794–13th November 1853), a millwright, was born at Newcastle upon Tyne, Northumberland. He married Mary Ann late Patrickson née Phalp (c.1808–75) on 21st October 1838 at Holy Trinity, Newington, London. She was born in Birmingham, Warwickshire. She married previously as Patrickson and had a daughter, Mary Ann Patrickson (born c.1832 at St Luke's, Middlesex), who was adopted into the Urwin family and was a dressmaker in 1851. Thomas was living with his family at 4 Richard Street, Lambeth, Surrey in 1851. Mary senior was living at 41 Agnes Street, Lambeth, Surrey in 1871. In addition to Margaret they had two other children:

- Sarah Urwin (1843–1922) was a machinist in 1871. She married Joseph Dunckley (1844–78) in 1878. He was born at Towcester, Northamptonshire. There were no children. Sarah was head of household at 7 Parade, Lambeth in 1881 and her sister Maria was living with her. By 1901 she had moved in with Maria and her family and remained there for the rest of her life.

- Maria Urwin (1850–1926) was also a machinist in 1871. She married Henry John Tubbs (1851–1901) in 1883. He was born at Ipswich, Suffolk and was a coach fitter (iron) in 1891, when they were living at 123 Princes Road, Lambeth. They had a son, Harry Leonard Tubbs, in 1886. She was head of household with her sister Sarah and son Harry at 9 Lorrimore Street, Walworth, London in 1901 and 1911.

John was living on High Road, Ilford when he married Edith Maynard in August 1904.

It is not certain where John was educated. It may have been at St Mary's Church Schools in Ilford (closed 1919–21) or at the local church school in Chadwell Heath (closed 1882–90). He moved to Cricklewood where he ran a corn and seed merchant's business.

John Sayer married Edith Louise née Maynard (1882–5th November 1958) on 15th August 1904 at Great Ilford. At the time she was living at 8 Empress Avenue in Ilford, with her brother John's family, and he was living at 239 High Road. They were living at 200 Cricklewood Lane, Hendon, Middlesex in 1911. They had six children:

THE CLOCKS AND WATCHES OF CAPTAIN JAMES COOK
1769-1969
By
Derek Howse and Beresford Hutchinson

Beresford Hutchinson, an antique clock restorer, was a director of The Museum of Soho Ltd 1992–2006 and The British Watch & Clockmaker's Guild 2002–06. He co-authored this book with Derek Howse.

- Olive Edith Sayer (15th August 1905–1970) married Charles Frank Hutchinson (1906–75) in 1933. They had two children – Beresford Hutchinson 1937 and John G Hutchinson 1940.
- Eric Maynard Sayer (24th March 1907–23rd March 1977) was a radio engineer in 1958. He died at 4 Lincoln Drive, Pyrford, Woking, Surrey, leaving effects valued at £1,384.
- Ivy Louise Sayer (18th December 1908–2001) married William John Baker (1903–2000) in October 1931. They had a son, David JM Baker (born 1936),

who married Susan JS Castle in 1964 and they had two children – Susanna Catherine L Baker 1966 and Richard William M Baker 1968.

- Dorothy Margaret Sayer (27th August 1910–24th April 1982) married George John Frank Allen (1908–78) in 1934. When she died at 25 Willowhayne Road, Angmering-on-Sea, West Preston, Sussex she left effects valued at £54,444. They had four children – Bridget M Allen 1938, Elizabeth A Allen 1940, Petrina J Allen 1948 and Alastair R Allen 1952.

- William John Sayer (17th September 1912–7th September 1979) married Winifred M Simpson (born 1917) in 1939. He died at 11 John Ray Gardens, Black Notley, Braintree, Essex.

John and Edith with their children Olive, Eric, Ivy, Dorothy and William. Joyce was not born until after John's death.

- Joyce Madeline Sayer (born 13th October 1918) married Herbert Crosskey (born 1914) in 1941. They had three children – Simon J Crosskey 1945, Penelope M Crosskey 1947 and Roland M Crosskey 1949. The marriage ended in divorce and she married Reverend Theodore William Durant Wright (1910–72) in 1968. Theodore had married Monica Westbury Corfield (born 1896) in 1934. Theodore and Joyce were living at The Vicarage, Penkridge, Staffordshire at the time of his death there on 23rd February 1972.

Edith's father, Henry Maynard (1843–91), was an apprentice living with his parents at 10 Queen Street, Spitalfields in 1861. He married Louisa née Eve (1850–96) in 1867. She was born at Writtle, Essex. Henry was a wood turner living with his family at 3 Albert Cottages, Mile End, London in 1871 and at 89 Pelham Street, London in 1881 and 1891. In addition to Edith they had six other children:

- John Midgley Maynard (1867–1948) was a traveller's assistant living with his parents in 1881 and later was a commercial traveller. He married Laura Hall (1865–1950) in 1890. They were living at 8 Empress Avenue, Ilford, London in 1901. They had two children – John Wilfred Marchmont Maynard 1892 and Irene Louise Maynard 1898.
- William Henry Maynard (1869–1930), a clergyman, married Susan Maude/ Maud Tedder (1869–1933) in 1896 at Dover, Kent. William was Curate of St Stephen, North Bow 1894–1903, Vicar of St Mary's, Stratford, Bow, London in 1901 and of St Peter's, Bethnal Green from 1903. They had a daughter, Kathleen Edith Maud Maynard (1899–1972). When William died Susan moved in with her daughter, Kathleen and son-in-law, Reverend Collett John Tovey (1884–1967), at St James' Vicarage, Fulham.
- Joseph Maynard (1871–74).

- Albert Edward Maynard (1874–1924) was a commercial clerk living with his parents in 1891. He married Eliza Jefkins (1873–1939) in 1897. He was an accountant with a church society in 1911, living with his family at 107 Sixth Avenue, Manor Park, East Ham, London. They had three children – Albert William Henry Maynard 1898, Stanley Cyril Maynard 1904 and Hilda Dorothy Maynard 1906.
- Arthur Eve Maynard (1876–1940) was a commercial clerk living with his parents in 1891. By 1901 he was a carrier's clerk living at 108 Woodlands Road, Ilford, Essex. He married Alice Fanny Field (born 1878) in 1904. Fanny had a daughter, Alice Emily Field, in 1900. They were living at 21 Marten Road, Walthamstow, Essex in 1911. They had three children – John Arthur Maynard 1906, Brian William Maynard 1908 and Ronald A Maynard 1914.
- Thomas Glasson Maynard (born 1891) was a stockbroker's clerk in 1911, living with his brother William and family. He married Dorothy Alice Roddis (1891–1963) in 1916. The marriage ended in divorce and Dorothy married Patrick Edwin Fell (1892–1974) in 1926 at St Martin in the Fields, London.

John's brother in law, William Henry Maynard, was Vicar of St Mary's, Stratford, Bow, which dates back to 1311. During the reign of Mary I many people were brought from Newgate to be burned at the stake in front of the church. The present building is a 14th century structure and the tower was added in the 15th century. Additions and replacements took place in 1794 and 1896. The church suffered considerable bomb damage during the Blitz and the bell tower was reconstructed after the war.

Patrick had married Dorothea Ray in December 1920 at Holy Trinity, Upper Chelsea and the marriage also ended in divorce. Dorothea married Allan S Wilkinson in 1925. Patrick, the son of Colonel Edwin James Fell, joined the Royal Navy on 15th May 1905 and was appointed midshipman on 15th May 1910. He was admitted to Chatham Naval Hospital with a sprained right ankle 1st-17th April 1912. Patrick was promoted acting sub lieutenant 15th September 1912, sub lieutenant 15th September 1913, lieutenant 15th July 1915 and lieutenant commander 15th July 1923. He was involved in a collision between HMS *Nereide* and an unknown steamer on 31st August 1914 and was cautioned to be more careful in future. Later he served on HMS *Cochrane, Hornet* and *Walker*. In December 1916 he was involved in a collision between HMS *Hornet* and SS *Norseman* and a note was made of his good service on this occasion. Appointed to command the destroyer HMS *Teviot* on 19th August 1918. He was granted permission to proceed abroad to the Riviera for one month on 18th December 1920 and was granted three months Half Pay when HMS *Shamrock* was reduced to Reserve. In October 1922 he failed to land a sample of cordite for testing and was cautioned to be more careful in future. In March 1925 the grounding of HMS

Tintagel was found to be due to his negligence and he received the displeasure of their Lordships. Joined fishery protection sloop HMS *Godetia* on 21st July 1925 and was admitted to Chatham Naval Hospital for three weeks from 30th January 1926 with measles. Appointed captain of the destroyer HMS *Worcester* on 1st August 1927 and captain of the minesweeper HMS *Selkirk* in the Fishery Protection Flotilla on 2nd September 1929. He also served at various times on HMS *Agamemnon*, *Bellerophon*, *Vivid*, *Whirlwind*, *Victory*, *Trenchant*, *Excellent*, *Steadfast*, *Dido*, *Hecla*, *Pembroke* and *Marshal Soult*, amongst others. He retired at his own request on 9th April 1931, although he last appears in the Navy List in July 1930. Patrick was re-employed as Secretary of the Mobilisation Committee, Devonport in 1938. He was sick on 13th April 1940 for a week with rubella. He was commended by C-in-C Plymouth for exceptional zeal and devotion to duty in a Special Order of the Day on 26th November 1945. Appointed Legionnaire of the American Legion of Merit for distinguished service to the Allied cause throughout the war (LG 28th May 1946). He was admitted to the Royal Naval Hospital Plymouth with varicose veins 27th November–14th December 1946 and retired on 13th March 1947 with the rank of commander. Patrick and Dorothy lived at Heronwood, Beckley, Battle, Sussex and at 25 Chesham Street, Chelsea. They had a son, Richard TE Fell, in 1929.

John enlisted under the Derby Scheme on 10th December 1915 and transferred to the Reserve. He was recalled on 25th July 1916 and went to France in December. Although there was no award, he was noted for exceptional bravery in August 1917 and may have been promoted lance corporal as a result. **Awarded the VC for his actions at Le Verguier, France on 21st March 1918, LG 9th June 1919.** The initial recommendation was made by his platoon commander, Lieutenant Claude Lorraine Piesse, on his return from captivity, and was supported by his CO, Lieutenant Colonel Hugh Chevalier Peirs. John was taken prisoner during his VC action and died of wounds at Le Cateau, France on 18th April 1918. He is buried in Le Cateau Military Cemetery (I B 59). The VC was presented to his widow by the King at Buckingham Palace on 26th July 1919. He is commemorated in a number of other places:

The American Legion of Merit is sixth in the order of precedence of US military awards. It is awarded for exceptionally meritorious conduct in the performance of outstanding services and achievements.

- John Sayer Close, Barking and Dagenham, dedicated in 2010.
- Named on the memorial at St Chad's Church, Chadwell Heath, Barking, Essex.
- Framed citation and replica VC at the Army Reserve Centre, 23 Guildford Road, Farnham, Surrey.
- A Department for Communities and Local Government commemorative VC paving stone was dedicated at Islington Memorial Green, Upper Street, Islington on 21st March 2018 to mark the centenary of his award.

John and Edith shortly after he enlisted.

John's grave in Le Cateau Military Cemetery.

John Sayer is commemorated on the war memorial within St Chad's Church, Chadwell Heath, which dates back to 1886.

Edith suffered great financial difficulty bringing up six children on her own. Her brother, Reverend Henry Maynard, wrote to various people, including Sir Edwin Cornwall MP, Sir James Craig MP at the Ministry of Pensions, Sir Frederick Milner and General Sir Ian Hamilton, seeking assistance. She moved to 35 Old London Road, Hastings, Sussex. She died at St Georges Hospital, Stafford, leaving effects valued at £966/0/10 and is buried in Hastings Cemetery, Sussex.

In addition to the VC John was awarded the British War Medal 1914–20 and Victory Medal 1914–19. His medals are held privately.

R/15089 RIFLEMAN ALBERT EDWARD SHEPHERD
12th Battalion, The King's Royal Rifle Corps

Albert Shepherd was born at Rowland Street, Senior Lane, Royston, near Barnsley, Yorkshire on 11th January 1897. His father, Noah Shepherd (1874–1947), was born at Dawley, Shropshire and his surname was registered as Ball. He married Laura née Darwin (1878–1909) at Barnsley in 1896. Noah was a pump man in a coalmine in 1901 and the family was living at 2 Court, 5 House, Hallam Street, Brightside Bierlow, Yorkshire. In 1911 he was a hewer and they were living at Dove Hill, Royston. Laura died due to complications with the birth of her daughter Laura. Albert had five siblings, one of whom died prior to 1911. Those known are:

- Bertha Shepherd (born 1898).
- Beatrice Annie E Shepherd (born 1902) married Leonard Land (1887–1931) in 1927 at Felkirk, near Barnsley, Yorkshire. He was a coalminer in 1911 boarding at South Hiendley, near Barnsley. They had a child, Jesse Land, also in 1927. Beatrice married Amos Stephens (c.1899–1966) in 1933 at Felkirk. They had a daughter, Verena M Stephens, in 1936.
- Jabez Shepherd (1905–96), a miner, was living at 11 Godley Street, Royston when he married Sylvia Gwendoline Bennett (1907–67) in 1926. They had five children – Irene Shepherd 1927, Jean Shepherd 1929, Lewis Shepherd 1930, Dennis Shepherd 1934 and Albert E Shepherd 1935.
- Laura Shepherd (born 1909) married Benjamin Eastwood (1909–39) in 1930 at Hemsworth. Laura and Benjamin had a son, Kenneth Eastwood, in 1933. Laura married Lawrence Cotton in 1941 and they had two sons – Laurence Cotton 1941 and Stewart Cotton 1948.

Royston is a suburban village of Barnsley, historically in the West Riding of Yorkshire and now in South Yorkshire. In the 1790s the Barnsley Canal was constructed and later a branch of the Midland Railway. Thereafter Royston had coalmines, clay works, brick works and more recently a coke works, which closed in 2014. The Doncaster Rovers footballer and comedian Charlie Williams was born there in 1927. Many of the miners who originally worked at Monkton Colliery came from the Midlands, as did Albert's paternal grandfather.

Albert's paternal grandfather was Joseph Ball (1853–1907), born at Dawley, Shropshire. He married Thursa (or Thurza/Thurya) née Bray (1853–1918), also born at Dawley, Shropshire, in 1874 at Wellington, Shropshire. He was a coal miner in 1881 and they were living at Montague Buildings, Conisbrough, Yorkshire. By 1891 he had changed the family name to Shepherd and they were living at Elm Street, Nether Hoyland, Yorkshire. They had moved to Foster's Gardens, Royston by 1901. In 1911 she was keeping house for her son Noah and his family at Dove Hill, Royston. In addition to Noah they had seven other children:

Dawley in Shropshire is now part of Telford. It is mentioned in the Domesday Book and had a castle until it was demolished in the 1640s. For over three centuries Dawley was a mining town for coal and ironstone. Clay extraction for industrial pipes, bricks and pottery had a major influence on the landscape. Dawley was the birthplace of Captain Matthew Webb (1848–83), the first person to swim the English Channel, in 1875.

- Fanny Elizabeth Ball (born 1877 at Dawley), later Shepherd, married Herbert Hill (born 1878), a steel smelter, in 1900 at Barnsley. They were living at 56 Earnshaw Street, Brightside Bierlow, Yorkshire in 1901.
- George Ball (born 1878 at Dawley).
- Jabez Shepherd (1881–1906) was born at Denaby, Yorkshire, registered at Doncaster as Sheppard. He was a coal miner. On 3rd September 1906 he cycled to Sheffield on a hot day and returned to Royston at 7.30 p.m. About three hours later he visited his fiancée, Ada Weston, and told her he had visited May Pickin, whom he had known since childhood, at Brightside, Sheffield. He said May had declared her love for him and would follow him anywhere, but he told her he did not love her. He was exhausted, hysterical and broke down in tears. He said May had broken his heart and complained his head and ear ached and that he *might be cold in the morning*. He gave Ada a card containing the words, *Lead, kindly light* and two rings off his fingers, kissed her and said goodbye. He then took a revolver from his pocket, which she seized but was not strong enough to prevent him wrestling it free and shooting himself through the right temple. He died at the scene. At an inquest at the Monckton Club, Royston on 11th September, May Pickin, a twenty-three year-old clerk at Messrs Colners outfitters, Market Place, Sheffield stated that Jabez had proposed to her in 1902, but she refused because her feelings for him were more like those of a brother. May denied Jabez had visited her that day and she had no idea of his feelings for her until he proposed in 1902. She had been courting another man for three years. Jabez began courting Ada Weston (born 1889) and they were reportedly engaged. Dr Eskrigge of Royston believed that the long day cycling in the heat had affected Jabez's mind and caused him to imagine things. The jury returned a verdict of *suicide whilst of unsound mind*.
- Rebecca Shepherd (born 1885 at Doncaster) was registered as Sheppard.
- Joseph William Shepherd (1887–1962), a coalminer hewer, married Alice Webb (born 1888), sister of Emily (see Larret Darwin below), on Christmas Day 1908. The two sisters were living at 41 Millgate Street, Royston and were married in the same church on the same day. Joseph and Alice were living at 2 Court, 6 House, Millgate Street, Royston in 1911. They had seven children – Joseph William Shepherd 1909, Horace Shepherd 1910, Mildred Shepherd 1911, Alice Hilda Shepherd 1916, twins Donald and Gladys Shepherd 1920 and Raymond Shepherd 1923.
- Hannah Shepherd (born 1891 registered as Shephard) married James Fellows (1887–1977), a coalminer hewer, in 1907 at Barnsley. He was born at Lower Gornal, Staffordshire. They were living at 6 Millgate Street, Royston in 1911. They had four children – Eunice May Fellows 1910, Annie Fellows 1914, Phyllis Fellows 1915 and Matilda Fellows 1917.
- Percy Shepherd (1895–1966), born at Birdwell, Yorkshire was registered at Wortley as Shephard. He was a pony driver below ground in 1911.

His maternal grandfather, Joseph Hague Darwin (1846–1925), born at Rotherham, married Elizabeth née Eaton (1850–90), born in Sheffield, in 1876. In 1881 he was a coal miner hewer and they were living at Stead Lane, Hoyland Nether, Yorkshire. He was living with his children there in 1891 and by 1901 was with his son-in-law, Noah and family, at 2 Court, 5 House, Hallam Street, Brightside Bierlow, Yorkshire. By 1911 he was a screen man above ground, living with his son-in-law, Noah and family, at 6 Dove Hill, Royston. In addition to Laura they had three other children:

- Larret Darwin (1879–1951), a coal miner, married Emily Webb (1885–1973) at Royston Parish Church on Christmas Day 1908. Her sister, Alice Webb, married the VC's uncle, Joseph William Shepherd, at the same time. Both were living at 41 Millgate Street, Royston at the time. Larret and Emily were living at Cross Lane, Royston in 1911. They had two sons, both named Joseph Darwin; the first was born and died in 1909 and the second was born in 1911.
- Possibly John William Darwin (born and died 1880).
- Blanch Darwin (1881–82).

Albert was educated at Royston West Riding School. In 1911 he was a pony driver at New Monckton Colliery, Barnsley. He enlisted on 18th August 1915 in 5th (Reserve) Battalion as a rifleman, although this was not an official rank until 1923. He was a keen cross-country runner and, as a boxer, was only beaten once in eleven bouts fought in the Army. He went to France after 31st December 1915. **Awarded the VC for his actions at Villers Plouich, France on 20th November 1917, LG 13th February 1918.** The VC was presented by the King at Buckingham Palace on 9th March 1918.

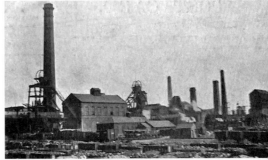

New Monckton Colliery, Barnsley, where Albert worked as a pony driver before the Great War.

Albert was presented with a gold watch and chain by the Patriotic Fund at Royston Palace, and with a bible by the scholars of the Primitive Methodist Chapel, with whom he was previously connected. A fund was also commenced to present him with War Bonds. He was promoted lance corporal on 28th August and corporal on 28th September 1918.

Albert was awarded the French Médaille Militaire, reputedly for

The Palace Cinema on the corner of Midland Road and Victoria Road in Royston opened in 1914 and had 712 seats. It is now a snooker club (Geograph).

actions on 10th October 1918, but his Battalion was out of the line that day, LG 17th March 1920. This was cancelled in the London Gazette of 21st January 1921 and replaced with the French Croix de Guerre. During his service he was wounded in the arm twice and gassed twice. As a result he received a pension. Albert was demobilised on 2nd January 1919 and was awarded the Silver War Badge (B/81750).

The Silver War Badge was issued to service personnel who had been honourably discharged due to wounds or sickness from September 1916. It was worn on the lapel badge in civilian clothes. They were individually numbered.

Albert Shepherd married Rosezillah née Tillman (1900–28th September 1925), born at Foleshill, Warwickshire, on 17th February 1919 at Royston, Yorkshire. They had a daughter, Mildred Shepherd, who was born and died in the third quarter of 1919. Rosezillah's father, Thomas Alfred Tillman (1880–1947), a coal miner, married Emma née Goodyer (1878–1948) in 1898. They were living at Hall Green, Foleshill, Warwickshire in 1901. By 1911 he was a contractor below ground and they were living at Godley Street, Royston, Yorkshire. In addition to Rosezillah they had seven other children:

- Charlotte Ann Tillman (born 1901) married Bert Pearman (1897–1969) at Barnsley in 1920. They had five children – Ronald Pearman 1921, Irene Pearman 1922, Bettina Pearman 1924, Rosezillah Pearman 1930 and Frank Pearman 1931.
- Alice Maud Tillman (born 1902) married Albert Edward Darbey (1899–1978) in 1921. They had two daughters, Constance Darbey 1921 and Nora Darbey 1925.
- Thomas Alfred Tillman (1905–06).
- Hilda Tillman (born and died 1908).
- Harold Tillman (1909–10).
- Richard A Tillman (born 1913) married Phyllis Wainwright in 1938. They had two sons – Derrick Tillman 1939 and Richard Tillman 1946.
- Lily Tillman (born and died 1919).

Albert Shepherd's first wife died in 1925 and is buried with her parents (Wakefield Family History Sharing).

Albert married Gladys Maud née Lees (8th January 1909–23rd October 1982) on 6th November 1926. They lived at 4 Oakwood Crescent, Royston and had five children:

- Clarence E Shepherd (born and died 1927).
- Kenneth Shepherd (1928–2008) married Edith Mary Field (1926–76) in 1952. They had a son, Alwyn Shepherd, in 1953.
- Eric Shepherd (born 1930) lived at 274 St Nicholas Avenue, Gosport, Hampshire.
- Lily Shepherd (born 1931).
- Mildred Shepherd (1939–44).

Gladys' father, Richard Lees (1859–1937), born at Whitwick, Leicestershire, was a coalminer. He was living with his father at 56 George Street, Hucknall Torkard, Nottinghamshire in 1901. He married Annie Maria née Jones (born c.1882 at Walsall, Staffordshire.) in 1902. They were living at 79 Milgate Street, Royston, Yorkshire by 1911. In addition to Gladys they had three other children:

- Richard Edward Lees (born 1903) married Edith Hickman (1906–63) in 1926. They had four children – Marjorie D Lees 1926, Doreen Lees 1930, Kenneth Lees 1934 and Enid Lees 1936.
- Joseph Lees (born 1905) married Ellen Wood in 1926. They had at least four children – Joyce Lees 1927, Albert E Lees 1928, Dennis Lees 1932 and Dorothy Lees 1936.
- Doris H Lees (1911–68) married Frederick Hunter (born 1904) in 1929. They had three children – Jean Hunter 1931, Ronald Hunter 1938 and Colin Hunter 1940.

Albert became a caretaker at Monckton Colliery offices and later joined the Corps of Commissionaires. He attended five VC reunions – VC Garden Party at Buckingham Palace on 26th June 1920, VC Dinner at the Royal Gallery of the House of Lords on 9th November 1929, Victory Day Celebration Dinner & Reception at The Dorchester, London on 8th June 1946, VC Centenary Celebrations at Hyde Park, London on 26th June 1956 and the 2nd VC Association Reunion at the Café Royal, London on 7th July 1960.

On 16th November 1929 Albert attended the funeral of John Crawshaw Raynes VC with fellow VCs George Sanders, Wilfrid Edwards, Fred McNess, Charles Hull, Albert Mountain, Frederick Dobson, Arthur Poulter, William Butler, Sam Meekosha and John Ormsby. He also attended a review of the Corps of Commissionaires at Buckingham Palace on 13th May 1959.

Albert died at his home at 4 Oakwood Crescent, Royston, near Barnsley on 23rd October 1966 and is buried in Royston Cemetery. He is commemorated in a number of other places:

Albert Shepherd's grave in Royston Cemetery (Memorials to Valour).

The French Croix de Guerre was first awarded in 1915 to individuals or units distinguishing themselves by acts of heroism. Some notable recipients include:

Josephine Baker – American born French dancer, singer and actress for her work in the Resistance.
Jacques Cousteau – pioneer diver and underwater filmmaker.
General Dwight D Eisenhower – Supreme Allied Commander during Operation OVERLORD.
Noor Inayat Khan and Violette Szabo – British SOE agents awarded the George Cross and executed by the Nazis.
Audie Murphy – actor and the most decorated US soldier of WW2, including the Medal of Honor.
General George S Patton – commander of US Third Army in the Second World War.
Theodore Roosevelt – son of President Theodore Roosevelt, awarded the Medal of Honor for his actions 6th June 1944 on Utah Beach.
James Stewart – actor for his role in the liberation of France as a USAAF colonel.
Major Richard D Winters – Easy Company, 506th Parachute Infantry Regiment, made famous by the TV series and book *Band of Brothers*.
Sergeant Alvin C York – American First World War Medal of Honor winner and subject of a film in 1941 starring Gary Cooper.

A 0-4-0 saddle tank locomotive (HC1784/47), constructed in 1947, carried nameplates bearing the inscription 'SHEPHERD VC'. It was used by the National Coal Board at Monckton Collieries in Royston until it was scrapped in November 1972. The nameplate is displayed in the Albert Shepherd VC Centre, Station Road, Royston.

Royston Civic Hall was renamed the Albert Shepherd VC Centre at a ceremony on 6th March 2015 by the Mayor of Barnsley. A commemorative blue plaque is fixed to the outside wall.

- The Albert Shepherd VC Centre, formerly Royston Civic Hall, on Station Road.
- Shepherd Way, Royston.
- Named on the memorial wooden archway to John the Baptist churchyard, Melbourn Street, Royston.
- Plaque on the War Memorial at John the Baptist Parish Church, Melbourn Street, Royston.
- The Department for Communities and Local Government decided to provide a commemorative paving stone at the birthplace of every Great War Victoria Cross recipient in the United Kingdom. Albert's stone was dedicated at the Town Hall Gardens, Church Street, Barnsley on 20th November 2017 to mark the centenary of his award.

In addition to the VC he was awarded the British War Medal 1914–20, Victory Medal 1914–19, George VI Coronation Medal 1937, Elizabeth II Coronation Medal

1953 and the French Croix de Guerre 1914–18 with Bronze Palm. It is believed that Albert never returned the Médaille Militaire when it was replaced by the Croix de Guerre in January 1921 and that is why both medals appear in his medal group, although officially he is only entitled to the Croix de Guerre. His medals were presented to the Royal Green Jackets Museum by his widow in June 1968. They are held by the Royal Green Jackets (Rifles) Museum, Peninsula Barracks, Romsey Road, Winchester.

LIEUTENANT COLONEL JOHN SHERWOOD-KELLY
The Norfolk Regiment, attached 1st Battalion, The Royal Inniskilling Fusiliers

John Kelly was born at Lady Frere, Queenstown, Cape Province, South Africa on 13th January 1880, an older twin with Hubert. John, also known as Jack, adopted the additional name of Sherwood later. His father, Captain John James Kelly (1850–1926), was born in Newbridge, Ireland. He served in the Frontier Armed and Mounted Police in 1868 and was one time Mayor of Lady Frere. He became the local Native Law Agent and was a fair man who gained a reputation for being even-handed. He opposed Cecil Rhodes in Parliament over dealings with local tribes and for not taking their customs and tribal laws into account. On the night of 8th/9th December 1874 John senior tied a rope to his waist and swam to the Italian barque *Nuovo Abele* (690 tons), which had foundered in the Chintsa River mouth. He saved ten lives (possibly more) and was awarded the Royal Humane Society's Bronze Medal. In 1878 the Frontier Armed and Mounted Police became the Cape Mounted Riflemen and John remained a member. John married Emily Jane née Didcott (1858–92) in 1877. She was born at Winchester, Cape Town, South Africa. On 8th August 1892 Emily was driving a cart at Lady Frere when the horse bolted and she was unable to control it. The cart turned over, landed on top of her and she was killed outright. John junior was distraught and the loss of his mother shaped the rest of his life more than any

Lady Frere in the Eastern Cape of South Africa, thirty miles northeast of Queenstown, was established in 1879. It was named after the wife of Sir Bartle Frere (1815–84), Governor of Cape Colony 1877–80.

The Chintsa River mouth where the Italian barque *Nuovo Abele* foundered in 1874. Parts of the ship's woodwork are still being found in the area. Inset is the Royal Humane Society's Bronze Medal, introduced in 1837, and awarded to people who have put their lives at great risk to save or attempt to save someone else (Håkon Thingstad).

Cecil Rhodes (1853–1902), a British businessman, mining magnate and politician in South Africa, was a fervent believer in British imperialism. He was Prime Minister of Cape Colony 1890–96, but was forced to resign after the disastrous Jameson Raid on the South African Republic (Transvaal). His British South Africa Company founded Rhodesia in 1895 (now Zimbabwe and Zambia), which was named after him. He set up the international postgraduate Rhodes Scholarships, funded by his estate, which continue to this day at Oxford University. By the end of 2016 there had been 7,776 scholars, including eight future heads of state – Wasim Saijad (Pakistan), Bill Clinton (USA), Dom Mintoff (Malta), John Turner (Canada), Norman Manley (Jamaica) and three Australian PMs, Bob Hawke, Tony Abbott and Malcolm Turnbull. Other Scholars include the astronomer Edwin Hubble and the singer/songwriter/actor Kris Kristofferson.

other single event. He became confrontational, angry and resentful. He had a small plaque erected in the church where she is buried, *She was a true Christian woman, noble, fond, loving affectionate mother and staunch friend. Jack, 8th August 1892.*

John senior married Selena Collins (died 1944) in 1894, having employed her as a governess and housekeeper. He raised the Lady Frere Company of local volunteers during the Second Boer War 1899–1902. During the influenza epidemic he delivered soup made by lady volunteers to ensure the local Xhosa villagers survived. John juniuor had twelve siblings from his father's two marriages:

- Emily Nuovo Abele Kelly (born 1878) at Queenstown, Cape Colony.
- Hubert (also seen as Hurbert) Henry Kelly (1880–93) was born a few minutes after John. He died on 21st July 1893 after falling from his horse.
- Olive Rebecca Kelly (born 1881) at Buffle Doorns, Cape Colony.
- Edward Charles Kelly (1882–1948), born at Buffle Doorns, Cape Colony, served in Montmorency's Scouts during the Boer War. He was employed in the civil service in Rhodesia when he enlisted in Hartigan's Horse during the Great War from September 1914 until July 1915. He served as a lieutenant, including some time in German South-West Africa. He paid his own passage to England and was living

at the Strand Palace Hotel, London when he applied for a commission on 27th July 1915. Hartigan recommended him by telegram. Commissioned in 3rd (Reserve) Norfolk at Walton, Felixstowe on 12th August and reported to the School of Instruction at St Mary's Home, Sea Road, Felixstowe on 16th August. He went to France and received a gunshot wound on 3rd July 1916 while attached

Winchester, Cape Town, South Africa where John's mother was born.

to 7th Suffolk. He embarked on SS *Panama* at Boulogne for Southampton on 8th July and was admitted to Reading War Hospital on 10th July. His address in Britain was c/o Mrs FH Hamilton, Margery Hall, near Reigate, Surrey and also 28 Alfred Place, South Kensington. A medical board on 20th July at Reading found him unfit for any service for two months. He was granted leave until 19th September and sailed on SS *Walmer Castle* on 22nd July for South Africa. A medical board on 11th October found him unfit for any service for three weeks and he was granted leave to 1st November. A medical board on 11th November found him fit for General Service and he joined 3rd (Reserve) Norfolk on 5th December. He was posted to 1st Norfolk in France in 1917 and became a company commander. A large party of the enemy gained a footing in his trench and he at once counterattacked at the head of his men, driving the enemy out and inflicting severe losses on them. The success of the attack was largely due to his fine example and leadership for which he was awarded the MC (LG 16th August 1917). He married Dallas Collie (1894–1989) in 1917 at St George, Hanover Square, London. She was born at Queenstown, Eastern Cape. They had at least a daughter, Nova DM Kelly, in 1918 at Wandsworth, London. On 12th September he was invited to dinner with the officers of 8th Leicestershire at Avesnes, France. On the way back to his unit, which was billeted at Beaucourt, he fell from his horse in Avesnes at 11.45 p.m. and was picked up by two soldiers at 5 a.m. next morning. A French lady heard the horse fall and it ran off leaving Edward lying on the ground. Others passed by ignoring him and she was frightened to go out alone. His skull was fractured and the vision in his right eye was affected. He embarked on 10th October at Rouen for Southampton and was admitted to the Empire Hospital, London on 12th October. A medical board at Millbank on 10th November found him permanently unfit for General Service and for Home Service for three months. He was granted leave until 1st December, but another medical board on 29th November recommended leave until 6th January 1918. A medical board on 13th February found him unfit for General Service for two months but fit for Home Service. A medical board on 13th March found him unfit for General Service permanently, but another medical board on 21st June found him fit for General Service and he rejoined 3rd (Reserve) Norfolk at Felixstowe. He claimed a wound gratuity for the fractured skull and loss of sight in his right eye, but it was rejected because he was not on duty. Later he claimed he was ordered in a note to see Lieutenant Colonel Utterson, CO 8th Leicestershire, and dinner was included. He could produce no written evidence but CSM E Rose of B Company, 1st Norfolk made a statement that he had seen the note from Utterson. However, CO 1st Norfolk, Lieutenant Colonel JWV Carroll, in his accident report is clear that Edward was not on duty. It was concluded that the accident was a joy ride and did not qualify for a wound gratuity. On 10th April 1919 he reported to the Repatriation Camp, Winchester. Other medical boards were ordered for 26th June and 10th September in London, but he did not attend either. He departed the Officers Wing, Repatriation Camp, Pirbright on 12th September for return to South Africa. He was demobilised on 8th October 1919 and relinquished his commission on 1st April 1920 retaining the rank of captain. He was eligible for an injury pension of £45 from 12th September 1919 to 11th September 1920. By June 1920 he was working for the Commissioner for Police in Kampala, Uganda, but was back in South Africa by February 1921.

- Percy Dennis Kelly (born 1885).
- Gertrude Margaret Kelly (1886–1935).
- Oswald Claude Kelly (born 1887).
- Clifford Terrence Kelly (born 1889) was educated at St Aidans College, Grahamstown, Cape Colony. He served for four years with the Natal Mounted Police and Cape Mounted Police as a trooper until discharged at his own request on 17th June 1909 on payment of £5. He then farmed in Rhodesia. On 24th January 1915 he applied for a commission in 2/6th Royal Sussex at Chiseldon Camp, Wiltshire giving his UK address as Margery Hall, Reigate, Surrey. He was 6′ tall and had previously had operations for appendicitis and a hernia. He was commissioned in 4th Royal Sussex on 10th August 1916 and was attached to 11th Battalion. On 30th September 1916 he left his unit suffering with abdominal trouble. He embarked at Boulogne for Dover on SS *St David* on 10th October and he had a haemorrhoid operation on 16th November. A medical board at Reading War Hospital on 5th December found him unfit for any service and he was granted leave to 9th January 1917. A medical board at Aylesbury on 15th January found he had recovered from the operation, but was suffering indigestion and was unfit for General Service for one month. A medical board at Tunbridge Wells on 17th February found him unfit for General and Home Service for three months and for light duties for two months. He was vomiting periodically and had stomach pains. It was recommended he be admitted for expert surgical advice. However, on 8th March 1917 he was demobilised and on 10th April 1917 he relinquished

his commission due to ill health (Silver War Badge 290597). Clifford was living at Chalfont Lodge, Chalfont St Peter, Buckinghamshire when he applied to the War Office for the return of his passport so that he could go home. In 1934 he wrote to the War Office for details of his VC brother's career. He was living at Macheke, South Rhodesia at the time.

- Ethel Mary Kelly (born 1890).
- Dorothy Elizabeth Kelly (born 1895).
- Henry James Kelly (born 1898).
- Patrick Dermot Kelly (born 1901).

John's paternal grandfather, James Kelly, of Newbridge, Co Kildare, Ireland, served in 11th Hussars (1613) and took part in the Charge of the Light Brigade in October 1854 during the Crimean War (Crimean Medal with clasps 'Alma', 'Balaclava', 'Inkerman' and 'Sebastopol'). He emigrated to South Africa in the 1860s. John's maternal grandfather was H Didcott, of Queenstown, South Africa. His wife's name is not known, but in addition to Emily they had two other children:

- Helen Mary Didcott married Frederick Howard Hamilton (Sir Frederick from 1936) (1865–1956), born at Whitechapel, London. He was educated at Mill Hill School and Caius College, Cambridge. He studied for the Bar at the Inner Temple before emigrating to South Africa in 1889, where he founded the *Zoutpansberg Review* in Pietersburg. He joined *The Star* in Johannesburg in 1890, becoming editor in 1895. He also had mining interests in Africa, Australia, and elsewhere. Frederick was sent from Johannesburg to Cape Town with Charles Leonard in late December 1895 to inform Cecil Rhodes of the postponement of the Jameson Raid. Returning to Johannesburg he was arrested and tried with the leaders of the Reform Committee, but was released on signing an undertaking not to take part in politics for a period of three years. His opposition to the Jameson Raid and other differences of opinion with those controlling *The Star* led to him resigning and he returned to Britain, where he became a successful financier. He was Chairman of the Executive Committee of the Liberal National Council and Vice President of the Royal Free Hospital. He married Mary Alice Forster Barrington-Ward née Smith (1884–1960) in 1941. Her father, Arthur Lionel Smith (1850–1924), was Master of Balliol College, Oxford. Mary was married previously to Frederick Temple Barrington-Ward (1880–1938) in 1908. Barrington-Ward was admitted to Lincoln's Inn as a barrister and served as Recorder of Hythe 1904–11, Recorder of Chichester 1914–25 and JP for Sussex 1923. He was appointed a Knight of the Garter in 1919. Frederick and Mary had a daughter, Sylvia Mary Barrington-Ward, in 1909.
- A second daughter, whose name is not known, married John James Kelly's brother.

John was educated at:

- Queenstown Grammar School until being expelled for his uncontrolled behaviour in 1895.
- Possibly Dale College, King William's Town, where he was also rebellious and was eventually expelled.
- St Andrew's College, Grahamstown from late 1896 and was expelled soon afterwards.

St Andrew's College (seen here in 1898), an Anglican boarding school for boys in Grahamstown, was founded in 1855 by the first Bishop of Grahamstown, John Armstrong. Famous alumni include:

Bevil Rudd – 1920 Antwerp 400m Olympic Gold Medallist.
James Thompson – 2012 lightweight coxless four Olympic Gold Medallist.
Peter van der Merwe – South African cricket captain 1965–67.
Sir Basil Schonland – the scientist who was involved in the development of radar.
James Henry Greathead – renowned for his work on the London Underground.
Brigadier Sir Miles Hunt-Davies – Private Secretary to the Duke of Edinburgh.
Charles Herbert Mullins VC.

After school John did not return home and volunteered for service with the British South Africa Police to deal with the Matabeleland Rebellion, which broke out on the border of Transkei in 1896. Soon after he enlisted in the Cape Police and in 1899 he was part of the mounted escort from Division 1 for the Governor of Cape Colony and High Commissioner for Southern Africa, Sir Alfred Milner GCMG KCB, when he visited Transkei. This small bodyguard included two other future VCs – William Bloomfield and Alexander Young. John was dismissed from the Cape Police for insubordination. He joined the Native Department in July 1899 as a result of his father's influence.

Two months later the Second Boer War broke out and John served in Colonel Herbert Plumer's column at the Relief of Mafeking on 17th May 1900 and also took part in operations in the Orange Free State, Transvaal and Rhodesia. He was promoted sergeant and was commissioned in 2nd Imperial Light Horse in the field on 8th January 1901. He resigned on 5th June 1901 after an argument with a senior officer and enlisted in 2nd Kitchener's Fighting Scouts, but was reduced to the ranks for insubordination in May 1902. John was Mentioned in General Herbert Kitchener's Despatch of 1st June 1902 for actions at Boschbult on 31st March 1902 (LG 18th

Alfred Milner, 1st Viscount Milner KG GCB GCMG PC (1854–1925), a statesman and colonial administrator, was influential in formulating foreign and domestic policy until the 1920s. As South African High Commissioner his arrogance and poor diplomacy were important factors in causing the Second Boer War 1899–1902.

The British South Africa Police was formed as a paramilitary force of mounted infantrymen in 1889 by Rhode's British South Africa Company. Until 1980 it was Rhodesia's police force. Officers were trained as policemen and soldiers until 1954 and members served in both world wars. It also provided units for the Rhodesian Bush War in the 1960s and 70s. Under Robert Mugabe the British South Africa Police became the Zimbabwe Republic Police in 1980. Seen here are the NCOs of a British South Africa Police company in 1890.

Herbert Charles Onslow Plumer (1857–1932) was commissioned in the 65th Regiment in September 1876. He served in India and in the Sudan on the 1884 Nile Expedition. After Staff College he was appointed Deputy Assistant Adjutant-General in Jersey in May 1890. In December 1895 he was appointed Assistant Military Secretary to General Officer Commanding Cape Colony. In 1896 he disarmed the local police force in Southern Rhodesia following the Jameson Raid. Later that year he commanded the Matabele Relief Force and returned to Britain as Deputy Assistant Adjutant-General at Aldershot in 1897. During the Second Boer War he raised a force of mounted infantry and led it during the Siege of Mafeking. Promoted colonel on 29th November 1900 and commanded a mixed force. He was promoted major general in August 1902 and commanded successively 4th Brigade, 10th Division and Eastern District. In 1904 he became Quartermaster-General. Command of 7th Division followed in April 1906 and 5th Division in Ireland in May 1907. Promoted lieutenant general in November 1908 and was appointed GOC-in-C Northern Command in November 1911. During the Great War he commanded V Corps and in May 1915 took command of Second Army. Plumer is best known for the outstanding victory at the Battle of Messines in June 1917. He was later C-in-C British Army of the Rhine, Governor of Malta and High Commissioner for Palestine in 1925. He retired in 1928 as Field Marshal, 1st Viscount Plumer.

July 1902). John resigned after the war and enlisted in the Somaliland Burgher Corps (No.32), serving in the Third Expedition against Muhammed Abdile Hassan (the Mad Mullah) November 1902–July 1903. By the end of the campaign John was a private again as a result of speaking out against his CO.

John returned to the Transkei and went into business as a trader and a recruiter of native labour for the mines in the Cape and elsewhere. He took part in the suppression of the Zulu Rebellion in 1906. In 1909 he was to give evidence in court, but delayed attendance to finish a tennis match. Summoned to appear immediately he appeared in tennis whites and the outraged judge ordered him to go away and come back dressed more appropriately and respectfully. John returned in morning coat, top hat and lavender coloured trousers. On

15th May 1912 he married Emily Sarah Lawlor née Snodgrass (1868–1931), born at Umtata, Cape of Good Hope, a wealthy widow previously married to Edward Lawlor in 1887. Emily's father, John Snodgrass (1843–1903), was born at Fort Beaufort, Cape, South Africa. He married Mary Polly née Wattrus (1849–1934), born at Ledbury, Herefordshire, England. Emily had cautiously drawn up a pre-nuptial agreement as the marriage ended in divorce soon afterwards.

Attracted by the chance of a fight, John is reputed to have travelled to Belfast in 1914 with his brother Edward and enlisted in the Sherwood Foresters under a false name, but no evidence has been found to substantiate this. On 31st August 1914 he enlisted in 2nd King Edward's Horse as a sergeant (985) at White City, London. He was described as a gentleman, 6′ ¼″ tall, weighing 186 lbs, with green eyes and fair hair. His brother Edward also enlisted. The brother of John's future wife also served in the unit. John applied for a commission in the cavalry or, failing that, any unit at the front. His permanent address was Box 39, Butterworth, Transkei, South Africa and his address for correspondence was c/o FH Hamilton Esq, Margery Hall, near Reigate.

John was commissioned in 3rd (Reserve) Battalion, Norfolk Regiment as a lieutenant on 4th November and was posted to 1/1st Norfolk Yeomanry (later 12th (Norfolk Yeomanry) Battalion, The Norfolk Regiment), at Woodbridge, Suffolk. On arrival it was apparent that he had more operational experience than any other officer and was appointed temporary major on 10th November to command a company. However, John quickly became frustrated and requested a transfer to get to the front.

He was posted to 1st King's Own Scottish Borderers and may have been in Egypt prior to serving at Gallipoli from 23rd July 1915. **Awarded the DSO for his actions at Chocolate Hill, Suvla on 21st August when, in spite of being wounded twice (including a gunshot to the right leg), he led his men to capture the enemy's position, LG 2nd February 1916.** He was evacuated on 22nd August 1915, to a hospital in Alexandria, Egypt and returned to duty on 15th September. On 28th October he was appointed to command 1st King's Own Scottish Borderers as an acting lieutenant colonel until 22nd January 1916. He became known as 'Bomb Kelly' because of his fondness for dangerous stunts and catapulting homemade bombs at the enemy trenches. He was wounded several more times during the campaign and was withdrawn temporarily from the front to command the 29th Division bombing school to pass on his expertise. **John was Mentioned in General Sir Ian Hamilton's Despatch dated 11th December 1915, LG 28th January 1916.** At the end of the campaign he was evacuated to Egypt and was appointed temporary lieutenant colonel on 22nd January and CO 1st King's Own Scottish Borderers on 2nd February 1916. He wrote to the War Office from Suez on 22nd February 1916 asking for a wound gratuity for his injuries on 21st August 1915. The claim was turned down on 22nd March as his injuries had not been severe enough. The 1st King's Own Scottish Borderers war diary records that John's predecessor as CO returned to resume command on 19th May 1916, having recovered from wounds. By then the Battalion was in France.

John spent some time in Britain to recover from his wounds, during which he married Nellie Elizabeth Crawford née Greene (1871–1971) on 22nd April 1916 at St Peter's Church, Cranley Gardens, Kensington. She met John through her brother, William, when both were serving in 2nd King Edward's Horse early in the war. Nellie was living at 21 Cranley Gardens, Kensington at the time. John gave his address as Margery Hall, Margate, Kent, where an aunt let him a flat. He gave his age as forty-two although he was only thirty-six. Nellie worked for the Red Cross during the war in a canteen in Paris.

John Sherwood-Kelly married Nellie Elizabeth Crawford Greene at St Peter's Church, Cranley Gardens, Kensington on 22nd April 1916.

There is a record of a daughter, Lee Sherwood Kelly, but it is not known who was the mother. Of nine offending letters written by John and intercepted by censors in Russia in 1919, three were to Mrs Cameron, Dunkerry Lodge, Minehead, Somerset. In one of these letters dated 26th July 1919 he wrote, *Give my Babe a huge hug & kiss for me* and *I long to see my Babe, news of her acts as a tonic to me*. He also realises that Mrs Cameron will not marry him. It is possible that Mrs Cameron was the mother of his daughter. Lee married Charles Henry Blood-Smyth (born 1927) on 26th February 1955, registered as Eileen Kelly. He was educated at Trinity College, Dublin and was living at 427 Fulham Road, London in 1955. They had three children all registered at Westminster, London – Lucinda Charlotte Fitzgerald Blood-Smyth 1959, Griselda Serena Sherwood Blood-Smyth 1961 and Henrietta Prudence Fitzgerald Blood-Smyth 1963.

Nellie's father, Hon George Henry Greene (1838–1911), was born at Collon, Louth, Ireland. He was the son of Lieutenant William Pomeroy Greene (1798–1845), a retired naval officer and Irish landowner, who sailed for Australia, arriving at Port Phillip, Victoria on 1st December in 1842. William entered the Royal Navy on 1st March 1810 and was aboard one of the ships (HMS *Northumberland* and *Myrmidon*) that took Napoleon into exile on St Helena. He was present at the Bombardment of Algiers by Lord Exmouth on 27th August 1816 and at the taking of Rangoon in the First Anglo–Burmese War in May 1824. He built a house at Woodlands, near Melbourne and founded the once well-known Woodlands Steeplechase. George was educated at Melbourne University 1855–58, where he was a renowned athlete and was one of the first five students to graduate. He was particularly interested in racing and bred the winner of the ten miles race at Wagga Wagga. He was also interested in boxing and cricket and he was a great lover of poetry. He purchased the Tooma Estate on the Upper Murray, New South Wales in partnership with his cousin, Mr McCartney, and Mr Kinleside. He also purchased Iandra Station and developed a prosperous wheat property. As a result he commenced building a village at Iandra, later known as Greenethorpe, and an ornate Edwardian mansion, which still exists. He was the founder of the 'share system' by which the landlord and the tenant farmer shared the profits rather than paying a fixed rent. George entered politics in his eighties and was elected Member of the Legislative Council of New South Wales for the Grenfell constituency on three occasions. He was known for his philanthropy, giving away hundreds of pounds anonymously annually. He married Ellen Elizabeth 'Nelly' née Crawford (died 1921), daughter of Colonel Crawford, Indian Army, in 1870. In addition to Nellie they had four other children:

John's father-in-law, George Henry Greene, was the fifth son of Lieutenant William Pomeroy Greene RN. In 1842 William chartered the *Sarah* to convey his household to Port Phillip, Victoria. They settled at Woodlands near Melbourne and George was one of the first five students to graduate from the University of Melbourne in 1858. He gained experience in New South Wales at Billabong station and was later part owner of Tooma and Marogle stations. He and his wife travelled the world for two years after selling their station interests in 1875. Returning to New South Wales, he bought Iandra estate (32,600 acres) near Grenfell for grazing and wheat growing. By 1911 Iandra had fifty share-farmers working 18,000 acres and there were 20,000 sheep. He represented Grenfell in the Legislative Assembly in 1889–91, July–October 1894 and in 1895–98. In April 1899 he was nominated to the Legislative Council to facilitate passage of a bill to have the Constitution put to a referendum.

- Georgina Marion Crawford Greene (1874–1941) married Captain Charles Edward Fox Webb RN (1863–1942) in 1907 at Hartley Wintney, Hampshire. He was Fleet Paymaster in 1911 and they were living at 32 Alhambra Road, Southsea, Hampshire. By 1937 they were living at Latimers, Weston Sub-Edge, Gloucestershire. They had a son, Patrick E Webb in 1914.
- George Cyril Crawford Greene (1878–1884).
- William Pomeroy Crawford Greene (1884–1959) was a farmer and stockbreeder who also served in 11th Light Horse, Australian Military Forces. After his father's death William moved to England, taking his sister Nellie with him. He was granted a temporary commission as a second lieutenant in 12th Reserve Regiment of Cavalry on 21st November 1914 and joined on 24th November. His address was Victoria Hotel, Aldershot and he nominated his brother in law, Fleet Paymaster Charles Webb RN, as his next of kin. William transferred to the Reserve Regiment 1st Life Guards for duty with 1st Life Guards on 19th May 1915, but rejoined on 3rd June because the number of officers required to replace casualties had been overestimated. He embarked at Folkestone on 24th

July, disembarked at Boulogne the same day and joined 13th Hussars on 25th July. He was appointed regimental transport officer 25th September–26th October. He embarked at Marseille on 27th June 1916 and disembarked at Basra, Mesopotamia on 26th July. William was admitted to 16th Casualty Clearing Station and later to hospital and the Officers' Convalescence Depot at Amara with tonsillitis 10th–27th January 1917. He was admitted to 23rd British Stationary Hospital at Amara on 28th January with inflamed glands in the neck and was discharged from the Officers' Hospital at Beit Naama on 26th February to rejoin 13th Hussars on 21st March. He was appointed acting captain while commanding a squadron 6th August–12th September. On 13th August he transferred to the Base for leave in Australia, but was admitted to 2nd British General Hospital at Amara on 25th August with sandfly fever and was discharged from 3rd British General Hospital at Basra on 5th September. He embarked at Basra for leave in Australia on 13th September. On the return he embarked on HT *Barpeta* in Bombay on 28th January 1918 and disembarked at Basra on 4th February, rejoining his unit on 18th February. William was promoted lieutenant on 27th March 1918 backdated to 1st July 1917. He was admitted to 119th Field Ambulance on 19th July with an undiagnosed fever and was treated at 23rd British Stationary Hospital, Amara and the Officers' Convalescence Depot, Baghdad until 22nd July, rejoining the unit on 29th July. He was again admitted to 119th Field Ambulance on 6th August with an undiagnosed fever and was treated at 23rd British Stationary Hospital, Amara and the Officers' Convalescence Depot, Baghdad until 18th August, rejoining the unit on 25th August. William transferred to the Base on 22nd February 1919 and embarked on HT *Shuja* for India en route for England on 19th March. He was demobilised on 23rd April 1919 and relinquished his commission on 1st April 1920, retaining the rank of lieutenant. His address was c/o Commercial Banking Company of Sydney Ltd, 18 Birchin Lane, London. William was Conservative MP for Worcester 1923–45. He returned to Australia, where he died on 10th June 1959 and is buried in Iandra Methodist Rural Youth Centre Cemetery (Greenthorpe Private Cemetery).

The Iandra estate prospered and in 1908 George Henry Greene began building Greenethorpe village at Iandra rail siding with forty houses for the share-farmers. In 1910 he completed this ornate mansion, built of reinforced concrete. Iandra had a store, post office, school, carpenter's and blacksmith's shops and a handling agent for farm machinery. In addition to sixty-one share-farmers, 350 men were employed on the estate. After George's death in 1911 and the departure of his family to Britain during the Great War, the property was sold to the Ianson family. In the 1950s it was sold to the Methodist Church and used as a home for delinquent boys. It is now owned privately and has been extensive renovated.

- Gladys Gwenlian Crawford Greene (born 1888).

John went to France in May 1916 and received a gunshot wound through the lung on 4th June while on a raid attached to 1st Royal Inniskilling Fusiliers. His life was saved by a stretcher-bearer named Jack Johnson. John was evacuated to Rouen where Nellie nursed him until he was evacuated through Southampton on 9th July to the London Hospital (Officers' Section), Whitechapel next day. A medical board on 20th July found him unfit for service for four months and recommended he would benefit from a sea voyage. He was granted three months sick leave and permission to proceed to South Africa with Nellie. Part of the trip involved a recruiting tour, an exhausting round of interviews, speaking engagements and dinners. John found it difficult to resist the attention of female admirers and his marriage began to break down. They returned to England in September, but he was declared unfit for any service for six weeks by a medical board on 19th October and was sent on leave until 29 November. His address was the Rubens Hotel, Buckingham Palace Road, London. He was awarded a very severe wound gratuity of £225 on 28th October. On 22nd November he was passed fit for Home Service. The DSO was presented by the King at Buckingham Palace on 29th November 1916.

John was posted to 3rd (Reserve) Battalion, King's Own Scottish Borderers at Duddingston Camp, Midlothian, Scotland on 1st December 1916, reverting to major. On 5th December he requested a transfer to 10th Norfolk, which had become 25th Training Reserve Battalion at Parkston, Dovercourt, Harwich, Essex, and joined on 8th January 1917. **Awarded the CMG, LG 1st January 1917.** The CMG was presented by the King at Buckingham Palace on 24th January 1917. In the meantime a medical board on 28th December found him unfit for General Service for two months and another on 26th January 1917 granted another wound gratuity of £112. A medical board on 17th February found him fit for General Service.

John returned to France on 19th March and was attached to 1st Royal Inniskilling Fusiliers, becoming CO on 29th March, replacing Richard Willis VC. Appointed acting lieutenant colonel while CO from 11th April. He was gassed on 15th April near Monchy-le-Preux, but remained at duty, and was slightly wounded on 18th July and also remained at duty. On 14th August he applied for a further gratuity for the wound he received in June 1916, but it was turned down as he had already received the full amount.

Awarded the VC for his actions at Marcoing, France on 20th November 1917, LG 11th January 1918. John was gassed on 5th December and had to relinquish command and acting lieutenant colonel. He was evacuated to a hospital at Le Tréport before being moved from Le Havre to Southampton on 23rd December. A medical board on 27th December found him unfit for any service for two months and recommended leave. The VC was presented by the King at Buckingham Palace on 23rd January 1918. Bernard Oppenheimer, the financier, offered £100 to the first five South African VCs and £50 to the first ten awarded the DSO. John directed that his money be donated directly to the Frontier Hospital in Queenstown. A medical board on 27th February found him unfit for General Service for six months and he was allowed to proceed on leave to South Africa. Nellie did not accompany him on this trip. He departed Devonport on HMT *Kenilworth Castle* on 12th March.

While in South Africa he undertook another recruiting tour, possibly at the invitation of General Botha. He fell foul of the South African authorities for a number of untactful remarks he made about the discipline of South African troops and for using injudicious language in a speech at East London. He was perceived by the British population to be too close to the Afrikaner Nationalists under Hertzog. He complained about not being paid his expenses, which he was assured would be forthcoming. In his defence, Brigadier General A Martyn CMG, Commanding Troops South Africa, said John was not a speechmaker and he made some remarks in the excitement of the moment, with no intention of becoming embroiled in politics.

John left Cape Town on SS *City of Karachi* on 6th June, in command of a contingent of recruits. When the ship stopped in Freetown, Sierra Leone, Major General CW Thompson CB DSO, Commanding Troops West Africa, held an enquiry at Military HQ on 21st June. Allegations had been made by Major CES King, a draft conducting officer (DCO), and Lieutenant Baxter, that John used language such as *damned South Africans* and *undisciplined rabble*. John had complained about slackness aboard and Major King allowing games and concerts all the time. He also had cause to speak to Baxter for having an NCO in his cabin. John apologised, which Baxter readily accepted, but King took some time to agree. Thompson concluded that Baxter should not have had an NCO in his cabin, but that Kelly was a man of violent temper and the South Africans were *up against it* from the start. Although a cordial relationship was unlikely to follow, the matter was settled and Thompson expected no further trouble on the journey. However, on arrival in England, Major King complained to the Director of War Recruiting in Cape Town about John's bullying and unseemly references to *damned South Africans*, poor discipline and describing the DCO staff as a rabble. The South African High Commissioner demanded action be taken, having been informed of the matter by the South African Minister of Defence. As a result John received a letter from the Army Council pointing out that had he displayed a little more tact in dealing with the situation the complaint would never have been made. As a result of this incident one official in March 1919 commented, *his tact is not on a par with his gallantry*.

John arrived in Britain on 8th July and was declared fit for General Service on 25th July, but his leave ran to 26th August and his address was again the Rubens Hotel, Buckingham Palace Road, London. He went to France on 7th September and was appointed acting CO of 12th Royal Scots Fusiliers on 10th September and acting lieutenant colonel and CO of 12th (Norfolk Yeomanry) Battalion, Norfolk Regiment 26th September 1918–30th April 1919. During this period he was temporarily commander of 94th Brigade from 3rd to 12th November. **John was Mentioned in General Sir Charles Monro's Despatch dated 6th March 1916 and General Sir Douglas Haig's Despatch dated 13th November 1916,**

LG 13th July 1916 and 4th January 1917 respectively. He was granted leave to Britain 26th November–3rd December 1918, 25th January–18th February 1919 and 13th–18th April, in addition to fourteen days local leave from 3rd March. On 30th April he was recalled for service in Russia. On 18th February 1919 his wife wrote to the War Office from 16 Levington Gardens, London seeking her husband's address as there were *several quite important matters to be discussed*. She was not aware if he was in England or not.

John volunteered for service with the Russian Relief Force in 2nd Hampshire. The Battalion contained men from a number of regiments and assembled at Crowbridge Barracks near Tunbridge Wells, Kent. Two weeks later it moved in haste to Tilbury to embark on SS *Stephen* on 13th May 1919. There were five others VCs aboard – Dudley Johnson, George Grogan, Archie White, Montagu Moore and Alfred Toye. The ship arrived off Archangel on 21st May. John was appointed acting lieutenant colonel and CO 2nd Hampshire on 27th May, the day he landed at Archangel, until 17th August.

George William St George Grogan was awarded the VC while a temporary brigadier general commanding 23rd Brigade during the Third Battle of the Aisne 27th–29th May 1918. He was commissioned in the West Africa Regiment and served in Sierra Leone in the 1898 Hut Tax War. He was seconded to the Egyptian Army in 1902 and in 1907 joined the King's Own Yorkshire Light Infantry, transferring to the Worcestershire Regiment in 1908. He commanded the 1st Battalion after the battle of Neuve Chapelle in March 1915. In 1919 he went with 1st Brigade of the Russian Relief Force. It was not until October 1923 that he was promoted substantive colonel and commanded 5th Infantry Brigade in 2nd Division. He was ADC to King George V 1920–26 and retired as honorary brigadier in 1926.

He immediately behaved provocatively by refusing to pay his own and his officers' mess bills in Archangel and appropriated the Base Depot Commandant's orderly room even though provision had been made for his unit. His unit lines were filthy and he refused to comply with orders for the disposition of his Battalion at a parade at Archangel for Grogan's Brigade on 27th May. At the King's birthday parade at Archangel he objected to the order he received and shouted profane language to his bandmaster.

John armed the barges used to transport his men up the Dvina River with all the automatic weapons available to the Battalion, in order to deter attack from the banks. The barges were known as 'Kelly's Mystery Ships'. The Battalion disembarked on 5th June and took over from an American unit. On the journey his behaviour was described as disgraceful by the transport officer and he was also extremely rude to the Americans. John began patrolling in earnest, leading some fighting patrols himself, but quickly realised the impossibility of making an impression on the Bolsheviks with such a small force. He was commended by the GOC for leading one of these patrols on 13th June, during which he personally killed three of the enemy. On 19th–20th June he was ordered to cooperate in an attack with 3rd Russian Rifles on the villages of Topsa and

Troitskoye. The Russians were to make the attack while John led two companies in an arduous nine miles march to get behind the Bolsheviks. After waiting for six hours under heavy fire, there was no sign of the Russians. John withdrew his force to avoid encirclement, but a little later the Russians attacked and took Topsa. During the march and subsequent retirement he made a number of critical remarks about the senior command in the presence of junior officers and soldiers, some of which drew laughter. He even mentioned the general was unfit to command a platoon. The signals officer cut into a line to allow him to speak to Brigadier General Graham and in the hearing of the column told Graham he had been shamefully let down. Other officers believed he pulled back prematurely and left the Russians with a poor impression. He also left the rest of the force in a poor position and appears to have lost his head. John claimed he did not know what was happening in his rear due to poor communications and felt compelled to withdraw to safeguard the Battalion. Brigadier General George Grogan VC, commanding 238th Special Brigade, appears to have understood John's decision, but General Ironside, commanding the force, decided that he had disobeyed orders. It is possible that John's nerve had gone as he became fearful at the noise of shellfire.

Grogan's patience with John eventually wore out. He was constantly unreasonable, insubordinate and his attitude to Grogan and his staff was unacceptable. His views appeared to be hardly sane and he lacked balance. He constantly questioned orders and criticised them in front of junior officers. Grogan interviewed him at the end of June. John appeared contrite and for a short while his behaviour improved. Grogan brought him before General Ironside who warned him formally as to his future behaviour and gave him one more chance. In July the Battalion left Grogan's command for the Vologda Railway Front. Except for one minor issue early on that was resolved quickly, Brigadier General Turner wrote that he never had cause for concern and Kelly was cordial, loyal and cooperative. His Battalion was efficient and well disciplined. However, Turner also reported to Ironside that Kelly had been far from satisfactory.

In late July, John was ordered to attack some Bolshevik blockhouses under cover of gas. He notified Turner that if left to him he would not attack, as it served no purpose other than to impress the unreliable White Russians. John again became openly critical of the staff and higher command in front of his men and in letters to friends, including the manager of the Rubens Hotel and Miss Pakeman of Towers House, Chesterfield Road, Eastbourne. These letters were intercepted by the censors and Grogan warned him about it but John ignored him. Ironside eventually persuaded General Lord Rawlinson, Commander-in-Chief Russia, to relieve John of command on 18th August, for criticism of the staff and commanders. In Ironside's opinion Kelly was hotheaded, quarrelsome and had had rows with everyone with whom he came into contact. His Battalion was well run and his men liked him but he was unsuitable for command in that situation. Before he left John submitted a detailed report to Rawlinson, countering the reasons why he was being relieved. He was sent home a few days later.

On returning to England John was still extremely angry and wrote three letters (5th & 12th September and 6th October) to the *Daily Express*, protesting about the futility of being in Russia and the competence of the high command, including the duplicity of Churchill, the Secretary for War, the architect of the intervention. The first letter was published on 6th September and the second on the 13th just after Churchill made a statement to the Commons on the issue. The final letter claimed the withdrawal from Russia had been accelerated by exposing Churchill's policy. John was staying at the Imperial Hotel in Hythe in mid–September and was reported for being extremely drunk in uniform and for molesting other guests. Also that month Mr Alfred Linton Barlow, an accountant in Felixstowe, was trying to trace him through the War Office, as he was indebted to a number of tradesmen in the town and had ignored all communications over the past four years.

Despite his excellent fighting record, patience with him had run out in the War Office. It was the opinion of a senior official that Ironside had 'let him off' by sending him home. A number of options were considered including trial, removal for misconduct and simply demobilising him, although the latter would have no adverse effect and was considered pointless. There was some caution because more senior officers had committed the same offence and had not been sanctioned, including Sir John French. The recommendation was to remove him for misconduct immediately and publicise this widely to show that such behaviour would not be tolerated. However, John continued to commit offences and the Secretary of State for War decided the case had to go to trial. The letters written from Russia could not be included as they had been dealt with when Ironside relieved John of command. The prosecution case was to concentrate on proving that he contacted the press without authority rather than becoming embroiled in the truth or otherwise of the allegations. There was provision in the Army Act for accusations against superiors to be investigated and John had chosen not to follow this legitimate route. He was ordered to report to HQ London District at Carlton House Terrace at 10 a.m. on Monday 13th October to be informed he would be tried and was placed in open arrest while attached to 1st Welsh Guards at Wellington Barracks. He was subsequently released from open arrest and allowed to continue living at the Rubens Hotel until the trial. The court martial took place on 28th October at Middlesex Guildhall. There were three charges under Section 40 of the Army Act, conduct to the prejudice of good order and military discipline, by communicating information to the *Daily Express*. He pleaded guilty and was severely reprimanded.

Middlesex Guildhall, where John was tried by court martial on 28th October 1919 and was severely reprimanded.

On 4th November John was admitted to Millbank Hospital due to his old chest wound. A medical board on 6th November found him unfit for General Service for three months and Home Service for two months. However, this was largely academic as he was demobilised on 11th November and was granted the rank of lieutenant colonel. He was viewed by the War Office as, *an abnormal officer with an ungovernable temper* and had narrowly avoided trial for assaulting a waiter at the Rubens Hotel a few years previously.

During the 1919 railway and transport workers strike John worked voluntarily as a stableman for Southern Railways at Blackfriars, London. He declined to accept the pay offered by the company and arranged for an equivalent sum to be paid to the Waifs and Strays Society. John separated from Nellie and lived in Windsor.

Queen Alexandra's Military Hospital, Millbank opened in July 1905. In the Great War it was a general hospital and afterwards was enlarged to 200 beds. It became the RAMC postgraduate school and there were strong ties with nearby Westminster Hospital. In 1957 the hospital was extended to 300 beds, but the hospital element closed in the 1970s when the Queen Elizabeth Military Hospital opened at Woolwich. The Royal Army Medical College remained until 1999.

The Divorce Court granted Nellie a decree of restitution of conjugal rights on 10th November. Despite the court proceedings, Nellie stood by him during his court martial in October 1919.

John attended the VC Garden Party at Buckingham Palace on 26th June 1920. On 22nd July the Divorce Court in London granted Nellie a decree nisi on the grounds of his misconduct and desertion. She gave evidence that the marriage was unhappy almost from the outset and John had stayed at a Bexhill hotel with a lady. John did not contest the case. The affair may have resulted in a child.

By 1922 John and Nellie had re-established some form of relationship and she supported him while he contested the 1923 and 1924 election campaigns. However, they became estranged again later. Letters to the War Office reveal he was in financial difficulties as claimants attempted to catch up with him. He was summoned to Windsor Court for non-payment of his gas bill. The judge gave him three months to settle the bill on account of his war record. In January 1922 Allan Hastings Fry, Royal Pavilion Studio, 68 East Street, Brighton wrote to the War Office seeking his address in connection with an unpaid 'considerable account'.

John contested the Parliamentary seat of Clay Cross for the Conservatives on 5th December 1923, but was beaten by 7,058 votes by the Labour candidate. By chance, during the election campaign the mother of Jack Johnson, the stretcher-bearer who saved John's life in 1916, introduced herself to Nellie and the two men were reunited. Undeterred he tried again in the 1924 General Election. During an election meeting on 24th October at Langwith an organised gang continually heckled him and one man named Watson called him a liar. The chairman appealed to the man to withdraw his offensive remark, but he repeated it, whereupon John stepped down and gave him a good thrashing to the applause of the audience. The man was ejected from the meeting, which then proceeded without further interruption. At the polls on 29th October, John was again beaten by the Labour candidate, this time by 6,549 votes.

John repeatedly tried to get back into the Army for service in Ireland, Turkey and China and wrote for support to Winston Churchill and the Prime Minister to no effect. He was simply too wild a character for a peacetime Army. In any case the Army was struggling to find employment for its regular officers and there was no place for a temporary officer with such a reputation for indiscipline. In July 1920 he tried to have a court of enquiry opened into Ironside's report on him. He may have been trying to get into the Royal Irish Constabulary at the time and wanted the report qualified or cancelled. In August 1925 he tried to gain a commission in the French Foreign Legion in order to take part in operations in Morocco. The War Office had no objection when asked by the French Embassy, but informed John that if he was successful he would have to relinquish his British rank. He was living at 16 Adam Street, Manchester Square, London at the time. Also in 1925 he tried to join the Army Educational Corps, but there were no vacancies and in any case he was unsuitable. In 1929 an official concluded that John was unlikely to find congenial employment until there was another war. By then his address was the Authors' Club, 2 Whitehall Court, London, of which he was a member. He lived at various times at The Deepdene, Dorking, Surrey and at Nutfield Cottage, Ascot, Surrey.

In 1925 a newspaper reported that he had reduced his golf handicap from maximum to scratch in only four months. In 1926 John became a Freemason, being Initiated into the Authors' Lodge (No.3456) on 20th October, was Passed to the Second Degree on 17th November and Raised to the Sublime Degree of a Master Mason on 19th January 1927. He

Charles Howard built a Palladian mansion on the site of The Deepdene at Dorking in the 1760s. In 1808 Thomas Hope, one of the richest men in England, bought The Deepdene and enlarged it with orangeries, conservatories, a library and galleries. The estate was extended by acquiring the Chart Park and Betchworth Castle estates. At one time the grounds stretched for twelve miles from Box Hill to Brockham. Towards the end of the century The Deepdene passed to the Duke of Newcastle, who let it to Lily, dowager Duchess of Marlborough. Her nephew, Winston Churchill, often visited her there. In the 1920s the estate was broken up. Some of the grounds were developed for housing and the house itself became a grand hotel. A bypass of the town ruined the gardens. The Deepdene was demolished in 1967.

Sir Arthur Philip Du Cros, 1st Baronet (1871–1955) attended a national school in Dublin and entered the civil service at the lowest-paid grade. In 1892 he joined his father and brothers in Dublin's Pneumatic Tyre and Booth's Cycle Agency, founded in 1889 by his father, Harvey du Cros, and JB Dunlop to exploit Dunlop's pneumatic tyre. Arthur was general manager and his brothers went to Europe and America to develop interests there. When JB Dunlop retired in 1895, Terah Hooley bought the business, by then named Pneumatic Tyre Co, for £3M and floated a new company on the stock market named The Dunlop Pneumatic Tyre Co. Arthur was joint managing director with his father, but Harvey was also chairman. In 1912 the Dunlop Pneumatic Tyre Company went out of business, but retained some financial commitments, and the name changed to The Parent Tyre Company Ltd. Arthur du Cros was managing director and deputy chairman and his family dominated the board. There was much financial impropriety

as Arthur found it difficult to distinguish between personal and company assets and used company funds for family investments and appointed family members to senior positions regardless of their ability. The company came close to bankruptcy and Arthur lost influence. He was dismissed after the 1921 depression. Arthur had entered politics in 1906 and in 1908 was elected MP for Hastings, succeeding his father. In 1909 he formed the Parliamentary Aerial Defence Committee to ensure funding for military aeronautical development and during the Great War he worked for the Ministry of Munitions. He was MP for Clapham 1918–22.

was Exalted into Royal Arch Masonry in the Authors' Holy Royal Arch Chapter on 23rd March 1927. On 31st October 1926 he and Oliver Brooks VC laid a wreath at the Cenotaph during the memorial service held on Horse Guards' Parade under the auspices of the Ypres League.

In March 1927 John tried unsuccessfully to secure employment in China through the War Office. He went to Bolivia that year to work for Bolivia Concessions Ltd in developing roads, railways and river transport. This was part of a plan to settle the area with British colonists and to open up contact for the first time between Buenos Aires and the Paraguayan River. The venture was later abandoned. John contracted malaria while there. In 1929 he became agent for Sir Arthur du Cros (1871–1955) at Craigweil House, Bognor Regis, Sussex. King George V had convalesced there from February to May 1929 and John hosted 13,000 people as they visited the rooms occupied by Their Majesties. John attended the VC Dinner at the Royal Gallery of the House of Lords, London on 9th November. He reportedly

Craigweil House was built by the Countess of Newburgh and was known as the Pavilion. In 1828 it was owned by the Reverend Henry Raikes and later by Captain Sir Alexander Dixie RN, who was at Trafalgar. The house passed through various owners until 1915, when it was sold to Sir Arthur du Cros, who enlarged it in 1919. King George V convalesced there from 9th February to 15th May 1929 while recovering from an operation. Following a fire in 1938 the house had to be demolished. Craigweil Estate was built in the grounds.

went to Tanganyika in September 1930, but contacted malaria after a few months and returned to Britain.

John Sherwood-Kelly died in a nursing home at 31 Queens Gate, Kensington, London on 18th August 1931 and is buried in Brookwood Cemetery, Woking, Surrey (Block 86, Grave 196296). Ernest Short (also a member of the Author's Club) of 52 Stanford Road, Kensington Court paid for and arranged the funeral as other relatives were in South Africa and unable to attend. The War Office advised that a formal military funeral was not permissible, but allowed military personnel to take part if Short covered their expenses and this was agreed. London District provided a bearer party (sergeant, corporal and twelve guardsmen), together with two drummers who played Last Post at the graveside. The 18 Pounder gun carriage was manned by the Royal Field Artillery and the Grenadier Guards provided a firing party (officer, warrant officer and eight soldiers). Aldershot Command provided the chaplain. The banners of the local British Legion accompanied the cortège on its way to Brookwood Cemetery. Appropriately the gravestone carries the words, *One who never turned his back but marched breast forward*.

The executor to his will was Elizabeth Coward, widow, and John left effects to the value of £390/19/5. His address was given as Washington Hotel, Curzon Street, Westminster. He is commemorated in a number of other places:

- Plaque at St Anne's Cathedral, Belfast, Northern Ireland.
- Named on one of eleven plaques honouring 175 men from overseas awarded the VC for the Great War. The plaques were unveiled by the Senior Minister of State at

Queen's Gate, Kensington.

John Sherwood-Kelly's grave in Brookwood Cemetery, Woking, Surrey (Findagrave).

The Castle of Good Hope, Cape Town.

the Foreign & Commonwealth Office and Minister for Faith and Communities, Baroness Warsi, at a reception at Lancaster House, London on 26th June 2014 attended by The Duke of Kent and relatives of the VC recipients. The South African plaque is at the Castle of Good Hope, Cape Town.

• The Secretary of State for Communities and Local Government, Eric Pickles MP announced that Victoria Cross recipients from the Great War would have commemorative paving stones laid in their birthplace as a lasting legacy of local heroes within communities. The stones would be laid on or close to the 100th anniversary of their VC actions. For the 145 VCs born in Australia, Belgium, Canada, China, Denmark, Egypt, France, Germany, India, Iraq, Japan, Nepal, Netherlands, New Zealand, Pakistan, South Africa, Sri Lanka, Ukraine and United States of America, individual commemorative stones were unveiled at the National Memorial Arboretum, Alrewas, Staffordshire by Prime Minister David Cameron MP and Sergeant Johnson Beharry VC on 5th March 2015.

In addition to the VC, CMG and DSO he was awarded the British South Africa Company's Medal 1890–97 with clasp 'Rhodesia 1896', Queen's South Africa Medal 1899–1902 with four clasps (Rhodesia, Orange Free State, Relief of Mafeking and Transvaal), King's South Africa Medal 1901–02 with two clasps (South Africa 1901 and South Africa 1902), Africa General Service Medal 1902–56 with clasp 'Somaliland 1902–04', 1914–15 Star, British War Medal 1914–20 and Victory Medal 1914–19 with Mentioned-in-Despatches Oakleaf. After his death his medals were probably with one of his brothers. In 1959 the South African National Museum of Military History paid £250 to John's sister-in-law, Mrs IH Kelly, for them. The VC is held by the National Museum of Military History, 22 Erlswold Way, Saxonwold, Johannesburg 2132, South Africa.

The British South Africa Company Medal (1890–97) was created by Queen Victoria for issue to troops engaged in the First Matabele War. In 1897 she sanctioned another medal for those engaged in the two campaigns of the Second Matabele War – Rhodesia in 1896 and Mashonaland in 1897. The medals are identical except for the name and date above the lion on the reverse, which denote the campaign for which the medal was issued.

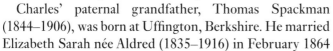

9522 SERGEANT CHARLES EDWARD SPACKMAN
1st Battalion, The Border Regiment

Charles Spackman was born at 46 Crefeld Road, Fulham, London on 11th January 1891. His father, Charles John Spackman (1866–1940), was a bricklayer's labourer. He married Eleanor Charlotte née Kempster (1869–1941) in 1890. They were living at 46 Crefeld Road, Fulham in 1891, by when she was an ironer. By 1901 she was a general laundress and they were living at 110 Bayonne Road, Fulham. Charles junior was an only child.

Charles' paternal grandfather, Thomas Spackman (1844–1906), was born at Uffington, Berkshire. He married Elizabeth Sarah née Aldred (1835–1916) in February 1864 at Kensington Parish Church, London. In 1871 he was a gasman and they were living at Reservoir Cottage, Kensington, London. By 1891 he was a French polisher and she was a charwoman and they were living at 72 Adeney Road, Fulham. By 1901 they were living at 26 Aintree Street, Fulham, by when she was a needlewoman. She was living alone at 11 Francis Street, Hammersmith, London in 1911. In addition to Charles they had four other children:

- Thomas Henry Spackman (1865–1907) was a prisoner at the Police Station, Bradfield Terrace, Fulham in 1881. He married Mary Ann Wright (1870–1906) in 1887. They were both hawkers in 1891, living at 5 Guivers Cottages, Fulham.
- Edward Richard Spackman (1868–1928) was a general labourer, living with his parents in 1891 and 1901. The marriage between an Edward Spackman and an Eliza Moysey was registered in the fourth quarter of 1912 at Fulham.
- Catherine 'Kate' Elizabeth Spackman (1871–1950) was an ironer in 1891 and a laundress living with her parents in 1901. She married George Leonard Jennings (1873–1921) in 1902. They lived at 15 Dawson Street, London. She was living at 11 Aviland Street, Fulham before being admitted to Fulham Hospital, St Dunstan's Road suffering from senility and died there on 3rd June 1950. They had nine children – twins George William Jennings and Thomas Jennings 1902, Leonard Jennings 1904, stillborn child 1905, Harry Jennings 1907, Sidney Jennings 1908, stillborn child 1910, Robert Ernest Jennings 1912 and Charles E Jennings 1913.
- Charlotte Louise Spackman (1873–74).

His maternal grandfather, James Kempster (c.1829–94), was born at North Mills, Hertfordshire. He married Caroline née Skinner (c.1828–82), born at Twerton, Devon, in 1862 at Kensington, London. He was a coal porter and the family was living at 52 Pembroke Road, Kensington in 1869. By 1871 they had moved to 16

Ashley Cottages, Kensington. James was living with his daughter Eleanor and her family in 1891. In addition to Eleanor they had two other daughters:

- Caroline Kempster (1864–1905).
- Sarah E Kempster (1866–1918) married Thomas John Gammon (1866–1936) in 1890. In 1901 he was a labourer on a barge and they were living at 11 Chelmsford Street, Fulham. They had eight children – Thomas John Gammon 1891, Henry John Gammon 1892, Ellen Beatrice Gammon 1894, Margaret Sarah Gammon 1898, Caroline Gammon 1899, Lilian Rose Gammon 1901, Edith Gammon 1905 and George Arthur J Gammon 1910.

Charles was educated at St Dunstan's School, Margravine Road, Fulham 1896–1905. He worked for the Imperial Tobacco Company, Palace Road, Fulham and was employed by Messrs Whiteley's from 1906. He enlisted in the Border Regiment on 5th January 1909 and was serving at Martinique Barracks, Bordon, Hampshire in 1911. Charles embarked for the Mediterranean Expeditionary Force in March 1915 and landed at Gallipoli on 25th April 1915 in 3 Platoon, A Company, 1st Border. The Battalion was evacuated to Mudros on 9th January 1916 and then to Egypt. He arrived in France in March 1916. **Awarded the VC for his actions at Marcoing, France on 20th November 1917, LG 11th January 1918.** The VC was presented by the King at Buckingham Palace on 23rd February 1918. **Awarded the French Médaille Militaire, LG 17th August 1918.**

Twerton, Devon where Charles' maternal grandmother was born.

Martinique Barracks at Bordon, Hampshire. The first camp at Bordon was laid out in 1899. As it expanded, individual barracks were named after battles in the Seven Years' War, the first two being St Lucia and Quebec. The camp at nearby Longmoor was built on boggy ground and in 1905 many of the huts were moved to Bordon to create Guadaloupe and Martinique Barracks. Bordon was then able to accommodate a complete infantry brigade. The first brick barracks, completed in 1907, housed two regiments of artillery and a riding school. Further expansion followed creating a veterinary hospital, RE lines and stables. Some of the hutted camps were demolished in the 1930s to make way for brick built barracks of a standard design, known as Sandhurst blocks, designed to house a battalion or regiment in one building. The hutted Martinique Barracks were renamed San Domingo Barracks and by 1967 had been demolished. Bordon and Longmoor camps were used by the Canadian Army in both world wars. After the Second World War Bordon became the main REME training centre until 2015.

Charles Spackman married Mary Alice née Copland (1894–14th January 1969) on 13th December 1919 at St Augustine's Church, Fulham. At the time she was a blouse-maker, living at 51 Filmer Road, Fulham, and he was living at 16 Moylan Road, Fulham. They had known each other since childhood. They were living at 21 Filmer Road in 1922 and had moved to 29 Durley Avenue, Pinner, Middlesex by 1937. They found it difficult to live on their old-age pensions there and moved to Southampton, Hampshire in 1958, where they lived at 32 Priory Road, Netley Abbey. Charles and Mary had five children:

Charles Spackman married Mary Copland in December 1919 at St Augustine's Church, Fulham. The church was built in 1916.

- Charles George Spackman (4th October 1920– May 1989) served in anti-aircraft artillery units during the Second World War. He married Edith B Smith in 1946 at Rugby, Warwickshire.
- George Edward Spackman (31st May 1926– August 2002) married Eleanor E Thulborn (1925–c.2011) in 1952. They had two children – Michael E Spackman 1958 and Malcolm M Spackman 1965.
- Marjory A Spackman (1928–48).
- Harold Albert Spackman (14th April 1930–13th August 1987) served in the Royal Marines. He married Bridget McShane (born 1933) in 1956 at Greenock, Renfrewshire. Harold was discharged on 27th May 1961 and was employed as a prison officer (medical) in London. They had two sons – Peter Charles Spackman 1958 and Stewart Spackman 1959.

Filmer Road, on the right, where Charles and Mary lived in the 1920s.

- David John Spackman (born 1932) married Kathleen V Clark in 1953. They were living at 32 Priory Road, Netley Abbey, Southampton in 1969. They had two children – Christopher J Spackman 1955 and Kathleen P Spackman 1959.

Mary's father, Albert Edward Copland (1868–1915), was born at Horstead, Norfolk. He married Alice née Holland (1871–1952), born at Bethnal Green, London, in 1894 at Fulham. In 1901 he was a boot maker and they were living at 34 Chelmsford Street, Fulham. By 1911 they had moved to 26 Filmer Road, Fulham. In addition to Mary they had six other children:

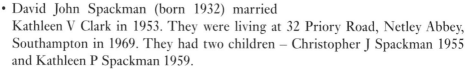

- Elizabeth Copland (1896–1922) was a dressmaker's assistant in 1911.
- George Copland (born 1898).
- Benjamin Copland (1899–1900).
- Emily Copland (1902–76).
- Annie Copland (1908–53) married Robert Thompson in 1929 and they had two daughters – Jean D Thompson 1934 and Wendy P Thompson 1938.
- Alice Copland (born 1911) married Thomas J Marshall in 1939 and they had at least two daughters – Elizabeth A Marshall 1947 and Alison M Marshall 1950.

After the war Charles was employed as a bank messenger. He joined the TA in 1925 as a sergeant in the Queen Victoria's Rifles. He volunteered for service on the outbreak of the Second World War and served as a sergeant major in the King's Royal Rifle Corps, based at Swindon, Wiltshire. After the war he was the caretaker at a coastal defence site.

Charles Spackman with the Prince of Wales, the future King Edward VIII. It is understood that this event was on Friday 6th October 1922.

Charles attended a number of VC reunions, including the Garden Party at Buckingham Palace on 26th June 1920, the VC Dinner at the Royal Gallery of the House of Lords on 9th November 1929, the Victory Day Celebration Dinner and Reception at The Dorchester, London on 8th June 1946, the VC Centenary Celebrations at Hyde Park, London on 26th June 1956 and the 2nd, 3rd, 4th and 5th VC & GC Association Reunions at the Café Royal, London in July 1960, 1962, 1964 and 1966. During the 1956 VC Centenary Celebrations he collected the autographs of all 269 VC holders present and presented them to the Netley Branch of the British Legion.

Charles Spackman died at Southampton General Hospital, Hampshire on 6th May 1969. His funeral, with full military honours, was at South Stoneham Church, Southampton on 9th May. The Border Regiment, King's Royal Rifle Corps, British Legion and National Provincial Bank were amongst those who sent wreaths. He was cremated at South Stoneham Crematorium, Stoneham Cemetery Road,

The Border Regiment Victoria Cross Memorial in Carlisle Cathedral (Memorials to Valour).

Swaythling, Southampton and his ashes were scattered in the Stoneham Garden of Remembrance (Bed 25, now Section 7 South). He is also commemorated:

* On the Border Regiment Victoria Cross Memorial, Carlisle Cathedral, Cumbria.
* A Department for Communities and Local Government commemorative VC paving stones was dedicated at Fulham War Memorial, All Saint's Church, Vicarage Gate, Fulham High Street on 20th November 2017 to mark the centenary of his award.

In addition to the VC he was awarded the 1914–15 Star, British War Medal 1914–20, Victory Medal 1914–19, Defence Medal, War Medal 1939–45, George VI Coronation Medal 1937, Elizabeth II Coronation Medal 1953, Efficiency Medal & Bar and the French Médaille Militaire. His eldest son, Charles, decided the medals should be sold a few months after his father's death as the family could not accept responsibility for safeguarding them. He did not consider giving the medals to his father's old Regiment because it no longer existed. The VC was sold at Glendinings on 17th December 1969 to the coin dealers Baldwin & Sons for £1,200. It is understood to be in Canada.

34328 GUNNER CHARLES EDWIN STONE
C Battery, 83rd Brigade, Royal Field Artillery

Charles Stone was born on 4th February 1889 at Street Lane, Belper, near Ripley, Derbyshire. His father, George Edward Stone (1857–1924), a coal miner, married Mary Ellen née Hunt (1856–1906) in 1877. She was a domestic servant in 1871 at Matlock Road, Belper. The family moved to a farm cottage in Sandbed Lane, Openwoodgate, Belper c.1895. Charles had twelve siblings, of whom ten are known:

* George Joseph Stone (born 1878) was registered as George William Stone. He was a farm labourer in 1891 and a wood machinist in 1901.
* Mary Hannah Stone (1879–1962) married her cousin, Charles Edward Poundall (1878–1961), in 1902. He was a coal miner hewer and they were living at Slepwood, Kilburn, Derbyshire in 1911.
* John William Stone (1880–1953), a coal miner, married Alice Walters (1880–1963) in 1901. They lived at 60 Over Lane, Belper and had two children – Norah Alice Stone 1902 and William Alfred Stone 1906. Norah married Jacob Byard in 1922, the brother of Joshua Byard, who married her aunt Edith – see below.

- Samuel Henry Stone (1882–1930) was registered as Samuel Edward Stone. He was a coal miner in 1901. He married Alice Eliza Booth (born 1878) in 1906. They had four children – Ivy May Stone 1908, Alice Elizabeth Stone 1910, Lois Ellen Stone 1912 and Ethel M Stone 1914.
- James Edward Stone (born 1885) was recorded as James Henry Stone in the 1891 Census. He was a coal miner in 1901.
- Thomas Frederick Stone (born 1887) was a coal miner, living with his brother John in 1911.
- Sarah Elizabeth Stone (1893–1963) married James William Hunt (1889–1966) in 1914. He served in the Royal Engineers during the Great War (490012 and 1521). They were living at 70 Pottery Houses, Kelbourne Road, Belper in 1952.

Albert Ernest Stone's grave in Vadencourt British Cemetery.

- Edith Ellen Stone (1895–1972) was a cotton spinner, living with her brother John in 1911. She married Joshua Byard (born 1893) in 1914. They had three children – Nora E Byard 1914, Stanley J Byard 1916 and Frank Byard 1919.
- Albert Ernest Stone (1897–1917) served as a sergeant in 4 Platoon, A Company, 2/5th Sherwood Foresters (200981). At Le Verguier, near St Quentin on 4th April 1917 his officer was wounded and he assumed command, but was killed leading his men. He is buried in Vadencourt British Cemetery, Maissemy, Aisne, France (IV B 16).
- Arthur Leonard Stone (1900–70) was living with his uncle, George Henry Hunt, at Millwood, Kirkby in Ashfield, Nottinghamshire in 1911. He married Alice Hall in 1923 and they had five children – Irene Stone 1925, Peter H Stone 1926, Mary Stone 1932, Doris Stone 1935 and Jill M Stone 1947.

Charles' paternal grandfather, William Stone (born c.1829), a potter, married Mary Ann née Gell (c.1833–99) in 1850 at Duffield, Derbyshire. They were living at Pottery, Belper in 1871 and 1881, by when he was a general labourer. William died in the period 1896–1900, when there were three deaths registered at Belper that could be him. In addition to George they had another eleven children:

- Hannah Stone (1850–1914) married William Poundall (1846–1932), a miner, in 1866. They were living at White Moor Hall, Belper in 1911. They had nine children – Mary Poundall 1866, Alfred Poundall 1868, Rosina Poundall 1871, George Henry Poundall 1872, Florence Poundall 1873, Henry Poundall 1875, Thomas Albert Poundall 1876, Charles Edward Poundall 1878 and Francis Christopher Poundall 1880.
- Anne Elizabeth Stone (1859–1935) died unmarried.

George Allen's name on the Loos Memorial.

- Martha Stone (1861–1929), a cotton spinner, married William Hardy Allen (1862–1926) in 1882 at St Alkmunds, Duffield. They were living at West Bank, Ambergate, Derby in 1915. They had ten children – Mary Ann Allen 1882, Flora Allen 1884, George Allen 1886, Ada Allen 1888, William Allen 1890, Fred Allen 1892, Arthur Allen 1895, Albert Allen 1899, May Allen 1901 and Lucy Allen 1907. George Allen served as a private in 12th Northumberland Fusiliers (7467) and was killed in action on 25th September 1915 (Loos Memorial, France – Panels 20–22).
- John Henry Stone (1864–93), a coal miner, married Sarah Ann Reader (1866–1936) in 1882. They had at least two children – John Henry Stone 1884 and Violet Stone 1890. Sarah married George Smales Cresswell (1858–1948) in 1896 and they had a son, George Smales Cresswell, the following year. They were living at The Pottery, Belper in 1891 and at 54 Sandbed Lane by 1911. George had married Hannah Spencer (1859–90) in 1880 and they had two children – Julia Smales Cresswell 1880 and Lily Smales Cresswell 1883.
- Charles Stone (born 1866) was a general labourer in 1881. He married Eliza Allen (born 1869) in 1886. He was a coal miner in 1891 and they were living at Station Road, Heanor, Derbyshire. They had two children – James Arthur Stone 1887 and Eliza A Stone 1888. The children were living with their maternal grandparents at 11 Holbrook Road, Belper at the time of the 1901 Census.
- Robert Stone (born 1868), a coal miner hewer, married Mary Hannah Munslow (1865–1934) in 1890. They were living at 56 Holbrook Road, Belper in 1911. They had four children – Horatio Nelson Stone 1893, Leonard Stone 1897, Robert Stone 1898 and Bernard Stone 1901.
- William Stone (born and died 1870).
- Fanny Stone (1873–1939), a cotton factory hand, married John Thomas Bott (1870–1929), a coal miner hewer, in 1891. They were living at The Green, Heage, Derbyshire in 1911. They had seven children including – Emma Bott 1892, Joel Bott 1897, Sarah Ann Bott 1899, John Thomas Bott 1901 and Catherine Bott 1902.

- Lucy Ellen Stone (1875–90).
- Susannah 'Susan' Stone (1876–1932) died unmarried.
- Samuel Stone (1879–1956), a coal miner hewer, married Elizabeth Annie West (1875–1932) in 1900. They were living at School House Hill, Heage in 1911. They had two children, including Annie Stone in 1909.

His maternal grandfather, Joseph Hunt (born c.1832 at Denby, Derbyshire), a coal miner, married Ellen née Blood (c.1835–94) in 1853. They were living in Street Lane, near Ripley in 1861. It is assumed that Joseph died before 1867. In addition to Mary Ellen they had four other children:

- Joseph Hunt (born c.1855) was a coal miner in 1871.
- John Hunt (1858–79) was a labourer in a brickyard in 1871.
- George Henry Hunt (1859–1933), an engine driver, married Sarah Ann Holloway (1860–1938) in 1883. They were living at Sutton Road, Hucknall under Huthwaite, Nottinghamshire in 1891, at Bentinck Cottages, Kirkby in Ashfield, Nottinghamshire in 1901 and at Millwood, Kirkby in Ashfield in 1911. They had nine children – Annie Mary Hunt 1884, Mary Hunt 1886, Helen Hunt 1889, George Henry Hunt 1892, John Edward Hunt 1894, Maggie Hunt 1895, Percival Hunt 1897, Hilda Hunt 1899 and Ida Hunt 1903.
- William Hunt (born 1861) was a coal miner in 1881.

Ellen married Luke Burgoyne (c.1826–92), a brick maker (also seen as Burgoin and Burgin), in 1867. Luke had married Lydia Briggs (c.1828–64) in 1847 and they had at least six children – Alfred Burgoin (sic) 1847, Ann Burgin (sic) 1852, Alice Burgoyne 1854, Sarah Burgoyne 1857, Lucy Burgoyne 1860 and Joseph Burgoyne 1862. Luke and Ellen were living at Street Lane, Ripley in 1871. At the time of the 1881 Census she was living with her parents at Street Lane. He appeared in the 1891 Census as a widower, living at Belper District Union Workhouse while Ellen was looking after her father, Joseph Blood, as his housekeeper at Street Lane.

Charles was educated at Street Lane School, Belper and Belper Pottery School. He worked as a coal miner at New Denby Hall Pit and later at Salterwood Colliery, near Ripley. Charles and his brother, Joseph, moved out of the family home and shared a house at Nottingham Road, Belper. Charles enlisted in the Royal Field Artillery at Sutton-in-Ashfield on 12th September 1914 and served with C Battery, 83rd Brigade in 18th (Eastern) Division. He was posted to Colchester, Essex for training. Due to severe shortages of equipment, drills were practised on a dummy wooden gun. He went to France on 25th July 1915 and was in action in all the major battles, serving as an officer's batman.

Awarded the MM for his actions on 28th October 1917, during the Battle of Passchendaele, when C Battery on the Poelcapelle road received several direct hits that caused many casualties but regardless of his own safety, he

Belper River Gardens.

Street Lane School, Belper.

Ripley market place in 1908.

Belper Pottery School.

tended the wounded, LG 4th February 1918. Awarded the VC for his actions near Benay, France on 21st March 1918, LG 22nd May 1918. He was promoted lance bombardier. The VC was presented by the King in the quadrangle at Buckingham Palace on 22nd June 1918. On returning to Belper after the investiture he was presented with a gold watch and chain plus £100 by local businessman, Mr HE Rawlings, at a reception at Belper River Gardens. The citizens of Ripley presented him with £100 in War Bonds at a ceremony in Ripley market place on 28th June. Charles was demobilised in January 1919.

Denby Hall Colliery later became a huge opencast site, closing in 1999.

He returned to his old job at Salterwood Colliery and took a keen interest in local athletics at Heage, near Belper, including coaching the local football team. Charles attended the VC Garden Party at Buckingham Palace on 26th June 1920 and was one of the VC Honour Guard at the burial of the Unknown Warrior at Westminster

Abbey on 11th November 1920. In 1923 he moved to Ashbourne and worked for Mr Clifford Etches at Heywood Farm. Whilst working there he saved a fellow worker, Miss Elizabeth Lees, from serious burns when her clothes caught light. He smothered the flames with his jacket. In 1924 he threw up the ball at the start of the second day of the Ashbourne Royal Shrovetide Football Match. The first day had been started by the Duke of Devonshire. That year he moved to Derby to work for Rolls Royce in the hardening shop and also in one of the foundries known as 'Dante's Inferno'. He lived at 32 Becket Well Lane, Derby and worked for Rolls Royce for twenty years. On 3rd June 1926 he attended the opening of the British Legion Club at Allenton. In 1929 he took the salute at a parade at Shrapnel Barracks, Woolwich, where he was greeted by his old commander in France, Brigadier W Evans, 18th Division Artillery. The Sergeant's Mess had a Stone Room in which he carved his name on a chair to commemorate his visit. He attended the VC Dinner at the Royal Gallery of the House of Lords, London on 9th November 1929. Whilst in London he learned that someone had masqueraded as him to obtain substantial financial assistance from a friendly society.

In 1940 Charles was introduced to King George VI during his visit to the Rolls Royce factory. Charles was presented with a hallmarked silver wristwatch by his Rolls Royce colleagues. During the Second World War he served in the Home Guard, probably in 13th Derbyshire (Derby & Borough) Battalion or 14th Derbyshire (Derby Works) Battalion. He

Heage United football team in 1921. Charles Stone, standing far left with the towel, was the trainer. On his left is H Stone (Treasurer), possibly Charles' brother, Samuel Henry Stone (George Sparham).

The Ashbourne Shrovetide Football Match (Royal from 1923) is played over two days on Shrove Tuesday and Ash Wednesday. It dates back to medieval times. Each day play commences at 2.00 p.m. and lasts until 10.00 p.m. If the ball is goaled before 5.30 p.m. play restarts from the town centre. The game is played throughout the town and there are no limits on the number of players. The game has been started by two Princes of Wales in 1928 and 2003. There are few rules. Murder and manslaughter are prohibited and unnecessary violence is frowned upon. The ball may not be carried in a vehicle and neither may it be hidden. Cemeteries, churchyards and the town memorial gardens are out of bounds, but otherwise just about anything goes.

was presented to the Duke of Edinburgh during a Royal Visit in June 1949.

Charles never married. He died in Derby City General Hospital of cardiac failure, diabetes and arteriosclerosis on 29th August 1952. A funeral service with

Rolls-Royce was formed in March 1906 and the Derby factory began production in early 1908. During the Great War the factory was extended to increase the production of aero engines.

Shrapnel Barracks was built in 1908 for a field artillery brigade. In the early 1970s the site was cleared for the building of Queen Elizabeth Military Hospital, which opened in 1977 with 456 beds in sixteen wards. The Hospital closed in 1995.

Charles Stone's grave in Belper Cemetery.

Derby City General Hospital.

full military honours was held at the British Legion in Strutt Street, Derby. He was buried in his mother's grave in Belper Cemetery, Derbyshire on 3rd September. He is also commemorated:

- On the Royal Artillery VC Memorial in the ruins of St George's Chapel, the former Garrison Church at Woolwich, Grand Depot Road, which was reduced to a roofless shell by a V1 in 1944.
- On the Royal Artillery VC Memorial in the Royal Artillery Tercentenary Chapel and Cloister, Larkhill, Wiltshire unveiled by Queen Elizabeth II on 26th May 2016.
- A Department for Communities and Local Government commemorative VC paving stone was dedicated at the War Memorial, Memorial Gardens, King Street, Belper on 21st March 2018 to mark the centenary of his award.

In addition to the VC and MM he was awarded the 1914–15 Star, British War Medal 1914–20, Victory Medal 1914–19 and George VI Coronation Medal 1937. The medals were donated to the Royal Regiment of Artillery Museum by his family. They were held at the Royal Artillery Museum, 'Firepower' in Woolwich, London until it closed in 2016. A new museum, close to the Royal Artillery Centre at Larkhill, is planned to open in 2020.

CAPTAIN WALTER NAPLETON STONE
3rd attached 17th Battalion (Empire), The Royal Fusiliers (City of London Regiment)

Walter Stone was born at 3 Lansdowne Place, Blackheath, Lewisham, London on 7th December 1891. His father, Edward Stone (9th October 1848–27th November 1918), a solicitor, born at Wellclose Square, St George in the East, London, married Emily Frances née Miéville (5th November 1853–28th January 1943), on 24th July 1874 at St Mary Hornsey Rise, Islington, London. They were living at 18 St John's Park, Islington in 1881 and by 1901 had moved to 3 Lansdowne Place, Blackheath. They also lived at 21 Vanbrugh Park, Blackheath, at 5 Finsbury Circus, London and at 41 Moorgate Street, London. Emily died at The Plaids, Tain, Ross-shire but was buried in the family grave at Greenwich Cemetery, London. She left effects valued at £2,124/16/5 to her daughters Dorothy and Marjorie. Walter had nine siblings:

- Edward Stone (14th March 1876–29th January 1946) served during the Second Boer War in South Africa with the West Australian Imperial Bushmen's Corps. He was commissioned in 2nd Dragoon Guards (Queen's Bays) on 15th March 1902. Edward was promoted lieutenant 29th April 1904, captain 27th November 1912 and major 21st April 1917. He was employed with the West African Frontier Force 16th May 1908–11th March 1913 and in France 15th August–5th

Walter's father, Edward Stone, was born at Wellclose Square, St George in the East, London.

St Mary Hornsey Rise, Islington, London, where Walter's parents married in 1874.

November 1914. He was employed at the Colonial Base Depot 21st January–September 1916 in the Egyptian Expeditionary Force and was wounded. He was appointed Staff Captain Home Forces 7th March 1917–1st May 1918, Brigade Major Home Forces 2nd May–18th December 1918 and Deputy Assistant Adjutant General, Eastern Command 19th December 1918–30th March 1919. He commanded No.4 Cavalry Depot 2nd April–30th October 1919. Edward went on to Half Pay on 17th August 1924 and last appears in the Army List in

The family grave in Greenwich Cemetery with inset details of the inscriptions.

January 1926. He married Dora Gertrude Williams (born 1887) on 29th April 1913. They were living at Ballardes Garden, 4 Church Street, Ewell, Surrey at the time of his death. He left effects valued at £5,683/14/4. Edward and Dora had two children:

   ° Dora Pamela Stone (1915–2003) married Dr Kenneth Prinz Pauli (1907–80) in 1941. He was granted a Regular Army Emergency Commission as a lieutenant in the Royal Army Medical Corps (101253) on 20th September 1939 and was promoted war substantive captain on 20th September 1940. He was appointed Examining Surgeon under the Factories Act 1937 for Mitcheldean, Gloucestershire on 13th February 1946. They had three children – Jennifer J Pauli 1942, Penelope Z Pauli 1944 and Edward C Pauli 1946.

   ° Edward Stone (1918–19).

• Arthur Stone (27th June 1877–2nd October 1918) graduated from King's College, Cambridge and became a solicitor, articled to his father. He was a skilled rifle shot and played football for Cambridge and Kent. He enlisted on a one-year engagement in the Special Reserve as a company sergeant major National Rifle Association musketry instructor (No.7) on 11th September 1914. On 15th October he applied for a commission from the School of Musketry, Bisley Camp, Surrey. He had previous service with the Clifton College contingent of the Gloucestershire Royal Engineers Volunteer Battalion 1892–96, Cambridge University Rifle Volunteers 1896–99 and the Inns of Court Rifle Volunteers Mounted Infantry 1899–1908. He was awarded the Territorial Efficiency Medal. He was commissioned in the Lancashire Fusiliers on 28th October 1914 and served as a temporary lieutenant colonel as CO 15th Battalion 5th October–22nd December 1916. Arthur was awarded the DSO (LG 22nd June 1918) and was also Mentioned in Despatches. He commanded 16th Battalion 5th April–16th July 1918 and again from 20th September 1918. He was killed in action on 2nd October 1918 and is buried in Hancourt British Cemetery,

Somme, France (B 12). The Battalion was commanded by Lieutenant Colonel James Neville Marshall MC from 12th October, who was awarded a posthumous VC for his actions on 4th November 1918.

- Edith Emily Stone (3rd September 1878–6th August 1941) married Cyril Arthur Priday (1879–1964) (brother of Thomas Oscar Priday, who married her sister Eleanor), a timber merchant of 23 Langlands Road, Sidcup, Kent on 1st January 1908. Cyril enlisted in the Inns of Court OTC (10865) on 11th January 1916 and transferred to the Class B Army Reserve next day. He was 5′ 7½″ tall and weighed 144 lbs. On 10th March 1917 he was mobilised in the Inns of Court OTC at Berkhamsted and was promoted successively unpaid lance corporal 31st May, corporal 12th June, unpaid lance sergeant 7th July and paid acting sergeant 8th November. On 8th February 1918 he was posted to the Household Brigade Officer Cadet Battalion, The Hall, Bushey, Hertfordshire and was commissioned in 3rd Oxfordshire and Buckinghamshire Light Infantry on 31st July. He was demobilised on 19th February 1919, promoted lieutenant on 31st January 1920 and relinquished his commission on 1st April 1920. Cyril and Edith lived at 6a Vanbrugh Terrace, Blackheath, Kent. They had a daughter, Joan Priday, in 1908.
- Reginald Guy Stone (9th February 1880–11th March 1946) was a naval cadet on HMS *Britannia* 15th January 1894–14th January 1896. He was promoted midshipman 15th June 1896, sub-lieutenant 15th December 1899, lieutenant 31st December 1901 and lieutenant commander 31st December 1909. He served on various ships and shore establishments – HMS *Revenge*, *Raleigh*, *St George*, *Alexandra*, *Pigeon*, *Pembroke*, *Cheerful*, *Angler*, *Hyacinth*, *Odin*, *Hardy*, *Havock*, *Orion*, *Superb*, *Vivid*, *Goldfinch*, *Blake*, *Nottingham*, *Europa*, *M18*, *Ladybird* and *Victory*. Although his reports were generally good, there were a number of adverse incidents. He incurred the severe displeasure of the Superintendent over a gambling dispute while serving on HMS *Angler*. He was limited to three glasses of spirits per day in 1910, the reason is not known, but his application to be appointed First Lieutenant of HMS *Liverpool* was refused. There was a collision at anchor between HMS *Nymphe*, *Goldfinch* and *Sheldrake* on 10th June 1913, resulting in him being cautioned to post an anchor watch in future when weather was threatening. On 1st April 1915 he was tried by court martial for stranding HMS *Goldfinch,* for which he was reprimanded. More positively he was Mentioned by C-in-C Salonika Force in his Despatch of 25th October 1917 for gallant conduct and distinguished services (LG 28th November 1917). Reginald was awarded the DSO (LG 17th May 1918) for services on the Mediterranean Station in the period ending on 31st December 1917. He returned to England on 5th April 1919 and the DSO investiture was at Buckingham Palace on 20th March 1920. Reginald retired at his own request on 1st June 1921, but his application for a step in rank on retirement was refused. He commuted £61 per year of his pension to raise £711/16/2, leaving £300 per year. He later commuted another £60 per year to raise a further £711/14/4. Reginald married Caroline Vere Fraser (1892–1975) on 24th April 1915 in Scotland. They had three children – Edward Reginald Stone 1916, Harry Walter Stone 1918 and

Caroline Mary M Stone 1921. Reginald was granted exemption from recall to naval service in 1939 as he was running a poultry farm singlehanded. He was admitted to Royal Naval Hospital, Invergordon with *paroxysmal tachycardia* 29th November 1944–5th January 1945.

• Dorothy Stone (2nd September 1881–24th April 1965) was a spinster living at Trosbie Cottage, 18 Milton Street, Brixham, Devon at the time of her death. Probate was granted to Pamela Croot Beresford née Stone. Effects were valued at £646.

• Marjorie Armine Stone (29th April 1884–1974) never married.

• Francis 'Frankie' le Strange Stone (14th June 1886–7th October 1938) was educated at Harrow, where he served in the school volunteers, and became a solicitor. He played rugby as a forward for Blackheath 1907–08 and 1913–14, the Barbarians during several tours, for Kent and for England against France at Stade Yves-du-Manoir, Colombes, near Paris, on 13th April 1914 in the last pre-war international. England won 39–13. He also served in the Inns of Court Rifle Volunteers Mounted Infantry for four years. When he enlisted he was described as 5' 11¼" tall and weighed 174 lbs. He rejoined the Inns of Court OTC (1028) on 24th August 1914, by when he was 6' 1" tall. Frankie was commissioned in 3rd (King's Own) Hussars (Special Reserve) with seniority backdated to 15th August 1914. On 8th December, while serving in 9th Reserve Regiment of Cavalry, a medical board at the Military Hospital Shorncliffe found him unfit for two months due to appendicitis (removed on 3rd December) and leave was granted until 7th February 1915. Further medical boards on 10th February, 10th March and 29th April found him unfit for one month, fit for Home Service and fit for General Service respectively. Promoted lieutenant on 6th July and later served in 4th Squadron Machine Gun Corps.

He attended a course with 177th Tunnelling Company RE 27th August–1st September 1916 and was posted to the Machine Gun Corps Training Centre as an instructor on 21st October. On 14th December he re-embarked for France and rejoined his unit on 17th December. Frankie was awarded the MC for his actions while serving with the brigade machine gun squadron. During an attack on his position he went from post to post under severe shellfire, superintending the work of the machine guns and making special dispositions against an assault. He had earlier carried out several dangerous daylight reconnaissances under enemy observation, to enable him to place his guns (LG 17th September 1917). On 3rd

Walter's brother, Francis le Strange Stone, played rugby for England against France in April 1914. Four members of that team were killed in the Great War, including the captain, Ronald Poulton-Palmer. Francis was awarded the MC in 1917.

December 1918 he was again posted to the Machine Gun Corps Training Centre as an instructor and was demobilised on 4th February 1919 from No.2 Dispersal Unit, Crystal Palace. He lived at 6 Duke Street Mansions, 41 Moorgate and 70 Duke Street, all in London. When he died he left effects valued at £6,406/17/5, with probate granted to his sister Eleanor and nephew Edward Reginald Stone.

- Phyllis Louisa Stone (10th May 1888–1975) was educated at Wycombe Abbey School, Buckinghamshire. She married Lieutenant William Henry Strickland Ball RN (1879–1939) on 14th April 1910. He was appointed midshipman on 15th October 1895 and saw action at Benin River, West Africa in 1897. He served on trawlers in the Firth of Forth during the Great War and was Mentioned in Despatches while serving on HMS *Forte*. By 1922 he was a commander and was appointed Assistant Inspector of Naval Ordnance, Torpedo Range, Weymouth, Dorset in 1923. They had a son, Peter Strickland Ball (1911–30), who was a RAF pilot officer. He was flying Avro 504N J9007 at No.2 Flying Training School at Digby, Lincolnshire on 9th September 1930, when his aircraft burst into flames after hitting a tree at Norton Heath, near Lincoln and he was killed. Phyllis married Group Captain Eugene Louis Gerrard CMG DSO RAF (1881–1963) on 1st June 1922. Rather unusually he appears in the Navy, Army and Air Force Lists at various times. He was commissioned in the Royal Marine Light Infantry on 1st September 1900 and was promoted lieutenant on 1st July 1901 and captain on 1st September 1911. He was awarded his wings on 2nd May 1911 (Certificate 76) and when the Central Flying School formed at Upavon, Wiltshire on 19th June 1912, he was one of the first instructors as a squadron commander with effect from 15th May 1912. Eugene held a number of flying records. He remained airborne for four hours and thirteen minutes with a passenger on 16th August 1911 and set two altitude records for pilot and passenger and then with two passengers in 1914. In the first, when he climbed to 10,000′, his passenger was Major Hugh Trenchard (later Marshal of the Royal Air Force Hugh Montague Trenchard, 1st Viscount Trenchard, 'Father of the Royal Air Force'). Eugene was appointed brevet major on 3rd January 1914. On 31st August he took command of No.1 Squadron Royal Naval Air Service and attacked the Dusseldorf airship sheds in a BE2a. Appointed temporary lieutenant colonel on 31st December 1914. He was awarded the DSO in June 1916 for services at Gallipoli while commanding a RNAS wing. Promoted major 6th June 1917. He commanded Eastbourne Air Station 22nd May 1916–31st July 1919. Eugene was promoted air commodore on 1st January 1923 and was appointed to command No.1 Group RAF

Eugene Louis Gerrard was commissioned in the Royal Marine Light Infantry on 1st September 1900 and retired from the Royal Air Force on 15th November 1929.

1923–24 and RAF Palestine from 1924. He commanded 1st Air Defence Group at 145 Sloane Street, London from 9th August 1927 and retired on 15th November 1929. He was also awarded the CMG and the Belgian Chevalier of the Order of Leopold. They were living at Centre Cliff Lodge, South Green, Southwold, Suffolk when he died in 1963, leaving effects valued at £151 to his widow. She was living at 20 Kings Hill, Great Cornard, Sudbury, Suffolk when she died in 1975, leaving effects valued at £11,293.

- Eleanor Whitney Stone (26th September 1890–1974) married Thomas Oscar Priday (1891–1977) (brother of Cyril Arthur Priday, who married her sister Edith) in 1912. Thomas was a cadet at the Royal Military College, Sandhurst and was commissioned in the Middlesex Regiment on 25th March 1911, but resigned his commission on 6th March 1912. He was commissioned in 1st South African Infantry and was appointed temporary captain and adjutant in 1st South African Infantry Brigade on 12th May 1916. He was wounded at Delville Wood, France on 16th July 1916. Thomas relinquished his commission on account of ill health caused by wounds on 7th May 1920. Eleanor and Thomas had a son, Richard A Priday, in 1922. Thomas was living at 35 Kensington Mansions, Trebovir, London at the time of his death, leaving effects valued at £40,077.

Walter's paternal grandfather, Thomas Stone (1812–93) was a solicitor and landowner, of Piddington and Finsbury Circus, London. He married Susanna née Hart (1820–1901) at Bridport, Dorset in 1843. They were living at Sutton Villas, 279 Camden Road, Islington in 1871 and had moved to 29 Lee Park, Lee by 1881. In addition to Edward they had eight other children:

- Elizabeth Susanna Stone (1847–1922) died unmarried while living at 13 The Paragon, Blackheath, London. She left effects valued at £3,151/13/1 to her sister Emily.
- Charles Stone (born 1850) was an articled clerk in a solicitor's office in 1871 and a solicitor by 1881. He married Alice Elizabeth Hart (1858–84) in 1882. She was the daughter of Edward Hart, Alderman of London and the sister of Edith Hart who married Charles' brother John below. They had a son, Charles Bede Stone, in 1883.
- Annie Mary Stone (1852–63).
- Emily Sarah Stone (1854–1931) died unmarried while living at 28 Kidbrooke Park Road, Blackheath, London. She left effects valued at £6,176/4/7.
- Fanny Margaret Stone (1855–87).
- John Morris Stone FRAS (1857–1930) was a law student at Lincoln's Inn and at St John's College, Cambridge (BA 1881, MA 1883). He married Edith Emily late Hubbuck née Hart (1867–1942) in 1895. She was the widow of Charles Alfred Hubbuck of Sydenham, the daughter of Edward Hart, Alderman of London, and the sister of Alice Hart who married John's brother Charles above. They were living at 73 Royal Parade, Eastbourne when he died in 1930, leaving effects

valued at £2,628/12/2 to his widow. She was living at 10 Jevington Gardens, Eastbourne when she died in 1942, leaving effects valued at £3,262/5/7. They had three children – John Leonard Stone 1896, Edith Alice Stone 1898 and Richard Stone 1899. John (later Sir John) Leonard Stone (1896–1978) enlisted in B Company, Inns of Court OTC (1250) on 23rd September 1914. He was 5′ 10¾″ tall and a law student. However, when he applied for a commission on 6th October he was only 5′ 8½″ tall and weighed 133 lbs. John was commissioned in 12th Worcestershire on 20th October and was promoted lieutenant on 1st April 1915. He received a gunshot wound to the left thigh during an attack at Krithia, Gallipoli while serving with X Company, 4th Worcestershire on 6th August 1915. He reached the Turkish trench with eight to ten men, reversed the parapet and opened fire on the enemy. The Turks counterattacked and John's men had no bombs and no reinforcements. All were killed except John and two others. He was knocked unconscious by a bomb and was carried to the rear as a prisoner of war by Lance Corporal D Lewis. During his captivity he communicated with the War Office using a code and supplied valuable information. He learned to speak Turkish fluently. On 22nd August 1918 he escaped from Haider Pasha Station, Constantinople with Captain EJ Fulton, 1st Lancers. They crossed the Bosphorus, reached San Stefano aerodrome and were about to get away in a Turkish aircraft when they were discovered. They managed to escape again but were betrayed on 5th September, as they were about to get away by boat across the Black Sea disguised as Turkish women. John escaped just before the Armistice and was not recaptured. For his services while a prisoner of war he was Mentioned in Despatches (LG 30th January 1920). He was sent to the Officers' Rest House, Salonika on 1st December 1918 and embarked for England on 4th December. On arrival he was sent on two months leave before reporting to the reserve unit. He was requested by General George Milne to be the Control Officer at Eski Shehr and disembarked at Salonika on 7th March 1919 and Constantinople on 13th March. John was admitted to 143rd Field Ambulance on 27th July, then 28th Division Collection Station and 82nd General Hospital on 29th July. On 11th November he was again admitted to 143rd Field Ambulance and 82nd General Hospital with urticaria (hives, a skin rash). He embarked at Constantinople for Britain on 24th February 1920 and relinquished his commission on 30th March. He was recalled for service in Turkey on 10th December 1920 and was appointed temporary captain on the General List on 14th December. He relinquished his appointment on the Sub-Commission of Organisation (Special Elements) on 9th August 1921 and was appointed Personal Assistant to Deputy Assistant Director of Requisitions and Hirings (Major General C McK Franks CB), Inter-Allied Requisition and Hiring Commission, Allied Forces of Occupation, Constantinople. John applied for a regular commission but was not successful at a time when the Army was reducing in size considerably, although Franks considered him to be an exceptional officer. Promoted captain on 10th August 1921. He was demobilised on 21st March 1922, while on leave in England from his post in Constantinople. He relinquished his commission, retaining the rank of captain. His addresses were 3 Stone Buildings, Lincoln's Inn, London and 50 Shooters Hill Road, Blackheath. He claimed movements expenses of £33/3/10, which he spent on going on leave (Orient Express Constantinople – London and travel allowances), arguing that he would not have done so had he not been on a two year engagement and would therefore have been eligible for the move home at public expense. John was called to the Bar at Gray's Inn in 1923, joined Lincoln's Inn Bar in 1931 and became a bencher of Gray's Inn in 1942. He served in the Home Guard until 1943 and was appointed the last British Chief Justice of the High Court of Bombay from 30th September 1943 until 1948. He was later Vice Chancellor of the County Palatine of Lancaster until 1963.

- Cecilia Emma Stone (1858–1956) died unmarried while living at Donabate, 82 St Georges Road, Cheltenham, Gloucestershire. She left effects valued at £14,280/11/9.
- Thomas Stephen Stone (1860–63).

His maternal grandfather, Andre (Andrew) Amédeé Miéville (1827–73), born in Switzerland of British parents, was a foreign banker. He married Emily née Dew (1825–89), born at Whitney, Herefordshire, in 1849. One of her brothers, Captain Armine Dew RA, was killed on 20th September 1855 at the Battle of the Alma. They were living at 7 Hill Road, Marylebone, London in 1851. By 1861 he was a shipping agent and they were living at 5 Bedford Place, Kensington. Later he was a stockbroker. By 1871 they had moved to 3 Ashley Villas, Finsbury and he was a retired stockbroker. Emily was living at 17 Beaumont Road, Islington in 1881 and at 35 Winchester Road, South Hampstead, London at the time of her death, leaving effects valued at £1,120/11/-. In addition to Emily they had six other children:

Walter's maternal grandfather, Andre Amédeé Miéville.

- Beatrice Margaret Miéville (1850–51).
- Edward Amédeé Miéville (1851–1902) was a merchant's clerk in 1871. He moved to America and married Helena Maude Mattoon (died 1931) in 1873 at Oswego, New York State. They had a son, Charles Amédeé Miéville, in 1876.
- Walter (later Sir Walter) Frederick Miéville (1855–1929) was educated at Christ's College, Finchley before becoming a civil servant in the Consular Service of the Foreign Office in 1874. His appointments included: HM Consul for Soudan 1st January 1882; HM Consul for the Province of Rio Grande do Sul and Santa Catarina, Brazil 21st April 1883; President of the Sanitary, Maritime and

Quarantine Board at Alexandria, Egypt 1884–87; special mission to Vienna, Berlin and Paris 1887; President of the Egyptian Maritime and Quarantine Board of Health; represented Egypt at the Sanitary Conference at Venice 1892 and Paris 1894; and Chairman of the Board of Land & Mortgage Company of Egypt. He was awarded the CMG 1887, Order of Osmanieh 2nd Class 22nd March 1897, Order of the Medjidie 2nd Class (LG 10th July 1891) and KCMG (LG 1st January 1898). Walter married Theodora Johanna Taylor (1860–1915) in 1882 at Lewisham, London. They were living at 68 Wilbury Road, Hove, Sussex in 1911, by when he was retired. There were no children.

Walter's uncle, Sir Walter Frederick Miéville KCMG.

- Charles Ernest Miéville (1858–1940) was in partnership with Arthur Gregory in Miéville and Gregory at 8 Drapers' Gardens, London. The partnership was dissolved by mutual consent on 29th April 1885 and Charles continued the business in his own name. He married Alice Huleatt Garcia Bampfield (1864–1934) in 1882. He was appointed Honorary Secretary of the Professional Golfers' Association and lived at 1 Freeland Road, Ealing Common, London before moving to 19 Creffield Road, Ealing Common by 1911, by when he was an estate agent. They had five children including – Alice Daisie Miéville 1884, Gladys Miéville 1889, Ernest Frederick Miéville 1891 and Eric Charles Miéville 1896.

- Roderick Napleton Miéville (1862–69).
- Herbert le Strange Miéville (born 1866) served in South Africa throughout the Second Boer War with 1st City (Grahamstown) Volunteers. He married Edith Ellen Goddard Watson in 1902.

Walter was educated at:

- Lindisfarne, Blackheath, London. He also played for Blackheath Rugby Club.
- Harrow School, Middlesex 1906–10, where he was a member of the Rifle Corps.
- Pembroke College, Cambridge 1910, but left before completing his degree.

Harrow School, founded in 1572, is one of the original ten public schools regulated by the 1868 Public Schools Act. Amongst its alumni are seven British Prime Ministers, including Robert Peel, Henry Palmerston, Stanley Baldwin and Winston Churchill, members of various royal families, Jawaharlal Nehru, first Prime Minister of India, and twenty VC and one GC winners. Other notables include Lord Byron, Wimbledon champions Spencer Gore and Frank Hadow, FA Cup founder Charles W Alcock, actor Benedict Cumberbatch, singer/songwriter James Blunt, rugby international Billy Vunipola and racing pundit John McCirick.

• Studied land surveying in Regina and Toronto, Canada, departing Liverpool for New York on RMS *Lusitania* on 27th April 1912.

Walter met Mabel Maud Jukes (born 19th October 1892 at St Catherine's, Ontario, Canada) in 1913 and they lived at 66 Bloor Street East, Toronto, Ontario. No record of a marriage has been found and all subsequent official documents give his father as his next of kin. Mabel and Walter had a son, Reginald Miéville Stone, born on 21st May 1914. Walter was a surveyor when he travelled to New York on RMS *Campania*, departing Liverpool, Lancashire on 17th January 1914. He returned to England at the outbreak of the Great War.

Mabel married Eric Oliver Gurney (born 17th May 1893 in London, England) on 25th September 1917 at Detroit, Michigan, USA. He was an auditor and bookkeeper living with his wife at 209 Lee Place, Detroit. He enlisted in 1st Depot Battalion, Western Ontario Regiment on 23rd October 1917 (2355490)

On Christmas Eve 1347, Edward III granted Marie de St Pol, Countess of Pembroke (1303–1377), a licence to found a new establishment in the university at Cambridge. It was known as the Hall of Valence Mary, later renamed Pembroke Hall and became Pembroke College in 1856. It is the third-oldest college of Cambridge University. The first chapel designed by Sir Christopher Wren is at Pembroke. Famous alumni include William Pitt, Prime Minister 1783–1801 and 1804–06, the author, Ian Fleming, and the organiser of the Great Escape, Roger Bushell. A number of comedians also attended the College – Tim Brooke-Taylor, Peter Cook, Eric Idle and Bill Oddie.

at London, Ontario, described as 5′ 10½″ tall, medium complexion, blue eyes, brown hair and his religious denomination was Roman Catholic. He was promoted corporal 5th December 1917, sergeant 22nd December 1917 and was discharged

When completed in 1907, RMS *Lusitania* was the largest ship ever built, but was overtaken by her slightly larger sister, *Mauretania*, shortly thereafter. *Lusitania* had double the passenger accommodation of her rivals and on her second transatlantic voyage she gained the Blue Riband for the fastest crossing. On her 202nd return Atlantic crossing she was torpedoed by a U-boat eleven miles off the southern Irish coast. She sank in eighteen minutes with the loss of 1,198 passengers and crew, including 128 American citizens. As a result public opinion in the USA began to shift against Germany and was a significant factor in bringing the Americans into the war in 1917.

on 4th December 1918 to 1600 Broadway, New York. In order to conceal that his mother was not married when he was born, Reginald was given his stepfather's name. Eric and Mabel were living at 10321 Bennockborn Drive, Cheviot Hills, Los Angeles, California and he registered for the US Forces in 1942 (2954). He was described as 6' tall, weighing 185 lbs, of ruddy complexion with blue eyes, brown hair and was employed by A&S Lyons (talent agency) at 356N Camden Drive, Beverly Hills, California.

Mabel's father, Elias Arthur Jukes (c.1852–1930), born at St Catherines, Lincoln, Canada, was a chemist. He married Alice Maud Mary née Birchall (1864–1945), also born in Canada, in 1891 at York, Ontario. She was living at Beverly Hills, Los Angeles, California, USA at the time of the 1940 US Census. In addition to Mabel they had another daughter, Gladys de Aguilar Jukes (1894–1951), who married Douglas Hartman Christian (born 1888) in 1919 in Chicago, Illinois. He was a salesman for Hornes Disappearing Beds Co at 175 West Jackson Boulevard, Chicago when he enlisted into the US Army on 5th June 1917 and served as a sergeant in 188th US Quartermasters Division.

Walter enlisted in the Inns of Court OTC on 9th November 1914 and joined the Royal Military College, Sandhurst on 29th December. He was commissioned in 3rd Royal Fusiliers on 12th May 1915 and went to France on 5th January 1916 to join 17th Battalion but was employed as the Staff Captain at HQ 5th Brigade. Promoted lieutenant on 7th March 1916 and was admitted sick to 9th Stationary Hospital, Le Havre on 23rd June. He was appointed acting captain 6th November 1916–10th January 1917 and 1st June–20th July 1917 while commanding a company and again on 21st July 1917. **Awarded the VC for his actions near Moeuvres, France on 30th November 1917, LG 13th February 1918.** He was killed during his VC action and is

Walter Stone's name on the Cambrai Memorial.

The Stone family headstone in Greenwich Cemetery.

Walter's name on the Stone of Remembrance in the Church of St Mary the Virgin, Shrewsbury, Shropshire. Inexplicably he is shown with the DSO and MC (Memorials to Valour).

commemorated on the Cambrai Memorial (Panel 3/4). The VC was presented to his parents by the King at Buckingham Palace on 26th July 1918. Walter is commemorated in a number of other places:

VC memorial plaque at Lewisham Shopping Centre, London.

- The Stone of Remembrance 1914–18 in the south transept of the Church of St Mary the Virgin, Shrewsbury, Shropshire.
- Family headstone in Greenwich Cemetery, Well Hall Road, South East London.
- Harrow School Speech Room with the other School VCs.
- Shropshire County Roll of Honour.
- Memorial plaque at Lewisham Shopping Centre, London unveiled by Philip Gardner VC in May 1995, commemorating fourteen VCs with local connections.
- Victoria Cross Memorial by the war memorial, High Street, Lewisham, South London.
- Victoria Cross Memorial, Civic Centre, Lewisham.

Pembroke College, Cambridge War Memorial.

- Royal Fusiliers panel in the Royal Memorial Chapel, Royal Military Academy, Sandhurst, Surrey.
- Named on the War Memorial, Pembroke College, Cambridge.
- The Department for Communities and Local Government decided to provide a commemorative paving stone at the birthplace of every Great War Victoria Cross recipient in the United Kingdom – Walter's stone was dedicated at Lewisham War Memorial on High Street on 30th November 2017 to mark the centenary of his award.

In addition to the VC he was awarded the British War Medal 1914–20 and Victory Medal 1914–19. The VC is held privately. Mabel is understood to have remained in Canada and later married Eric Oliver Gurney, an American citizen.

LIEUTENANT HARCUS STRACHAN
Fort Garry Horse, Canadian Expeditionary Force

Harcus Strachan was born on 7th November 1884 at Grange Terrace, Borrowstounness, Linlithgow, West Lothian, Scotland. His given names are also seen as Henry Mateus. His surname is pronounced 'Strawn' and he was annoyed if addressed otherwise. His father, William Strachan (c.1846–1908), born at Kirkpatrick Durham, Kirkcudbrightshire was a fiscale clerk in 1861 and a lawyer's clerk in 1871, lodging at 1 Bank Street, Dunse, Berwickshire. He was living at 24 High Street, Linlithgow when he married Isabella Thomson née Veitch (born 1848 at Polwarth, Berwickshire) on 19th February 1874 at 24 Prince Albert Buildings, Edinburgh. Midlothian. By 1881 William had become a solicitor and was living with his family at Grange Terrace, Borrowstounness. By 1891 they were living at Grahamsdyke Road, Holywood, Carriden, Borrowstounness. He was appointed Sheriff-Clerk of Linlithgowshire and died on 31st January 1908. Isabella emigrated to Canada with some of her children in 1908 and settled on a homestead at Chauvin, Alberta. In 1916 she was living nearby at Ribstone, Alberta. Harcus had six siblings:

Kirkpatrick Durham, Kirkcudbrightshire, where Harcus' father was born.

- William Andrew Strachan (1874–1901).
- Hannah Jane Catherine Strachan (born 1876).
- Alexander Veitch Strachan (1878–1961) was a mechanical engineer by 1901. He married Margaret Morris Davidson (1877–1947) in 1908.
- Grace Mary Strachan (1880–1963) was a pupil teacher in 1901. She married Francis Ord Mickel (1862–1936), a timber merchant, at Holywood, Carriden in 1907. He was later managing director of a hosiery manufacturing business. They were living at Norham, Carriden, Borrowstounness in 1911. They had a son, Patrick Lizars Mickel, in 1910.
- Norman Philip Strachan (1887–1976) went to Canada with his mother in 1908 and farmed there.
- May Isabella Strachan (born 1889) went to Canada with her mother and was living in New Westminster, British Columbia in 1982.

The Royal High School is one of the oldest schools in the world, dating back to at least 1128. By 1378 it was the Grammar School of the Church of Edinburgh. In 1566 Mary Queen of Scots transferred control from Holyrood Abbey to the Town Council of Edinburgh and James VI granted it royal patronage about 1590. By the early 19th century the School had gained an international reputation and attracted foreign students. It was the model for

the English High School of Boston, the first public high school in the USA in 1821. The School had many locations in Edinburgh, the most famous on Regent Road was in use from 1829 until 1968, when it moved to its current site at Barnton. During the First World War 1,024 former members served in the armed forces of whom 180 died. The School gained over 100 gallantry awards, including two VCs, the other being awarded to Philip Bent. Another VC was awarded to John Cruikshank in the Second World War. The School has numerous famous alumni including: architect, Robert Adam; inventor, Alexander Graham Bell; Labour politician and Foreign Secretary, Robin Cook; comedian, Ronnie Corbett; and author, Walter Scott. The building on Regent Street was to be the site of a devolved legislature for Scotland, but it failed to gain sufficient support in 1979. The building was subsequently used for various political committees and as offices for Edinburgh City Council. Following Scottish devolution in 1999, the former school was considered for the Scottish Parliament, but it was established on a new site at Holyrood. Since then a number of proposals have been made for its use, including home for a Scottish National Photography Centre and a luxury hotel.

Harcus' paternal grandfather, William Strachan (born c.1808 at Balmaghie, Kirkcudbrightshire) was a labourer, living at Poplar Cottage, Holywood, Dumfriesshire with his sister Jean (born c.1798), who was acting as housekeeper. He married Mary née McMillan. By 1871 he was living at Woodland Porter's Lodge with Agnes Kirkpatrick, a servant. He was a farmer in 1874.

His maternal grandfather, Andrew Veitch (1808–72), was born at Symington, Lanarkshire. He married Hannah née Harkness (born c.1816 at Gladsmuir, Haddingtonshire) in 1845. Andrew was a head gardener in 1851 and they were living at Polwarth, Marchmont, Berwickshire. They were still there in 1861. He died on 22nd February 1872 at Royal Edinburgh Asylum, Edinburgh, Midlothian. In addition to Isabella they had four other children:

• Alexander William Veitch (born 1846) who died in infancy.
• Alexander Veitch (1850–85) married Isabella Gardner in 1878.
• Andrew Veitch (1853–1922) may have married Marion Todd (1857–89) in 1885 and Wilhelmina Sutherland (1870–1954) in 1891, both at St Giles, Edinburgh.
• Robert Veitch (born 1856).

Harcus was educated at:

• Borrowstounness Academy, Linlithgow, West Lothian. While there he was a member of 1st Borrowstounness Company, Boys' Brigade.

The University of Edinburgh was founded in 1582 and is the sixth oldest in the English speaking world. It was originally a college of law. Amongst its alumni are twenty-one Nobel Prize winners. It currently admits about 6,300 students per year. Its numerous famous alumni include:

Charles Darwin – naturalist who formulated the theory of evolution.
Joseph Lister – pioneer of antiseptic surgery.
Alexander Graham Bell – inventor of the telephone.
British Prime Ministers – Gordon Brown, Lord Palmerston and Lord John Russell.
Authors – Arthur Conan Doyle, Robert Louis Stevenson, JM Barrie and Walter Scott.
Poet – William Wordsworth.
MI5 Director – Stella Rimington.
First President of Tanzania – Julius Nyerere.
Captain Eric 'Winkle' Brown CBE DSC AFC RN (1919–2016) holds the world record for flying 487 aircraft types and for undertaking 2,407 aircraft carrier take-offs and 2,271 landings.

- Royal High School Edinburgh, Midlothian. In 1902–04 he was a member of the Rugby XV and Cricket XI. He created a school record in 1902 for throwing the cricket ball 109 yards.
- University of Edinburgh, where he studied medicine.

Harcus emigrated to Canada with his mother in 1909 and became a homesteader at Chauvin, Alberta. He left the farm in the hands of his mother, brothers and sisters when he attempted to enlist in

Chauvin began as a railroad siding in 1908, named after George Von Chauvin, a railroad official. In 2016 its population was 335.

Canada, but failed an eyesight test. He sailed to England, intending to join the London Scottish but instead enlisted as a trooper at the Canadian Cavalry Depot, Canterbury, Kent on 15th July 1915 (15585). He was described as a rancher, 5′ 11″ tall, weighing 158 lbs, with dark complexion, grey eyes, dark hair and his religious denomination was Presbyterian. He gave his birth date as 7th November 1887. An index card in his service record indicates that he was in 7th Canadian Mounted Rifles in October 1915. In December 1915 it was decided to replace 2nd King Edward's Horse in the Canadian Cavalry Brigade in France with a Canadian regiment. The Fort Garry Horse formed at Shorncliffe, Kent in January 1916 from personnel of the Canadian Cavalry Depot. Harcus transferred to the Regiment on 21st January and was promoted lance corporal on 1st February. His assigned pay from February 1916 was sent to his sister, Mrs FO Mickel, Norham, Borrowstounness, West Lothian until he was commissioned, when it went to the Bank of Montreal, 9 Waterloo Place, London.

Lieutenant FMW Harvey VC.

Harcus sailed for France with the Regiment on 24th February, arriving at Le Havre next day. Promoted corporal 16th April, lance sergeant 16th June and sergeant on 23rd June. Elements of the Regiment were first in action on 13th/14th July. Harcus was commissioned as a lieutenant in the Fort Garry Horse on 22nd (later backdated to 1st) September 1916. He was granted leave 26th January–5th February 1917 and also leave to Paris 27th February–3rd March. During the first leave he became a Freemason, Initiated into Douglas Lodge (No.409), Borrowstounness, Linlithgow, West Lothian on 22nd January 1917.

The Canadian Cavalry Brigade took part in an attack on Guyencourt-Saulcourt on 27th March 1917, during which Lieutenant FMW Harvey of Lord Strathcona's Horse was awarded the VC. It was the first major action involving the entire brigade mounted. **Awarded the MC for his actions in May 1917 commanding a party in an attack on enemy outposts in the area of Somerville Wood and Max Wood, south of St Quentin, France; they captured eight prisoners and killed many more without suffering a single casualty, LG 16 August 1917.** During a raid on 8th July he received gunshot wounds to his right arm and thigh and was also gassed. He was admitted to 2nd Canadian Field Ambulance and 55 then 34 Casualty Clearing Stations next day. Harcus was discharged to his unit on 14th July but was admitted to 12th Stationary Hospital at Étaples on 24th July with the same wounds. He moved to 8th General Hospital at Rouen on 26th July, followed by 8th Michelham Convalescence Home at Dieppe 8th–22nd August. He was discharged to the Base Depot at Étaples and rejoined his unit in the field on 30th August. Harcus was granted ten days' leave at the family home 7th–19th September.

Awarded the VC for his actions near Masnières, France on 20th November 1917, LG 18th December 1917 and correction 26th March 1918. Appointed temporary captain on 20th November and was granted thirty-one days leave from 31st December. The VC and MC were presented by the King at Buckingham Palace on 16th January 1918. He was presented with a silver rose-bowl by the pupils and staff at the Royal High School, Edinburgh on 24th January 1918. On 4th February he returned to the Canadian Cavalry Reserve Depot at

Harcus Strachan at the head of his squadron of Fort Garry Horse on 30th November 1917.

Shorncliffe. Leave to Canada was granted on compassionate grounds from 23rd February until 23rd April, extended to 23rd May. He returned to Britain on SS *Grampian*, rejoining the Canadian Cavalry Reserve Depot on 5th June. He returned to France on 25th June and rejoined the Fort Garry Horse on 6th July. Appointed temporary major on 1st August. Harcus was granted leave from 26th November and rejoined the unit on 22nd December. He was granted another fourteen days leave from 1st April 1919 and returned to Britain on 18th April. Harcus was released from the Canadian Forces on 30th April in order to join British forces in Archangel,

SS *Grampian* (10,187 tons) docked at Glasgow, was one of the largest vessels in the Allan Line, completed by Alexander Stephen & Sons of Linthouse in 1907. She was gutted in a fire during a refit at Antwerp in 1921 and was scrapped in 1925.

Russia. On one of his furloughs he was presented with a sword of honour by the town of Borrowstounness, Linlithgow, West Lothian. Lord Rosebery was present during the presentation.

Following military service Harcus returned to Edmonton, Alberta to resume farming. In 1921 he attempted to enter Federal politics on behalf of the Liberal Party for the Wainwright constituency but was defeated. He was appointed a field supervisor at the Canadian Bank of Commerce at Calgary and Toronto. Harcus also continued service in the Militia. Appointed lieutenant in 19th Alberta Dragoons on 2nd August 1920. Promoted captain 9th September 1921 and major as second-in-command 19th Alberta Dragoons on 10th April 1922. He transferred to 15th Canadian Light Horse in 1926 and to 2nd Reserve Regiment on 22nd November 1927. On 4th January 1936 he was appointed Honorary ADC to the Governor General. He transferred to the Reserve of Officers (15th Alberta Light Horse) on 15th December 1936.

Harcus married Bessie Lorena Sterling (10th May 1903–21st February 1964) in Calgary in 1928. She was born at Selma, Hants County, Nova Scotia and was working in the bank at Chauvin when they married. They had four children:

- Jean Joyce Strachan married King Gilmour and they had at least a son, Robert.
- Robin Strachan.
- Robert Strachan.
- May Strachan.

Bessie's father, Herbert Huntington Sterling (1854–1918), a builder and carpenter, married Deborah 'Dibby' Elizabeth née Dotten (1856–1944). They were living at Maitland, Hants County, Nova Scotia in 1901. By 1906 they were living at Township 30, Range 27, west of the fourth meridian (Longitude 110°) on the Alberta-Saskatchewan border and were still there in 1911. When Dibby died her address was 323 Regina Street, New Westminster, British Columbia. In addition to Bessie they had six other children:

- Edward James Sterling (1888–1956) married Eileen Susie Hurry (born 1904).
- Margaret May Sterling (1890–1906).
- Elveria (also seen as Alvera) Birdena Sterling (1892–1956) married Elmer Albert Edgar (born 1888) in 1913 and they had a daughter, Dorothy Gwendolyn Moore, in 1921.
- Leonard Banks Sterling (1894–1973) married Laura Roger Kent (born 1899).
- Ruby Ellen Sterling (1898–1970) was unmarried, living at 317–3rd Avenue, New Westminster, British Columbia in June 1955.
- Hervey (also seen as Harvey) Chandler Sterling (1900–75) married Elsie Emily Scoville (1903–64) in 1928. They were living at 2506 West 3rd Avenue, Vancouver, British Columbia in 1955.

Harcus attended the VC Dinner at the Royal Gallery of the House of Lords, London on 9th November 1929. He was one of six VCs presented to King George VI and Queen Elizabeth at the Alberta Legislature during the Royal couple's visit to the Province in 1939. He rejoined the Canadian Army at the outbreak of the Second World War as a lieutenant colonel with 15th Alberta Light Horse. Appointed major with the South Alberta Regiment, Canadian Active Service Force. In July 1940 he was appointed lieutenant colonel to command the Edmonton Fusiliers. Harcus served in Europe and returned to the Reserve of Officers on 27th October 1944. He transferred to the Retired List on 4th July 1946. Harcus was appointed ADC to the Governor General of Canada and retired in 1950. He and Bessie then moved from Toronto to Vancouver, British Columbia. He attended the VC Centenary Celebrations at Hyde Park, London on 26th June 1956. Harcus was one of seven VC pallbearers at the funeral of Michael O'Rourke VC at Mount Lehman, British Columbia on 10th December 1957.

Harcus Strachan died at the University of British Columbia Hospital, Vancouver on 1st May 1982. Aged ninety-seven years and 175 days, he was the longest-lived VC holder. He requested no funeral service and was cremated at North Vancouver Crematorium, 1505 Lillooet, Vancouver, British Columbia. His ashes were scattered near the Rose Garden Columbarium at Boal Chapel Memorial Gardens in North Vancouver. Harcus is commemorated in a number of places:

- Named on a Victoria Cross obelisk to all Canadian VCs at Military Heritage Park, Barrie, Ontario dedicated by The Princess Royal on 22nd October 2013.

The Canadian VC memorial plaque (back right) outside the British High Commission in Ottawa (Memorials to Valour).

The Fort Garry Horse Memorial at Masnières.

Mount Strachan.

- Named on one of eleven plaques honouring 175 men from overseas awarded the VC for the Great War. The plaques were unveiled by the Senior Minister of State at the Foreign & Commonwealth Office and Minister for Faith and Communities, Baroness Warsi, at a reception at Lancaster House, London on 26th June 2014 attended by The Duke of Kent and relatives of the VC recipients. The Canadian plaque was unveiled outside the British High Commission in Elgin Street, Ottawa on 10th November 2014 by The Princess Royal in the presence of British High Commissioner Howard Drake, Canadian Minister of Veterans Affairs Julian Fantino and Canadian Chief of the Defence Staff General Thomas J Lawson.

The 49 Cent postage stamps issued by Canada Post on 21st October 2004.

- Mount Strachan on the outskirts of Vancouver, British Columbia was named in 1918.

The Canadian Volunteer Service Medal was awarded to military personel who completed eighteen months voluntary active service between 3rd September 1939 and 1st March 1947. A silver clasp with a maple leaf was awarded for sixty days service outside Canada. Eligibility was extended in 2001 to members of the auxiliary services, merchant mariners, Corps of Canadian Fire Fighters who served in Britain during the Blitz, Overseas Welfare Workers, Voluntary Aid Detachments, Ferry Command pilots and British Commonwealth Air Training Plan instructors. Members of the Royal Canadian Mounted Police were added in 2003.

- Cambrai Company, Army Foundation College, Harrogate comprises six platoons named after VC winners in the Battle of Cambrai, including 10 (Strachan VC) Platoon.
- Harcus Strachan Lake, Manitoba named in November 2013.
- His VC action was featured in Issue No.343 of the Victor Comic entitled *The Charge of the Fort Garry Cavalry*, dated 16th September 1967.
- His portrait hangs in Parliament House, Ottawa.
- Display in the Fort Garry Horse Museum, Winnipeg.
- Fort Garry Horse Memorial on the banks of the St Quentin Canal at Masnières dedicated on 11 June 2004.
- Plaque on the York Cemetery VC Memorial, West Don River Valley, Toronto, Canada dedicated on 25th June 2017.
- Two 49 cents postage stamps in honour of the 94 Canadian VC winners were issued by Canada Post on 21st October 2004 on the 150th Anniversary of the first Canadian VC's action, Alexander Roberts Dunn VC.
- The Department for Communities and Local Government decided to provide a commemorative paving stone at the birthplace of every Great War Victoria Cross recipient in the United Kingdom. A commemorative stone for Harcus was dedicated at Borrowstounness War Memorial at the junction of Stewart Avenue and Church Wynd on 20th November 2017 to mark the centenary of his award.
- Boys' Brigade VC & GC Memorial, National Memorial Arboretum, Alrewas, Staffordshire.

In addition to the VC and MC he was awarded the British War Medal 1914–20, Victory Medal 1914–19, Canadian Volunteer Service Medal 1939–45, War Medal 1939–45, George VI Coronation Medal 1937, Elizabeth II Coronation Medal 1953, Canadian Centennial Medal 1967 and Elizabeth II Silver Jubilee Medal 1977. The VC was acquired by the Canadian War Museum on 28th November 2017.

50842 LANCE CORPORAL JOHN THOMAS
2/5th Battalion, The Prince of Wales's (North Staffordshire Regiment)

John Thomas was born at Higher Openshaw, Manchester, Lancashire on 10th May 1886. He was also known as Thomas. His father, Edward Thomas (c.1832–95), a boot maker, was born at St Andrew's, Worcester. He married Elizabeth 'Eliza' née Crellin (born c.1851 at Malew, Isle of Man), a nurse, on 15th September 1877 at St Simon's, Salford, Lancashire. Edward was almost certainly married before and had at least three children – Anne Thomas 1862, Edward Thomas 1864 and Alice Thomas 1869. Edward

John's family was living on Ashton Road, Openshaw in 1891.

The clock tower and market house in Ledbury, Herefordshire, where John's paternal grandmother was born.

and Eliza were living at 30 Barlow Street, Bradford, Manchester in 1881 and at 428 Ashton Road, Openshaw in 1891. John had three sisters:

- Maggie May Thomas (1878–1918), born at Ballahick, Malew, Isle of Man, married Noah Brown (1874–1962) in 1898. He was a lamp man with the railways in 1901 when they were living at 115 Margaret Street, Ardwick, Manchester. He was later a stableman with Midland Railway. Maggie had been admitted to Lancaster Lunatic Asylum by 1911 and died there on 16th March 1918. Maggie and Noah had a daughter, Ada Brown, in 1904. Noah married Emma Page (born 1874) in 1924.

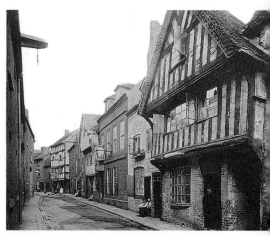

Fish Street, Worcester, where John's paternal grandparents were living in 1851.

- Mary Ellen 'Nellie' Thomas (born 1879) married Thomas Haslam Rostron (born 1873) in 1897. They emigrated to Boston, Massachusetts, USA in June 1900 and were living at Methuen Precinct 1, Essex County, Massachusetts in 1910. They had three children – Nellie Rostron 1899, Annie Rostron 1902 and Frederick Rostron 1905.
- Charlotte 'Lottie' Thomas (1883–1963) married Benjamin Aldred (1880–1956), a driller in an iron works, in 1904. They were living at 10 Egerton Street, Openshaw in 1911. They had four children – Charlotte Aldred 1905, Lily Aldred 1908, Benjamin Aldred 1909 and Joshua Aldred 1910.

William Laslett bought the old Worcester City Gaol in 1867 and used the cells as almshouses, as seen in this picture. In 1912 the site was cleared and new almshouses were constructed in mock-Tudor style.

Samuel Cunard, a Nova Scotian, was awarded the first British transatlantic steamship contract in 1839 and formed the British and North American Royal Mail Steam-Packet Company. It dominated Atlantic travel until it came under pressure from rivals in the 1870s and reorganised as the Cunard Steamship Company. In 1902 the British Government provided Cunard with loans and a subsidy to build two new large liners. Post-WW1 Cunard faced new competition from German, Italian and French companies and in 1934 the British Government helped Cunard finish *Queen Mary* and start a new liner, *Queen Elizabeth*, on the condition that the company merged with the failing White Star line to form Cunard-White Star Ltd. The company name reverted to Cunard Line in 1950, by when it had regained its position as the largest transatlantic passenger line. By the late 1950s passenger ships were increasingly unprofitable due to the introduction of jet airliners. As a result Cunard concentrated on cruising holidays but at the time of writing the company was the only one still operating a scheduled passenger service between Europe and North America.

John's paternal grandfather, Edward Thomas (c.1795–1883), born at Powick, Worcestershire, married Ann née Treherne (c.1798–1870), born at Ledbury, Herefordshire, on 8th November 1819 at Claines, Worcester. In 1851 they were living at 8 Fish Street, St Alban, Worcester, when he was a shoemaker and general dealer and she was a shoe binder. In 1881 he was living at 32 Lasletts Almshouses, Worcester. In addition to Edward they also had, Eliza Thomas, born c.1832.

His maternal grandfather, Daniel Crellin, a publican, married Margaret née Taubman (born c.1827 at Malew, Isle of Man) on 7th June 1845 at Patrick, Isle of Man. In addition to Eliza they had three other children:

• John Crellin (born c.1846) was a carpenter in 1871, living with his father and stepmother at Rushden, Isle of Man.
• Catherine Crellin (born c.1849 in England).
• Margaret Crellin (born c.1850).

It is assumed that Daniel and Margaret divorced as he later married Catherine (born c.1824 at Arbory, Isle of Man). They were living at 31 Main Street, Rushden, Isle of Man in 1871.

After John's parents died he and two sisters were cared for by relatives. He was educated at St Barnabus' Church School, Openshaw and was employed as a merchant seaman with the Cunard Shipping Company in Liverpool. He enlisted in 3rd (Special Reserve) Battalion, South Lancashire Regiment on 13th October 1908 (791). On 7th June 1909 he enlisted in the Army Service Corps as a transport driver (T/27643), transferred to the Reserve in 1912 and returned to work for Cunard.

On the outbreak of war he was recalled and went to France on 9th August 1914. He was wounded and evacuated to England, where he was taken on the strength of 87th Training Reserve Battalion (TR69988) on 22nd May 1917. On recovering he transferred to 2/5th North Staffordshire on 7th July. He was promoted lance corporal.

Awarded the VC for his actions near Fontaine-Notre-Dame, France on 30th November 1917, LG 13th February 1918. The VC was presented by the King at Buckingham Palace on 23rd March 1918. In the same month he is reported to have been blown up and concussed at Bullecourt, for which he received a partial disability pension of 9/4 per week after the war. On 27th March he was presented with a gold watch and an illuminated address by the Mayor of Manchester at a civic reception. John was promoted corporal and transferred to 3rd (Reserve) Battalion on 10th December. He was discharged on 15th February 1919 and was awarded the Silver War Badge (495063).

Saint Matthew's Church on the quay at Douglas, where John Thomas married Amelia Wood in June 1919. It was built between 1895 and 1908 to replace the previous church on the site.

John Thomas married Amelia née Wood (25th July 1896–16th November 1980) on 11th June 1919 at Saint Matthew's, Douglas, Isle of Man. Their address was Bridge House, Bridge Road, Douglas. They had six children:

- Irene Thomas (21st June 1920–4th December 2005) married William Swindells in 1946. They had a daughter, Jean Swindells, in 1952.
- John Thomas (born 31st December 1921).
- Edward Thomas (twin with Henry) (born 1924).
- Henry Thomas (twin with Edward) (born 1924).

The North Western Road Car Company formed in 1923 from existing bus services and acquired other bus companies thereafter. It operated services in Cheshire, Lancashire, West Riding of Yorkshire, Derbyshire and Staffordshire as well as some express coach services to London, North Wales and Yorkshire.

Willys Overland Crossley only existed from 1919 to 1934, but had factories in Stockport, Berlin and Antwerp to produce cars, buses and trucks. In 1925 sales of two new models did not reach expectations and the company had to sell the Avro aircraft company to survive. Both overseas factories were forced to close in the Depression and the company went into voluntary liquidation in 1933, although there was some production into 1934, when the Stockport factory seen here was sold to the Fairey Aviation Company.

- Barbara Thomas (twin with Ruth) (born 1929).
- Ruth Thomas (twin with Barbara) (born 1929), married Alan Reilly in 1955 and they had two sons – Allan W Reilly 1959 and Robert P Reilly 1961.

Two of his sons are reported to have served in the Special Air Service during the Second World War. Amelia's father, Henry Wood (1866–1942), born at Prestbury, Cheshire, married Eliza née Poole (1866–1948), born at Risbridge, Suffolk, in 1887. In 1901 he was a corporation gas works stoker and they were living at Hulme, Lancashire. By 1911 they had moved to Stretford Road, Hulme. In addition to Amelia they had another nine children, including Harry Wood 1888, Florence Wood 1891, William Wood 1894, Ernest Wood 1898, Ethel Wood 1900 and Gladys Wood 1904.

John Thomas' grave in Stockport Borough Cemetery.

Post-war John was employed as a storekeeper by Willys Overland Crossley Motors in Manchester and later as a bus driver for North Western Road Car Company. His last job was machine moulder in a rubber works. He gave up work in November 1947 due to ill health. John attended a number of VC reunions – Garden Party at Buckingham Palace on 26th June 1920, VC Dinner at the Royal Gallery of the House of Lords, London on 9th November 1929 and the Victory Day Celebration Dinner and Reception at The Dorchester, London on 8th June 1946. He was present at the dedication of the war memorial in St Peter's Square, Manchester in 1924 and was one of five VCs introduced to Lord Derby. Although he found walking difficult he was in the welcoming committee at Altrincham Town Hall when Private Bill Speakman VC returned home from Korea on 30th January 1952. John was also present, with other VCs, at the Coronation Parade of Queen Elizabeth II on 2nd June 1953.

John Thomas died at his home at 33 Lowfield Road, Stockport, Cheshire on 28th February 1954 and is buried in Stockport Borough Cemetery (LB 550). Amelia was living at 15 Osborne Road, Stockport at

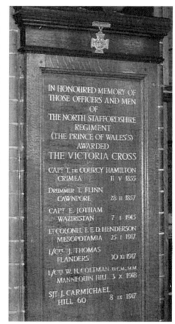

The memorial to North Staffordshire Regiment VCs in the Garrison Church at Whittington Barracks, Lichfield (Memorials to Valour).

Manchester's Cenotaph in St Peter's Square in the 1920s.

The 1914 Star was awarded to members of the British Expeditionary Force, including Indians and a few Canadians, who served in France and Belgium between 5th August and midnight on 22nd/23rd November 1914, the last day of the First Battle of Ypres. The clasp, sown onto the ribbon, was awarded to those who had been under fire or were within enemy artillery range in the same period. The medal became known as the Mons Star and recipients are known as Old Contemptibles. A total of 365,622 medals were awarded. The precise number of clasps is unknown as it had to be claimed personally by the recipient and a large number died during the course of the war or failed to apply. Those who served in France and Belgium from 23rd November 1914 until 31st December 1915 received the 1914–15 Star. The 1914 Star was never awarded singly, but came with the British War Medal and Victory Medal, collectively known as 'Pip, Squeak and Wilfred' after popular comic strip characters.

the time of her death on 16th November 1980, leaving effects valued at £17,658. John is commemorated in a number of other places:

- Victoria Cross Memorial, Garrison Church of St George, Whittington Barracks, Tamworth Road, Lichfield, Staffordshire.
- The Department for Communities and Local Government decided to provide a commemorative paving stone at the birthplace of every Great War Victoria Cross recipient in the United Kingdom. A commemorative stone for John was dedicated at Manchester Cenotaph, St Peter's Square, Manchester on 14th October 2016 to mark the centenary of his award.

In addition to the VC he was awarded the 1914 Star with 'Mons' clasp, British War Medal 1914–20, Victory Medal 1914–19, George VI Coronation Medal 1937 and Elizabeth II Coronation Medal 1953. He once absent-mindedly left his VC on a bus, but it was handed to lost property and returned to him. The VC is held privately.

CAPTAIN RICHARD WILLIAM LESLIE WAIN
A Battalion, Tank Corps

Richard Wain was born at 4 Victoria Square, Penarth, Glamorganshire, Wales on 5th December 1896. His father, Harris Wain (1866–1925), born at Brynmawr, near Ebbw Vale, was educated at Magdalene College, Oxford and became a solicitor. He practised at Bank Buildings, 98 St Mary Street, Cardiff and later at Llandaff, Glamorgan. He married Florence Emily née Tucker (1866–1938), born at

Abergavenny, Monmouthshire, in 1894. She was educated at South Hill House School, Lyncombe and Widdicombe, Somerset. They were living with his parents in 1901 at The Knoll, Sully, Glamorganshire. By 1911 they had moved to 7 The Green, Llandaff and to Woodside, 4 The Avenue, Llandaff by 1917. At various times they also lived at Hillside, Llanishen, Cardiff, at 94 Newport Road, Cardiff and at 22 Plasturton Avenue, Canton, Cardiff. When Harris died, in 1925 he left effects valued at £2,018/3/5 to his widow. Florence was living at 56 Albert Road, Bolton, Lancashire when she died, leaving effects valued at £2,831/15/7 to her daughter Elsie.

Richard's paternal grandparents lived at The Knoll, Sully, Glamorganshire (Rightmove).

Richard had a sister, Elsie Madeline Wain (1896–1962), who was educated at Howell's School in Landaff and at Caldersyde Girls' School, Seascale, Cumberland. She enlisted in Queen Mary's Army Auxiliary Corps on 20th July 1918 (45973). She volunteered for immobile clerical duties, having been employed by the Ministry of Labour's Employment Department for two and a half years. She was described as 5′ 2½″ tall, of slight build, with hazel eyes, fair hair, a mole on her left cheek and her religious denomination was Church of England. She was posted to 534th Agricultural Company, Labour Corps at Ely Racecourse, Cardiff and was discharged on termination of her engagement on 10th July 1919. She married John Thomas Victor Webster (1885–1973), born at Londonderry, Ireland in 1920 and they had a daughter, Pamela Mary Webster, in 1923. He entered the Royal Navy on 15th January 1903 and was promoted midshipman 15th January 1904, sub lieutenant 30th October 1906, lieutenant 30th October 1908, acting lieutenant commander 30th June 1916, lieutenant commander 30th October 1916, commander 30th October 1924 and captain

The Wain family was living at The Green, Llandaff in 1911.

The family also lived at 22 Plasturton Avenue, Canton, Cardiff (Rightmove).

(retired) 30th October 1935. He served aboard HMS *Vivid, Black Prince, Centurion, Albion, Vengeance, Andromeda, Indus, Vulcan, Impregnable, Temeraire, Galatea, Cardiff, Victory, President, Chatham, Durban, Drake, Caroline, Racer* and *Diomede*. John served on the China Station 3rd November 1903–17th January 1905 and was reprimanded in July 1908 for negligence in handling a secret document. He was Secretary to Rear Admiral Sir Edwyn Alexander-Sinclair CB MVO 15th October 1917–1st September 1919, who commanded 6th Light Cruiser Squadron from HMS *Cardiff* and led the surrendered German Fleet into internment at Scapa Flow. John was awarded the DSO, LG 27th June

Richard, top right, with his parents and sister (Derek Wain).

1919. He was in hospital at Plymouth and Peebles with rheumatism and arthritis 5th September 1919–27th January 1920. Appointed to the Intelligence Department at the Admiralty 5th August 1920–31st March 1922, then served in the New Zealand Naval Intelligence Department in Wellington 1st July 1922–30th October 1924. He again served on the China Station 2nd November 1926–4th June 1929, then returned to New Zealand as Secretary to the Naval Board & Secretary to Commodore Commanding New Zealand Station (Commodore Geoffrey Blake) 7th June 1929–12th September 1932). Returning to Britain, he was Secretary to 4th Sea Lord (Rear Admiral Geoffrey Blake) at the Admiralty 13th September 1932–17th February 1935. His last appointment was Supply Duties at Devonport 18th February–2nd August 1935 and he retired on 30th October. On 25th August 1939 he was recalled as paymaster commander and served at

Richard's paternal grandfather was proprietor of the Griffin Hotel, Brynmawr in 1871.

Richard Wain was proprietor of the Royal Hotel, St Mary's Street, Cardiff in 1881. It opened in July 1866 and is now Grade II listed. On 13th June 1910, two days before Captain Robert Falcon Scott's expedition to Antarctica departed, a fundraising dinner for the expedition took place there.

Larne as Base Supply Officer until reverting to the Retired List on 26th January 1945. Elsie and John were living at Windover, Ballygalley, Larne, Northern Ireland when she died, leaving effects valued at £1,794/18/6.

Richard's paternal grandfather, Richard Wain (1833–1903), born at Strand, London, married Elizabeth née Edmonds (c.1826–92), born at Caerleon, Caernarvon, in 1859 at Lambeth, London. In 1861 she was a housekeeper and he was a butler for John Rowland, proprietor of an iron mine, at Aberystruth, Monmouthshire. He was proprietor of the Griffin Hotel, Brynmawr, Brecknockshire in 1871, the Royal Hotel, St Mary's Street, Cardiff in 1881 and the Penarth Hotel, Glamorgan in 1891. In addition to Harris they had three other children:

- Madeline Cecilia Wain (1860–82) died unmarried.
- Richard Edmund Thomas Wain (1862–68).
- William Henry Wain (1864–65).

Elizabeth died on 5th April 1892 and Richard married Elizabeth née Jackson (c.1830–1909) in June 1893 at St George, Hanover Square, London. She was born at Westling, Gloucestershire and had not been married previously. They retired to The Knoll, Sully, Glamorgan and were living there with his son, Harris and family, in 1901. When Richard died he left effects valued at £9,397/8/7.

His maternal grandfather, William Tucker (c.1833–81), born at Abergavenny, Monmouthshire, married Emily née Jackson (1840–1929) in 1861. She was born at Gloucester. William was proprietor of the Double Greyhound Hotel, Abergavenny. In addition to Florence they had five other children:

- William Hunt Tucker (1862–67).
- Kate Elizabeth Tucker (1864–1915) married Alfred Jenkins (born c.1855), a mechanical engineer, in 1885. They were living at Sunny Bank, Abergavenny in 1911, by when he was a wine and spirit merchant. They had three children – Caroline 'Cassie' Victoria Jenkins 1887, Phyllis Emily Jenkins 1890 and Horace A Jenkins 1895.
- Frederick John Tucker (1868–1940), a veterinary surgeon, was living at 5 Whitecross Street, Monmouth in 1901. He married Jane Bell (1870–1953) in 1903 at Brampton, Cumberland. They were living at 58 Monnow Street, Monmouth in 1911 and at Lanercost, 597 Crewe Road, Wistaston, Cheshire in 1939. When he died in 1940 he was living at 87 Monnow Street, Monmouth and he left effects valued at £1,025/17/3 to his widow. She was living at Lanercost, Wistaston at the time of her death on 10 August 1953 at Crewe, Cheshire. They a son, Reginald Frederick Tucker (1904–39), who served in the Royal Engineers (76666). He was a lieutenant in the Supplementary Reserve Category A from 6th August 1938 and was promoted captain on 13th September 1939. Reginald died on 25th September 1939 (Brest (Kerfautras) Cemetery, France – 40 9 1).

- Tom Henry Tucker (1871–80).
- George Edwin Tucker (1877–78).

Emily married Thomas Harrill Tomkins (1856–1911) in 1885. He was a corn merchant's cashier in 1891 and they were living at Carlton House, Avenue Road, Abergavenny. By 1911 they had moved to Hawkhurst, Abergavenny, by when he was an auctioneer.

Richard was educated at Llandaff Cathedral School and St Bees School in Cumberland September 1911–July 1914. He was a member of the OTC and was at summer camp when war broke out. He intended going to Oxford University.

He enlisted in 1/7th Welch (Cyclist) in September 1914 and transferred to 16th Middlesex (Public Schools Battalion) (1276) on 30th December. He was commissioned in 25th (Reserve) Battalion, Manchester Regiment on 3rd July 1915 and was posted to 17th Battalion at Belton Park, Grantham, Lincolnshire on 16th July. He moved to Larkhill on Salisbury Plain, Wiltshire in September and the Battalion went to France in November, but he did not follow until March 1916, when he joined A Company. The Battalion was at a training area at Picquigny near Amiens for ten days from 18th June before moving to assembly trenches south of Cambridge Copse and northeast of Maricourt on the Somme. In the attack on 1st July he was wounded in the leg during the advance on Montauban and was evacuated through the regimental aid post, a field ambulance and a casualty clearing station back to Britain where he was hospitalised. During his recovery he returned to his parents in Cardiff and also visited his old school at St Bees.

Llandaff Cathedral School's most famous pupil was the storywriter Roald Dahl. Other famous alumni include Simon Hughes, Liberal Democrat MP, Deputy Party Leader 2010–14 and Minister of Justice 2013–15, and the singer Charlotte Church.

St Bees School was founded in 1583 by the Archbishop of Canterbury, Edmund Grindal. Two other old boys were awarded the VC during the Great War – John Fox-Russell and William Leefe Robinson. During the Second World War, Mill Hill School was evacuated to St Bees from London and the two schools ran together but independently. The school became coeducational in 1978 and in 2008 a preparatory department opened. However, the school closed in the summer of 2015. Famous alumni include Commodore John Charles Keith Dowding who commanded the ill-fated PQ-17 Convoy in the Second World War and Rowan Atkinson the comedian, writer and actor.

Richard was promoted temporary lieutenant on 12th July and acting captain on 12th November. He transferred to A Battalion, Heavy Branch, Machine Gun

Corps (Tank Corps from 28th July 1917) and was on a course at No.3 Army Gas Training School for five days. In February 1917 A Battalion went through a period of intensive training at Éclimeux, west of Arras, including day and night driving, wearing gas helmets and gas drills, unhitching and various weapons. He was granted ten days leave in Paris in April and moved to Ouderdom, Belgium in late May, by when the Battalion had been equipped with the new Mark IV Tank. Richard took part in the Battle of Messines on 7th June, commanding tank A5 in A (or 1) Company, in support of 33rd Brigade. The Company was in reserve initially, but later in the day

During the Great War a large training camp was established at Belton Park and it became the Depot fo the Machine Gun Corps. In January 1942 the RAF Regiment was established with its first Depot at Filey, but it moved to Belton Park later in 1942 and closed in 1946.

overcame a number of machine gun positions. One man in his tank was injured by a shell fragment that penetrated the side plate. In July he was sent to the Central Workshops at Teneur for a week, possibly in connection with the development of fascines to enable tanks to cross wide trenches.

On 22nd August Richard became a section commander. Two days later he was slightly wounded but remained with the unit. During the Battle of the Menin Road Ridge on 22nd September, he led his section forward over very difficult ground, although there was little for them to do. Captain Clement Robinson of C Company was awarded a posthumous VC for his actions on 4th October. A week later the Battalion moved by rail to Wailly for training with fascines. Richard was granted leave to Britain that day and rejoined the Battalion on 22nd October.

Awarded the VC for his actions near Marcoing, France on 20th November 1917, LG 13th February 1918. He was killed during the VC action and was buried where he fell, next to his tank, *Abu-Ben-Adam II*, with Lieutenant Christopher Duncan MC. The grave was lost after the war and he is commemorated on the Cambrai Memorial, Louverval, France – Panel 13. As he never married the VC was presented to his parents by the King at Buckingham Palace on 20th April 1918. He is commemorated in a number of other places:

Richard Wain's name on the Cambrai Memorial.

- Cambrai Company, Army Foundation College, Harrogate comprises six platoons named after VC winners in the Battle of Cambrai, including 9 (Wain VC) Platoon.
- Named on the family grave at St John's Churchyard, Sully, Glamorgan.

Llandaff War Memorial.

The family grave in St John's Churchyard, Sully, Glamorgan (Memorials to Valour).

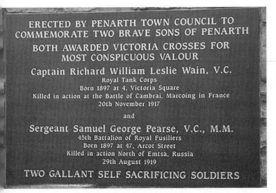

ERECTED BY PENARTH TOWN COUNCIL TO
COMMEMORATE TWO BRAVE SONS OF PENARTH
BOTH AWARDED VICTORIA CROSSES FOR
MOST CONSPICUOUS VALOUR
Captain Richard William Leslie Wain, V.C.
Royal Tank Corps
Born 1897 at 4, Victoria Square
Killed in action at the Battle of Cambrai, Marcoing in France
20th November 1917

and

Sergeant Samuel George Pearse, V.C., M.M.
45th Battalion of Royal Fusiliers
Born 1897 at 47, Arcot Street
Killed in action North of Emtsa, Russia
29th August 1919

TWO GALLANT SELF SACRIFICING SOLDIERS

Memorial at Penarth Town Council's West House to
Richard Wain VC and Samuel Pearse.

The VC memorial plaque at St Bees School
(Dougsim).

- Plaque at St Bees School, Cumberland.
- Llandaff War Memorial, Llandaff Cathedral Green, Glamorgan commemorates the 105 men of Llandaff and the Cathedral School who died during the Great War.
- Llandaff Cathedral School War Memorial plaque commemorates fifty-six masters and old boys of Llandaff Cathedral who fell in the Great War. The memorial was funded by the estate of Lieutenant JR Hall, one of those commemorated.
- Plaque at Penarth Town Council's West House unveiled in April 2008, commemorating Captain Richard William Leslie Wain VC and Sergeant Samuel George Pearse VC MM.

The British War Medal was instituted on 26th July 1919 for all ranks who served for twenty-eight days in an operational theatre between 5th August 1914 and 11th November 1918, or died on active service before the completion of this period. Eligibility was extended to 1919–20 for mine-clearing at sea and operations in North and South Russia, eastern Baltic, Siberia, Black Sea and Caspian Sea. Many veterans were awarded the 1914–15 Star, British War Medal and Victory Medal. They became known as Pip, Squeak and Wilfred after a strip cartoon published in the Daily Mirror from 1919 to 1956.

Richard Wain's VC action appeared in three editions of the Victor, including this one in December 1964.

• Wain Close, Penarth, Glamorgan, Wales on a housing development at Penarth Heights, is off Gibson Way, named after Wing Commander Guy Gibson VC. The next street along is Pearse Close, after Sergeant Samuel George Pearse VC MM.
• His VC action was featured in three issues of the Victor Comic:
   ° No.198 entitled *The Courage of Captain Wain*, dated 5th December 1964.
   ° No. 710 entitled *A V.C. for the Tanks*, dated 28th September 1974.
   ° No.1250 entitled *A True Story of Men at War*, dated 2nd February 1985.
• The *More Men of Glory* series by Macdonald Hastings in 1959 entitled *The Twenty-year-old Who Believed in Tanks*.
• Wain Road, Bovington Camp, Dorset.
• Display at the Tank Museum, Bovington, Dorset.

In addition to the VC he was awarded the British War Medal 1914–20 and Victory Medal 1914–19. The medals are held privately.

LIEUTENANT SAMUEL THOMAS DICKSON WALLACE
C Battery, 63rd Brigade, Royal Field Artillery

Samuel Wallace was born at Holmhill, Thornhill, Dumfriesshire, Scotland on 7th March 1892. His father, John William Wallace (1860–1946), a farmer, married Catherine Jane née Dickson (1867–1940) on 4th June 1891 at Drumcruil, Durisdeer. They lived at Ford, Thornhill, Dumfriesshire. In 1901 she was living with her children at Wallace Hall, Dumfries. Samuel had two siblings:

- Quinton Wallace (1893–1959) was a farmer.
- Katherine Wallace (1894–1974) married John Herbert Murray (born 1890), a farmer, in 1921. They had at least one child, a daughter.

Samuel's paternal grandfather, Samuel Wallace (1810–84), a farmer, married Susan née Reid (1823–89), born at Dalmellington, Ayrshire, in 1851. In 1871 they were living at Auchenbrack, Dumfries on a farm of 9,600 acres, employing twenty-four men, ten women and three boys. By 1881 they had moved to Holmhill, Morton, Dumfries running a farm of 500 acres, employing nine men, five women, a cook and a housemaid. In addition to John they had seven other children:

Samuel's paternal grandmother, Susan Reid was born at Dalmellington, Ayrshire.

- James Reid Williamson Wallace (1852–1922), a farmer, married Harriet Montgomery Craig (1877–1928) in 1900.
- Robert Wallace (born 1853).
- Samuel Williamson Wallace (1855–1932) married Ellen Cameron (c.1864–1915) in 1893.
- Janet 'Jessie' McAdam Wallace (1856–1936) died unmarried.
- Margaret Williamson Wallace (1858–1939) died unmarried.
- Quintin McAdam Wallace (1861–92) was a surgeon. He married Marion Jane Brown (born 1865) in 1890 at The Grand Hotel, Glasgow. In 1889 he was working at North Hospital, Liverpool, Lancashire. They were living at 59 Grange Mount, Birkenhead, Cheshire in 1891.
- Walter Scott Wallace (1866–1935), a mechanical engineer, married Margaret Jane Wilson (c.1868–1924) in 1891. They had two children – Walter Williamson

Wallace 1892 and Dorothy Susan Reid Scott Wallace 1894.

His maternal grandfather, Thomas Dickson (1821–1905) married Catherine née Moffat (born 1835) in 1856. She was boarding at 12 Great King Street, Edinburgh, Midlothian in 1851. He was a farmer of 950 acres at Drumcruilton, Durisdeer, Dumfriesshire in 1861, employing ten men, eight women and four boys. By 1881 he was farming 500 acres and was employing four men, three girls and two boys. In 1901 they were living at Eccles House, Penpont, Dumfriesshire. In addition to Catherine they had five other children:

Samuel's maternal grandparents were living at Penpont, Dumfriesshire in 1901.

- Jane Dickson (born 1859).
- Sarah Dickson (born 1862).
- Agnes Dickson (1869–1946) married John Borland (1857–1927), a farmer, in 1896. They had five children – Robert Borland 1897, Catherine Pretoria Borland 1900, John Borland 1903, Thomas Dickson Borland 1905 and Mary Fergusson Borland 1906.
- Alice Dickson (born 1873) married Robert Primrose (1872–1958), a farmer, in 1904. They had two children – Robert Primrose 1905 and John Dickson Primrose 1906.
- Frances Jessie Dickson (1877–1966).

Samuel was educated at:

- Crossford School, Glencairn, Dumfriesshire.
- Dumfries Academy, Dumfriesshire 1903–10.
- East of Scotland Agricultural College, Edinburgh, Midlothian.
- University of Edinburgh 1911–14 (BSc Agriculture), where he was a member of the OTC April 1912–October 1914. He was a medallist in structural and field geology and agricultural chemistry, gaining first class certificates in these subjects as well as in veterinary science and forestry.

Dumfries Academy was founded in its present form in 1804, but dates back to 1330. It was a grammar school until 1983. Famous alumni include:

Sir James Anderson – captain of SS *Great Eastern* when she laid telegraph cables across the Atlantic 1865–66.
Sir James M Barrie – author of *Peter Pan*.
John Laurie – Shakespearean and film actor, best known for his part as Private Frazer in the television series *Dad's Army*.
Neil Oliver – archaeologist, author and television presenter.

Samuel was commissioned on 13th October 1914 in A Battery, 64th Brigade RFA. He went to France in May 1915 and was promoted lieutenant on 1st July

1917. **Awarded the VC for his actions at Gonnelieu, France on 30th November 1917, LG 13th February 1918.** His former school had a day off on hearing of his award. When home on leave he was given a reception, passing through a guard of honour of Dumfries Academy's Cadet Corps. Boy Scouts and Girl Guides were also on parade. A Girl Guide presented him with a fitted suitcase from the pupils, teachers and managers as a token of their admiration. In his speech he thanked them for their kindness. One pupil sang *There's a Land* and all later sang *Rule Britannia*, followed by a final vote of thanks by the Rector. The VC was presented by the King outside Buckingham Palace on 31st July 1918.

Samuel was employed under the Home Office according to the Army List from November 1917 until March 1919. Appointed acting captain 3rd September–1st November 1918 and 1st December 1918 while a battery second-in-command. He relinquished his commission on 18th February 1919 and retained the rank of lieutenant. He last appears in the Army List in June 1920.

He entered the Indian Agricultural Service and became Deputy Director of Animal Husbandry in Central Province from February 1919. While in India he served in the Calcutta Light Horse, Auxiliary Force (India) and trained the Nagpur Volunteer Rifles, taking an active part in suppressing civil disturbances.

Samuel Wallace married Margaret Nöel née Edenborough (25th

The Calcutta Light Horse was raised in 1872 as part of the Cavalry Reserve of the Indian Army and disbanded following independence in 1947. Its most famous exploit came in 1943 when Lieutenant Colonel Lewis Henry Owain Pugh (1907–81), of SOE's Force 136, led a small force of the Regiment to destroy the German merchant ship, *Ehrenfels*, which was transmitting Allied shipping positions to U-boats from Mormugao harbour in Portugal's neutral territory of Goa. The incident was revealed in the 1978 book *Boarding Party – The Last Action of the Calcutta Light Horse*, and in the 1980 film, *Sea Wolves*, starring Gregory Peck as Pugh. The picture of the officers of the Regiment in 1944 shows at least two of the men who took part in the action – Colonel WH Grice, seated centre, and Captain Sandys Lumsdaine, seated far left. Lewis Henry Owain Pugh was the cousin of Lieutenant Colonel Lewis Pugh Evans, Black Watch attached 1st Lincolnshire, who was awarded the VC for his actions near Reutel, Belgium on 4th October 1917.

Nagpur is at the centre of India and has the Zero Mile Stone, which was used by the British to measure all distances within the Indian subcontinent.

December 1903–23rd February 1975) at Nagpur on 17th October 1925. The marriage was conducted by Eyre Chatterton, Bishop of Nagpur. They had a daughter, Margaret Wallace, born on 10th February 1927 at Bungalow No.16, Public Works Department, Nagpur.

Margaret's father, Claude Edenborough (1862–1927), was a publisher who frequently travelled to New York on business. He married Ethel Norton née Dawson (born 1868) in 1902. They were living at Chewton Common, Highcliffe, Christchurch, Hampshire in 1911 and at 29 St Georges Mansions, London in 1919. By 1922 they had moved to Hillcote, 81 Woodland Avenue, Guildford, Surrey and later to Bramshott Cottage, Park Road, Woking, Surrey. Claude died on 17th January 1927 at Nagpur, leaving £4,704/11/4 to his widow.

Samuel and Margaret returned from India in 1932. He was commissioned as a pilot officer in the Administration and Special Duties Branch RAFVR on 29th August 1940 (85327). He was stationed at Langham Camp, North Norfolk and also served at RAF Turnhouse, Edinburgh on station defence duties. Promoted flying officer on 29th August 1941. Following a number of courses he became an instructor at No.1 Ground Defence Gunnery School, Ronaldsway, Isle of Man in October 1941. Appointed acting flight lieutenant December 1941 and promoted flight lieutenant on 1st September 1942. He transferred to the RAF Regiment on its formation on 1st February 1942 and was posted to No.3 RAF Regiment School, Douglas, Isle of Man in July as a gunnery instructor. In January 1943 he was posted to No.1 RAF Regiment School, Filey, Yorkshire. On 21st August he transferred back to the Administrative and Special Duties Branch

Filey holiday camp was being built for Billy Butlin in 1939, when it was taken over by the Air Ministry as RAF Hunmanby Moor. No.1 RAF Regiment School was there until February 1943 when it moved to Belton Park, Lincolnshire. About 4,000 of the 5,500 West Indians recruited into the RAF as ground crew in the Second World War were trained there in 1944. Butlin's holiday camp opened in June 1945 and at its peak accommodated 11,000 visitors. It had its own railway station until 1977. It is understood that Paul McCartney made his first stage appearance there in a talent contest with his brother during a family holiday. Butlins' closed in 1983.

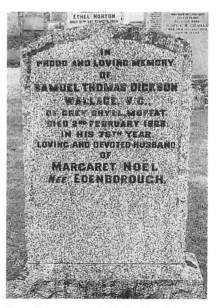

Samuel's gravestone in Moffat New Cemetery.

The Defence Medal was awarded for non-operational service in the Armed Forces, Home Guard, Civil Defence and other civilian services during the period 3rd September 1939–2nd September 1945. In the United Kingdom this included military personnel in headquarters, training bases and airfields until 8th May 1945 and members of the Home Guard from 14th May 1940 until 31st December 1944. The length of qualifying service varied depending upon where and in what role an individual served. In the United Kingdom the requirement was three years or ninety days in a Mine/Bomb Disposal Unit.

due to ill health and served at HQ 54 (Training) Group. Samuel relinquished his commission due to his health on 26th December 1943. He took an appointment with the Ministry of Agriculture in Lincolnshire 1944–47 before returning to Moffat, where they lived at Grey Ghyll.

Samuel attended the VC Centenary Celebrations at Hyde Park, London on 26th June 1956. He died at Moffat, Scotland on 2nd February 1968 and is buried in Moffat New Cemetery. He is commemorated in a number of other places:

- Royal Artillery VC Memorial in the ruins of St George's Chapel, the former Garrison Church at Woolwich, which was reduced to a roofless shell by a V1 in 1944.
- Cambrai Company, Army Foundation College, Harrogate comprises six platoons named after VC winners in the Battle of Cambrai, including 12 (Wallace VC) Platoon.
- Memorial park bench at St Andrew's Church, Moffat, Dumfries and Galloway.
- Memorial to Distinguished Artillery Officers in Old College, Royal Military Academy, Sandhurst.
- Plaque dedicated at Tynron War Memorial on 20th November 2017. Samuel lived there for some time.
- The Department for Communities and Local Government decided to provide a commemorative paving stone at the birthplace of every Great War Victoria Cross recipient in the United Kingdom. A commemorative stone for Samuel was dedicated at the Joseph Thomson Memorial, Thornhill, Dumfries & Galloway, Scotland on 20th November 2017 to mark the centenary of his award.
- Plaque dedicated at Moffat Town Hall on 20th November 2017.
- The Royal Artillery VC Memorial in the Royal Artillery Tercentenary Chapel and Cloister, Larkhill, Wiltshire, unveiled by Queen Elizabeth II on 26th May 2016.

In addition to the VC he was awarded the 1914–15 Star, British War Medal 1914–20, Victory Medal 1914–19, Defence Medal, George VI Coronation Medal 1937 and Elizabeth II Coronation Medal 1953. The VC is held by the Royal Artillery Museum.

Sources

The following institutions, individuals and publications were consulted:

Regimental Museums

Royal Warwickshire Regimental Museum, Warwick; RHQ The Argyll and Sutherland Highlanders, Stirling; The Royal Gloucestershire, Berkshire and Wiltshire Regiment Museum, Salisbury; Museum of the Manchesters, Ashton-under-Lyne; Museum of the Northamptonshire Regiment, Northampton; Royal Green Jackets Museum, Winchester; HQ Scots Guards, London; Royal Inniskilling Fusiliers Regimental Association, Enniskillen, Co Fermanagh; Green Howards Museum, Richmond, Yorkshire; RHQ Prince of Wales's Own Regiment of Yorkshire, York; Border Regiment and Kings Own Royal Border Regiment Museum, Carlisle; Canadian War Museum, Ottawa; Royal Artillery Historical Trust; The Tank Museum.

Individuals

Graham Adams, Doug and Richard Arman, David Baker, Katrina Barling, Captain Robert Bonner, Marjorie Buntin, Maj John Cotterill, Adrian De Wind, Norman J De Wind, Josh DeWind, David Fletcher, George Gamble, Doug Gee, Colin Godley, Tony Grant, Ray Harding, Robert Harrison, Brian Hawkins, Terry Hissey, Peter M James, Donald Jennings, Tom Johnson, Alan Jordan, Marilyn King, Steve Lee, Anne Lehmkuhl, David Linnell, Alasdair Macintyre, Andrew MacLehose, Nigel Marshall, T McAlister, Lt Col ND McIntosh, Nick Metcalf, Susan Mills, Jane Murfin, Tony Newcombe, FJ Lascelles Pallin, Richard Perkins, David Rodgers, Peter Rothwell, Derek Seaton, Margaret Self, Stephen Sellick, Mrs DW Shaw, Peter Silk, George Sparham, Iain Stewart, Vic Tambling, Tim Vaughan, Lt Col Les Wilson MBE.

Record Offices, Libraries and Local Museums

Nuneaton Library.

Schools and Universities

Alloa Academy; Balliol College Oxford; Bristol Grammar School; Christ's Hospital, Horsham; Edinburgh University; Eton College; Harrow School; King's College, London; Oundle School; Pennal School, Machynlleth, Merionethshire; Uppingham School.

Divisional Histories

The Guards Division in the Great War. C Headlam. Murray 1929. Two volumes.
The History of the Second Division 1914–18. E Wyrall. Nelson 1921. Two volumes.
A Short History of the 6th Division August 1914–March 1919. Editor Maj Gen T O Marden. Rees 1920.
The Eighth Division in War 1914–18. Lt Col J H Boraston and Capt C E O Bax. Medici Society 1926.
History of the 12th (Eastern) Division in the Great War 1914–18. Editor Maj Gen Sir A B Scott. Compiler P M Brumwell. Nisbet 1927.
History of the 17th (Northern) Division. A H Atheridge. University Press 1929.
The 18th Division in the Great War. Capt G H F Nichols. Blackwood 1922.
The History of the 19th Division 1914–18. E Wyrall. Arnold 1932.
A Short History of the 19th (Western) Division 1914–18. Anon. John Murray 1919.
The History of the 20th (Light) Division. Capt V E Inglefield. Nisbet 1921.
The 25th Division in France and Flanders. Lt Col M Kincaid-Smith. Harrison 1919.
The Story of the 29th Division – A Record of Gallant Deeds. Capt S Gillon. Nelson 1925.
The History of the 36th (Ulster) Division. C Falls. Linenhall Press 1922.
The History of the 40th Division. Lt Col F E Whitton. Gale & Polden 1926.
The History of the 51st (Highland) Division 1914–18. Maj F W Bewsher. Blackwood 1921.
The Story of the 55th (West Lancashire) Division. Rev'd J O Coop. Liverpool Daily Post 1919.

Brigade Histories

A Short History of the 5th Infantry Brigade. Maj G D P Young. Forces Press 1965.
History of the 50th Infantry Brigade 1914–19. Anon. Oxford University Press 1919.
The 54th Infantry Brigade 1914–18 – Some Records of Battle and Laughter in France. E R. Gale & Polden 1919.

Regimental/Unit Histories

The Royal Artillery War Commemoration Book. Anon. G Bell 1970.
History of the 359th (4th West Lancashire) Medium Regiment Royal Artillery (TA) 1859–1959. Anon. Liverpool 1959.
History of the Royal Regiment of Artillery, Western Front, 1914–18. Gen Sir M Farndale. Dorset Press 1986.
ARTYVICS – The Victoria Cross and The Royal Regiment of Artillery. Marc J Sherriff. Witherbys, Aylesbury St, London.
Tunnellers, The Story of the Tunnelling Companies Royal Engineers during the World War. Capt W Grant Grieve & B Newman. Herbert Jenkins 1936.

History of the Corps of Royal Engineers, Volume V, The Home Front, France, Flanders and Italy in the First World War. Anon. Institute of the Royal Engineers 1952.

The Grenadier Guards in the Great War of 1914–18. Lt Col Sir F Ponsonby. Macmillan 1920. Three volumes.

The Scots Guards in the Great War 1914–18. F Loraine Petre, W Ewart and Maj Gen Sir C Lowther. Murray 1925.

A Guide to the Queen's Regiment. G Blaxland. Elvy & Gibbs.

History of the Queen's Royal Regiment Volume VII. Col H C Wylly. Gale & Polden 1925.

The Story of the Royal Warwickshire Regiment. C L Kingsford. Country Life 1921.

The East Yorkshire Regiment in the Great War 1914–19. E Wyrall. Harrison 1928.

The Green Howards in the Great War 1914–19. Col H C Wylly. Butler & Tanner 1926.

The Green Howards – For Valour 1914–18. Anon. Published 1964.

The History of the Green Howards – 300 Years of Service. G Powell. Arms and Armour 1992.

The Royal Inniskilling Fusiliers in the World War. Sir F Fox. Constable 1928.

The Gloucestershire Regiment in the Great War 1914–18. E Wyrall. Methuen 1931.

The Slasher, A New Short History of the Gloucestershire Regiment 1694–1965. Anon.

The Worcestershire Regiment in the Great War. Capt H Fitzm Stacke. G T Cheshire 1929.

The Border Regiment in the Great War. Col H C Wylly. Gale & Polden 1924.

Tried and Valiant, The History of the Border Regiment 1702–1959. D Sutherland. Leo Cooper 1972.

The Northamptonshire Regiment 1914–18. Regimental Historical Committee. Gale & Polden.

Four VCs in Forty Months, The Proud Record in World War One of the 6th (Service) Battalion The Northamptonshire Regiment. G Moore. G Moore 1979.

The Die Hards in the Great War, A History of the Duke of Cambridge's Own (Middlesex Regiment). E Wyrall. Harrison 1926–30. Two volumes (1914–16 and 1916–19).

The Annals of the King's Royal Rifle Corps, Volume V The Great War. Maj Gen Sir S Hare. John Murray 1932.

The King's Royal Rifle Corps Chronicles 1914, 1915, 1916 and 1917.

History of the Manchester Regiment, Volume II 1883–1922. Col H C Wylly. Forster Groom 1925.

16th, 17th, 18th and 19th Battalions The Manchester Regiment (1st City Brigade), A Record 1914–18. Anon. Sherratt & Hughes 1923.

Manchester Pals, 16th–23rd Battalions The Manchester Regiment. M Stedman. Leo Cooper 1994.

Faithful, The Story of the Durham Light Infantry. S G P Ward. Nelson 1962.

The Durham Forces in the Field 1914–18, Volume II The Service Battalions of the Durham Light Infantry. Capt W Miles. Cassell 1920.

Officers of the Durham Light Infantry 1758–1968 (Volume 1 – Regulars). M McGregor. Published privately 1989.

Seaforth Highlanders. Editor Col J Sym. Gale & Polden 1962.

The History of the First 7 Battalions The Royal Irish Rifles in the Great War, Volume II. C Falls. Gale & Polden 1925.

Argyllshire Highlanders 1860–1960. Lt Col G I Malcolm. Halberd Press.

Fighting Highlanders – The History of the Argyll and Sutherland Highlanders. P J R Mileham. Arms and Armour Press 1993.

Machine Guns, Their History and Tactical Employment (Being also a History of the Machine Gun Corps 1916–22). Lt Col G S Hutchinson. MacMillan 1938.

Official History of the Canadian Army in the First World War – Canadian Expeditionary Force 1914–19. Col GWL Nicholson 1962.

Canada in Flanders. Sir Max Aitken 1916.

With the Indians in France. Gen Sir James Willcocks 1920.

The New Zealand Division 1916–1919. A Popular History Based on Official Records. Col H Stewart CMG DSO MC. Whitcombe & Tombs Ltd, Auckland 1921.

General Works

A Bibliography of Regimental Histories of the British Army. Compiler A S White. Society for Army Historical Research 1965.

A Military Atlas of the First World War. A Banks & A Palmer. Purnell 1975.

The Soldier's War 1914–18. P Liddle. Blandford Press.

Into Battle 1914–18. E Parker. Longmans 1964.

The Times History of the Great War.

Topography of Armageddon, A British Trench Map Atlas of the Western Front 1914–18. P Chasseaud. Mapbooks 1991.

Before Endeavours Fade. R E B Coombs. Battle of Britain Prints 1976.

British Regiments 1914–18. Brig E A James. Samson 1978.

Orange, Green and Khaki, The Story of the Irish Regiments in the Great War 1914–18. T Johnstone. 1992.

Biographical

The Dictionary of National Biography 1901–85. Various volumes. Oxford University Press.

The Cross of Sacrifice, Officers Who Died in the Service of the British, Indian and East African Regiments and Corps 1914–19. S D and D B Jarvis. Roberts Medals 1993.

Australian Dictionary of Biography.

Whitaker's Peerage, Baronetage, Knightage & Companionage 1915.

The Roll of Honour Parts 1–5, A Biographical Record of Members of His Majesty's Naval and Military Forces who fell in the Great War 1914–18. Marquis de Ruvigny. Standard Art Book Co 1917–19.

The Dictionary of Edwardian Biography – various volumes. Printed 1904–08, reprinted 1985–87 Peter Bell Edinburgh.

Fire-Eater: the Memoirs of a VC. Alfred Pollard. 1932.

Dictionary of Canadian Biography.

Valiant Hearts. Atlantic Canada and the Victoria Cross. John Boileau. Nimbus Publishing, Halifax, Nova Scotia 2005.

Specific Works on the Victoria Cross

The Register of the Victoria Cross. This England 1981 and 1988.

The Story of the Victoria Cross 1856–1963. Brig Sir J Smyth. Frederick Muller 1963.

The Evolution of the Victoria Cross, A Study in Administrative History. M J Crook. Midas 1975.

The Victoria Cross and the George Cross. IWM 1970.

The Victoria Cross, The Empire's Roll of Valour. Lt Col R Stewart. Hutchinson 1928.

The Victoria Cross 1856–1920. Sir O'Moore Creagh and E M Humphris. Standard Art Book Company, London 1920.

Victoria Cross – Awards to Irish Servicemen. B Clark. Published in The Irish Sword, summer 1986.

Heart of a Dragon, VC's of Wales and the Welsh Regiments 1914–82. W Alister Williams. Bridge Books 2006.

Devotion to Duty, Tributes to a Region's VCs. J W Bancroft. Aim High 1990.

For Valour, The Victoria Cross, Courage in Action. J Percival. Thames Methuen 1985.

VC Locator. D Pillinger and A Staunton. Highland Press, Queanbeyan, New South Wales, Australia 1991.

The VC Roll of Honour. J W Bancroft. Aim High 1989.

A Bibliography of the Victoria Cross. W James McDonald. W J Mcdonald, Nova Scotia 1994.

Canon Lummis VC Files held in the National Army Museum, Chelsea.

Recipients of the Victoria Cross in the Care of the Commonwealth War Graves Commission. CWGC 1997.

Victoria Cross Heroes. Michael Ashcroft. Headline Review 2006

Monuments to Courage. David Harvey. 1999.

Beyond the Five Points – Masonic Winners of The Victoria Cross and The George Cross. Phillip May GC, edited by Richard Cowley. Twin Pillars Books, Northamptonshire 2001.

Irish Winners of the Victoria Cross. Richard Doherty & David Truesdale. Four Courts Press, Dublin, Ireland 2000.

Our Bravest and Our Best: The Stories of Canada's Victoria Cross Winners. Arthur Bishop 1995.

A Breed Apart. Richard Leake. Great Northern Publishing 2008.

A Tiger and a Fusilier: Leicester's VC Heroes. Derek Seaton. Norwood Press 2001.

Other Honours and Awards

Recipients of Bars to the Military Cross 1916–20. J V Webb 1988.

Distinguished Conduct Medal 1914–18, Citations of Recipients. London Stamp Exchange 1983.

Recipients of the Distinguished Conduct Medal 1914–1920. RW Walker.

The Distinguished Service Order 1886–1923 (in 2 volumes). Sir O'Moore Creagh and E M Humphris. J B Hayward 1978 (originally published 1924).

Orders and Medals Society Journal (various articles).

Burke's Handbook to the Most Excellent Order of the British Empire. A Winton Thorpe (Editor). Burke Publishing Co Ltd, London 1921.

South African War – Honours and Awards 1899–1902.

Honours and Awards of the Indian Army: August 1914–August 1921. 1931.

University and Schools Publications

Harrow Memorials of the Great War Volume 5. Medici Society 1920.

Official Publications and Sources

History of the Great War, Order of Battle of Divisions. Compiler Maj A F Becke. HMSO.

History of the Great War, Military Operations, France and Belgium. Compiler Brig Gen Sir J E Edmonds. HMSO. Published in 14 volumes of text, with 7 map volumes and 2 separate Appendices between 1923 and 1948.

Location of Hospitals and Casualty Clearing Stations, BEF 1914–19. Ministry of Pensions 1923.

List of British Officers taken Prisoner in the Various Theatres of War between August 1914 and November 1918. Compiled from Official Records by Messrs Cox & Co, Charing Cross, London 1919.

London Gazettes

Census returns, particularly for 1881, 1891, 1901 and 1911.

Births, Marriages and Deaths records in the Family Records Centre, Islington, London.

Australian service records in the National Archives of Australia.

Service records from the Library and Archives of Canada.

Service records in Archives New Zealand.

Officers and Soldiers Died in the Great War.

National Archives

Unit of Formation War Diaries under WO 95

Military maps under WO 297.

Medal Cards and Medal Rolls under WO 329, 372 and ADM 171.

Royal Navy service records under ADM 11, 29, 196, 240, 336, 337 and 354.
Army service records under WO 25, 76, 97, 339, 363, 365 and 374.
RAF service records under Air 76 and 79.

Official Lists

Navy Lists.
Army Lists – including Graduation Lists and Record of War Service.
Air Force Lists.
Home Guard Lists 1942–44.
Indian Army Lists 1897–1940.
India List 1923–40.

Reference Publications

Who's Who and Who Was Who.
The Times 1914 onwards.
The Daily Telegraph 1914 onwards.
Kelly's Handbook to the Titled, Landed and Official Classes.
Burke's Peerage.

Internet Websites

History of the Victoria Cross – www2.prestel.co.uk/stewart – Iain Stewart.
Commonwealth War Graves Commission – www.yard.ccta.gov.uk/cwgc.
Scottish General Registry Office – www.origins.net/GRO.
Free Births, Marriages and Deaths – www.freebmd.com
Memorials to Valour – http://www.memorialstovalour.co.uk
Nick Metcalf – account of VC action of Edmund De Wind. – http://www.nickmetcalfe.
co.uk/my-family-in-the-first-world-war-part-4-robert-thompson/

Periodicals

This England magazine – various editions.
Coin and Medal News – various editions.
Journal of The Victoria Cross Society
Gun Fire – A Journal of First World War History. Edited by AJ Peacock, but no longer
published
Stand To – journal of the Western Front Association.

Useful Information

Accommodation – there is a wide variety of accommodation available in France. Search on-line for your requirements. There are also numerous campsites, but many close for the winter from late September.

Clothing and Kit – consider taking:

Waterproofs.
Headwear and gloves.
Walking shoes/boots.
Shades and sunscreen.
Binoculars and camera.
Snacks and drinks.

Customs/Behaviour – local people are generally tolerant of battlefield visitors but please respect their property and address them respectfully. The French are less inclined to switch to English than other Europeans. If you try some basic French it will be appreciated.

Driving – rules of the road are similar to UK, apart from having to drive on the right. If in doubt about priorities, give way to the right, particularly in France. Obey laws and road signs – police impose harsh on-the-spot fines. Penalties for drinking and driving are heavy and the legal limit is lower than UK (50mg rather than 80mg). Most autoroutes in France are toll roads.

Fuel – petrol stations are only open 24 hours on major routes. Some accept credit cards in automatic tellers. The cheapest fuel is at hypermarkets.

Mandatory Requirements – if taking your own car you need:
Full driving licence.
Vehicle registration document.
Comprehensive motor insurance valid in Europe (Green Card).
European breakdown and recovery cover.
Letter of authorisation from the owner if the vehicle is not yours.
Spare set of bulbs, headlight beam adjusters, warning triangle, GB sticker, high visibility vest and breathalyzer.

Emergency – keep details required in an emergency separate from wallet or handbag:
Photocopy passport, insurance documents and EHIC (see Health below).
Mobile phone details.
Credit/debit card numbers and cancellation telephone contacts.
Travel insurance company contact number.

Ferries – the closest ports are Boulogne, Calais and Dunkirk. The Shuttle is quicker, but usually more expensive.

Health

European Health Insurance Card – entitles the holder to medical treatment at local rates. Apply online at www.ehic.org.uk/Internet/startApplication.do. Issued free and valid for five years. You are only covered if you have the EHIC with you when you go for treatment.

Travel Insurance – you are also strongly advised to have travel insurance. If you receive treatment get a statement by the doctor (*feuille de soins*) and a receipt to make a claim on return.

Personal Medical Kit – treating minor ailments saves time and money. Pack sufficient prescription medicine for the trip.

Chemist (*Pharmacie*) – look for the green cross. They provide some treatment and if unable to help will direct you to a doctor. Most open 0900–1900 except Sunday. Out of hours services (*pharmacie de garde*) are advertised in Pharmacie windows.

Doctor and Dentist – hotel receptions have details of local practices. Beware private doctors/hospitals, as extra charges cannot be reclaimed – the French national health service is known as *conventionné*.

Rabies – contact with infected animals is very rare, but if bitten by any animal, get the wound examined professionally immediately.

Money

ATMs – at most banks and post offices with instructions in English. Check your card can be used in France and what charges apply. Some banks limit how much can be withdrawn. Let your bank know you will be away, as some block cards if transactions take place unexpectedly.

Credit/Debit Cards – major cards are usually accepted, but some have different names – Visa is Carte Bleue and Mastercard is Eurocard.

Exchange – beware 0% commission, as the rate may be poor. The Post Office takes back unused currency at the same rate, which may or may not be advantageous. Since the Euro, currency exchange facilities are scarce.

Local Taxes – if you buy high value items you can reclaim tax. Get the forms completed by the shop, have them stamped by Customs, post them to the shop and they will refund about 12%.

Passport – a valid passport is required.

Post – postcard stamps are available from vendors, newsagents and tabacs.

Public Holidays – just about everything closes and banks can close early the day before. Transport may be affected, but tourist attractions in high season are unlikely to be. The following dates/days are public holidays:

1 January
Easter Monday
1 May
8 May
Ascension Day
Whit Monday
14 July
15 August
1 & 11 November
25 December

In France many businesses and restaurants close for the majority of August.

Radio – if you want to pick up the news from home try BBC Radio 4 on 198 kHz long wave. BBC Five Live on 909 kHz medium wave can sometimes be received. There are numerous internet options for keeping up with the news.

Shops – in large towns and tourist areas they tend to open all day. In more remote places they may close for lunch. Some bakers open Sunday a.m. and during the week take later lunch breaks. In general shops do not open on Sundays.

Telephone

To UK – 0044, delete initial 0 then dial the rest of the number.

Local Calls – dial the full number even if within the same zone.

Mobiles – check yours will work in France and the charges.

Emergencies – dial 112 for medical, fire and police anywhere in Europe from any landline, pay phone or mobile. Calls are free

British Embassy (Paris) – 01 44 51 31 00.

Time Zone – one hour ahead of UK.

Tipping – a small tip is expected by cloakroom and lavatory attendants and porters. Not required in restaurants, when a service charge is included.

Toilets – the best are in museums and the main tourist attractions. Towns usually have public toilets where markets are held; some are coin operated.

Index

Notes:

1. Not every person or location is included. Most family members named in the Biographies are not.
2. Armed forces units, establishments, etc are grouped under the respective country, except for Britain's, which appear under the three services – British Army, Royal Air Force and Royal Navy. Royal Naval Division units appear under British Army for convenience.
3. Newfoundland appears under Canada although not part of it at the time.
4. Cemeteries/Crematoria, Cathedrals, Churches, Hospitals, Schools, Trenches, Universities and Commonwealth War Graves Commission appear under those group headings.
5. All orders, medals and decorations appear under Orders.
6. Belgium, Britain, France and Germany are not indexed in the accounts of the VC actions as there are too many mentions. Similarly England, Britain and United Kingdom are not indexed in the biographies.